101 8

D1321575

Environmental
and Natural
Resources
Economics

ONE WEEK LOAN

Environmental and Natural Resources Economics

Theory, Policy, and the Sustainable Society

3rd edition

Steven C. Hackett

M.E.Sharpe

Armonk, New York
London, England

Library of Congress Cataloging-in-Publication Data

Hackett, Steven C., 1960–
  Environmental and natural resources economics : theory, policy, and the sustainable society /
Steven C. Hackett.—3rd ed.
    p. cm.
  Includes bibliographical references and index.
  ISBN 0-7656-1472-3 (cloth : alk. paper) — ISBN 0-7656-1473-1 (pbk. : alk. paper)
    1. Environmental economics. 2. Environmental policy. 3. Natural resources.
  4. Sustainable development. I. Title.

HD75.6.H33 2006
333.7—dc22   2005024132

For Mary

Contents

List of Tables and Figures

Tables

Figures

Preface

This textbook provides an accessible yet rigorous treatment of environmental and natural resource economics, as well as the emerging subject of sustainability and sustainable development. This third edition is built on the foundation of more than ten years of classroom experience working with and learning from thousands of students at Humboldt State University and other institutions. These include undergraduate majors in business, economics, environmental science, forestry, natural resources planning, and master's degree students from the environment and community, environmental systems, and natural resource graduate programs. Many of the noneconomists I have taught have little in the way of prior training in economics, and approach the topics covered in this textbook with a healthy dose of skepticism. As a result, this book was designed to balance accessibility, breadth, and rigor, with the goal of creating a valuable learning experience for students coming from economics as well as interdisciplinary programs focused on environmental science, resource management, and public policy. Provocative issues are raised with the intention of stimulating interest and generating constructive debate. Chapters 1–11 can be used to cover a traditional one-semester course in environmental and resource economics. A nontraditional course on the economics of a sustainable society can be built around chapters 1–3 (economic fundamentals), followed by chapters 12–16 (issues in the economics of a sustainable society), likely in combination with outside materials. In a graduate course I find it productive to assign spreadsheet simulation exercises to help cement a better understanding of the workings and comparative-static properties of the economic models presented in the chapters.

There are a number of topics that can be added or subtracted based on the nature of the course being taught. For example, chapters 1–3 introduce basic principles, and are included to make the book accessible to those who do not have a prior background in economics. If this book is to be used in an upper-division undergraduate course for economics majors, students can cover these quickly as a review. Those who are teaching an introductory course can skip the mathematical models on dynamic efficiency in chapter 5 and on the bioeconomics of marine capture fisheries in chapter 6 and focus on the concepts. Since this textbook was designed for diverse student readers, the content covers both mainstream economic topics and topics that lie at the boundary with other disciplines. Examples of the broader approach can be seen in the coverage of philosophy in chapter 2, marine fisheries in chapter 6, the science of climate change in chapter 11, and the extensive material on sustainability in chapters 12–16. The textbook makes extensive use of citations to original material in each chapter, thus providing a starting point for those wishing to pursue further study on a topic (such as for term papers or theses). Since many of these scholarly works, policy studies, and government research documents are available on the Internet, an annotated set of Internet links is provided at the end of each chapter.

Those who are new to environmental and natural resource economics must develop a new technical vocabulary. To make that process easier and less frustrating, technical terms introduced for the first time are italicized, with definitions provided in an extensive glossary included at the end of the textbook.

A considerable amount of new material was added in creating the third edition of this textbook. While every chapter was substantially revised, the more significant changes are highlighted below. Chapter 6 was added to provide a marine fisheries application for the conceptual material in chapter 5 that covers the economics of renewable resources and of common-pool resource dilemmas. Somewhat more advanced mathematical models of natural resource economics were added in chapters 5 and 6, and more advanced spreadsheet simulation exercises were added at the end of chapters 3, 4, 5, 6, and 7. A more extensive treatment of supply and demand was added to the material on market capitalism in chapter 3, some of which was moved out of chapter 4. The material in chapter 11 on global climate change was substantially updated, as research and public policy have changed rapidly since the second edition was written in 2000. Internet links at the end of each chapter were updated, and new problems were added at the end of most chapters. The glossary has also been expanded for the third edition, and there are many new figures and tables. An updated Internet site accompanies this textbook (http://www.humboldt.edu/~envecon). Readers will find helpful applications such as audio clips, Excel-based interactive simulations, lecture outlines, sample essays, annotated Internet links, and much more.

I would like to acknowledge the support and understanding of my family during the summers of 2004 and 2005 when I was writing the third edition of this textbook. My colleagues Dan Ihara, Michal Moore, Yo Nagai, and David Narum have used this textbook in their classes and offered many helpful suggestions that I have addressed in this third edition. I have also received helpful input from my colleagues Chris Dewees, Dave Hankin, and Lin Ostrom. Amber Jamieson and Jocelyn Godinho provided capable student research assistance. I would also like to thank the many students who have used this book in the classroom and have offered me valuable insights and constructive criticism that are reflected in this third edition.

Part I

Theory and Fundamentals

1

Introduction to Environmental and Natural Resources Economics

Introduction

Traditionally, economists learned very little about the environment, and environmental scientists and resource managers learned very little about economics. Yet economic and environmental systems interact in many important ways, and an increasing number of economists, scientists, and resource managers are finding that they need to work in an interdisciplinary fashion in order to understand these interactions and develop effective public policy. This book provides a foundation for you to learn more about a wide variety of problems and policies at the interface of economic and environmental systems. Economic systems derive many valuable inputs (some commodified, some free) from the ecological, hydrological, geological, atmospheric, and other systems and processes of Earth. For example, essential *ecosystem services* such as nutrient cycling, sink functions of wetlands, and the hydrological cycle have economic value, and methods are being developed to measure these values. Economic activity can have negative impacts on the functional integrity of these natural systems and processes, though in some cases these impacts can be substantially reduced or even eliminated through careful public policy. Environmentally harmful activity can be reduced (or environmentally benign activity can be increased) by changing the incentives of people and businesses through the use of taxes, subsidies, ecolabels, deposit/refund systems, and liability, or through the use of caps, bans, and technology standards. Markets for emission credits can be used in conjunction with emissions caps to reduce the cost of compliance with environmental regulation. While industry groups will oftentimes exert political influence to reduce or overturn costly environmental regulations, under some circumstances firms have an incentive to lobby to impose more stringent environmental regulation on their industry. These are just a few of the topics addressed in this book. As Berry (1987) observes, "the thing that troubles us about the industrial economy is exactly that it is not comprehensive enough, that, moreover, it tends to destroy what it does not comprehend, and that it is dependent upon much that it does not comprehend" (pp. 54–55). It is hoped that this book will help introduce economists to relevant and important environmental issues, and to help resource and environmental specialists develop a basic competency in economics.

There are a number of themes covered in this book that usually come together under the heading of environmental and natural resources economics, and there are some that are still new and developing. A primary focus of this book is on *environmental economics,* which analyzes the economic basis for pollution problems, as well as the policies designed to resolve pollution. Much of the work in environmental economics studies the application and performance of incentive regulatory practices, such as pollution taxes, liability, or cap-and-trade systems. Some environmental economists also develop or apply methods for estimating the benefits of environmental improvements or the costs of pollution externalities. Others study the political economy of environmental policy. Another important focus of this book is on *natural resource economics,* which has traditionally addressed problems of governing common-pool natural resources, of finding dynamically optimal rates of renewable or nonrenewable resource extraction, and of the workings of resource and energy markets. Fossil or renewable energy resources and policy are an important area of study in natural resource economics. More recently *ecological economics* has emerged as an area of study focused on understanding the economics of *natural capital* and the ecosystem goods and services that flow from it. Another more recent area of inquiry, *the economics of a sustainable society,* includes efforts at identifying, modeling, and measuring the contribution of economic activities to a more sustainable society. Sustainability studies focus on understanding the interactions between economy, community, and environment over the long term, and on using this information to fashion policies that move us closer to a sustainable society. While some of these topics are complex, the book is also designed to be accessible to readers who may have little in the way of an economics background, but who possess a compensatory motivation to learn.

There are threads of economic theory that connect the various chapters of this book. One of these is the principle of pollution taxation, first introduced with externality theory in chapter 4. Various policy experiments in pollution taxation are described in chapter 10. More ambitious programs of ecological tax reform that call for a comprehensive shifting of taxes from beneficial activities such as employment to pollution and resource degradation are described in chapter 13. Another thread is the concept of dynamic efficiency, which is an adaptation of static efficiency concepts to resource allocation problems over multiple time periods into the future. The theoretical concept is developed with regard to nonrenewable resources in chapter 5 and is also applied to benefit/cost analysis in chapter 7. The concept arises again in chapter 13, where it is related to the challenge of making sustainability policy today that generates benefit and cost flows in the future. Related to the concept of dynamic efficiency, Hotelling rents occur when future demand for a scarce and depletable resource is reflected in current prices and represent the difference between the price and the marginal extraction cost of a resource. A theoretical model is developed in chapter 5 and applied again in chapter 14, where it is shown how reinvestment of Hotelling rents contributes to sustainability. Finally, the problem of governing common-pool resources (resources such as fisheries that are used by multiple people and are subject to depletion from overuse), first presented as a theoretical concept in chapter 5, is revisited in application to marine capture fisheries in chapter 6, and again in chapter 16 in the context of self-governance of localized common-pool resources.

The section that follows introduces some basic economic concepts. This section will help build a conceptual foundation for those who are new to economics. Readers with a prior background in economics may find it to be a useful review.

Fundamental Concepts

Many people approach economics with a preconceived notion of what economics is about. An example is the common tendency to equate economics with commercial activity and the stock market. These notions are embedded in our culture and in the various news media. The purpose of this section is to develop a clearer understanding of what economics is about. Let's start out by defining economics. *Economics* is the study of how scarce resources, goods, and services are allocated among competing uses. The key issue in economics is that the choice problem of *how* to allocate is implied by the condition of scarcity, and so economy or minimization of waste occurs when resources are allocated to their highest-valued use. Thus at the center of economics is scarcity. *Scarcity* means not having enough of something to provide for all that is wanted. The condition of scarcity implies that not all goals can be attained at the same time. While some aspects of scarcity are social constructs, or are created or heightened by advertising, others are unavoidable aspects of life.

Examples of scarce resources:

- A candy bar offered to a classroom full of hungry students.
- A given hour of your time.
- A popular campground at a mountain lake.
- Old-growth trees in a national forest.
- Your money income.
- Clean water in rivers.
- Fish in a fishery.
- Your attention.
- Tax revenues flowing to a city government.
- A predator's energy and time.
- Net earnings at a profit-maximizing firm.

In each of the cases given above, there is a choice problem necessitated by a condition of scarcity. It is interesting to note that the economic problem of allocating scarce resources in the context of competing uses is not unique to humans. Other forms of life also respond to conditions of scarcity, and one can argue that natural selection tends to favor those organisms that are most successful in allocating their time and energy in the context of scarcity. Scarcity is one of the fundamental aspects of our world, both inside and outside of markets. Scarcity makes choice unavoidable. Since so many aspects of our world involve choices necessitated by a condition of scarcity, economics is fundamental and ever-present in most everything we do, whether we are aware of it or not. When you choose to buy a slice of pizza instead of a bowl of vegetarian chili for lunch, that choice is an economic decision. When the Forest Service chooses to manage a particular watershed to protect wilderness-dependent species rather than for logging or intense recreation, then that choice is also an economic decision.

Since scarcity forces us to make choices from a set of alternatives, on what basis can we rank the various alternatives and choose the best one? Economic analysis requires a system of value from which we can compare alternatives and so distinguish good from less good allocations. Every day you make economic choices that involve ranking alternatives. From a cognitive point of view, many people develop decision rules and rules-of-thumb that simplify the process of ranking and choosing alternatives to such an extent that we are no longer consciously aware of those choices being made.

Much of government policy making involves the ranking of alternatives. Since people have different values, the best economic choice for one is not necessarily the best for another. As a consequence, environmental policy conflicts often have their basis in value conflicts, though they may be popularly cast as conflicts between economy and environment.

While economics is a very broad field of study, there is a tendency to more narrowly equate economics with commercial activity. For example, consider the following hypothetical headline: *"The decision to manage a segment of national forest as wilderness rather than as a timber production area is a rare example of the environment winning out over economics."* The headline writer seems to be implying that wilderness values are noneconomic, confusing commerce with economics. This implication is false. The time and money that people spend in traveling to wilderness areas for recreation is scarce, as is the time and money spent by those who lobby and advocate for wilderness protection. People who do not visit wilderness areas nevertheless may value their existence. Wilderness areas also provide valuable ecosystem services and natural resources that flow beyond the wilderness boundary, such as clean air, fresh water, wildlife, and plants. These and other wilderness benefits are no less economic than the price of admission to Disneyland or the revenues generated from a timber harvest. While markets are a prominent way of making allocation choices in the context of scarcity, economics encompasses the study of both market and nonmarket allocation of scarce resources. As Power (1996) observes, economic analysis of the environment is challenging and important precisely because its value is not conveniently revealed in a market and thus is subject to inappropriate use. Even wilderness area management itself is partly an economic problem. Managers have limited budgets to allocate for science and maintenance, and allocating a popular section of wilderness for threatened and endangered species habitat may require sharp cutbacks in recreational visitation. And so it should be clear that the lack of a market for wilderness does not mean that it has no economic value. In chapter 7 you will learn about various methods that have been developed for measuring the value of resources and other aspects of the environment that are not traded in markets and so lack a market price as an indicator of value.

Continuing our example, protecting wildlands as a designated wilderness area means that certain extractive activities such as logging, mining, and ski area development cannot occur. Suppose that the next best use of the area could be measured by the net revenue generated from timber harvest. Then this net revenue is part of the cost of wilderness protection, in this case referred to as an *opportunity cost*. When something scarce is allocated to one particular use, the opportunity cost of that choice is the value of the best alternative that had to be given up. Everything that is scarce and so requires an allocation choice has an opportunity cost. We can evaluate the rationality of a particular choice by comparing the benefits that it generates relative to its opportunity cost. *Economic rationality,* as the term is used in this book, refers to behavior that is intended to be consistent with the values and objectives of the decision maker, given the information that is available to the decision maker. Or more simply, economic rationality refers to choices made in the context of scarcity where the benefits to the decision maker are perceived to exceed cost. There are several issues that should be addressed at this point. First, rational and reasonable do not mean the same thing. One person's rational choice may not seem reasonable to another who does not share the same values. Second, underlying the notion of economic rationality is the view that people (and economic organizations) are optimizers who have the objective of maximizing net value. In the context of markets, for example, consumer theory starts from the premise that consumers wish to maximize their overall level of satisfaction, or utility, as constrained by their income and by market prices, while firms wish to maximize their profits. From an economic point of view, however, optimizing behavior is not limited to market exchanges designed to improve material well-being; to think that is to confuse optimization with self-interest. Optimization more generally involves the process of ranking alternative uses of one's time, energy, attention, resources, or income based on a particular set of values and preferences, and then selecting the alternative that yields the greatest increase in net value. Thus, allocating scarce time and energy as a volunteer, a voter, or an activist can be entirely rational, optimizing behavior for those who care a great deal about their community.

The concepts of scarcity and opportunity cost can be illustrated in a *production possibilities frontier (PPF)*. In the simple illustrative example given in Figure 1.1, we have an economy that has a set of resources (land, labor, capital) that can be used to produce various combinations of food and clothing outputs.

The PPF in Figure 1.1 represents all the possible combinations of food and clothing that can be produced in a given time period when available resources are fully and efficiently employed. When resources are wasted, such as when discrimination results in women being unable to obtain certain types of jobs for which they are qualified, we are inside rather than on the PPF, such as at point A in Figure 1.1. As we move along a PPF and increase the production of one good, such as clothing, we must shift resources away from producing the other good, food. The opportunity cost of a given increase in clothing is reflected in the amount of food (and the value we place on it) that is given up to produce more clothing. For example, the movement from point B to point D

Figure 1.1 **Production Possibilities Frontier**

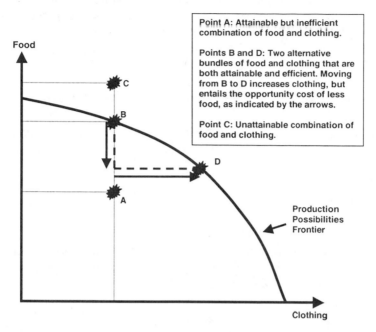

Point A: Attainable but inefficient combination of food and clothing.

Points B and D: Two alternative bundles of food and clothing that are both attainable and efficient. Moving from B to D increases clothing, but entails the opportunity cost of less food, as indicated by the arrows.

Point C: Unattainable combination of food and clothing.

along the PPF in Figure 1.1 results in an increase in clothing and a corresponding decrease in food. The "bowed-out" shape of the PPF is based on the idea that the economic resources used to produce food and clothing are at least somewhat specialized. As a result, each additional unit of clothing production entails a larger and larger opportunity cost, as resources that are more productively deployed for food production are redirected to clothing production. In economics this is referred to as the *Law of Increasing Opportunity Cost*. Outward shifts in the PPF occur when more resources are available or when better technologies are developed that increase the productivity of a given resource. Preferences for food and clothing determine which combination along the frontier is produced in this highly simplified economy.

So what situations do *not* have an economic dimension? The answer is those things that are not scarce. Value systems, love, friendship, aspects of culture, and spirituality are, or at least can be, outside of economics because it is not clear that they are subject to scarcity. The range of possible thoughts and ideas is also not subject to scarcity, though it is clear that a person's cognitive capacities are scarce and thus subject to economics. Moreover, the assertion that economics is fundamental to the human experience does not necessarily imply that economists can measure and model everything of value that is affected by environmental and natural resources policy. In addition, the moral, ethical, and spiritual implications of a particular allocation problem may supersede the use of economic tools for determining what the proper allocation might be. This does not invalidate economic analysis, but acknowledges that social and political factors may play an equal or a greater role in determining how a society ultimately chooses to allocate resources.

Some Reasons for Optimism and Some Reasons for Concern

In terms of trends there are reasons for both optimism and concern. Let's first consider some reasons for being optimistic regarding economics and the environment.

Reasons for Optimism

One reason for being optimistic is that regulations such as the Clean Air Act and its amendments have led to substantial progress being made in reducing nationwide emissions of the key air pollutants. For example, the U.S. Environmental Protection Agency (EPA) reported that between 1983 and 2002 emissions of nitrogen oxides fell by 15 percent, emissions of volatile organic compounds fell by 40 percent, emissions of sulfur dioxide fell by 33 percent, emissions of carbon monoxide fell by 41 percent, and emissions of lead fell by 93 percent. Moreover, there is evidence that our investment in clean air has generated substantial net economic benefits as well. In their benefit/cost analysis on the Clean Air Act, the EPA found that over the period from 1970 to 1990, each dollar of compliance cost generated approximately $44.40 in economic benefits, largely from improved human health (U.S. EPA 1997).

Another reason for optimism is the decline in toxic releases since the initiation of the Toxic Release Inventory (TRI) Program. Specifically, the Emergency Planning and Community Right-to-Know Act of 1986 requires firms to report releases of many different toxic chemicals. Emissions of the toxic chemicals originally included in the inventory declined by 55 percent between 1988 and 2001. Moreover, new chemicals and new facilities have been added to the inventory, and total output of the industries covered by the TRI has increased by 40 percent since 1991 (Pacific Research Institute website). Analysis by Maxwell, Lyon, and Hackett (2000) indicates that beginning in 1989 there was a highly significant downward shift in the relationship between the value of manufacturing output and toxic releases, indicating cleaner production.

The increasing cost-effectiveness of reducing sulfur dioxide emissions in the EPA's Acid Rain Program offers another reason for optimism. As described in greater detail in chapter 10, the Acid Rain Program includes a novel approach to regulation that allows firms with lower cleanup costs to contract to perform cleanup for firms with very high cleanup costs. This market contracting process occurs in the context of a substantial overall reduction in allowed sulfur dioxide emissions. Carlson et al. (1998) estimate that allowance trading in the Acid Rain Program achieved cost savings of $700 million to $800 million a year over what could have been expected from a command and control program with a uniform emission-rate standard.

Optimists have had their positions supported by the failure of the predictions regarding the exhaustion of many important nonrenewable resources provided by Meadows et al. (1972). In their publication *Limits to Growth* (1972), Meadows et al. applied an exponential function for resource consumption to the known reserves of various energy and mineral resources. These analysts arrived at the conclusion that resources such as copper, gold, lead, mercury, natural gas, petroleum, silver, tin, and zinc would all be fully depleted by the year 2000. Petroleum provides about 40 percent of the world's energy, and the prospect that we were going to run out brought substantial attention to the Club of Rome. In fact, none of these predictions actually came true. One factor that was not addressed in the analysis was the prospect of exploration and discovery of new reserves. For example, the world's proven petroleum reserves nearly doubled between the time of the analysis and 1994, and estimates of world recoverable reserves increased from 600 billion barrels in 1940 to as much as 2.3 trillion billion in 1995 (Campbell 1995). The 1973 OPEC (Organization of Petroleum Exporting Countries) oil embargo resulted in higher prices, which in turn spurred exploration and development of new reserves. Another factor is technological progress that lowers the cost of extraction and so tends to increase reserves. A third factor is the ability to substitute more abundant resources for those that become extremely scarce and expensive. These issues are discussed in greater detail in chapter 5.

Another reason for optimism is that there is relatively little evidence in favor of pollution haven–driven trade. In their comprehensive review of the literature on environmental regulation and international trade, Copeland and Taylor (2004) refer to the idea "that a tightening up of pollution regulation will, at the margin, have an effect on plant location decisions and trade flows" as the *pollution haven effect* (p. 9). In other words, pollution regulation, along with many other factors, influences the pattern of international trade. They note that this idea derives from economic theory and is supported by recent empirical research. Copeland and Taylor use the term *pollution haven hypothesis* to describe the notion that free ("liberalized") trade *will* result in pollution-intensive industry shifting from countries with stringent regulations to countries with weaker regulations. They note that economic theory does not strongly support the pollution haven hypothesis because many other factors, in addition to pollution regulation, affect trade flows. Moreover, Copeland and Taylor note that "there is little convincing evidence to support the pollution-haven hypothesis. While there is evidence of a pollution-haven *effect,* it is only one of many factors that determine trade patterns, and there is no evidence that it is the dominant factor" (p. 67).

Finally, while there have been localized job losses, such as at lumber mills dependent upon timber sales from national forests where harvests have been reduced, the evidence generally suggests that there is little to no national-level trade-off between jobs and environmental protection. It has been argued that environmental protection measures have led to widespread shutdown of manufacturing plants, encouraged the flight of U.S. manufacturing overseas, and reduced domestic investment in new jobs by hampering productivity growth. In fact, the aggregate data suggest that environmental regulations have not been a major source of aggregate job losses. The U.S. Department of Labor has compiled information on layoffs in which employers are asked to list the primary cause of layoffs. During the period from 1990 to 2000, for example, employers blamed environmental regulations as the leading cause of mass layoffs in less than 0.12 percent of all mass layoffs nationwide (Bureau of Labor Statistics website).

In the Pacific Northwest (including northwestern California) the impact of logging on the environment has been a major ideological issue dividing communities in the region. In 1994 President Clinton approved the Northwest Forest Plan, which protected spotted owl habitat by reducing logging by more than 80 percent on federal lands in the region. Social divisions in the region have been worsened by long-term timber-related job losses, with questions raised about the extent to which environmental restrictions or market-driven economic restructuring of the industry are to blame. In a study designed to address this question, the U.S. Forest Service (2005) reports that 30,000 timber-related jobs were lost in the Pacific Northwest region between 1990 and 2000, and of this total, 11,000 occurred after 1994. According to this draft Forest Service report, only 400 of the 11,000 timber jobs lost in the Pacific Northwest since 1994 can be directly attributable to reduced logging activity under the Northwest Forest Plan. The vast majority of timber-related job losses in the region, according to this report, are attributable to economic restructuring in the timber industry that would have occurred regardless of the Northwest Forest Plan's restrictions. Most of these job losses have been focused in heavily impacted timber-dependent rural communities, many of which still have not recovered from the economic restructuring of the timber industry. As the authors of the draft report note:

Many factors can influence the stability of forest-based communities. . . . Demand for wood and commodity prices fluctuates; alternative sources of supply are available; some firms prefer locating close to large labor markets rather than in geographically isolated areas; mills compete for timber supply; communities compete for jobs; wood products manufacturing technology changes; and other federal and state policies affecting the business climate change. All of these forces can affect jobs in the timber industry, and neither agencies nor communities have much influence over them. (U.S. Forest Service 2005, p. 18)

In contrast, the region's urban centers have experienced dramatic growth and real estate price appreciation. As Power and colleagues (1995) have observed, a key factor driving the Pacific Northwest's vibrant economy is the region's attractive social and natural environment. In this sense, environmental protection can be seen as a form of investment in the region's economic future, though this view provides little solace to declining timber-dependent communities in the region.

Reasons for Concern

While there have been many notable environmental success stories in the United States and elsewhere, there are also many reasons for concern. One reason for concern is the potential for catastrophic change in the global climate because the increased burning of fossil fuels creates so-called greenhouse gases that trap heat and may warm the earth's biosphere. As described in much greater detail in chapter 11, possible scenarios include rising sea levels and inundation of populous low-lying areas such as the Ganges and Nile Deltas, and desertification of vital cereal grain–producing areas, both of which would result in mass hunger and dislocation as well as a more rapid loss of biodiversity. Some degree of action on carbon dioxide emissions is justified as a type of insurance premium in the context of uncertain but potentially large future impacts. Yet while the benefits of controlling greenhouse gas emissions remain uncertain, diffuse, international in scope, and cast in the future, the costs of such control are easier to calculate, threaten our lifestyles, and are cast in the present, which makes it politically difficult to enact meaningful greenhouse gas control policy.

Another reason for concern is the continued loss of habitat for many of the world's species of animals and plants. Balmford et al. (2002) estimated that between 1992 and 2002 the world's biomes experienced a mean annual decline of 1.2 percent. As a consequence, "the capacity of natural systems to deliver goods and services upon which we depend is decreasingly markedly"

(p. 952). They estimate that this mean annual decline in the world's biomes "costs the human enterprise, in net terms, on the order of $250 billion" (p. 952). In other words, the economic gain from land conversion is outweighed by the lost value of the ecosystem goods and services. Balmford et al. contend that there are three reasons why economically inefficient habitat conversion continues: (1) we lack information on the quantity and the value of the ecosystem goods and services provided by wildlands; (2) the major benefits associated with retaining intact natural systems are external to market systems; (3) perverse government tax and subsidy policies exaggerate the private benefits from land conversion. They argue that globally, the subset of subsidies that are both economically and ecologically perverse totals between $950 billion and $1.95 trillion each year.

Finally, many of the world's environmental and natural resources problems are linked to failures of democratic process and empowerment, disproportionate consumption of resources by the rich, and large numbers of very poor people living in fragile environments. Very poor regions and countries are the least resilient to stresses and shocks such as prolonged droughts and political instabilities. With few options, the response to these shocks often leads to intensified deforestation, farming on unstable slopes and nutrient-poor rain forest soils, and other forms of resource degradation as well as migration to crowded and highly polluted urban areas. Poor and politically disenfranchised people are subjected to massive environmental degradation in places such as Ogoniland in Nigeria. Two-thirds of the world's illiterate people are women, and there is a strong inverse relationship between women's educational attainment and fertility, and yet worldwide female illiteracy rates actually increased from 58 percent in 1960 to 66 percent in 1985.

What inference can we draw from these examples of policy successes and areas of concern? Clearly we have made some progress, and environmental and natural resources economics has played a role in some of those successes. Just as clearly, we are faced with enormous challenges worthy of our best efforts.

Overview

This book is divided into three parts. Part I introduces basic concepts about the role of values and ethics in economics and public policy, the economics of market allocation, externality theory, natural resource economics, and an application to marine capture fisheries management and policy. We will learn that indeed there is an unavoidable subjective element to how we rank the choices that are available to us with regard to the environment. We will explore the economics of market capitalism, and learn about the conditions that are required for a well-functioning competitive market. This discussion will extend into the development of the supply and demand market model and the concepts of equilibrium and efficiency. The theory of the perfect market will serve as a benchmark against which we can evaluate various market failures. A more detailed treatment is given to the market failures associated with positive and negative externalities, and how idealized regulatory interventions can internalize these externalities and enhance efficiency. Our focus will then turn to the economics of renewable and nonrenewable natural resources, and the dilemmas associated with common-pool resources. The unifying themes in this first section of the book are core concepts and theoretical models.

The second part of this textbook is focused on the economics of environmental and natural resource policy. We will start out by applying some of the tools of renewable-resource economics and the economics of common-pool resource dilemmas to marine capture fisheries. We will then turn to a discussion of the concepts and methodological approaches of benefit/cost analysis, which is a common way of expressing economic tradeoff information in public policy analysis. Unfortunately we cannot assume that policy is fashioned in the public interest, and thus to understand policy outcomes, we explore the political economy of policy formation. Moreover, once we have public policy rules, we cannot assume that people and businesses will automatically comply with them. As a result, we will consider the economics of enforcement and compliance assurance. Next we turn to the economics of incentive regulation. Economists have been refining their models for efficient regulation to introduce incentives for polluters, and the EPA and other government agencies have increasingly been experimenting with these incentive regulatory schemes. The second part of this textbook ends with an analysis of the science, economics, and public policy associated with climate-change policy. To a greater extent than the other material in this section of the textbook, climate-change policy must contend with some degree of scientific uncertainty, irreversibility of impact, and the international scope of the problem. Global climate change is also an area in which policymakers must acknowledge that impacts will occur over a very long time horizon, an issue that provides a bridge to the material on sustainability in the last portion of the book.

The economics of a sustainable society, the topic of Part III of this textbook, is about sustaining economy, community, and environment over a long-term time horizon. Unlike environmental and natural resources economics, sustainability introduces a significant role for community and issues of empowerment, demographic change, poverty, and social justice.

After a brief introduction, the material begins with a chapter covering the linkages between poverty, growth in population and economic activity, and the integrity of environmental and resource systems. Once we develop a basic understanding of how social, economic, and environmental factors interact, we will then discuss policies that are better targeted at improving and sustaining the quality of people's lives over time. One example is the movement for sustainable development, which is the subject of an entire chapter. Making sustainable development operational calls for methods and strategies for sustainable production and consumption. Particular attention is paid to the economics of renewable energy resources and technologies, and policies designed to promote more sustainable production and consumption. The final chapter investigates concepts, methods, and case studies related to sustainable local communities. Special attention will be paid to linkages between local people and the local common-pool natural resource systems on which they depend.

It is hoped that this book fosters not only a better understanding of economics and the environment but also an appreciation of the challenges and rewards of forming environmental and resource policy in a diverse society.

Summary

- Environmental economics focuses attention on pollution problems and on policies to resolve them. Attention is also given to measurement of benefits and costs, and to understanding the political economy of environmental policy. Natural resources economics studies the problems of governing common-pool natural resources, of dynamically optimal rates of resource extraction, and of resource markets. Many natural resource economists focus on the economics and public policy of renewable and nonrenewable energy resources and technologies. The sustainability movement is concerned with maintaining or enhancing ecological integrity, economic vitality, and democratic political and social institutions over time.
- Economics is the study of how scarce resources are allocated among competing uses. Something is said to be scarce when, at a zero price, more is wanted than is available. Something scarce can be allocated to a variety of different uses. When one use is chosen, the opportunity cost of that choice is the value of the next best alternative, which was given up. A rational choice from among competing options is anticipated to yield benefits that exceed the opportunity cost.
- There are a number of reasons for optimism. Environmental policies

have generated substantial improvements in air quality in the United States, and production methods are becoming cleaner. There does not seem to be much support for the argument that environmental protection results in overall job loss in the United States. While production facilities have moved from the United States to Mexico and other developing countries, there is not strong evidence that pollution havens overseas are the primary driver for observed trends in international trade and in plant relocations.

- Yet there are important areas of concern, including loss of habitat, global warming, and impacts due to various government failures.

Review Questions and Problems

1. You are an investigative reporter covering the issue of a trade-off between jobs and the environment. Your assignment is to write a 500-word column that provides:

    a. a brief overview and description of the concept of a jobs versus environment trade-off;

    b. an explanation of situations in which environmental protection has resulted in job losses;

    c. a summary of the evidence for a jobs versus environment trade-off using national-level (macroeconomic) data (see discussion in the text in the chapter);

    d. a conclusion that summarizes the jobs versus environment story and perhaps strays a bit into the political economy of who benefits from this persistent myth.

2. Price is a simple indicator of value for things traded in markets. Yet if the economic problem also applies to something like a wilderness area, which has no price to indicate value, then how are we to assign value to it? In your answer, consider the following:

    a. Think of some specific indicators of the monetary value of a wilderness area that an analyst could measure.

    b. What are some monetary indicators of the opportunity cost of wilderness preservation?

    c. If we were to make a decision regarding how to manage the land area under analysis based on the information you provided in (a) and (b) above, what other elements of value might be omitted and thus not be reflected in the policy decision?

3.   Classroom debate activity: Debate consists of reasoned arguments for or against a given proposition. Form two groups in your class (affirmative and negative) for the purpose of debating the following proposition: *Resolved: Environmental regulation impairs the international competitiveness of U.S. manufacturers.* Members of each group should be given a week or so to research the issues. The debate will occur in a panel, moderated by your professor. Two members of each group will serve as panelists, and any additional group members can serve as researchers. There are a variety of different ways to structure a debate, one of which is the Michigan cross-examination method:

a.   The first affirmative panelist presents the affirmative case (6 minutes).
b.   The first affirmative panelist is cross-examined by the second negative panelist (4 minutes).
c.   Questions from the audience are put to the members of the affirmative team (5 minutes).
d.   The first negative panelist presents the negative case (6 minutes).
e.   The second affirmative panelist cross-examines the first negative panelist (4 minutes).
f.   Questions from the audience are put to the members of the negative team (5 minutes).
g.   The second negative panelist summarizes the negative case (2 minutes).
h.   The second affirmative panelist summarizes the affirmative case (2 minutes).

Internet Links

Economic Report of the President (http://w3.access.gpo.gov/eop/): Extensive source of up-to-date U.S. economic information.

Environmental Protection Agency's National Center for Environmental Economics (NCEE) (http://yosemite.epa.gov/ee/epa/eed.nsf/pages/ homepage): The NCEE analyzes relationships between the economy, environmental health, and environmental pollution control.

Federal Reserve Economic Data (www.stls.frb.org/fred/index.html): Comprehensive source of U.S. economic data.

FedStats (http://www.fedstats.gov/map.html): This site provides easy access to the full range of statistics and information produced by over seventy agencies of the U.S. government.

Food and Agriculture Organization (www.fao.org/): A UN organization offering extensive research reports and databases having to do with agriculture, economics, fisheries, forestry, human nutrition, and sustainable development.

Major Schools of Economic Thought (http://www.frbsf.org/publications/ education/unfrmd.great/greattimes.html): An easy-to-read summary produced by the Federal Reserve Bank of San Francisco.

Textbook Internet Site (www.humboldt.edu/~envecon): Includes lecture outlines, extensive annotated Internet links, interactive Excel-based simulations, audio clips, interactive quizzes, and much more.

World Resources Institute (www.wri.org/): The World Resources Institute provides information, ideas, and solutions to global environmental problems. They publish the authoritative biennial *World Resources.*

References and Further Reading

Balmford, A., A. Bruner, P. Cooper, R. Costanza, S. Farber, R. Green, M. Jenkins, P. Jefferiss, V. Jessamy, J. Madden, K. Munro, N. Myers, S. Naeem, J. Paavola, M. Rayment, S. Rosendo, J. Roughgarden, K. Trumper, and R. Turner. 2002. "Economic Reasons for Conserving Wild Nature." *Science* 297: 950–54.

Berry, W. 1987. *Home Economics.* San Francisco: North Point Press.

Bureau of Labor Statistics (http://www.bls.gov/).

Campbell, C. 1995. "The Next Oil Price Shock: The World's Remaining Oil and Its Depletion." *Energy Exploration and Exploitation* 13 (1): 19–44.

Carlson, C., D. Burtraw, M. Cropper, and K. Palmer. 1998. "Sulfur Dioxide Control by Electric Utilities: What Are the Gains from Trade?" Resources for the Future Discussion Paper 98–44.

Copeland, B., and M. Taylor. 2004. "Trade, Growth, and the Environment." *Journal of Economic Literature* 42 (March): 7–71.

Goodstein, E. 1994. "Jobs and the Environment: The Myth of a National Trade-off." Paper. Washington, DC: Economic Policy Institute.

Jaffe, A., S. Peterson, P. Portney, and R. Stavins. 1995. "Environmental Regulation and the Competitiveness of U.S. Manufacturing." *Journal of Economic Literature* 33 (March): 132–63.

List, J., and C. Co. 2000. "The Effects of Environmental Regulations on Foreign Direct Investment." *Journal of Environmental Economics and Management* 40: 1–20.

Maxwell, J., T. Lyon, and S. Hackett. 2000. "Self-Regulation and Social Welfare: The Political Economy of Corporate Environmentalism." *Journal of Law and Economics* 43 (2): 583–618 .

Meadows, D.H., D.L Meadows, J. Randers, and W. Behrens. 1972. *The Limits to Growth.* New York: Universe Books.

Moore, C., and A. Miller. 1995. *Green Gold: Japan, Germany, the United States, and the Race for Environmental Technology.* Boston: Beacon Press.

Pearce, D., and J. Warford. 1993. *World Without End: Economics, Environment, and Sustainable Development.* Oxford: Oxford University Press.

Porter, M. 1991. "America's Green Strategy," *Scientific American* 264: 168.

Power, T. 1995. *Economic Well-Being and Environmental Protection in the Pacific Northwest: A Consensus Report by Pacific Northwest Economists.* Missoula: University of Montana.

———. 1996. *Environmental Protection and Economic Well-Being: The Economic Pursuit of Quality.* 2nd ed. Armonk, NY: M.E. Sharpe.

U.S. Environmental Protection Agency. 1997. *The Benefits and Costs of the Clean Air Act, 1970–1990.* Washington, DC: U.S. EPA.

U.S. Forest Service. 2005. *Northwest Forest Plan: The First Ten Years, Socioeconomic Monitoring Results,* Volume I: *Key Findings.* Available at www.reo.gov/monitoring/10yr-report/social-economic/final-report.html.

2

Value Systems and Economic Systems

Introduction

Economics is concerned with the problem of allocating scarce resources among competing uses. When something is scarce, allocating it to one use means we forgo the opportunity for another use, creating an opportunity cost. An allocation is good when it generates net benefits that exceed the opportunity cost. Thus, at the most basic level, economics is about understanding opportunity costs. All human societies are confronted with this fundamental problem. Throughout time and around the globe, societies have been motivated by widely different social and philosophical value systems for determining benefits and costs and so have had different answers to the question of what a *good* way to allocate things might be. As a consequence we have observed many different kinds of economies. Understanding economic systems provides insight into otherwise inexplicable aspects of our lives and the choices that we make.

In this chapter we will investigate several fundamental questions related to human values and economic systems. We will first consider the basis for distinguishing a good economy from a bad one, or a good allocation choice from a bad one. A response to this question might be that a good economy is more efficient than a bad one, producing things of value with a minimum of waste, and allocating resources to their highest-valued use, and indeed few would deny that efficiency is a central element of a good economy. But the judgment of what constitutes a wasteful resource allocation, and how we determine highest-valued use, depends critically on the value system of the judge. Even more fundamental is the question of whether an action (for example, policy protecting old-growth forest) is to be judged on its intrinsic rightness or based on the measurable benefits and costs that might result from the allocation. We will also consider the problem of determining the proper balance between individual self-interest and the common good. We will conclude the discussion of value systems by presenting contrasting perspectives on the basis for and the merits of private property rights systems.

We will then turn to a discussion of some fundamental issues associated with economic systems and methods. One of these has to do with different methods of economic analysis. One branch of economic analysis is based on the Western scientific method of describing, explaining, and predicting observable empirical phenomena. A set of "best methods" for describing observable phenomena has evolved that is generally accepted by the community of economic practitioners, and analyses that properly follow these best methods yield findings that generate little in the way of disagreement. For example, the hypothesis that a per-unit tax on firms will result in a short-run increase in price and reduction in volume of trade can be evaluated empirically, and this form of positive analysis can also tell us the amount by which price rises and volume of trade declines. Another branch of economic analysis proposes a set of "best choices" based on particular normative systems of value. Thus, a profit-maximizing corporation can be advised of a system of compensation designed to best align the incentives of its employees with the maximization of profit for the firm. Alternatively, a government can be advised as to the best use of an old-growth forest based on the utilitarian value system of benefit/cost analysis. It is important to distinguish these forms of analysis; while the former yields something we can think of as fact, the latter naturally generates disagreements among economists who articulate arguments derived from widely different systems of value.

We will conclude the discussion of economic systems by describing the fundamental choices required of all societies by the condition of scarcity, regardless of the value system or criteria for efficiency that are employed. These choices are responses to the basic economic questions of (1) what should we allocate resources to produce (e.g., produce board feet of timber or wildlife habitat), (2) by what method should we produce (i.e., choice of engineering or management system), and (3) who receives what is produced? The fundamental issues discussed in this chapter provide a broad foundation for the analysis of markets, market failure, and social policy that is to follow in the remainder of the book.

Fundamentals of Ethical Systems

Societies are frequently confronted with policy decisions that must be made because of scarcity. Examples include the allocation of budget monies and the management of public land, water, and wildlife. These policy decisions affect both human and nonhuman communities. Because of scarcity, any choice made by policymakers will have an opportunity cost. What are the values that will be used to rank policy alternatives? From an economic point of view, a decision is good when it generates net value that exceeds the opportunity cost. Yet different value systems will lead to a different ranking of alternatives and so will provide different answers to the question of which course of action is best. As you can see, in order to make good economic decisions we need value systems to rank alternatives. When individuals make choices in the context of scarcity they are guided by their own values and preferences, as well as by those of their culture. In order to make public policy decisions that serve the interests of the public, however, the economic and political aspects of policy making must embody society's shared or dominant values, or aggregate individual values and preferences. This is one reason why social institutions, such as those that provide the structure for political and economic choices and interactions, embody the shared or dominant values of the societies from which they evolve.

Ethics is a branch of philosophy that is concerned with moral duty and ideal human character. Morals are defined to be principles of right and wrong, of good and bad. Ethical systems either describe particular shared values, or provide a method for arriving at an aggregation of individual values and preferences. Different ethical systems lead to different economic choices. There are two traditional classes of ethics, deontological and teleological, which are described below.

Deontological Ethics

Ethical systems in the deontological tradition develop theories of action based on duty or moral obligation. Under this system, an action is judged by its *intrinsic rightness* and not by the extent to which it serves as an instrumentality in furthering one's goals or aspirations. Immanuel Kant, one of the best-known proponents of this ethical system, argued in *Metaphysics of Morals* (1785, p. 96) that there are two types of *imperatives* or rules that command or direct our proper behavior:

> All imperatives command either hypothetically or categorically. The former presents the practical necessity of a possible action as a means of achieving something else which one desires (or which one may possibly desire). The categorical imperative would be one which presented an action as of itself objectively necessary, without regard to any other end.

As O'Brien (1996) points out, a hypothetical imperative commences with a statement such as "If we want to limit acid rain, we ought to reduce emissions of sulfur dioxide and nitrogen oxides." Kant would refer to this as a practical reason for taking an act. Kant's major contribution to the development of deontological ethics is the notion of a categorical imperative. Unlike a hypothetical imperative that appeals to reason, a categorical imperative asserts that a particular action is intrinsically necessary without regard to the outcome or ends that might possibly derive from the act. Thus, from the perspective of a categorical imperative, one could argue that a person should never treat another person as a mere means to an end or a goal. The basis for ethical behavior, according to Kant, was for autonomous people to freely submit themselves to the same rules that they would prescribe for others, in which case individual autonomy would lead to cooperative harmony.

Perhaps one of the best-known "neo-Kantians" is John Rawls, who developed the theory of justice as fairness. *Justice* here means the principle of rightness of action. Rawls (1971) conceived of justice as arising from a state of ignorance. In particular, Rawls proposed the following thought experiment. If people could select some principle of justice (for example, that society has the duty of assisting the less fortunate) before they were aware of their own status and position, then under this "veil of ignorance" people would not be biased toward justice systems that favor their particular situation. In the "original position" that exists prior to the revelation of differences in status and position, people would naturally agree on the intrinsic value of a justice system that favors the least advantaged in society. Rawlsian justice is deontological because the ethics of justice determine rightness of action as a categorical imperative. The link between Kant and Rawls can be seen in the following quote from Kant's *Foundations:* "There is, therefore, only one categorical imperative. It is: Act only according to the maxim by which you can at the same time will [i.e., make happen] that it should become a universal law" (p. 101).

Both Aldo Leopold's land ethic and Bill Devall's conception of ecosophy, or earth wisdom, can be considered examples of deontological ethical systems, calling for ecosystem protection as a categorical imperative. The deep-ecology movement promotes ecosophy by way of becoming grounded "through fuller experience of our connection to earth" (Devall and Sessions 1985). In 1984 Naess and George Sessions articulated a set of deep-ecology principles (Devall 1988):

- The well-being and flourishing of human and nonhuman life on Earth have value in themselves (intrinsic value). These values are independent of the usefulness of the nonhuman world for human purposes.

- Richness and diversity of life forms contribute to the realization of these values and are also values in themselves.
- Humans have no right to reduce this richness and diversity except to satisfy vital needs.
- The flourishing of human life and cultures is compatible with a substantial decrease of the human population. The flourishing of nonhuman life requires such a decrease.
- Present human interference with the nonhuman world is excessive, and the situation is rapidly worsening.
- Policies must therefore be changed. The changes in policies affect basic economic, technological, and ideological structures. The resulting state of affairs will be deeply different from the present.
- The ideological change is mainly that of appreciating life quality (dwelling in situations of inherent worth) rather than adhering to an increasingly higher (material) standard of living. There will be a profound awareness of the difference between big and great.
- Those who subscribe to the foregoing points have an obligation directly or indirectly to participate in the attempt to implement the necessary changes.

We have seen that deontological ethical systems lead to expressions of categorical imperatives that prescribe certain necessary actions. Deontological ethics can serve to guide social policy for those circumstances for which members of society share the same values. In diverse societies, however, policies based on one group's system of intrinsic value may be oppressive to those holding different values. If a community or society lacks common ground on a set of deontological principles, then an alternative that is investigated below would be to aggregate individual preferences.

Teleological Ethics

Telos is a Greek term for end or purpose. Under teleological systems of ethics, an action is judged not by its intrinsic value but by the extent to which the action has instrumental value in providing advancement toward a desirable end. If an action is instrumental in yielding a desirable end, then generally the action itself is ethical. Thus the ethical focus is on goals rather than actions. Central to teleological systems is the notion of *consequentialism,* which argues that the moral worth of actions or practices is determined solely by the consequences of the actions or the practices (Beauchamp and Bowie 1979). This ethical system was advocated by Aristotle and later by religious philosophers exploring natural law ethics and utilitarian philosophers such as David Hume, Jeremy Bentham, and John Stuart Mill. To avoid the obvious criticism that under teleological ethics "the end justifies the means," Aristotle argued that one must instead look at each individual action and justify it in terms of its own goal. Of the various teleological ethical traditions, the one most relevant to environmental and natural resources economics is utilitarianism.

Under this system of teleological ethics, the merits of an action (e.g., a social policy) are evaluated by considering the total benefits (utility) and the total costs (disutility) created by the action for human society. Under *act utilitarianism* a social rule is followed if, after adding up the utility and the disutility the rule will cause for all members of society, the net utility is positive. Thus this rule is sometimes imprecisely characterized as providing "the greatest good for the greatest number." This is not always true, however, because it is possible that the utilitarian-ethical policy will generate large benefits to a few and very small costs to many. Another problem with utilitarianism is that it can be used to impose the tyranny of the majority. Act utilitarianism can therefore be used to justify throwing a virgin into a volcano if it is believed that such an act will save a village from the ravages of an eruption. Utilitarian ethics is teleological because the merit of a rule is judged by its effect, or ends, rather than by the intrinsic rightness of the act itself independent of any possible outcome or end.

Utilitarian principles are prominent in contemporary policy analysis. In diverse societies where people cannot agree on the intrinsic merits of certain actions, as is required by systems of deontological ethics, utilitarianism offers an alternative that provides for the weighing of aggregate policy impacts across diverse elements of society.

A Closer Look at Utilitarianism

Much of the traditional economic perspective on social policy has utilitarianism as its normative base, perhaps because economists prefer to avoid commitment to a particular deontological system and the intrinsic values that obtain. Benefit/cost analysis is a common method of policy analysis that derives from a utilitarian ethical system. Thus it is worthwhile to consider utilitarianism in greater detail. Utilitarianism as a means of social progress in economics was perhaps best articulated by Jeremy Bentham, a younger contemporary of Adam Smith (who professed the "natural utilitarianism" of decentralized market processes). As Beauchamp and Bowie (1979) point out, Bentham was particularly dissatisfied with the legal theories of William Blackstone, which served to justify the British legal system. In particular, Bentham thought that the British system of ranking crimes was wrong because it was based on an "abstract moral theory" rather than on the unhappiness, misery, or disutility a crime caused to other members of society. Thus in Bentham's view the punishments prescribed by law should be proportionate to the disutility created by the crime and not based on notions of intrinsic rightness or morality. In his book *Principles of Morals and Legislation* (1790), Bentham described utility as the principle that approves or disapproves of actions according to their tendency to increase or decrease an individual's pleasure. Bentham was a hedonist and so believed that pleasure is the only intrinsic good or end against which acts are to be evaluated. As W.H. Auden (1962) observed, "pleasure is by no means an infallible critical guide, but it is the least fallible."

While Smith argued in *Wealth of Nations* that in many commercial contexts the social welfare was best met through the invisible hand of the market, Bentham identified conditions in which members of society needed to act collectively to resolve social problems such as disease, waterworks, and so forth. These were rather radical ideas at the time. Bentham's notion of utilitarianism is conceptually very simple: Suppose that each person in society is affected by a set of possible policy options. For each option, the utility gains to those benefiting from the policy, as well as the disutility (utility losses) to those being harmed by the policy, are to be added up to arrive at net social utility. The utilitarian-ethical policy is the one that maximizes net social utility relative to all the other options under consideration. Bentham therefore conceived of what we now call cardinal utility, which means that pain and pleasure can be reduced to a positive or a negative number for each person, and the social engineer can measure these numbers and simply add them up. Therefore, one person's unhappiness with a policy yields a utility number that can be directly compared to the utility number for someone else's happiness. As you can see, the concept of cardinal utility is based on the notion that utility is objectively measurable and comparable across individuals. From a mathematical perspective social utility is computed using something called a *social utility function*. Utilitarian policy analysis calls for the computation of net social utility for each of the new policies under consideration, and the utilitarian-ethical policy option is the one (if any) that generates the largest increase in net social utility relative to the status quo. Note that status quo means "the current way of doing things."

Amartya Sen (1987) reduced utilitarianism to three fundamental elements:

- *Welfarism:* The "goodness" of a proposed rule depends on utility information. In other words, the goodness of a proposed rule is determined by the utility or disutility that it creates among members of society.
- *Sum ranking:* The utility information regarding any proposed rule is

assessed by looking only at the sum total of all the individual utilities associated with the rule. In other words, in evaluating a proposed rule, utilitarianism requires that we add up the utilities and the disutilities that it creates among all members of society.

- *Consequentialism:* Every rule choice must ultimately be evaluated by the goodness of the consequent state of affairs (the "ends" it moves us toward). In other words, under utilitarianism the ethical policy is the one that generates policy outcomes ("ends") that lead to the largest net social utility.

Utilitarianism also allows for the evaluation of efficiency. There are two different efficiency criteria commonly used by economists for evaluating social policy.

The *Pareto efficiency criterion* is named after Vilfredo Pareto, an early economist, and it imposes a stringent requirement for any change from the status quo. As an example, suppose there are five policy alternatives to the status quo being considered. In order to determine whether any of them is Pareto efficient we must evaluate the impacts of each policy alternative on every member of society. If a policy alternative makes any member of society worse off than under the status quo, then that policy alternative is eliminated from further consideration. Continuing our example, suppose that four of the five policy alternatives are eliminated because they make one or more members of society worse off relative to the status quo. Thus there is only one policy alternative that makes some people better off and nobody worse off than under the status quo. This policy alternative is said to be Pareto efficient relative to the status quo.

Unfortunately, few real-world policy alternatives can pass the Pareto criterion since it is so difficult to assure that nobody is made worse off than under the status quo. Because of this, economists consider the Pareto efficiency criterion to be biased toward preserving the status quo. This can create a serious social conflict when many in society see the status quo as being unethical from a deontological perspective. A historically important example is slavery in the United States. Slavery was widely seen in the North as being unethical from a deontological perspective, but a policy alternative of ending slavery would make slave owners worse off than under the status quo, and thus would have failed the Pareto efficiency criterion. These arguments may help you understand why the Pareto efficiency criterion is rarely used in policy analysis.

An alternative approach that is more widely used is simply to rank policy alternatives based on net social utility, as originally conceived by the utilitarians, and to do away with the requirement that nobody be made worse off relative to the status quo. This less rigorous efficiency criterion was proposed by economists Kaldor (1939) and Hicks (1939). Going back to our original example of five policy alternatives to the status quo, we would no longer eliminate four of the five because they made some members of society worse off. Instead, according to the Kaldor-Hicks efficiency criterion, we must compute net social utility (adding up the gains and the losses for each member of society) for each policy alternative to the status quo. The policy alternative that generates the largest gain in net social utility is the Kaldor-Hicks-efficient policy alternative. This also corresponds with the utilitarian-ethical policy alternative.

The Kaldor-Hicks efficiency criterion is sometimes referred to as being potentially Pareto efficient because the potential exists for those made better off under a policy change to compensate those made worse off and thus share the net benefits with all members of society. We actually see crude attempts at this sort of compensation scheme in certain social policies that make some people worse off. For example, consider the Clinton administration's preservation scheme for the northern spotted owl, which limited the harvest of old-growth trees and thus made some local timber-dependent communities in the Pacific Northwest worse off. The Northwest Economic Adjustment Initiative, an element of the Northwest Forest Plan, allocated $1.2 billion in general tax dollars to retrain dislocated workers, assist local businesses, diversify the economy of the region, enhance community infrastructure and technical capacity, and restore watersheds and create short-term jobs through a "Jobs in the Woods" program. If those made worse off under a policy alternative that is Kaldor-Hicks efficient could be fully compensated, then the policy alternative would also satisfy the Pareto efficiency criterion.

As you may have guessed, it is not possible to directly compare one person's level of utility to that of another, and thus to construct a true social utility function as envisioned by the classical utilitarian philosophers. Because of this, economists and others who wish to rank policies based on a utilitarian ethic usually approximate utility and disutility with estimates of monetary benefits and costs. The implicit assumption is that since a dollar is a measure of value in markets, the utility that one person can derive from a dollar (in terms of the available goods and services that can be purchased with the dollar) is the same as that of another. While this is a convenient assumption that allows economists to conduct benefit/cost analysis, there is no reason to believe it is true. In fact, many economists believe that the utility that a person derives from the purchasing power of a dollar declines as the person's income rises. In other words, a dollar creates less of a utility gain to a billionaire than to a homeless mother with a hungry child. We will discuss these and other issues related to benefit/cost analysis in greater detail in chapter 7.

The fundamental economic problem of allocating scarce resources among competing ends exists regardless of whether society subscribes to a deontological or a teleological system of ethics. The dilemma of endangered species protection offers a good illustrative example. The existence of an endangered species is subject to scarcity, since protection and restoration of a species and the habitat it requires involves opportunity costs associated with development activities and alternative uses of protection and restoration funds. In a society that views the existence of a species as being of intrinsic value (deontological ethics), the categorical imperative calls for actions that make at least minimal provision for habitat preservation regardless of cost. The fact that the species is of intrinsic value places its habitat above the value of human appropriation, unless perhaps the development is required to prevent loss of human life (a potentially higher intrinsic value). In a society that views the existence of a species as being subject to a utilitarian calculus, the allocation problem is resolved by benefit/cost analysis, and the opportunity cost is the value of whichever option (species protection or development) yields the next highest net benefits. The difference in cases is not whether an economic problem exists but how that problem is to be resolved.

Self-Interest, the Common Good, and Social Order

One of the central dilemmas that all societies must confront is how to maintain social order and thus balance the sometimes conflicting imperatives of self-interest and the common good. Hobbs (1651, p. 27–28), for example, argued that unless there exists a "common power" to keep people "in awe," the natural state of human society is one of war and conflict:

> Hereby it is manifest that during the time men live without a common power to keep them all in awe, they are in that condition which is called war; and such a war as is of every man against every man.... Whatsoever therefore is consequent to a time of war, where every man is enemy to every man, the same consequent to the time wherein men live without other security than what their own strength and their own invention shall furnish them withal. In such condition there is no place for industry, because the fruit thereof is uncertain: and consequently no culture of the earth; no navigation, nor use of the commodities that may be imported by sea; no commodious building; no instruments of moving and removing such things as require much force; no knowledge of the face of the earth; no account of time; no arts; no letters; no society; and which is worst of all, continual

fear, and danger of violent death; and the life of man, solitary, poor, nasty, brutish, and short.

If we assume for a moment that Hobbs is right, then what is this common power that keeps people in awe and prevents violent and destructive conflict? Some argue that this is the role of religion. As Fukuyama (1999) argues, in Western society, "Christianity first established the principle of the universality of human dignity, a principle that was brought down from the heavens and turned into a secular doctrine of universal human equality by the Enlightenment" (p. 80). Others, such as sociologist Max Weber, argue that social order in an industrialized society must come from the rational bureaucracy of a strong centralized government.

It should be pointed out, however, that self-interest and the common good are not always in conflict, and that war and conflict may not be our natural state. As you will learn in greater detail in chapter 3, Adam Smith argued that self-interested interaction in a well-functioning competitive market will yield outcomes that are consistent with the common good. Moreover, it is argued that many small preindustrial communities around the world were self-organizing and thus did not need external religious or bureaucratic structures.

In the case of social order in modern industrial society, Fukuyama (1999, p. 58) observes:

> The modern liberal state was premised on the notion that in the interests of political peace, government would not take sides among the differing moral claims made by religion and traditional culture. Church and State were to be kept separate; there would be pluralism in opinions about the most important moral and ethical questions, concerning ultimate ends or the nature of the good. Tolerance would become the cardinal virtue; in place of moral consensus would be a transparent framework of law and institutions that produced political order. Such a political system did not require that people be particularly virtuous; they need only be rational and follow the law in their own self-interest.

This transparent framework of law and institutions must be supplemented by at least a minimum level of *social capital.* As we shall discuss in greater detail in chapter 12, social capital, according to Putnam (1993), refers to the features of social organization including networks, norms, and trust that facilitate coordination and cooperation for mutual benefit. Putnam recognized that in regions with high social capital, residents are engaged in public issues, trust one another, make and keep commitments, engage in reciprocity, and obey laws. Social and political institutions tend to be organized horizontally, rather than hierarchically, and solidarity, civic participation, and integrity all tend to be highly valued. Putnam has observed that while social capital seems to be a precondition for economic development and effective government, it tends to be underprovided by private agents. Thus, the culture of individualism that is reinforced by the modern liberal state undermines the shared values and the contribution to social capital that creates social order.

Along the same lines, there have been a number of studies indicating that classroom exposure to the model of the self-interested maximizer in economics affects student and faculty attitudes toward voluntary contributions. Frank, Gilovich, and Regan (1993) analyzed the responses to a questionnaire from 576 college and university professors from a variety of disciplines. Frank and his colleagues found that economists were among the least generous of the group. For example, 9.3 percent of the economics professors gave no money to charity, relative to a range of between 1.1 and 4.2 percent in other surveyed fields. Additional support is offered by the work of Marwell and Ames (1981). In a series of laboratory experiments, Marwell and Ames studied voluntary contributions in a simulated environment in which the contributions are used to create public goods that benefit the group as a whole. Economics students were found to donate less than half as much as students from other disciplines. Finally, Carter and Irons (1991) studied the "ultimatum game," in which one person decides how to share a pool of money with another, and the other person can either accept the allocation or throw away the entire pool of money. Economics majors were far more likely to allocate all but a cent or two to themselves relative to nonmajors, who more commonly split the pool of money equally. These findings are also consistent with those of Kahneman, Knetsh, and Thaler (1986). These studies offer some remarkable evidence that exposure to the model of the self-interested maximizer does indeed encourage self-interested behavior outside the confines of markets where such behavior is most likely to be appropriate.

Private Property

So far, we have discussed different conceptions of ethics, which provide a guide to our relations with others, and of social capital, which serves as the foundation for social order and helps resolve the conflict between self-interest and the common good. Western notions of private property and its origins also provide useful insights into our relationship with one another and with the natural world. The origin and implications of private property rights can be found in the liberal society described by John Locke and the civil society of Jean-Jacques Rousseau and other Enlightenment philosophers. Let's take a moment to consider these two perspectives on the origin and implications of private property.

Locke and the Liberal Society

The liberal society is articulated in John Locke's *Two Treatises on Government* (1690). Locke sees the fundamental goal of society as providing opportunities for people to exercise their talent and effort in the creation of valuable personal property and the well-being that derives from this property. In his conception of private property rights, Locke's Christian cosmology provides as self-evident truth that God gave Earth to man in common. He then sets out to explain that God also gave man the capacity and the imperative to make the best use of God's gift in satisfying man's "support and comfort." Completing the construct, Locke (pp. 77, 81) concludes:

> Every man has a Property in his own Person. . . . The Labor of his Body, and the Work of his Hands, we may say, are properly his. Whatsoever then he removes out of the State that Nature hath provided, and left it in, he hath mixed his Labor with, and joined to it something that is his own, and thereby makes it his Property. It being by him removed from the common state nature placed it in, hath by this Labor something annexed to it, that excluded the common right of other Men. . . . [Y]et there are still *great Tracts of Ground* to be found, which (the Inhabitants thereof not having joyned with the rest of Mankind, in the consent of Use of their common Money) *lie wasts,* and are more than the People, who dwell on it, do, or can make use of, and so still lie in common.

It is interesting to see some of the concepts of what later came to be the U.S. Homestead Act of 1862 articulated in the writings of Locke, such as the requirement in the Homestead Act for "actual settlement and cultivation" in order to patent a claim on otherwise "unappropriated" public land. We also gain insight into our cultural past by reading the argument Locke gives for denying aboriginal people a private property right, which seemingly provided a justification for the taking of aboriginal lands.

Rousseau and the Civil Society

In *Discourse on Inequality* (1755), French philosopher Jean-Jacques Rousseau argued that an early golden age of social cooperation, interdependence, and freedom existed prior to the emplacement of private property regimes that underlie the civil society. From Rousseau's perspective, contemporary civil society, and the private property rights systems that are its foundation, alienate people from nature, lead to greater and greater inequality, and ultimately are responsible for wars and other destructive conflicts. The transformation from the early natural state to contemporary civil society occurred as human enlightenment led to the refinement of skills for the modification of nature. Perhaps following Locke, Rousseau saw the introduction of private property as occurring when a person applied his or her skill to create something of value from nature, such as a hut or shelter. Family societies formed around these dwellings and were bound together by mutual attachment and freedom. Specialization and teamwork in hunting and gathering led in turn to abundant leisure time, which could be filled by the development of tools and other conveniences. This is the point at which Rousseau first sees the evils of civil society, as tools and other conveniences "degenerated into real needs, . . . and men were unhappy to lose them without being happy to possess them" (p. 67).

Rousseau (pp. 70–72) goes on to argue that:

> To the poet it is gold and silver, but to the philosopher it is iron and grain that made men civilized and brought on the downfall of the human race. . . . When men were needed for smelting and forging iron, others had to feed them. . . . Since the artisans required food in exchange for their iron, the others finally found means of using iron to increase the amount of food available. . . . The division of land necessarily followed from its cultivation, and once property had been recognized it gave rise to the first rules of justice. . . . It is work alone that gives a farmer title to the produce of the land he has tilled, and consequently to the land itself. . . . If this possession is continued uninterruptedly from year to year, it is easily transformed into ownership. When the ancients, says Grotius, called Ceres "the lawgiver" and gave the name Thesmaphoria to a festival celebrated in her honor, they implied that the division of land had produced a new kind of right: the right of property, different from that which derives from natural law. . . . Things in this state might have remained equal if abilities had been equal. . . . It is thus that natural inequality [skills, effort, etc.] gradually becomes accentuated by inequalities of exchange, and differences among men, developed by differences in circumstances, became more noticeable and more permanent in their efforts, and begin to influence the fate of individuals in the same proportion.

Rank and position in society, according to Rousseau, are gauged by property and power to coerce others. Freedom was lost, as people became slaves to the social demands for property, leading to "competition and rivalry on the one hand, opposition of interests on the other, and always the hidden desire to profit at the expense of others. All these evils were the first effect of property, and the inseparable accompaniments of incipient inequality" (pp. 72–73).

Society must balance individual liberty against environmental and community integrity. Where a particular society ends up depends on the evolution of its culture, laws, values, and economic, social, religious, and political institutions. All along the spectrum from communal living to libertarian anarchy, there will be economies that are *alike* in that they provide ways of allocating things that are scarce, but which *differ* in how that allocation occurs. Moroever, each ethical system implies its own economic system. Thus, we have Amish and Mennonite communities that have social and religious constraints that limit the scope of market exchange within and outside their communities. Many scarce resources, goods, and services in these communities are allocated in the form of gifts or based on need, and the social structure provides considerable insurance in a nonmarket context. These communities produce much of what they need and so engage in only a limited trade for imports with the greater U.S. economy. In contrast, most U.S. communities have a secular consumer culture, rely much more completely on markets for the exchange of goods and services, and for the provision of insurance, and goods and services are allocated based on willingness to pay. Economies of scale and the extensive use of markets to allocate scarce resources, goods, and services imply that these communities tend to specialize in producing a narrow range of products and engage in extensive trade outside the community to meet their needs and desires. These examples illustrate how economic systems and institutions embody a community's dominant values.

On Positive and Normative Economics

So what is the nature of our economy, and what should we do to change it? In responding to these questions, it is useful to consider an illustrative example. Suppose that policymakers are considering taxing products whose production or consumption generates pollution. Two questions that arise are: (1) what can we expect to be the observable effects of this tax in the short and long term, and (2) should we do it?

Economics has two methodologically distinct branches that speak to these questions. *Positive economics* is a method of analysis based on the Western scientific tradition of modeling the world and then subjecting these models to empirical testing using data from "out there" in the world. A set of best methods for empirical research has evolved that allows for internal and external validation of these models. Consequently, economists can broadly agree on how good a positive economic model is by how well the data support it. Modeling improves through a process of scientific evolution in which weak and falsified models are sloughed off. Thus positive economics seeks to explain the observable. Because the real world is hopelessly more complex than we can ever hope to model comprehensively, a positive analyst must focus on what are thought to be the most important elements of the phenomenon being studied. The selection process by which researchers determine what is important enough to include in their models and what can be ignored is subject to normative interpretation, deriving in part from the culture and the values of the research community, as well as the role of the researcher in that community.

As an example, positive economic analysis might use empirical methods to estimate the impacts of a pollution tax on electricity prices, electricity consumption, and pollution emissions. But what of the myriad other effects of the tax, the values of which are difficult to measure, compare, and agree on? For example, one might argue that the value of protecting personal liberty exceeds the net benefits of remediating pollution. Another might argue that knowingly allowing firms' pollution to harm people without compensation is unethical to such a degree that pollution should be taxed even if the net benefits of remediating pollution are negative. *Normative economics* is about identifying what a person, a firm, or a society *should* do. Note that a *norm* is defined as a rule or an authoritative standard. Economic policy recommendations are a form of *normative analysis,* and such an analysis is how economists would try to answer the second question above.

Economic Questions That All Societies Must Answer

Society's dominant values determine how we answer the *three fundamental economic questions:*

- *What* goods and services are produced, including what "services" we derive from natural resources systems (e.g., wilderness or timber)?
- *How* they are produced, involving issues like technology, pollution, and harvest techniques?
- *Who* gets things, involving issues like the extent to which prices or other factors are used to allocate and whether the rich subsidize the poor?

In the next chapter we will learn about how a pure system of market capitalism answers the three fundamental economic questions.

Summary

- Economics is concerned with finding good ways (oftentimes termed "efficient" ways) of allocating things (e.g., goods, services, resources, time, land, air, and water) that are scarce.

- How we judge the meaning of *good* or *efficient* depends on our value or ethical system(s).
- There are deontological and teleological systems of ethics, among others, and different specific forms within each of these two categories. Such ethical systems underlie all we do in economics, because they provide the basis for ranking alternatives and determining opportunity cost.
- We live in a diverse, pluralistic society in which honorable people subscribe to different ethical perspectives and therefore differ in their perception of what fairness and justice means and thus what the relative value of different things might be.
- A fundamental challenge is to forge durable social policy in the context of this diversity.
- Modern, mainstream, Western-style economics has utilitarianism as its normative base. Utilitarianism as a normative underpinning is not *required* of economic systems, however. Economic systems built on natural law ethical underpinnings were quite common in the Middle Ages in Europe and likely in village economies in many primary societies.
- Social capital forms the foundation for social order and the capacity to resolve conflicts between self-interest and the common good. A culture of self-interested individualism is promoted by market capitalism and democracy, and yet this culture can undermine the structure of social capital.
- Positive economics is concerned with using scientific methods to describe the world around us, while normative economics is concerned with articulating what we should do.
- The three fundamental economic questions that all economies must answer are what to produce, how to produce, and for whom to produce.

Review Questions and Problems

1. The Endangered Species Act calls for the protection and recovery of listed species independent of cost. It has been argued that the act needs to be modified to incorporate benefit/cost analysis.

    a. Describe the ethical conflict at the heart of this debate.
    b. Is benefit/cost testing of species protection necessary for the act to be economically rational, or is this an argument based in utilitarian as opposed to deontological ethics?

2. How do you think the three economic questions would be answered in a pure market system of allocation? Be precise. How do you think the three economic questions would be answered in a commune? What are

some of the advantages and the disadvantages of these two economic systems?

3. Classroom debate activity: Debate consists of reasoned arguments for or against a given proposition. Form two groups in your class (affirmative and negative) for the purpose of debating the following proposition: *Resolved: All social policy should be utilitarian-ethical.* Members of each group should be given a week or so to research the issues. The debate will occur in a panel, moderated by your professor. Two members of each group will serve as panelists, and any additional group members can serve as researchers. There are a variety of different ways to structure a debate, one of which is the Michigan cross-examination method:

    a. The first affirmative panelist presents the affirmative case (6 minutes).

    b. The first affirmative panelist is cross-examined by the second negative panelist (4 minutes).

    c. Questions from the audience are put to the members of the affirmative team (5 minutes).

    d. The first negative panelist presents the negative case (6 minutes).

    e. The second affirmative panelist cross-examines the first negative panelist (4 minutes).

    f. Questions from the audience are put to the members of the negative team (5 minutes).

    g. The second negative panelist summarizes the negative case (2 minutes).

    h. The second affirmative panelist summarizes the affirmative case (2 minutes).

4. In his book *Moral Sentiments,* Adam Smith (1759; p. 25) says: "And hence it is, that to feel much for others and little for ourselves, that to restrain our selfish, and to indulge our benevolent affections, constitutes the perfection of human nature." Compare that statement to this famous quote from Smith's *Wealth of Nations:* "by directing that industry in such a manner as its produce may be of the greatest value, he intends only his own gain, and he is in this, as in many other cases, led by an invisible hand to promote an end which was no part of his intention. . . . By pursuing his own interest he frequently promotes that of the society more effectually than when he really intends to promote it. I have never known much good done by those who affected to trade for the public good." Can you reconcile these two statements from Smith? For example, is Smith suggesting that the morality of self-interest depends on the context, or that the ends (the public good) justify the means? As a take-home assignment you can read both books on-line at the Internet link below.

Internet Links

Internet Classics Archive (http://classics.mit.edu/Browse/index.html): Free on-line classic texts, primarily of Greco-Roman origin.

McMaster University Archive for the History of Economic Thought (www.economics.mcmaster.ca/ugcm/3113/): Free full-text books on the Internet by authors such as Aristotle, Locke, Ricardo, Rousseau, and Smith who wrote about economics. This is a good place to get primary source material.

References and Further Reading

Aristotle. 1984. *The Nicomachean Ethics.* In *The Complete Works of Aristotle,* ed. J. Barnes. Princeton, NJ: Princeton University Press.

Auden, W.H. 1962. *The Dyer's Hand, and Other Essays by W.H. Auden.* New York: Random House.

Beauchamp, T., and N. Bowie. 1979. *Ethical Theory and Business.* Englewood Cliffs, NJ: Prentice Hall.

Bentham, J. 1790. *An Introduction to the Principles of Morals and Legislation.* Oxford: Clarendon Press.

Carter, J., and M. Irons. 1991. "Are Economists Different, and If So, Why?" *Journal of Economic Perspectives* 5 (Spring): 171–77.

Devall, B. 1988. *Simple in Means, Rich in Ends.* Salt Lake City: Peregrine Smith.

Devall, B., and G. Sessions. 1985. *Deep Ecology: Living As If Nature Mattered.* Salt Lake City: Peregrine Smith.

Ekelund, R., and R. Hebert. 1983. *A History of Economic Theory and Method.* 2nd ed. New York: McGraw-Hill.

Frank, R., T. Gilovich, and D. Regan. 1993. "Does Studying Economics Inhibit Cooperation?" *Journal of Economic Perspectives* 7 (Spring): 159–72.

Fukuyama, F. 1999. "The Great Disruption: Human Nature and the Reconstitution of Social Order." *Atlantic Monthly* 283: 55–80.

Hicks, J. 1939. "The Foundations of Welfare Economics." *Economic Journal* 49: 696.

Hobbs, T. 1651. *Leviathan.* Reprinted in *Leviathan / Thomas Hobbes,* ed. R. Tuck. New York: Cambridge University Press, 1991.

Kahneman, D., J. Knetsch, and R. Thaler. 1986. "Fairness and the Assumptions of Economics." *Journal of Business* 59 (October, part 2): s285–s300.

Kaldor, N. 1939. "Welfare Propositions in Economics." *Economic Journal* 49: 549.

Kant, I. 1785. "The Categorical Imperative." In *Foundations of the Metaphysics of Morals,* tr. Lewis Beck. Upper Saddle River, NJ: Prentice Hall, 1959. Reprinted in *Thinking About the Environment,* ed. M. Cahn and R. O'Brien. Armonk, NY: M.E. Sharpe, 1996.

Locke, J. 1690. *Two Treatises on Government.* Reprinted in *Thinking About the Environment: Readings on Politics, Property, and the Physical World,* ed. M. Cahn and R. O'Brien. Armonk, NY: M.E. Sharpe, 1996.

Marwell, G., and R. Ames. 1981. "Economists Free Ride, Does Anyone Else? Experiments on the Provision of Public Goods, IV." *Journal of Public Economics* 15 (June): 295–310.

O'Brien, R. 1996. "Law, Property, and the Environment: An Introduction." In *Thinking about the Environment: Readings on Politics, Property, and the Physical World,* ed. M. Cahn and R. O'Brien. Armonk, NY: M.E. Sharpe.

Piderit, J. 1993. *The Ethical Foundations of Economics.* Washington, DC: Georgetown University Press.

Putnam, R. 1993. *Making Democracy Work: Civic Traditions in Modern Italy.* Princeton, NJ: Princeton University Press.

Rawls, J. 1971. *A Theory of Justice.* Cambridge: Harvard University Press.

Rousseau, J-J. 1755. *Discourse on the Origin and Foundation of Inequality Among Mankind.* Reprinted in *Thinking about the Environment: Readings on Politics, Property, and the Physical World,* ed. M. Cahn and R. O'Brien. Armonk, NY: M.E. Sharpe, 1996.

Sen, A. 1987. *On Ethics and Economics.* New York: Basil Blackwell.

Smith, A., 1759. *The Theory of Moral Sentiments.* London: A. Millar.

Yezer, A., R. Goldfarb, and P. Poppen. 1996. "Does Studying Economics Discourage Cooperation? Watch What We Do, Not What We Say or How We Play." *Journal of Economic Perspectives* 10 (Winter): 177–86.uu/

3

The Economics of
Market Allocation

Introduction

In this chapter, we will learn the fundamentals of neoclassical market microeconomics, with particular attention to the conditions that are required for the existence of a well-functioning competitive market. In the process, we will develop a model of supply and demand. We will also learn what it means to say that this market will efficiently allocate scarce resources in equilibrium. The conditions required for such a market to function may fail to hold, however, and so we will find out how markets are distorted and efficiency is impaired by these market failures. This basic understanding of market economics will then form the analytical framework for the chapter that follows, which reviews the theory of externalities and forms the economic argument for environmental regulations.

Market Capitalism

Market capitalism is a socioeconomic system in which scarce resources (and the goods and services into which they are transformed) are allocated by way of a complete set of *decentralized markets*. As used here, the term *decentralized* means that systemwide resource allocation occurs because of many individual market transactions, each of which is guided by self-interest. Adam Smith's famous "invisible hand" of the market refers to the remarkable outcome of efficient systemwide resource allocation that results from individual self-interest rather than the "visible hand" of socialist systems in which allocation decisions are made by centralized planners at some level of community or government control. While in all systems other than slave states, individuals own their own labor, under capitalism individuals rather than governments or collectives also own the other factors of production—land and capital. Thus the three economic questions identified in chapter 2—(1) what to produce, (2) how to produce, and (3) for whom goods and services are produced—are answered under capitalism by (1) goods and services demanded by the consumer, (2) using the least-cost production technology, and (3) those consumers with the willingness to pay. A central tenet of neoclassical microeconomic theory is that a well-functioning competitive market in equilibrium is efficient. This result serves as the theoretical foundation for normative arguments about the merits of the market system of allocation. But what conditions must be met in order to have a well-functioning competitive market?

Conditions Required for a Well-Functioning Competitive Market

A *well-functioning competitive market* has the following properties:

- There are well-defined and enforceable *property rights* that characterize the ownership of resources, goods, and services (described in detail in chapter 4).
- There is a functioning *market* institution that is made up of the various rules governing how buyers and sellers interact, particularly how price and other terms of trade are set. Examples range from ascending price art or livestock auctions to posted prices at grocery stores.
- There are large numbers of buyers and sellers, each of which is small relative to the overall market. Consequently, no individual buyer or seller has *market power*—the capacity to affect market price by manipulating the quantity they purchase or sell.
- Buyers and sellers are unable to *collude* and form organizations (e.g., *cartels*) that can affect market price by coordinating member firms' collective purchase or sales quantities.
- There are no positive or negative *externalities* (described below and in chapter 4).
- There is the potential for low-cost entry by new sellers or buyers, which further limits the potential for market power by incumbent firms. Exiting the market (e.g., "going out of business") can occur at low cost due to production equipment and other capital having a high salvage value, which reduces the risk of entering the market.
- *Transaction costs,* such as legal fees, taxes, or regulatory costs that must

be paid before an economic exchange is transacted, are sufficiently low that they do not choke off mutually satisfactory transactions.

- Information on characteristics such as the quality, availability, pricing, and location of goods and services is available at low cost to market participants.

There are probably no real-world markets that perfectly satisfy these requirements. It has sometimes been argued that certain agricultural and natural resource commodity markets come closest. *Market failure* occurs when one or more of the above conditions for a well-functioning competitive market are not met in a substantial way. We will discuss this in detail below. Before we address market failure, however, we need to consider the concepts of market demand and supply, equilibrium, and efficiency.

Market Demand and Supply

Markets are made up of a number of buyers and sellers trading a particular type of good or service, and an institution governing how buyers and sellers communicate and trade. Let's assume for now that all the conditions are met for a well-functioning competitive market. Below we will develop the theory of demand and short-run supply. If you have already been exposed to these ideas in a microeconomic theory course, you may want to skip ahead.

Market Demand

In neoclassical microeconomic theory, demand originates from a set of buyers known as *consumers* who are assumed to have the objective of maximizing their overall level of satisfaction, or utility, but are constrained in this endeavor by their budget and by market prices. In other words, each consumer tries to get as much utility as possible given his limited budget and the market prices for various alternative goods and services. Each unit of each good or service provides the consumer with an increment of utility known as *marginal utility*. For example, in economic jargon the satisfaction one gets from eating a slice of pizza represents the marginal utility from that slice of pizza. Economists assume that when more than one unit of a good is consumed in a reasonably short period, the marginal utility of each successive unit consumed will decline. This phenomenon is referred to as the *Law of Diminishing Marginal Utility*. Continuing our pizza example, if several slices of pizza are eaten for dinner, the second slice will provide less marginal utility than the first, and the third slice will provide less marginal utility than the second. Can you think of any circumstances

Table 3.1

Hypothetical Example of a Consumer's Marginal Utility from Successive Quantities of Different Lunchtime Meal Alternatives

Quantity consumed per week	Marginal Utility			
	Pizza slice	Sub	Egg roll	Burrito
1	8	28	18	24
2	7	26	16	22
3	6	24	14	20
4	5	22	12	18
5	4	20	10	16
6	3	18	8	12
7	2	8	6	6
8	1	4	4	4
9	0.5	2	2	1

where marginal utility would continuously increase rather than decrease as more and more is consumed?

In the simplest version of the economic model of consumer choice, consumers are assumed to be fully informed of the marginal utility and the price of each unit of all the various goods and services available to them, and fully expend their budget during the time under consideration. As utility maximizers constrained by a limited budget, consumers make successive purchase decisions that generate the largest marginal utility per dollar spent. This should make sense, since if one were to add up the marginal utility from these purchases, the result would be the largest possible total utility that could be gained from the total expended budget. For example, consider the marginal utility that one might get from different quantities of various lunch alternatives during a typical week, as shown in Table 3.1. One can see that this hypothetical consumer experiences diminishing marginal utility for each lunch alternative. If each menu item costs $4, and the consumer has a budget of $24 per week to spend on eating out at lunch, what combination of lunchtime meals will maximize her utility given her $24 budget?

Recall that as utility maximizers, consumers will make successive purchase decisions that generate the largest marginal utility per dollar spent. Since each menu item costs $4, one can simply divide each marginal utility figure in Table 3.1 by $4 to get marginal utility per dollar spent. Our consumer's first choice will be to buy a sub, which generates 7 units ("utils") of utility per dollar spent. After eating the sub, say on Monday, what will be her choice on Tuesday? In this case, she will buy another sub, as the second sub of the week generates 6.5 units of utility per dollar spent. On Wednesday, she is indifferent between her third sub of the week and her first burrito, so suppose that she flips a coin and buys her third sub of the week, and her first burrito of the week on Thursday. Likewise, on Friday and Saturday she will buy her second burrito of the week and her fourth sub of the week. After having had six lunches out this week she has spent all of her weekly lunch budget and has purchased four subs and two burritos, which generated 146 units of total utility for her this week. Could you have her purchase a different combination of lunchtime meals and get more than 146 units of utility for her $24?

Now let's suppose that the following week our consumer has the same marginal utility for different quantities of various lunch alternatives as shown in Table 3.1, and has another $24 to spend, but the burrito stand has reduced the price of burritos to $2. How will this lower price affect our consumer's utility-maximizing choice of lunchtime meals? First we need to recompute marginal utility per dollar spent. Since pizza slices, subs, and egg rolls are still $4 each, then just as before we divide these marginal utility numbers by $4. Since burritos are now $2 each, however, we divide the marginal utility numbers for burritos by $2, thereby doubling the marginal utility per dollar spent relative to when burritos were $4 each. Following the consumer choice procedure that we used before, we find that our consumer will be eating more food than the previous week. In particular, this week she will start out by buying five burritos (say, for example, two on Monday, two on Tuesday, and one on Wednesday), then buy three subs (say, for example, one each on Thursday, Friday, and Saturday), and then go back to the burrito stand and buy her sixth burrito of the week (say on Sunday). Therefore, when the price of burritos decreased from $4 to $2, our consumer increased her weekly burrito purchases from two to six.

This example illustrates a number of important points related to consumer demand. Notice that as the price of burritos declined, the number of burritos eaten per week by the consumer increased. Usually there is an inverse relationship between the price of a good or service and the *quantity demanded* by consumers. This inverse relationship price and quantity demanded is so common that economists refer to it as the *Law of Demand*. Consider a diagram with price on the vertical axis and weekly quantity on the horizontal axis. In this diagram we can draw two points, one indicating a price of $4 and a quantity demanded of burritos, and another indicating a price of $2 and a quantity demanded of burritos. If we were to draw a line connecting these two points, we would have estimated this consumer's *demand curve* for burritos, as shown in Figure 3.1. Each point on this demand curve represents the maximum amount of money the consumer is *willing to pay* for the indicated quantity of burritos.

The demand curve in Figure 3.1 shows the relationship between price

Figure 3.1   **Individual Consumer Demand for Burritos**

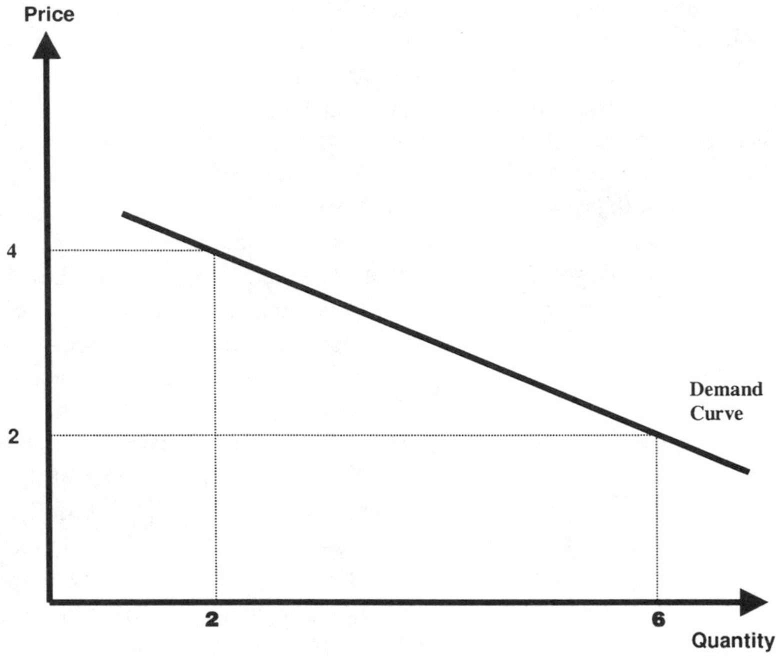

of burritos and the quantity of burritos demanded by the individual consumer, assuming that the consumer's budget, meal preferences, and the
price of the various menu items all remain unchanged. If the consumer's
budget, her preferences for various meal alternatives, or the price of other
lunch foods were to change, then her consumer choice behavior would
also change, resulting in an entirely new demand curve. For example, suppose that her budget or the price of one or more of the other foods were to
increase. Then normally we would expect that her demand for burritos
would increase, which would be illustrated by a new demand curve drawn
to the right of the old demand curve in Figure 3.1. In other words, for a
given burrito price, her quantity of burritos demanded would increase. The
reverse is also true—if her budget or the price of one or more of the other
menu items were to decrease, then we would normally expect to see her
demand for burritos decrease.

   There are many consumers who go out to eat at lunch, many of whom
have a demand curve for burritos. If we were to add up the quantity of burritos
demanded by all consumers at each price, we would get the market demand
curve for burritos. Therefore, the market demand for burritos will increase if
there are more consumers who like to eat burritos.

Market Supply

Sellers are assumed to be firms that have the objective of maximizing profit in neoclassical microeconomics. Analogous to demand, a *supply curve* is a graphical relationship between price and quantity supplied. We will be focusing on production in the economic *short run,* the time period for a firm during which one or more inputs, usually land or capital, are fixed. For example, capital is fixed over the time period of an equipment or office space lease. Likewise, land is fixed over the growing season once it is planted with a crop. In order to understand supply in the short run, we first need to look at a firm's short-run production and short-run cost. Note that the appendix to this chapter provides a simple calculus treatment of marginal cost and supply.

The *Law of Diminishing Marginal Returns* characterizes production in the short run. This law states that as more and more of a variable input is added to a fixed input, the *marginal productivity* of each successive unit of variable input will eventually become smaller. For example, each new worker hired (variable input) to work in a restaurant kitchen (fixed input) will result in increased production of food (the marginal product of labor), as shown in Table 3.2. The Law of Diminishing Marginal Returns indicates that each successive kitchen worker hired will result in smaller and smaller increases in food production. In fact, it is possible that marginal productivity could eventually become zero or negative if the kitchen gets too crowded. Would a profit-maximizing restaurant knowingly hire additional workers if the marginal product of those additional workers were zero or negative?

Now let's introduce cost. Suppose that each worker generates $100 per day in wages and employment benefits, and each unit of food produced can be sold at a price of $5. In this case each unit of food sold generates *marginal revenue* of $5. It is usually the case that marginal revenue is equal to the product's sales price in competitive markets. This is because the seller is a price taker and is unable to affect market price by varying the level of product sold. To keep the example simple, if unrealistic, we will assume that labor is the only cost associated with producing food at the restaurant. *Marginal cost* is equal to the change in total cost caused by an incremental change in output. Marginal cost tells us how much total cost increases when we increase the quantity of output by one unit. In our simplified example, where an increase in food output is generated by hiring another kitchen worker, marginal cost is found by dividing the $100 of additional daily labor cost for the new worker by the marginal product of this new worker. How many workers would be optimal for a profit-maximizing restaurant to hire? Economists use the method of *marginal analysis*

Table 3.2

Hypothetical Example of Restaurant Production in the Short Run

Workers per day	Marginal product of labor	Total product
1	30	30
2	28	58
3	26	84
4	24	108
5	22	130
6	20	150
7	18	168
8	16	184
9	14	198
10	12	210

Table 3.3

Hypothetical Example of Daily Production, Cost, and Profit

Number of workers	Marginal product of labor	Total output	Marginal cost	Total cost	Marginal revenue (price)	Total revenue	Profit (total revenue – total cost)
1	30	30	3.33	100	5	150	50
2	28	58	3.57	200	5	290	90
3	26	84	3.85	300	5	420	120
4	24	108	4.17	400	5	540	140
5	22	130	4.55	500	5	650	150
6	20	150	5	600	5	750	150
7	18	168	5.56	700	5	840	140
8	16	184	6.25	800	5	920	120
9	14	198	7.14	900	5	990	90
10	12	210	8.33	1000	5	1050	50

Note: Marginal cost is the change in total cost divided by marginal product. We assume here that each worker is paid $100 per day, there are no other production costs, and each unit of marginal product (units of food) is sold at a price of $5.

in these sorts of problems. Perhaps it is easiest to understand by starting with no kitchen workers, then successively increasing the kitchen staff by one worker, and then comparing marginal revenue (price) and marginal cost, as shown in Table 3.3.

The first kitchen worker hired generates 30 additional units of food per day. Marginal cost is equal to the change in total cost ($100 for the worker) divided by the first worker's marginal product (30 units of food), or $3.33 per unit of food. Marginal revenue is equal to $5 (the price per unit of food).

Table 3.4

Hypothetical Example of Daily Production, Cost, and Profit When Menu Price Increases

Number of workers	Marginal product of labor	Total output	Marginal cost	Total cost	Marginal revenue (price)	Total revenue	Profit (total revenue − total cost)
1	30	30	3.33	100	6.25	187.50	87.50
2	28	58	3.57	200	6.25	362.50	162.50
3	26	84	3.85	300	6.25	525	225
4	24	108	4.17	400	6.25	675	275
5	22	130	4.55	500	6.25	812.50	312.50
6	20	150	5	600	6.25	937.50	337.50
7	18	168	5.56	700	6.25	1050	350
8	16	184	6.25	800	6.25	1150	350
9	14	198	7.14	900	6.25	1237.50	337.50
10	12	210	8.33	1000	6.25	1312.50	312.50

Note: Marginal cost is the change in total cost divided by marginal product. We assume here that each worker is paid $100 per day, there are no other production costs, and each unit of marginal product (units of food) is sold at a price of $6.25.

Since marginal revenue is greater than marginal cost, it is profitable to hire the first kitchen worker. Would profit increase if a second kitchen worker is added? The marginal product of the second worker is 28, implying that the marginal cost of producing an additional unit of food when the second worker is hired is equal to $100/28 = $3.57. Since marginal revenue ($5) again exceeds marginal cost ($3.57), profits are increased when a second worker is hired. Marginal analysis suggests that profits will be the maximum possible when you stop adding new workers where marginal revenue equals marginal cost. In our example, profit is maximized at an output of 150 units of food, which occurs when six workers are employed.

Now suppose that the price per unit of food increased to $6.25. How would this change the restaurant's profit-maximizing level of food output? First, note that the only things that change are price, marginal and total revenue, and profit, as shown in Table 3.4. Following the same marginal analysis procedure, we find that eight kitchen workers will result in 184 units of food produced per day, which maximizes profit. Thus, an increase in the price of food results in an increase in the quantity of food supplied by the restaurant. *Under competitive market conditions where sellers are price takers, firms supply along their marginal cost curve.* In other words, we have shown that a firm's profit-maximizing output level occurs where price equals marginal cost. When price rises, profit-maximizing firms respond by

Figure 3.2   **A Competitive Firm's Marginal Cost Curve Is Also Its
Short-Run Supply Curve**

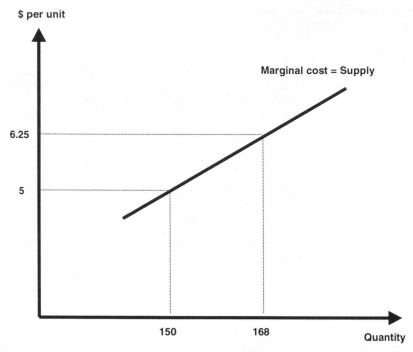

increasing their output level. Higher prices are required to overcome rising marginal costs, which in turn occur due to the Law of Diminishing Marginal Returns. Since a supply curve shows the relationship between price and quantity supplied, the firm's supply curve is its marginal cost curve, as illustrated in Figure 3.2.

An increase in marginal cost, which might occur due to higher labor costs, will cause the firm's supply curve to shift inward to the left, which is known as a decrease in supply. Likewise, a decrease in marginal cost, which might occur due to lower labor costs, will cause the firm's supply curve to shift outward to the right, which is known as an increase in supply. In chapter 4 we will look at how supply is affected when firms are able to reduce their marginal costs by using cheaper, polluting production methods. In our supply example, we can assume that there are many restaurants, each of which has a supply curve for prepared food. If we were to add up the quantity of food supplied by all restaurants at each price per unit of food, we would get the market supply curve for the type of restaurant meal. Therefore, the market supply of this food will increase if new restaurants open in the same area.

Figure 3.3 **Supply and Demand**

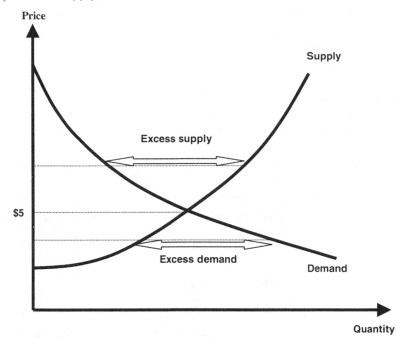

Market Equilibrium and Efficiency

We have determined that utility, product prices, and limited consumer budgets determine consumer demand for goods and services. We have also determined that profit-maximizing firms in a competitive market supply along their short-run marginal cost curves. We also learned that market demand is found by horizontally summing all consumers' quantity demanded associated with each price, and that market supply is found by horizontally summing all firms' quantity supplied associated with each price. We will now address the concept of equilibrium in a well-functioning competitive market, and how resources are efficiently allocated in equilibrium.

Market Equilibrium

Consider the supply and demand curves shown in Figure 3.3. If you like, you can consider this a well-functioning competitive market for a particular type of lunchtime meal. Note that at a price above $5, there is an *excess supply,* meaning that quantity supplied exceeds quantity demanded. When there is excess supply, market forces lead to a reduction in price. For example, if a retailer overestimated demand for a new line of clothing, then unsold inventory would result unless price were reduced, perhaps through a clearance sale. In contrast, at a price below $5, there is an *excess demand,* meaning that quantity demanded exceeds quantity supplied. When there is excess demand, market forces lead to an increase in price. For example, if a retailer or manufacturer underestimated demand for a new toy, then quantity demanded would far outstrip quantity supplied unless price was increased.

Market equilibrium occurs at a price where the quantity supplied by sellers equals the quantity demanded by consumers. Because quantity supplied equals quantity demanded, there is neither excess supply nor excess demand. This state of affairs is referred to as an equilibrium because the price and the volume of trade will stay the same over time until some factor influencing buyer or seller market behavior changes, which will then necessitate a period of adjustment as price seeks its new equilibrium level. If markets are frequently buffeted by shifts in buyer or seller behavior, price may be nearly continuously shifting.

Efficient Resource Allocation

The generic definition of *efficiency* is the condition of producing something beneficial or valuable with a minimization of waste. There are many different ways that the word "efficient" is used, such as fuel-efficient, time-efficient, and Pareto-efficient, and this multitude of different ways of specifying efficiency can be confusing. For example, mutually satisfactory market transactions, such as those that occur in well-functioning competitive markets, satisfy the Pareto criterion compared to the status quo of no trade. Can you explain why?

The concept of efficient resource allocation ultimately rests on how we measure the welfare of market participants. Buyers have a maximum price they are willing to pay for a given quantity of the good, as represented by points along their demand curve, and receive a gain from trade called *consumer surplus* when their willingness-to-pay value is larger than the price they had to pay. When people "get a bargain" at an auction or a garage sale, they are experiencing consumer surplus. Since the market demand curve represents the willingness-to-pay values of all the buyers in the market, total consumer surplus is approximated by the area in Figure 3.4 between the demand curve and market price. To be technically correct, an exact measure of consumer surplus requires an income-compensated demand curve. Exploration of this technical issue goes beyond the scope of this textbook, but interested readers are encouraged to pursue the topic in most any intermediate microeconomic theory textbook.

Figure 3.4 **Consumer and Producer Surplus**

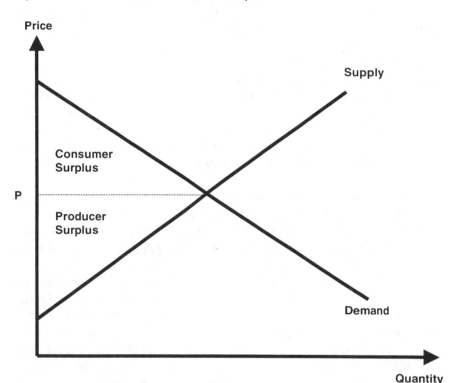

Sellers receive a symmetrical gain from trade, called *producer surplus,* when market price exceeds those costs that must be covered to make a sale worthwhile. Producer surplus is the area in Figure 3.4 between the supply curve and market price. Producer surplus is essentially profit to the producer before fixed costs are taken into account. The sum of consumer and producer surplus is referred to as *total surplus,* or the total *gain from trade* in this market. We measure the overall *welfare* of the market participants based on total surplus.

Now we are going to develop the important concept of a well-functioning competitive market being efficient. In the context of market analysis, *resources are efficiency allocated* when the welfare of the market participants (as measured by total surplus) is maximized. In other words, resources are efficiently allocated when market participants receive the maximum possible gains from trade. Resources are efficiently allocated at the equilibrium market price because in a well-functioning competitive market there is neither excess supply nor excess demand, and so there are neither too many nor too few units of the good or service produced. If price were above the equilibrium level, we would have excess supply, and so the amount actually traded (equal to quantity demanded) would be less than the quantity traded at the equilibrium price, thereby reducing total surplus. If price were below the equilibrium level, we would have excess demand (also known as a shortage), and so the amount traded (equal to quantity supplied) would be less than the quantity traded at the equilibrium price, thereby reducing total gains from trade (total surplus). As a result, when there is either excess supply or excess demand, some mutually satisfactory transactions are prevented from occurring that would have generated consumer and producer surplus, which is why nonequilibrium prices are inefficient.

While there is a tendency to ignore the functioning of markets, or to take them for granted, Hayek (1937, 1945) focused attention on the fact that the price system in competitive markets provides a unique means of conveying and exploiting information. While Adam Smith argued that the self-interested interaction of many buyers and sellers results in efficient production and allocation, Hayek went further by observing that markets are the only way of bringing together the widely dispersed information necessary for efficient production and allocation. Hayek said that the reason why centrally planned socialist systems have such great difficulties is that they require the central planners to embody all the information held by producers and consumers in markets. In setting prices and quantities, and in choosing technologies and levels of employment, the central planner must somehow know the willingness-to-pay of all consumers, the production costs of all sellers, and the most efficient means of organizing production. Planners must also know how to adjust prices and quantities in response to external factors such as fluctuations in the price of substitutes, consumer income, input price changes, regulatory impacts, new technologies, changes in the workforce, and weather. The appropriate adjustment to prices, quantities, and methods of production relies upon the knowledge held by large numbers of independent consumers and producers, and according to Hayek, it is not possible for central planners to gather, process, and act upon this dispersed knowledge. According to this view, prices, quantities, and methods of production will reflect dispersed information only when they are determined in competitive markets.

Unfortunately, the conditions required for efficient markets are not always met. For example, if consumers are misled by exaggerated quality claims, then demand for the good is overstated, leading to excessive consumption and negative gains from trade for those who later realize that their willingness to pay based on actual quality is less than the price they paid. If sellers can shift costs to society as a whole by polluting rather than paying for cleanup, then (as we will learn in chapter 4) the market supply curve will be shifted out to the right and excessive consumption occurs. In either case, the market's failure to integrate knowledge is not so different from the failings of Hayek's central planners. When markets fail to be efficient, there is an economic argument for some form of government intervention, such as regulation.

Market Failure

Most markets are less than perfectly efficient. When these inefficiencies are substantial, we refer to such a state as a *market failure.* Let's consider some of the possible sources of market failure.

Monopoly, Cartels, and Market Power

A *monopoly* exists when there is a single seller in a market. A *cartel* is a group of colluding sellers that collectively act like a monopolist. Competition fails under either of these conditions. In order to raise price and profit, a monopolist or a cartel will need to reduce output from the competitive level. This can be more difficult for cartels because the reduction in output must be coordinated among all cartel members. If a monopolist or a cartel is successful in reducing output relative to the competitive equilibrium level, price will rise along the demand curve. Since price rises, monopolists and cartel members are able to transform some consumer surplus into producer surplus. Since output must be reduced in order for price to rise above competitive levels, the decline in output implies that some mutually satisfactory transactions that produce consumer and producer surplus do not occur. By how much will monopolists and cartels reduce output relative to competitive levels? A point will eventually be reached beyond which the producer surplus lost from further reducing output will outweigh the producer surplus gained from the resulting increase in price. Because monopolies and cartels produce less than the competitive equilibrium level of output, resources are not efficiently allocated in the market (too small a quantity is produced), and the sum of producer and consumer surplus is less than in the competitive equilibrium. In addition, from an equity or fairness perspective, monopolized or cartelized markets give undue power to the sellers. The government intervention in the United States occurs by way of state and federal *antitrust laws,* which provide criminal and civil sanctions for monopolized or cartelized markets.

Externalities

As we shall discuss in detail in chapter 4, *externalities* are unpaid-for benefits or uncompensated costs that impact society as a by-product of production and exchange. The term *externality* refers to the fact that these benefits or costs are not reflected in market demand and supply. *Positive externalities* are external benefits generated from production and exchange and enjoyed without payment by members of society. An example would be the benefits received by neighbors when homeowners beautify their yards and adjoining roads and sidewalks. Since those who benefit from positive externalities do not pay for them, their willingness-to-pay is not included in market demand, and accordingly market demand is too small. In the example given above, the market for landscaping materials and services will produce an inefficiently small quantity because the external benefits enjoyed by the neighbors are not reflected in market demand. Other examples of positive externalities include the external benefits from vaccinations for infectious disease (reduced likelihood of epidemic), the external benefits from literacy and education in a democratic society (more informed voting and civic participation), and the external benefits from land stewardship practiced by farmers, ranchers, and timberland owners (reduced likelihood of flooding, improved groundwater quality, open space, etc.). In each case the buyers in the market receive private benefits, but there are also external benefits that are not included in the market, which is why an inefficiently small quantity is produced by the market.

Negative externalities are external costs generated from production and exchange and borne without compensation by members of society. The prime example is pollution generated as a by-product of producing electricity. Profit-maximizing firms in otherwise well-functioning competitive markets have an incentive to pollute if doing so allows them to reduce their own costs and thus raise their profits. As will be explored in detail in chapter 4, since firms that emit external costs do not have to pay these costs, the market supply curve is too large, and too large a quantity is produced in the market. In the example given above, the market for electricity will produce an inefficiently large quantity of electricity because the external costs borne by people and the environment are not reflected in market supply. Consequently, even well-functioning competitive markets can be inefficient when there are substantial pollution externalities.

Government intervention for positive externalities takes the form of a subsidy to consumers (or producers). For example, a city or county government might provide subsidized vaccinations for infectious disease, provide free or subsidized education, and use tax dollars to purchase conservation easements to subsidize appropriate land stewardship from farmers, ranchers, and timberland owners. In the case of negative externalities, government regulations take the form of state and federal environmental regulations that impose criminal and civil penalties, taxes, or outright bans on polluters.

Common-Pool Resources and Public Goods: Collectively Produced and/or Consumed Goods

Some goods and services have the characteristic that individual property rights are not assigned, and so they are collectively produced and/or consumed. Examples include parks, highways, emergency services, marine fisheries, rivers, groundwater basins, air, public radio, wilderness areas, and recreation sites. The two categories of collectively consumed goods that are relevant to this book are *common-pool resources* and *public goods*. A common-pool resource (CPR) is distinguished by the characteristics that (1) it is difficult to exclude multiple individuals who appropriate from the resource stock, and (2) the resource features rivalry in consumption or subtractability, meaning that resource units appropriated by one subtract from what is available to others. In contrast, while it is difficult to exclude multiple individuals who benefit from public goods, these goods differ from CPRs in that they lack rivalry in consumption. Thus a coastal fishery is a CPR because fish are harvested by one subtract from what is available to others at a given point in time, while public television broadcasts are public goods because one person's reception of the broadcast does not subtract from what is available to other viewers.

These goods tend to be underproduced and/or overconsumed when they are allocated in markets. For human-made goods that are collectively consumed, such as public radio and television, self-interested individuals have an incentive to *free ride* on the provision efforts of others. Since few are willing to pay for something that they believe will be provided by others, market demand for these goods and services is far too low, leading to an inefficiently small quantity provided in markets. How many of us listen to public radio or watch public television, but rely on others to support it? Because the inputs that people provide, such as effort or financial contributions, are privately owned, while the output is collectively consumed, provision of the good is a positive externality and thus is underprovided in market systems. If the benefits flowing to free riders were included in the market, such as through compulsory taxes or user fees, market demand would shift out, and a larger equilibrium quantity would result. Thus, free riding leads to an inefficiently low quantity provided through the market. Appropriate government intervention may be public provision by way of taxes or compulsory user fees, such as the use of taxes to fund the Corporation for Public Broadcasting.

While the problem of underprovision affects both CPRs and public goods, the problem of overconsumption is specific to CPRs. Those who appropriate from CPRs such as ocean fisheries, oil fields, groundwater basins, and congested roads and public parks have an incentive to overuse the good, which can lead to deterioration unless rule systems are put into place to limit use. This process is sometimes known as the *tragedy of the commons*. At the heart of the tragedy of the commons is an *appropriation externality,* where an individual's appropriation activity yields benefits to the individual, but imposes the cost of reduced resource availability on all appropriators. Since these incentives operate on all who use the CPR, the appropriation externality leads to a race to appropriate resource units. In this case appropriate government intervention may take the form of rules and regulations limiting use and harvest from CPRs. CPRs (and to lesser extent public goods) will be discussed in detail in chapters 5 and 16.

Imperfect Information

If people are poorly informed of product quality, safety, or availability, then their willingness-to-pay is distorted, which in turn implies that market demand is either too large or too small. Consequently, either too much or too little is produced relative to the full-information benchmark, leading to inefficient resource allocation. For example, if buyers are poorly informed about a product's quality prior to purchase, there is an incentive for a "fly-by-night" seller to overstate quality. In this case, demand is overstated because buyers think quality is higher than it actually is, and so the equilibrium quantity traded is inefficiently large. If employers understate workplace hazards, then the supply of labor to these employers will be overstated, leading to a wage below what workers would demand if true workplace safety were known. If market participants do not resolve the imperfect information problem through such things as product warranties and reputation, then either government or nongovernment organizations may intervene by providing information. Examples include content labels required on processed food, or product testing services provided by the Consumer Union.

Fairness, Equity, and Distributive Justice

The efficiency properties of well-functioning competitive markets have nothing to say about the underlying fairness with which resources, wealth, and income are distributed in society. Such a market is efficient because it maximizes the available gains from trade, yet others in society may place a high value on the good or service being produced but lack the income to be able to represent this value as willingness to pay. Yet it can also be argued that it is fair that those who work harder, produce more, or find innovative ways to cut costs or save energy should be compensated for their added contributions. If this is not the case, then there is no financial incentive to work harder or innovate. Since capabilities and access to education and skills are unevenly endowed in the population, rewarding productivity leads to inequality in society. Moreover, those who succeed can provide their children with a better start, resulting in intergenerational inequalities as well. *Economies of scale in production*, sunk costs associated with entry and exit (e.g., new product promotional costs), and government-created franchise monopolies and patents can all lead to concentrations of a few firms in many markets, resulting in a weakening of the competitive process. Balancing incentives and equality is one of the central dilemmas with which all societies are confronted.

Perspectives on Market Failures and Government Intervention

As we can see, there are almost no examples of real-world markets that do not have some degree or another of market failure, often of various dimensions and degrees. From an economic perspective, then, there is potential for regulatory intervention of some kind to resolve market failures in most markets. Such intervention, however, can itself create problems and distortions. Thus, when we see an opportunity for a regulatory intervention because of market failure, it is also worthwhile to consider whether the form of intervention being contemplated truly makes us better off. The particular form that regulations take may at times be more a reflection of political expediency than economic efficiency, a condition sometimes referred to as government failure. We will discuss this point in chapter 8, which addresses the topic of political economy, and in chapter 10, which focuses on incentive regulation.

Summary

- We have defined *capitalism* as an economic system based on the use of a complete set of "decentralized markets" to allocate scarce resources, goods, and services. (This as opposed to socialist systems, in which allocation decisions are centralized at some level of community or government control.) Individuals (or other private entities) own capital, and production and employment decisions are decentralized.
- It has been pointed out that there have been no true tests of pure, *laissez-faire* market capitalism (fully unregulated) in recent history. It is unlikely to be in the best interests of society as a whole to practice pure laissez-faire capitalism because of market failures and because of inequalities heightened by capitalism.

- A well-functioning competitive market is the primary benchmark for evaluating market failures and the need for public policy intervention. For a market to be well-functioning and competitive, there must be many individual buyers and sellers, each of whom is small relative to the overall market. Market entry and exit costs must be inconsequential. Current and potential market participants must be fully informed of prices, qualities, and location; transaction costs must be low. There must be no collusion among the market participants. There can be no consequential positive or negative externalities.
- When any of the above conditions is substantially absent, a *market failure* has occurred, meaning that the market no longer meets the conditions for being well functioning and competitive.
- Economists argue that market failures are a central justification for public policy intervention in market capitalist systems if these interventions are designed to correct for the market imperfections and the interventions do not create a larger distortion than the market failure itself.
- Consumer demand can be derived from the level of their utility over various alternative products, their budget constraint, and product prices. Horizontally summing the quantity demanded of all consumers at a given market price results in the market demand curve.
- In a well-functioning competitive market, a firm's short-run supply curve is equal to its marginal cost curve. Horizontally summing the quantity supplied by all sellers at a given market price results in the market supply curve.
- We discussed the theoretical requirements for efficient markets to be in *equilibrium,* namely that the quantity supplied by sellers equals the quantity demanded by buyers at the prevailing price, so there is neither a shortage nor a surplus.
- The equilibrium market allocation is *efficient* because neither too much nor too little is produced, and thus there is no waste. Another aspect of efficiency is that total surplus (gains from trade) is as large as possible, with none wasted, meaning that the sum of producer and consumer surplus is maximized.
- In the next chapter we shall discuss market failures based on externalities and the role of this form of market failure in justifying environmental regulation.

Review Questions and Problems

1. Consider the demand and supply for used science textbooks. Suppose that the used-textbook market is competitive, with supply given by

$P = 10 + .1Q$ and demand given by $P = 100 - .08Q$. Solve for the competitive market equilibrium price and quantity of used textbooks in this market. Determine the quantity of shortage or surplus that would occur if a price ceiling (maximum allowable price) of \$35 were imposed on this market. Describe why the market fails to be efficient in the context of this ceiling and what market participants commonly do to overcome the inefficiency caused by official prices below the equilibrium market price. If the intention is to help low-income students, compare the effects of the price ceiling to an alternative scheme of giving \$25 purchase vouchers to low-income students. In your answer, consider the effect of the vouchers on the demand for textbooks.

2. Starting with a supply and demand diagram as in Figure 3.1, identify producer and consumer surplus in the competitive equilibrium. Now suppose that sellers form a cartel and wish to increase producer surplus. Illustrate in your diagram how a reduction in output will (i) transform some consumer surplus into producer surplus, and (ii) result in a reduction in total surplus due to the loss of some mutually beneficial transactions.

3. Classroom debate activity: Debate consists of reasoned arguments for or against a given proposition. Form two groups in your class (affirmative and negative) for the purpose of debating the following proposition: *Resolved: Due to overwhelming market failures, the invisible hand of the market must be directed by the visible hand of government regulation.* Members of each group should be given a week or so to research the issues. The debate will occur in a panel, moderated by your professor. Two members of each group will serve as panelists, and any additional group members can serve as researchers. There are a variety of different ways to structure a debate, one of which is the Michigan cross-examination method:

a. The first affirmative panelist presents the affirmative case (6 minutes).
b. The first affirmative panelist is cross-examined by the second negative panelist (4 minutes).
c. Questions from the audience are put to the members of the affirmative team (5 minutes).
d. The first negative panelist presents the negative case (6 minutes).
e. The second affirmative panelist cross-examines the first negative panelist (4 minutes).
f. Questions from the audience are put to the members of the negative team (5 minutes).
g. The second negative panelist summarizes the negative case (2 minutes).
h. The second affirmative panelist summarizes the affirmative case (2 minutes).

4. Classroom role-play activity: Before class, the instructor makes ten seller cards (3x5 note cards), with opportunity cost values written on them. The lowest opportunity cost card should be $1, and have them escalate in $1 intervals so that the highest opportunity cost card is $10. Likewise, make ten buyer cards with maximum willingness-to-pay values written on them. The highest willingness-to-pay card should be $16, with the other cards declining in $1 intervals so that the lowest willingness-to-pay card is $7. Each card represents a single unit of a fictitious good that can be bought or sold. These cards induce a step-function supply and demand curve that can be shown to class after the activity. Hand these cards out in class. Explain that students will be role playing as buyers and sellers. It is vital to the activity that (i) sellers not sell below the opportunity cost value on their cards, (ii) buyers not buy at a price above the maximum willingness-to-pay value on their cards, (iii) students seek to maximize their gains from trade, and (iv) students with a card engage in only one transaction of a single unit of the fictitious good in the trading round. The instructor serves as auctioneer and conducts a double-oral auction on a chalkboard, where improving buyer bid prices must rise, and improving seller ask prices must decline. Conduct at least five trading rounds, with students swapping cards after each round, and then show the induced supply and demand curves to class. If students follow the rules above, then auction market trading should result in an approximation of the equilibrium price and quantity, even when traders don't see supply or demand curves.

5. Spreadsheet simulation: Suppose that supply is given by the equation $P = c + dQ$, and demand is given by the $P = a - bQ$.

    a. Create a spreadsheet file with these supply and demand equations. Let $a = 2000$, $b = 1$, $c = 100$, and $d = 2$.

    b. Plot the supply and demand curves for different P and Q parameter values in a fully labeled diagram.

    c. Solve for equilibrium price and quantity (P^* and Q^*) in the same sheet (carefully label your answer) using the parameters in 5a above.

    d. Build a table showing different (comparative-static) values for P^* and Q^* when a is 1000, 2000, and 3000, and when c is 50, 100, and 200. Provide a brief narrative economic interpretation of the change in a values and the change in c values and their impact on equilibrium price and quantity.

Internet Links

Antitrust Division of the U.S. Department of Justice (www.usdoj.gov/atr/index.html): The mission of the Antitrust Division is to promote and protect the competitive process through the enforcement of the antitrust laws. The antitrust laws apply to virtually all industries and to every level of business, and they prohibit a variety of practices that restrain trade, such as price-fixing conspiracies, corporate mergers likely to reduce the competitive vigor of particular markets, and predatory acts designed to achieve or maintain monopoly power.

Consumer Products Safety Commission (www.cpsc.gov/): An independent agency of the U.S. government, the CPSC helps keep American families safe by reducing the risk of injury or death from consumer products.

Federal Trade Commission (www.ftc.gov/): The Federal Trade Commission enforces a variety of federal antitrust and consumer protection laws, and seeks to ensure that the nation's markets function competitively and are vigorous, efficient, and free of undue restrictions. The commission also works to enhance the smooth operation of the marketplace by eliminating acts or practices that are unfair, deceptive, or threaten consumers' opportunities to exercise informed choice.

European Union Competition Policy Website (http://europa.eu.int/comm/ competition/index_en.html).

Hayek Research Website (www.hayekcenter.org/friedrichhayek/ research.html).

History of Economic Thought Website (http://cepa.newschool.edu/het): Produced by the New School for Social Research, here you can read about the whole spectrum of economic thought.

International Association for the Study of Common Property (www.indiana.edu/~iascp/): Lots of useful material related to common-pool resources and the ownership regime of common property.

Writings of Adam Smith (www.economics.mcmaster.ca/ugcm/3113/smith/ index.html).

Writings of Alfred Marshall (www.economics.mcmaster.ca/ugcm/3113/ marshall/index.html).

References and Further Reading

Hayek, F. 1937. "Economics and Knowledge." *Economica N.S.* 4: 33–54.
⎯⎯⎯. 1945. "The Use of Knowledge in Society." *American Economic Review* 35 (September): 519–30.

Ostrom, E. 1990. *Governing the Commons: The Evolution of Institutions for Collective Action*. Cambridge: Cambridge University Press.

Rosser, J.B., and M.V. Rosser. 1995. "The Theory and Practice of Market Capitalism." In *Comparative Economics in a Transforming World Economy*. Burr Ridge, IL: Irwin.

Scherer, F.M., and D. Ross. 1990. *Industrial Market Structure and Economic Performance*. 3rd ed. Boston: Houghton Mifflin.

Viscusi, W., J. Vernon, and J. Harrington. 2000. *Economics of Regulation and Antitrust*. Cambridge, MA: MIT Press.

Appendix: A Calculus-based Derivation of Supply Curves

This appendix is intended for those who have a calculus background but who have not had a microtheory course in which they have derived a competitive firm's supply curve. Supply curves result from firms in competitive markets trying to maximize profits. A firm in a perfectly competitive market is assumed to be relatively small compared to the size of the overall market. As a consequence, an individual firm will take the market price as a fixed parameter and vary its output to maximize its profits. In particular, for a competitive firm, profits are given by

Profit = total revenue (TR) – total cost (TC).

In the short run, total revenue is simply equal to market price multiplied by the firm's output ($TR = PQ$). Likewise in the short run, total costs will have a functional form such as

$$TC = a + bQ + cQ^2.$$

Note that a is the fixed cost of production, like the debt service on a factory, while b and c are coefficients for variable cost $bQ + cQ^2$. Note that variable costs increase with output Q.

Note that marginal cost (MC) in our simple example above is $b + 2cQ$ (the partial derivative of TC with respect to Q), meaning that as Q grows, so does MC. Why? Recall from the text that in the short run a firm will eventually experience congestion of its fixed facilities as it tries to increase output, which means that marginal costs increase with increases in output. Similarly, marginal revenue (MR) is simply P, the market price.

A competitive firm selects its sales quantity, Q, to maximize profit:

Figure 3.5 **Profit-Maximizing Output**

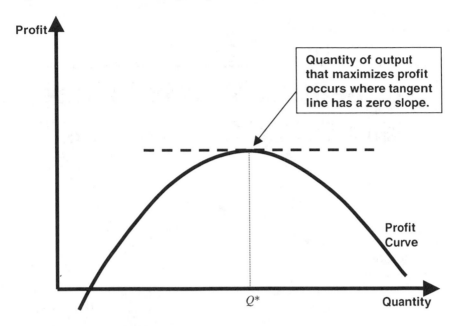

Profit

> Quantity of output
> that maximizes profit
> occurs where tangent
> line has a zero slope.

Profit
Curve

Q^* Quantity

$\text{Profit} = PQ - a - bQ - cQ^2.$

Note that since total revenue is linear, while total cost is convex, there is an output level at which this profit function attains a unique maximum. As shown in Figure 3.5, the profit function first rises, reaches a peak, and then falls. The profit curve has a slope of zero at its peak, meaning that the derivative of the profit function with regard to Q is equal to zero. At this point a one-unit increase in Q will generate marginal revenue that is equal to marginal cost. We can use this property of the profit function to determine the profit-maximizing output level Q^*. If you take the partial derivative of the profit function with respect to Q, and set this equation equal to zero, you will find that $P = b + 2cQ$. Since marginal revenue is equal to price for a competitive firm (the derivative of total revenue with respect to Q is equal to P), this equation simply shows us that the profit-maximizing output level occurs where marginal revenue equals marginal cost. As market price changes, the firm sets quantity supplied where market price equals marginal cost. Therefore, a firm's supply curve is its marginal cost curve.

4

Externalities, Market Failures, and Policy Interventions

Introduction

In this chapter, we continue the discussion of markets, market failures, and efficiency from chapter 3 by evaluating the economic theory of externalities. We will evaluate externalities in the context of an otherwise well-functioning competitive market system. *Externalities* are positive or negative impacts on society that occur as a by-product of production and exchange. These effects are called externalities because they are not included in the factors that underlie market supply and demand, and their omission leads to the market failing to efficiently allocate resources. The inefficiency due to externalities can be used as a justification for government intervention in otherwise well-functioning competitive market systems. Externality problems are not unique to market systems, however, as illustrated by the profound pollution that occurred in the former Soviet Union and its Eastern European satellite states.

In the section that follows, we will begin with a discussion of positive externalities, the distortion they create in the market, and possible policy interventions that have the potential for enhancing market efficiency. Next, we will turn to negative externalities. Because pollution is such a persistent and encompassing problem, we will evaluate the source and the consequences of negative externalities in detail.

Positive Externalities

Consider pastureland near a growing urban area that can be used for livestock grazing or converted into new housing, schools, roads, and retail development. Pastureland produces benefits for local residents such as open space, vistas, wildlife habitat, and temporary floodwater storage. If local residents receive these benefits without having to pay for them, then those benefits are external to the market process. Pastureland is bought and sold in markets, however, and the market demand for pastureland is based on the *private benefits* that flow to the buyers, such as revenues from grazing cattle, stabling horses, producing hay, or selling to a developer. Consequently, the market demand for pastureland ignores the external benefits received by others who do not pay for them. Since market demand does not reflect the external benefits of intact pastureland that flow to society, the market process will allocate *less than the socially optimal amount* of such land as pasture, leading to excessive agricultural land conversion and urban sprawl.

A *positive externality* can be defined as an unpaid-for benefit enjoyed by others in society that is generated as a by-product of production and exchange. Positive externalities are also known as external benefits. For example, as a by-product of purchasing a college education, a college student produces external benefits to society in the form of being an informed voter and a resourceful citizen. Likewise as a by-product of a parent vaccinating her child for infectious disease, an immunized child reduces the likelihood of a disease epidemic spreading to others in society. The pastureland example above offers yet another example of a positive externality.

While positive externalities are nice for those who benefit from them, otherwise well-functioning competitive markets are not very good at providing them. Recall from chapter 3 that well-functioning competitive markets in equilibrium are efficient. When there are substantial external benefits, however, those efficiency properties fail. Specifically, when buyers in a market purchase goods, the market demand for the good reflects the private benefits that flow to the buyers. Since those who receive positive externalities do not pay for them, market demand does not include external benefits. The sum of private benefit and external benefit is called *social benefit*. Figure 4.1 indicates how the demand curve based only on private benefits is smaller than (to the left of) the demand curve based on social benefits. The vertical difference between the private-benefit and the social-benefit demand curves is *marginal external benefit,* or the external benefit per unit of output, as indicated by the letter "C" in Figure 4.1. In the pastureland example, marginal external benefit would be the external benefits from an additional acre of intact pastureland (open space, vistas, wildlife habitat, and temporary floodwater storage). The marginal concept will be developed more completely for the case of negative externalities later in the chapter.

As shown in Figure 4.1, the market demand curve based on social benefits exceeds (lies to the right of) the market demand curve based only on private

Figure 4.1   **Positive Externalities and Market Failure**

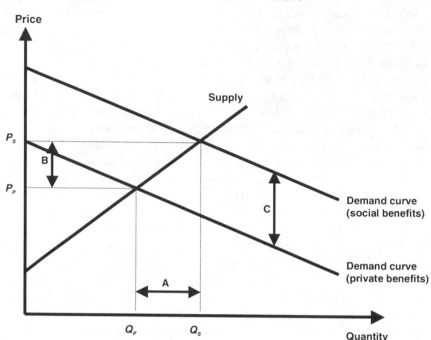

benefits. Since buyers' willingness-to-pay only reflects their private benefits, only the market demand based on private benefits will exist in the market. Since the demand based on private benefits is smaller than the demand based on social benefits, an otherwise well-functioning competitive market will underprovide those goods (pastureland, education, vaccinations) that generate positive externalities. This underprovision is indicated by the letter "A" in Figure 4.1. If society intervened in the market by using tax revenues to subsidize buyers, then market demand would reflect social benefits and the efficient quantity of those goods (pastureland, education, vaccinations) that generate positive externalities. For example, in the case of pastureland, many counties have open space districts that tax residents and use those tax revenues to purchase *conservation easements*. When a farmer sells a conservation easement on her land, she and any future owner no longer have a right to convert the pastureland to housing, roads, or other developments that might impair the open space and ecological services provided by the land. By purchasing the easement, society internalizes the positive externality.

It should be noted that not all positive externalities are limited to distorting the market demand curve. One well-known example is a *technology spillover.* For example, the Apollo space program led to the development of many new products and technological innovations that spilled over into commercial market applications. Similarly, military and National Science Foundation–sponsored efforts helped to create the basic Internet structure, which has transformed the way that people communicate and conduct business. Technology spillovers are unpaid-for benefits, and many of them reduce production costs, enhance productivity, and thus shift out the supply curve. Commercial buyers in the market for research and technology only take into account the private benefits that they hope to receive, and not beneficial technology spillovers, and thus there is an inefficiently small amount of basic research conducted by private enterprise. This is one reason why government subsidizes basic research that has the potential for technology spillovers.

Negative Externalities

Consider cabinet manufacturers that can use two alternative production processes for making finished cabinets. Process A costs the firm less than nontoxic process B, but process A allows toxic volatile organic compounds from the wood-finishing process to escape into the atmosphere. These volatile organic compounds contribute to smog and thus impose *external costs* on people who breathe the polluted air but who are not compensated for these harms. Since process A has lower *private costs,* profit-maximizing firms will usually choose it over the nontoxic alternative, which allows them to supply furniture at lower prices to consumers. Since the supply of cabinets in the competitive furniture market does not reflect the external costs borne by members of society, the market process will allocate more than the socially optimal amount of cabinets when they are produced with the more polluting technology.

A *negative externality* can be defined as an uncompensated harm to others in society that is generated as a by-product of production and exchange. Many negative externalities occur as a by-product of market transactions. Pollution is the prime example of a negative externality, as illustrated in the cabinet example above. The harms created by pollution are known as external costs. As we will see below, when market exchange generates negative externalities, market supply fails to reflect the true social cost of producing the good generating the externality, and so too much of the good is produced.

Following Scitovsky (1954), one can draw a distinction between *technological* and *pecuniary* externalities, and when economists refer to externalities, they usually mean technological externalities. A pecuniary externality occurs, for example, when a new firm enters a market. This entry will initially increase market supply and will tend to reduce market price, reducing the profit of other sellers. This is a negative pecuniary externality because it affects the profits or financial circumstances of another individual or firm, and the harm is directly transmitted by way of the market process. From an economic perspective, however, pecuniary externalities do not generate a misallocation of society's scarce resources, and thus are not considered a market failure. In contrast, a technological externality is a "peculiarity of the production function" (Scitovsky 1954, p. 145) in which the production process generates external costs such as pollution, whose harms are not directly transmitted by way of the market process. As we shall show below, technological externalities such as pollution do in fact result in a misallocation of society's scarce resources and so represent a form of market failure. When we refer to externalities in this textbook, we will mean the technological form rather than pecuniary form.

Before we address how negative externalities result in market failure, let's take a moment and look at the important topic of property rights and negative externalities.

Property Rights and Negative Externalities

If negative externalities are uncompensated harms generated as a by-product of production and exchange, why don't those who bear these costs simply use the legal process to sue polluters for damages? The common-law tradition in the United States and elsewhere protects the integrity of property rights. Property rights represent an enforceable authority to undertake particular actions in specific circumstances (see Commons 1968). Thus if someone is known to have dumped garbage on your front yard, this act is punishable (through criminal and/or civil penalties) because it impairs the value of your property. Certain aspects of our environment, including the air, ocean, wildlife, and groundwater, were not traditionally owned by anybody, and so damage to them did not directly impair the value of someone's property. Consequently, the common law did not provide criminal and/or civil penalties for damage to valuable but unowned aspects of the natural world. Both government and common property rights regimes have been developed to prevent degradation of valuable resources that are not privately owned (see Bromley 1989 and Ostrom 1990).

Schlager and Ostrom (1992) identify five important property rights that when bundled together make up ownership:

- *Access:* The right to enjoy benefits of the property that do not subtract from benefits that others can enjoy, such as walking along the beach.

Authorized entrants have access rights, such as those that are purchased with entry fees at national parks.

* *Withdrawal:* The right to withdraw the product of the property, such as harvesting fish from a fishery. Authorized users have both access and withdrawal rights, such as those that are acquired with the purchase of a fishing license or a firewood gathering permit from a national forest.
* *Management:* The right to regulate use and improvements. Ostrom (1997) uses the term *claimant* to refer to those who hold access, withdrawal, and management rights, such as farmers who participate in the management of government-owned irrigation systems.
* *Exclusion:* The right to determine who has access and who can be excluded from using the property. Ostrom (1997) uses the term *proprietor* to refer to those who hold access, withdrawal, management, and exclusion rights. Citizens of Swiss villages that possess and govern their own common property pastures and forests are proprietors in this sense.
* *Alienation:* The right to sell or lease. "Owners" possess all the rights of proprietors along with the right of alienation. Private property falls under this category, though owners can also be governments or communities.

We can see that there is more to property rights than ownership. It is not unusual to unbundle a portion of these rights and assign them to nonowners. For example, someone with a valid fishing or hunting license is an authorized user with certain rights to harvest fish and game, while government retains proprietary rights to the wildlife in a public trust capacity. *Usufructuary rights* refer to certain use and withdrawal rights granted to property that is owned by others. For example, treaties ceding Indian lands to the federal government sometimes include clauses granting Indian tribes usufructuary rights for hunting, fishing, and gathering on the ceded lands. These arrangements reflect a melding of precontact Indian customary *land tenure* systems governing the harvest of resources from land and water, and Euro-American property rights systems. Likewise, the right to appropriate from navigable waters in the United States is a usufructuary right, with the waterway itself being owned by government in a public trust capacity. California water law is built on the notion that the right of property in water is usufructuary. California Water Code section 102 provides that "[a]ll water within the State is the property of the people of the State, but the right to the use of water [usufructuary rights] may be acquired by appropriation in the manner provided by law."

We have already discussed the role of conservation easements as a mechanism for internalizing positive externalities. When a conservation easement is sold or donated by a landowner, the landowner is voluntarily transferring certain withdrawal and management rights tied to specified types of development to the easement buyer (usually a not-for-profit land trust). Easements are thus a set of legally enforceable property rights, and usually they are permanent and "run with the land," and thus are binding on all future landowners. The owner of the easement is responsible for monitoring and enforcing the terms of the easement. The seller of the easement retains ownership, but no longer has the right to, say, subdivide the land for housing or commercial develop-ment, or to use clearcut timber harvest methods. Conservation easements are commonly used to protect the external benefits (viewsheds, floodwater reten-tion, wildlife habitat) associated with "working landscapes"—farms, ranches, and private timberlands—while continuing to allow the farmer or rancher to live on the land and work the land, and keeping the lands privately owned and on the tax rolls. An additional benefit to the landowner is that the sale or donation of an easement by definition reduces the development-based value of the land, which can substantially reduce property tax (and inheritance tax) liability. In the United States, nearly 2.6 million acres of land have been pro-tected using conservation easements owned by local or regional land trusts. Some areas under strong development pressure, such as the San Francisco Bay area, have open space districts with the authority to levy taxes to fund the purchase of conservation easements.

Property rights scholars distinguish four different classes or regimes of property rights based on who holds these rights:

- *Private property rights:* Rights held by individuals and business enter-prises, usually with a legally recognized owner.
- *Common property rights:* Rights held by an identified group of proprietors.
- *State property rights:* Rights held by government.
- *Open access:* No specific property rights recognized, and thus the re-source is open to all under the common-law rule of capture with no capacity for management or exclusion.

As we saw in chapter 2, property rights to land and other resources originate from open-access conditions. Property rights can originate from being first in time with a valid claim for an unallocated open-access resource (such as the Homestead Act for land, or the prior appropriation doctrine for water in the frontier west). Property rights can also originate by conquest (taking of other people's property), the assertion of government regulatory rights, or capture (removing resource units from an open-access or a common property resource such as water, marine fisheries, or oil and gas). As Hanna (1996, p. 385) states: "Property rights regimes do not exist as two opposing types but rather as com-binations along a spectrum from open access to private ownership. . . . Second, no single type of property rights regime can be prescribed as a remedy for [all] problems of resource degradation and overuse. . . . The key attribute of an effective property rights regime is that it is context-specific, reflecting environmental, economic, social, and political conditions."

Prior to the advent of environmental regulations, some types of pollution harms to private, common, or state property were punishable (at least in theory) under traditional common law as trespass or as nuisances. Meiners and Yandle (1998), for example, describe some cases in which common-law penalties were extended to pollution affecting proprietors holding riparian water rights. In his more comprehensive historical treatment of the topic, however, McEvoy (1986) observes that this sort of enlightened application of common-law remedies to resource and environmental harms was not the norm in nineteenth-century America.

For our purposes, it is important to observe that pollution or other harms to open-access resources such as breathable air were not usually punishable under common law. Therefore, if a profit-maximizing firm could avoid cleanup costs by polluting an open-access resource, there was generally no common-law legal penalty to deter such an action. The same was true if those who held private, common, or state property rights were unable to enforce their rights. This problem with the common law and open-access resources led to the development of environmental regulations. By vesting government with the authority to manage and excluding certain uses of a resource, environmental regulation establishes a system of property rights to formerly open-access resources. We can see, then, that an important step in protecting the environment is assigning appropriate property rights. The type of property rights regime that is appropriate depends on factors such as the nature of the resource, the culture and values of society, and the costs of monitoring and excluding use. For example, resources such as air, oceans, groundwater, and fisheries are *fugitive resources,* meaning that it is difficult or impossible to brand individual resource units or partition the stock of the resource into individually owned parcels. Fugitive resources are less likely to be private property and more likely to be common property, state property, or open access.

In the material that follows, we will explore how negative externalities lead to market failure.

Social Cost as the Sum of Private and External Cost

Let's now return to our cabinet manufacturing example. Suppose the firm chooses to use the cheaper but more polluting process A, as described earlier. For example, the negative externalities could be volatile petroleum

Table 4.1

Marginal Private, External, and Social Costs

Output of Cabinets	1. Marginal Private Cost	2. Marginal External Cost	Marginal Social Cost (1 + 2)
100	2	3	5
200	3	3	6
300	5	3	8
400	7	3	10
500	10	3	13
600	13	3	16
700	17	3	20
800	23	3	26

distillates used in inexpensive stains and preservatives. Moreover, assume that a lower-bound estimate of the harms caused by the use of this preservative (the cost of impaired health and damage to the environment, for example) is $3 on a per-cabinet basis. This $3 is an external cost per unit of output, commonly referred to as a *marginal external cost*. Marginal external cost can be difficult to estimate, and to keep the following example simple we will assume that marginal cost is constant. Assume that nontoxic, pollution-free wood preservatives are more costly, and so in the absence of regulation (and environmentally concerned consumers), the profit-maximizing woodshop chooses to use the cheaper, more polluting wood stain and preservative.

Social cost refers to a fuller accounting of the costs of production and exchange. Social cost is equal to the sum of *private cost* borne by producers and *external cost* borne by affected members of society in the form of pollution harms. Likewise, *marginal social cost* is the sum of *marginal private cost* and *marginal external cost*. Since marginal external cost is a constant $3 in our example, then at each level of output of cabinets marginal social cost is $3 greater than marginal private cost. A hypothetical numerical example of marginal private cost, marginal external cost, and marginal social cost is given in Table 4.1, while Figure 4.2 provides a diagrammatic example of marginal private, external, and social cost curves. It is assumed here that marginal external cost is constant in order to keep the example simple, but in the real world marginal external cost might increase or decrease with the quantity produced. (Why?)

Recall our discussion of supply curves from chapter 3. In that chapter, we described supply/demand equilibrium for the case of a well-functioning competitive market. Now we are relaxing that assumption and allowing for market failure in the form of negative externalities. When there are external costs there are two market supply curves. One of these supply curves is operational in the

Figure 4.2 **Marginal Private Cost, Marginal External Cost, and Marginal Social Cost**

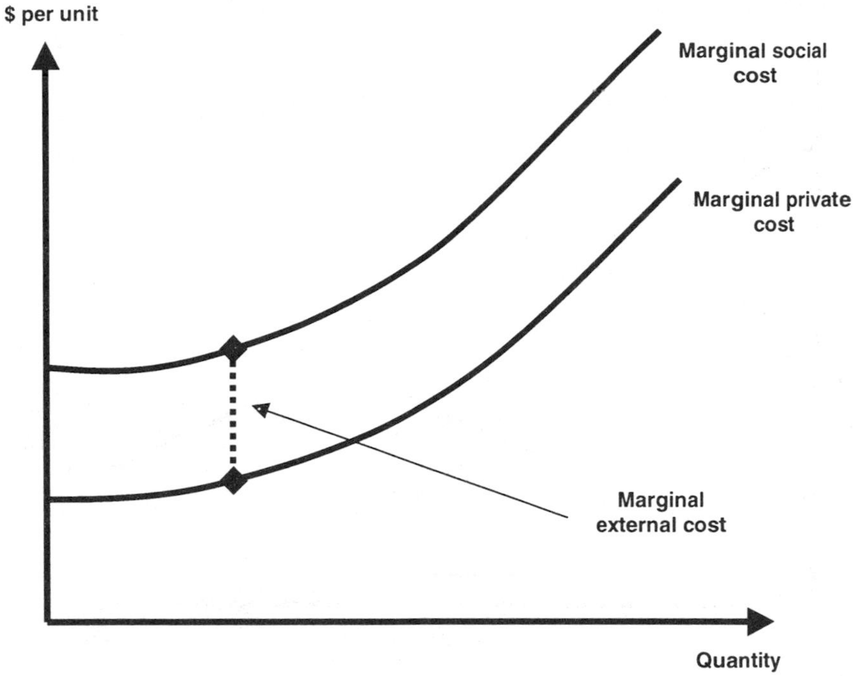

market when firms are allowed to freely pollute. This is the supply curve derived from the firms' marginal private costs. The other supply curve is based on marginal social costs, which considers both private and external costs. Therefore, the vertical difference between these two supply curves is the dollar amount of marginal external cost. The supply curve based on marginal social costs will only be operational if firms internalize the external costs of production. These two supply curves are illustrated in Figure 4.3. We will find out in the next section of the chapter that if firms are allowed to freely pollute, otherwise well-functioning competitive markets fail to efficiently allocate resources (cabinets in our example). We will also learn that government intervention in the form of a tax equal to marginal external cost will cause firms to internalize external costs and supply along the social-cost supply curve.

Competitive Markets Are Inefficient When There Are Negative Externalities

Figure 4.3 illustrates a well-functioning competitive market for a good or service, such as cabinets, with two possible supply curves. As noted above,

Figure 4.3 **Negative Externalities and Market Failure**

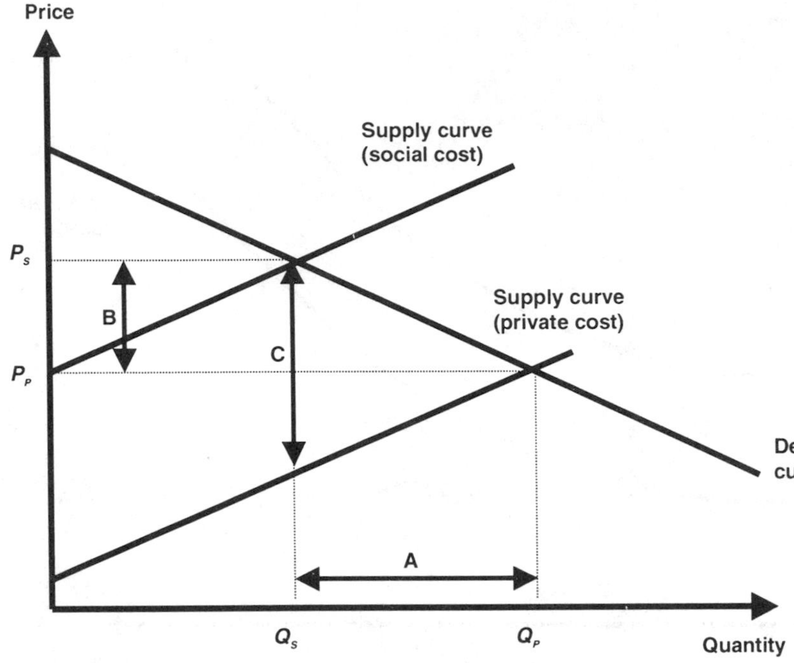

one supply curve is based on firms' marginal private costs, with marginal external costs borne by the environment and society. The other supply curve is based on marginal social costs. This latter supply curve is operational only if firms are made to internalize their negative externalities.

As shown in Figure 4.3, the quantity of cabinets produced where the private-cost supply curve crosses the demand curve is the market equilibrium quantity when firms are allowed to freely pollute, indicated by Q_P in Figure 4.3. The corresponding equilibrium price when there are unresolved negative externalities is indicated by P_p in Figure 4.3. In contrast, the quantity of cabinets produced where the social-cost supply curve crosses the demand curve is the market equilibrium quantity when firms are forced to fully internalize all their external costs, indicated by Q_S in Figure 4.3. P_S in Figure 4.3 indicates the corresponding equilibrium price when there are unresolved negative externalities.

Therefore, when firms can freely pollute they will supply along the private-cost supply curve, leading to an equilibrium quantity of the good or service being produced and sold that is larger than when firms are made to supply along the social-cost supply curve. This difference in output is denoted by the letter A in Figure 4.3 and reflects excess production that occurs in competitive markets where firms are allowed to freely emit negative externalities. Moreover, when firms can freely pollute and supply along the private-cost supply curve, the equilibrium market price P_p only reflects marginal private cost, whereas when negative externalities are internalized the equilibrium market price P_S reflects the full marginal social cost of production. The difference in these two equilibrium prices is denoted by the letter B in Figure 4.3, and indicates the distortion of the price signal sent to consumers in the marketplace. This distorted price signal creates an incentive for consumers to buy too much of the good or service in question. As we will see in a moment, the market is not efficiently allocating scarce resources when there are unresolved negative externalities.

Why is output Q_S, where the social-cost supply curve crosses the demand curve, the efficient level of output? To answer this question we need to think about the gains from trade and external costs. We also need to use some simple geometry. Figure 4.4 will be our guide. Suppose firms are allowed to freely pollute, and so they supply along the private-cost supply curve, yielding an equilibrium price and quantity as shown in Figure 4.4. The buyers and the sellers receive a gross gain from trade equal to the large triangle *abc* in Figure 4.4. Recall from chapter 3 that the portion of this triangle above the dashed price line is a simplified approximation for consumer surplus, while the portion below the price line is producer surplus.

Since firms are freely polluting, however, there are external costs that we have not yet taken into account. The parallelogram *bcde* in Figure 4.4 gives us the total dollar figure for the harms to human health and the environment caused by negative externalities. In our simplified example, total external cost is equal to marginal external cost (height *cd* or *be,* which gives us external cost for each cabinet) multiplied by the equilibrium quantity of cabinets produced when firms operate on the private-cost supply and freely pollute (length $0Q_p$ along the horizontal axis). After accounting for total external costs, the true net gains from trade to all members of society when firms freely pollute is area *abc* minus area *bcde*.

Now suppose that firms are forced by regulatory intervention or market reputation to internalize their external costs and supply along the social-cost supply curve. As we will learn in the next section of this chapter, one way to internalize negative externalities is by way of a Pigouvian tax equal to marginal external cost. When firms supply along the social-cost supply curve, equilibrium output is found at point *f,* where the social-cost supply curve crosses the demand curve, as shown in Figure 4.4. Since firms have paid the tax to society they have (at least in theory) compensated society for their pollution, and thus have internalized the external costs. In this case, the total

Figure 4.4   **Negative Externalities and Inefficient Resource Allocation**

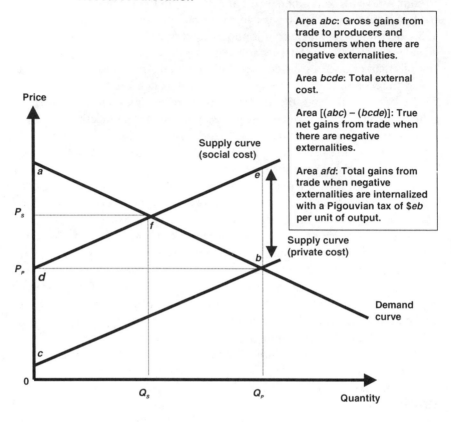

> Area *abc*: Gross gains from trade to producers and consumers when there are negative externalities.
>
> Area *bcde*: Total external cost.
>
> Area [(*abc*) − (*bcde*)]: True net gains from trade when there are negative externalities.
>
> Area *afd*: Total gains from trade when negative externalities are internalized with a Pigouvian tax of $*eb* per unit of output.

gains from trade when firms fully internalize their external costs are given by the triangle *afd*.

So now let's return to our question of why output set where the social-cost supply curve crosses the demand curve is the efficient level of output. We will continue to make use of Figure 4.4 in our analysis. The reason is that area *afd*, the gains from trade when negative externalities are fully internalized and firms supply along the social-cost supply curve, is larger than area [(*abc*)–(*bcde*)], the true gains from trade to all members of society when firms freely pollute. In other words, internalizing externalities improves the welfare of society. The difference between area *afd* and area [(*abe*)–(*bcde*)] is the little triangle *bfe*, known in microeconomic theory as *deadweight social loss,* and it represents the resource allocation inefficiency caused by negative externalities. In our simple linear example, deadweight social loss is a triangle with a base equal to the difference in equilibrium output $(0Q_P - 0Q_S)$ and a height equal to marginal external cost eb.

Allowing firms to pollute for free amounts to society granting these firms a production subsidy on each cabinet produced. Since society bears the external costs when firms freely pollute, members of society subsidize production along the private-cost supply curve. The amount of this implicit subsidy per cabinet is equal to marginal external cost eb in Figure 4.4. Some of this subsidy is passed along to consumers in the form of a lower product price $(0P_P - 0P_S)$. Whenever firms freely pollute or cause environmental harm in otherwise competitive markets, firms are being subsidized by society and consumers are sharing in this subsidy by way of a lower product price. This subsidy makes it particularly difficult for cleaner alternative technologies to succeed in the marketplace. If one firm were to adopt a more expensive clean technology, it would be at a price disadvantage in the marketplace relative to other firms. Unless consumers recognize and reward products made with the use of cleaner technologies, such firms will struggle and fail in the competitive marketplace. As we will see in the next section of the chapter, Pigouvian taxes eliminate this subsidy and enhance market efficiency.

Pigouvian Taxes: The Theory of Policy Interventions for Negative Externalities

Economist A.C. Pigou suggested that the solution to the problem of negative externalities is to place a tax on each unit of output that is equal to marginal external cost. Accordingly, taxes on each unit of output (such as cabinets) equal to marginal external cost are called Pigouvian taxes. Therefore, if we tax firms $3 per cabinet in our example, an amount equal to the marginal external cost from producing each cabinet, two things will happen. First, the social-cost supply curve will become operational in the market, since firms are now paying both marginal private cost and marginal external cost. As a consequence fewer cabinets will be produced, and each cabinet will sell at a price that reflects the marginal social cost of production. Consequently, firms and consumers in the market internalize negative externalities, and society is reimbursed for bearing the external costs of production. By internalizing negative externalities, Pigouvian taxes enhance the allocative efficiency of markets, as shown in Figure 4.4.

Second, profit-maximizing firms will now have an incentive to look for ways to reduce the Pigouvian tax element of their production costs. Of course, one way to do so would be to lobby for removal of the regulation. Assuming that the regulation is stable, however, firms will have an incentive to look for ways to reduce their emissions. Suppose first that a nontoxic alternative wood preservative is available that costs firms $2 more than the standard toxic alternative. Since the firm no longer emits pollution, it is no longer liable for the Pigouvian tax. In this case the Pigouvian tax will cause firms to immediately switch to the nontoxic alternative, emissions will be eliminated, firms will no longer by charged a Pigouvian tax, and the private-cost supply curve will shift upwards by $2 to form a new "clean production" supply curve.

Now suppose that a nontoxic alternative wood preservative is available that costs firms $4 more than the standard toxic alternative, and that also eliminates their emissions and thus eliminates the need for a Pigouvian tax. The problem is that since the cleaner production technology is more expensive than the Pigouvian tax, firms will see the tax as a part of the "cost of doing business" and will not adopt the nontoxic alternative. Note that some emissions are eliminated even if firms do not adopt the nontoxic alternative, since market equilibrium output is lower under the Pigouvian tax. Yet even if the nontoxic wood preservative raised costs by more than $3 per cabinet, a Pigouvian tax would encourage research and development to find a cost-effective way of producing a toxics-free wood preservative.

We can see that Pigouvian taxes change the incentives of producers and consumers in the market. Of course, taxes are also a way to generate government revenue. Ideally, these revenues would go toward compensating people harmed by pollution and remediating environmental damage caused by the pollution that is being taxed. In practice, there is no guarantee that the political process will generate environmental policies that are consistent in this manner.

Figure 4.3 illustrates how firms and consumers share in the cost increase when a Pigouvian tax is imposed on producers. If firms were to pay the full social cost of production, price would be P_S, while if firms can avoid the marginal social cost of production, market price would be P_P. If firms were to pay the full social cost of production, consumers would pay an extra $[P_S - P_P]$ for each cabinet they buy. Since demand for the good is downward sloping, firms cannot pass along all of the Pigouvian tax to consumers; firms retain a portion of the tax, which reduces their profit. This analysis also illustrates the reverse, namely, that when firms can freely pollute in the absence of environmental regulations, consumers share in the cost savings in the form of lower prices. The fewer the number of substitutes available for a product the steeper is the demand curve for the product (such as gasoline), and therefore the larger is the share of the Pigouvian tax passed on to consumers.

In principle, we can argue for government regulatory intervention in the case of pollution externalities based on efficiency alone. Namely, resources are not efficiently allocated because too much of the good is produced when externalities remain unresolved. There is also a fairness argument: unless we have a positive externality that requires subsidy, why should society have to absorb part of a firm's costs? While economists generally accept the theory of externalities, not all agree that externalities are very large or important. Indeed, if external costs are small and insignificant, then little is lost by simply ignoring them as minor side effects of the wealth generated by markets. While this may be true in some cases, it does not appear to be at all universally true. For example, as mentioned in chapter 1, recent estimates by the U.S. Environmental Protection Agency (1997) indicate that the Clean Air Act of 1970 created substantial benefits in the form of avoided external costs. In particular, between 1970 and 1990 the Clean Air Act is thought to have prevented an estimated $22.2 trillion in pollution harms to human health, agriculture, and the environment in constant 1990 dollars. As will be described in detail in chapter 6, these benefits were substantially larger than the costs. Thus externalities can indeed be very large and are worthy of well-designed environmental regulatory policy.

In the real world, measurement of external costs must take into account the relationship between the action (e.g., pollution) and the impact (e.g., diminished human health), and between the impact and economic cost (e.g., healthcare expenditures, the value of foregone production, and the value assigned to diminished quality of life). An example of estimated external costs per unit of output is shown for the case of various European countries in Table 4.2. Moreover, social policy often reflects political expediency as well as economic efficiency. In chapter 10, we will return to the idea of intervening in markets to mitigate the effects of pollution. In that chapter, we will focus on the more general notion of *pollution taxes* as a tool of environmental policy. Pollution taxes differ from the theoretically ideal Pigouvian tax in that the former may not fully internalize negative externalities due to difficulties in measuring marginal external costs and due to interest group rivalry and political expediency in the policy-making process. Also in chapter 10 we will discuss the notion of command-and-control regulation as an alternative to taxation. Command-and-control regulation limits the quantity of pollution emissions at the source, and frequently specifies the emissions-control technology to be used. Another alternative to Pigouvian taxes is to let the polluters and those impacted by pollution negotiate with one another and resolve their conflict without government intervention, a process called Coasian contracting, in honor of economist Ronald Coase. The effectiveness of direct contracting relative to regulation is a policy issue addressed in detail in chapter 7.

Table 4.2

External Costs (in Euro Cents) per Kilowatt-Hour of Electricity Generated from Various Energy Sources

Country	Coal	Oil	Natural Gas	Biomass	Wind
Belgium	4–15		1–2		
Denmark	4–7		2–3	1	0.1
France	7–10	8–11	2–4	1	
Germany	3–6	5–8	1–2	3	0.05
Italy		3–6	2–3		
Spain	5–8		1–2	3–5	0.2
United Kingdom	4–7	3–5	1–2	1	0.15

Source: European Commission (2003)

Summary

- Positive externalities are unpaid-for benefits to society generated as a by-product of production and exchange. When there are important positive externalities, market demand based on the private benefits of buyers understates the full social benefits of the good or service generating the external benefit. Consequently, too little of the good or service generating the positive externality is produced in otherwise well-functioning competitive markets. Subsidies represent a form of policy intervention that can enhance market efficiency. Positive externalities can also affect the supply curve, such as when there are technology spillovers.

- While the legal system is designed to protect property, open-access resources are not protected under law from pollution harms and thus are subject to degradation. The legal system does not function perfectly, of course, and so pollution harms to people, their homes, and other valuable objects that are property do regularly occur. One problem is in determining the source of the pollution when there may be very large numbers of emitters, as is the case with automobile exhaust.

- Negative externalities are uncompensated harms to society generated as a by-product of production and exchange. Profit-maximizing firms have an incentive to transform private costs into negative externalities (external costs) in the absence of regulation or reputation effects. When there are important negative externalities, market supply based on private costs to sellers is too large, leading to too much of the good or service generating the negative externalities being produced in otherwise well-functioning competitive markets. Pigouvian taxes represent a form of policy intervention that can enhance market efficiency.

- In the real world, it is difficult to craft Pigouvian taxes due to (i) practical problems measuring marginal external costs without controversy, and (ii) the influence of rival interest groups and political expediency in the policy-making process.

Review Questions and Problems

1. Suppose that there are 100 identical competitive firms, each of which supplies a quantity where price equals marginal cost. Therefore if marginal cost is $10 + Q$, each individual firm's supply curve is given by $P = 10 + Q$. Since there are 100 such firms, the market supply curve is $P = 10 + .01Q$. Also assume that market demand is given by $P = 100 - .005Q$. Note that Q refers to the quantity of some good, like shoes.

   a. Solve for the competitive market equilibrium price and quantity.
   b. Suppose now that in part 1a above firms were freely polluting by emitting marginal external costs equal to a constant $20 for each unit of output produced. Based on this information we know that each firm's social-cost supply curve is given by $P = 30 + Q$, and the social-cost market supply is given by the function $P = 30 + .01Q$. With demand as given above, solve for the competitive equilibrium when firms must internalize their external costs, such as through a Pigouvian tax.
   c. Based on the correct answers to parts 1a and 1b, calculate the amount by which quantity is too large and price is too low when firms can freely pollute and supply along the private-cost supply curve. Calculate the monetary value of total external cost when firms can freely pollute (the area between the two supply curves up to the quantity traded based on the private-cost supply) and the monetary value of deadweight loss. In what specific way are resources inefficiently allocated when firms can freely pollute?
   d. Suppose that government intervention occurs in the form of a $20-per-unit Pigouvian tax imposed on polluters. Also suppose that firms can eliminate their emissions of pollution, and thus avoid the Pigouvian tax, by using a different input that increases marginal private costs by $10 per unit. Will firms pay the Pigouvian tax and continue to pollute, or will they adopt the more expensive clean technology? More challenging: What will be the new market equilibrium price and quantity traded with the more expensive, pollution-free input? Do the benefits of cleanup exceed the cost? How would your answer change if the input increased marginal private costs by $30?

2. Write a one-page essay in which you explain why, in the absence of government subsidies, competitive markets underproduce goods that feature positive externalities. Be sure to provide an example of a good that generates a positive externality, explain the nature of the external benefits and the two demand curves, and describe how they lead to different market equilibria. Draw and carefully label a diagram to illustrate your arguments.

3. Write a one-page essay in which you explain why, in the absence of government environmental regulation, competitive markets overproduce goods whose production involves the creation of negative externalities. Be sure to provide an example of a good that generates a negative externality, explain the nature of the external costs and the two supply curves, and describe how they lead to different market equilibria. Describe why allowing firms to pollute amounts to a production subsidy, and why this is inefficient, creating an economic motive for government policy intervention. Draw and carefully label a diagram to illustrate your arguments.

4. Describe the various reasons why it might be difficult for government interventions to perfectly resolve positive and negative externalities. Address the problem of measurement as well as the workings of the political process.

5. Classroom debate activity: Debate consists of reasoned arguments for or against a given proposition. Form two groups in your class (affirmative and negative) for the purpose of debating the following proposition: *Resolved: Landowners whose property is diminished in commercial value due to environmental regulations should be fully compensated by the government regulatory authority.* Members of each group should be given a week or so to research the issues. The debate will occur in a panel, moderated by your professor. Two members of each group will serve as panelists, and any additional group members can serve as researchers. There are a variety of different ways to structure a debate, one of which is the Michigan cross-examination method:

  a. The first affirmative panelist presents the affirmative case (6 minutes).
  b. The first affirmative panelist is cross-examined by the second negative panelist (4 minutes).
  c. Questions from the audience are put to the members of the affirmative team (5 minutes).
  d. The first negative panelist presents the negative case (6 minutes).
  e. The second affirmative panelist cross-examines the first negative panelist (4 minutes).
  f. Questions from the audience are put to the members of the negative team (5 minutes).

g. The second negative panelist summarizes the negative case (2 minutes).
h. The second affirmative panelist summarizes the affirmative case (2 minutes).

6. Spreadsheet simulation (more advanced): Suppose that demand is given by $P = a - bQ$, private-cost supply is given by $P = c + dQ$, and marginal external cost equals "e."

a. Solve for the algebraic "free market" equilibrium price and quantity $(P^{\#}, Q^{\#})$, total external cost, deadweight social loss, and true net gains from trade. These are found using the private-cost supply curve and the demand curve, and are "reduced-form" solutions described entirely as algebraic expressions of parameters a, b, c, and d. Place these labeled equations in your spreadsheet.

b. Solve for the algebraic "socially optimal" equilibrium price and quantity (P^*, Q^*) and true net gains from trade. Assume that negative externalities are fully internalized and offset by a Pigouvian tax that is used to compensate those harmed by pollution, and to restore the environment. These are found using the social-cost supply curve (private cost $+ e$) and the demand curve, and are "reduced-form" solutions described entirely as algebraic expressions of parameters a, b, c, and d. Place these labeled equations in your spreadsheet.

c. Using the following parameters ($a = 2000$, $b = 1$, $c = 100$, $d = 2$, and $e = 300$), plot demand, social-cost supply, and private-cost supply in a diagram for different values of price and quantity in a fully labeled diagram. Provide a brief narrative economic interpretation of the two different equilibria shown in your diagram.

d. For the parameter values in 6c above, derive the numerical values for $P^{\#}$, $Q^{\#}$, P^*, Q^*, total external cost, deadweight social loss, and true net gains from trade, using the equations in 6a and 6b.

e. Perform sensitivity analysis on deadweight social loss by varying the parameter value for "e" ($e = 100, 300, 500$). Provide a brief narrative economic interpretation.

Internet Links

EPA's National Center for Environmental Economics (http://yosemite1.epa.gov/ee/epa/eed.nsf/pages/homepage): You can access a wide variety of EPA economic studies, including the benefit/cost analysis of the Clean Air Act cited in the text.

Environmental Externalities in Electric Power Markets: Acid Rain, Urban Ozone, and Climate Change (www.eia.doe.gov/cneaf/pubs_html/rea/feature1.html): An article by John Carlin, sponsored by the U.S. Energy Information Administration.

External Costs Associated with Electricity and Transport (www.externe.info/externpr.pdf): Data on average external cost per kilowatt-hour for various European countries, from the European Commission.

Negative Externalities Audio Clip (www.humboldt.edu/~envecon/audio/1.ram): A brief audio clip of the author describing negative externalities.

Oil Slickers: How Petroleum Benefits at the Taxpayer's Expense (www.ilsr.org/carbo/costs/truecosttoc.html): An article by Jenny B. Wahl, sponsored by the Institute for Local Self-Reliance. Particularly relevant is Section V on the environmental and health costs of petroleum.

Private and Common Property Rights (http://allserv.rug.ac.be/~gdegeest/2000book.pdf): Article by Elinor Ostrom in the on-line *Encyclopedia of Law and Economics* that clearly distinguishes private property, common property, open-access regimes, and common-pool resources.

Pollution Taxes (http://allserv.rug.ac.be/~gdegeest/2500book.pdf): Article by Britt Groosman in the on-line *Encyclopedia of Law and Economics.*

Nuisance (http://allserv.rug.ac.be/~gdegeest/2100book.pdf): Article by Timothy Swanson and Andreas Kontoleon in the on-line *Encyclopedia of Law and Economics.*

The Common Law: How It Protects the Environment (www.perc.org/publications/policyseries/commonlaw_full.php?s=2): Article by Roger Meiners and Bruce Yandle, sponsored by the Political Economy Research Institute, describing how the common law can be effective in protecting the environment.

The Real Price of Gasoline (www.icta.org/projects/trans/): A study produced by the International Center for Technology Assessment on the external costs of gasoline.

References and Further Reading

Ayres, R., and A. Kneese. 1969. "Production, Consumption, and Externalities." *American Economic Review* 59 (June): 282–97.

Baumol, W. 1972. "On Taxation and the Control of Externalities." *American Economic Review* 62 (June): 307–22.

Baumol, W., and W. Oates. 1988. *The Theory of Environmental Policy.* 2nd ed. Cambridge: Cambridge University Press.

Bromley, D. 1989. *Economic Interests and Institutions: The Conceptual Framework of Public Policy.* Oxford: Basil Blackwell.

Coase, R. 1960. "The Problem of Social Cost." *Journal of Law and Economics* 3 (October): 1–44.

Commons, J. 1968. *Legal Foundations of Capitalism.* Madison: University of Wisconsin Press.

European Commission. 2003. *External Costs: Research Results on Socio-Environmental Damages due to Electricity and Transport.* Brussels, Belgium: European Communities.

Hanna, S. 1996. "Property Rights, People, and the Environment." In *Getting Down to Earth: Practical Applications of Ecological Economics,* ed. R. Costanza, O. Segura, and J. Martinez-Alier. Washington, DC: Island Press.

McEvoy, A. 1986. *The Fisherman's Problem: Ecology and Law in the California Fisheries, 1850–1980.* London, UK: Cambridge University Press.

Meiners, R., and B. Yandle. 1998. "The Common Law: How It Protects the Environment." PERC Policy Series Paper PS-13.

Ostrom, E. 1990. *Governing the Commons: The Evolution of Institutions for Collective Action.* Cambridge: Cambridge University Press.

———. 1997. "Private and Common Property Rights." Section 2000, *Encyclopedia of Law and Economics* (Internet publication http://encyclo.findlaw.com/lit/2000art.html).

Schlager, E., and E. Ostrom. 1992. "Property Rights Regimes and Natural Resources: A Conceptual Analysis." *Land Economics* 68 (3): 249–62.

Scitovsky, T. 1954. "Two Concepts of External Economies." *Journal* of *Political Economy* 62 (April): 143–51.

Tietenberg, T. 1996. *Environmental and Natural Resource Economics.* 4th ed. New York: HarperCollins.

U.S. Environmental Protection Agency. 1997. *The Benefits and Costs of the Clean Air Act, 1970–1990.* Washington, DC: U.S. EPA.

Young, O. 1982. *Resource Regimes: Natural Resources and Social Institutions.* Berkeley: University of California Press.

5

The Economics of Natural Resource Systems, Part I: Theory and Concepts

Introduction and Overview

Environmental economics is primarily concerned with identifying externalities and evaluating regulatory policies designed to control them. Traditionally, natural resources economics has been concerned with the optimal use and management of natural resource systems. An element of nature is a natural resource when it is directly useful to people, or when human technology can utilize it to form something valuable. For example, petroleum bubbling up through the ground and fouling soil used to be considered a nuisance to farmers until the development of refining and internal combustion engine technology transformed this material into a valuable natural resource. As will be shown below, the price of a natural resource reflects the relative scarcity of the resource and the availability of substitutes, and acts as a driver for technological innovation. Increasing scarcity will tend to increase the resource's price and promote the production and consumption of substitutes. This process is illustrated by the increased production and consumption of coal and natural gas (and increased research and development spending on alternative energy) following the oil price shocks in the mid-1970s caused by the Organization of Petroleum Exporting Countries (OPEC) oil embargo.

   The best methods for managing a given natural resource system depend upon factors such as relative resource prices, available substitutes, environmental impacts, societal values, and the physical characteristics of the resource. For example, some natural resource systems—such as oil fields, natural gas fields, coal beds, and other fossil-fuel energy resources—are inherently *nonrenewable*. The question of interest for nonrenewable resource systems has to do with optimal extraction rates over time: should the resource be depleted immediately, very gradually, or not at all? In this chapter, we will investigate the conditions required for efficient extraction of a nonrenewable resource over time. Many nonrenewable mineral resources such as iron and aluminum are also recyclable, in which case current primary production creates its own future competition in the form of increased secondary (recycled) supplies. We will review this issue and consider the incentives and the legal treatment of recyclable resource monopolists.

Another class of natural resource system is comprised of the renewable resources associated with the self-regulating elements of life on earth. Issues associated with renewable resources—such as pasturage, forests, groundwater basins, rivers, the air, fisheries, and wildlife populations— include the *maximum sustained yield* that can be harvested from the resource without depleting the productive capacity of the resource system. Private ownership has been suggested as a way of preventing the depletion of commercially valuable resources such as timber and pasturage. Private ownership is not a panacea, however, since private ownership does not resolve harms to aspects of the environment that lack commercial market value. Moreover, resource systems having *common-pool* characteristics, such as the stocks of air, groundwater, stratospheric ozone, and marine fisheries, are difficult to partition as private property. In this chapter, we will look at the economics of common-pool resources and the tragedy of the commons in detail. In chapter 6 we will look at marine fisheries management as a practical application of the economics of common-pool resources. Additional coverage of common-pool resources from the perspective of local self-governance is provided in chapter 16.

Less obvious but no less important from an economic standpoint are the various *ecosystem services* such as fresh water provided by the hydrological cycle, fertility provided by topsoil, and oxygen provided by plants. Another vital ecosystem service is the *sink capacity* of the biosphere—its capacity to absorb human wastes. Examples of sink functions include the capacity of rivers, wetlands, and other bodies of water to absorb waste, and the capacity of aquatic and terrestrial ecosystems to absorb carbon dioxide generated as a byproduct of the burning of fossil fuels. Ecosystem services can be thought of as the flow of benefits that derive from the stock of natural capital. The economics of ecosystem services is a new and emerging area of study that will be briefly surveyed below.

Allocating Nonrenewable Resources

Examples of nonrenewable natural resources include:

- oil fields
- natural gas fields
- coal beds
- mineral deposits

In fact, nonrenewable resources are in large part synonymous with mineral and fossil fuel energy resources. The term *nonrenewable* means that the resource system ultimately has a *fixed stock* (fixed size of total "reserves") within the human timeframe. Nonrenewable resources can be further divided into two categories:

- nonrenewable, nonrecyclable (fossil-fuel energy resources)
- nonrenewable, recyclable (some mineral resources such as iron and aluminum and gold)

Let's begin by considering the nonrecyclable group.

The Industrial Organization of Energy Delivery in the United States

When oil and natural gas were first developed on a large scale in the United States, there was a need to invest in interstate pipelines to transport these fuels from production fields to refineries (oil) or residential and industrial distribution (gas). Many fields were served by only a single pipeline because of economies of scale in pipe diameter, and the common practice was for joint ownership of producing field and pipeline, which then sold the bundle of fuel and transportation service. To prevent monopoly prices being charged on this bundle, the Natural Gas Act of 1938 resulted in producer/pipeline entities being subjected to public utilities–style regulation of prices (i.e., price is used to recover allowed capital expenditures, variable costs, and a "normal" rate of return on capital investment). This pricing system began to break down following the oil price shocks caused by the OPEC oil embargo in 1973–74; administered prices designed for cost recovery could not adapt to rapid price fluctuations following the embargo. At the same time, the development of transportation network interconnectivity increasingly gave end users access to a variety of potentially competitive producers.

The new system that has emerged for natural gas is very similar to that which also exists for oil and which is emerging for electricity as well. In this system, end users purchase the product (gas, oil, or electricity) under competitive market conditions and then separately contract for transportation and delivery services, aspects of which still have monopoly characteristics and so are regulated under public utility principles. As Lyon and Hackett (1993) have shown, this form of partial energy market deregulation makes the problem of transportation system load balancing in the context of continuous and decentralized injections and withdrawals more complex. There are more transactions and an increased need for system coordination to reduce the potential for negative *network externalities,* which are more likely in partially deregulated systems. Negative network externalities occur when consumer/producer transactions impose harms on overall system function, leading to excess or inadequate pipeline pressure for gas or oil, or the potential for power surges or blackouts in electric transmission and distribution grids.

The spectacular failure of partial deregulation of California's electricity markets highlights by its absence the importance of a well-functioning competitive market for a product with few substitutes. While California has been criticized by industry observers for NIMBYism ("not in my backyard") when it comes to the construction of new power plants, perhaps an even more important failure was the institutional structure of the electric power market. Developed in the mid-1990s when there was a large excess generating capacity, and when Californians were paying higher-than-average regulated electricity rates, deregulation was seen as a way for industrial and other consumers to access cheaper electric power. The public utilities were encouraged to sell their power plants to independent power producers as a way to create a larger number of power sellers and promote competition. Retail electricity rates were cut by 10 percent but remained fixed, while wholesale electricity prices were set each day in the California Power Exchange (Cal PX) market, subject to network load balancing done by the California Independent System Operator (CAISO). Fixed retail rates and floating wholesale rates were an element of the deregulation plan lobbied for by public utilities anticipating profit due to what were then very low wholesale electricity prices.

In the first few years the California deregulation plan worked, though the economic boom of the late 1990s increased baseload demand, which in combination with no new plants being built resulted in much of the excess generating capacity being eliminated. Moreover, economic growth in neighboring states reduced the generating capacity that could be imported from out of state. Then, during hot summer days when demand increased to within several percentage points of available generating capacity, independent power producers and brokers discovered they could game the market in various ways and trigger emergency prices that were many times higher than had existed prior to deregulation. For example, an independent power producer could take a power plant offline for bogus maintenance, trigger emergency pricing, and then bring the plant back online at much higher prices. Perhaps the most infamous villain of the California energy crisis, however, was Enron.

As the *New York Times* reported on May 7, 2002, "[e]lectricity traders at Enron drove up prices during the California power crisis through questionable techniques that company lawyers said 'may have contributed' to severe power shortages." Examples of Enron market gaming tactics include:

- *Death Star:* "Enron gets paid for moving energy to relieve congestion without actually moving any energy or relieving any congestion" (excerpted from Enron memos, December 2000).
- *Loadshift:* Enron created "the appearance of congestion through the deliberate overstatement" of power to be delivered (excerpted from Enron memos, December 2000).
- *Fatboy:* Documents provided by Enron state that its "Fatboy" trading strategy included parking energy on El Paso Electric's system (excerpted from El Paso Electric federal lawsuit settlement).
- *Ricochet:* Enron bought energy from the Cal PX and exported it to El Paso Electric; El Paso sold it back to Enron, and Enron resold it back to the CAISO in the real-time market (excerpted from El Paso Electric federal lawsuit settlement).

As a result, Californians paid billions of dollars more for electricity than they would have under the previous system of regulation. Various independent power producers and brokers such as Enron have been the target of federal and state prosecution efforts.

The Theory of Dynamically Efficient Nonrenewable Resource Pricing

An important economic problem we now turn to is how to allocate a fixed stock of resource, such as oil or natural gas, efficiently over time. If we were to develop the stock of oil reserves rapidly, current prices would decline, but as the stock is rapidly exhausted, prices in the future will also rapidly increase. Yet these high future prices give owners of oil an incentive to reduce current production in order to have oil to sell in the future at these high prices. Recall from chapter 3 that well-functioning competitive markets are efficient in the sense that they maximize total surplus—consumer surplus plus producer surplus. Harold Hotelling (1931) and other economists have derived a similar efficiency criterion, known as *dynamic efficiency,* for determining the optimal balancing of current and future sales in a competitive natural resource market. Before we consider dynamic efficiency, however, we must first develop some tools for measuring the present value of payments made or received in the future.

Present Value Analysis

Most of us can acknowledge that an individual would rather have $1,000 today than in the future. Reasons include the ability to spend the money right away and avoid higher future prices due to inflation, or the opportunity to invest the money now and receive interest or dividend income. The higher value placed on receiving $1,000 today rather than in the future reflects the fact that a future payment is *discounted* or diminished when considering its *present value*. For example, suppose that the lowest interest rate that a lender is willing to accept in order to make a one-year loan of $1,000 is 10 percent. This information tells us that the lender is indifferent between having $1,000 today (the present value) and being repaid $1,100 in one year (the future value). The future value of today's $1,000 will increase with the interest rate and with the length of time of the loan. There is another way of looking at this relationship. Suppose someone was going to receive $1,100 exactly one year in the future, but the person needed that money in the present. What is the smallest amount of money that that person would take right now in return for giving up the inheritance next year? The answer to this question is that person's present value of the future $1,100 inheritance. Economists use the term *discount rate* to refer to the rate of time preference (such as an interest rate) that equates present value and future value. The formula for determining the present value (PV) of a stream of payments into the future is as follows:

PV of a stream of future payments $= \Sigma_i$ ($ payment, i years from the present)$/(1 + r)^i$, $i = 0, 1, 2, \ldots, n$.

Note that Σ_i means summation over all i time periods," while i refers to the number of years from the present that a particular payment is received, and r refers to the discount rate. Interest rates or the average (risk-adjusted) rates of return available from portfolios of stocks are examples of discount rates.

If there is just one payment to be made in a future period that is i years from the present, as in our $1,000 example above, then the PV of the single future payment is found as follows:

PV of a single future payment $= $ ($ payment, i years from the present)$/(1 + r)^i$.

Continuing our $1,000 example above, suppose that the discount rate is 10 percent. Then using the formula above, $i = 1$, $r = 0.1$, and the PV of $1,000 to be received next year is $\$1{,}000/(1.1)^1 = \$909.09$. In other words, if the discount rate is 10 percent, then one is indifferent between $909.09 received today and $1,000 received in one year. Another way to look at this is to note that if you took $909.09 today and invested it in a bond that pays 10 percent interest, then in one year your $909.09 will have grown to be $1,000.

Dynamic Efficiency

A resource market is dynamically efficient when the sum of total surplus (in PV terms) is maximized over the entire time horizon in which the resource is allocated. We will now consider a very simple example of a competitive market for oil to illustrate how one can solve for the dynamically efficient allocation of the resource in question. We will see that the dynamically efficient allocation is also an equilibrium in that producers have no incentive to reallocate resource sales from one year to the next.

There are a number of assumptions that we need to keep in mind as we work through the analysis. We assume that there is a well-functioning competitive market for the resource in question, and that market participants are fully and completely informed of current and future demand, marginal cost, discount rate, available supplies, and price.

To keep the example simple there will only be two periods in the analysis—the present time, referred to as year 0, and year 1. For the sake of simplicity, we will also assume that the marginal cost of producing oil is constant and equal to $5 per barrel. As we learned in chapter 4, marginal cost is the basis for the competitive market supply curve. Since marginal cost is constant at $5, the market supply curve for the resource in question is also constant at $5. Finally, we assume that market demand is the same in each of the two periods.

Let the demand for oil in a given year be given by the following expression:

$$P = 20 - .5q.$$

Note that q refers to quantity of oil in barrels. We will assume that there is a fixed quantity—Q_{tot}—equal to 40 barrels of oil that can be allocated over the two years, and that people in this market use a 15 percent discount rate.

In order to provide a basis for comparison with the dynamically efficient solution, let's first suppose that market participants in year 0 fully ignore the consequences of their actions on year 1 supplies, prices, and profit. Then in

Figure 5.1 **Total Surplus, Year 0**

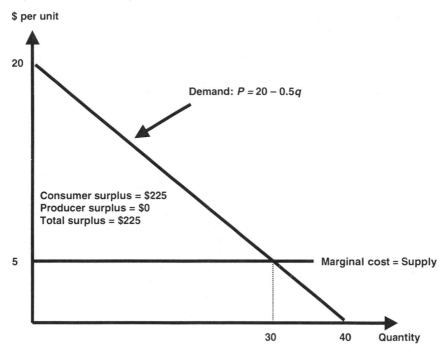

$ per unit

20

Demand: $P = 20 - 0.5q$

Consumer surplus = $225
Producer surplus = $0
Total surplus = $225

5 ──────────────────── Marginal cost = Supply

30   40   Quantity

year 0 the competitive market equilibrium quantity of oil traded is found at that price ($5) where supply equals demand:

$$20 - .5q = 5.$$

Solving for q we find that 30 barrels of oil would be traded in year 0. If we now substitute 30 for q in the demand equation, we can confirm that equilibrium price is $5. Note, however, that we have only left 10 barrels of oil for consumption in year 1.

As we can see in Figure 5.1, if market participants ignore the future, then in year 0 total surplus in this market is:

$$.5(15 \times 30) = \$225.$$

Note that the entire total surplus in year 0 is made up of consumer surplus (recall from chapter 3 that this represents a simplified approximation for the exact value for consumer surplus). Producer surplus equals zero because firms are selling at price equal to marginal cost. Since market participants have

Figure 5.2   **Total Surplus, Year 1**

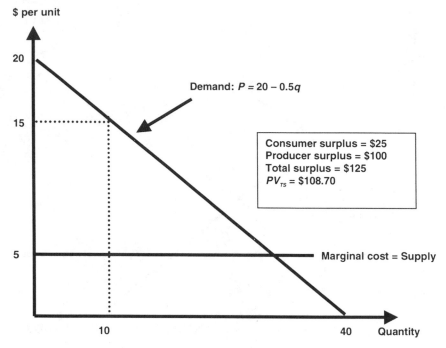

ignored the future period, there are only 10 barrels of oil available for year 1.

With only 10 barrels of oil supplies available, we can determine the price of oil in year 1 by substituting 10 for q in our demand equation:

$$20 - (.5 \times 10) = \$15.$$

In year 1 consumer surplus is considerably smaller ($25), while producer surplus is considerably larger ($100), as illustrated in Figure 5.2, and consequently total surplus in year 1 is $125.

The sum of total surplus (in PV terms) over the two time periods is:

$$\$225/(1.15)^0 + \$125/(1.15)^1 = \$333.70.$$

Is the sum of total surplus (in PV terms) when market participants in year 0 ignore their gains from trade in year 1 the maximum available? Have we achieved the dynamically efficient allocation of the resource stock? Are we in a dynamic equilibrium? As we will see below, the answer is no. To help build your intuition, suppose that you were a seller of oil in the market above, but you no longer ignored prices and profit in year 1. If you knew that today's price of $5 would rise to next year's price of $15, would you want to hold off selling some oil today and save some for next year? The answer is yes. Note that the *marginal profit* from selling a barrel of oil is $(P - MC)$. The marginal profit from selling a single barrel of oil in year 0 is $0, since the $5 price equals marginal cost. If instead you were to save that one barrel of oil and sell it in year 1, price in year 1 would be $(20 - 0.5 \times 11) = $14.50 and the *PV* of marginal profit in year 1 would be $(14.5 - 5)/(1.15)^1$, which equals $8.26. Clearly, a profit-maximizing firm that is fully informed of current and future market conditions has an incentive to shift this barrel of production from year 0 to year 1. Therefore, the allocation of 30 barrels of oil in year 0, and 10 barrels of oil in year 1, is not in a dynamic equilibrium. We will show below how to find the dynamic equilibrium, and we will show that this equilibrium is dynamically efficient and maximizes the sum of total surplus (in *PV* terms).

The dynamically efficient equilibrium with full information on current and future market conditions is one in which the marginal profit of selling a barrel of oil today is equal to the *PV* of marginal profit from selling a barrel of oil next year (and in any future years). Economist Harold Hotelling (1931) developed a rule for finding the dynamically efficient solution to resource allocation problems such as ours. The rule for dynamic efficiency, called *Hotelling's rule,* requires that marginal profit $(P - MC)$ in year 0 must equal the *PV* of $(P - MC)$ in year 1 (and in any other future years). Hotelling's rule simply formalizes our intuition that dynamic equilibrium occurs when the marginal profit from selling a unit of the resource is the same today as it is in a future period. As you might expect, if there are more than just two periods, then Hotelling's rule requires that the PV of $(P - MC)$ be equal across all time periods in which the resource is to be allocated. When this condition holds, the sum of total surplus (in *PV* terms) over all time periods in which the resource is to be allocated will be maximized.

One can solve the dynamic resource allocation problem using the mathematics of optimization, or by repeated experiment. Since the reader is not assumed to possess advanced mathematics, we will demonstrate the method of repeated experiment. First, let's develop some intuition. We already know that 30 barrels in year 0 and 10 barrels in year 1 is not a dynamic equilibrium since firms will not produce these quantities in these years. We also know that a firm can increase its profit by reducing production below 30 barrels in year 0 and increasing production above 10 barrels in year 1. Since future profits (and gains from trade in general) are discounted, do you think that the dynamically efficient solution will lead to (i) a larger share of the total resource being consumed in year 0 than in year 1, (ii) an equal share of the total resource being consumed in years 0 and 1, or (iii) a smaller share of the total resource being consumed in year 0 than in year 1?

Since future payoffs are discounted relative to the present, market participants will generally prefer to get a larger share of their gains from trade now rather than later, which means a larger share of the total resource is produced and consumed in year 0, as in (i) above. Moreover, the higher the discount rate the stronger the preference for current over future profit (or gains from trade), and the less that will be saved for future production and consumption. Therefore, the dynamically efficient solution to our problem will involve allocating more of the total oil stock in year 0 than in year 1.

The *repeated experiment* method simply involves trying different divisions of the resource and testing the allocation using Hotelling's rule. For example, given the intuition we developed above you might start out trying 22 barrels in year 0 and 18 barrels in year 1. Now you should test this allocation by computing the *PV* of $(P - MC)$ in the two years to see if they are equal. With 22 barrels in year 0, price in year 0 is $9 and the *PV* of $(P- MC)$ in year 0 is $4. With 18 barrels in year 1, price in year 1 is $11 and the *PV* of $(P- MC)$ in year 1 is $5.22. Therefore, an allocation of 22 in year 0 and 18 in year 1 does not meet Hotelling's rule. When Hotelling's rule is not met, you should allocate more resource to the period in which the *PV* of $(P - MC)$ is larger, and again check to see if Hotelling's rule is satisfied. Continue this process until you zero in on a sufficiently precise solution.

The *exact solution* to this problem derives from the mathematics of optimization. Some of the key steps in this process require higher mathematics than is assumed to be known by many readers. Suppose that demand in each of two periods is given by the following equation:

$$P = a - bq.$$

Marginal extraction cost (*MC*) is a constant and equal to "*c*," which implies that total extraction cost is *cQ*. As before, the constant discount rate is given by "*r*." Since *MC* is constant the supply curve is horizontal, and total surplus is equal to the area under between the demand curve and *MC* (this is the same total surplus [TS] as the area between the supply and demand curves that we first explored in chapter 3). Integral calculus can be used to show that this total surplus is given in algebraic form by the following equation:

$$TS = aq - bq^2/2 - cq$$

The optimization problem is to choose an allocation of the fixed resource stock over each of the time periods under analysis in order to maximize the sum of *TS*, in *PV* terms, for each of the time periods. Since we are maximizing the sum of *TS*, in *PV* terms, this solution is dynamically efficient. The optimization problem is constrained by the fact that the total resource allocated over time cannot exceed the fixed stock available. Derivative calculus is used to identify the optimal allocation. If there are only two time periods under analysis (periods 0 and 1), then the optimal solution satisfies the following two equations:

$$a - bq_0 - c)/(1+r)^0 = (a - bq_1 - c)/(1+r)^1$$
and
$$q_0 + q_1 = Q_{tot}$$

The solution to these equations will provide the exact solution to the problem of identifying the dynamically efficient allocation of the fixed resource stock. In the example we have been working on, $a = 20$, $b = 0.5$, $c = 5$, $r = 0.15$, and $Q_{tot} = 40$. As a result, the exact solution to our particular problem satisfies the following two equations:

$$(15 - 0.5q_0)/(1.15)^0 = (15 - 0.5q_1)/(1.15)^1$$
and
$$q_0 + q_1 = 40$$

With two equations and two unknowns (q_0 and q_1), we can make use of the fact that $q_0 = 40 - q_1$ from the second equation and substitute $40 - q_1$ for q_0 into the first equation, which reduces the problem to one equation that can be solved for q_1. Once q_1 is found we can then solve for $q_0 = 40 - q_1$.

Using this method in our problem, it can be shown that the exact solution involves selling 20.7 barrels of oil in year 0, in which case market price in year 0 is $20 - (.5 \times 20.7) = \$9.65$, and the marginal profit ($P - MC$) from selling the last barrel of oil in year 0 is $4.65. This allocation is illustrated in Figure 5.3. We would then have the remaining 19.3 barrels of oil to sell in year 1 at a price of $10.35. Therefore, you can see that consuming more today and less in the future causes price to rise over time. In year 1 the PV of ($P - MC$) is $\$5.35/(1.15)^1$, or $4.65, which is the same as in year 0, as shown in Figure 5.4. Since marginal profit in PV terms is equal in the two time periods, Hotelling's rule is satisfied.

This is a dynamic equilibrium because sellers have no incentive to shift sales from one year to the next, since marginal profit in PV terms is equal in the two time periods. The sum of total surplus (in PV terms) over the two years is $374.14 in the dynamic equilibrium. One cannot rearrange the allocation of the 40 units of resource in our problem between year 0 and year 1 and generate any more than $374.14 in total surplus (in PV terms over the

Figure 5.3   **Dynamically Efficient Solution, Year 0**

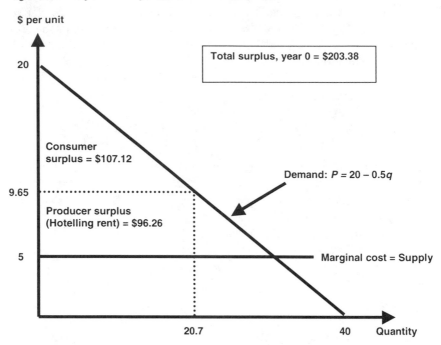

two years), which indicates that this dynamic equilibrium also results in dynamically efficient resource allocation. One can see, however, that the sum of total surplus (in *PV* terms) is larger in the dynamic equilibrium than when 30 barrels are allocated to year 0 and 10 to year 1.

This brings us to an important insight. When a nonrenewable resource is abundant, then consumption today does not involve an opportunity cost of forgone marginal profit in the future, since there is plenty available for both today and the future. As the resource becomes increasingly scarce, however, consumption today involves an increasingly high opportunity cost of forgone marginal profit in the future. Therefore the profit created by this form of resource scarcity is called *Hotelling rent* (also known as *resource rent* or by the Ricardian term *scarcity rent*). Hotelling rent is economic profit that can be earned and can persist in certain natural resource cases due to the fixed supply of the resource. Hotelling rent generated in year 0 by our dynamically efficient solution is illustrated in Figure 5.3. Due to fixed supply, consumption of a resource unit today has an opportunity cost equal to the present value of the marginal profit from selling the resource in the future. This opportunity cost limits current supply, which in turn elevates current

Figure 5.4   **Dynamically Efficient Solution, Year 1**

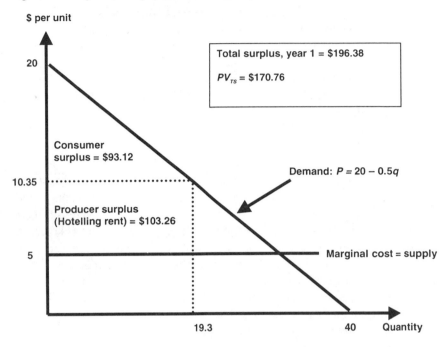

price above marginal cost, creating the rent. Likewise, marginal Hotelling rent is defined to be the marginal profit received from a unit of the scarce resource, $(P - MC)$. As a resource becomes increasingly scarce relative to current and future demand, this scarcity is revealed in higher and higher marginal Hotelling rent.

Applying this analysis to the world petroleum market is complicated by several factors. First, proven and recoverable reserves have increased over time due to new discoveries, and changes in technology have allowed for recovery of stocks that had been considered unrecoverable in the past. Second, the world petroleum market has not been well functioning and competitive. The OPEC cartel has had periods of success in artificially limiting quantity supplied in order to raise price, and the United States and other countries have distorted competitive supply conditions by providing massive subsidies for oil production and shipment through both tax policy and militarization of key foreign production areas and shipping routes (more on this topic in chapter 13). Third, petroleum usage generates large unresolved negative externalities in the form of pollution and climate change (see chapters 4 and 11) that distort competitive supply conditions in the world petroleum market. Many petroleum experts believe that *peak oil,* the point at which world oil production peaks, either has already occurred or will occur soon. Uncertainty exists because it is possible that new reserves will still be discovered, and that reserves reported by oil companies and governments may be distorted by market or cartel incentives to overstate stocks. Once peak oil production is reached, rising future demand will be confronted with declining future quantities supplied, and Hotelling-style pricing equilibria are likely to become manifest in the global market.

As a final point, note that the discount rate has a powerful impact on the dynamically efficient allocation of the scarce resource. For example, a zero percent discount rate indicates that people are indifferent between a payment today and a payment in the future. If you replaced the 15 percent discount rate with a zero percent discount rate in the example given above, then you should be able to prove to yourself that the dynamically efficient solution results in an equal division of the resource over time. As the discount rate rises, however, people increasingly prefer receiving their gain from trade in the present rather than in the future. Therefore, the higher the discount rate the larger the share of the resource consumed in the present rather than in the future. At the limiting case of an infinite percent discount rate (indicating that people place no value on a future payment, such as those who hold that the world will end after today), then the dynamically efficient solution is to consume all of the resource today. Therefore, the notion of sustaining a resource for future generations relies upon people today having relatively low discount rates. This topic will be addressed in detail at the end of chapter 13.

The simple two-period model with stable per-period demand and constant marginal cost yields valuable insights into the way that a scarce resource is efficiently allocated across time by a competitive resource market. Those interested in the more general *N*-period analysis with increasing marginal costs and substitute resources may wish to consult Tietenberg (2006). We will return to the topic of Hotelling rents in chapter 13, where a model of sustainable economic development is presented in which reinvestment of these rents in natural or human-made capital, such as by way of a resource depletion tax, contributes to sustainability.

Allocating Recyclable Resources

Many resources such as paper, plastic, and metal are recyclable. One interesting aspect of recyclable resources is that salvaged or recycled resource acts as a substitute for virgin resource. Suppose for a moment that virgin and recycled sources for a resource result in an identical commodity (e.g., aluminum ingots). Suppose further that the supply of resource commodity gen-

Figure 5.5 **Commodity Market with Costly Recycled and Cheaper Virgin Supplies**

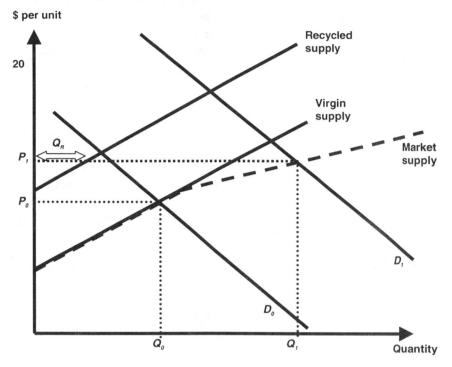

erated from recycling involves higher marginal cost due to additional collection, sorting, and shipping, and that these exceed any energy cost savings that may accrue due to reduced processing costs for the recycled resource. In this case the commodity market will have three supply curves—one for the recycled source, one for the virgin source, and the market supply curve that represents the horizontal sum of these two supply curves. This circumstance is illustrated in Figure 5.5. Two different cases are explored. With low commodity demand (D_0 in Figure 5.5), equilibrium price P_0 is everywhere below the minimum price required to supply commodity from recycled sources. In this case, firms (or recycling centers) cannot afford to supply recycled material due to its higher marginal cost, and the entire equilibrium market quantity Q_0 is generated from virgin material. Under this unfortunate circumstance recycling will only occur if the higher collection, sorting, and shipping costs are subsidized. In contrast, with high commodity demand (D_1 in Figure 5.5), equilibrium price P_1 results in a total equilibrium market quantity Q_1, a portion of which (Q_R, as indicated by the arrow in Figure 5.5) is generated from recycled material. In this case higher market demand enables results in an equilibrium market price that is sufficiently high as to support market-based recycling without subsidy.

An interesting problem for metals cartels and monopolists is in setting production levels and prices for primary resources, knowing that these prices and production levels directly affect future competition from secondary (recycled) resources. Excessive current production of a durable resource or good will increase the future used or recycled supplies that act as substitutes for future primary production. Consider the problem of the manufacturer of a durable good such as a textbook. College textbook authors and publishers can mitigate the level of future competition in the used-textbook market by producing new editions of the book. Thus, long before a textbook is obsolete, the authors and publishers will find the cheaper used-textbook supplies squeezing out sales of new textbooks and so will have an incentive to introduce new editions to make the existing stock of used books obsolete. This is an example of planned obsolescence. Now consider the problem of the producer of metals and other durable resources. In the case of metals, a higher level of current production assures a higher secondary scrap market supply. As the stock of scrap grows, the supply of (new + used) metal grows, driving down price.

This is very similar to the story of Alcoa in the early decades of the twentieth century. Alcoa had about 90 percent of the virgin aluminum market in the United States (smelted from bauxite ore) and competed against recycled material Alcoa had produced in previous years. Since current production creates a negative (pecuniary) externality on future profits, the optimal amount of metal to supply in the current year reflects not only the current year's profits but also the present value of all impacts on (forecasted) future profits. Gaskins (1974) was able to show that in this circumstance Alcoa had an incentive to produce less than the optimal monopoly output of primary aluminum in order to mitigate future secondary aluminum competition. Alcoa was found guilty of monopolization of the U.S. aluminum market in 1945. Judge Learned Hand argued in the decision that "the competition of 'secondary' must therefore be disregarded, as soon as we consider the position of 'Alcoa' over a period of years: it was as much within 'Alcoa's' control as was the production of the 'virgin' from which it had been derived" (in Gaskins 1974, p. 254).

Even though Alcoa did not have a full monopoly in the (new + scrap) aluminum market, Hand argued that Alcoa was able to use its monopoly in the virgin aluminum market to control the supplies of its scrap supplier rivals and thus exert market power in the (new + scrap) market.

Economists such as Milton Friedman have commented on the Alcoa decision by pointing out that the secondary market would eventually have curtailed Alcoa's monopoly in the primary market. Yet Gaskins (1974) found that if aluminum demand is growing, as has been the case, then demand growth almost totally mitigates the procompetitive effect of the secondary market, which supports Judge Hand's decision.

Allocating Renewable Resources

Unlike nonrenewable resources such as minerals, renewable resources are a part of the self-regulating process of the living planet. Removing some trees, fish, groundwater, forage, or dissolved oxygen in a river will not result in permanent destruction of the resource stock. Renewable resources can be depleted, however, if use exceeds the *maximum sustainable yield* over extended periods of time. Substantial work has been done on establishing maximum sustained yield from various renewable resource stocks, the results of which underlie disciplines such as fisheries and forest management. The notion underlying maximum sustained yield is to identify the largest harvest rate (a "flow" variable) that can be sustained indefinitely from the existing resource stock. A complicating factor is that resources on the living planet are not independent of one another—harvest of one affects availability of another. Thus a harvest rate consistent with maximum sustained yield of one resource (say, timber) can affect the level of the stock of another resource (say, a fishery or wildlife).

This challenge of balancing multiple interdependent resource uses and maximum sustained yield of a renewable resource is illustrated by the U.S. Forest Service (USFS). The USFS is a federal agency created by the Organic Act of 1897 and charged with managing federally owned lands, largely forested, for multiple uses. Gifford Pinchot, an early leader of the USFS, gave direction to USFS employees by arguing that multiple use meant that all resources occurring on national forest lands—wilderness/recreation, watershed, timber, wildlife—had equal standing. Prior to the 1950s it was rare for timber harvesting to adversely affect the other resources occurring on the national forest lands. During the 1950s, however, the amount of timber harvested nationally more than doubled, as did recreational visitation. Thus, conflicts began to arise between those who thought that timber harvest should be the primary product of the national forests and those who believed that protection of other resource values was the highest priority.

In 1960 the Multiple-Use Sustained Yield Act formally stated as law Pinchot's argument that all resource values had equal standing and arose in part because of negative public reaction to the unconstrained timber harvesting being conducted by USFS personnel. Respect for nontimber resource values was further strengthened by passage of a series of laws during the

1960s and early 1970s. The Wilderness Act of 1964 allows Congress and the president to grant formal wilderness protection under federal law to certain tracts of federal land, and was a landmark law in recognizing nontimber resource values. The National Environmental Policy Act of 1970 formally requires the USFS and other agencies to conduct environmental impact analysis and to provide for public participation. The Endangered Species Act of 1973 requires that projects such as logging in the national forests be contingent on there being no adverse impact on any species listed as endangered or threatened and requires mitigation for adverse impacts to these species. The Resource Planning Act of 1974 requires the USFS and similar agencies to propose long-term objectives and to construct long-term resource plans consistent with these objectives. Concerns about the harms caused by clear-cutting led to the passage of the National Forest Management Act of 1976, which requires the USFS to create a forest plan for each national forest. This plan provides key direction to timber harvest volumes, methods, and locations, and explicitly requires a plan for managing nontimber resources. Forest plans are contentious and allow for public comment and appeal, and so take a great deal of time to develop, but nearly all projects are now open to public review and appeal.

According to the U.S. Forest Service (1995), $130.7 billion in gross domestic product were created by national forests in the year 2000. Of that, $97.8 billion derives from recreation, plus $12.9 billion from fish and wildlife benefits. The combined recreational and fish/wildlife values account for 85 percent of the total economic value generated by U.S. national forests. Only $3.5 billion will be generated by timber harvest. Similarly, of the estimated 3.3 million jobs directly or indirectly generated by activity in the U.S. national forests for the year 2000, recreation and fish/wildlife accounted for 87.7 percent of the total. Recreational visitor-days totaled 730 million in 1993, nearly a quarter of which occurred in California, and overall recreational use is projected to increase 63 percent by 2045. The budget process is still largely driven by timber harvesting, however; while recreation accounts for 75 percent of the economic benefits generated by national forests, only 21 percent of the Forest Service budget goes to support this activity.

Allocating Common-Pool Resources

As we first discussed in chapter 4, many natural resource systems are not partitioned by private property rights. These resources may be held as state property or common property (among a defined user group), or they may simply be open-access. This ownership status may be based on tradition or culture, or because certain resource stocks such as air, groundwater, or open-ocean fisheries are fugitive resources that cannot effectively be partitioned and privately owned.

When a resource stock is not partitioned by private property rights, there is potential for rivalry among those who *appropriate* (harvest resource units) from the resource stock. A common-pool resource (CPR) has the following general characteristics:

- It is difficult to exclude multiple individuals from appropriating from the resource stock, such as is the case when the resource stock is not partitioned by a well-defined and enforced private property rights regime.
- The resource features rivalry in consumption, or subtractability, meaning that resource units appropriated by one party subtract from what is available to others.

Since multiple individuals (*appropriators*) appropriate resource units from the CPR, subtractability implies that appropriation by one imposes an external cost on all other appropriators. This external cost may take the form of less abundant fish in a fishery, less fodder for livestock in a pasture CPR, less water in an aquifer CPR, or less oil in an oil field CPR. This external cost in a CPR is called an *appropriation externality*. Note that a *pure public good* differs from a CPR in that it lacks rivalry in consumption. For example, public television and radio broadcasts do not feature rivalry in consumption because one person's reception does not usually impair the ability of someone else to receive the same broadcast.

As Gordon (1954) and others since then have shown, in the absence of effective *institutions* (rule structures) that limit appropriation from a CPR, people will over-appropriate from the CPR relative to the level of appropriation that would be efficient for the group as a whole. For example, if a commercially valuable CPR could be transformed into a privately owned renewable resource, then the resource owner would select the dynamically efficient appropriation level each year. As with nonrenewable resources described earlier in the chapter, the efficient level of appropriation sustains the resource and generates the largest possible present value of Hotelling rent.

Gordon constructed a simple model of a commercially valuable common-pool resource under open-access conditions to illustrate the problems associated with appropriation externalities. Gordon's model helps us understand the economics of CPR depletion, such as in many of the world's marine capture fisheries. The diagram for Gordon's model differs from the standard supply and demand diagrams we have worked with so far. In Gordon's model, the problem is to find the optimal amount of effort input E instead of the optimal quantity of output Q. Appropriation effort refers to inputs such as capital and labor that are applied to harvesting resource units from the CPR. To keep the example simple, assume that the market price of the resource being harvested is not affected by the amount of effort applied to the fishery. For the same reason we assume that *marginal effort cost (MEC)* and *average effort cost (AEC)* are constant. *MEC* is the increase in total cost from an additional unit of effort, while *AEC* is total cost divided by the total amount of effort applied to resource harvest. For example, constant *MEC* and *AEC* imply that the cost of operating an oil well or a fishing boat for an hour remains constant.

The economic benefits from effort are measured by revenue generation. As with effort cost, there are two important revenue measures for effort—*marginal revenue product (MRP)* and *average revenue product (ARP)*. *MRP* is simply the change in total revenue caused by an additional unit of effort, while average revenue product is total revenue divided by the total amount of effort applied to resource harvest. For example, the revenue generated by operating a fishing vessel for an additional hour is *MRP,* while ARP is the average amount of revenue generated by an hour of vessel operation. Low levels of total appropriation effort do not harm the productivity of the resource stock, and so *ARP* and *MRP* are both high when total effort E is low. For example, if a fishery has not been fished very much, then a vessel can catch many fish in an hour of effort. As total appropriation effort grows, however, the resource stock declines, and so both *MRP* and *ARP* decline. *MRP* declines more sharply than *ARP* because *MRP* reflects revenue generated by an additional unit of effort on an increasingly depleted resource, while *ARP* reflects the average of revenue from both abundant and depleted resource conditions. Declining *MRP* pulls *ARP* down, however, just as a bad set of semester grades will pull down a student's cumulative grade point average.

As shown in Figure 5.6, the group-optimum (efficient) level of appropriation effort E^* occurs where *MEC = MRP.* The intuition is similar to the reasoning behind why a profit-maximizing firm in a competitive market will supply a quantity of output where market price equals marginal cost in chapter 4. Starting at zero effort, one can incrementally increase effort in one-unit intervals and compare *MRP* to *MEC*. As long as *MRP > MEC* then an additional unit of effort will increase profit. If *MRP = MEC,* then further effort will cause *MRP < MEC,* which will cause profit to decline. The efficient level of appropriation effort leads to maximum Hotelling rent to be shared by all the appropriators. This simplified one-diagram model reflects the dynamic efficiency result developed earlier in the chapter. Under conditions of open-access, or when other property rights regimes fail, individual appropriators are unable to work together to limit total effort and maximize Hotelling rent. If one appropriator were to limit effort, someone else would simply harvest the resource units. The result is that Hotelling rent is fully

Figure 5.6 **CPR Appropriation: Full Rent Dissipation Versus Group Optimum**

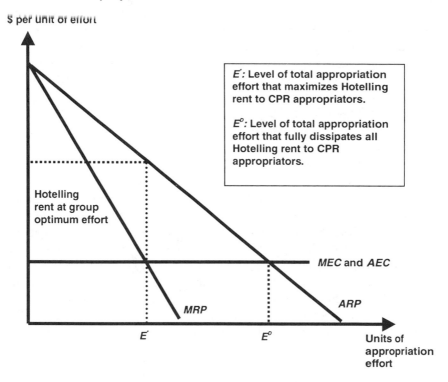

$ per unit of effort

E′: Level of total appropriation effort that maximizes Hotelling rent to CPR appropriators.

E⁰: Level of total appropriation effort that fully dissipates all Hotelling rent to CPR appropriators.

Hotelling rent at group optimum effort

MEC and AEC

MRP

ARP

E′   E⁰

Units of appropriation effort

dissipated, which occurs as an outcome of rivalry among individual appropriators. Rents are fully dissipated at the level of total effort E^D where $AEC = ARP$, because at this point the average cost of a unit of effort equals the average revenue produced by that effort, yielding zero profit or rent. Note that if you multiply both AEC and ARP by total effort E^D you get total cost (TC) = total revenue (TR), which means that $TR - TC = 0$.

Gordon's model also indicates that managing a CPR for maximum net social return results in a lower level of effort than what is required to produce the CPR's maximum sustainable yield (MSY). To see this, note that maximum sustainable yield in Gordon's model occurs at a level of total effort where total product appropriated from the CPR is maximized. Therefore, at MSY the marginal product of a unit of effort is zero. Since the market price of the harvested product is assumed constant, then MRP at MSY is also zero. Consequently, MSY in Gordon's model occurs at the point in Figure 5.4 where MRP becomes equal to zero by crossing the horizontal axis. Recall that the socially efficient level of appropriation effort occurs where $MEC = MRP$. Since MEC is greater than zero, the efficient level of appropriation effort for the appropriators as a group is actually less than what would occur if the CPR were managed for MSY. In the case of a fishery, the implication is that the efficient level of effort for the fishers results in a larger stock of fish being maintained in the fishery than what is required for MSY. In contrast, the open-access outcome is not only economically inefficient, but also biologically inefficient because it results in a smaller stock of fish being maintained in the fishery than what is needed to achieve MSY. We will discuss the economic and policy issues associated with marine capture fisheries in detail in chapter 6.

The dilemma with CPRs is that, unlike the invisible hand of Adam Smith's competitive market, self-interested behavior in a CPR does not yield the efficient outcome. Suppose a village has a common pasture for grazing livestock but lacks effective rules for governing the number of cattle that villagers graze on the pasture. In addition, suppose that the pasture is currently being used at its carrying capacity. If a villager adds one more milk cow to the village pasture, the villager gains 100 percent of the benefit of increased milk production, but also creates an appropriation externality of reduced forage and a deteriorating pasture condition shared by all who graze livestock on the pasture. If all villagers act in the same manner, the result will be destruction of the commons. As Hardin (1968, p. 1244) argues:

> The rational herdsman concludes that the only sensible course for him to pursue is to add another animal to his herd. And another; and another. . . But this is the conclusion reached by each and every rational herdsman sharing the commons. Therein is the tragedy. Each man is locked into a system that compels him to increase his herd without limit—in a world that is limited. Ruin is the destination toward which all men rush, each pursuing his own best interest in a society that believes in the freedom of the commons.

Along the same vein, Gordon (1954, p. 135) concludes:

> There appears, then, to be some truth in the conservative dictum that everybody's property is nobody's property. Wealth that is free for all is valued by no one because he who is foolhardy enough to wait for its proper time of use will only find that it has been taken by another.

Or for the case of fishery CPRs:

For years, [Sam] Novello had made a decent living off the abundant groundfish—cod, haddock, yellowtail flounder—that he hauled up off the Atlantic Ocean floor. He used nets with a large-enough mesh size to allow juvenile fish to pass through, and worked the best spots sparingly with his tows. "I didn't know I was a conservationist until somebody told me," he says, "but I believed in only taking the interest out of the bank." But Novello watched many of his competitors make three times as much money depleting vast areas and keeping thousands of pre-spawning-size fish. And he has never forgotten the disdainful words of a local dealer: "What are you, stupid? One boat is gonna save every fish in the sea?" So, he adds sadly, "Finally I said, OK, I'll fish like everybody else does." (Russell 1996, p. 125)

Recall from chapter 3 that the process of rent dissipation in CPRs is referred to as the *tragedy of the commons,* a term coined by Garrett Hardin. The theory behind Hardin's tragedy of the commons is illustrated using a simple strategic model in the appendix at the end of this chapter.

In the past, many economists have argued that the solution to the tragedy of the commons is to assign private property rights. In developing their arguments, these economists have often assumed that an open-access property rights regime is in force, meaning that there are no rules limiting use. While indeed transforming an open-access resource into a private property resource will attenuate the tragedy of the commons when privatization is desirable and feasible, increasingly those who study CPRs argue that appropriately designed common property regimes may also work to prevent this tragedy from occurring. Elinor Ostrom and her colleagues have argued that the grim picture of CPR governance failure is not at all universal and that in fact there are many examples of long-enduring, sustainable local CPR systems around the world. Bromley (1992) provides additional case study analysis that supports Ostrom's argument. Ostrom and her colleagues sought to learn what makes these systems successful and to develop a set of design principles from them that can guide the design of new CPR systems as well as predict CPR success.

Ostrom's central idea is that localized CPR systems can be durable and sustainable in situations in which open-access conditions are displaced by a common property regime established and governed by the local people who depend on the CPR. Sustainable self-governance calls for a set of rule systems or institutions that define the physical boundaries of the CPR. These institutions also specify the people who are allowed to use the CPR, the methods and extent of appropriations from the CPR, the methods and financing of monitoring systems, a system for resolving conflicts, and a set of sanctions that are proportionate with the importance of the transgression. An additional characteristic of successful self-governance is that the rule structures must be capable of adapting to changing circumstances, such as those driven by weather cycles or population growth. As Sethi and Somanathan (1996) point out, a key element of the success of local self-governance is the ability of the resource-dependent community to establish codes of conduct and to impose sanctions such as cultural isolation and expulsion from the community upon those who violate these rules of conduct. Local self-governance of CPRs will be addressed again in chapter 15 in the context of sustainable local communities; those who would like to further pursue this issue may want to jump ahead.

It is interesting to consider factors that might explain why some resources are held as common rather than private property. Clearly, some resource stocks such as fisheries, groundwater basins, and mobile wildlife are not conducive to being partitioned as private property. Moreover, in his study of common property systems in Swiss alpine villages, Netting (1981) identified five environmental variables that tend to lead to resources being held as common rather than private property:

- The value of the harvestable resource is low per unit of area.
- The amount of harvestable resource is highly variable.
- Investment in improvements yields a relatively small increase in productivity of the resource.
- Overall costs can be reduced if people can coordinate activities such as herding livestock or processing dairy products.
- Fence, road, and other building costs can be reduced when done on a larger scale.

There is evidence that this pattern also held for primary societies. McEvoy (1986), for example, observes that highly productive locations for catching salmon along the Klamath River in northwest California were privately owned by individuals or partners in the Yurok tribe before contact with whites. As private property, these productive fishing spots could be transferred by way of market-like exchanges, and others were excluded from fishing at or immediately below the spot. Yurok land that was farther from settlements or that was less productive for catching fish had lower economic value and was recognized as a common-property or an open-access resource.

Ostrom and her colleagues have also used laboratory experimental techniques to evaluate aspects of CPR theory. Laboratory conditions replicate the key *incentives* of the model under investigation with cash payments to participants, and these cash payments vary based on the appropriation or other decisions that they make. An important element of this research work has been to determine the role of face-to-face communication in creating "social capital" and informal rule systems that can prevent the dissipation of Hotelling rents. Some of the basic results of this research include:

- When participants appropriate from a commons but are unable to cooperate or communicate with one another, the result is that most or all Hotelling rents are dissipated, as predicted by the tragedy of the commons, yielding the rent dissipation outcome in Figure 5.4 (see Ostrom, Walker, and Gardner 1992; and Ostrom, Gardner, and Walker 1994).
- When these participants are allowed to communicate with one another but cannot form enforceable agreements, they usually develop informal rule structures that coordinate reduced appropriation and generate most or all of the potential Hotelling rents shown in Figure 5.4, even though the agreements were not enforceable (see Ostrom, Walker, and Gardner 1992; Ostrom, Gardner, and Walker 1994).
- When some participants pay to acquire a larger appropriation capacity (e.g., buy a big fishing vessel), the informal rule systems devised through face-to-face communication tend to allocate quotas proportionate with appropriation capacity, which also matches the available evidence from field CPR systems featuring heterogeneity (see Hackett, Schlager, and Walker 1994).

Group discussion and communication have been found to be a major factor in resolving many social dilemmas such as the tragedy of the commons. Orbell, van de Kragt, and Dawes (1988) find evidence that communication fosters the creation of a group identity, leading to a displacement of egoism for group regardfulness, and allows for consensual promise making, where discussion of the collective benefits of cooperation motivates consensus agreements on limiting resource dissipation by way of promised behavior.

Ecosystem Services and Natural Capital

Imagine trying to set up a fully functional enclosed ecosystem like Biosphere 2 on the moon. What ecosystem services would such an enclosed system need to include? What geological, atmospheric, and biophysical relationships would need to be replicated? And like Noah, we would also need to know what species of plants, animals, fungi, bacteria, and other life forms to include. Unlike Noah we would also need to know how many to bring, which to group together, and what their life requirements are. Daily (1997) includes the following as essential ecosystem services:

- Purification of air and water
- Mitigation of floods and droughts
- Detoxification and decomposition of wastes
- Generation and renewal of soil and soil fertility
- Pollination of crops and natural vegetation
- Control of agricultural pests
- Dispersal of seeds and translocation of nutrients
- Maintenance of biodiversity for uses such as agriculture, medicine, and industry
- Protection from the sun's ultraviolet rays
- Partial stabilization of climate
- Moderation of wind, wave, and temperature extremes
- Support of diverse human cultures
- Provision of aesthetic beauty and intellectual stimulation

Costanza et al. (1997) include seventeen such ecosystem services in their comprehensive study. Clearly, it would be very complex and expensive to replicate these ecosystem services on the moon. Since most ecosystem services occur outside of commercial markets, for the most part, we take them for granted, and they are assumed not to have economic value. Costanza et al. (1997) observe that "ecosystem goods (such as food) and ecosystem services (such as waste assimilation) represent the benefits human populations derive, directly and indirectly, from ecosystem functions" (p. 253). These ecosystem services represent flows of materials, energy, and information from the stock of *natural capital.* Natural capital consists broadly of the stock of nonrenewable resources, renewable resources, and the elements and relationships embodied in ecosystem functions. Depletion of an element of natural capital, such as when fishery stocks are drawn down, implies that the corresponding flow of harvestable fish also declines. Both constructed and human capital, and more generally all the world's economies, rely upon the functional integrity of natural capital.

The economic value of ecosystem services will be touched upon in chapter 7, and the extent to which technology can develop substitutes for natural capital will be addressed in chapter 14.

Resources for the Future: Factors Affecting Future Resource Scarcity

Are we going to be experiencing growing resource scarcity in the future, as nonrenewable resources run out, renewable resources are depleted, and the integrity of earth's ecosystem services is fatally compromised? Alternatively, will market price and technology seamlessly guide society to the more efficient use of existing resources and develop alternatives for those that are depleted? In addition, what is the role of population?

Thomas Malthus, in his book *An Essay on the Principle of Population* (1798), argued that growth in human population would outstrip the natural resource endowment of the planet. Malthus's arguments were originally focused on the land resource and food production. Malthus believed in the notion of *absolute resource scarcity*, meaning that most important natural resources have no substitutes available now, and technology cannot create substitutes. While in Malthus's view food production could indeed grow, this growth would be outstripped by the growth in human population. Because of absolute scarcity, human society will eventually exceed the "carrying capacity" of planet earth, leading society to collapse. Many ecologists have been heavily influenced by Malthusian thought. "Neo-Malthusians" have generalized the Malthusian argument to include an overall statement about the natural environment, human population growth, and quality of life.

The argument from mainstream natural resources economics is that when adequate property rights have been assigned and enforced, and a resource is allocated through competitive markets, Hotelling's rule indicates that price will reflect the relative scarcity of the resource. Specifically, the scarcer the resource, the larger the Hotelling rents, and thus the higher will be the price of the resource. Therefore, market price offers a good indication of overall scarcity. Technological change has allowed us to reduce consumption of increasingly scarce resources by identifying more resource-efficient technologies and by utilizing substitute resources. The energy crisis of the mid- and late 1970s offers another lesson: higher oil prices spurred domestic production of coal and natural gas, and created an incentive for R&D into alternative energy sources such as solar and wind. Many people were able to reduce their energy use substantially through home insulation and adapting to lower household temperatures, as well as car-pooling and riding public transportation to work. Energy inputs per dollar of produced goods and services have declined substantially in many industrialized countries. A further argument made by many economists is that there is relatively little evidence of growing Hotelling rents in natural resource markets. The inflation-adjusted prices of coal; oil; natural gas; metals such as aluminum, iron, and copper; and basic foodstuffs such as wheat, soybeans, and cattle have not increased, and in many cases have actually declined over the last thirty years, despite the rapid growth in human population.

Economists argue that Malthus assumed *static technologies,* meaning that resource productivity would remain at 1798 levels. Perhaps Malthus took this position because he largely preceded the rapid technological change that was associated with the industrial revolution. In any event, by ignoring the role of technology in increasing resource productivity and facilitating the development of substitutes, Malthus failed to predict that in fact from his time to the present, food production actually outgrew human population.

Global resource prices may provide a false indication of resource scarcity, however. As Cohen (1996) points out, prices can provide a false indication of resource scarcity for at least two reasons. First, prices do not provide information on the scarcity of open-access resources or poorly enforced state and common property resources being depleted due to tragedy of the commons. Second, resource prices may decline because production shifts to countries where the lack of environmental taxes and regulation leads to a larger proportion of the external costs of resource extraction, use, and disposal not being reflected in price. A third reason one can offer for why prices do not provide a comprehensive indication of resource scarcity is that many important resources and ecosystem services are not and cannot be directly provided for and protected by the individual actions of buyers and sellers in a market. One example is the ecosystem service of atmospheric gas regulation (such as the CO_2/O_2 balance and stratospheric O_3 for protection from ultraviolet radiation). Atmospheric gas regulation cannot easily be partitioned and sold as private property in the market. In the absence of government intervention and a coordinated effort the necessary changes in fuel and land use would not happen. Therefore, market price will not fulfill its role as the signaler of scarcity and depletion, and technology is unlikely to offer us satisfactory substitutes.

Economists such as Anderson and Leal (1991) argue that inadequate resource protection occurs because of an inappropriate property rights regime, and they suggest that the solution is privatization when possible. Yet the stocks of fresh air, marine fisheries, groundwater, stratospheric ozone, biodiversity, and many other resources cannot effectively be partitioned as private property. In addition, it is not clear that a resource such as topsoil fertility is conserved in privately owned farms, or that non-income-generating aspects of the environment such as old-growth-dependent species are adequately protected in privately owned forest lands. Even for those resources for which privatization can effectively reverse degradation, it is not at all clear that such a move would be consistent with community values. For example, in societies with highly unequal distributions of wealth, the privatization solution will put park and open-space access beyond the reach of people with low or modest incomes. Ostrom and others have shown that private property regimes are not necessary for sustainable resource management; common property regimes can sustain natural resources when they are governed by locally devised and maintained rule structures.

This debate between ecologists and economists over the changing nature of scarcity led to a rather famous bet. In 1980, economist Julian Simon and ecologist Paul Ehrlich made a highly publicized bet on whether the price of a set of metals selected by Ehrlich (copper, chrome, nickel, tin, and tungsten) would rise, remain constant, or fall by 1990. One thousand dollars' worth of these metals was bought in 1980. Ehrlich agreed to pay Simon the difference between the 1980 and 1990 value of this quantity of metals if their aggregate (inflation-adjusted) market price declined, while Simon agreed to pay Ehrlich the difference between the 1980 and 1990 value of these metals if their aggregate (inflation-adjusted) market price rose. In 1990, Ehrlich paid Simon $576.07, indicating that the inflation-adjusted aggregate price of the metals had fallen from $1,000 to $423.93. Ehrlich lost his bet because new resources were discovered, substitutes were developed for those that had become scarce, and some metals markets became more competitive. The outcome of this bet would have been different if they had bet on factors such as urban sprawl and biodiversity.

Summary

- For something to be a natural resource means that it is an aspect of earth's endowment that is useful to people in some way. A natural resource has either direct value or value contingent upon the existence of technology that transforms the raw resource into something useful. Thus petroleum was not a valuable resource until the internal combustion engine technology, combined with the technology for cracking petroleum into refined products such as gasoline, allowed it to be converted into something useful to people.
- Nonrenewable resources are fixed in total quantity and thus are said to have a fixed stock that does not recharge over the human timeframe. Fossil fuels and mineral resources are examples of nonrenewable resources. If steady declines in supply or increases in demand are anticipated in the future, economists have argued that market forces will mitigate against a sudden price shock or "running out" of the resource in question. The reason is that resource owners anticipating higher future prices will have an incentive to sell less today in order to have more to sell at higher future prices. Consequently current prices will also rise. Higher current prices in turn cause people to conserve on use of the resource and provide incentive for R&D into technology to make use of alternative resources, such as substituting solar energy for oil, as well as into more resource-efficient technologies. Of course if unanticipated supply or demand shocks occur, or if

there is political manipulation of the process, this rational adjustment may not occur.

- Dynamic efficiency occurs in resource markets when the *PV* of surplus is maximized. According to Hotelling's rule, this occurs in nonrenewable, nonrecyclable resource markets when the *PV* of marginal Hotelling rent $(P - MC)$ is equalized over time. If marginal extraction costs remain relatively constant over time, the implication of Hotelling's rule is that the price rises over time. This increase in price will spur conservation and the development of substitutes.

- Recyclable resources such as glass, paper, and metals have a primary market where the original resource is sold and a secondary or recycled market where the salvaged resource is resold. Resources in the primary market must thus compete against resources from the secondary market. A monopoly or cartel that controls a recyclable natural resource must anticipate future competition from the secondary market when it sets output. Excessive production today will result in excessive competition from the secondary market in the future.

- Renewable resources are aspects of the living planet and can regenerate themselves under sustained-yield management, or become depleted when yield rates exceed the maximum that can be sustained. Natural resource systems are usually a complex of interdependent elements, and the maximum sustained yield of one element may result in overharvest in the impact on another related resource. An example is overharvest of timber in its effects on watershed and fisheries resources.

- Common-pool resources (CPRs) are resources for which it is difficult to prevent multiple individuals from harvesting resource units, and resource units harvested by one are not available for another. Thus CPRs differ from private goods, where it is possible to exclude others from use, and pure public goods like public radio, where my use does not impair your use. Garrett Hardin coined the term *tragedy of the commons* to refer to the situation in which individuals overuse the commons because of the presence of appropriation externalities: if you graze more cattle, you get the financial gain, while the damage to the common pasture is borne by everyone in the community. Elinor Ostrom has argued that the tragedy of the commons can be (and has been) avoided through the construction and maintenance of carefully crafted CPR governance structures.

- Ecosystem services, such as the supply of fresh water, soil fertility, and climate regulation, are the benefits that human society receives, both directly and indirectly, from ecosystem functions. Costanza and colleagues observe that these ecosystem services represent flows of materials, energy, and information from the stock of *natural capital.*

• The argument has raged over whether or not there is growing resource scarcity because of growing population, as Malthus originally argued. In fact, the price of many marketed natural resources such as coal, oil, natural gas, forest products, seafood, and pasturage has not risen as rapidly as some predicted and in many cases has actually fallen. This has reinforced the arguments of the technological optimists such as Julian Simon. On the other hand, in many parts of the world, ecosystem services as well as common-property and open-access resources are being depleted. There is truth in both camps: human ingenuity has indeed offset substantial amounts of resource limitations with technological advances, but many unique and irreplaceable resources are under increasing pressure, and many are failing.

Review Questions and Problems

1. Suppose that in the oil example given in the chapter for dynamic efficiency, all else remains the same except that the discount rate r rises from 15 percent to 30 percent. Using the technique shown in this chapter (p. 94), determine how this increase in the discount rate will change the dynamically efficient allocation of oil across the two periods, and how it will change the size of the marginal Hotelling rent on each barrel of oil.

2. Suppose that in the oil example given in the chapter for dynamic efficiency, all else remains the same except that now there are 60 barrels of oil rather than only 40. Using the technique shown in this chapter (p. 94), determine how this increase in the availability of oil affects the dynamically efficient allocation of oil across the two periods and how it will change the size of the marginal Hotelling rent on each barrel of oil.

3. Carefully define a common-pool natural resource relative to both private goods and pure public goods. Provide an example. Use this example to explain the tragedy of the commons. If resource users can govern themselves, what sort of rules might prevent the commons from becoming damaged from overuse?

4. Explain why the pure Malthusian outcome has not occurred, despite rapid population growth since Malthus's time (1798). Carefully list the factors that would explain why some resources have not grown increasingly scarce and why some have substantially degraded. The role of technology and the possibility of substitution should be at the center of your explanation.

5. Suppose there is a groundwater basin that is being drawn from faster than it is being recharged from its aquifer, resulting in dropping water tables in the area. Explain the different ways that people improve this situation.

6. Spreadsheet simulation (more advanced): Suppose that demand is given

by the equation $P = 200 - Q$, and supply is given by the equation $P = 10$. Suppose that the total resource stock $Q_{tot} = 100$, and that it can be consumed over two periods (0 and 1). Place these equations and other information into a spreadsheet.

a. Solve for the dynamically efficient resource allocation for $r = 0, 0.05, 0.10, 0.2$, and 0.5. Note that from the exact solution we have $q_0 = (bQ_{tot} + r(a - c))/b(2 + r)$, and $q_1 = Q_{tot} - q_0$.

Build a table with columns showing "r," "q_0," "q_1," "PV of marginal profit period 0" and "PV of marginal profit period 1." There will be five rows, one for each "r" value above. Confirm that Hotelling's rule is satisfied in each case. Provide a brief interpretation of the impacts of rising discount rates on the dynamically optimal price and quantity path over time.

b. Now suppose that $Q_{tot} = 70$. Build a second table like the one in 6a above. Provide a brief narrative economic interpretation of the impact of a smaller resource stock on the dynamically efficient allocation of the resource, as well as prices and marginal profit.

Internet Links

Association for the Study of Peak Oil and Gas (www.peakoil.net): Learn more about independent assessments of when we will reach global peak oil production.

California's Independent Electricity System Operator (www.caiso.com): Learn about partial deregulation of California's electric energy industry.

Economic Sustainability and Scarcity of Natural Resources (www.rff.org/ issue_briefs/PDF_files/tahvonen_naturalres.pdf): Olli Tahvonen of the Finnish Forest Research Institute in Helsinki traces the history of economic thinking about scarcity of natural resources and the sustainability of economic growth. This is June 2000 Resources for the Future *Issue Brief.*

Food and Agriculture Organization (www.fao.org/): The United Nations Food and Agriculture Organization (FAO) is an excellent source of information on important agricultural and natural resources, including fisheries and forests. The FAOSTAT datebase (http://apps.fao.org/) is particularly valuable.

Food and Agriculture Organization's Forestry Department (www.fao.org/ waicent/FAOINFO/Forestry/Forestry.htm): A good overview of global forestry issues.

Forest and Rangeland Ecosystem Science Center (http://fresc .fsl.orst.edu): Learn more about forests and rangeland resources.

Hotelling's Rule Audio Clip (www.humboldt.edu/~envecon/audio/2.ram): A brief audio clip of the author describing Hotelling's rule.

International Association for the Study of Common Property (www.indiana.edu/~iascp/): A good place to learn more about systems of governance for common-pool resources.

Malthus Website (http://socserv2.socsci.mcmaster.ca/~econ/ugcm/3113/ malthus/index.html): Read his original work on population.

Rangeland **(http://uvalde.tamu.edu/rangel/home.htm):** A publication of the Society for Range Management.

World Resources Institute (www.wri.org/): Excellent source of global information on the state of the world's natural resources.

World Resources Institute's Sustainable Agriculture Site (www.wri.org/ wri/sustag/): Learn more about sustainable agriculture.

References and Further Reading

Adelaja, A., B. McCay, and J. Menzo. 1998. "Market Power, Industrial Organization, and Tradable Quotas." *Review of Industrial Organization* 13: 589–601.

Anderson, T., and D. Leal. 1991. *Free Market Environmentalism.* San Francisco: Pacific Research Institute.

Barnett, H., and C. Morse. 1963. *Scarcity and Growth.* Baltimore: Johns Hopkins University Press (for Resources for the Future).

Bromley, D., ed. 1992. *Making the Commons Work.* San Francisco: ICS Press.

Brown, L., ed. 1995. *State of the World 1995.* New York: Norton.

Ciriacy-Wantrup, S., and R. Bishop. 1975. "'Common Property' as a Concept in Natural Resources Policy." *Natural Resources Journal* 15: 713–27.

Cohen, J. 1996. "Ecologists Ask Economists: Is the Price Right?" *Scientist* (18 May): 11.

Costanza, R., R. d'Arge, R. de Groot, M. Farber, M. Grasso, B. Hannon, K. Limburg, S. Naeem, R. O'Neill, J. Paruelo, R. Raskin, P. Sutton, and M. van den Belt. 1997. "The Value of the World's Ecosystem Services and Natural Capital." *Nature* 387: 253–60.

Daily, G., ed. 1997. *Nature's Services: Societal Dependence on Natural Ecosystems.* Covelo, CA: Island Press.

Ehrlich, P. 1968. *The Population Bomb.* New York: Ballantine Books.

Ehrlich, P., and J. Holden. 1971. "Impact of Population Growth." *Science* (March): 1212–17.

Eichhorn, W., R. Henn, K. Neumann, and R.W. Shephard, eds. 1982. *Economic Theory of Natural Resources.* Würzburg, Germany: Physica-Verlag.

Gaskins, D. 1974. "Alcoa Revisited: The Welfare Implications of a Secondhand Market." *Journal of Economic Theory* 7: 254–71.

Gordon, H.S. 1954. "The Economic Theory of a Common-Property Resource: The Fishery." *Journal of Political Economy* 62 (April): 124–42.

Hackett, S., E. Schlager, and J. Walker. 1994. "The Role of Communication in Resolving Commons Dilemmas: Experimental Evidence with Heterogeneous Appropriators." *Journal of Environmental Economics and Management* 27: 99–126.

Hardin, G. 1968. "The Tragedy of the Commons." *Science* 162 (13 December): 1243–48.

Hotelling, H. 1931. "The Economics of Exhaustible Resources." *Journal of Political Economy* 31: 137–75.

Keen, E. 1988. *Ownership and Productivity of Marine Fishery Resources: An Essay on the Resolution of Conflict in the Use of the Ocean Pastures.* Blacksburg, VA: McDonald and Woodward.

Lyon, T., and S. Hackett. 1993. "Bottlenecks and Governance Structures: Open-Access and Long-Term Contracting in Natural Gas." *Journal of Law, Economics, and Organization* 9 (October): 380–98.

McEvoy, A. 1986. *The Fisherman's Problem: Ecology and Law in the California Fisheries, 1850–1980.* London: Cambridge University Press.

Malthus, T. 1798. *An Essay on the Principle of Population.* London (reprinted for the Royal Economic Society by MacMillan & Co. Ltd. London, 1926).

Netting, R. 1981. *Balancing on an Alp: Ecological Change and Continuity in a Swiss Mountain Community.* New York: Cambridge University Press.

Olson, M. 1965. *The Logic of Collective Action.* Cambridge: Cambridge University Press.

Orbell, J., A. van de Kragt, and R. Dawes. 1988. "Explaining Discussion-Induced Cooperation." *Journal of Personality and Social Psychology* 54 (5): 811–19.

Ostrom, E. 1990. *Governing the Commons: The Evolution of Institutions for Collective Action.* Cambridge: Cambridge University Press.

Ostrom, E., R. Gardner, and J. Walker. 1994. *Rules, Games, and Common-Pool Resources.* Ann Arbor: University of Michigan Press.

Ostrom, E., J. Walker, and R. Gardner. 1992. "Covenants with and without a Sword: Self Governance Is Possible." *American Political Science Review* 86: 128–45.

Owen, O. 1985. *Natural Resource Conservation: An Ecological Approach.* New York: Macmillan.

Russell, D. 1996. "Fisheries in Crisis (Part II)." *E Magazine* 7 (September–October).

Sethi, R., and E. Somanathan. 1996. "The Evolution of Social Norms in Common Property Resource Use." *American Economic Review* 86 (September): 766–88.

Simon, J. 1981. *The Ultimate Resource.* Princeton: Princeton University Press.

Smith, V.K., and J. Krutilla, eds. 1982. *Explorations in Natural Resource Economics.* Baltimore: Johns Hopkins University Press (for Resources for the Future).

Terry, J. 1993. *The Use of Individual Quotas in Fisheries Management.* Paris: Organization for Economic Cooperation and Development.

Tietenberg, T. 2006. *Environmental and Natural Resources Economics.* 7th ed. Boston: Pearson Addison Wesley.

U.S. Forest Service. 1995. *The Forest Service Program for Forest and Rangeland Resources: A Long-Term Strategic Plan.* Draft 1995 RPA Program. Washington, DC: U.S. Forest Service.

Weber, P. 1995. "Protecting Oceanic Fisheries and Jobs." In *State of the World 1995.* New York: Norton (for Worldwatch).

Wiggins, S., and G. Libecap. 1987. "Firm Heterogeneities and Cartelization Efforts in Domestic Crude Oil." *Journal of Law, Economics, and Organization* 3 (Spring): 1–25.

Appendix: The Prisoner's Dilemma and the Tragedy of the Commons

The tragedy of the commons is most likely to occur under the conditions of open-access or other poorly designed and enforced property rights regimes. The tragedy of the commons outcome results from strategic behavior—behavior that an individual engages in based on how other people are expected to behave or respond. At the heart of the tragedy of the commons is the belief that if one were to conserve the common-pool resources, others will take what was conserved, and the CPR will still degrade. Mathematicians refer to situations like this, in which people are taking strategic actions based on how other people are expected to behave or respond, as *games,* and the theory used to analyze the outcomes of such situations is referred to as *game theory.*

The tragedy of the commons can be described by a more general game called the prisoner's dilemma. In the prisoner's dilemma there are two prisoners, Chang and Adams, who are being investigated in regard to a crime punishable with a fine. Unless one or both of them confess, there is insufficient evidence to convict them, and they will go free and pay no fine. If one of the prisoners were to confess and provide evidence to implicate the other, while the other claims innocence, then the prisoner who confesses will receive a $500 cash reward, while the prisoner claiming innocence will be convicted of a crime and have to pay a $5,000 fine for lying and claiming innocence. If both confess, then they both will be convicted of a crime, but because they confessed, each will only have to pay a $1,000 fine. The prisoners are separated and do not know how the other will respond to this situation and are unable to coordinate their actions. Assume that the implicated prisoner cannot later punish the other prisoner for providing evidence.

Table 5.1

Strategic Form of the Prisoner's Dilemma Game

	Chang Claims Innocence		Chang Confesses	
Adams claims innocence	A: $0	C: $0	A: −$5000	C: $500
Adams confesses	A: $500	C: −$5000	A: −$1000	C: −$1000

Note: "A" denotes Adams's payoff, while "C" denotes Chang's payoff.

The *payoff structure* that forms the incentives for this game is summarized in Table 5.1.

In this situation, each prisoner is confronted with the choice of "confess" or "claim innocence" and with a conjecture of what the other prisoner will do. To determine the Nash equilibrium to this game (named after John Nash, a game theorist), first consider the options available to Chang. Chang knows that if Adams confesses, then Chang will be fined $5,000 if he claims innocence or fined $1,000 if he also confesses. In this circumstance, Chang is best off to confess. If instead Adams claims innocence, then Chang will receive a $500 cash reward for confessing or get off free and pay $0 fine if he also keeps quiet. In this circumstance, Chang is also best off to confess. Thus, Chang has what is known as a *dominant strategy* of confessing. This strategy is referred to as being dominant because Chang will confess regardless of what Adams does.

Now consider Adams, whose situation is exactly the same as that of Chang. If Adams thinks Chang will confess, then Adams will be fined $5,000 if he claims innocence or fined $1,000 if he also confesses. In this circumstance, Adams is best off to confess. If instead Adams believes that Chang will claim innocence, then Adams will receive a $500 cash reward for confessing or get off free and pay $0 fine for also claiming innocence. In this circumstance, Adams is also best off to confess. Thus, Adams also has a dominant strategy of always confessing regardless of what Chang does.

The Nash equilibrium outcome of the prisoner's dilemma is (confess, confess), and both parties are fined $1,000. Note that this outcome is inefficient relative to the (claim innocence, claim innocence) outcome, in which both parties pay no fine, but that outcome is not an equilibrium because both parties have an incentive to defect and confess if they think the other will claim innocence.

You may already see that the strategic structure of the prisoner's dilemma game is also that of the CPR dilemma. If we rename this game CPR dilemma, the strategy of "claiming innocence" is renamed "sustainable use," and the strategy of "confessing" is renamed "resource depletion." Thus the equilibrium of the CPR dilemma game is (resource depletion, resource depletion), which is inferior to that of (sustainable use, sustainable use). If Adams believes that Chang will use the resource sustainably, Adams's dominant strategy is to capture the resources left by the other and deplete the resource. Chang has the same dominant strategy, which yields the tragedy of the commons outcome of the CPR dilemma game.

Of course, in the context of a CPR dilemma, the payoffs from (sustainable use, sustainable use) will be positive rather than the $0 payoff used in the prisoner's dilemma game for (claim innocence, claim innocence). Nevertheless, the same result will occur with positive payoff values in the upper left cell of the bimatrix table, as long as the payoff to confessing given that the other is claiming innocence is larger than the payoff when both claim innocence.

Possible methods of avoiding the tragedy of the commons outcome include (1) changing the payoff structure of the game, (2) repeated play, and (3) cooperative rather than noncooperative decision making. The payoff structure of the game can be changed, for example, if there is a CPR governance structure that imposes substantial sanctions on those who violate the sustainable use rules and deplete the resource (akin to prisoners' being able to credibly threaten to punish those who "rat" and implicate others through confession). Under repeated play, it may be possible for the value of future sustainable use to weigh against depleting the resource today, though this may require an effectively infinite horizon of repeated play. If the noncooperative nature of the game is transformed into a cooperative game through some form of CPR governance structure, then the jointly optimal outcome can be realized through coordination.

Part II
Policy

6

The Economics of Natural Resource Systems, Part II: Marine Capture Fisheries

Introduction

From an economic standpoint, a *fishery* refers to the interaction of human harvest activities, environmental conditions, and the population dynamics associated with one or more species of fish. The term *capture fishery* refers to the enterprise of catching wild marine or inland fish, which can be contrasted with *aquaculture,* or fish farming. As was described in chapter 5, capture fisheries frequently have the characteristics of common-pool resources. Consequently, unconstrained rivalry among fishery participants, such as under the property rights system of open access, can result in the depletion of the resource and the economic rents that fishery participants derive from that resource. Therefore, the assignment of property rights, particularly the rights of management and exclusion, is an essential element of sustaining fisheries. While some localized capture fisheries are held as common property (see chapter 15), most of the world's major marine capture fisheries are state property, with some level of government responsible for regulating harvest.

The focus of this chapter will be on the interaction of biological, economic, and regulatory circumstances in marine capture fisheries. We will start out by considering world trends in marine capture fisheries. We will then develop a bioeconomic model of a fishery, a dynamic approach that links together the biological conditions in the fishery to the economic circumstances of the participants. Next, we will consider some conventional, non-quota-based fishery regulations, including their intended and unintended consequences. The problems of overcapitalization and derby conditions that plague many of these systems will serve as a motivation for the consideration of quota-based regulatory systems. The biological and economic conditions in marine capture fisheries are impacted in various ways by aquaculture operations, which is where we will end our discussion in this chapter.

World Trends

Perhaps the best source of information for world trends is the United Nations Food and Agriculture Organization (FAO), and the statistics given below derive from the FAO (United Nations FAO, hereafter FAO, 2002). The total quantity of landings from marine and freshwater capture fisheries (excluding China) grew from around 20 million metric tons in 1950 to a peak of 83 million metric tons in 1989, and ranged between 70 and 80 million metric tons between 1996 and 2001. Marine capture fisheries represented approximately 90 percent of these total capture fishery landings between 1996 and 2001, and peak production from marine capture fisheries (omitting China) was 75.5 million metric tons in 1995. China is believed to have overstated its landings, particularly during the 1990s, and so world statistics are frequently cited with China omitted. The northwest Pacific, west central Pacific, southeast Pacific, and northeast Atlantic regions dominate worldwide landings from marine capture fisheries, and total harvest from these regions has grown or remained steady since 1970. China increasingly dominates the harvest from the northwest Pacific region, and is thought to be the world's largest harvester from marine capture fisheries. Anchoveta was by far the dominant species landed from marine capture fisheries in 2000, though landings of this species fluctuate considerably year to year due to ocean conditions.

The FAO (2002) notes that global fishing pressure continues to increase, the number of underexploited and moderately exploited fishery resources continues to decline slightly, the number of fully exploited stocks remains relatively stable, and the number of overexploited, depleted, and recovering stocks is increasing slightly. An estimated 25 percent of the major marine fish stocks or species groups for which information is available are either underexploited or moderately exploited. About 47 percent of the main stocks or species groups are fully exploited and are therefore producing catches that have reached, or are very close to, their maximum sustainable limits. Approximately 18 percent of stocks or species groups are reported as being overexploited. Prospects for expansion or increased production from these stocks are negligible, and there is an increasing likelihood that stocks will decline further and catches will decrease, unless remedial management action is taken to reduce overfishing conditions. The remaining 10 percent of stocks have become significantly depleted, or are recovering from depletion and are far less productive than they used to be or could be. As a result, landings from about 75 percent of the world's major marine fish stocks are expected either to remain constant or to decline in the future.

Changes in landings from major marine capture fisheries occur due to both human and environmental causes. For example, the biomass of some *benthic* or groundfish species groups such as cod, flounder, halibut, and rockfish (found on or near the seafloor) may not recover very easily after heavy harvest. Many groundfish are long-lived, do not become sexually mature for many years, and are slow to reproduce. Examples include the northwestern Atlantic cod fishery and the eastern Pacific groundfish fishery. The Grand Banks and Georges Bank fisheries in the northwest Atlantic had once been some of the world's most productive groundfish fisheries and yet are now essentially closed following their collapse. The formerly dominant species of groundfish—including flounder, cod, haddock, and hake—have been fished down to a small fraction of their previous abundance. The Georges Bank codfish catch peaked at more than 60,000 metric tons in 1983 and declined to nearly 20,000 metric tons by 1994.

The Atlantic cod fishery in eastern Canada had for centuries been an economic mainstay for fishery-dependent communities, especially in Newfoundland and Labrador. While annual landings in the nineteenth century ranged between 150,000 and 400,000 metric tons, annual landings of cod reached a peak during the 1960s at nearly two million metric tons. Eastern Canada's annual cod landings declined dramatically during the 1970s, and by 1977 had fallen below 500,000 metric tons. Declining cod landings continued into the early 1990s, at which time Canada's cod fishery was widely seen as being in crisis. In 1993 Canada announced that all major cod fisheries would be suspended, and that quotas for other groundfish species would be sharply restricted in 1994. The moratorium was maintained indefinitely beyond its May 15, 1994, scheduled termination, and it was estimated that up to 35,000 fishery participants and plant workers were put out of work as a result of these closures (Canadian Department of Fish and Oceans website). In 1998, Canada announced a five-year, $730-million program called the Canadian Fisheries Adjustment and Recovery Plan to address the permanent downsizing of the Atlantic groundfish fishery. At that time Canada's fisheries minister noted that Atlantic groundfish stocks could take many years (possibly decades) to rebuild, and that even then, the industry would not be able to support the same number of fishermen and fishery workers.

The cod catch in the northwestern Atlantic peaked in the 1960s at about

1.43 million metric tons per year, declined to 644,000 metric tons per year in the 1980s, and collapsed to only 48,000 metric tons in 1994. Similarly, the 1997 catch of cod, hake, and haddock in the northwest Atlantic was only 16.5 percent of the 1990 catch (FAOSTAT database). The National Marine Fisheries Service reports that in 1965 cod, haddock, hake, and flounder made up more than 70 percent of the common fishes in the Gulf of Maine. By 1992 dogfish and skate (less desirable species of fish) made up more than 75 percent of the common fish in these waters. The collapse of New England cod stocks is estimated to have eliminated at least 20,000 regional fishing-related jobs, as well as an estimated $349 million in annual revenues (Weber, 1994; McGinn, 1998). The New England Fishery Management Council (NEFMC) estimates that recent groundfish catches of 120 million pounds (valued at $105 million) could increase by approximately a factor of four (to 425 million pounds, with a value estimated at $425 million), if New England's groundfish fishery were fully restored to potential levels (NEFMC, 2002). Restoration of slow-growing groundfish stocks would involve additional fishing restrictions and economic hardships for participants in these fisheries.

A similar pattern has developed on the west coast of the United States in the Pacific groundfish fishery. The 1976 Magnuson Fishery Management and Conservation Act displaced foreign factory trawlers with domestic vessels within the newly established 200-mile exclusive economic zone in federal waters. As Young (2001) points out, programs such as the Investment Tax Credit, Fishing Vessel Obligation Guarantee Fund, and Capital Construction Fund encouraged investment in new vessels, though at the time there was poor information on what harvest rates the stocks could sustain. Fishermen responded by dramatically increasing the number of vessels in the west coast fleet during the late 1970s, while increasingly sophisticated technology made both existing and new vessels more efficient at harvesting fish. During the early 1980s the west coast shrimp and salmon fisheries declined, and many vessels shifted to the groundfish fishery. In 2000 the Scientific and Statistical Committee of the Pacific Fishery Management Council estimated that about 70 percent of the fishing vessels in west coast groundfish were redundant (Pacific Fishery Management Council 2000). This overcapitalization was seen as the fundamental cause of many problems in the fishery. In 2003 President Bush signed into law the Pacific groundfish vessel buyback program, which retired 35 percent of the groundfish trawl permits held during the 1998–2001 base years, accounting for 36.5 percent of all the trawl-caught Pacific groundfish.

In contrast to groundfish, the biomass of some *pelagic* species groups such as anchoveta, pilchards, sardines, and squid (found in the open ocean off the seafloor) fluctuates due to oceanic conditions such as the El Niño cycle. This cycle features a warming of the ocean surface in the eastern tropical Pacific that occurs every four to twelve years when upwelling of cold, nutrient-rich water does not occur. These types of marine animals are relatively short-lived and fertile, and can potentially recover from heavy harvest over a period of years or decades. As reported by McEvoy (1986) in his history of California fisheries, in the 1932–33 fishing season the west coast sardine fishery reached its estimated maximum sustainable yield of approximately 250,000 to 300,000 tons. The majority of the sardine fishery occurred in California waters, and there were 570 vessels fishing for sardine off the California coast in 1936. By the 1936–37 fishing season, the sardine catch had increased to nearly 800,000 tons. While California sardine processors began as canneries (thus John Steinbeck's *Cannery Row* set in Monterey), increasingly sardines were being reduced into fishmeal and oil for use as animal feed and fertilizer. Despite the lack of any sort of conservation measures, the sardine catch managed to hold at between 500,000 and 600,000 tons through the 1945–46 season.

By 1947 the number of vessels pursuing sardines in California waters had nearly doubled to 1,100. Spawning failed in 1949 and 1950, and by the early 1950s total landings on the west coast of the United States fell to slightly less than 15,000 tons. With high demand for sardines as feedstock for fertilizer, pressure turned to the Peruvian anchoveta fishery, which like the California sardine fishery went through a brief boom followed by collapse in the early 1970s. Following the same trend, the North Sea herring catch peaked at more than 1 million tons in 1966–67. By 1977 the catch was less than 40,000 tons, and a ban was placed on harvest in 1978. Both the California sardine fishery and the Peruvian anchoveta fishery experienced a recovery in the late 1990s into 2000. Total sardine landings in California were 62,600 tons in 1999, and maximum sustainable yield of Pacific sardines off the west coast of the United States is estimated to be about 22 percent of the spawning biomass (Wolfe, Smith, and Bergen 2001).

In April 1994 the U.S. National Academy of Sciences (NAS) concluded that excessive fishery harvest had caused drastic reductions in many of the preferred species of edible fish. Moreover, the NAS reported that changes in the composition and abundance of marine flora and fauna had been extensive enough to endanger the functioning of marine ecosystems. While the NAS recognized that fishing was only one of a number of different negative human impacts on the marine environment, overfishing was considered the most important single impact. Similarly, the FAO has concluded that substantial damage has occurred to the marine environment, and to the economies that depend on the fishery resource.

With these issues in mind, we will now develop a dynamic bioeconomic model of a fishery, following an approach similar to that of Hartwick and Olewiler (1998).

Bioeconomic Model of a Fishery

Suppose that $X(t)$ is the stock or biomass of economically valuable fish at time t, and $F(X)$ is the biological growth function for the stock over time (from a calculus standpoint, think of this as the instantaneous growth rate of X, equal to dX/dt). $F(X)$ reflects the rate of net recruitment (number of new fish entering a fishery, net of fish removed from the fishery). Suppose that for the particular species in question $F(X)$ can be described by a *logistic function:*

$F(X) = rX(1 - X/k)$.

Note that r is interpreted as the rate of growth of X when the stock X is nearly zero. Note that k is interpreted as the maximum value for the stock (carrying capacity) for a given habitat. Thus:

$X = k \rightarrow F(X) = 0$.

As shown in Figure 6.1, the flow of harvestable fish from the fish stock—(measured by $F(X)$— starts out small when the stock is small, and then rises to the maximum sustainable yield (MSY) at F_{MAX}. The flow of harvestable fish at first grows as the stock of fish grows due to the small stock only exploiting a small portion of the available food and habitat, thus allowing for substantial reproductive success and recruitment of new fish into the stock. Beyond X_{MSY} the flow of harvestable fish then falls as the stock increases toward k. The flow of harvestable fish eventually declines as the stock increases beyond X_{MSY} because the large stocks of fish increasingly exploit the available food and habitat, thereby limiting reproductive success and recruitment of new fish into the stock. $X = k$ is the biological equilibrium where habitat is fully exploited and the population is presumably in balance with nonhuman predation, so that no net growth can occur.

Now let's introduce human harvest rate H into the model and develop the idea of the *bioeconomic equilibrium.* We can use the bioeconomic model to relate harvest rates to the growth rate of the fish stock. A bioeconomic equilibrium occurs where $H = F(X)$ and the net growth rate of the stock is equal to zero. We can identify several different cases that relate harvest rate to the flow of harvestable fish. For our first case, suppose that the harvest rate ex-

Figure 6.1   **Biological Mechanics of a Fishery**

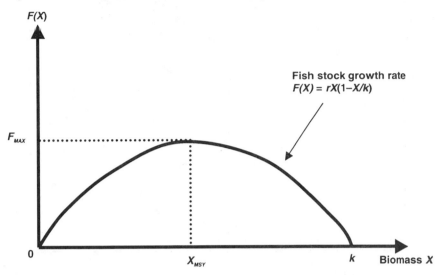

ceeds the maximum sustainable flow of harvestable fish ($H > F_{MAX}$). In this case the net growth rate of the fish stock, $F(X) - H$, will be negative and the stock will decline. This harvest rate is not sustainable, and if it is not re-duced, the bioeconomic equilibrium will feature the elimination of the fish stock ($X = 0$), at which point $H = F(0) = 0$.

In our next case, suppose that the harvest rate H is set equal to F_{MAX}, as shown in Figure 6.2. Since the harvest rate is equal to maximum sustainable yield from the fishery, won't this assure that the fishery will be sustained over time? It ends up that it depends critically on the size of the fish stock at the time that the harvest rule is put into place. If the fish stock X is larger than X_{MSY} at the time that the harvest rule is put into place, then we can see in Figure 6.2 that $F(X) < F_{MAX}$, which means that the actual flow of harvestable fish is less than the maximum sustainable yield. Since $H > F(X))$ we know that the net growth rate of the fish stock will become negative and the stock will decline. Unlike the first case, however, the stock will stop shrinking at $H = F_{MAX}$, indicating that the bioeconomic equilibrium occurs at X_{MSY} If the fish stock X is smaller than X_{MSY}, however, then once again we can see in Figure 6.2 that $F(X) < F_{MAX}$, which means that the actual flow of harvestable fish is less than the maximum sustainable yield. Since $H > F(X))$ we know that the net growth rate of the fish stock will become negative and the stock will decline, and the stock will be fully depleted unless the harvest rate is reduced. Thus another bioeconomic equilibrium occurs at $X = 0$ at which point $H = F(0) = 0$.

An interesting third case is illustrated in Figure 6.3, and features a harvest

Figure 6.2   **Bioeconomic Equilibria with $H = F_{MAX}$**

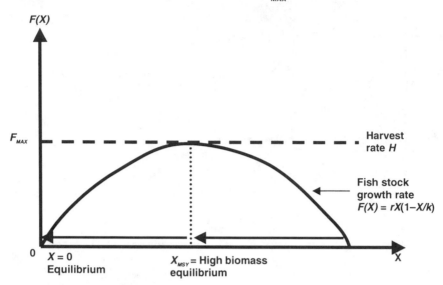

rate $H < F_{MAX}$. In this case there are three bioeconomic equilibria. One of these occurs at X_H. If at the time this harvest rule is put into place the stock of fish is greater than X_H, then $H > F(X)$ and we know that the net growth rate of the fish stock will become negative and the stock will decline. The stock will stop shrinking at $H = F(X_H)$, indicating that the bioeconomic equilibrium occurs at X_H. If the time this harvest rule is put into place the stock of fish is such that $X_L < X < X_H$, then we can see in Figure 6.3 that $H < F(X)$ and we know that the net growth rate of the fish stock will become positive and the stock will grow. The stock will stop growing at $H = F(X_H)$, indicating again that the bioeconomic equilibrium occurs at X_H. Thus, we can see that the high biomass equilibrium is stable for a relatively wide range of stock levels.

A second bioeconomic equilibrium exists at X_L, but it only occurs when $X = X_L$, at which point $H = F(X_L)$. To see this, note that if $X_L < X < X_H$, then we get the high biomass equilibrium as was shown in the previous paragraph. Moreover, if $X < X_L$ then $H > F(X)$ and the net growth rate of the fish stock will be negative and the stock will decline. This harvest rate is not sustainable, and if it is not reduced, then the (third) bioeconomic equilibrium will occur at $X = 0$, at which point $H = F(0) = 0$.

So far, we have assumed that the harvest rate is constant. To be more realistic, consider the following *harvest function:*

$$H(t) = G[E(t), X(t)].$$

Figure 6.3   **Bioeconomic Equilibria With $H < F_{MAX}$**

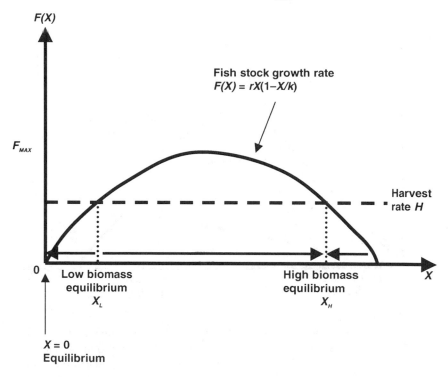

This harvest function tells us that the harvest rate H is a function of the size of the fish stock X and the level of fishing effort E at time period t. Recall that fishing effort is a measure of the inputs (such as deckhands, vessel, gear, fuel, and bait) applied to catching fish. The harvest equation is simply a special form of a production function, which in microeconomic theory relates the transformation of inputs into outputs. For a given level of effort, we would expect that an increase in fish stocks would result in an increase in harvest (in calculus terms, that $dH/dX > 0$). Likewise, for a given stock level, we would expect that an increase in effort would result in an increase in harvest (in calculus terms, that $dH/dE > 0$). The Law of Diminishing Marginal Returns would suggest that in the short run, with the stock level fixed, it would require successively larger and larger increments of effort to generate successive increases in harvest of a given size.

Figure 6.4 illustrates the bioeconomic equilibria that we first considered in Figure 6.3, but now with two harvest functions. Harvest function H_1 assumes a relatively low level of total effort E_1 applied by participants in the fishery, and shows the level of harvest increasing linearly with increases in the size of the fish

Figure 6.4   **Bioeconomic Equilibria With Two Different Levels of Fishing Effort**

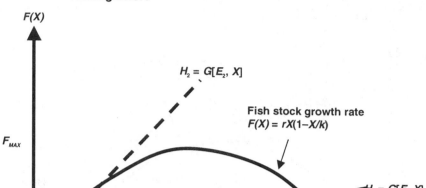

stock. Harvest function H_2 is like the first, but assumes a relatively high level of total effort E_2. Let's assume that E_1 corresponds to the group-optimum level of effort identified in chapter 5, while E_2 corresponds to the level of effort that fully dissipates total Hotelling rents among the participants in the fishery. For a given size of the fish stock on the horizontal axis, the greater level of fishing effort assumed in H_2 results in a larger harvest rate (measured on the vertical axis) than in H_1. You can see this in Figure 6.4 by assuming that fish stocks are at X_L, and then noting that $H_1 = G[E_1, X_L] < H_2 = G[E_2, X_L]$.

Figure 6.4 reveals an important point. Each of the harvest functions has its own bioeconomic equilibrium where harvest rate H equals fishery growth rate $F(X)$. The high biomass equilibrium is associated with the lower, group-optimum level of effort E_1, while the low biomass equilibrium is associated with the higher, rent-dissipating level of effort E_2. Interestingly, however, both of the bioeconomic equilibria result in the *same* equilibrium harvest rate H^*. Therefore, we can see that the bioeconomic equilibrium associated with E_1 is clearly better for the fishery participants because it generates the same level of harvest with less effort. As a result, we can clearly see that the group-optimum bioeconomic equilibrium is also more economically efficient than the equilibrium associated with full rent dissipation, as the former generates the same level of output as the latter, but with fewer inputs employed. Moreover, we can also see in Figure 6.4 that the group-optimum solution also results in a higher steady-state stock of fish than the equilibrium associated with full rent dissipation. Note that if fish are sufficiently valuable, stocks grow slowly, and if fishing effort is sufficiently cheap, it is possible for the harvest function associated with full rent dissipation to be so steep as to lie strictly above $F(X)$. In this unfortunate case the bioeconomic equilibrium occurs at $X = 0$, where the fish stock is exterminated.

While this bioeconomic model does not fit the biomechanics of all fisheries, it provides a relatively simple illustration of the dynamic interaction between fish stocks and human harvest rates. We will now turn to a discussion of fishery management practices and the intended and unintended impacts that they have had on stocks, fishery participants, and others.

Fishery Management

Traditional regulatory schemes used in marine capture fisheries in the United States and elsewhere include *output controls, technical measures,* and *input controls.* Examples of output controls include total allowable catch (TAC) for the fishery and trip or bag limits on vessel landings. Examples of technical measures include restrictions on fish size and sex. Examples of input controls on effort, the oldest type of fishery management tool, include gear restrictions, vessel licenses, and seasonal restrictions. Most fisheries are managed using a combination of such measures. In many cases, these regulatory tactics have proved to be ineffectual in sustaining fishery stocks and have led to a number of harmful unintended consequences for both fishers and consumers.

Consider, for example, the historical management practice used for Alaskan halibut and sablefish, which involved establishment of a TAC, gear restrictions, and seasonal restrictions. This set of management tools was typical of many other fisheries. Since fishers do not have a property right to a share of the TAC, they respond to limited seasons by acquiring more gear and larger vessels so that they can capture more fish in a shorter period of time during the open season. The result is an intense race for fish, or *derby*, which in turn may require regulators to further reduce the season openings. The central Gulf of Alaska halibut fishery, which has accounted for between one-third and one-half of the total U.S. and Canadian catch since 1977, offers an illustrative example of induced derby effects. The halibut season length fell from over 150 days in the early 1970s to 2–3 days in the early 1990s, while the total catch approximately tripled (National Research Council 1999).

Derby conditions can occur without a TAC as long as there is a relatively fixed quantity of fish available for capture. For example, California's Dungeness crab fishery restricts harvest to male crabs with carapace diameter of at least 6.25 inches during a season opening that begins in late fall and runs into mid-summer. The fishery has been fully and intensely exploited for at least forty years. Approximately 80 to 90 percent of the legal-sized male crabs are harvested each season. Despite this intense harvest and high variability in abundance, most scientists and industry participants feel that current regulations are adequately protecting the crab resource. Dewees et al. (2004) estimate that 171,090 traps were deployed in California's crab fishery in December 2000. While there have been no other estimates of California trap numbers since the 1975–76 season, Didier (2002) estimated that from 1971–72 through 1975–76 California trap numbers averaged 29,115. Thus there was nearly a sixfold increase in trap deployment in the California Dungeness crab fishery from the mid-1970s to 2000. An economic analysis of the combined California/Oregon/Washington fishery indicated that 60,000 traps would maximize the net economic value of the fishery (PMFC 1978), while Dewees et al. (2004) estimated that in 2000 there were more than six times this number of traps being fished in the combined fishery. Overcapitalization has contributed to derby conditions in this fishery, and in recent years, approximately 80 percent of total annual landings in California are made in a few weeks in December (Hankin and Warner 2001). This intense race has led to glutted markets, increased densities of crab traps on the fishing grounds, and fishing in dangerous conditions leading to loss of lives and vessels.

Derby fisheries suffer from a number of problems. First, derbies create an incentive for fishery participants to acquire larger vessels and more gear than they would otherwise need, thus leading to overcapitalization. Second, the large pulse of fish landings, followed by long periods of inactivity, requires that the fish be frozen and sold throughout the year, which can yield a lower-quality product than live or fresh fish, and a more highly concentrated and thus less competitive processing industry structure (Casey et al. 1995; Hackett et al. 2003). Hackett et al. (2005) show that the processing sector serving a derby fishery will tend to be highly concentrated, featuring a small number of large processors. Moreover, the need to invest in specialized and location-specific processing capital equipment can serve as a means of limiting entry and maintaining some degree of market power to dictate low ex-vessel prices paid to fishermen. (These are termed "ex-vessel" prices because they mediate the sale of fish off the vessel to the primary processor).Third, the race for fish can induce fishing in hazardous seas and unnecessary loss of life. In their Census of Fatal Occupational Injuries, the Bureau of Labor Statistics (BLS) lists commercial fishing as the single most deadly occupation in the United States. The BLS reports that in the five-year period 1992–96 there were 140 fatalities per 100,000 fishers in the United States compared to the national average of five fatalities per 100,000 for all occupations.

Overcapitalized fishery participants loaded down with debt can put enormous political pressure on policymakers setting catch limits. There are practical difficulties involved with reducing excess fishing capacity. One practical difficulty is that of measurement. Some gear and vessels can be deployed in different fisheries, which makes it difficult to attribute a given amount of fishing capacity to a particular fishery. Moreover, attempts at reducing fishing capacity in one fishery can result in vessels and gear shifting to another fishery. For example, efforts made by some developed countries to reduce fishing capacity have led to the relocation of vessels to the fisheries of other (usually developing and least developed) countries. This does not constitute a reduction in capacity on a global scale. Moreover, the open-access nature of high seas fisheries creates a particularly difficult situation with respect to the control of fishing capacity. In the 1982 United Nations Convention on the Law of the Sea, in particular, the issue of fishing capacity is largely ignored (FAO 1998). As the FAO (1990, p. 78) observes:

> The relative failure of international management to establish sustainable fisheries in many areas, despite the high quality of the research base sometimes provided, is clearly demonstrated by the dwindling resources, excessive catching capacity [number and size of boats and gear], uncontrolled transfers of fishing effort between resources and oceans, and depletion of many highly valuable resources. . . . The fact that uncontrolled development of fishing effort leads to disaster has now been widely acknowledged in the scientific literature and by high level fisheries management and development authorities.

As we shall see in the next section of this chapter, there are a number of new alternative management schemes that address excess capacity, the race for fish, and the overfished status of many marine capture fisheries.

Individual Quotas

A key problem with both open-access fisheries and traditional fishery management tools is that fishers do not have any property rights to a share of the available fishery stock prior to capture. Because fishers do not have a property right to fish until capture, the harvest by one vessel imposes a *rule of capture* externality on all others by reducing the remaining stock of fish. When the rule of capture externality is operating, fishery participants have an incentive to overcapitalize in vessel, crew, and gear (Casey et al. 1995). We have also seen that the rule of capture externality promotes a race for fish that leads to diminished product quality and increased fishing hazards. A number of alternative management regimes have recently been implemented to address some or all of these deficiencies of traditional management. Some of the more prominent examples are summarized in Table 6.1 and will be discussed below.

Table 6.1

Quota-Based Management Systems for Marine Capture Fisheries

Management regime	Purpose	How it works	Examples	Discussion
Individual Fishing Quota (IFQ)	Eliminate derby, reduce over-capitalization, increase economic efficiency	Quota shares to total allowable catch (TAC) allocated to individual fishers; may be transferable	Alaskan halibut and sablefish, Australian blue fin tuna, Icelandic herring and cod, New Zealand fisheries, U.S. Atlantic surf clam and ocean quahogs	Establishment of initial quota shares may be contentious; must be feasible to set TAC and monitor landings; concentration of ownership is an issue
Individual Vessel Quota (IVQ)	Eliminate derby, reduce over-capitalization, increase economic efficiency	Similar to IFQ except that shares are allocated among registered vessels instead of individuals	British Columbian halibut, sablefish, and groundfish; Norwegian fisheries	Similar to IFQ
Community Fishing Quota (CFQ)	Promote community cohesiveness and other goals	Quota shares to TAC allocated to a community defined by geography, cultural identity, or some other factor(s)	Chatham Islands and Maori communities in New Zealand; Sambro, Nova Scotia	Like the closely related Community Development Quota system, CFQs promote community cohesion
Effort Quota (EQ)	Reduce effort and increase economic efficiency	Quota shares to effort, including inputs such as crustacean traps, or time at sea; may be transferable	Washington Dungeness crab pot licenses, Florida spiny lobster crab trap certificates, scallop fleet days-at-sea limits	Only effective in controlling total catch if there are no substitutes for the restricted input, and input productivity is predictable and stable

Sources: National Research Council (1999); Organization for Economic Cooperation and Development (1997).

Individual quotas (IQs) were first implemented in Iceland and New Zealand in the early 1980s, and since then have been implemented in an increasing number of fisheries around the world (Wilen 2000). IQs assign a share of the TAC to individual fishers (IFQs), vessels (IVQs), or communities (CFQs). Those who hold quota shares own a share of the TAC. Therefore, the fishing season does not end until all quota shares are filled, subject to biological constraints. By assigning rights prior to capture, IQs eliminate the rule of capture externality. As a result, derby conditions and the incentive for over-capitalization are either substantially reduced or eliminated. Reduction or elimination of derby conditions implies that the pulse of landings that occurs due to the derby is instead spread out over a longer period of time. Reducing overcapitalization increases the *economic efficiency* of the fishing industry by reducing the total cost of harvesting a given quantity of fish. IQs can also be transferable or tradable, which can introduce further gains in economic efficiency. When IQs are tradable in a competitive market setting, economic theory suggests that quota will flow to its highest-valued use. This is particularly important in overcapitalized and depleted fisheries in which quota shares are too small to allow for economically efficient and profitable vessel operation. In this case tradable quota shares will tend to be concentrated on a subset of the original fishing fleet that can operate efficiently and profitably. Those who exit the fishery can at least receive the value of their quota share. An IQ operating on an isolated fishery undergoing consolidation can result in vessels simply being redeployed in some other less-regulated fishery, which reduces the global benefits of a tradable IQ.

There is some evidence that IQs have improved overall economic conditions in fisheries, as well as in the processing industry complexes that serve as the primary market for these fisheries. In the Atlantic surf clam/ocean quahog fishery, imposition of an IQ system in late 1990 resulted in a decrease in excess capacity and a consequent increase in economic efficiency (National Research Council 1999). The number of vessels working the Atlantic surf clam/ocean quahog fishery fell by at least 50 percent following the imposition of IQ fishery management. Likewise, the imposition of IQs on the Icelandic herring fishery increased economic efficiency, reduced the number of vessels from 200 to 29, and increased the profitability of fishing firms (National Research Council 1999). Along these same lines, the OECD (1997) reports that imposition of IQs in Australia's bluefin tuna fishery resulted in a 70 percent reduction in vessel numbers and an estimated fourfold increase in Hotelling rent.

Moreover, as Matulich, Mittelhammer, and Reberte (1996) and Hackett et al. (2005) observe, displacement of derby fisheries through the imposition of IQ fishery management also has implications for the structure and performance of the associated fish processing industry. Matulich, Mittelhammer, and Reberte (1996) show that IQ fishery management will harm incumbent fish processors, but assume that seafood product forms do not change. Hackett et al. (2005) use a similar modeling approach, but take into account that derby conditions and resulting pulse of landings necessitate freezing or canning, and that spreading out landings through IQ fishery management allows for an increase in production of fresh seafood products. They cite research showing that in many (though not all) circumstances, consumers value fresh seafood products at least as much as similar preserved products. Consequently, unlike Matulich, Mittelhammer, and Reberte, they find that after IQ fishery management is put into place, processors no longer need extensive capital in the form of freezers and canning equipment, potentially allowing for entry by new and smaller fresh-fish processors. The implication is that there will be more buyer competition for the catch coming out of the fishery, which in turn raises ex-vessel prices and improves economic conditions in the fishery. While incumbent processors may be made worse off, they may also convert their operations to the less costly and perhaps more valuable processing of fresh seafood products. To the extent that consumers prefer fresh to frozen or canned seafood, additional economic value is created even further downstream due to the change in product forms.

There is evidence to support the predictions that derive from the Hackett et al. (2005) model. For example, IQs in New Zealand have reduced overcapitalization in vessels and gear (Clark 1993). IQs have also eased the derby characteristic of some New Zealand fisheries and has resulted in increased export sales of more valuable live product such as rock lobster. Perhaps the best example comes from the British Columbian halibut fishery. The imposition of IQs in British Columbia's halibut fishery resulted in the percentage of halibut landings sold as a higher-valued fresh product to increase from 42 percent to 94 percent, thereby raising ex-vessel prices and profitability (Casey et al. 1995). A summary of the changes in seafood product forms, processing industry structure, and ex-vessel prices observed in actual fisheries that have displaced derby conditions and the associated pulse of landings by way of IQ fishery management is presented in Table 6.2.

Since an IQ grants the owner a right to catch a fixed percentage of the TAC, the price of an IQ should reflect the present discounted value of the expected flow of Hotelling rents from the quota. Therefore rising quota share prices indicates an increase in Hotelling rents, which can be attributable to increasing economic efficiency and the sustainable management of the fishery. For example, the price for renting Icelandic cod fishing quota increased from $0.05 to $0.09 per kilogram in 1984 to approximately $1 per kilogram in 1994. Similarly, the price of quota shares in many of New Zealand's fish-

Table 6.2

Effects of Derby Reduction, Resulting from IQ Fishery Management, on the Seafood Processing Industry

Location	Fishery	Ex-vessel price	Number of processors	Proportion product fresh
British Columbia	Halibut and sablefish	+	+	+
Alaska	Halibut and sablefish	+	+	+
Iceland	Cod	+	−	+
New Zealand, Australia	Rock lobster	+	+	Increased live
Scotia-Fundy, Canada	Groundfish	+	−	+

Source: Hackett et al. (2005).

eries has increased. For example, the average sales price of abalone quota increased from $NZ50,000 per metric ton in 1991 to approximately $NZ190,000 per metric ton in 1994 (National Research Council 1999).

There are a number of issues that can make IQs difficult to implement. First, it must be possible to establish a TAC on the fishery, which from a biological point of view may be difficult. Moreover, it must be feasible to monitor landings to prevent cheating on quota shares. Second, quota shares must be allocated to individuals, vessels, or coastal communities, and the initial quota allocation can be contentious. A common practice is to allocate initial quota shares based on historical landings. If conflict already exists on the fishery due to significant capacity differences in vessels or due to recent entry by vessels displaced from other fisheries, this conflict is likely to be manifested in initial quota assignments. Conflict can also occur over whether processors are to be allocated quota shares. Moreover, if individual quotas are being allocated, there is an issue over whether crewmembers should receive quota shares, which introduces further problems due to poor documentation of crewmember tenure on the fishery. Third, a decision must be made about whether IQs are to be tradable. If IQs are to be tradable, then a determination must be made regarding who is allowed to purchase quota shares and whether there is to be an upper limit on quota holdings by an individual, vessel, or community. Limits on quota shares were not established on the IQs for the Atlantic surf clam/ ocean quahog fishery, which led to some degree of ownership concentration and concerns about market power and rapid declines in total employment (National Research Council 1999). Fourth, some see IQ systems as a giveaway of public resources to private individuals, and so a decision must be made over whether some sort of auction or tax should be used to reclaim Hotelling rent from fisheries, and to fund monitoring and enforcement.

Effort quotas have been used to limit effort and reduce overcapitalization in fisheries. Most of the effort quotas used in the United States have been trap certificate programs in pot fisheries for crustaceans such as Dungeness crab and spiny lobster. In the case of trap certificates, a total number of traps for the fishery is established, and trap quota shares or certificates are usually assigned to fishers based on individual landings history in the fishery. As with IQs, trap certificates can be tradable. Effort quotas have also been used for Atlantic groundfish and scallops through fleetwide "days-at-sea" limitations (National Research Council 1999). While effort quotas can reduce over-capitalization and to some degree temporally spread landings, they do not establish rights to fish prior to capture and thus do not resolve all of the negative aspects of derby fisheries.

Unfortunately, there is even less information available on the performance of effort quotas such as trap certificate programs than there is on IQs. A trap certificate program was instituted in 1992 for the Florida spiny lobster fishery. The purpose of the program was to stabilize the fishery and increase yield per trap by reducing the total number of traps. Because of the trap certificate program, the number of spiny lobster traps decreased by 42 percent, from the 940,000 reported in 1991–92 prior to the certificate program, to 544,000 in the 1998–99 season (Milon, Larkin, and Lee 1998). They also report an increasing, though still small, degree of concentration in the spiny lobster fishing industry. As a result of the reduction in traps the average price of individual trap certificates sold to nonfamily members rose from about $5 in 1994 to about $20 in 1998 (Milon, Larkin, and Lee 1998).

Aquaculture

While most of the world's marine capture fisheries have reached or exceeded full exploitation, aquaculture, or fish farming, continues to grow in both absolute levels and as a percentage of total fish production. According to the FAO (2002), aquaculture's contribution to global supplies of fish, crustaceans, and molluscs continues to grow, increasing from 3.9 percent of total production by weight in 1970 to 27.3 percent in 2000. In 2000, aquaculture provided over 36 percent of the world's food fish supplies. Aquaculture is growing more rapidly than all other animal food-producing sectors. World-wide, the sector has increased at an average compounded rate of 9.2 percent per year since 1970, compared with only 1.4 percent for capture fisheries and 2.8 percent for terrestrial farmed meat production systems. Approximately one-third of the shrimp consumed in 1996 were produced by aquaculture, and 60 percent of all salmon consumed in 2003 was farmed. Freshwater aquaculture production represents approximately 60 percent of total aquaculture production. While freshwater aquaculture is dominated by finfish production such as carp, shellfish dominate marine aquaculture. In 2000 China was by far the dominant producer of farmed fish in the world, producing nearly 68 percent of total world aquaculture production; 82 percent of world aquaculture production occurs in lower-income food-deficit countries. High-value aquaculture species include giant tiger prawns, Pacific cupped oysters, various carp, and Atlantic salmon.

While aquaculture is an important source of food in food-deficit countries, in some cases aquaculture can harm wild fishery stocks. For example, some shrimp farmers engage in large-scale "biomass fishing"—fine-mesh net fishing that catches large numbers of the juveniles from wild fishery stocks. The construction of pens for coastal fish or shrimp farms accounts for a substantial proportion of the decline in the world's mangrove ecosystems, which are essential as nurseries for many species of fish and as natural water filtration systems. For example, Nixon (1996) reports that approximately 75 percent of the original mangrove forest existing in the Philippines in the 1920s is gone, with the trees harvested for lumber and the sites commonly transformed into shrimp farms. Safina (1994) reports that the farming of groupers, milkfish, and eels requires that hatchlings be captured from wild stocks because they cannot be bred in captivity, which puts further pressure on wild stocks. The density of fish in aquaculture facilities increases the potential for diseases to spread, which increases the risk of lost production to operators and creates the potential for the spread of disease to wild stocks.

In addition to impacts on marine ecology, aquaculture also has economic impacts on marine capture fisheries. Consider, for example, the case of farmed and wild salmon. The "farming" of salmon in net pens set up in protected coastal areas was pioneered commercially in Norway in the 1970s. The original perception was that farmed salmon would reduce pressure on wild stocks and provide economic opportunities for coastal communities impacted by declining wild stocks. Industry observers note that the idealistic vision for salmon farming was based on small-scale operations producing farmed fish at prices above those that prevailed for salmon from capture fisheries. Yet high prices and increasing consumer demand under competitive conditions in the world seafood market elicited large-scale entry by new salmon aquaculture operators in coastal countries with suitable ocean conditions around the world, including Canada, Chile, Iceland, Ireland, the Netherlands, and Scotland. Falling prices forced operators to exploit economies of scale, causing the industry to consolidate into a relatively small number of large operators, and these cost-cutting moves resulted in further downward pressure on prices. Farmed salmon is now an international protein commodity that competes directly with salmon from wild stocks, as well as beef, chicken, and other protein products.

According to the *Alaska Salmon Industry Baseline Study* (Alaska Department of Community and Economic Development 2003), in Alaska, where salmon farming is banned, wild salmon from the state's stocks have been significantly displaced in the world market by farmed salmon. In 1980 wild Alaskan salmon represented 43 percent of all the salmon consumed worldwide, and farmed salmon represented only 1 percent of world consumption. Over the following twenty-one years, the market share captured by wild Alaskan salmon declined steadily while that of farmed salmon increased. By 2001 wild Alaskan salmon held only a 19 percent share of the world salmon market. This study goes on to note that the development of large-scale salmon farming roughly tripled overall salmon consumption and transformed product preferences.

While the wild salmon market was traditionally for canned or frozen as a "headed and gutted" product, with a small, seasonal fresh salmon component, farmed production provided fresh fish year round to consumers. The attractiveness of farmed salmon to retailers and secondary processors stemmed from a number of factors, including overall quality, consistency of supply, and elimination of inventory requirements. Moreover, the strong U.S. dollar made farmed salmon imports from Canada, Chile, and Norway even more price-competitive, while reducing the price competitiveness of wild Alaskan salmon exports to Japan. The result has been a price squeeze on Alaskan salmon fishermen and processors. Currently industry participants from salmon capture fisheries are focusing on providing quality fresh product and emphasizing the environmental and possible health benefits of consuming wild salmon.

Summary

- From an economic standpoint, a *fishery* refers to the interaction of human harvest activities, environmental conditions, and the population dynamics associated with one or more species of fish.
- The term *capture fishery* refers to the enterprise of catching wild marine or inland fish, which can be contrasted with *aquaculture,* or fish farming.
- As was described in chapter 5, capture fisheries frequently have the characteristics of common-pool resources. Consequently, unconstrained rivalry among fishery participants, such as under the property rights system of open access, can result in the depletion of the resource and the economic rents that fishery participants derive from that resource.
- Total landings from marine and freshwater capture fisheries (excluding

China) grow from around 20 million metric tons in 1950 to a peak of 83 million metric tons in 1989, and ranged between 70 and 80 million metric tons between 1996 and 2001.

- Global fishing pressure continues to increase, the number of underexploited and moderately exploited fishery resources continues to decline slightly, the number of fully exploited stocks remains relatively stable, and the number of overexploited, depleted, and recovering stocks is increasing slightly. Landings from about 75 percent of the world's major marine fish stocks are expected either to remain constant or to decline in the future.
- A bioeconomic equilibrium occurs when the harvest rate equals the growth rate of fish stocks. With a logistic stock growth function, if the harvest rate is set below the maximum sustainable yield, a given level of harvest can be generated from high and low levels of effort. The group-optimum level of total effort applied to a fishery maximizes total Hotelling rent for fishery participants.
- Marine fishery management programs that allow participants to compete for shares of a fixed total quantity of available fish (such as with a TAC) often become overcapitalized and feature a race for fish, or derby, that results in temporally compressed landings, reduced profits for participants, a more highly concentrated processing industry, and at times less desirable frozen products.
- In contrast, marine fishery management that allocates quota shares of a fixed TAC to participants do not become overcapitalized and do not feature derby conditions. If these individual quotas are transferable, then remaining vessels can operate efficiently even in depleted fisheries, though there is the potential for concentrated quota ownership.
- In 2000 aquaculture provided over 36 percent of the world's food fish supplies. Aquaculture is growing more rapidly than all other animal food-producing sectors.
- While the farming of filter-feeding animals such as oysters can improve water quality, there are significant environmental problems associated with shrimp and salmon aquaculture.

Review Questions and Problems

1. Research project: Identify an interesting fishery not covered in this chapter and write a three-page essay that describes (i) trends in landings, (ii) key fishery management milestones, and (iii) prices and other economic conditions in the fishery. Evaluate how well fishery management has performed in terms of protecting the resource and providing for the needs of fishermen,

processors, fishery-dependent communities, and consumers.

2. California's Dungeness crab fishery includes relatively small vessels that each fish an average of approximately 150 traps, medium-sized vessels that each fish an average of 250 traps, and large vessels that each fish an average of 450 traps. If the overall economic performance of this fishery would be improved by reducing the number of traps fished, what is the maximum number of traps that each vessel should be allowed to fish? What are the pros and cons of a single trap limit for all vessels versus a trap limit that varies proportionately with vessel size? Who are the winners and the losers in each case?

3. In what way is a company town, where workers can be employed only by a single firm, similar to the case of a monopsony processor that buys all the fish from commercial fishermen in a coastal region? How would prevailing wages (or fish prices) compare to markets where there are more employers (or fish processors)?

4. Spreadsheet simulation (more advanced): Suppose that stock growth is given by $F(X) = aX - bX^2$, where $(a = r, b = r/k)$. Note that steady-state harvest $H = E[a/b - E/b]$. If for simplicity we assume that $P = 1$ and total costs are given by $TC = cE$, then the *open-access equilibrium* occurs where $TR = TC$, implying that $E[a/b - E/b] = cE$, or $E^0 = a - bc$. The *group optimum equilibrium* occurs where $MR = MC$. With $P = 1$, then $MR = a/b - 2E/b$. Thus the group-optimum equilibrium occurs where $a/b - 2E/b = c$, or $E^* = a - bc$ /2. Assuming that $a = 1000$, $b = 1$, $p = \$1$, $c = \$100$:

    a. Solve for the "group-optimum" and "open-access" equilibrium values for E, X, and H.

    b. Create a table that shows $F(X)$ values for 50-unit increments of X (starting at $X = 0$ up to $X = 1000$). Plot the $F(X)$ values from the table in a fully labeled diagram and show the "group optimum" and "open access" equilibrium values for X on the horizontal axis, and for H on the vertical axis.

Internet Links

Food and Agriculture Organization's Fisheries Department (www.fao.org/fi/default.asp): The place to access various reports on the state of the world's marine capture fisheries, inland fisheries, and aquaculture.

National Marine Fisheries Service (www.nmfs.gov/): Learn about federal regulation of U.S. marine capture fisheries.

World Resources Institute (www.wri.org/): Excellent source of global information on the state of the world's natural resources.

References and Further Reading

Alaska Department of Community and Economic Development. 2003. *Alaska Salmon Industry Baseline Study*. Alaska Department of Community and Economic Development. www.dced.state.ak.us/oed/seafood/pub/BaseLineStudy.pdf.

Canadian Department of Fish and Oceans. A Recent Account of Canada's Atlantic Cod Fishery. www.dfo-mpo.gc.ca/kids-enfants/map-carte/map_e.htm.

Casey, K., C. Dewees, B. Turris, and J. Wilen. 1995. "The Effects of Individual Vessel Quotas in the British Columbia Halibut Fishery." *Marine Resource Economics* 10: 211–30.

Clark, I. 1993. "Individual Transferable Quotas: The New Zealand Experience." Marine Policy, September 17: 340–42.

Dewees, C., K. Sortais, S. Hackett, M. Krachey, and D. Hankin. 2004. "Racing for Crabs: Costs and Management Options in California's Commercial Dungeness Crab Fishery." *California Agriculture* 58 (October–December): 186–93.

Didier A. 2002. "The Pacific Coast Dungeness Crab Fishery." Paper, Pacific States Marine Fisheries Commission, Gladstone, OR.

Hackett, S. 2002. "An Economic Overview of the California Wetfish Industry Complex." In *California's "Wetfish" Industry: Its Importance Past, Present and Future*, ed. D. Pleschner-Steele. Santa Barbara, CA: California Seafood Council.

Hackett, S., M. Krachey, S. Brown, and D. Hankin. 2005. "Derby Fisheries, Individual Quotas, and Transition in the Fish Processing Industry." *Marine Resource Economics*, 20 (1) (April): 47–60.

Hackett, S., M. Krachey, C. Dewees, D. Hankin, and K. Sortais. 2003. "An Economic Overview of Dungeness Crab (*Cancer magister*) Processing in California." *California Cooperative Oceanic Fisheries Investigations Reports* 44: 86–93.

Hankin, D., and R. Warner. 2001. "Dungeness Crab." In *California's Living Marine Resources: A Status Report*, ed. W. Leet, C. Dewees, R. Klingbeil, and E. Larson. Sacramento: California Department of Fish and Game.

Hartwick, J., and N. Olewiler. 1998. *The Economics of Natural Resource Use*. 2nd ed. Reading, MA: Addison-Wesley.

Matulich, S., R. Mittelhammer, and C. Reberte. 1996. "Toward a More Complete Model of Individual Transferable Fishing Quotas: Implications of Incorporating the Processing Sector." *Journal of Environmental Economics and Management* 31: 112–28.

McEvoy, A. 1986. *The Fisherman's Problem: Ecology and Law in the California Fisheries, 1850–1980*. London: Cambridge University Press.

McGinn, A.1998. "Rocking the Boat: Conserving Fisheries and Protecting Jobs." Worldwatch Paper 142. Washington, DC: Worldwatch Institute.

Milon, J., S. Larkin, and D. Lee. 1998. "The Performance of Florida's Spiny Lobster Trap Certificate Program." Paper, Gainesville: Florida Sea Grant College Program.

National Research Council. 1999. *Sharing the Fish: Toward a National Policy on Individual Fishing Quotas*. Washington, DC: National Academy Press.

New England Fishery Management Council. Frequently asked questions. www.nefmc.org.

Nixon, W. 1996. "Rainforest Shrimp." *Mother Jones* 21 (March–April): 31–35, 71–73.

OECD. 1997. "Towards Sustainable Fisheries: Economic Aspects of the Management of Living Marine Resources." Paper, Paris: OECD.

Pacific Fishery Management Council, Scientific and Statistical Committee (SSC). 2000. *Overcapitalization in the West Coast Groundfish Fishery: Background, Issues and Solutions.* www.pcouncil.org/Groundfish/ssc_report_all.pdf.

Pacific Marine Fisheries Commission (PMFC). 1978. "Dungeness Crab Project of the State–Federal Fisheries Management Program." Portland, OR: Pacific Marine Fisheries Commission.

Ruitenbeek, H. 1996. "The Great Canadian Fishery Collapse: Some Policy Lessons." *Ecological Economics* 19 (November): 103–6.

Russell, D. 1996. "Fisheries in Crisis (Part II)." *E Magazine* 7 (September–October).

Safina, C. 1994. "Where Have All the Fishes Gone?" *Issues in Science and Technology* 10 (Spring): 37–43.

United Nations Food and Agriculture Organization (FAO). 1990. *Yearbook of Fishery Statistics.* Rome: United Nations Food and Agriculture Organization.

_____. 1998. *Yearbook of Fishery Statistics.* Rome: United Nations Food and Agriculture Organization.

———. 2002. *The State of World Fisheries and Aquaculture.* Rome: United Nations Food and Agriculture Organization.

Weber, P. 1994. "Net Loss: Fish, Jobs, and the Marine Environment." Worldwatch Paper 120. Washington, DC: Worldwatch Institute.

Wilen, J. 2000. "Renewable Resource Economists and Policy: What Differences Have We Made?" *Journal of Environmental Economics and Management* 39: 306–27.

Wolfe, P., P. Smith, and D. Bergen. 2001. "Pacific Sardine." In *California's Living Marine Resources: A Status Report*, ed. W. Leet, C. Dewees, R. Klingbeil, and E. Larson. Sacramento: California Department of Fish and Game.

Young, Richard. 2001. "Buying Back the Groundfish Fleet." Fisherman's Marketing Association. www.trawl.org.

7

Measurement and Analysis of Benefits and Costs

Introduction: Benefit/Cost Analysis

This chapter provides an overview of the methods used to measure the benefits and the costs of environmental protection, as well as a description of benefit/cost analysis (BCA). The goal is to introduce the reader to these concepts and the ways in which they have been applied in assessing proposed projects, policy changes, and man-made damages to the environment. Readers interested in going beyond this introductory treatment and developing the technical skills required to conduct nonmarket valuation studies, cost assessments, and other elements of benefit/cost analysis can begin with the citations list and Internet links to technical studies listed at the end of the chapter.

Enhancing environmental conservation and restoration entails opportunity costs. Examples of these opportunity costs include the economic value of harvested timber, fishery, or mineral resources left undeveloped; the profitable investment opportunities lost when firms are required to invest in pollution-control machinery and equipment; and the alternative use of tax revenues allocated by government for increased monitoring and enforcement. While there are many philosophical and conceptual problems with benefit/cost analysis (which we will explore below), policy decisions are made in the context of scarcity, and so policy decisions entail opportunity costs. Informed decision making ultimately requires that we rank alternatives and confront the net benefits of one policy option with the opportunity cost of that choice. Unless society can agree that certain environmental policies are intrinsically right, it is very difficult to avoid some form of benefit/cost analysis of social policy.

While costs are frequently measured in monetary terms, many of the benefits of environmental policy derive from improvements in aspects of the environment and human health that are not traded in markets, and so their value is not expressed in monetary terms. Thus a common metric is needed in order to compare the "apples and oranges" of benefits and costs. People routinely make the "apples and oranges" comparison of benefits and costs for themselves based on their values and preferences. When someone buys a good or service, they are comparing money cost with the utility or pleasure of the good that they anticipate receiving in exchange. If people know the quality of the good before purchase, then we can use the money that they spend on a good or service as a measurable indicator of their unmeasurable utility. If we aggregate the money spent on a particular good or service by all buyers, we can get a (perhaps crude) measure of the aggregate social utility generated by that good or service. Nevertheless, what if we are trying to measure the social utility of protecting an aspect of the natural environment that is not bought or sold in markets? We will discuss various techniques for measuring the value of nonmarketed environmental amenities later in this chapter.

Another metric for aggregating utility is provided by political systems. In democratic systems, we can use voting patterns as a binary indicator of the relative utility that voters have for various political candidates or ballot measures. Of course, because all human societies feature inequalities of wealth and power, both markets and politics are flawed instruments for measuring social utility. Benefit/cost analysis usually uses money as a measure of utility, and thus monetizing benefits and costs is an important aspect of such an analysis. In chapter 8 we shall discuss political economy, which evaluates policy alternatives based on preferences revealed through voting and political influence.

Jules Dupuit offers one of the earliest discussions of benefit/cost analysis in his book *On the Measurement of the Utility of Public Works* (1844). Dupuit argued that the output of a project (e.g., water generated by a water filtration system) multiplied by per-unit market price gives an estimate of the minimum social benefit of the project. Some consumers are willing to pay more, but this information may not be available for valuation purposes. One of the first applications of BCA was in the U.S. Flood Control Act of 1936. In this legislation, Congress declared that the benefits associated with federal projects, "to whomsoever they may accrue," should exceed costs. While benefits were supposed to exceed costs, no consistent methods were offered for measuring these benefits and costs. The Corps of Engineers, Soil Conservation Service, Bureau of Reclamation, and so on, all used different approaches. In 1950 the Federal Interagency River Basin Committee issued a publication called *Pro-*

posed Practices for Economic Analysis of River Basin Projects, also known as the "green book," which provided a uniform best-practices guide for various agencies involved with public projects.

In the current environmental policy debate, benefit/cost analysis has become a highly charged, controversial issue. Some wish to increase the use of benefit/cost analysis in order to enhance the efficiency of government regulation. It can be argued, however, that benefit/cost analysis is inappropriate as the single deciding policy factor in many circumstances where its use is proposed. Elements of this argument include:

- Using benefit/cost analysis as the single deciding factor in setting policy assumes implicitly that the values of all objects and states of affairs are commensurable, meaning that they can be ranked based on a single characteristic of value such as money or utility. Yet issues of fairness, ethics, and spirituality may not be commensurable with monetized costs or benefits. Can we compare the value of a unique sacred place to the revenues and jobs created by logging, mining, or grazing the site?
- Scientists and others do not fully understand the interdependencies in ecosystems, and so when we do benefit/cost analysis on one element of the ecosystem (for example, on preserving a particular species or damming a segment of river), we cannot understand the benefit/cost implications for all the other elements of the ecosystem. In other words, social and ecological systems may be too complex to quantify comprehensively through benefit/cost analysis.
- Some of the benefits of environmental improvements include the reduced loss of human life. Placing an infinite value on a human life in benefit/cost analysis would lead to the conclusion that all of the world's resources should be allocated toward prevention of any one death, an unlikely choice of social policy. Yet if we measure the value of a human life based on income generation, then the analysis will tell us that a life in a rich country is worth more than one in a poor country. In this case benefit/cost analysis will yield the unethical conclusion that it is "efficient" to dispose of toxics and other life-threatening pollutants in low-income countries because lives saved in rich countries are worth more than lives lost in poor countries. For example, Bowland and Beghin (1998) estimated that the value of a statistical life saved in Santiago, Chile, due to reduced air pollution is approximately $600,000, which is only about 12.5 percent of the $4.8 million value of an American statistical life used by the U.S. Environmental Protection Agency (EPA 1997). The Nazis applied similar "efficiency" arguments regarding the differential value of human lives to justify the euthanasia of groups such as

the disabled. Thus, benefit/cost analysis can lead to environmental discrimination and racism.

- When we use benefit/cost analysis to evaluate projects or policies that affect future generations, we must somehow decide on how to bring the benefits and costs accruing to these future generations into the present. While discounting clearly makes sense in individual behavior, if we apply discounting to benefit/cost analysis, are we robbing future generations to benefit the present? Moreover, since we do not know the values and preferences of future generations, we must project our own upon them.

- When we monetize benefits and costs without regard to who receives them, we are implicitly assuming that a dollar generates the same incremental gain in pleasure or marginal utility to all people. Yet this is not generally true when wealth is highly unequally distributed; for example, a $10 gain to a mother with a hungry child likely generates substantially higher marginal utility than it would to a billionaire. Thus, policies that generate the greatest net monetary benefit may in fact generate a substantially inefficient level of human happiness when we assume that the marginal utility of money is the same for all people.

While it is clear that monetization and benefit/cost analysis capture at best only parts of the total impact of a policy, and so should not be considered a sole guide to policy, data on benefits and costs can be informative and valuable. Along these lines Munda (1996) and others argue for *integrated environmental assessment,* which combines benefit/cost analysis with other ecological, social, and political factors in environmental policy analysis.

Efficiency

An economic process is said to be efficient if it produces something of value with a minimum of waste. What we mean by waste, however, depends on our norms and objectives. For example, if the objective is to maximize profit, then a timber company will want to use least-cost harvest methods to prevent the waste of potential profit. Doing so, however, may result in damage to the ecosystem of the affected area. Yet since the objective is to maximize profit, damage to the ecosystem is not counted as waste; in this context, waste would be defined as lost profits created by more costly sustainable forestry practices. On the other hand, if the objective were sustainable forestry, then a clear cut would create waste because it would damage aspects of the ecosystem that are integral to sustainable forestry practices. In the specific context of benefit/cost analysis, efficiency refers to the extent to which a particular policy improves upon status quo social utility as measured by net (monetary) benefits.

If there is a range of possible policy options, then the efficient policy option is the one that generates the largest improvement in social utility. As was discussed in chapter 2, there are two different criteria for judging the efficiency of social policy. The *Kaldor-Hicks efficiency criterion* states that the efficient policy option generates the largest net monetary benefits relative to the other policy alternatives. In contrast, the more restrictive *Pareto efficiency criterion* states that an efficient policy option makes some people better off and nobody worse off when compared to the status quo. The Pareto criterion is considered nearly impossible to satisfy in actual policy analysis, and so Kaldor-Hicks is the usual efficiency criterion used. While the usual method of performing benefit/cost analysis is to maximize the present value (PV) of net monetary benefits (as described below), an alternative method is to select policies that generate the greatest amount of monetary benefit for each dollar of cost; called the *benefit/cost ratio method*. The ratio method tends to favor smaller projects, while the net monetary benefit method tends to favor larger projects. In the presentation that follows, we will assume that the Kaldor-Hicks efficiency criterion is applied to the PV of net benefits.

Maximizing Net Present Value (PV)

The concepts of PV and dynamic efficiency were first introduced in chapter 5. Here we will apply the PV methodology to benefit/cost analysis. To calculate the PV of net benefits, we must first estimate the flow of benefits and costs from various project alternatives for each year into the future. Then we choose an appropriate discount rate (the rate of interest charged if you loan money for a year rather than use that money yourself) and compute the PV of the net benefits for each year into the future. As we learned in chapter 5, we can calculate the PV of net benefits as follows:

$$PV_{NB} = (B_0 - C_0)/(1 + r)^0 + (B_1 - C_1)/(1 + r)^1 + \ldots + (B_n - C_n)/(1 + r)^n$$

Note that C = cost in a given time period, B = benefit in a given time period, r = discount rate, and n is the end period of the project in years from the present. $(B_1 - C_1)$, for example, refers to net benefits received one year from the present. The expression $(1 + r)^n$ means that the sum $(1 + r)$ is taken to the nth power.

Discounting will tend to undermine those policies that have large up-front costs, and benefits that are cast into the future, such as with green-

Table 7.1

Hypothetical PV of Costs and Benefits for Control of Sulfur Dioxide Emissions (in millions of dollars)

1. Percentage of sulfur dioxide emissions eliminated	2. Total cost	3. Marginal cost (change in 2 divided by change in 1)	4. Total benefit	5. Marginal benefit (change in 4 divided by change in 1)	6. Marginal net benefit (5 minus 3)	7. Total net benefit (4 minus 2)
10	30	3	500	50	47	470
20	80	5	970	47	42	890
30	160	8	1,370	40	32	1,210
40	310	15	1,700	33	18	1,390
50	560	25	1,950	25	0	1,390
60	920	36	2,100	15	−21	1,180
70	1,400	48	2,175	7.5	−40.5	7,75
80	2,010	61	2,205	3	−58	1,95
90	2,760	75	2,220	1.5	−73.5	−5,40
100	3,670	91	2,225	.5	−90.5	−1,445

house gas emissions control and global warming. To see this, note that the PV of $100 of benefit received fifty years from now, using a standard 10 percent discount rate, is only 85 cents. Therefore 85 cents deposited today in a financial investment paying 10 percent interest will compound in value to $100 in fifty years. If the federal government routinely uses a 10 percent discount rate, then spending more than 85 cents on a policy today that will generate $100 of benefits fifty years from now will not pass a benefit/cost test. This subject will be discussed in more detail in chapter 13.

An Illustrative Example of Benefit/Cost Analysis

Acid rain in the eastern United States and Canada is caused by sulfur dioxide emitted from sources such as the smokestacks of coal-fired power plants. Acid rain (and other forms of acid deposition) lowers the pH of soil, streams, and water bodies, thereby reducing biotic productivity and at times even killing entire species of animals and plants. We can consider a variety of different levels of sulfur dioxide control. Benefit/cost analysis can be used to determine the policy alternative that yields the largest net monetary benefit. Consider the hypothetical PV of costs and benefits (in millions of dollars) associated with each incremental 10 percent reduction in sulfur dioxide in Table 7.1. Assume for a moment that the monetary values given in the table fully measure the benefits and the costs associated with controlling sulfur dioxide emissions.

Figure 7.1 **Level of Pollution Control That Maximizes Total Net Benefit Occurs Where Marginal Benefit Equals Marginal Cost**

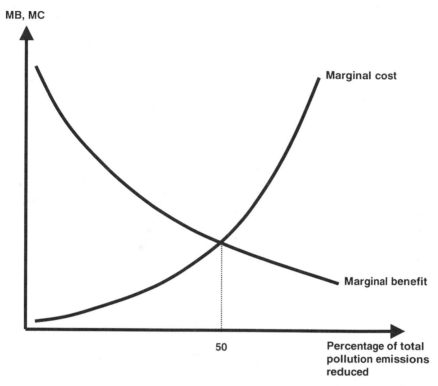

MB, MC

Marginal cost

Marginal benefit

50

Percentage of total pollution emissions reduced

Figures 7.1 and 7.2 illustrate the relationship between marginal benefits and costs, and total net benefits. When an additional increment of pollution abatement generates marginal benefits that exceed marginal cost, then marginal net benefit is positive, and therefore total net benefit increases with additional cleanup. At some point, an increment of additional pollution abatement will generate a marginal benefit that is equal to marginal cost, which means that marginal net benefit is zero, and total net benefit remains unchanged. Any further increment of additional pollution abatement will generate marginal benefit that is less than marginal cost, which means that marginal net benefit is negative, and total net benefit declines. Therefore, total net benefit is maximized when marginal benefit equals marginal cost. This illustrates a more general analytical tool used in microeconomics, called *marginal analysis,* which helps us identify a maximum (such as the maximum total net benefit in Table 7.1) by evaluating marginal benefits and marginal costs. The *equimarginal principle* states that the optimal allocation occurs when marginal benefit equals marginal cost. Recall that we used mar-

Figure 7.2   **Total Net Benefit Curve**

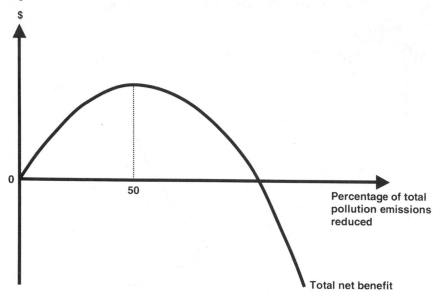

ginal analysis in chapter 4 to find the competitive market supply curve using the "price equals marginal cost" rule.

The efficient level of sulfur dioxide pollution control is found where total net benefits are maximized, which in the example above happens to occur at the 50 percent level of control. To see how we arrive at the conclusion that the 50 percent level of pollution control maximizes total net benefits, apply the methodology described in the preceding paragraph. Note that as one begins the first increment of the cleanup process, marginal net benefits are positive, meaning that the initial 10 percent increment of cleanup adds marginal benefits that exceed marginal cost. Therefore, the first 10 percent increment of cleanup causes total net benefits to increase. Likewise, as long as an additional increment of cleanup generates positive marginal net benefits they will continue to increase total net benefits. At some point, marginal net benefits will become zero, which corresponds to maximum total net benefits. When the marginal net benefits of further cleanup become negative (which occurs when the level of pollution abatement increases from 50 to 60 percent in the example above), total net benefit declines with any additional pollution reduction. Consequently, in our example the efficient level of sulfur dioxide pollution control occurs at the 50 percent level of control.

Note that in our example the marginal costs of cleanup are rising, while the marginal benefits are falling. While this does not always have to be the case, we generally expect marginal costs to rise. For example, the first 10 percent reduction in sulfur dioxide may be accomplished by rather inexpensive replacement of low-sulfur for high-sulfur coal in coal-burning electric generator facilities. Yet the last 10 percent reduction in sulfur dioxide (from 90 percent control to complete elimination of all sulfur dioxide emissions) may require the immediate elimination of all fossil fuel burning in the world, which would entail an enormous short-term cost. We may expect the marginal benefits of sulfur dioxide control to decline; the first 10 percent reduction occurs in a highly polluted situation, while the last 10 percent reduction may have little noticeable effect because the environment can naturally assimilate that last 10 percent of emissions.

It has been pointed out that we may not need regulations to achieve the efficient level of pollution control described above. In particular, economist Ronald Coase argued that the efficient outcome might also be realized if we assign and enforce property rights and allow people to resolve pollution disputes through negotiation. We will consider this point in detail below.

The Coase Theorem

The Coase theorem is based on a very simple and intuitive argument. Suppose that environmental protection or enhancement benefits one group of people and imposes costs on another. If the benefits of environmental protection exceed the costs, then the positive total net benefits from cleanup can be thought of as a pie to be divided between members of society. The size of the pie is maximized at the efficient level of pollution control, such as the 50 percent level of control in the example in the preceding section of the chapter. Suppose that all stakeholders involved with a localized pollution problem are cognizant of the efficient level of pollution control. The Coase theorem simply states that a way to achieve this efficient outcome would be to (i) determine who holds the relevant property rights and (ii) arrange for a payment that makes it mutually satisfactory for all parties to adopt the efficient pollution-control outcome.

For example, suppose there is an auto body shop near a new housing development in the process of being built. The city's nuisance law has a threshold of 125 decibels, and the auto body shop emits 120. In this case, the auto body shop holds the relevant property rights and can legally operate. Suppose that there are two ways to eliminate the noise. One is to move the auto body shop at a cost of $300,000, and the other is to install sound-absorbing materials in the shop for $100,000 that will eliminate the bothersome noise. Also suppose that eliminating the noise will result in a $1 million increase in residential property values in the development. In this case, the installation of sound-absorbing materials is efficient, generating a $900,000 pie to be divided. With the rights held by the auto body shop, the Coase theorem simply states that the efficient outcome can be realized by having the developer enter into a legally binding contract with the auto body shop in which the developer pays to install the sound-absorbing material.

Now suppose that the auto body shop is exceeding the decibel threshold for residential areas. Now the residential developer holds the relevant property rights. As before, the efficient solution is to install sound-absorbing materials in the auto body shop. With the rights held by the developer, the Coase theorem states that the efficient outcome can be realized by having the auto body shop enter into a legally binding contract with the developer in which the auto body shop pays to install the sound-absorbing material. This remains less expensive than moving the shop, and generates considerable net benefits to society. Either way, the efficient outcome is achieved by way of a negotiated contract, without government regulatory intervention.

What Coase and other economists found interesting is that the same overall social efficiency gain will result regardless of who "owns" the right to control the environmental improvement. Under certain conditions, it does not matter who holds the property rights. In particular, this Coase theorem result will hold under the following conditions:

- It is feasible to assign property rights to aspects of the environment such as clean air, water, and earth.
- There are positive net benefits from environmental improvement.
- The *transaction costs* of coordinating people and conducting the negotiation process are low.
- There is no *free-rider problem* in gathering payment funds from a group of stakeholders.
- Any agreement that is reached is legally enforceable.

In addition to the problems mentioned at the start of the chapter concerning monetization and benefit/cost analysis, transaction costs and free riding also plague Coasian contracting. *Transaction costs* are simply the costs associated with arranging a transaction. In the case of Coasian contracting, the cost of bringing together and coordinating large numbers of stakeholders would require large expenditures for coordination and communication. *Free riding* refers to behavior in which people receive benefits from the creation of a public good or a common-pool resource but choose not to make a voluntary contribution toward the production of those goods. Transaction costs and free riding tend to become larger as more and more people are included in the negotiation process.

For example, suppose that we tried to use Coasian contracting to resolve the problem of halocarbons damaging the earth's stratospheric ozone layer. Billions of people benefit and would need to either be compensated or make a payment, depending upon who holds the relevant rights. The cost of coordinating such negotiations would entail prohibitive transaction expenses. In addition, with large numbers of people benefiting from a cleaner environment trying to pool money to buy out a major polluter, a self-interested individual may say, "The plan will work even if I don't pay my $50," with the result (possibly) being a failure of collective action. For these reasons, Coasian contracting is far more likely to be used for small-scale environmental problems involving small numbers of affected individuals, such as neighbors working out problems over a fence. When large numbers of people are involved, government intervention can reduce transaction costs and the free-rider problem that would otherwise exist under Coasian contracting.

Operationalizing Benefit/Cost Analysis in U.S. Environmental Policy

Since Executive Order 12044, issued by President Jimmy Carter in 1978, federal regulations such as those for protecting health, safety, and the environment are required to be cost-effective, and federal agencies must quantify the benefits and costs for the various regulations that they administer. As Viscusi (1996) points out, this cost-effectiveness test did not tend to screen out inefficient methods of regulatory administration because alternative regulatory methods were rarely identified. Since Executive Order 12291, issued by President Ronald Reagan in 1981, the federal government must show that regulations pass a benefit/cost test. In an important U.S. Supreme Court case dealing with the Occupational Safety and Health Administration (OSHA) cotton-dust regulation in the workplace, however, the Court argued that the legislative mandate placed a feasibility test rather than a benefit/cost test on such regulation (*American Textile Manufacturers' Institute v. Donovan*, 452 U.S. 490 [1981]). In *UAW v. OSHA*, 938 F.2d 1310 (DC Circuit, 1991), the U.S. Court of Appeals allowed that OSHA was not foreclosed from using a benefit/cost test in the promulgation of its regulations. Viscusi reports that many federal regulatory agencies currently interpret their mandate as exempting them from the executive orders regarding benefit/cost testing. In Executive Order 12866, the Clinton administration broadened the definition of benefits in Reagan's executive order to acknowledge the difficulty of monetizing all relevant regulatory benefits.

The Safe Drinking Water Act (SDWA), reauthorized in 1996, now requires the Environmental Protection Agency (EPA) to utilize benefit/cost analysis for new regulations. While the SDWA requires the EPA to publish these benefit/cost analyses, it does not bind the EPA to reject regulations based on their failure to pass a benefit/cost test. The Clean Air Act (CAA) amendments of 1990 required the EPA to conduct a benefit/cost analysis of the original CAA of 1970. In its report, the EPA (1997) states that the benefits of the CAA between 1970 and 1990 had a central estimate of $22.2 trillion in constant 1990 dollars. Only a subset of the known negative externalities associated with air pollution was included, primarily adverse human health effects, along with some agricultural and visibility impacts. Due to resource and data limitations, improvements in ecological and other conditions were not quantified in the assessment. For this reason, the estimated benefits can be considered understated. Estimates of the direct costs of complying with the CAA during this period are approximately $0.5 trillion in constant 1990 dollars. Thus each $1 of compliance cost to the economy is estimated to have generated over $44 in benefits. It is interesting to point out that the original CAA was widely seen as being more costly than necessary. The CAA amendments of 1990 included an experiment in incentive regulation (to be discussed in chapter 10) as a means of reducing these compliance costs.

Now that we understand the concepts and the practices of benefit/cost analysis, we will turn to a discussion of the methods for measuring benefits and costs.

Measuring Benefits

Overview

People derive many benefits from ecosystems and natural resources, ranging from recreation to wildlife habitat and from food and raw materials production to nutrient cycling and soil formation. For example, swamps and other wetlands used to be considered of little value and were frequently drained for agricultural uses. More recently, ecologists have identified many vital ecosystem functions performed by these areas, and economists have developed tools for estimating the monetary value of these functions. In a comprehensive study attempting to estimate the value of various ecosystem and natural resource services, for example, Costanza et al. (1997) report that the nutrient-cycling function of estuaries generates annual benefits worth $11,100 to $30,100 per hectare, while the water-supply function of swamps and floodplains yields annual benefits worth $7,600 per hectare. Likewise, Balmford et al. (2002) found that the economic value of the services derived from intact and fully functioning tropical mangrove ecosystems (Thailand) and wetlands (Canada) exceeded the economic value of activities such as shrimp aquaculture (Thailand) or intensive farming on "reclaimed" wetlands (Canada). This section of the chapter provides an overview of the various techniques that economists have applied to measuring the benefits of environmental and natural resources.

To introduce the economic problem of measuring benefits, consider the example of particulate emissions. Particulate matter will cause some harms to commercially valuable goods and services. These damages will be manifested in changes in market conditions that can be gauged using standard supply and demand analysis. For example, as we will consider in detail in the next section of the chapter, risk assessment methods can be used to measure the harms to human health caused by breathing a certain quantity of particulate matter. Premature death and illnesses lead to lost earnings that can be quantified when assessing the benefits of reducing particulate matter. Particulate matter also damages exterior paint and necessitates the cleaning of exterior walls and windows of buildings. Reduced particulate emissions in a particular area will likely increase real estate values in a predictable way, as people will find the area more desirable to live in. Moreover, when visual aesthetics are an important part of a local economy, such as with tourism in the Grand Canyon area, then reduced ambient concentrations of particulate matter will generate measurable increases in tourism-based income. There may also be measurable improvements in crop yields. More generally, environmental cleanup will generate some benefits to things whose value is revealed in markets.

As we have seen in the discussion above and in previous chapters, well-functioning competitive markets are useful because they reveal value. For goods and services that are marketed, we can derive consumer surplus from market demand and thereby estimate the net value of the good or service to consumers. Nevertheless, pollution such as particulate matter also affects people and ecosystems in ways that cannot be deduced directly from market impacts. The measurement process is more difficult when trying to determine the benefits provided by conserving or restoring nonmarketed aspects of the environment because there is no market price or wage to indicate value. Thus, economists have developed methods of nonmarket valuation to estimate the demand for environmental conservation and restoration. Before we address the various methods of demand estimation for nonmarketed environmental qualities, however, we must first consider how to deal with situations in which environmental improvements result in reductions in health and safety risks.

A particular challenge associated with policies such as toxic emissions control is that many of the benefits to society are in the form of reduced

probabilities or *risks* that an individual member of society will suffer measurable harm, such as contracting cancer or some illness associated with the
pollution emissions. Thus quantitative risk assessment is an important element of measuring benefits.

Measuring the Health and Ecological Benefits of Regulation: Quantitative Risk Assessment (QRA) and the Value of a Statistical Life (VSL)

Many environmentally damaging practices such as pollution generate harms
to human health that are recognizable in overall populations, but which have
uncertain effects on any single individual. A natural example is the emission
of toxic pollution into air or water, which elevates the risk of a person contracting cancer, emphysema, or various reproductive disorders. In this case,
one way to view the harm is the elevated likelihood of a person becoming ill
or dying. Thus, a benefit of environmental protection is the reduction in the
probability of a person experiencing specific adverse health effects. Health
risk assessment provides a basis for quantifying the benefits of different regulatory options. Likewise, ecological risk assessment is used to evaluate the
potential adverse effects that human activities have on the plants and animals
that make up ecosystems.

The National Research Council (NRC 1983) defined risk assessment as
including some or all of the following components (paradigm): hazard identification, dose-response assessment, exposure assessment, and risk characterization. The EPA's National Center for Environmental Assessment (NCEA)
Internet site describes the risk assessment and management paradigm:

> *Risk Assessment* is the process used to evaluate the degree and probability
> of harm to human health and the environment from such stressors as pollu-
> tion or habitat loss. The risk assessment process, as proposed by the Na-
> tional Academy of Sciences (NAS) in 1983, consists of:
>
> - **Exposure Assessment**—describing the populations or ecosystems exposed
>   to stressors and the magnitude, duration, and spatial extent exposure
> - **Hazard Identification**—identifying adverse effects (e.g., short-term ill-
>   ness, cancer) that may occur from exposure to environmental stressors
> - **Dose-Response Assessment**—determining the toxicity or potency of
>   stressors
> - **Risk Characterization**—using the data collected in the first three steps
>   to estimate and describe the effects of human or ecological exposure to
>   stressors

Risk Management entails determining whether and how risks should be managed or reduced. It is based on the results of the risk assessment as well as other factors (e.g., public health, social, and economic factors). Risk management options include pollution prevention or control technologies to reduce or eliminate the pollutant or other stressor on the environment. The environmental or public health impacts resulting from risk management decisions must then be monitored so that any necessary adjustments can be made.

The EPA has developed risk assessments for a variety of different pollutants, such as mercury, particulate matter, and dioxin, as well as guidelines for various human health and ecological risks. For example, the guidelines for neurotoxicity risk assessment establish principles and procedures to guide EPA scientists in evaluating pollutants that may pose neurotoxic risks, and inform EPA decision makers and the public about these procedures. In contrast, the EPA's guidelines for ecological risk assessment are designed and conducted to provide information to risk managers about the potential adverse effects of different management decisions. Ecological risk assessments are used to support many types of management actions, including the regulation of hazardous waste sites, industrial chemicals, and pesticides, or the management of watersheds or other ecosystems affected by multiple nonchemical and chemical stressors. While risk assessment focuses on the analysis and interpretation of data, acquiring the appropriate data for use in the process is critical, and risk assessment may stop until necessary data are obtained. The EPA describes the process as being more often iterative than linear, since the evaluation of new data or information may require revisiting a part of the process or conducting a new assessment.

Risk assessments play a direct role in the formulation and economic assessment of environmental policy. For example, section 108 of the Clean Air Act (CAA) directs the administrator of the EPA to list pollutants that may reasonably be anticipated to endanger public health or welfare, and to issue air quality criteria for them. The air quality criteria are to reflect the latest scientific information useful in indicating the kind and extent of all exposure-related effects on public health and welfare that may be expected from the presence of the pollutant in ambient air. As was mentioned earlier in the chapter, environmental regulations such as those governing air quality are increasingly being evaluated using benefit/cost methodology. A good example is the EPA (1997) study of the benefits and costs of the CAA between 1970 and 1990, which was required under the 1990 CAA Amendments. The dominant benefit identified in that study was reduced premature mortality due to reductions in particulate matter, which contributed $16.6 trillion of the estimated mean benefits of $22.2

trillion (in constant 1990 dollars), or approximately 75 percent of the total economic benefit. Nevertheless, how do researchers go from risk assessment of a pollutant such as particulate matter to the economic value of premature mortality prevented by regulation? The answer is the *value-of-statistical-life* (VSL) approach described below.

There are a number of different ways to estimate the economic value of a statistical premature death avoided due to environmental regulation. Most of these use information on people's willingness to pay for a reduction in the probability of premature death. For example, one can use survey methods to solicit hypothetical willingness-to-pay information from respondents (described in detail in the section on contingent valuation) regarding changes in the likelihood of premature death. One can also conduct wage-risk studies to estimate the additional compensation demanded in the labor market for riskier jobs. In particular, when jobs are similar in most all respects except that one entails a higher risk of some harm, then competitive labor markets (with well-informed workers) are expected to yield a "wage premium" paid to those workers who accept the higher risk of premature death or workplace injury. Of course these wage premiums may not be observed if some workers are misinformed of risk, the labor market is not competitive, or if some people are naturally less averse to risk than others. In one example of a wage premium, Olson (1981) estimated that, all else being equal, a 10 percent increase in the probability of a nonfatal workplace accident is associated with a 9.1 percent increase in wage. Workers in jobs of average risk—1 in 30 of a nonfatal accident—received on average $2,200 more per year in income when compared to workers with similar educational attainment in virtually riskless jobs. These numbers can be translated into the value of a statistical life, as will be shown below.

Let's see how wage premiums paid for accepting riskier work environments can be used in the VSL approach. Suppose that a wage-risk study estimates that when the annual risk of premature death on the job increases by 0.0001 (1 in 10,000), workers receive an annual wage premium of $550 as compensation for this added risk. Assume that all other work characteristics are held constant. If we assume that those workers are fully informed and the labor market is competitive, then we can expect the following equation to hold:

Wage premium = (value of statistical life) × (increased probability of death).

Thus, with a bit of algebraic rearranging, we get:

Value of statistical life = (wage premium) ÷ (increased probability of death).

Plugging in an increased probability of death of 0.0001 and a $550 wage premium we arrive at a value of a statistical premature death avoided of $5.5 million.

Based on twenty-six wage-risk and hypothetical willingness-to-pay studies, the EPA (1997) estimated a mean value of a statistical premature death avoided to be $4.8 million (in constant 1990 dollars). Controversy surrounds the VSL approach used by the EPA (1997). For example, while most of the twenty-six studies used by the EPA in arriving at the VSL figure of $4.8 million involved the value of risks to middle-aged working people, those who die prematurely from particulate matter are more likely to be aged and past their working years. Moreover, job-related risks are more likely to be borne voluntarily, and involve the risk of sudden and catastrophic death, while pollution-related risks are borne involuntarily, and involve the risk of longer periods of disease and suffering. Other controversies regarding the VSL approach have to do with differences in wages and earnings between rich and poor countries. In poor countries with low wages, labor markets will pay smaller wage premiums for a given increase in risk of death than in rich countries, implying that a statistical life is more valuable in a rich country than in a poor country. As mentioned at the start of the chapter, the study by Bowland and Beghin (1998) offers a good example of VSL differences across rich and poor countries. They estimated that the value of a statistical life saved in Santiago, Chile, due to reduced air pollution is approximately $600,000, which is only about 12.5 percent of the $4.8 million value of an American statistical life used by the EPA (1997). The logic of benefit/cost analysis might then suggest locating hazardous life-threatening industrial activity and toxic wastes in the poorest regions of the world, which many would consider an unacceptable example of environmental injustice. While there are many problems with the VSL approach, simply ignoring the economic cost of premature death and leaving it out of benefit/cost analysis leads to a substantial underestimate of the benefits of environmental conservation and restoration.

An alternative approach taken by Tengs et al. (1995) is to evaluate the cost of regulatory intervention per statistical life-year saved by the intervention. This type of analysis allows policymakers to allocate regulatory resources to those interventions that generate the largest number of statistical life-years saved per dollar of intervention. To arrive at cost per statistical life-year saved, Tengs and her colleagues took the total cost of a regulatory intervention and divided by the number of statistical life-years saved by that intervention. They found, for example, that the cost per statistical life-year saved was only $69 for mandatory seatbelt use laws but was $920 for mandatory smoke detector laws. Chlorination of drinking water generated a cost per life-year of $3,100. Banning asbestos water pipe insulation generated a cost per life-year of $65,000, while banning amitraz pesticide use for pears generated a figure of $350,000 and the ozone-control program in southern California generated a cost per life-year of $610,000. Banning asbestos in packing generated a cost per statistical life-year saved of $5 million, and seismic retrofitting of buildings in earthquake-prone areas generated a cost per life-year of a whopping $18 million. It is important to note that the approach taken by Tengs et al. assumes that the saving of statistical life-years is the only benefit produced by the regulatory intervention, when in fact preventing premature death is only part of the benefit of many of these regulations. Nevertheless, their work offers useful guidance on the most cost-effective ways to save lives through regulatory intervention. It also illustrates how risk assessment can be used to provide information on the cost-effectiveness of various regulatory interventions without having to establish a particular value of a statistical life.

We will now address different types of values that people assign to various aspects of the environment that are not directly traded in markets. Once we have categorized these values, we will consider the various methods that economists have devised to measure these values. These nonmarket valuation methods can be used to estimate the benefits of various types of environmental improvements such as limiting pollution, restoring watersheds, or preserving parkland, open space, and agricultural working landscapes.

Categories of Nonmarketed Environmental Benefits: Use and Nonuse Values

Use Values

Use value represents the utility enjoyed by people who directly use some aspect of the environment. For example, a bird sanctuary yields use value to bird watchers and to those who use the area as an open space (walking, jogging, and observing the view). Likewise, a backcountry area provides use value to hunters, hikers, backpackers, and equestrians, and the ocean shore provides use value to surfers and fishers.

Nonuse Values

Nonuse values, also known as passive-use values or existence values, reflect value that people assign to aspects of the natural environment that they care about but do not use in a commercial, recreational, or other manner. For example, someone might value the existence of grizzly bear habitat in Alaska but have no interest in actually visiting such wildland habitat. Existence values are controversial because they are difficult to measure. As we will see in the next section of the chapter, survey research methods have developed to measure nonuse values. One type of nonuse value is option value. Option value is prominent when (1) there is uncertainty over the ultimate environmental impact of a given activity, and (2) that impact is irreversible. The classic example is large-scale tropical rain forest destruction, where thousands of species of plants and animals are made extinct before people even understand them and their possible beneficial role in medicine, foodstuffs, and so forth. Preservation has option value—it gives us time to learn about the possible services that are provided to people by the rain forest. Another is greenhouse gas production, where changes in the atmosphere are irreversible on the scale of human generations, and the extent and ultimate impact of global warming are not fully known. There is an option value to controlling greenhouse gas emissions today until we learn about their impact on our life-support systems.

Measuring Nonmarketed Environmental Benefits: The Contingent Valuation Method (CVM)

The CVM involves the use of survey questionnaires to elicit hypothetical willingness-to-pay information. The CVM was first proposed by Ciriacy-Wantrup (1947), who recognized that some aspects of soil erosion (e.g., clogging of shared irrigation channels) have the attributes of a negative externality that is not borne as a cost by the individual farmer. He did not actually conduct a CVM. A Harvard Ph.D. student named Rob Davis did the first actual CVM study in his dissertation, where he attempted to value nonmarketed aspects of the Maine woods (hunting and recreation values). In his study, he compared the results of the CVM against the travel cost method (described below) for the same area and found that the two methods arrived at remarkably similar valuations. Finally, since CVM studies are one of the few ways to measure nonuse values, they became popular following the publication of a highly influential paper by environmental economist John Krutilla (1967) that endorsed the "real" nature of existence and other nonuse values.

An important event that hastened the development of best methods in contingent valuation was the damage assessment following the March 1989 *Exxon Valdez* oil spill disaster in Prince William Sound, Alaska. The description that follows borrows heavily from Portney (1994). The oil tanker *Exxon Valdez* struck Bligh Reef in Prince William Sound and punctured its hull, causing 11 million gallons of crude oil to spill into the ocean. A CVM analysis was conducted by Carson et al. (1992) for the state of Alaska to determine lost existence value for U.S. residents. Carson et al.'s analysis yielded an estimate of $3 billion in lost existence value. In 1991 a lawsuit by the federal government and the state of Alaska against Exxon was settled for $1.15 billion. Because the case was settled out of court, it is impossible to know whether the study by Carson et al. influenced the size of the settlement.

The federal Oil Pollution Act of 1990 was passed in response to the *Exxon Valdez* oil spill, and a part of this legislation directed the National Oceanographic and Atmospheric Administration (NOAA) to draft regulations governing damage assessment. NOAA was pressured by environmentalists to have lost nonuse values be fully compensable damages and to use the CVM to measure them. Oil companies and others strongly lobbied against the inclusion of nonuse values and the CVM in damage assessment. In response to these conflicting pressures, NOAA asked Nobel laureates Kenneth Arrow and Robert Solow to chair a panel of experts (including Paul Portney) to advise NOAA on the CVM. NOAA wanted an answer to the question of whether the CVM is capable of providing estimates of lost nonuse values that are reliable enough to be used in natural resource damage assessments. The NOAA panel completed its report in early 1993.

The NOAA panel concluded that CVM analysis, conducted appropriately, "can produce estimates reliable enough to be the starting point of a judicial process of damage assessment, including lost passive-use values." Nevertheless, what was the panel's view of an appropriately conducted CVM study? The panel established a set of guidelines for future CVM studies aimed at producing reliable estimates of lost existence values for the purposes of damage assessment or regulatory policy. These guidelines have contributed to the development of the modern CVM survey, which is organized as follows:

1. Clearly identify the contingency to be studied. In the case of estimating lost existence values in damage assessment, the NOAA panel guidelines call for eliciting willingness to pay (WTP) to prevent a future incident rather than the minimum compensation required for damages that have already occurred. Examples of environmental or resource contingencies include land management policy or river and stream habitat restoration.
2. Perform a pretest in which you survey a small focus group. The pretest can be used to identify problems with the survey instrument and to determine the likely range of WTP values.
3. Use these preliminary values to make up a survey instrument. The survey instrument must accurately and clearly inform people of the precise nature of the anticipated effects of the contingency. The survey instrument must use a referendum-style format in eliciting WTP information.

A *referendum* is a vote in which people are asked to make a dichotomous choice (yes or no) regarding a political question. Therefore, the survey should ask respondents how they would vote if faced with a referendum proposal in which the specific environmental improvement is to be paid for by a specific increase in taxes or higher product prices. As Portney (1994) observes, the NOAA panel reasoned that people are frequently confronted with decisions involving specific posted prices, and that stated responses are more likely to reflect actual valuations than if confronted with an open-ended question asking maximum WTP. The survey instrument must remind respondents that an affirmative WTP response reduces funds that the respondent will have to spend on other goods and services. The survey instrument must remind respondents of the availability of substitutes for the environmental improvement being proposed. For example, if the CVM is evaluating WTP to enhance salmon habitat in a stream, the survey instrument should inform respondents of other stream habitat that already exists. The survey instrument should include follow-up questions to ensure that respondents understood the issues and questions in the survey, and to determine the reasons for their response.

4. Use repeated random sampling techniques with a different dollar amount for each random sample of people to be surveyed. The NOAA panel guidelines call for the use of personal interviews rather than telephone interviews when possible. Telephone interviews are considered to be preferable to mail surveys.

5. Analyze the data using relevant statistical techniques to estimate a demand curve (WTP function), which relates percentage of "yes" responses to each of the surveyed WTP values, holding other reported factors such as income, age, sex, educational attainment, and concern for the environment constant.

One would normally expect that the higher the WTP value asked to one of the random samples of people, then the smaller would be the frequency of "yes" responses. Thus if one plots WTP on the "y" axis and frequency of "yes" responses on the "x" axis, one would expect to observe an inverse relationship in the responses to the questionnaire. Thus one can estimate a demand curve for the environmental amenity under analysis by relating WTP values to percentage of "yes" responses, as shown by the generic curve in Figure 7.3. An estimate of consumer surplus—the net economic value of the environmental improvement—can then be derived from this demand curve.

Contingent valuation is far more complex than the brief overview above would suggest. One should be fully versed in survey design and methodol-

Figure 7.3 **Nonmarket Demand for an Environmental Amenity Estimated from the Contingent Valuation Method**

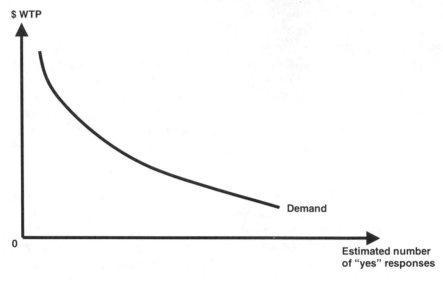

ogy, as well as *econometric* methods, before taking on a CVM study. The researcher needs to know the geographic scope of the population to be surveyed, as well as the variables required for demand estimation, before constructing the survey questionnaire. Moreover, the econometric techniques required for demand estimation are more complex than one might normally encounter in more conventional economic analysis. The interested reader is referred to the excellent primer on contingent valuation by Boyle (2003).

Examples of CVM Studies

Loomis (1996) performed a CVM study on the benefits of removing dams and restoring the Elwha River in Washington State. Loomis used a modern dichotomous-choice voter referendum form of CVM study to obtain estimates of willingness to pay for removing two dams on the Elwha River on the Olympic Peninsula in Washington State and restoring the ecosystem, with particular attention to the benefits of enhancing the salmon runs. Loomis found that mean annual value per household was estimated to be $59 in Clallam County, Washington, and $73 for the rest of Washington State. The aggregate benefits to the residents of the state of Washington were estimated to be $138 million annually for ten years.

Loomis (1987) used the CVM to quantify nonmarketed environmental benefits from enhancing natural aquatic conditions. In this case, the problem was to determine the public trust values of Mono Lake in California at alternative lake levels. Loomis found that the economic benefit to California residents of preserving Mono Lake could conservatively be estimated to be $1.5 billion annually. Purchase of replacement water and power would cost Los Angeles $26.2 million per year. Thus, on efficiency grounds the reallocation of water for maintenance of public trust values in Mono Lake could be warranted.

California has lost more than 90 percent of its historic wetlands, the largest percentage of any state in the United States. Allen et al. (1992) surveyed the literature to determine low, median, and high valuations for the various "services" provided by wetlands, including flood control, water supply, water quality, recreation, commercial fisheries, and wildlife habitat. Their overall median annual benefit was estimated to be $9.96 billion.

Schultze et al. (1983) used the CVM to study the economic benefits of visual quality in the Grand Canyon. A large coal-fired electricity-generating plant impaired visibility in the Grand Canyon and other nearby natural areas. Schultze et al. surveyed residents of Albuquerque, Denver, Los Angeles, and Chicago to determine the maximum a household would be willing to pay in higher entry fees or higher utility bills to maintain the park's visual quality. The average figure was $7 to $10 per month per household, leading to an aggregate estimate (taking into account socioeconomic household characteristics) of $6 billion per year. Note that for 99 percent of the households, these represent "existence" values rather than direct consumption values, as only about 1 percent visit the parks—an indication of the important role of nonuse values.

Walsh, Gillman, and Loomis (1982) used the CVM to determine how much people value allocating an additional 2.6 million acres as federal wilderness in Colorado. Their survey was designed to gain insight into the relative importance of key value areas—use, option, and existence. On average, recreation was worth $18.50 per visitor-day—yielding a total of $28 million per year. Passive-use values (existence, option) totaled $135 million per year. This totals into the billions when one calculates present value of this stream of benefits into the future.

Bell, Huppert, and Johnson (2003) used the CVM to estimate local coastal residents' willingness to pay for restoration and enhancement of coho salmon habitat in five Oregon and Washington estuaries. Those surveyed lived within thirty miles of the estuaries targeted for enhancement—Grays Harbor and Willapa Bay in Washington, and Tillamook Bay, Yaquina Bay, and Coos Bay in Oregon. The specified annual household cost on the mail questionnaires varied randomly from $5 to $500 based on a uniform distribution. Mean willingness to pay by "high-income" Washington residents surveyed ranged between \$117 and \$122, while that of "low-income" Washington residents ranged between \$76 and \$79. Results were much more variable for Oregon residents, and in some cases estimated willingness-to-pay values were not significantly different from zero. They also found that public confidence in the effectiveness of the enhancement programs is inextricably linked to people's willingness to pay for these programs.

The CVM Debate

Despite the advances that have occurred in CVM technique, economists are somewhat divided over the usefulness of the CVM in measuring value and guiding policy. The *Journal of Economic Perspectives* published a symposium on the usefulness of the CVM in its fall 1994 issue. A number of the issues discussed in that symposium by Diamond and Hausman (1994) and Hanemann (1994) are summarized below.

A key problem with CVM analysis, as claimed by Diamond and Hausman (1994), is the *embedding effect*. Embedding refers to the research methodology of comparing the value of a particular good, such as protection of a mountain lake, to a more inclusive good, such as protecting an entire mountainous region that includes the lake. The embedding effect occurs when willingness-to-pay responses for the particular good (protecting the mountain lake) are approximately equal to the willingness-to-pay responses for the more inclusive good (protecting the entire mountainous region). Diamond and Hausman (1994) observe that the embedding effect arises from the nonexistence of individual preferences for the good in question and from the failure of respondents to consider the effects of their budget constraints in hypothetical willingness-to-pay surveys. Hanemann (1994) disputes the argument by Diamond and Hausman (1994) that CVM studies are prone to embedding effects. Hanemann observes that the studies used by Diamond and Hausman (1994) in making their argument violate the NOAA panel guidelines in a number of important ways, and therefore argues that the evidence for the embedding effect does not apply to properly conducted CVM studies. Diamond and Hausman (1994) state that "embedding still infects even very recent work done by experienced contingent valuation analysts who were well aware of the problem" (p. 52), and conclude that the embedding effect implies that responses in CVM studies reflect "warm glow" feelings rather than true WTP.

Another problem identified in some CVM studies is a difference in responses between WTP for an environmental improvement and willingness to accept payment in return for giving up the environmental improvement. Economic theory suggests that WTP and willingness to accept (WTA) should be nearly the same, differing slightly due to income effects. Usually WTP is considerably less than WTA for the same environmental improvement, which is inconsistent with the economic theory of consumer choice. Hanemann (1994) observes that the WTP-WTA gap is seen in CVM studies that violate the NOAA panel guidelines by using "open-ended" payment questions that solicit the respondent's WTP rather than a "closed-ended" fixed WTP value in referendum format that respondents are given the dichotomous choice of either accepting or rejecting.

All surveys are vulnerable to *response effects,* in which small changes in wording or order of survey questionnaire material can cause significant changes in survey responses. As Hanemann (1994) states, "surveys, like all communication, are sensitive to nuance and context and are bound by constraints of human cognition" (p. 27). Nevertheless, surveys are a central source of data for "traditional" economic analysis and include the Current Population Survey, Consumer Expenditure Survey, Monthly Labor Survey, and Panel Study on Income Dynamics. Therefore, if these sorts of response effects are a reason to cast doubt on CVM studies, they should also cast doubt on the large number of other survey-based data sets used by economists.

Another criticism of the CVM is that the survey process itself creates the values reported as empirical data—people just make something up when asked. The standard view of rational humans in economics is based on people's having a preexisting valuation map in their heads that ranks all the possible choices available in contemporary markets, yet as Hanemann (1994) points out, this view is inconsistent with much of the contemporary research in cognition. The issue is whether the preferences are stable, and recent studies support this (comparing values over time). One can also argue that there is the potential for *strategic bias* in CVM survey data, in which people may inflate their stated values because they do not have to "put their money where their mouth is." This is one of the reasons why the NOAA panel called for closed-ended, referendum-style WTP questions. Moreover, some referendum-style CVM studies have compared the hypothetical responses to actual parallel referenda and have found that in modern CVM studies there is often no significant difference in responses. See the "cannot be verified" criticism below.

Critics of the CVM also argue that ordinary people are ill trained for valuing the environment in a referendum-style format. Note, however, that training is not a criterion for voting in democratic systems, and one could make the argument that there is at least a core of rationality in voter behavior. Critics also argue that responses to hypothetical contingent valuation questions do not match responses in real situations. As a result, the NOAA panel stated that a "critically important contribution could come from experiments in which state-of-the-art CV studies are employed in a context where they can in fact be compared with 'real' behavioral willingness to pay for goods that can actually be bought and sold" (Arrow et al. 1993). As Hanemann (1994) has noted, real-world voting behavior, in which voters choose whether to tax themselves to fund an environmental or other improvement, may be the closest nonexperimental test of the contingent valuation method. In an earlier study, Carson, Hanemann, and Mitchell (1987) compared survey responses with voter choices on a California bond issue addressing clean water. Aggregate survey responses only matched aggregate voter choices when "undecided" survey responses were allocated as 40 percent "yes" and 60 percent "no."

In a somewhat more recent study, Vossler et al. (2003) sought to address the NOAA panel's suggestion by conducting research on the question of whether respondents report the same decisions in nonbinding surveys as they do in actual elections. They studied a November 1995 Corvallis, Oregon, referendum to raise open-space funds. The amount of additional property tax a person had to pay for open space was $0.35 per $1,000 of assessed property value. Majority approval of the referendum would generate $950,000 annually for five years for the purchase of open-space lands. Just prior to the election, in mid-October 1995, researchers conducted random telephone surveys of Corvallis residents. Vossler and colleagues found that the telephone survey only matched aggregate voter choices when all "undecided" survey responses were coded as "no." They also found estimated annual willingness to pay for open space from actual voting behavior to be $48.89, which was not statistically different from the mean willingness to pay of $49.67 from CV survey data when "undecided" responses are coded as "no."

In addition to the above-mentioned problems with the CVM, there is also the problem of whether people understand the ecosystem function of the particular aspect of the environment subject to the CVM analysis. The ecosystem role of an element of the environment may not be known unless or until it is destroyed. It is also clear that many people do not want to participate in a process of monetizing the environment, just as Christians would not want to monetize the value of their faith.

Measuring NonMarketed Environmental Benefits: The Travel Cost Method (TCM)

The TCM was first proposed by economist Harold Hotelling in a 1947 letter to the U.S. Park Service, in which he suggested that the full cost of visiting a park must necessarily include the cost of getting there. The TCM is useful for measuring active-use values of place-based aspects of the environment

like lakes, rivers, beaches, and wilderness areas used for recreational purposes. The TCM offers a way of measuring the value of a nonmarketed recreational resource by using data on trip costs incurred by people who visit the
area. Studies that estimate the value of a single site estimate a downward
sloping site demand curve in which price is the trip cost and the quantity
demanded is the number of trips taken to the site in a given time period. The
area under the site demand curve is consumer surplus, a measure of the economic value of accessing the site for recreational purposes. If access to the
recreational use of a site has been curtailed due to a chemical spill or development, for example, then the TCM can be used to assess economic damages to
recreationalists. Likewise, TCM values can be used to weigh the benefits and
costs of a proposed change in resource management. As with the contingent
valuation method described above, this section of the chapter will only provide a general overview of the methodology. The empirical estimation of
nonmarket values is complex, and readers interested in a more detailed expo-
sition might start with Parsons (2003) or Loomis and Walsh (1997).

The single-site model estimates the number of trips taken by a person
over a year (or season of use) as a function of the cost incurred to get to the
site, as well as personal characteristics (age, sex, income, experience level)
and travel cost to alternative sites. These explanatory variables are usually
gathered using survey research methods. Following Parsons, we can describe
the following steps in a single-site TCM study:

1. Define the boundaries of the site to be studied.
2. Define the recreational uses and season(s) of use.
3. Develop a sampling strategy for surveying recreational users.
4. Specify a demand estimation model, including all the variables to be
   used in that model.
5. Address the issue of multiple purpose recreational trips.
6. Design and conduct the survey.
7. Measure trip cost.
8. Estimate site demand using trip cost and data from the survey.
9. Calculate the access value of the site.

Decisions, assumptions, and estimates must be made at each step. For
example, some sites host multiple recreational uses, such as rivers where
people swim, sunbathe, fish, and engage in boating. A travel cost study may
focus on certain types of recreational uses, or researchers may be able to
aggregate similar classes of recreational use. A key decision regarding sampling strategy is whether to conduct on-site surveys of visitors, or a random
survey of the overall population. On-site surveys have the advantage of be-

ing better targeted, requiring fewer survey solicitations to get the desired sample size. On the other hand, on-site surveys omit from the sample people who take zero trips during the time period under study, which impairs the estimation of the vertical intercept of the site demand curve. Likewise, an on-site survey strategy will oversample frequent visitors ("endogenous stratification"). The researcher must correct her econometric model for these problems. Off-site surveys of the overall population can avoid these problems, but a very large number of surveys must be sent out in order to receive back a sufficiently large sample of completed questionnaires from recreationalists who visit the site. Moreover, off-site surveys require the researcher to make some assumptions about the geographical scope of the "market" containing site visitors. As mentioned earlier, the researcher will develop a demand model that explains the number of site visits as a function of the visitor's trip cost "price," income, trip cost to substitute sites, and other visitor characteristics that might influence their frequency of visits.

A further complication in using the TCM has to do with whether trip cost was expended for the sole purpose of visiting the recreational site under study, or whether the trip encompassed multiple purposes including other sites or visiting friends or family along the way. Parsons (2003) suggests that if the nature of the study is to focus on day-use trips, then one can usually assume that the trip cost is single-purpose in nature. In contrast, if the recreational use identified in the second step involves one or more overnight stays, the researcher should include the question of single-purpose or multiple-purpose travel in the questionnaire. The researcher can then choose whether to drop multiple-purpose trips from the data set, or develop a more complicated demand model that explicitly incorporates multiple purposes for travel. As with the CVM, those considering the use of the TCM should have a background in survey methods and design, which goes beyond the scope of this book. In addition to introductory material, the questionnaire will include questions for the variables identified in step 4, as well as the number of site visits over the time period in question and detailed questions on trip cost and other aspects of the most recent visit, which are presumably easiest for the subject to recall.

Trip cost includes the cost of travel, opportunity cost of time, and other direct expenditures required for a site visit. Travel cost via automobile would be measured as the product of round-trip distance multiplied by the average cost per mile from an authoritative source such as the U.S. Department of Transportation. The opportunity cost of a visitor's time is difficult to estimate and represents a large portion of the economic value estimated from the TCM. Many researchers make the assumption that some portion of time in transit and at the site involves the opportunity cost of forgone earnings from

Figure 7.4   **Nonmarket Demand for a Recreational Site Estimated from the Travel Cost Method**

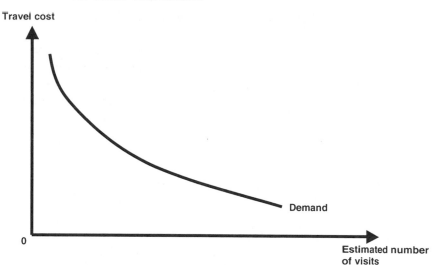

work, though this is obviously flawed for retired people, students, the unemployed, and those with paid vacation time. It is difficult to apportion part of the capital cost of recreational gear and equipment owned by the recreationalist to a particular trip. While rental rates on equipment can be used to estimate equipment and gear costs on a per-trip basis, many researchers omit these costs altogether. Once the data are tabulated from returned surveys, the researcher uses econometric techniques to estimate a site demand function such as the one shown in Figure 7.4.

Let's take a moment and consider the results of some TCM studies. Sohngen (2000) used the TCM to estimate the economic value of access to beaches on Lake Erie in Ohio. Sohngen estimated that on average a visitor received between $25 and $38 each day in access value (consumer surplus). Englin and Shonkwiler (1995) used the TCM to estimate the economic value to hiking in the Cascade mountain range of Washington and Oregon. Their preferred estimate was that an average hike generated between approximately $16 and $24 (1985 dollars) in net benefits. Using similar methodology Casey, Vukina, and Danielson (1995) estimated a mean consumer surplus per visit of approximately $513 for hiking in the Grandfather Mountain Wilderness Preserve in North Carolina. This large value for consumer surplus occurs in part because the opportunity cost of time revealed by individual visitors was quite high, averaging nearly $47 per hour. Bell and Leeworthy (1990) used the individual survey approach to estimate the recreational economic value of

Florida's beaches. They gathered data on days spent on the beach, expenses incurred while visiting, the cost of recreationalists' travel to Florida, as well as other factors that influence visiting the beach such as age, children, income, and perceived quality of such an experience. Using the statistical technique of multiple regression analysis, they were able to isolate the impact of travel cost and number of beach visits. The average tourist spent nearly five days on the beach and spent on average $85 per day. From this information, Bell and Leeworthy estimated average daily consumer surplus of $38. With 70 million tourists annually visiting the Florida beaches, these beaches were found to yield a lower-bound estimate of $2.7 billion annually in active-use value.

Measuring Nonmarketed Environmental Benefits: Hedonic Regression Method (HRM)

As Taylor (2003) notes, hedonic regression techniques can be used to estimate the value of product quality attributes in markets that feature product differentiation. If instead all products were identical, then one could not use regression analysis to estimate the impact of varying a product's quality attributes. HRM is most commonly used to evaluate the contribution of environmental attributes of housing, including view, air quality, proximity to parks, and neighborhood safety. While these environmental attributes are not directly traded in markets, they are aspects of a house's location and as such are inextricably bundled with the market value of a house. The term "hedonic" refers to people assigning value to product attributes that induce pleasure, while the term "regression" refers to an econometric technique for estimating these values.

For example, suppose that there are a large number of otherwise identical homes in a community and they all have backyards bordering on undeveloped land, the scenic and recreational quality of which is marred by illegal dumping of old appliances and tires. Suppose that the equilibrium price of these homes is $100,000. Now suppose that a portion of the undeveloped land is county property, and the county cleans up its property, installs a gate, and manages the area as protected parkland. We would expect that those homes with backyards bordering on the parkland would now be more desirable than those homes adjacent to the illegal dump. At the old equilibrium price, therefore, we would expect an excess demand for the more desirable homes, which would result in a new, higher equilibrium price for those homes bordering the parkland. Suppose that in the new equilibrium, the houses bordering the dump are still priced at $100,000, while those bordering the parkland are now priced at $400,000. The $300,000 difference in home prices represents the implicit price that homebuyers are willing to pay for the incremental improvement in a home's quality attributes resulting from proximity to land that has been cleaned up and protected as parkland.

Since real-world houses have many quality attributes that vary from location to location, there are few simple natural experiments such as the hypothetical example given above. Suppose we can quantify these quality attributes (e.g., size, age, condition, lot size, air quality, presence or absence of view, distance to parks and schools, crime rates, and the like) in a data set that includes sales prices. Then we can use the econometric tool of regression analysis to estimate a model that explains sales price as a function of each quality attribute. This is the first stage of hedonic regression analysis. We can use this first-stage analysis to estimate how a quantitative improvement in environmental quality (all else held constant) increases the value of a home. This increase in the value of the home represents the implicit price of the incremental increase in the quality attribute. In the second stage of hedonic regression analysis, researchers use implicit price information to estimate the demand curve for the environmental attribute. As shown in Figure 7.5, the attribute demand curve shows the relationship between implicit attribute price and the quantity of the attribute demanded.

Consider some examples of the use of the HRM. Pollard (1982) found that, holding other characteristics constant, Chicago apartments with views of Lake Michigan commanded on average a 26 percent rental price premium. Given that housing typically accounts for 20–25 percent of an individual's income, the amenity value of scenic beauty was worth a sacrifice of 5–6 percent of overall income. Grimes (1983) estimated that land fronting on Lake Michigan sold at prices twice as high (on a per-acre basis) as land just 500 feet inland. As the distance from the lake increased to 1,500 feet, the value fell to one-fifth that of lakefront property. Brown and Pollakowski (1977) found that, holding constant other factors such as house size and age, on average a house within 300 feet of Lakes Washington, Green, or Haller commanded a price premium of approximately $24,800 (1993 dollars) relative to houses farther away from the lakes. Brookshire et al. (1982) estimated that the hedonic value of clean air in the Los Angeles area was approximately $381 (1993 dollars) per month for locations with more direct access to fresh air off the Pacific Ocean (not necessarily beachfront). Diamond (1980) estimated that approximately 7.5 percent of the value of a home in Boston was based on the crime characteristics of its location. More recent studies have used the HRM to estimate the attribute demand for local parks (Shultz and King 2001) and for air quality (Sieg et al. 2000).

Readers interested in learning the specific steps involved with hedonic regression analysis will need to have a solid understanding of econometric

Figure 7.5   **Nonmarket Demand for an Environmental Attribute Estimated from the Hedonic Regression Method**

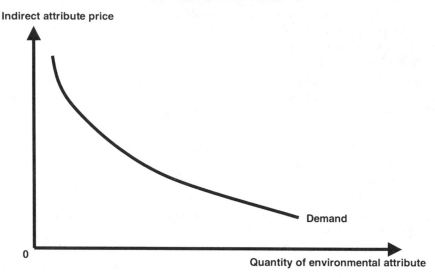

analysis, and are encouraged to review the excellent primer on the HRM by Taylor (2003).

Other Valuation Approaches

Several additional valuation approaches can be used to estimate the value of environmental improvements such as pollution reduction or land restoration or preservation. In this section, we will consider the ways in which defensive behavior and damage costs indicate value, followed by an exploration of the technique of benefits transfer and a brief discussion of replacement cost.

Defensive behavior refers to actions taken by people to reduce their exposure to harm caused by pollution, diseases, and other hazards. For example, suppose that a leaking garbage dump creates a plume of contaminated groundwater that adversely affects wells used for residential water supplies. If residents respond to groundwater contamination by building water tanks and having uncontaminated water trucked in, then these actions are examples of defensive behavior. The cost of the defensive behavior—purchases of water tanks and water—reveals something about the economic value of the environmental quality attribute of clean, safe household water supplies. Dickie (2003) develops a model (based on Harrington and Portney 1987) in which defensive behavior is a substitute for pollution reduction. He shows that if defensive behavior is cheap and effective, or when pollution has little impact on health, then people will have a lower willingness to pay for pollution reduction. Likewise, if defensive behavior is expensive or ineffective, or if pollution has a large impact on health, people will have a higher willingness to pay for pollution reduction.

Continuing our water contamination example above, suppose that if the residents had not taken defensive action, then they would have experienced harms to their health. The direct expenditures required to treat illnesses suffered by residents and their pets or livestock that is caused by contaminated water, as well as indirect costs associated with foregone earnings and productivity when residents are ill, all represent *damage costs*. If residents know in advance that they are being exposed to water contamination and understand both damage costs and the cost of defensive behavior, then economically speaking we would expect that residents would only bear damage costs if they are cheaper than the cost of defensive behavior. Of course, many contamination cases are not detected in time to avoid damage costs, which makes the question moot.

Conducting original research on nonmarket valuation is complex, costly, and time-consuming, and relatively few specialists have the expertise to do this sort of work. When budget or time limitations restrict the ability to conduct original nonmarket valuation research, in some circumstances one can use the technique of *benefits transfer*. As Rosenberger and Loomis (2003) note, the term "benefits transfer" is an informal term used by economists for the practice of adapting information derived from an existing study to a new setting or context. One can transfer specific numerical estimates, such as an estimate of willingness to pay, or one can transfer an entire estimated function, such as those described for CVM, TCM, and HRM. As Rosenberger and Loomis suggest, in most cases the researcher needs to first define the characteristics of the context under study, and then conduct a broad and thorough literature review to find related original research, both published and unpublished. The researcher should then screen the original research studies to identify those of high quality that best correspond to the context under study.

While transferring specific numerical estimates is simpler than an entire function, specific numerical estimates cannot be adjusted for significant differences between the context of the original research and the current study context. Transferring an entire function usually increases the precision of benefits transfer, but involves more steps. One must gather data on the current study context to use as inputs to the function being transferred in order to get a tailored estimate. The transfer of an entire function assumes that the statistical relationship between the dependent and independent variables from the original study will hold for the new context. This may not be the case.

In chapter 6, we touched on the topic of ecosystem goods and services. The nonmarket value of ecosystem services, such as natural nutrient cycling and filtering, can be valued using *replacement cost* (or avoided cost) methods that price the service provided in terms of equivalent man-made services (Folke 1991). Perhaps one of the best examples is given by the Catskill/ Delaware watershed, which provides most of New York City's drinking water supplies. The 1989 Federal Safe Drinking Water Act's Surface Water Treatment Rule requires filtration of public surface water supplies, but managers can receive a waiver from the rule if they can meet standards for waterborne disease contamination, phosphorus loads, and turbidity in their waters without filtration. The city of New York was able to get a filtration waiver from the EPA through a commitment to watershed restoration and protection. Therefore, it has been argued that the natural filtration processes in their watershed can be valued based on the avoided capital and operating costs of a filtration plant.

With a sense of how benefits are estimated, we will now turn to the subject of measuring and assessing the costs of complying with environmental and natural resource regulations.

Measuring Costs

In this section of the chapter, we will consider a number of different concepts related to the cost of complying with environmental and natural resource regulations. We will begin by investigating direct costs, followed by indirect costs.

Direct Costs

Direct costs of compliance with environmental and natural resource regulations are the visible consequence of compliance. They include the capital costs of investment in appropriate equipment (e.g., smokestack scrubbers, wastewater treatment), operating and maintenance costs of this capital equipment, and personnel costs (e.g., equipment operators, monitors, regulatory compliance staff). Direct costs also include forgone revenue flows that can be directly attributable to regulation. For example, streamside buffer zones required in timber harvest operations in California reduce the quantity of harvestable timber available to the firm. Consequently, an element of direct regulatory cost must include the forgone net revenue flows due to harvest restrictions. Likewise, restrictions on development of wetlands and other environmentally sensitive lands generate a direct cost in the form of forgone net revenue flows. Direct costs are borne by government agencies, firms, and consumers. According to Pizer, Morgenstern, and Shih (2001), direct expenditures for environmental protection in the United States are estimated to exceed $150 billion annually, or about 2 percent of GDP. They note that reported expenditures in the manufacturing sector reflect expenses that the plant manager identifies with environmental protection. It is likely that this accounting of direct costs omits opportunity costs in the form of forgone revenue flows due to natural resource regulation. There is also the possibility that cost accounting systems used by firms themselves may inadequately accumulate direct costs of compliance with environmental regulation.

Each year between 1973 and 1994, and again for a one-year pilot study in 1999, the Census Bureau reported on pollution abatement costs and expenditures (PACE) (omitting opportunity costs). In the earlier series of reports, PACE was divided into spending on pollution abatement (about 90 percent of total PACE), government regulation and monitoring, and research and development (the latter two are about 10 percent of total PACE). Pollution abatement *capital expenditures* by manufacturing establishments with twenty employees or more amounted to $7.88 billion in 1994. Of this total, $7.58 billion was attributable to a particular media: $4.31 billion for air, $2.43 billion for water, and $838 million for solid/contained waste. *Operating costs* related to pollution abatement activities totaled $20.67 billion. Of this amount, $18.77 billion was attributable to a particular medium: $6.14 billion for air, $7.03 billion for water, and $5.60 billion for solid/contained waste. Spending for the nonmedia and "other" category was $1.90 billion.

The 1999 PACE survey differed from the earlier PACE surveys described above. While these changes prevent direct comparisons to earlier surveys, the Census Bureau states that the changes were designed to better reflect industry terminology and enhance the accuracy of the survey estimates. The survey collected data on pollution abatement and prevention capital expenditures and operating costs for air, water, solid waste, and multimedia. The survey also collected data on disposal, recycling, site cleanup, habitat protection, environmental monitoring, and testing and administrative costs as well as other payments, such as permits, fees, fines, penalties, and tradable permits bought or sold. Of these, habitat protection, monitoring and testing, administrative expenses, permits, fees, fines, and penalties were not collected in the earlier PACE surveys. According to the Census Bureau, 1999 pollution abatement *capital expenditures* by regulated industry amounted to $5.81 billion, three quarters of which was borne by the manufacturing sector. Of this total, $3.46 billion was attributed to air, $1.80 billion to water, $361.9 million to solid waste, and $182.3 million to multimedia. Pollution abatement *operating costs* amounted to $11.86 billion in 1999, and 86 percent of these costs were borne by the manufacturing sector. Of this total, $5.07 billion was attributed to air, $4.59 billion to water, $2.01 billion to solid waste, and $195.5 million to multimedia.

Viscusi (1996) reported that of the estimated $500 billion in annualized regulatory costs in the U.S. economy from all forms of regulation, about one-half are attributable to paperwork costs. Of the estimated $200 billion in annualized direct regulatory costs to business and elsewhere, about one-half can be attributed to environmental regulations.

Indirect Costs

In addition to direct costs, environmental regulations also impose various kinds of *indirect costs,* sometimes known as hidden costs. The indirect costs, or secondary costs, of complying with environmental and natural resource regulations occur as a side effect or consequence of direct expenditures in compliance efforts. For example, expenditures for complying with environmental or natural resource regulation may "crowd out" other productive investments, discourage investment in more efficient production technologies, and reduce operational flexibility, thereby further reducing future productive output, profits, and (in aggregate) economic growth. This value of this reduced future economic output would represent an indirect cost of regulation. Moreover, cost-accounting systems (from which direct compliance cost information is drawn) may fail to properly accumulate significant elements of materials, managerial, and certain overhead costs that should be allocated to compliance with environmental and natural resource regulations.

The study by Joshi, Krishnan, and Lave (2001) provides a good example of indirect cost analysis. They studied the full economic cost of compliance with environmental regulations using plant-level data from fifty-five steel mills, as well as structured interviews of corporate-level managers and plant-level accountants. While the U.S. steel industry had experienced a 58 percent decline in production between 1974 and 1995, and industry blamed a portion of this decline on the cost of environmental regulations, direct compliance costs in this industry were estimated to be less than 5 percent of total cost. While some may see this as unwarranted scapegoating of environmental regulations, Joshi et al. found that a $1 increase in the visible (direct) cost of environmental regulation is associated with an increase in total cost (at the margin) of $10–11, of which $9–10 are hidden or indirect.

Indirect benefits (negative indirect costs) may also be generated because of direct expenditures in compliance efforts. In this case, for example, reported environmental costs may overstate true economic costs due to complementarity between pollution-control technologies and other production activities, meaning that the total cost of jointly producing goods and a cleaner environment is lower than if each were produced separately. Therefore, when direct compliance costs are reported by themselves, they overstate true economic costs because they do not take into account indirect benefits in the form of increased productivity. The Porter hypothesis (named after its proponent, Professor Michael Porter) suggests that these sorts of indirect benefits will be generated by direct environmental compliance expenditures. The idea is that regulations require a firm to reexamine its production processes, which in turn results in a probability of innovative new processes or technologies being found that produce indirect benefits (Porter and van der Linde 1995). In addition, a second strand to this theory (discussed in chapter 1) adds that environmental regulation in particular may lead to improved competitiveness, as pollution represents wasted resources that could be more effectively used. Therefore, according to the Porter hypothesis, regulation that requires reduced pollution therefore inherently favors processes that are more productive.

Pizer, Morgenstern, and Shih (2001) used empirical methods to explore the relationship between reported direct expenditures in compliance with environmental regulations and indirect costs or benefits in the manufacturing sector. Their study focused on a large plant-level data set at the four-digit standard industrial classification (SIC) level, and used a cost function modeling approach that treated both environmental compliance and nonenvironmental production activities as distinct, unrelated cost-minimization problems for each plant. They then explored the possibility that these activities are, in fact, related by including reported direct regulatory expenditures in the cost function for nonenvironmental output. In contrast with Joshi et al., they found that reported direct environmental expenditures tended to generate indirect benefits in some industries and indirect costs in others. Their strongest results focused on the four most heavily regulated industries in the United States, where they found that each dollar of reported direct environmental expenditure resulted in eighteen cents of indirect benefit, with a standard error of forty-two cents. This is equivalent to saying that total direct and indirect costs associated with compliance with environmental regulation rise by eighty-two cents for every dollar increase in reported direct environmental expenditures.

In 1999, the Environmental Law Institute convened a conference on cost, innovation, and environmental regulation. Proceedings from that conference (Environmental Law Institute 1999) suggest that the design of environmental regulation exerts a significant effect on the cost of compliance. The conference proceedings note that a central problem with U.S. environmental and natural resource regulations is that the design of emissions standards based on "available" or "feasible" control technologies under the Clean Water Act and Clean

Air Act strongly discourages innovation. The proceedings also noted that small changes in regulatory standards are unlikely to trigger the reexamination of a firm's production processes that is central to the creation of indirect benefits in the Porter hypothesis. Specifically, significant increases in the stringency of regulatory standards, combined with flexibility in how firms comply, are most likely to promote innovation and the generation of indirect benefits.

In an earlier study, the EPA (1997) reported on estimated indirect macro-economic impacts from the Clean Air Act (CAA) during the period from 1970 to 1990. These impacts were estimated from a general-equilibrium economic model that evaluated the feedback effects of the CAA regulatory controls relative to a hypothetical no-control scenario. They grouped these macroeconomic impacts into two broad classes: sectoral impacts and aggregate impacts. The EPA (1997) reported that compliance with the CAA had the greatest sectoral impacts on large energy producers and consumers, particularly those sectors that relied most heavily on consumption of fossil fuels. Production costs increased more for capital-intensive industries than for non-capital-intensive industries due to a projected increase in interest rates. Interest rates were projected to have been increased by the CAA because the CAA required significant investment in capital PACE that increased the demand for loanable funds. Indirect regulatory impacts on the electric utility industry were estimated to have generated a 2 to 4 percent increase in consumer prices and a resulting 3 to 5 percent reduction in output by 1990. Many other manufacturing sectors saw an output reduction effect in the 1 percent range. A key aggregate impact of the CAA was an estimated one-twentieth of 1 percent annual reduction in economic growth due to CAA-mandated investment in capital PACE reducing the level of investment available for capital formation. Consequently, GNP was estimated to have been reduced by 1 percent ($55 billion) relative to the no-control scenario.

There are also potential microeconomic impacts on certain capital-intensive industries. Environmental regulations may not only increase the cost per unit (e.g., per piece of furniture, per BTU of electricity), but perhaps more important they increase *fixed costs* (those costs that do not vary with how much a firm produces, such as the cost of scrubbers on smokestacks). When fixed costs increase substantially, it requires that a firm have a larger output level to maintain profitability. Thus large fixed costs can lead to market structures with fewer, larger firms (increased market concentration). Firms gain larger market shares because each is compelled to expand production capacity in order to cover these additional fixed costs. Unless demand for the goods these firms produce somehow changes, firms will merge, reducing the number of competitors and reducing the degree of rivalry. Pashigian (1984) found that, all else being constant, industries with higher burdens of environmental regulation also had more rapid growth in mean plant size and more rapid decreases in the number of production facilities in an industry, compared to less regulated firms. To illustrate the role of increased fixed costs on market concentration, consider the following example.

Suppose that a wood table manufacturing firm has an annualized fixed cost of $100,000 (production equipment, facility, owner's time), while on average, each table has $50 worth of wood and labor and fasteners and stain in it. What is the breakeven output level of this firm if market demand is such that tables sell for $300 each? To answer this, note that breakeven occurs when output is such that the average table costs $300 to produce. Currently, on average, each table costs $50 in variable costs, so we need to find the output level at which fixed cost on average is $250 per table. This is found by computing the following:

$100,000/x = $250, x = 100,000/250 = 400 tables.

Therefore, the firm breaks even at an output of 400 tables per year, has positive economic profits for output greater than 400 tables, and suffers negative economic profits for output less than 400 tables.

Suppose that there are ten firms each producing 400 tables, so at the market level there are 4,000 tables per year sold at around $300 each. In addition, suppose that each firm must install a collection chamber that increases its annualized fixed cost from $100,000 to $500,000. Assuming that market demand does not change, the new break-even output level for a firm is:

$500,000/x = $250, x = 2,000 tables.

Note that the market will only absorb 4,000 tables at a price of $300 per table (and even less at table prices greater than $300), so *at most* the market can support only two firms where it used to support ten firms at the prevailing price. Now these two firms will each be as big as the five former firms, and will hire many of the workers laid off by those exiting the industry.

The potential problem with a reduced number of firms in this industry is that many believe a smaller number of competitor firms are more likely to collude. The argument is that it is much easier to police cheating with only two firms than with ten. Thus, we may see price rise above $300. As price rises, market quantity demanded falls. So the cartel must choose its price carefully, based on how sensitive consumers are to price increases (factors: number of substitutes, etc.). For example, if price rises to $400 per table, the breakeven output for each firm is:

$500,000/x = $350, x = 1,429 tables.

So as long as market demand is relatively price-inelastic so that quantity demanded is more than twice the single-firm break-even output (more than 2,857), these remaining firms will enjoy positive economic profits rather than just breaking even. With fewer firms, however, the industry is more susceptible to collusion. Thus, an indirect cost associated with environmental regulation that requires substantial new fixed-cost investments in pollution control is that market concentration rises, competition falls, and firms may be able to exercise more market power, making consumers worse off. Moreover, with less competition there may be less pressure to minimize costs (X-inefficiency), further raising consumer prices.

In closing, recall from chapter 1 that some argue that another indirect cost of environmental regulations is overall job loss, the export of production facilities to "pollution havens," and declines in productivity and competitiveness in international trade. It was shown in the introductory chapter of this book that these arguments have little currency when confronted with empirical research on the job and productivity implications of environmental regulations. In particular, pollution control and clean technologies tend to be labor-intensive, and the exportation of production facilities to low-income countries has primarily been driven by enormous labor cost differences rather than environmental regulations. Finally, there is little evidence that environmental regulations are responsible for more than a small fraction of the decline in productivity growth rates experienced in the United States.

Summary

- Benefit/cost analysis is the way in which utilitarian concepts of ethical social policy are operationalized in policy making. In this context, an environmental or other policy is said to be efficient if it generates the greatest net benefit to society.
- The Kaldor-Hicks criterion for efficiency judges a policy based on the extent to which aggregate net benefits to society are maximized.
- The more restrictive Pareto criterion for efficiency requires that any change from the status quo not only generate positive net benefits, but also not make any member of society worse off. Thus, the Pareto efficiency criterion is concerned with how benefits and costs are distributed in society, while the Kaldor-Hicks criterion is not.
- A requirement of benefit/cost analysis is that benefits and costs be measurable and comparable on a common metric.
- Dynamic efficiency occurs when the policy option is selected that generates the largest PV of net benefits or, alternatively, that generates the largest PV of benefits per PV dollar of cost.

- It is particularly challenging and important to measure the benefits of proposed regulations for protecting or enhancing aspects of the natural environment that are not marketed. The reason is that in well-functioning competitive markets, price provides extensive information on the value of the object being traded. In particular, one can estimate a demand curve for the good and estimate consumer surplus, the excess of maximum willingness to pay over and above the price actually paid.
- Economists have developed a number of techniques for measuring the benefits of environmental protection and enhancement that are not directly traded in markets. These methods include quantitative risk assessment of pollutants affecting human health and various methods for measuring the value of environmental conservation, including the contingent valuation method, the travel cost method, and the hedonic regression method.
- Quantitative risk assessment uses health data to determine the relationship between pollution or workplace hazards and the statistical likelihood of mortality or morbidity in a given-sized population. This information can then be compared to the cost of incremental reductions in various pollutants or workplace hazards, and thus regulatory policies can be made consistent with one another.
- The contingent valuation method is the only one of the three that is capable of measuring passive-use values such as existence and option values. A disadvantage of this method, however, is that data are gathered by way of a hypothetical survey. Nevertheless, studies indicate that well-constructed surveys using the dichotomous-choice referendum format perform remarkably well in parallel studies with actual referenda.
- The travel cost method offers a way of acquiring information on the active-use value that people assign to an area. The data are based on actual expenditures rather than hypothetical surveys, but cannot measure passive uses in which people do not travel to an area.
- The hedonic regression method is also based on actual expenditures and measures the indirect value of individual environmental attributes associated with something that is marketed, such as the value of safety or a scenic view associated with residential real estate.
- The cost of defensive behavior associated with avoiding pollution and other harms provides an indication of the value of pollution reduction, as can damage costs borne when people cannot or do not take action to avoid harm.
- Benefit transfer is an approach designed to use information from existing studies in estimating benefit values for a new study. Benefit transfer may be faster, cheaper, and simpler than conducting an original valuation study.

- Replacement cost can be used to assign economic value to nonmarketed ecosystem services, such as water filtration services provided by a natural watershed. Were the watershed to be impaired through resource extraction or development, the value of the lost filtration service could be measured by way of the cost of a constructed filtration facility.
- The cost of environmental regulation can be divided into direct and indirect costs. Direct compliance costs include visible pollution abatement and expenditures by firms, consumers, and government, as well as opportunity costs that can be attributed directly to regulation.
- There are also a variety of different indirect costs that represent either hidden compliance costs or result as feedback effects from environmental regulation, such as reduced rates of investment in productive capital, lower rates of productivity growth, reduced output, higher interest rates, reduced economic growth rates, and allocative inefficiencies due to market power in more concentrated industries.
- Many factors limit the applicability of benefit/cost analysis in environmental regulatory applications. For example, ethical, spiritual, and religious values cannot be reasonably quantified. Benefits are oftentimes diffuse and, because they are not traded in markets, do not have prices that reveal value, making them difficult to measure comprehensively. In addition, it may be difficult to attribute environmental improvements to a single action. Moreover, the benefits (or costs) to future generations of people affected by current regulations are discounted as a requirement for dynamic efficiency, but this discounting biases us away from policies with up-front costs and benefits enjoyed by future generations. It is impossible to know what preferences future generations will have regarding the environment. Aggregate benefits and costs may not be equitably distributed, and a dollar will generate substantially more utility for a poor person than for an extremely wealthy person. The impact of environmental regulations is not easy to estimate with certainty, and so risk assessment is often required.

Review Questions and Problems

1. Make up a hypothetical table for the cleanup of some pollutant as in the present chapter to illustrate the use of the efficiency standard and benefit/cost analysis. Set up your table with:

- the first column showing equal 10 percent increments of reduction in the pollutant;

- the second column showing the *total* (cumulative) cost of cleanup up to that point;
- the third column showing the *marginal* cost of cleaning up for each 10 percent increment;
- the fourth column showing the *total* (cumulative) benefit of cleanup;
- the fifth column showing the *marginal* benefit of cleanup for each 10 percent increment;
- the sixth column showing the *marginal* net benefit (marginal benefit/ marginal cost) for each 10 percent increment;
- the seventh column showing the *total* (cumulative) net benefit (total benefit/total cost).

a. Construct and carefully label your table.
b. Carefully graph your marginal benefits and marginal costs data.
c. Briefly explain why the trend in marginal benefits and marginal costs in your table makes sense for the pollutant you are using in your example (e.g., why you might have diminishing marginal benefits and increasing marginal costs, or constant marginal benefits and increasing marginal costs).
d. Identify the level of cleanup that yields the maximum possible total net benefit. Briefly describe the conditions that must be true for this level of cleanup to be truly socially optimal. In other words, for what reasons is it true that existing "best methods" may still undermeasure or overmeasure benefits or costs?

2. Do some library research and find a study that uses nonmarket valuation techniques to measure the benefits of some natural resource or environmental amenity. Likely journals include the *Journal of Environmental Economics and Management, Land Economics,* or *Ecological Economics.* Write a one-page review of the study, including the target area of analysis, the methods used, the research findings, and any policy implications.

3. Discuss the advantages and disadvantages of the different methods addressed in this chapter for measuring the nonmarket value of environmental amenities in the context of valuing a neighborhood park. Which method, or combination of methods, would you use and why?

4. Access the Internet site for the National Center for Environmental Assessment (http://cfpub1.epa.gov/ncea /). Find a risk assessment report for a particular toxic pollutant and summarize the findings. What was the role of economics in the assessment? How has the risk assessment affected regulatory policy?

5. Access the Internet study *Dying Too Soon: How Cost-Effectiveness*

Analysis Can Save Lives (www.ncpa.org/studies/s204/s204.html) by Professor Tammy Tengs. If the value of a statistical life is approximately $5 million, and if preventing premature death is the only benefit of the regulation, then based on Tengs's cost-effectiveness analysis what are some examples of regulatory interventions that fail the benefit/cost test? How might your answer change if there are other benefits associated with the regulatory intervention? How might your answer change if the value of a statistical life is considerably lower, such as in a developing country?

6. Use the Internet or your library and find an environmental impact statement (EIS) that addresses an important management or policy change, and that contains a socioeconomic element with a benefit/cost analysis. Write a report that summarizes the elements of the benefit/cost analysis, including the types of nonmarket and market-based valuation methods employed, the types of cost included, and the discount rate used to calculate the present value of net benefits.

7. Spreadsheet simulation (more advanced): Consider the following simplified fitted TCM linear regression equation: VISITS = 50,000 + 0.5*INC + 50*TCSUB − 100*TCTARGET, where VISITS is the annual number of visits to the target area under study, INC = per capita personal income, TCSUB = travel cost to a substitute destination, and TCTARGET = travel cost to the target area. Suppose that the mean value of INC is $50,000, the mean value of TCSUB is $500, and the mean value of TCTARGET is $200. Enter all this information into a spreadsheet.

   a. What does the fitted TCM regression forecast as the annual number of visits to the target area when the independent variables are evaluated at their mean value?
   b. Create a table with two columns, one labeled "travel cost" and one labeled "estimated number of visits." Continue to use the mean values for INC and TCSUB in the regression equation, but now progressively increase the mean value of TCTARGET in $10 increments. This will tell us the marginal effect of an increase in the travel cost "price" on the estimated number of visits. Record (TCTARGET + $10 increment) and the associated forecast number of visits in each row of the table. Stop adding increments of $10 to the mean value of travel cost when the forecasted number of visits reaches zero.
   c. Plot these data in a diagram where the "y" axis is labeled "travel cost" and the "x" axis is labeled "estimated number of visits." Label the curve as the "resource demand curve." It should be downward-sloping and linear.
   d. Use geometry to calculate the area under this resource demand curve

and above the $200 average travel cost "price" line. This figure represents a simplified estimate of the net economic recreational use value (consumer surplus) derived from the target area. Provide a brief narrative economic interpretation of your findings. Given that the mean value of TCTARGET can be interpreted as the average actual "price" paid for the recreational experience, explain why the area under the resource demand curve represents a simplified estimate of the consumer surplus derived from recreational visitation.

Internet Links

EPA's *Guidelines for Preparing Economic Analyses* **(http:// yosemite.epa.gov/ee/epa/eed.nsf/webpages/Guidelines.html):** The *Guidelines* provide guidance on analyzing the economic impacts of regulations and policies, and assessing the distribution of costs and benefits among various segments of the population, with a particular focus on disadvantaged and vulnerable groups.

EPA's National Center for Environmental Economics (NCEE) (http:// yosemite1.epa.gov/ee/epa/eed.nsf/pages/homepage): The NCEE analyzes relationships between the economy, environmental health, and environmental pollution control.

National Center for Environmental Assessment (http://cfpub1.epa.gov/ ncea/): A division of the EPA's Office of Research and Development, the National Center for Environmental Assessment serves as the national resource center for the overall process of human health and ecological risk assessments. This includes the integration of hazard, dose-response, and exposure data and models to produce risk characterizations.

Resources for the Future's Cost/Benefit Analysis Website (www.rff.org/ rff/Cost-BenefitAnalysis.cfm): Access a large number of research reports and other studies on benefit/cost analysis as it relates to the environment and natural resources.

Dying Too Soon: How Cost-Effectiveness Analysis Can Save Lives (www.ncpa.org/studies/s204/s204.html): Work by Professor Tammy Tengs on the cost effectiveness of various regulations in which she divides the total cost of a regulatory intervention by the number of statistical life-years saved by the regulation. Site sponsored by the National Center for Policy Analysis (NCPA Policy Report 204).

Studies of the Environmental Costs of Electricity (www.emanifesto.org/ OTAEnvironmentalCost/): An accessible description of the methods and the role of environmental cost studies for electricity, from the Office of Technology Assessment (U.S. Congress).

Survey of Pollution Abatement Costs and Expenditures (www.census.gov/ econ/www/mu1100.html): PDF file provides access to the Pollution Abatement Costs and Expenditures report from the Census Bureau, covering the years 1973–94, and the one-year 1999 pilot study.

References and Further Reading

Allen, J., M. Cunningham, A. Greenwood, and L. Rosenthal. 1992. *The Value of California Wetlands: An Analysis of Their Economic Benefits.* Berkeley: The Campaign to Save California Wetlands.

American Textile Manufacturers' Institute v. Donovan, 452 U.S. 490 (1981).

Arrow, K., R. Solow, E. Leamer, P. Portney, R. Radner, and H. Schuman. 1993. "Report of the NOAA Panel on Contingent Valuation." *Federal Register* 58: 4601–4614.

Balmford, A., A. Bruner, P. Cooper, R. Costanza, S. Farber, R. Green, M. Jenkins, P. Jefferiss, V. Jessamy, J. Madden, K. Munro, N. Myers, S. Naeem, J. Paavola, M. Rayment, S. Rosendo, J. Roughgarden, K. Trumper, and R. Turner. 2002. "Economic Reasons for Conserving Wild Nature." *Science* 297: 950–54.

Bayless, M. 1982. "Measuring the Benefits of Air Quality Improvements: A Hedonic Salary Approach." *Journal of Environmental Economics and Management* 9: 81–99.

Bell, F., and V. Leeworthy. 1990. "Recreational Demand by Tourists for Saltwater Beach Days." *Journal of Environmental Economics and Management* 18 (3): 189–205.

Bell, K., D. Huppert, and R. Johnson. 2003. "Willingness to Pay for Local Coho Salmon Enhancement in Coastal Communities." *Marine Resource Economics* 18: 15–31.

Bowland, B., and J. Beghin. 1998. "Robust Estimates of Value of a Statistical Life for Developing Economies: An Application to Pollution and Mortality in Santiago." Working paper, Department of Economics, Iowa State University. Available at www.econ.iastate.edu/research/abstracts/NDN0012.html.

Boyle, K. 2003. "Contingent Valuation in Practice." In *A Primer on Nonmarket Valuation,* ed. P. Champ, K. Boyle, and T. Brown. Dordrecht, Netherlands: Kluwer Academic Publishers.

Brookshire, D., W. Schulze, M. Thayer, and R. d'Arge. 1982. "Valuing Public Goods: A Comparison of Survey and Hedonic Approaches." *American Economic Review* 72 (1): 165–77.

Brown, G.M., and H. Pollakowski. 1977. "The Economic Valuation of Shoreline." *Review of Economics and Statistics* 59 (3): 272–78.

Carson, R., W. Hanemann and R. Mitchell. 1987. "The Use of Simulated Political Markets to Value Public Goods." Discussion Paper 87-7, Department of Economics, University of California, San Diego.

Carson, R., R. Mitchell, W. Hanemann, R. Kopp, S. Presser, and P. Ruud. 1992. *A Contingent Valuation Study of Lost Passive Use Values Resulting from the Exxon Valdez Oil Spill.* Report to the attorney general of the state of Alaska. Prepared by Natural Resource Damage Assessment, Inc., La Jolla, CA.

Casey, J., T. Vukina, and L. Danielson. 1995. "The Economic Value of Hiking: Further Considerations of Opportunity Cost of Time in Recreational Demand Models." *Journal of Agricultural and Applied Economics* 27: 658–68.

Champ, P., K. Boyle, and T. Brown, eds. 2003. *A Primer on Nonmarket Valuation.* Dordrecht, Netherlands: Kluwer Academic Publishers.

Ciriacy-Wantrup, S.V. 1947. "Capital Returns from Soil Conservation Practices." *Journal of Farm Economics* 29 (November): 1181–96.

Clawson, M. 1959. "Methods of Measuring the Demand for and Value of Outdoor Recreations." Reprint 10, Resources for the Future, Washington, DC.

Costanza, R., R. d'Arge, R. de Groot, S. Farberk, M. Grasso, B. Hannon, K. Limburg, S. Naeem, R. O'Neill, J. Paruelo, R. Raskin, P. Sutton, and M. van den Belt. 1997. "The Value of the World's Ecosystem Services and Natural Capital." *Nature* 387 (May 15): 253–60.

Cummings, R., D. Brookshire, and W. Shultze, eds. 1986. *Valuing Environmental Goods: An Assessment of the Contingent Valuation Method.* Totowa, NJ: Rowman and Allanheld.

Diamond, D. 1980. "Income and Residential Location: Muth Revisited." *Urban Studies* 17: 1–12.

Diamond, P., and J. Hausman. 1994. "Contingent Valuation: Is Some Number Better Than No Number?" *Journal of Economic Perspectives* 8 (Fall): 45–64.

Dickie, M. 2003. "Defensive Behavior and Damage Cost Methods." In *A Primer on Nonmarket Valuation,* ed. P. Champ, K. Boyle, and T. Brown. Dordrecht, Netherlands: Kluwer Academic Publishers.

Dupuit, J. 1844. *On the Measurement of the Utility of Public Works.* In *Readings in Welfare Economics,* Volume 12, ed. K. Arrow and T. Scitovsky. Homewood, IL: Richard D. Irwin, pp. 255–83.

Englin, J., and J. Shonkwiler. 1995. "Modeling Recreation Demand in the Presence of Unobservable Travel Costs: Toward a Travel Price Model." *Journal of Environmental Economics and Management* 29: 368–77.

Environmental Law Institute. 1999. *Proceedings of the Conference on Cost, Innovation and Environmental Regulation: A Research and Policy Update.* Washington, DC: Environmental Law Institute.

Folke, C. 1991. "The Societal Value of Wetland Life-Support." In *Linking the Natural Environment and the Economy: Essays from the Eco-Eco Group,* ed. C. Folke and T. Kaberger. Dordrecht, Netherlands: Kluwer Academic Publishers.

Grimes, O. 1983. "The Influence of Urban Centers on Recreational Land Use." In *The Economics of Urban Amenities,* ed. D. Diamond and G. Tolley. New York: Academic Press.

Grossman, G., and A. Krueger. 1991. "Environmental Impacts of a North American Free Trade Agreement." Woodrow Wilson School of Public Affairs Discussion Paper 158.

Hanemann, W.M. 1994. "Valuing the Environment Through Contingent Valuation." *Journal of Economic Perspectives* 8 (Fall): 19–43.

Harrington, W., and P. Portney. 1987. "Valuing the Benefits of Health and Safety Regulation." *Journal of Urban Economics* 22: 101–12.

Joshi, S., R. Krishnan, and L. Lave. 2001. "Estimating the Hidden Costs of Environmental Regulation." *Accounting Review* 76 (2): 171–98.

Knetsch, J. 1995. "Assumptions, Behavioral Findings and Policy Analysis." *Journal of Policy Analysis and Management* 14 (1): 78–89.

Krutilla, J. 1967. "Conservation Reconsidered." *American Economic Review* 56 (September): 777–86.

Loomis, J. 1987. "Balancing Public Trust Resources of Mono Lake and Los Angeles' Water Right: An Economic Approach." *Water Resources Research* 23 (August): 1449–56.

———. 1996. "Measuring the Economic Benefits of Removing Dams and Restoring the Elwha River: Results of a Contingent Valuation Survey." *Water Resources Research* 32 (February): 441–47.

Loomis, J., and R. Walsh. 1997. *Recreational Economic Decisions: Comparing Benefits and Costs.* State College, PA: Venture Publishing.

Mitchell, R., and R. Carson. 1989. *Using Surveys to Value Public Goods: The Contingent Valuation Method.* Washington, DC: Resources for the Future.

Moore, C., and A. Miller. 1995. *Green Gold: Japan, Germany, the United States, and the Race for Environmental Technology.* Boston: Beacon Press.

Moss, S., R. McCann, and M. Feldman. N.d. *A Guide for Reviewing Environmental Policy Studies: A Handbook for the California Environmental Protection Agency.* Sacramento: California Environmental Protection Agency.

Munda, G. 1996. "Cost–Benefit Analysis in Integrated Environmental Assessment: Some Methodological Issues." *Ecological Economics* 19 (November): 157–68.

Naroff, J., D. Hellman, and D. Skinner. 1980. "Estimates of the Impact of Crime on Property Values: The Boston Experience." *Growth and Change* 7 (January): 24–30.

National Research Council. 1983. *Risk Assessment in the Federal Government: Managing the Process.* Washington, DC: National Academy Press.

Oak Ridge National Laboratory, Center for Transportation Analysis. 1999. *Transportation Energy Data Book.* 19th ed. Chapter 5. Available at www.cta.ornl.gov/data/tedb19/Chapter_5.pdf.

Odum, H.T., and E.C. Odum. 1976. *Energy Basis for Man and Nature.* New York: McGraw-Hill.

Olson, C. 1981. "An Analysis of Wage Differentials Received by Workers on Dangerous Jobs." *Journal of Human Resources* 16 (2): 165–68.

Parsons, G. 2003. "The Travel Cost Model." In *A Primer on Nonmarket Valuation*, ed. P. Champ, K. Boyle, and T Brown. Dordrecht, Netherlands: Kluwer Academic Publishers.

Pashigian, P. 1984. "The Effects of Environmental Regulation on Optimal Plant Size and Factor Shares." *Journal of Environmental Economics and Management* 28 (April): 1–28.

Pearce, D., and J. Warford. 1993. *World without End: Economics, Environment, and Sustainable Development.* Oxford: Oxford University Press.

Pizer, W., R. Morgenstern, and J. Shih. 2001. "The Cost of Environmental Protection." *Review of Economics and Statistics* 83: 732–38.

Pollard, R. 1982. "View Amenities, Building Heights and Housing Supply." In *The Economics of Urban Amenities,* ed. D. Diamond and G. Tolley. New York: Academic Press.

Porter. M., and C. van der Linde 1995 "Green and Competitive: Ending the Stale-
mate." *Harvard Business Review* September–October· 397–425.

Portney, P. 1994. "The Contingent Valuation Debate: Why Economists Should Care."
Journal of Economic Perspectives 8 (Fall): 3–17.

Power, T. 1996. *Environmental Protection and Economic Well-Being*. 2nd ed. Armonk,
NY: M.E. Sharpe.

Randall, A. 1994. "A Difficulty with the Travel Cost Method." *Land Economics* 70:
88–96.

Rosenberger, R., and J. Loomis. 2003. "Benefit Transfer." In *A Primer on Nonmarket
Valuation*, ed. P. Champ, K. Boyle, and T. Brown. Dordrecht, Netherlands: Kluwer
Academic Publishers.

Rutledge, G., and C. Vogan. 1995. "Pollution Abatement and Control Expenditures,
1993." *Survey of Current Business* 75 (May): 36–45.

Sassone, P., and W. Schaffer. 1978. *Cost–Benefit Analysis: A Handbook*. New York:
Academic Press.

Schultz, S., and D. King. 2001. "The Use of Census Data for Hedonic Price Estimates
of Open Space Amenities and Land Use." *Journal of Real Estate Finance and
Economics* 22: 239–52.

Schultze, W., D. Brookshire, E. Walther, K. MacFarland, M. Thayer, R. Whitworth,
S. Ben-David, W. Malm, and J. Molenar. 1983. "The Economic Benefit of Pre-
serving Visibility in the National Parklands of the Southwest." *Natural Resources
Journal* 23 (1): 149–73.

Sieg, H., V. Smith, H. Banzhaf, and R. Walsh. 2000. "Estimating the General Equilibrium Benefits of Large Policy Changes: The Clean Air Act Revisited." NBER
Working Paper 7744. Available at www.nber.org/papers/w7744.

Sinden, J. 1988. "Empirical Tests of Hypothetical Biases in Consumers' Surplus Surveys." *American Journal of Agricultural Economics* 32: 98–112.

Sohngen, B. 2000. "The Value of Day Trips to Lake Erie Beaches." Unpublished
report, Department of Agricultural, Environmental, and Development Economics,
Ohio State University.

Subcommittee on Benefits and Costs, Federal Inter-Agency River Basin Committee.
1950. *Proposed Practices for Economic Analysis of River Basin Projects*. Washington, DC: U.S. Government Printing Office.

Taylor, L. 2003. "The Hedonic Method." In *A Primer on Nonmarket Valuation*, ed. P.
Champ, K. Boyle, and T. Brown. Dordrecht, Netherlands: Kluwer Academic Publishers.

Tengs, T., M. Adams, J. Pliskin, D. Safran, J. Siegel, M. Weinstein, and J. Graham.
1995. "Five-Hundred Life-Saving Interventions and Their Cost-Effectiveness." *Risk
Analysis* 15: 369–90.

UAW v. OSHA, 938 F.2d 1310 (DC Circuit, 1991).

U.S. Bureau of the Census, Current Industrial Reports. 1996. *Pollution Abatement
Costs and Expenditures, 1994, MA200(94)-1*. Washington, DC: U.S. Government
Printing Office.

U.S. Environmental Protection Agency. 1990. *Environmental Investments: The Cost
of a Clean Environment*. Report of the Administrator of the Environmental Protection Agency to the Congress of the United States, EPA-230–11–90–083. Washington, DC: U.S. Environmental Protection Agency.

———. 1997. *The Benefits and Costs of the Clean Air Act, 1970–1990*. Washington,
DC: U.S. Environmental Protection Agency.

U.S. Water Resources Council. 1983. *Economic and Environmental Principles and Guidelines for Water and Related Land Resources Implementation Studies.* Washington, DC: U.S. Government Printing Office.

Viscusi, W. 1996. "Economic Foundations of the Current Regulatory Reform Efforts." *Journal of Economic Perspectives* 10 (Summer): 119–34.

Vossler, C., J. Kerkvliet, S. Polasky, and O. Gainutdinova. 2003. "Externally Validating Contingent Valuation: An Open Space Survey and Referendum in Corvallis, Oregon." *Journal of Economic Behavior and Organization* 51: 261–77.

Walsh, R., R. Gillman, and J. Loomis. 1982. *Wilderness Resource Economics: Recreational Use and Preservation Values.* Denver: American Wilderness Alliance.

Wendling, R., and R. Bezdek. 1989. "Acid Rain Abatement Legislation: Costs and Benefits." *OMEGA International Journal of Management Science* 17 (3): 251–61.

8

The Political Economy of
Environmental Regulation and
Resource Management

Introduction: What Is Political Economy?

Political economy is not a unified discipline. Political economy was the term originally used to describe the discipline of economics. Adam Smith, Karl Marx, and John Stuart Mill, for example, were deeply concerned with the interconnectedness of social, economic, and political phenomena. Much of the focus was on what we might now call the economics of public policy. In contemporary usage, political economy is distinct from the discipline of economics in that it is more interdisciplinary in nature, draws upon related fields such as law and political science, and often has a broader scope. Within microeconomics, political economy is an approach used to understand how political and legal institutions influence the economic behavior of people, firms, and markets, as well as the economics of how interest groups influence the formation of laws and regulatory policy. From the standpoint of international economics, political economy is concerned with understanding how national policies influence international trade, investment, and finance, with the processes that lead to the formation of international economic treaties and institutions, and with the economic consequences of these laws and institutions. These relatively recent approaches to political economy—sometimes referred to as the *new political economy*—borrow economic approaches for modeling incentives as a way to understand the political and economic forces that shape public policy. In contrast to the economic approach, political scientists have a tradition of viewing political economy as a means for analyzing economic and power relationships among nation-states. Many sociologists use a framework for political economy drawn from Marx to understand how the structure of production influences the social interaction of individuals and groups. The political economy framework used by anthropologists provides an understanding of the relationship between the capitalist system and local cultures around the world. The role and functioning of the market economy in a social context is perhaps the most important relationship studied in all the various branches of political economy. A comprehensive presentation of the full range of thought on political economy is beyond the scope of this chapter. Instead, we will focus on the application of new political economy theory to environmental economics, policy, and the collective-choice problems associated with the governance of common-pool resources (CPRs).

In chapter 4 we developed the economic theory of efficiency-enhancing environmental regulation. But since environmental regulation is an outcome of political processes, the nature of environmental regulation will reflect the economic forces at work in the political process. Therefore, new political economy models can help us understand how regulation comes about. Rational-choice models of political economy develop a linkage between the institutional structure of the political process, the preferences of decision makers, and the preferences of those affected by regulation. We will see, for example, that the process of developing environmental regulation can be modeled in a supply and demand framework. The supply and demand framework is not the only way to model environmental political economy, and we will consider a number of other approaches, including those addressing the governance of locally self-governed common-pool resources. Studying political economy also helps us understand cases of *government failure,* in which policymakers fail to design environmental policies that adequately resolve market failures at reasonable cost. Therefore, while market failures provide a theoretical or conceptual justification for regulatory intervention, one must also critically evaluate the efficiency of the regulatory intervention itself. Such a critical evaluation can help us understand why existing regulatory schemes do not function as expected and can thus be a first step in the design of more effective regulatory incentives and institutions.

In this chapter we will first develop a political-economic model of the regulatory process that uses supply and demand methodology. Next, we will describe some of the more important models of political economy that have been developed by economists studying the regulatory process. We will then discuss how these models have been applied to the political economy of environmental regulation, to the governance of CPR systems, and to the process of forming international environmental accords.

Economic Models of Political Economy and the Regulatory Process

Introduction

Economists who study the political process are interested in explaining government policies as a function of (1) optimizing, *rational choice* behavior by the policymakers (behavior consistent with optimizing over some set of objectives), (2) modified by incentives from various sources, and subject to (3) political and other institutions (the rules of the game). Ordeshook (1990) has argued that the extension of this rational choice paradigm to politics, which is the foundation of thought in political economy today, represents a case of imperialism (expansion of territory using power) by microeconomic theorists such as Arrow (1951) and Olson (1965).

Political economy models can be used to help explain and predict policy outcomes. For example, consider the choice between a state government gathering revenues through a sales tax or an income tax. Sales taxes tend to be more *regressive,* meaning that they take a larger percentage of the income of poor people relative to rich people. The reason is that poor people spend a much larger share of their income on items subject to sales tax than rich people, who save and invest a substantial portion of their income. In contrast, income taxes are usually graduated, and so taxes take a larger share of the income of rich people, making them *progressive.* Thus, income taxes will tend to be the preferred method of taxation for political candidates who position themselves to represent the interests of low-income people, while sales taxes will tend to be the preferred method of taxation for candidates who represent upper-middle-class and wealthy people. Thus, in those states where the very poor have a very low voter participation rate, and so represent a minority of voters, one could predict that the tax structure will tend to make greater use of sales taxes relative to income taxes.

Early work in the rational-choice approach to political economy by Buchanan and Tullock (1962) led to the creation of the branch of political economy known as the *public choice school of thought.* Instead of assuming that politicians select policies that best serve the public interest, traditional public choice models start from the premise that politicians, like other economic agents, are motivated by incentives such as ideology, wealth, reelection, and power. From this foundation, one can model the supply of legislation or administrative rules. For example, Kalt and Zupan (1984) find that the voting behavior of legislators can be explained as a function of both individual ideology and the requirement to satisfy the economic and other interests of the constituents whose votes are needed to remain in office. While factors such as ideology, reelection, and the like help us understand the supply of regulation, legislative and administrative outcomes also depend on the institutional structure within which these activities occur. Shepsle and Weingast (1987) offer an accessible survey of the work that has been done on the institutional structure of the U.S. Congress. For example, issues such as party control, seniority, the role of committees and committee chairs, voting rules, and other aspects of procedure are important elements in understanding legislative outcomes. A different institutional structure governs the administrative rule-making process.

While some economists and political scientists were studying the behavior of legislators and others on the supply side of regulation, a number of economists associated with the Chicago school of economics were developing a political economic model of the demand for regulation. Stigler (1971) argued generally that firms will lobby legislators for regulation when such regulation provides (1) direct monetary subsidies, (2) constraints on substitute products or subsidies on complementary products, (3) easier price-fixing/collusive atmosphere, and (4) incumbent firms with the ability to control entry by potential new rivals. Together with the work of Peltzman (1976), Stigler is credited with the development of the *capture theory of regulation.* In this model, firms (or others) capture the regulatory process because each firm potentially bears a high cost if regulation constrains its behavior, so each firm has a lot at stake. In contrast, while the public as a whole has a lot at stake, generally, any one person has only a very small stake in the regulatory process and so has little incentive to invest resources in affecting the regulatory process. At the same time, there are comparatively few firms relative to the overall public, so the cost of organizing the firms is low compared to the cost of organizing the public. As a result, firms have both the incentive and the better opportunity to invest resources successfully in lobbying for favorable regulation. As with the later work of Becker (1983), the capture theory of regulation ignores the supply side of the regulatory process, and assumes that regulation is an outcome of interest group competition.

There is evidence consistent with the capture theory of regulation. One example is revolving-door deals, in which high-level regulators and other officials leave government and find high-level jobs in the same industry that they had been responsible for regulating. While it is difficult to prove a causal relationship between regulatory decisions and future employment, careful attention to the interests of regulated industries can be a highly lucrative career-building strategy for senior government regulators. Sanjour (1992) provides a remarkable accounting of the possible revolving-door relationship between the Environmental Protection Agency (EPA) and the hazardous waste industry. For example, Sanjour reports that chief EPA administrator William Ruckelshaus became a director of Weyerhauser, Monsanto, and CEO of Browning Ferris, all regulated by the EPA. Chief EPA administrator Douglas Costle became chair of Metalf and Eddy, a Superfund contractor. Chief EPA administrator Lee Thomas became CEO of Law Environmental, a hazardous waste firm. Similarly, various deputy administrators, acting administrators, assistant administrators, and regional administrators, as well as enforcement attorneys, gained high-level employment in hazardous waste firms such as Waste Management, Chemical Waste Management, Browning Ferris, and Rollins Environmental Services. Likewise, Greenberg (1993) found that 80 percent of top EPA officials who had worked with toxic waste clean-ups and left the government between 1980 and the time of his study joined firms holding Superfund clean-up contracts or having consulted with or given legal advice to companies about dealing with Superfund. More generally, Lewis (1998) found that between 36 and 40 percent of senior staffers serving members of key congressional budgetary committees left to become registered lobbyists between 1991 and 1996. In a July 1999 news release, the group Common Cause reported that 128 former members of Congress were lobbyists in 1998, and that at least 22 percent of lawmakers leaving office became lobbyists in the 1990s, compared to only 3 percent in the 1970s.

Additional support for the capture theory of regulation comes from a 1997 *Los Angeles Times* analysis of political giving by major U.S. corporations. That report found that the largest contributors tended to be those most heavily regulated by government or most dependent upon government for subsidies (Vartabedian 1997). Clearly, these firms have a high demand for favorable regulation. By the same token, firms with a reputation for sound management, and which therefore have a relatively lower demand for favorable regulation, were found to be below-average contributors. From a sectoral point of view, the largest political contributors came from the financial, military, oil, telecommunications, and tobacco industries.

The Political Market for Regulation

In this section of the chapter, we will see how the two strands of the rational-choice theory of political economy described in the preceding section can be brought together in a simple equilibrium supply and demand framework. Since regulation may have its origins in both legislation and administrative rules, we will use the term "regulator" to refer to the agent (either legislator or administrator) who participates in the production of regulation. We will assume a competitive market in which the equilibrium level of effective support for a particular regulation is the outcome of interaction between interest groups and regulators. This section of the chapter is loosely based on the work of Keohane, Revesz, and Stavins (1999).

The demand for regulation derives from the various groups whose interests are served by regulation. Since regulation is a public good, and since political influence is costly, individuals are unlikely to find it worthwhile to participate on their own. Interest groups are effective because they pool the resources of many individuals and reduce the total cost of lobbying activity. Since regulation is a public good, however, interest groups suffer from free-riding problems (Olson 1965). Effective interest groups are able to overcome the free-rider problem by offering membership benefits such as solidarity, access to regulators, and information. Interest groups organize around a common set of preferences, and therefore express a groups' willingness to pay for effective support of a regulation that reflects the marginal utility derived from the regulatory outcome. This willingness to pay is manifested as political currency that includes money payments, votes, volunteer effort, and endorsements. Stigler (1971) and Peltzman's (1976) capture theory of regulation focuses on the advocacy behavior of regulated firms, and suggests that interest groups are most likely to be successful in affecting regulatory outcomes when individual members have a large willingness to pay for favorable regulation, and when the interest group is able to effectively organize and focus its collective preferences.

Those who study the demand for regulation characterize several specific types of interest groups. Firms often organize themselves in trade associations. As Stigler and Peltzman observed, these trade associations are likely to seek regulations that reduce their production costs, provide subsidies, erect entry barriers and constrain substitutes, and provide an environment more conducive to collusion. Environmentalists organize themselves into groups that lobby for regulation that conserves or restores the environment. Likewise, consumers may organize themselves into interest groups seeking lower product prices and product quality assurance, and workers may organize into interest groups seeking more jobs, higher pay, and better working conditions.

In terms of environmental interest groups, Agnone (2004) performed an analysis of 406 pro-environmental bills passed by Congress between 1960 and 1994. He found, for example, that taking to the streets to demonstrate and protest is more effective than working inside the system to influence the passage of pro-environment legislation in the United States. The actual impact of individual protest acts on whether legislation passes is relatively small, with each protest event that occurs in a given year increasing the number of pro-environment bills passed by about 2.2 percent. Thus in a year in which twenty protests occurred, about 44 percent more pro-environment bills would be approved. Moreover, the impact of individual protest actions is small compared to which party controls Congress, and whether or not it is an election year. Agnone's research indicates that a piece of environmental legislation has a 75 percent better chance of passage when Democrats control both houses of Congress, and a bill is more than 200 percent more likely to be passed in a congressional election year.

As Keohane, Revesz, and Stavins (1999) argue, the supply of regulation has three components, each reflecting the cost of supplying effective support for a particular regulatory outcome. First, the supply of regulation is a function of the opportunity cost of the time and effort invested by the regulator in shepherding environmental legislation or administrative rules through the political process. Second, the supply of regulation is a function of the psychological cost of supporting regulation that may be in opposition to the personal preferences of the regulator. It is possible that this cost becomes negative if the regulation is in accord with the regulator's personal preferences. Third, the supply of regulation is a function of the opportunity cost of supporting regulation that can impair the regulator's probability of reelection or reappointment. As with the regulator's personal preferences, this opportunity cost can become negative if the regulation is in accord with the interests of the regulator's constituency and thus increases the likelihood of reelection or reappointment. Each of these three components of the supply of regulation affects the utility of the regulator.

The equilibrium concept as it applies to a supply and demand model is described in chapter 3. In this more complex political market, the price of a unit of effective support, denominated in political currency, reflects the marginal willingness to pay for the groups whose interests are reflected in the demand curve. The equilibrium quantity of effective support is found where the demand for regulation intersects the supply of regulation, as shown in Figure 8.1. What factors might displace this equilibrium and cause an increase or a decrease in the equilibrium level of effective support for a particular regulation? An increase in demand might occur, for example, if a new interest group joins the coalition demanding the regulation. All else equal, an increase in demand would cause an increase in the equilibrium level of effective support. Likewise, if polls indicate that constituents more strongly favor the regulation then this would increase the supply of regulation and therefore increase the equilibrium quantity of effective support. Each regulatory alternative will have its own supply and demand, and thus will have its own equilibrium level of effective support. Different regulatory alternatives will derive their demand from a different mix of interest groups, and will derive their supply from different regulator opportunity costs.

Nevertheless, how do these equilibrium levels of effective support relate to regulatory outcomes? That is the role of political institutions. For example,

Figure 8.1   **The Political Market for Regulation**

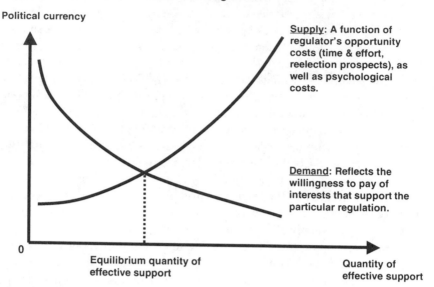

the rules of governance may require a threshold level of equilibrium support in a legislature in order for a particular regulation to become law. In the case of administrative rule-making processes, the process may involve selecting from among regulatory alternatives based on which receives the largest level of equilibrium support.

The Political Economy of Environmental Regulation: A Selective Survey

In this section, we will review a number of studies that have used the tools of political economy to evaluate environmental regulation. One issue has to do with determining the political economy of how pollution-control laws are implemented by the EPA and other relevant administrative agencies. Implementation involves diverse elements of government, including enforcement policy, field monitoring, sanctioning decisions, and legal activity. Downing (1981) has studied the political economy of the process of implementing pollution-control laws, and his model includes three groups: the polluter, those bearing the pollution costs, and the regulatory agency. The first two groups invest resources to influence the regulatory agency. Downing assumes that the manager(s) of the regulatory agency have the twin objectives of maximizing agency budget and discretionary control and of improving environmental quality. Polluters, and those suffering from pollution, invest resources in influencing the politicians who set the agency budget, and thus indirectly control the level of pollution-control activity.

This is a useful structure for analyzing the role of interest groups in determining the nature of particular environmental policies. For example, this model indicates that there is a feedback effect between the type of environmental regulation we observe (e.g., effluent fees, technology forcing) and the pattern of lobbying pressure exerted by the regulated firms. Milliman and Prince (1989) studied a polluting firm's incentives for spending money on research and development (R&D) to find innovative and less expensive ways of meeting the requirements of pollution-control laws. One relationship they studied was the way in which firms that succeeded in finding an innovative and lower-cost means of complying with pollution-control laws might influence the introduction of even more stringent environmental regulations. They argue, "firms, not regulatory agencies, often initiate [environmentally friendly] innovation and diffusion" (p. 248).

What sort of influence might such a firm with a cost-reducing innovation exert on policymakers? Hackett (1995) investigated the question of whether polluting firms would ever have an incentive to lobby policymakers for more restrictive regulation of their own industry and used a Stigler-style model of regulatory influence. This counterintuitive scenario can actually occur when doing so would raise the cost of rival firms more than the firm's own cost, as argued by Salop et al. (1984). In Hackett's model, firms are engaged in a patent race to develop less expensive methods of clean production technology. The incentive to engage in this patent race need not be some external threat from the government. Instead, the winner(s) of the patent race have found a much cheaper method of clean production than other industry members, and so have an incentive to lobby government for pollution-control regulations. Such regulations raise their costs as well but they raise production costs of noninnovating rivals by much more. As a result, the innovating firms have a cost advantage in the regulated setting, which increases their profits.

The viewpoint offered above is that there are circumstances in which polluting firms actually have an incentive to invest money in pollution-control R&D and, if successful, to lobby for more restrictive environmental laws. There are other, somewhat less benign, reasons why firms might engage in voluntary pollution abatement. In particular, Maxwell, Lyon, and Hackett (2000) look at the situation in which polluting firms face the possibility of more restrictive environmental laws in the future. They use a demand-side political economy model in which rival interest groups compete with one another to influence policymakers, as in Becker (1983). They find that if the cost of organizing those harmed by pollution to lobby for more restrictive environmental law is sufficiently high, the polluting firms may have an incentive to engage voluntarily in clean-up activities. Nevertheless, how much voluntary overcompliance will firms select? The answer is just enough to keep those suffering from pollution from organizing, but less than what the firms think they would be forced to clean up if they had to compete in the influence process. Consequently, firms are able to foreclose the influence process through some voluntary pollution control.

Maxwell, Lyon, and Hackett (2000) use data on the Toxics Release Inventory (TRI) to evaluate whether declines in the cost of organizing political resistance to pollution emissions lead to a greater threat of increased government regulation, driving firms to self-regulate and reduce emissions. The TRI requires firms to self-report their emissions of certain toxic compounds and thus works to lower the information cost to citizen groups that lobby government for stricter regulations. Since the TRI was instituted in 1989, toxic emissions per unit of manufacturing output have steadily declined, which is consistent with Maxwell, Lyon, and Hackett's prediction. Moreover, states such as California that have a very high density of self-identified environmentalists are shown to have a more rapid reduction in toxic emissions per unit of manufacturing output than states with a lower density of environmentalists. Thus, by simply providing information on pollution emissions, the TRI makes it easier for citizens to threaten polluters with more stringent regulation, which in turn works to lower emissions by way of voluntary self-regulation in order to attenuate the threat of more stringent regulation.

We will now look at applications of political economy that have been used to explain successes and failures in CPR governance.

The Political Economy of Locally Self-Governed Common-Pool Resources

We have discussed a number of different ways that the techniques of political economy have been used to help explain environmental laws and their implementation. The techniques of political economy can also be applied to appropriator groups that form self-governing organizations for managing CPR systems. One of the clearest applications of this methodology is in understanding how appropriator groups solve the problem of internally allocating harvest rights when overall harvest must be reduced in order to protect the productive capacity of the CPR.

Buchanan and Tullock (1962) have argued that the percentage of voters needed for a voting organization (e.g., a legislature or a condominium owners association or a group of groundwater pumpers) to reach agreement has important cost implications. Building on this notion, Hackett (1992) studied voting rules in CPR systems in which the appropriators differ in one or more important ways. For example, from prior use, some groundwater pumpers may have drawn very large volumes of water from the aquifer, while others may have appropriated only very small volumes. Suppose that the CPR system has been abused from overuse, and the appropriators have just self-organized to reduce overall appropriation levels in order to manage the CPR more sustainably. The question is how the overall reduction in use will be divided among the individual appropriators.

Rule systems that change the original *status quo shares* redistribute wealth from one type of appropriator to another, and are therefore more likely to generate conflict. For example, suppose that a groundwater basin is found to be in overdraft and new rules are developed to reduce the daily quantity of water to be withdrawn from the aquifer. Wealth will be redistributed from historically small appropriators to historically large appropriators if all appropriators must cut back by the same number of gallons per day. Wealth will be redistributed from large appropriators to small ones if groundwater quota shares of equal size are assigned without regard to historical pumping levels. In contrast, a rule system that requires all appropriators to cut back by the same *percentage* from historical use levels is neutral and does not redistribute wealth. Self-governed CPR appropriators must resolve this distributional conflict in order to achieve more sustainable use of the CPR.

The larger the percentage of voters required to reach agreement on a distributional rule, the *more inclusive* the voting rule. The extreme case would be a consensus rule. Hackett (1992) developed a model that identifies the following trade-off: heterogeneous groups with highly inclusive voting rules will take a longer time to reach agreement because such voting rules make it easier to block agreements. This delay allows the CPR to continue to decline in productivity. Distributional rules that are approved, however, are less likely to result in large redistributions of wealth relative to the status quo, and so individual appropriators are less likely to fight and violate such rules, reducing future monitoring and enforcement costs. In contrast, *less inclusive* voting rules, such as a simple majority rule, are more likely to result in a redistribution of wealth from the minority to the majority of voters, and so repair of the CPR system is not delayed. Yet if the majority does manage to pass highly redistributive rules, the agreement is more likely to be fought and violated by the minority in the future, resulting in higher monitoring and enforcement costs.

Thus self-governed yet highly heterogeneous CPR appropriator groups may have to trade off delay costs against higher monitoring and enforcement costs when they devise their voting rule. Hackett, Schlager, and Walker (1994) used laboratory experimental techniques to look at how groups resolve this problem. Laboratory experiments such as this have people role-play the interactions of CPR appropriator groups. The incentive to take this seriously is created by using cash payments to re-create the incentives that are present in naturally occurring CPR systems. The advantage of laboratory techniques is that they allow researchers to test the hypotheses of models for which data are not available from naturally occurring sources. Hackett, Schlager, and Walker created heterogeneity in appropriator size—large appropriators had the capability (and the history) of harvesting a much larger volume from the CPR than the small appropriators harvest. After allowing appropriators to abuse the CPR, they were given the opportunity to communicate freely and devise a sharing rule to (1) reduce overall harvest on the CPR and (2) allocate these reduced harvest rights among the appropriators themselves. Hackett, Schlager, and Walker found that this form of heterogeneity did not seriously deter appropriators from forming successful sharing rules. When large appropriators had to pay for their added harvest capacity, sharing rules allocated larger harvest shares to them relative to those with smaller harvest capacity. These proportionate sharing rules were seen as being fair and prevented the large-capacity appropriators from cheating on the agreement.

There have been a number of field studies as well. For example, the effects of appropriator heterogeneity and voting rules on the performance of CPR governance structures have been looked at for the case of oil and gas fields by Wiggins and Libecap (1985) and Libecap and Wiggins (1985). As Wiggins and Libecap (1985) point out, "[c]onflict over estimated lease values and unit shares [sharing rules] is the heart of the contracting problem" (p. 372). Self-governance on oil and gas fields with many individual mineral rights holders is important, because excessively rapid competitive "pumping races" deplete the natural pressurization in the oil pocket that allows the oil to be brought to the surface. They found, for example, that self-governance was far more successful in the state of Wyoming, where oil fields are primarily on federal land and federal policy encourages agreements prior to pumping when heterogeneities could set in. By 1975, 82 percent of Wyoming oil came from fields with sharing rule agreements and controls on overpumping. Agreements were far less common in Texas, where pumping could occur prior to talks on self-governance, allowing heterogeneities to set in. Moreover, unanimity is required for agreement in Texas. As a result, while major oil fields were developed in Texas in the late 1920s and early 1930s, only 20 percent of the state's overall oil production came from self-governed pumpers by 1975. Oklahoma, in contrast to Texas, allowed for legally binding sharing rule agreements when at least 63 percent of the pumpers (weighted by acreage of mineral rights) agreed to a sharing rule. By

1975, nearly 40 percent of Oklahoma oil came from fields with sharing rule agreements and controls on overpumping. Thus, heterogeneity and highly inclusive voting rules both contribute to delay in forming effective CPR governance structures.

Libecap and Wiggins (1985) also investigated the political economic effects of large- and small-firm oil field appropriator groups on the form of state and federal oil field quota rules. They found evidence that state and federal resource allocation rules vary as a function of the political influence of these two appropriator groups. In Texas, small lease owners were numerous and influential; they successfully delayed productivity-enhancing oil field CPR rules that favored large lease owners. On the other hand, the federal government is both a large lease owner and a supplier of rules for oil fields on public lands and so selected rules that favored large lease owners.

Johnson and Libecap (1982) provide a similar analysis of CPR governance structures designed to resolve overuse and to allocate harvest rights. They studied the Texas shrimp industry, where fishers "vary principally with regard to fishing skill" (p. 1005). There is also a biological interdependence between inshore and offshore fisheries, where the productivity of the offshore fishery depends in part on number of shrimp that migrate there from shallower inshore waters. While fishers' unions and trade associations developed along the U.S. coast to limit entry in order to control overfishing, a series of Supreme Court decisions during the 1940s interpreted these as cartel agreements (cartels like the Organization of Petroleum Exporting Countries [OPEC], for example, are illegal under U.S. law), and required that they be dismantled. Johnson and Libecap point out that heterogeneity in skill created conflict over the type of government fishery regulations the various fishers preferred: "For example, total effort [in catching fish] could be restricted through uniform quotas for eligible fishermen. But if fishermen are heterogeneous, uniform quotas will be costly to assign and enforce because of opposition from more productive fishermen" (p. 1010).

Field research generally indicates that rules linking CPR output shares to an appropriator's size and historical level of CPR harvest (number of fishing boats, acres under irrigation) or contribution (effort or financial contributions for upkeep or monitoring and enforcement) are far more common than rules that simply divide CPR output equally. There is an aspect of fairness in rewarding greater contributions with larger shares, and sharing rules that differ markedly from historical use patterns tend to undermine individual cooperation with group efforts directed at improving the conditions of the commons.

Thus we have seen that the techniques of political economy and public choice are helpful in understanding the problems and challenges associated with successful self-governance of localized CPRs as well as the nature of the rule structures these groups develop. Heterogeneity and highly inclusive voting rules for reaching agreement explain a substantial amount of the delays, high costs, and failures of CPR governance. These problems occur because incompatible incentives of individuals create distributional conflict, and highly inclusive voting rules increase the strategic power of individual appropriators to hold up agreements for special treatment.

The Political Economy of International Environmental Accords: The Case of the Montreal Protocol

The methods of political economy can also be used to help us understand the nature of international environmental accords. One of the most prominent of these is the Montreal Protocol, which sets an international schedule for the banning of chlorofluorocarbons (CFCs) and related chemicals that deplete atmospheric ozone. Oye and Maxwell (1995) offer a comprehensive political economic analysis of the Montreal Protocol, and we will draw heavily upon their work in this case study.

Oye and Maxwell argue that successful environmental management occurs when narrow, self-interested behavior is also consistent with the common good, and thus those interested in the common good should look for opportunities to foster these linkages. This is something like Adam Smith's notion that the *invisible hand* of the marketplace transforms narrowly self-interested behavior into efficient outcomes. In particular, their case study analysis of the Montreal Protocol and other environmental agreements indicates that environmental regulations work most effectively when they create benefits for those firms being regulated.

Theoretical Foundation

Consider two different regulatory situations. One of these we shall refer to as Olsonian cases, using the terminology developed by Oye and Maxwell for regulatory situations matching those described in the work by Olson (1965) on privileged groups. In Olsonian situations regulatory benefits are diffuse, spread thinly across many entities, while regulatory costs are concentrated, weighing heavily on a few entities. In Olsonian situations the many who receive relatively small benefits from regulation have little incentive to invest in policy influence activities, and moreover, as Stigler argued, they also face high organizational and coordination costs because of their large numbers. On the other hand, the few who bear a particularly heavy regulatory burden (e.g., large polluting firms) have an incentive to organize opposition and by being small in number also face smaller organizational costs. Thus in

Olsonian situations it is more difficult to get stable systems of regulation, meaning that regulatory controls for protecting the environment, for example, are relatively likely to be overturned due to the lobbying efforts of the few who bear the costs.

In contrast to Olsonian regulatory situations are Stiglerian cases, named after Nobel Prize–winning economist and regulatory scholar George Stigler. Recall that in Stiglerian situations the benefits of regulatory controls are concentrated heavily on a few entities, while the costs are rather thinly spread across many entities. Regulatory controls are more stable in Stiglerian situations because the influence advantage falls to those who benefit from the regulation, while those who would like to overturn the regulation have relatively little incentive to do so, and face high organizational costs.

Oye and Maxwell argue that the Montreal Protocol case features constraints on substitute products or subsidies on complementary products, and the ability of an incumbent firm to control entry by potential new rivals. These conditions exist because the protocol, which outlawed CFC production by the year 2000, gave a particularly strong advantage to firms like DuPont that came up with CFC alternatives over their rivals that did not. In particular, Oye and Maxwell find that the "DuPont and Imperial Chemical Industries, Ltd. (ICI) experience with restrictions on CFC's represents a classic Stiglerian illustration of producers benefiting from regulations mandating product substitution" (pp. 193–94). The material below closely follows that of Oye and Maxwell.

Case Study: The International Political Economy of CFC Control

Halocarbons, two prominent forms of which are CFCs and halons, are substances that combine chlorine, fluorine, iodine, and bromine. CFCs were invented in the 1930s and up to the 1970s were considered one of the most successful products of the chemical industry. In particular, CFCs are stable, easy to produce, and have wide application in refrigeration, as aerosol propellants, and in industrial cleaning and manufacturing uses. In an important study published in 1974 in the journal *Nature,* however, scientists Molina and Rowland argued that CFCs could reach the upper atmosphere through surface turbulence, despite their heaviness. Once in the stratosphere, time ultraviolet radiation would cause the CFCs to decompose into free chlorine, each molecule of which is capable of consuming large quantities of stratospheric ozone. Moreover, CFCs can persist in the atmosphere for 100 or more years. In 1976 the U.S. National Academy of Sciences (NAS) called for elimination of all nonessential uses of CFCs. In contrast, the British Department of the Environment was much more cautious, calling for further research before any regulatory actions. In the face of state-level bans and rising consumer concerns motivated by environmental activism in the United States, firms such as Johnson Wax announced in 1975 that they would voluntarily phase out CFCs in aerosol applications. Other U.S. consumer products companies followed. In 1978 the United States—along with Canada, Denmark, Norway, and Sweden—banned the use of CFCs as aerosol propellants. Interestingly, in Great Britain 80 percent of CFC use in the late 1970s was in aerosol applications, while in the United States air conditioning made up approximately 50 percent of CFC use. ICI, at the time Britain's largest single manufacturing firm and a major producer of CFCs, would thus have been disproportionately harmed by an aerosol ban, which Britain opposed.

In 1979 the NAS estimated that a 16 percent reduction in the ozone layer would result in several thousand more cases of skin cancer each year, both fatal and nonfatal, and the reduction in ozone would harm crop yields. Following this, the Carter administration's EPA sought to reduce U.S. production of CFCs further and pressed European countries to also ban aerosol and other nonessential applications of CFCs. Only token regulation followed. Thus weak European regulation together with the U.S. ban on aerosol applications led to less U.S. production and in fact to a manufacturing overcapacity in the United States, while in Britain expensive new production facilities were being added to accommodate its increased share of worldwide CFC production.

By the early 1980s the new Reagan administration was opposed to further CFC controls. Moreover, the new scientific evidence coming in during the early 1980s supported the more cautious British perspective on CFCs; for example, the NAS adjusted downward its estimate of ozone layer reductions from 16 percent to 2–4 percent in 1984. Low-level international negotiations commenced, culminating in the Vienna Convention, which called for the international community to control ozone-depleting chemicals eventually but lacked specific measures. The research programs begun in the mid-1970s for CFC alternatives by DuPont and ICI were discontinued in the early 1980s because of a lack of a market for CFC alternatives at the time.

This rather rosy picture of CFCs and ozone depletion was smashed by Farman, Gardiner, and Shanklin's 1985 study, also published in *Nature,* in which they reported for the first time that there was a hole in the stratospheric ozone layer in the Antarctic polar vortex. This information was widely reported and public awareness was high, and like Rachel Carson's book *Silent Spring,* it resulted in a translation of public concern into policy. The U.S. position in reopened international negotiations was that CFCs should be totally phased out by 1995. Importantly, DuPont adopted the position in

1986 that international regulations should limit worldwide production to then-existing *levels*. Thus, DuPont revealed a willingness to shift its capacity to the manufacture of CFC alternatives. In contrast, the British government argued for a cap at existing production capacities. The British were quite concerned about protecting ICI, which had recently invested in profitable new CFC production facilities, while in the United States DuPont and other CFC makers were continuing to experience excess capacity in older facilities, low profit margins, and the very real possibility of an outright domestic production ban.

Thus DuPont wanted an international restriction so that ICI would be disproportionately harmed. The CFC alternatives market promised profit-making opportunities for DuPont, which had developed CFC alternatives. Production of these alternatives would require substantial fixed-cost (capital) investment in precision manufacturing facilities, which would eliminate smaller producers and would thus likely feature higher profit margins for DuPont. The new chemicals were projected in the mid-1980s to sell for between five and ten times the price of CFC 11 and 12, so major users (e.g., the automotive and appliance industries) would not voluntarily switch without government regulation.

Note here the Stiglerian nature of the situation. Financial benefits were concentrated on DuPont, while the costs were spread across many manufacturers. Yet since the increased cost of the CFC alternatives was still only a small fraction of overall manufacturing cost, their cost burden was relatively small. These costs could be further mitigated by a phase-in period to allow manufacturers time to adjust compressors and other technologies to the CFC alternatives. This transition would require a public/private coordination that DuPont was eager to provide. Thus DuPont saw that it needed to promote this regulation to create a profitable new market for itself, which would benefit DuPont more than ICI.

Representatives of twenty-four countries signed the Montreal Protocol on Substances That Deplete the Ozone Layer, agreed to under the auspices of the United Nations, in 1987. The Montreal Protocol called for the twenty-four signatory countries to reduce CFCs and halons by 50 percent relative to 1986 levels. Two weeks after the signing of the Montreal Protocol, new evidence was presented by the National Aeronautics and Space Administration (NASA)/World Meteorological Organization (WMO) Ozone Trends Panel that substantially more ozone depletion was occurring over mid- and high-northern latitudes during winter than had been anticipated by earlier science. Within ten days of the NASA/WMO study's release, DuPont announced plans to eliminate CFC production voluntarily and to speed transition to CFC alternatives. ICI later followed DuPont's lead. At a European Community meeting in March 1989, British officials attempting to look good by proposing an 85 percent reduction in CFCs by 1999 were upstaged by representatives from other European countries, who forced an agreement for signatory countries to phase out production of CFCs completely by 2000. The agreement became known as the London Revisions to the Montreal Protocol, and was signed in June 1990. The London Revisions call for high-CFC-consuming signatory countries to end CFC production and consumption by 2000. Some countries have unilaterally used an accelerated phase-out schedule; for example, the United States committed to a complete phase-out by the end of 1995. The London Revisions also included a phase-out of carbon tetrachloride by 2005 and established a schedule for phasing out halogenated CFCs (HCFCs).

While developing countries argued that 80 percent of CFC consumption was by developed countries, it was clear that the Montreal Protocol would be jeopardized if developing countries refused to ratify it. Accordingly, the London Revisions gave low-CFC-consuming countries a ten-year grace period on the phase-out of CFCs. As Alberty and VanDeveer (1996) have observed, these exemptions were required to get key developing countries to support the agreement. Moreover, Alberty and VanDeveer go on to report that India and China later refused to ratify the Montreal Protocol unless an additional side agreement was reached in which rich countries would provide a fund to be used to subsidize the costs of installing technologies for utilizing CFC alternatives in poor countries. As a consequence, the London Amendments created this multilateral fund, and estimates at the time were that approximately $2 billion would be required. Alberty and VanDeveer report that while rich signatory countries originally pledged $240 million if India and China were to sign, actual contributions are far below the pledges. Nevertheless, these side payments from rich to poor countries have become a model for international environmental agreements, such as those attempted for climate change and biodiversity.

CFCs produced in developing countries like China and India and smuggled into developed countries where their production is banned was a problem in the early years of the phase-out, but more recent estimates indicate that much of the smuggling has been curtailed. For example, the *Economist* (1995) reported that CFC production in developing countries increased 87 percent following the phase-out, and exports by 1,700 percent, between 1986 and 1993. The EPA (1999) estimates that between 7.5 and 15 million pounds of Freon (CFC 12 or R 12) was smuggled into the United States each year between 1994 and 1995. The *Economist* article estimated that 20 percent of all CFCs in use in 1995 had been bought on the black market. Since then the U.S. government has clamped down on smuggling. The EPA (1999) estimates that between 5 and 10 million pounds of Freon were smuggled into the United States each year between 1996 and 1997. By mid-1997, 2 million pounds of Freon had been impounded by U.S. Customs, and by the end of February 1999 over ninety individuals and businesses had been charged for smuggling into the United States. The remaining stockpile of Freon in the United States was estimated to be between 24 and 48 million pounds at the beginning of 1999. As the price of the dwindling stocks of Freon continues to rise, the cost of converting to Freon substitutes will become increasingly attractive.

As we have seen, international regulations mandating a CFC ban offered firms like DuPont the Stiglerian solution of new and more profitable markets, which because of higher fixed costs would be more concentrated and thus less competitive than the former CFC marketplace. The financial cost of adjusting to CFC alternatives was diffuse across the many consumer products companies and was still only a small part of overall manufacturing costs, weakening the companies' incentive to organize resistance.

Summary

- Political economy is a method of analyzing the incentives, institutions, and outcomes of governance problems.
- Environmental laws and policies are outcomes of political processes, and so political economy can be used to explain why particular laws and policies occur. The techniques of political economy are also useful in helping us understand cases of "government failure" to design environmental policies that adequately resolve market failures at reasonable cost. Such a critical evaluation can help us understand why existing regulatory schemes do not function as expected and can thus be a first step in the design of more effective regulatory incentives and institutions.
- Economists who study the political process are interested in explaining government policies as a function of (1) optimizing, rational choice behavior by the policymakers (behavior consistent with optimizing over some set of objectives) and (2) behavior modified by incentives, subject to (3) political and other institutions (the rules of the game).
- Stigler (1971) is credited with the development of the capture theory of regulation. In this model, firms (or others) capture the regulatory process because each firm potentially bears a high cost if regulation constrains its behavior, so each firm has a lot at stake. In contrast, while the public as a whole has a lot at stake, generally any one person has only a very small stake in the regulatory process and so has

little incentive to invest resources in affecting the regulatory process. At the same time, there are comparatively few firms relative to the overall public, so the cost of organizing the firms is low compared to the cost of organizing the public. As a result, firms have both the incentive and the better opportunity to invest resources in lobbying for favorable regulation.

- There is evidence consistent with the capture theory of regulation—for example, the infamous revolving-door deals, in which high-level regulators (EPA administrators, for example) leave government and find high-level jobs in the same industry that they had been responsible for regulating.

- Economists have modeled the regulatory process using the tools of political economy by developing a supply and demand framework. The supply of regulation reflects the opportunity cost of effort in developing and shepherding regulation, the psychological cost of supporting regulation that may be inconsistent with the regulator's preferences, and the impacts on the likelihood of reelection. The demand for regulation reflects the willingness to pay of groups that aggregate the interests of those who receive a benefit from regulation. The equilibrium level of effective support for a particular regulation occurs where the supply and the demand for regulation intersect.

- While firms generally have an incentive to lobby for less environmental regulation, there are situations in which firms might actually lobby for more regulation. A firm may lobby for regulation when the regulation would raise its rivals' costs more than its own. Firms may also engage in voluntary clean-up when doing so gives those suffering from pollution just enough relief to keep them from organizing to lobby for regulations that are even more restrictive.

- Political economy models can also be used to explain the sharing rules and voting rules used by self-governing CPR appropriator groups. Heterogeneity in appropriator characteristics and the requirement that nearly all appropriators agree before rules are implemented are two of the leading causes of rule failure in oil, gas, and fishery CPR systems.

- The balance of pressure from various interest groups can also be used to explain the nature of international environmental accords. Oye and Maxwell (1995) show that the Montreal Protocol agreement on control of chlorofluorocarbons (CFCs) was driven by scientific information and pressure by DuPont to phase out CFCs. DuPont's pro-phase-out position is consistent with Hackett's model, since DuPont had developed CFC alternatives and saw an opportunity to dominate in the CFC alternatives market.

Review Questions and Problems

1. Consider the supply and demand model of the political market for regulation described in the chapter. How would the equilibrium level of effective support change if industry groups opposing regulation conducted a successful advertising campaign that cast doubt among the public on the factual basis for the environmental problems addressed by the regulation? Be specific about demand and supply shifts.

2. Suppose that "gunk" is a pollution by-product of manufacturing computer processors. Environmental activists propose regulation to limit emissions of gunk. The proposed regulation leads to pollution-control costs that are heavily concentrated upon the small number of firms that produce computer processors. Control costs under the proposal are estimated to be approximately $100 million per manufacturing facility per year. The benefits of reduced gunk emissions are thinly spread out among the 12 million or so people who live in the region where computer processors are manufactured. It is estimated that each of the 12 million people living near a facility will typically incur around $50 per year in external costs associated with uncontrolled gunk emissions, mostly from occasional mild coldlike symptoms, but gunk is not known to be linked to any deaths, debilitating injuries, or birth defects.

    a. Using Oye and Maxwell's terminology, is this an example of a "Stiglerian" or an "Olsonian" regulatory situation? Carefully explain your reasoning.

    b. Describe the most likely political economic outcomes of proposed gunk-control regulation. Will regulation occur? If so, what form might it take, and how stable will it be? Carefully explain your reasoning.

3. Suppose that the standard industry process for transforming wood chips into pulp for paper manufacturing leads to "badstuff" being flushed into adjacent bodies of water. Badstuff is estimated to create health- and food-related external costs of nearly $1 billion per year and is widely known to elevate cancer risks and birth defects in many localized "hot spots" around the country. Several firms have patented a new process for making pulp that eliminates badstuff pollution. While this patented new process is more expensive than the current industry standard process, it is much, much cheaper than other existing methods of badstuff-free pulp processing. These firms would like to make money from the patent by leasing the technology to other pulp makers and so have an incentive to lobby for more stringent environmental regulations in order to create a market for their new tech-

nology. Because the benefits of cleaning up badstuff are large and concentrated on people who live in the hot-spot areas, pressure groups have developed around environmental groups, physicians' groups, sport fishers, surfers, rafters, and concerned parents of small children. The firms that have developed a badstuff-free pulp-processing technology also have a concentrated benefit in more stringent regulation and have begun a high-profile lobbying and public information campaign in partnership with the other pressure groups.

   a. How might this scenario be different from that described in problem (1) above? Using Oye and Maxwell's terminology, what aspects of this scenario is more Stiglerian than that in problem (1)? Carefully explain your reasoning.

   b. Describe how the most likely political economic outcome of proposed badstuff-control regulation might differ from that of gunk-control regulation in problem (1) above. Carefully explain your reasoning.

   4. Alberty and VanDeveer (1996) have compared the political economics of the Montreal Protocol to that of international attempts at controlling greenhouse gas emissions. Greenhouse gases, primarily carbon dioxide, are emitted from the burning of fossil fuels, especially coal. While North America and Western Europe have been responsible for approximately 60 percent of the human-caused increase in atmospheric carbon dioxide, developing countries such as India and China that will be developing their coal resources are expected to surpass the emissions levels of rich countries in the first third of the twenty-first century. These countries interpret attempts at controlling their coal-based economic development as another example of rich countries trying to keep poor countries from raising incomes and attaining international power.

   a. Relative to the Montreal Protocol, is the international effort to control greenhouse gases more Stiglerian or Olsonian in nature? Why might the political economic outcomes be different from that of CFCs?

   b. In the late 1990s, BP Amoco and Royal Dutch Shell left the Global Climate Coalition, an industry association that has lobbied heavily against the Kyoto Protocol for limiting greenhouse gases, and have have signed on with the pro-treaty group International Climate Change Partnership. How might this development change your answer in 4a above? You can access information on the Business Environmental Leadership Council on the Internet site for the Pew Center on Climate Change (www.pewclimate.org/belc/index.html) to learn more about the corporations that are supporting action on global warming.

5. Go to the Opensecrets.org website (www.opensecrets.org) and research the most recent campaign finance profile of one or more members of the U.S. Senate or House of Representatives. As of 2005, this site also provides a link to the legislation sponsored by the legislator you selected (from the Library of Congress's thomas.loc.gov website). See if you can discern a relationship between the pattern of campaign contributors and the pattern of legislation sponsored by the legislator you selected. See if your results are consistent with the interest group performance evaluations at Project Vote Smart (www.vote-smart.org).

Internet Links

Center for Public Integrity (www.publicintegrity.org): A nonprofit, nonpartisan educational organization that conducts investigative reporting on the role and influence of campaign contributions in the political process.

Lost in Transit: Global CFC Smuggling Trends and the Need for a Faster Phase-Out (http://usembassy.state.gov/ircseoul/wwwf4095.pdf): A 2003 report by the Environmental Investigation Agency, a nonprofit NGO based in London and Washington, D.C., committed to investigating and exposing environmental crime.

Montreal Protocol for Substances That Deplete the Ozone Layer (www.unep.org/ozone/montreal.htm): The primary site for information on the Montreal Protocol, maintained by the United Nations Environment Program.

Opensecrets.org—The Online Source for Money in Politics Data (www.opensecrets.org): This site provides comprehensive information on campaign contributions and is provided by the Center for Responsive Politics. The Center for Responsive Politics is a nonpartisan, nonprofit research group based in Washington, D.C., that tracks money in politics and its effect on elections and public policy.

Project Vote Smart (www.vote-smart.org): Project Vote Smart is a nonpartisan organization offering an Internet library of factual information on candidates for public office at the federal and state level. Coverage is provided in five basic areas: backgrounds, issue positions, voting records, campaign finances, and performance evaluations made by various special interest groups.

The Positive Political Economy of Instrument Choice in Environmental Policy (www.rff.org/Documents/RFF-DP-97-25.pdf): An informative description of environmental political economy by Nathaniel O. Keohane, Richard L. Revesz, and Robert N. Stavins.

References and Further Reading

Agnone, J. 2004. "Explaining Federal Environmental Policy: The Impact of the U.S. Environmental Movement." MA Thesis, Department of Sociology, University of Washington, Seattle, Washington.

Alberty, M., and S. VanDeveer. 1996. "International Treaties for Sustainability: Is the Montreal Protocol a Useful Model?" In *Building Sustainable Societies,* ed. D. Pirages. Armonk, NY: M.E. Sharpe.

Alt, J., and K. Shepsle, eds. 1990. *Perspectives on Positive Political Economy.* Cambridge: Cambridge University Press.

Arrow, K. 1951. *Social Choice and Individual Values.* New Haven: Yale University Press.

Becker, G. 1983. "A Theory of Competition among Pressure Groups for Political Influence." *Quarterly Journal of Economics* (August): 371–400.

Birney, P.W., and A.E. Boyle. 1992. *International Law and the Environment.* Oxford: Oxford University Press.

Bromley, D.W. 1989. *Economic Interests and Institutions: The Conceptual Foundations of Public Policy.* Oxford: Basil Blackwell.

———. 1991. *Environment and Economy: Property Rights and Public Policy.* Oxford: Basil Blackwell.

Buchanan, J., and G. Tullock. 1962. *The Calculus of Consent: Logical Foundations of Constitutional Democracy.* Ann Arbor: University of Michigan Press.

Dasgupta, P. 1992. *An Enquiry into Well-Being and Destitution.* Oxford: Clarendon Press.

Dasgupta, P., and K.-G. Maler. 1992. *The Economics of Transnational Commons.* Oxford: Clarendon Press.

———, eds. 1993. *Poverty, Institutions and Environmental-Resource Base.* Development Research Program No. 39, London School of Economics.

Downing, P. 1981. "A Political Economy Model of Implementing Pollution Laws." *Journal of Environmental Economics and Management* 8: 255–71.

Dryzek, J. 1987. *Rational Ecology: Environment and Political Economy.* London: Basil Blackwell.

Economist. 1995. "Holed Up." 337 (December 9): 63.

Engelberg, S. 1995. "Wood Products Company Helps Write a Law to Derail an E.P.A. Inquiry." *New York Times,* April 26, A16.

Falk, R. 1989. *Revitalizing International Law.* Ames: Iowa State University Press.

Farman, J., B. Gardiner, and J. Shanklin. 1985. "Large Losses of Total Ozone in Antarctica Reveal Seasonal ClO_x/No_x Interaction." *Nature* 315 (16 May): 207–10.

Gamman, J.K. 1994. *Overcoming Obstacles in Environmental Policymaking.* Albany: State University of New York Press.

Greenberg, E. 1993. *Toxic Temptation: The Revolving Door, Bureaucratic Inertia and the Disappointment of the EPA Superfund Program.* Report 12, Center for Public Integrity, Washington, DC.

Gunderson, L.H., C.S. Holling, and S. Light. 1995. *Barriers and Bridges to Renewal of Ecosystems and Environment.* Boston: Kluwer Academic Publishers.

Hackett, S. 1992. "Heterogeneity and the Provision of Governance for Common-Pool Resources." *Journal of Theoretical Politics* 4 (July): 325–42.

———. 1995. "Pollution-Controlling Innovation in Oligopolistic Industries: Some Comparisons between Patent Races and Research Joint Ventures." *Journal of Environmental Economics and Management* 29 (November): 339–56.

Hackett, S., D. Dudley, and J. Walker. 1995. "Heterogeneities, Information, and Conflict Resolution: Experimental Evidence on Sharing Contracts." In *Local Commons and Global Interdependence,* ed. R. Keohane and E. Ostrom. London: Sage.

Hackett, S., E. Schlager, and J. Walker. 1994. "The Role of Communication in Resolving Commons Dilemmas: Experimental Evidence with Heterogeneous Appropriators." *Journal of Environmental Economics and Management* 27: 99–126.

Johnson, R., and G. Libecap. 1982. "Contracting Problems and Regulations: The Case of the Fishery." *American Economic Review* 72: 1005–22.

Kalt, J., and M. Zupan. 1984. "Capture and Ideology in the Economic Theory of Politics." *American Economic Review* 74(3): 279–300.

Keohane, R., and M. Levy, eds. 1993. *Institutions for the Earth.* Cambridge, MA: MIT Press.

Keohane, R., and E. Ostrom, eds. 1995. *Local Commons and Global Interdependence.* London: Sage.

Keohane, R., R. Revesz, and R. Stavins. 1999. "The Positive Political Economy of Instrument Choice in Environmental Policy." In *Environmental and Public Economics: Essays in Honor of Wallace Oates,* eds. A. Panagariya, P. Portney, and R. Schwab, pp. 89–125. London: Edward Elgar, Ltd.

Lewis, C. 1998. *The Buying of the Congress: How Special Interests Have Stolen Your Right to Life, Liberty, and the Pursuit of Happiness.* Washington, DC: Center for Public Integrity.

Libecap, G., and S. Wiggins. 1985. "The Influence of Private Contractual Failure on Regulation: The Case of Oil Field Unitization." *Journal of Political Economy* 93: 690–714.

Maxwell, J., T. Lyon, and S. Hackett. 2000. "Self-Regulation and Social Welfare: The Political Economy of Corporate Environmentalism." *Journal of Law and Economics* 43: 583–618.

Milliman, S., and R. Prince. 1989. "Firm Incentives to Promote Technological Change in Pollution Control." *Journal of Environmental Economics and Management* 17: 247–65.

Molina, M., and F. Rowland. 1974. "Stratospheric Sink for Chlorofluoromethanes: Chlorine Atom Catalysed Destruction of Ozone." *Nature* 249 (28 June): 810–12.

Olson, M. 1965. *The Logic of Collective Action.* Cambridge, MA: Harvard University Press.

Ordeshook, P. 1990. "The Emerging Discipline of Political Economy." In *Perspectives on Positive Political Economy,* ed. J. Alt and K. Shepsle. Cambridge: Cambridge University Press.

Oye, K., and J. Maxwell. 1995. "Self-Interest and Environmental Management." In *Local Commons and Global Interdependence,* ed. R. Keohane and E. Ostrom. London: Sage.

Peltzman, S. 1976. "Toward a More General Theory of Regulation." *Journal of Law and Economics* 19 (August): 211–48.

Porter, G., and B.W. Brown. 1995. *Global Environmental Politics.* 2nd ed. Boulder, CO: Westview Press.

Salop, S., D. Scheffman, and W. Schwartz. 1984. "A Bidding Analysis of Special Interest Regulation: Raising Rivals' Costs in a Rent Seeking Society." In *The Political Economy of Regulation: Private Interests in the Regulatory Process,* ed. R. Rogowsky and B. Yandle. Washington, DC: Federal Trade Commission.

Sands, P.H. 1990. *Lessons Learned in Global Environmental Governance.* Washington, DC: World Resources Institute.

Sanjour, W. 1992. *What EPA Is Like and What Can Be Done about It.* Washington, DC: Environmental Research Foundation.

Shepsle, K., and B. Weingast. 1987. "The Institutional Foundations of Committee Power." *American Political Science Review* 81: 85–104.

Staniland, M. 1985. *What Is Political Economy?* New Haven: Yale University Press.

Stigler, G. 1971. "The Theory of Economic Regulation." *Bell Journal of Economics and Management Science* 2 (Spring): 3–21.

Stone, A., and E. Harpham, eds. 1982. *The Political Economy of Public Policy.* London: Sage.

U.S. Environmental Protection Agency. 1999. *Report on the Supply and Demand of CFC-12 in the United States.* Washington, DC: Environmental Protection Agency.

Vartabedian, R. 1997. "Troubled Corporations Are Top Political Donors: Analysis Shows Big Givers Often Have Poor Reputations or Are Being Probed." *Los Angeles Times.* Reprinted in the *San Francisco Examiner,* September 21, A-5.

Wiggins, S., and G. Libecap. 1985. "Oil Field Unitization: Contractual Failure in the Presence of Imperfect Information." *American Economic Review* 75 (June): 368–85.

9

Motivating Regulatory Compliance: Monitoring, Enforcement, and Sanctions

Introduction

To what extent do government administrative agencies monitor and enforce environmental regulations? Is there sufficient deterrence to prevent large-scale noncompliance by polluting industries? To answer these and other questions, we will first look at the economics of crime and then turn to a more detailed description of how the EPA and other agencies actually administer environmental law. We will also discuss the role of market-based reputational enforcement, voluntary compliance programs, and citizen lawsuits in creating an incentive for compliance.

The Economics of Crime

Law enforcement agencies have limited budgets and must choose the best way of allocating these scarce resources among competing ends. Some law enforcement activities are driven by legislative and other mandates, others by political pressure. From an economic point of view, the efficient method of allocating law enforcement resources is to evaluate enforcement benefits and costs. For example, analysis of crime records may indicate that the incidence of property crime is highest during summer months and lower in the winter. In contrast, alcohol-related automobile accidents may peak around popular holidays. A police department that assigns a fixed number of personnel to property crime and drunk-driving deterrence throughout the year may instead find that seasonally adjusting the allocation of these enforcement resources can reduce the incidence of crime without increasing the overall law enforcement budget. Given that government funds are scarce, it is important from the perspective of society that law enforcement resources be spent efficiently. A municipal government, for example, must allocate its tax income over a set of obligations to its citizens that include road building and maintenance, operation of public schools, law enforcement, and fire control, among others. Increasing the budget share allocated to law enforcement necessarily reduces the budget share allocated to other uses.

To illustrate the economics of law enforcement, consider the following example. To begin, suppose that law enforcement receives a very small budget share, while other municipal programs are well funded. In this case, there may be a relatively high level of crime, and so the *marginal benefits* of increasing law enforcement spending by some increment (such as hiring a new police officer) will tend to be high. Given that other municipal activities are relatively well funded, then shifting resources from other programs to fund this increase in law enforcement leads to a marginal opportunity cost of this shift (the foregone benefits of the money being spent on roads, schools, etc.) that is likely to be relatively low. In this case, spending more on law enforcement entails high marginal benefits and low marginal costs, and so from an economic perspective would seem to make sense.

Now suppose that law enforcement receives a very large share of the municipal budget, while other programs are relatively poorly funded. In this case, the level of criminal activity is likely to be relatively low, as the high level of law enforcement activity will tend to create deterrence, and so the marginal benefits of increasing the law enforcement budget even more may be low. Given that other municipal activities are poorly funded, if we were to shift some additional resources away from these programs to fund additional law enforcement, the marginal opportunity cost of this shift will be relatively high. In this case, spending more on law enforcement entails low marginal benefits (there is already substantial crime deterrence from existing law enforcement activities) and high marginal costs, and thus would not seem to make sense from an economic perspective.

This hypothetical example illustrates several general relationships that economists consider to be important in determining the efficient level of law enforcement activity. First, the marginal benefits of law enforcement spending are presumed to start out high but to decline as more and more resources are allocated to law enforcement activities. Second, the marginal opportunity cost of law enforcement spending may start out low but will rise as more and more resources are allocated away from other beneficial uses to fund

Figure 9.1   **Optimal Level of Crime Control**

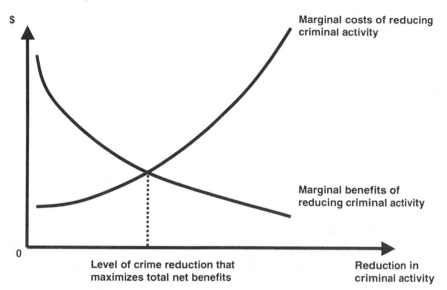

additional law enforcement. From a conceptual perspective, as marginal benefits decline and marginal costs rise, there will be a level of law enforcement spending where marginal benefits equal marginal costs. This is another application of the equimarginal principle, first used in chapter 4 to describe a firm's optimal (profit-maximizing) output level, and later used in chapter 6 in the discussion of the optimal (net benefit-maximizing) level of environmental protection or improvement. In the case of the economics of law enforcement, when resources are allocated to law enforcement up to the point where marginal benefit equals marginal cost, then total net benefits (total benefit minus total cost) will be largest. Any further law enforcement spending will generate marginal benefits that are smaller than marginal costs, which reduces total net benefits in a manner similar to that shown in chapter 6. If society is using an efficiency standard, then the optimal level of law enforcement spending occurs where net benefit is maximized and marginal benefit equals marginal cost, as illustrated in Figure 9.1.

The Economics of Deterrence

A primary goal of law enforcement is to create an adequate *deterrent* to criminal activity. Deterrence is complex, and involves the probability of being caught (detected), the probability of being punished (sanctioned) once you have been detected, followed by the prospect for various penalties (sanctions) being imposed, and the perpetrator's preferences regarding risk, among other factors. Before continuing, we need to address the subject of *risk preference*. One's risk preference regarding a particular risky situation falls into one of three categories. To understand these, suppose you are offered the following choice: (a) $1,000, or, (b) based on outcome of the flip of a fair coin, either $0 (heads) or $2,000 (tails). Of course, the coin is not tossed until after you choose between (a) and (b). Note that the *expected value* of (B) equals 0.5*$0 + 0.5*$2,000 = $1,000, which equals the guaranteed value of (a). A risk-averse person prefers (a) over (b), even though they have the same expected value, since choice (a) avoids risk. A risk-neutral person is indifferent between (a) and (b), as they have the same expected value. A risk-loving person will prefer (b) over (a), even though they have the same expected value, since choice (b) includes risk. A person's risk preference usually varies across different types of choices. It is common to assume that large firms are risk-neutral, though this is not necessarily the case.

Let's first look at deterrence in the context of risk neutrality. To create a sufficient deterrent against violating environmental law, enforcement systems must create an *expected penalty* (the expected value of the gamble of being detected as a lawbreaker and being sanctioned) that exceeds the economic gain from violating environmental law. People, organizations, and firms that are risk-neutral can be thought of as seeking to maximize the expected net benefits from their activities. The economic gain from violating environmental law may include the avoided cost of compliance, higher revenues (such as from illegally harvesting fish, game, or timber for commercial gain), competitive advantage over rival firms, or higher utility (such as from illegally riding a four-wheel-drive truck in sand dunes that are home to endangered plovers). Sanctions can include various levels of fines, damage claims, the disutility of confinement (such as jail or prison), as well as the costs of restitution and court expenses. To keep the analysis simple, we will assume that the only sanction is a fixed monetary fine.

In the case described above, deterrence in any given time period requires that the following relation must exist for a risk-neutral firm:

Expected penalty > economic gain.

And:

Expected penalty = [probability of detection] × [probability of being sanctioned given detection] × $ sanction.

If a person contemplating violating environmental law is risk-averse, but faces the same circumstances described above that deterred a risk-neutral person from breaking the law, will the risk-averse person also be deterred? The answer is yes, since the risk-averse person gains disutility from risk itself, and will therefore be even more strongly deterred by the risk of being sanctioned than the risk-neutral person. In contrast, a risk-loving person may not be deterred unless the expected penalty is far greater than the economic gain from violating the law (why?). In general, adequate deterrence exists when potential environmental lawbreakers evaluate the expected benefits and costs of violating the law and find that the crime does not pay.

In practice, different people, firms, or organizations will have different subjective views of the probability of being detected, and of being sanctioned. As a result, in a given circumstance some risk-neutral or risk-averse people may fail to be deterred because they have the most "optimistic" views of the chances of being detected or sanctioned. As a result, we cannot make generalizations about whether a given level of environmental law enforcement, prosecution, and sanction will fully deter all environmental crimes. One indicator of whether a given law enforcement system is achieving successful deterrence is the recidivism rate—that is, the extent to which past offenders lapse back into past patterns of lawbreaking behavior.

As a final point, our analysis so far has assumed economic rationality, meaning that people, firms, and organizations are able to perceive and weigh benefits and costs, and choose the path that provides the highest net benefits. In practice, crimes also occur due to mental derangement from powerful emotions, drugs, or mental illness. Rational economic models of deterrence are invalid when a person's mind is clouded by factors such as acute anger, methamphetamine abuse, or severe psychosis.

As we have noted, sanctions against lawbreaking activity are only realized when the lawbreaking activity is detected. If a law enforcement agency does not spend much time on monitoring, then a proportionately higher sanction must be available in order to keep the *expected penalty* the same. Figure 9.2 illustrates an equal expected penalty curve, showing that as the probability of successful detection falls, the sanction must rise to keep the expected penalty constant.

It is tempting to think that in practice we could maintain a given level of deterrence by reducing monitoring activities and increasing sanctions, as shown in the upper left-hand portion of the curve in Figure 9.2. This would save public funds that would otherwise be needed for monitoring activity by police or wardens. The problem with this idea is that in the event that a violation is detected, courts may not be willing to impose large statutory penalties for modest violations. To do so would violate the legal norm that

Figure 9.2   **Equal Expected Penalty Curve**

$ sanction

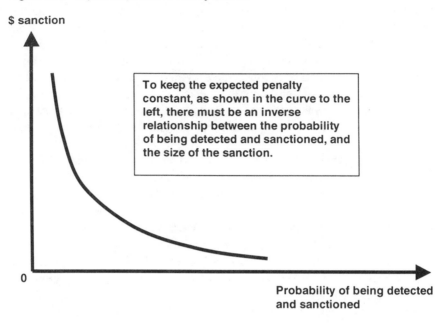

To keep the expected penalty constant, as shown in the curve to the left, there must be an inverse relationship between the probability of being detected and sanctioned, and the size of the sanction.

0

Probability of being detected and sanctioned

penalties should be proportionate to the violation. Moreover, if we reduce the intensity of polluter monitoring relative to other forms of law enforcement, then to maintain deterrence, we may have to impose sanctions on moderate levels of pollution that are larger than the sanctions for more intensely monitored violations such as violent crime. In actual practice, judges and politicians will be unlikely to support large sanctions for modest violations, and therefore it is unlikely to be feasible to operate on the upper left-hand portion of the equal expected penalty curve. If society holds to the legal norm of penalties being proportionate to the harms, then deterrence will be maintained only when society commits sufficient resources to monitoring activity.

It is sometimes argued that the sanction imposed on polluters should be equal to the economic gain from polluting. Yet deterrence will fail if we ignore the probability of detecting and sanctioning polluters. For example, suppose that by being out of compliance with pollution laws, a firm can save $10 million for certain each year in pollution-control costs. Suppose that the statutory penalty is set equal to the economic gain to the polluter from being out of compliance (in this case $10 million). Also assume that there is a 75 percent chance that the firm will be detected as being out of compliance and a 90 percent chance that a judge will impose the sanction if the violation is detected. Has effective deterrence been created? No, because the expected benefit of polluting is $10 million each year; the expected cost of polluting is:

$$0.75 \times 0.90 \times \$10 \text{ million} = \$6.75 \text{ million}.$$

Thus in the example above it pays to be out of compliance, and no effective deterrence has been created. Even if the firm is risk-averse and places a subjective probability of 85 percent rather than 75 percent on the likelihood of detection, it still pays to pollute.

Criminal Penalties and Incarceration Versus Fines and Monetary Damages

Fines and monetary damage claims usually result in lower social costs than incarceration, as Becker (1968) has argued, because society must pay to keep someone behind bars, because criminal cases are more expensive to prosecute and more difficult to prove, and because the person is no longer generating taxable income. But there are a variety of reasons why fines may not generate sufficient deterrence:

- Statutory fines may be too low to provide a deterrent given existing levels of monitoring.
- The value of the lawbreaker's assets may be smaller than the fine.
- Violators may have a subjective probability of being caught that is less than the actual probability.
- Monitoring and penalties may be based on violators having a neutral attitude toward risk, when some violators may actually have a preference for risk.
- Fines may be bargained down in out-of-court settlements, or administrators and judges may fail to impose adequate penalties when violations are observed. Russell (1990) finds, for example, that from 1977 to 1983 the average fine per notice of violation (NOV) issued across various states was less than $100 in many cases and rarely exceeded $2,000. He reported that in many cases firms received fines in fewer than 10 percent of the instances in which a state agency issued an NOV.
- A large component of a fine can often be shifted to insurers, consumers, or taxpayers. For example, monetary damages reduce corporate income and thus can be used as a corporate tax write-off.

A clear advantage of incarceration is that it cannot be shifted, as can fines. Moreover, successful criminal prosecutions create quite a bit of publicity, and the adverse publicity may generate an additional market-based reputational cost for the environmental criminal. On the other hand, there are problems with using criminal sanctions and incarceration to create deterrence. As mentioned above, criminal sanctions impose incarceration costs on society, and the families of those who are incarcerated will experience a loss of income. In addition, criminal sanctions have a higher burden of proof (beyond a reasonable doubt) than do administrative fines or monetary penalties generated from civil lawsuits (preponderance of evidence). As a result, criminal cases are more costly to prosecute and may be less likely to succeed in passing the higher burden of proof. Another problem with criminal sanctioning is that apparently judges have been hesitant to impose prison terms for environmental crimes. In particular, Cohen (1992) finds that out of a sample of 116 cases of firms successfully prosecuted for environmental crime in federal courts from 1984 to 1990, executives were sentenced to prison terms in only 25 (fines were issued in the remainder). Of these 25 cases of prison terms being imposed, 23 were from "small" firms of less than $1 million in sales or with fewer than 50 employees. Finally, many have criticized the "club fed" minimum-security facilities at which many environmental and other "white-collar" criminals are imprisoned as not promoting much in the way of deterrence.

As Segerson and Tietenberg (1992) argue, the traditional penalty structure used in enforcement of environmental laws has involved monetary penalties imposed on firms rather than fines and prison terms imposed on individuals. The effectiveness of this approach in changing the behavior of employees who violate company policies on compliance with environmental law depends critically on firms being able to impose adequate internal sanctions on those employees responsible for the violation. In their model of internal firm organization, Segerson and Tietenberg find that traditional penalties operate efficiently only when employee behavior is fully observable and the firm's compensation structure is sufficiently flexible that it can shift penalties onto guilty employees. Yet the same incentives can be provided by directly penalizing the employee. In practice, however, these conditions are unlikely to be met. Segerson and Tietenberg show that incarceration can be the socially efficient form of deterrence mechanism in more "real-world" circumstances.

Market-based Reputational Enforcement and Voluntary Overcompliance

As we have seen, fines, monetary damages, and criminal penalties are coercive, costly, and will sometimes fail to foster deterrence. Market reputation provides an alternative method of aligning the incentives of firms with those of society. We know, for example, that many corporations care about how they are perceived, as evidenced by the substantial image advertising budgets of many oil, forest products, chemical manufacturing, and other corporations. A particularly striking example is offered by a 1996 civil rights settlement against Texaco. Texaco was involved in a civil rights lawsuit brought by several black employees. After approximately two and a half years without a settlement, an incriminating tape surfaced in November 1996 that strongly supported the claims of the black employees. Black leaders such as Jesse Jackson threatened boycotts. Eleven days after the recording surfaced, and with mounting press coverage of the boycott threats, Texaco settled for $176 million. This costly settlement was widely seen as a way for Texaco to limit harm to its corporate reputation.

Market reputations are most likely to foster deterrence in an environmental context when the following conditions are met:

- Objective information is available on the environmental performance of firms at low cost.
- Consumers and environmentalists can be organized into an effective interest group capable of boycotting environmentally harmful products.
- Quality substitute products are readily available.
- A boycott imposes meaningful costs on firms with a poor environmental record, and meaningful benefits on firms with a strong environmental record. These costs and benefits may derive from price premia or product market shares that derive from the image of the brand or the firm.

In the context of a profit-maximizing firm, reputational enforcement occurs when the economic benefits that derive from that reputation exceed the economic benefits from "cheating" on its reputation. For example, suppose that the gain to a firm from cheating on its reputation is the present value of annual savings from less rigorous environmental performance. There is a cost to cheating, however, which is that consumers discover that the firm no longer warrants a reputational price premium for its product, and price thereafter is lower than before. In this case, it pays for the firm to continue investing in its "reputational asset" (the firm's image and good name) through strong environmental performance when the present value of annual savings from less rigorous environmental performance is smaller than the expected present value of the portion of the firm's future profit stream that depends upon an intact reputational asset. There are a variety of practical problems that constrain the effectiveness of reputational enforcement, however, including the ability of firms to hide destructive practices through subcontrac-

Table 9.1

Sample Programs, EPA Partners for the Environment

Program	Description
Agricultural programs:	
AgSTAR	Promotes the use of biogas recovery systems to methane emissions at dairy and swine operations.
Pesticide Environmental Stewardship	Promotes integrated pest management and reduces pesticide risk in agricultural and nonagricultural settings.
Air quality programs:	
Indoor Environments	Promotes simple, low-cost methods for reducing indoor air-quality risks.
Energy efficiency and global climate change programs:	
Climate Leaders	Encourages companies to develop long-term comprehensive climate change strategies and set greenhouse gas (GHG) emissions reduction goals.
Energy Star	Maximizes energy efficiency in commercial, industrial, and residential settings by promoting new building and product design and practices.
Landfill Methane Outreach	Reduces methane emissions from landfills by installing products to capture gases and produce electricity, steam, or boiler fuel.
Natural Gas STAR	Encourages natural gas industry to reduce leaks through cost-effective best management practices.
Voluntary Aluminum Industrial Partnership	Reduces perflouorocarbon gas emissions (a potent and long-lived greenhouse gas) from aluminum smelting.
Labeling programs:	
Consumer Labeling Initiative	Promotes easier-to-read labels on household cleaners and pesticides to improve consumer safety.

tors or overseas production, and limits to the number of boycotts that consumers can juggle at any given time.

An increasing number of corporations are finding that an environmentally friendly reputation serves as a substitute for conventional advertising. For example, the Environmental Protection Agency (EPA) has a wide variety of voluntary pollution-control programs, described collectively as "Partners for the Environment." A sample of nationwide Partners for the Environment programs is given in Table 9.1. As the material in the table indicates, the Partners for the Environment programs are focused on producing environmental improvements that are not currently required by regulation. A key benefit received by participating firms is the ability to self-identify as being in

Pollution prevention programs:

Design for the Environment	Helps businesses incorporate environmental considerations into the design of products, processes, and technical and management systems.
Green Chemistry	Promotes the design of chemical products and processes that reduce or eliminate the use and generation of hazardous substances.

Regulatory innovation programs:

Performance Track	Recognizes and encourages top environmental performance among private and public facilities that goes beyond compliance with regulatory requirements to achieve environmental excellence.

Waste management programs:

Carpet America Recovery Effort	Aims to increase the amount of recycling and reuse of postconsumer carpet, and reduce the amount of carpet going to landfills.
WasteWise	Encourages business, government, and institutional partners to reduce municipal solid waste through waste prevention, recycling, and buying/manufacturing products with recycled content, benefiting their bottom lines and the environment.

Water programs:

Adopt Your Watershed	Challenges citizens and organizations to join EPA and others who are working to protect and restore rivers, streams, wetlands, lakes, groundwater, and estuaries.

Source: U.S. EPA (www.epa.gov/partners/).

"overcompliance" with environmental law and thereby improve their reputation. This reputational benefit has been explicitly stated on the EPA Partners Internet site: "showing statistically that your organization saved thousands of gallons of water or prevented thousands of tons of waste sends a clear 'green' message to your customers."

Energy Star is one of the more prominent of these voluntary overcompliance programs. According to the EPA (2003b), in 2003 the Energy Star program saved about 110 billion kilowatt hours of electricity and 20,000 megawatts of peak power, the amount of energy required to power about 20 million homes. To earn the Energy Star label on products, manufacturers must meet strict energy efficiency guidelines set by the federal government. In 2003, more than

1,400 manufacturers met Energy Star requirements across a total of 28,000 individual product models in over 40 product categories. Through 2003, Americans had bought more than one billion Energy Star–qualified products.

The 33/50 program was the first of the EPA voluntary overcompliance programs, and it was designed to reduce the 1.5 billion pounds of seventeen high-priority toxic chemical emissions identified in the 1988 Toxic Release Inventory by 33 percent in 1992 and by 50 percent in 1995. A total of 1,300 firms signed up with the 33/50 program, and toxic emissions were ultimately reduced by 55 percent from 1988 levels. Once the goals were reached, the program was discontinued.

Arora and Cason (1995) find that those firms that participate in the EPA voluntary overcompliance programs tend to be large firms in less concentrated industries (more "competitive"), and that *public recognition* (i.e., reputation) is an important element in fostering participation. The research nonprofit organization Resources for the Future (1997) evaluated the performance of the EPA's Common Sense Initiative, 33/50 program, and Project XL, along with several other environmental, health, and safety programs. The researchers argue that these voluntary programs for the most part have had only a peripheral impact on solving important pollution problems. While some of the voluntary programs have had a positive impact, particularly 33/50, they argue that it is difficult to create strong incentives for industry action in the absence of legislation.

Private Auditing

There is a growing movement to have firms and other organizations develop environmental management systems that utilize private, third-party audits of their emissions and wastes. These include programs by the EPA, various states, and the International Organization for Standardization (ISO 14001). Independent third-party auditing companies conduct environmental audits, with neutrality similar to that of auditors of financial statements for the shareholders of publicly traded corporations. There are a number of reasons why firms may want to utilize private third-party environmental audits. One is that the audit may reveal substandard practices that significantly elevate the chances of an environmental disaster, such as the *Exxon Valdez* oil spill, which can cost a firm enormous amounts of money in fines and damage claims. For example, having a certified environmental management system utilizing neutral third-party environmental auditors demonstrates a higher standard of care, which from a legal perspective can shield a company from punitive damage claims. Moreover, failure to reveal a publicly traded corporation's excessive exposure to such financial hazards to its shareholders can result in the firm's being further exposed to class-action lawsuits brought by shareholders. Audits can also help companies identify areas where costly waste of energy or materials can be reduced.

A potential problem with environmental audits can arise if the information can be used to fine a company or sue for damages resulting from discovery of past noncompliance or past tortious acts. To maintain the incentive for environmental auditing, currently a number of states grant environmental audit privilege, which means that the right to employ a private third-party environmental auditor is deemed more important from a policy perspective than the information generated by the audit. This is the privilege given to disclosure to one's spouse or attorney or priest. Some states grant amnesty to firms that discover violations of environmental law using an environmental management system and correct the problems causing the compliance failure.

In 2000 the EPA issued final policy guidelines for auditing and self-policing. As Pfaff and Sanchirico (2004) note, the EPA audit policy serves as a guideline for federal prosecution and settlement negotiation. From a technical standpoint, the policy concerns the component of fines linked to the significance or "gravity" of the offense. As Pfaff and Sanchirico report, under the EPA audit policy the gravity component of a fine is eliminated when a firm discovers a violation through an internal audit program, voluntarily discloses the violation within 21 days of discovery without prompting, corrects the violation within 60 days, takes steps to prevent recurrence, and cooperates with the EPA throughout. In order to eliminate the gravity component of a fine, the violation cannot be part of a pattern of repeated violations or be one that has caused or may cause "serious harm."

Pfaff and Sanchirico (2004) provide evidence that the vast majority of violations uncovered from self-audits represent relatively minor reporting or record-keeping violations, rather than actual emissions violations, and question whether the EPA's audit policy provides sufficient incentives for firms to report serious emissions violations. Since the policy represents a guideline, not an enforceable promise of reduced fines, firms may be hesitant to report serious emissions violations voluntarily. Moreover, the policy does not cover the economic benefit component of fines, and thus may not offer sufficient incentive to report. As a final point, Pfaff and Sanchirico note that firms may volunteer relatively insignificant violations to distract regulator attention from more serious, undisclosed violations.

Incentive Enforcement Systems

Unlike environmental audits, which are designed to help firms identify wasteful and hazardous processes, incentive enforcement systems are designed to give polluting firms an incentive to comply with environmental regulations, thus reducing monitoring and enforcement costs while maintaining deterrence. To illustrate how they work, consider the following regulatory scheme. The Clean Water Act, the 1990 Clean Air Act (CAA) amendments, and the enabling legislation for the Toxics Release Inventory all require that firms monitor and self-report their emissions. Falsifying is a criminal offense, primarily followed up on by citizen groups in citizen lawsuits. Moreover, both the EPA and the Department of Justice have developed incentive policies in which those who self-report and resolve environmental violations can qualify for reduced or suspended penalties.

Economists have also researched the question of incentive-based enforcement systems. For example, consider the following system:

- Firms self-report their emissions and pay fines if they exceed allowed emissions.
- The government monitors more vigorously the lower the reported level of emissions.
- If actual emissions exceed reported emissions, the firm pays additional pollution fines plus an additional fine for having made a false claim.

The advantage of this scheme, devised by Malik (1993), is that with some level of government monitoring and an adequate penalty for falsification, the scheme gives firms an incentive to report their actual emissions and lowers the cost of government monitoring efforts.

EPA Enforcement

The Office of Regulatory Enforcement in the EPA's Office for Enforcement and Compliance Assurance works with states, EPA regional offices, tribes, and other federal agencies to ensure compliance with the nation's environmental laws through facility inspections, civil enforcement actions, and compliance assistance and incentives. The EPA does not have the resources to monitor all pollution sources for compliance with environmental law. Monitoring resources tend to be focused on the major point sources of air and water pollution. In the case of water pollution discharges, for example, the EPA requires by law that the firms submit a record of the nature of the discharge to the EPA and that each firm report the status of its compliance with the pollution permit that it has been given.

The nature and the source of the pollution affect the feasibility of effective enforcement. Hazards that arise on a decentralized basis—such as toxic wastes, agricultural runoff, radon in homes, and asbestos in buildings—

oftentimes pose substantial enforcement problems because of the large number of pollution sources involved and the difficulty in monitoring the responsible parties. The process of screening chemicals and regulating the sale of commercially produced chemicals is a relatively easy monitoring function for the EPA, as is the process of monitoring the use of hazard-warning labels.It is much more difficult to monitor to assure that hazardous products are used appropriately. Moreover, the disposal of chemical containers and the dilution of insecticides are among the decentralized activities that pose nearly insurmountable monitoring problems. Providing hazard information and hoping that people adopt the appropriate ethic may be all that an administrative agency can do in such cases. In order to increase the impact of the federal government's enforcement efforts, both the EPA and the Department of Justice have recently instituted incentive policies in which firms and individuals that self-report and resolve violations can qualify for reduced or suspended penalties.

EPA compliance monitoring involves the following range of activities:

- Surveillance: a pre-inspection activity that consists of obtaining general site information prior to actually entering the facility. Examples may include ambient sampling at the property line or observations of activity at the site.
- Inspections (on site): may include record reviews, observations, sampling, or interviews.
- Record reviews: may be conducted at EPA, state or local offices, or at the facility, and may or may not be combined with fieldwork. Records may be derived from routine self-monitoring requirements, inspection reports, citizen/employee tips, or remote sensing.
- Investigations:generally more comprehensive than inspections and may be warranted when an inspection or record review suggests the potential for serious, widespread, and/or continuing civil or criminal violations.

In terms of EPA sanctions, there are two options:

- Impose administrative penalties, which are legislatively established in environmental law, and are usually modest in size and limited in terms of the circumstances in which they can be levied.
- Refer cases to the Department of Justice for criminal or civil prosecution.

The EPA's Office for Enforcement and Compliance Assurance has established specific enforcement policies for air, water, and other pollution media. The various policies contain the special designation of "significant noncompliers" for facilities that commit the worst offenses; the air program calls them "high-priority violators." The exact criteria for significant noncompliers vary with each statute. For example, under the Resource Conservation and Recovery Act, operating a treatment, storage, or disposal facility without a permit classifies the facility as a significant noncomplier. Within the framework of these enforcement policies, the EPA periodically establishes national enforcement and compliance priorities based on new scientific knowledge, social and political pressures, and the extent to which performance goals are being met.

An analysis contained in EPA (2003a) was critical of the effectiveness of EPA enforcement efforts. The report noted that data for enforcement efforts by the EPA and the states for the period 1999–2001 show that only a low percentage (9–13 percent) of enforcement actions were taken in a timely and appropriate manner, only 39–40 percent of formal actions resulted in penalties, and average penalties that were imposed were low (about $5,000 per action). One of the recommendations from EPA (2003a) was to establish a Facility Watch List. The EPA anticipates that the Facility Watch List will be a key effort to address significant noncompliance at the facility level, since it identifies facilities that have been in significant noncompliance for lengthy periods with no apparent formal enforcement response from the EPA or the relevant state.

As an agency of the administrative branch of the federal government, the EPA and its enforcement efforts are politicized and tend to reflect the priorities of the president. External events such as the terrorist attacks on September 11, 2001, can change law enforcement priorities to the detriment of environmental enforcement. Data from the George W. Bush administration of the EPA indicate, for example, that the number of EPA civil referrals to the Department of Justice declined from previous levels, as did the total dollar value of civil lawsuit settlements and the number of facilities inspected by the EPA.

It is important to note that the majority of environmental enforcement activity in the United States is carried out by state environmental agencies, since most states have received authority from the EPA to administer federal environmental laws under EPA oversight. Of course, states also administer and enforce their own state laws. There is considerable variation in the vigor with which states enforce environmental laws. Some states have a strong record of performance in following EPA mandates, while others are relatively lax. In the latter case, there may be inadequate compliance monitoring, and when violations are detected, those responsible for enforcement may rarely respond with meaningful penalties.

Before we turn to civil and criminal referrals to the Department of Justice, it is useful to see how legislation creates administrative penalty tools for the EPA. For example, under the 1990 Clean Air Act amendments, the EPA was granted additional administrative authority to assess penalties without filing a court case and involving the Department of Justice. This administrative authority allows the EPA to order payment of penalties of up to $200,000 and/or order that violations be corrected. Those who receive an EPA order can appeal to an administrative law judge. The EPA can also issue "field citations" of up to $5,000 per day to violators when an EPA inspector finds certain types of violations, such as nonfunctioning monitoring equipment. These new authorities allow the EPA to act on smaller cases without having to incur the time and expense of a federal court action. The amendments also expand the notion of "emergency actions" to include threats to the environment, rather than specifically to human health. These emergency orders have fines that range from $5,000 to $25,000 per day, and add a criminal penalty of up to five years in prison for knowingly violating an emergency order. Other criminal penalties include five years for knowingly and seriously violating the CAA, doubled for second offenses; fifteen years for knowingly releasing hazardous air pollution that places people in imminent danger of death or bodily injury; one year for negligent releases; one year for tampering with a monitoring device; and the criminalization of the falsification of pollution data.

Selected Civil and Criminal Case Summaries from the Department of Justice

The civil and criminal case summaries in this section are taken from Department of Justice records and press releases.

A 2005 settlement will require Weyerhaeuser Company to clean up the Plainwell Mill and 12th Street Landfill in Plainwell, Michigan, which are portions of the Kalamazoo River Superfund site. Weyerhaeuser will pay $6.2 million, which the EPA will use to fund the clean-up of polychlorinated biphenyl (PCB) contamination in the Kalamazoo River. Weyerhaeuser is one of several companies responsible for PCB contamination at the Kalamazoo River Superfund Site, which includes the mill, the landfill, a portion of the Kalamazoo River, and other areas. The PCB contamination at the site resulted primarily from paper companies that produced and processed PCB-containing carbonless copy paper along the river between the 1950s and 1970s. The EPA estimates that there are hundreds of thousands of pounds of PCBs in the soil and sediment at the site. Investigations at the site indicate that PCB contamination has had an adverse impact on bird and fish populations. For several decades, fish consumption advisories have urged consumers to limit the type and amount of fish that they eat from the river.

A 2004 settlement gained by the U.S. Department of Justice in collaboration with the State of Indiana resulted in eight companies having to pay nearly $60 million to restore natural resources in the Grand Calumet River and Indiana Harbor Canal. In addition to the payments that will be made to fund restoration projects in the waterway, the companies have agreed to set aside for habitat protection 233 acres of land that contain important fish and wildlife habitat. Led by the Indiana Department of Environmental Management and the U.S. Department of Interior through its Fish and Wildlife Service, a team of seven federal and state agencies had been working since 1996 to determine the extent of natural resource damages from a century of industrial releases of oil and other hazardous substances into the waterway. Studies showed that the releases contaminated the river's water and streambed, affecting migratory birds, fish, invertebrates, and aquatic insects.

A 1999 settlement with seven heavy-duty diesel engine manufacturers led to the largest Clean Air Act penalty up to that time. The settlement resolved charges that the companies violated the CAA by installing software that allowed engines to meet EPA emission standards during testing but disabled the emission control system during normal highway driving. The settlement is expected to prevent 75 million tons of nitrous oxide air pollution over the next twenty-seven years and reduce such emissions from diesel engines by one-third by 2003. The initiative also resulted in an $83.4 million penalty payment, the largest civil environmental penalty imposed up to that time.

In 1999 the Fourth Circuit Court of Appeals upheld imposition of a Clean Water Act (CWA) civil penalty in excess of $12 million, the largest penalty awarded under the CWA up to that time. The appellate court affirmed a lower court ruling that Smithfield Foods and its subsidiaries violated the CWA by discharging illegal levels of phosphorous, ammonia, cyanide, and fecal coliform from their slaughterhouse into the Pagan River in Virginia. The court held that an agreement between the company and the state of Virginia that allowed Smithfield to exceed its permit limits did not excuse Smithfield's violations because the agreement was not part of the permit approved by EPA and because Virginia's state law was not comparable to the federal law.

In 1999 the District Court in Arkansas entered final judgment for the United States in the amount of $100.5 million, plus future costs, concluding eighteen years of litigation at the Vertac Superfund Site. The Vertac Site, the location of an herbicide manufacturing plant that operated from the 1960s to the 1980s and manufactured, among other things, Agent Orange, was one of the worst dioxin-contaminated sites in the country. This was the largest adjudicated Superfund judgment up to that time.

In January 1999 Buddy Frazier and his associates, Chance Gaines and James Bragg, were sentenced to prison for thirty, thirty-three, and twenty-four months, respectively, for multiple asbestos work practice and worker identification violations in connection with the demolition of a manufacturing building in Marshfield, Wisconsin. The defendants had recruited untrained homeless men from a community kitchen in Chattanooga, Tennessee, obtained fraudulent asbestos training identification cards for these workers, and directed them to strip asbestos pipe insulation without first wetting the material, thereby exposing them to the severe health risks associated with asbestos inhalation. In connection with this prosecution, the Environment and Natural Resources Division of the Department of Justice launched a nationwide project with the EPA and the National Coalition for the Homeless to halt the exploitation of homeless and itinerant workers for illegal asbestos work.

In 1998 the Department of Justice entered into a consent decree with the FMC Corporation resolving numerous violations of the Resource Conservation and Recovery Act (RCRA) at an FMC facility on the Shoshone-Bannock tribe's Fort Hall Indian Reservation in Pocatello, Idaho. The facility is the world's largest producer of elemental phosphorus, which is used in detergents, beverages, foods, synthetic lubricants, and pesticides. The most serious of the RCRA violations involved mismanagement of phosphorus wastes in ponds. The wastes burn vigorously when exposed to the air, and also generate toxic gases that can cause serious health and environmental problems. FMC agreed to spend approximately $158 million to settle this case as well as another $11.8 million as a civil penalty, the largest obtained under RCRA up to that time.

In September 1996 U.S. District Court Judge Hector Laffitte sentenced three corporations—Bunker Group Puerto Rico, Bunker Group Incorporated, and New England Marine Services—to each pay a $25 million fine and complete a five-year term of corporate probation. On April 25, 1996, a federal jury convicted the companies of sending out an unseaworthy vessel, negligently discharging oil, and failing to notify the Coast Guard that a hazardous condition existed on the vessel. As a result, 750,000 gallons of oil were spilled into the waters off Puerto Rico and onto its popular Escambron Beach at the height of the tourist season in January 1994. At the time, this was considered one of the largest fines ever imposed for an environmental crime.

California Enforcement

Most states have environmental laws that mirror those at the federal level. California offers a good illustration. Most California environmental statutes contain provisions allowing for criminal liability of both firms and individuals who violate these statutes. Civil liability in the form of civil penalties and injunctive relief can also be imposed. Criminal penalty provisions are included in the following California environmental and other related statutes (and their federal counterparts):

- The Porter-Cologne Water Quality Control Act (federal counterpart: Clean Water Act). California is authorized to implement the provisions of the CWA in its state waters. California law provides for substantial felony penalties for knowingly violating its own Porter-Cologne Water Quality Control Act.
- California Clean Air Act (federal counterpart: Clean Air Act and amendments). The California Clean Air Act provides for criminal penalties for violation of a permitee's emissions permit. The criminal sanction is increased if the violation occurred knowingly or as a result of negligence. An emission that causes or threatens serious bodily injury or death can result in a fifteen-year prison term and a fine of up to $1 million.
- The Hazardous Waste Control Act (federal counterpart: Resource Conservation and Recovery Act). Under California law, criminal penalties exist for failure to properly transport, store, handle, or maintain records of hazardous waste. This law also provides for civil liability and injunctive relief that can be imposed cumulatively with the criminal penalties. Violations that result in great bodily injury or cause a substantial probability of death can result in up to three years in prison and fines of $250,000 per day of violation.
- The Hazardous Substances Account Act (federal counterpart: Comprehensive Environmental Response, Compensation, and Liability Act [CERCLA]). Under California law, criminal penalties exist for failing to report a release, or a threatened release, of a hazardous material, for particular failures to file disposal reports, and for certain record-keeping violations. Penalties for subsequent violations range up to fines of $50,000 per day and imprisonment for two years.
- California Corporate Criminal Liability Act. Also known as the "be a manager, go to jail" law, it makes corporations and their managers criminally liable when they fail to warn their employees of, or report to a California regulatory agency, the existence of "serious concealed dangers of which the corporation and its managers have actual knowledge. . . . A serious concealed danger is normal or foreseeable use of a product or practice that creates a substantial probability of death, great bodily harm, or serious exposure to an individual to whom the danger is not readily apparent" (Pen C sect. 387[b][3, 4]). Up to three years in prison and fines of $25,000 can be imposed on individuals, and fines of up to $1 million can be imposed on corporations ("Criminal Penalties and Considerations" 1993).

Compliance

The Clean Water Act, the 1990 Clean Air Act amendments, and the enabling legislation for the Toxics Release Inventory all require that firms monitor and self-report their emissions. Falsifying is a criminal offense, primarily followed up on by citizen groups in citizen lawsuits.

One issue is initial compliance—has the firm installed the necessary technology and/or established the necessary monitoring/control functions? Another issue is compliance over time—"continuous" compliance. There are no comprehensive estimates of the extent of continuous compliance. There are indications, however, that while initial compliance rates tend to be high (80–90 percent), continuous compliance rates are much lower, approximately 45 percent or so (Russell 1990). Why might compliance rates be exaggerated? Perhaps because the EPA had commonly relied upon pre-announced on-site inspections of stationary/point-source polluters, which gives firms an opportunity to install, fix, or turn on pollution-control equipment. Typical inspection rates are once a year, with the inspection usually restricted to making sure that pollution-control equipment is functioning properly.

According to the EPA (1999), regional EPA staff conducted 23,237 inspections in 1998, an increase of 19 percent over 1997. Nevertheless, these inspections covered only 1.7 percent of the 1,366,634 core regulated facilities that were required to comply with environmental regulation (or just 0.29 percent of all core and noncore regulated facilities). The EPA found a wide range of different rates of significant noncompliance with environmental regulations in 1998. For example, 11.8 percent of automobile assembly facilities, 19 percent of pulp manufacturers, 45 percent of petroleum refineries, and 72.7 percent of integrated iron and steel mills were found to be in significant noncompliance with air quality regulations. Overall, in 1998 the EPA estimated that 7 percent of air pollution sources were found to be in significant noncompliance, though a review by the inspector general suggests that violations are underreported. Approximately 20 percent of waste combusters and landfill operators were in significant noncompliance with the Resource Conservation and Recovery Act, and about one-third of tank owners and operators are likewise out of compliance with the Underground Storage Tank program requirements. Finally, about one-quarter of all drinking water systems are out of compliance with the Safe Drinking Water Act.

Mintz (2004) reports there were 20,417 EPA field inspections in 2000 and 17,668 in 2002. This decline may reflect a change in law enforcement priorities following the September 11th terrorist attack, or the different political priorities of the George W. Bush administration relative to the Clinton administration. According to the EPA (2003a), approximately 25 percent of major facilities were in significant noncompliance with their Clean Water Act (CWA) permits at any given time. Moreover, that rate of significant non-compliance had effectively remained constant since 1994.

Citizen Suits

Most environmental laws have provisions that allow for private citizens to sue polluters for violating statutes. The possibility of citizen lawsuits leverages government enforcement efforts by empowering people who are directly harmed by pollution to do something about it. These suits can force compliance, may require damages restitution, and can impose sanctions as well—for hazardous waste (RCRA) and Superfund (CERCLA). Successful citizen lawsuits are difficult, however, because of the evidentiary requirements. Such suits have been most common in Clean Water Act cases where monthly self-reporting is required and where private citizens can monitor waterways. Citizen suits are very important because they can counteract political pressure brought to bear on the EPA and the revolving-door motive for ignoring pollution violations.

Prior to the 1990 CAA amendments, citizens could only sue violators to force compliance; under the 1990 amendments, citizen suits can include cash penalties, which, if the suits are successful, go into an enforcement fund. Congress authorized awards of up to $10,000 to citizens who provide information leading to criminal convictions or civil penalties for violation of the CAA. Unfortunately, state and federal employees are exempt. Recent state law in Arizona has eliminated the right of citizens to sue a company for polluting private or public property. The public may still sue the state to take action, but only if the state agrees that there has been a violation. Thus if the state decides to ignore violations, citizens in Arizona no longer have recourse through citizen suits.

Summary

- The economics of crime is such that the marginal benefits decline as more and more enforcement effort is exerted, while the marginal costs tend to rise. As a result, the level of enforcement activity that maximizes total net benefits will generally imply less than complete prevention of illegal activity.
- Fines and prison time are the common ways that state and federal agencies enforce environmental laws. While fines generate fewer social costs and can be imposed with a lower burden of proof, prison time cannot be shifted onto insurance companies, consumers, or taxpayers, and can have a substantial deterrent effect on individuals.

- Deterrence occurs when crime does not pay. In the context of risk-neutrality, deterrence occurs when the expected penalties associated with a violation exceed the economic gains from being out of compliance. The expected penalty is the monetary or criminal sanction, weighted by the probability of detection and the probability of the penalties actually being imposed given detection. Since the probability of being caught and penalized is less than 100 percent, the actual penalties that are imposed must exceed the gain from being out of compliance.
- In practice, it is difficult to know whether a given level of compliance monitoring and a given penalty structure is sufficient to create deterrence for particular firms, organizations, and members of the public. People (and managers of firms and organizations) have different preferences for risk and different, subjective, views of the probability of being caught and of being punished. Moreover, not all environmental law violators are economically rational, and consequently may not respond in their own best interest to the legal incentives for compliance.
- Market reputations can also play a role in providing an incentive for firms to be "environmentally friendly." Consumer boycotts are one example, and voluntary overcompliance programs such as the EPA's Green Lights Program can act as substitutes for image advertising. Consumers must be environmentally conscious and well informed for these reputational systems to function.
- Incentive schemes have been developed and implemented in laws such as the Clean Water Act that require self-reporting and provide for penalties for false reporting. These schemes have the potential for generating deterrence while saving the government some monitoring costs.
- Citizen lawsuit provisions of environmental and natural resource protection laws give members of the public legal standing to sue alleged lawbreakers. These provisions can provide an important source of deterrence.

Review Questions and Problems

1. Suppose that a firm can increase its profits by $1 million each year by choosing not to comply with environmental regulations. The firm is a risk-neutral expected profit maximizer. The probability that the firm will be detected and found to be out of compliance is 40 percent, and the probability that a judge will impose a penalty given detection is 75 percent. If the only penalty is a fine, what is the minimum fine necessary to get this firm to comply with environmental regulations?

2. Suppose that a firm can increase its profits by $2 million each year by

choosing not to comply with environmental regulations. The firm is a risk-neutral expected profit maximizer. The firm anticipates that if it is detected and found to be out of compliance, it will have to pay a penalty of $3 million. If the only penalty is this fine, what is the minimum probability of detection and being fined necessary to get this firm to comply with environmental regulations?

3. Economist Gary Becker (1968) has argued that fines are a more efficient form of penalty than prison terms. While fines can be calibrated to create deterrence, prison terms create higher social costs because they eliminate a person's productive income and require society to pay tens of thousands of dollars annually to hold the person in prison. Give some reasons why there may be economically good arguments for making environmental violations punishable by prison terms.

4. Go to the Internet site for the Environmental and Natural Resources Division of the U.S. Department of Justice (www.usdoj.gov/enrd). Going beyond the examples given in the textbook, find an example of a recent and significant civil penalty or criminal sentence being imposed for violation of environmental. law. Summarize the key elements of the case, including the name of the company or individual, the relevant environmental law, the nature of the violation, and the penalty imposed.

Internet Links

Code of Federal Regulations (CFR) (www.access.gpo.gov/nara/cfr): Read about actual monitoring procedures and administrative and criminal penalties embedded within various environmental regulations. The Clean Air Act, for example, is contained in Chapter 85 of Title 42 of the CFR.

Cornell University Legal Information Institute's Coverage of Environmental Law (www.law.cornell.edu/topics/environmental.html): Read about federal and state statutory environmental law, major federal and state court decisions having to do with the environment, and international environmental law.

Environmental and Natural Resources Division of the Department of Justice (www.usdoj.gov/enrd): "The nation's environmental lawyer." Areas of responsibility include litigation concerning the protection, use, and development of the nation's natural resources and public lands; wildlife protection; Indian rights and claims; clean-up of the nation's hazardous waste sites; the acquisition of private property for federal use; and defense of environmental challenges to government programs and activities.

Environmental Investigation Agency (www.eia-international.org): The Environmental Investigation Agency (EIA) is an independent, international campaigning organization committed to investigating and exposing environmental crime.

EPA Compliance and Enforcement Portal (www.epa.gov/compliance): Source of information on compliance monitoring and enforcement efforts.

EPA Partners for the Environment Programs (www.epa.gov/partners): Read more about EPA-sponsored voluntary overcompliance programs.

EPA Enforcement Actions, Criminal Referrals, and Settlements (http:// cfpub.epa.gov/compliance/newsroom/): Read about administrative actions, penalties, and criminal referrals by the EPA.

References and Further Reading

Arora, S., and T. Cason. 1995. "Why Do Firms Overcomply with Environmental Regulations? Understanding Participation in EPA's 33/50 Program." Working paper, University of Southern California, Los Angeles.

Becker, G. 1968. "Crime and Punishment: An Economic Approach." *Journal of Political Economy* 78: 169–217.

Cohen, M. 1992. "Environmental Crime and Punishment: Legal/Economic Theory and Empirical Evidence on Enforcement of Environmental Statutes." *Journal of Criminal Law and Criminology* 82–84: 1053–1108.

"Criminal Penalties and Considerations." 1993. *California Civil Practice—Environmental Litigation.* San Francisco: Bancroft-Whitney Law Publishers.

Cushman, J. 1996. "States Shield Businesses from Ecological Liability." *San Francisco Examiner*, April 7, A-2.

Klein, B., and K. Leffler. 1981. "The Role of Market Forces in Assuring Contractual Performance." *Journal of Political Economy* 89 (August): 615–41.

Magat, W., and K. Viscusi. 1990. "Effectiveness of the EPA's Regulatory Enforcement: The Case of Industrial Effluent Standards." *Journal of Law and Economics* 33 (October): 331–59.

Malik, A. 1993. "Self-Reporting and the Design of Policies for Regulating Stochastic Pollution." *Journal of Environmental Economics and Management* 24: 241–57.

Mintz, J. 2004. "'Treading Water': A Preliminary Assessment of EPA Enforcement During the Bush II Administration." *Environmental Law Reporter* 34: 10,933–53.

Pfaff, A., and C. Sanchirico. 2004. "Big Field, Small Potatoes: An Empirical Assessment of EPA's Self-Audit Policy." *Journal of Policy Analysis and Management* 23(3): 415–32.

Polinsky, A., and S. Shavell. 1979. "The Optimal Tradeoff Between the Probability and Magnitude of Fines." *American Economic Review* 69: 880–91.

Resources for the Future. 1997. "Voluntary Incentives Are No Shortcut to Pollution Abatement." *Resources* 126 (Winter): 18.

Russell, C. 1990. "Monitoring and Enforcement." In *Public Policies for Environmental Protection,* ed. P. Portney. Washington, DC: Resources for the Future.

Russell, C., W. Harrington, and W. Vaughn. 1985. *Enforcing Pollution Control Laws.* Washington, DC: Resources for the Future.

Segerson, K., and T. Tietenberg. 1992. "The Structure of Penalties in Environmental Enforcement: An Economic Analysis." *Journal of Environmental Economics and Management* 23: 179–200.

Tietenberg, T., ed. 1992. *Innovation in Environmental Policy: Economic and Legal Aspects of Recent Developments in Liability and Enforcement.* Cheltingham, U.K.: Edward Elgar.

U.S. Environmental Protection Agency. 1999. *Enforcement and Compliance Assurance: FY 1998 Accomplishments Report.* Washington, DC: EPA.

———. 2003a. *A Pilot for Performance Analysis of Selected Components of the National Enforcement and Compliance Assurance Program.* Washington, DC: EPA.

———. 2003b. *Protecting the Environment—Together: Energy Star and Other Voluntary Programs, Climate Protection Partnerships Division, 2003 Annual Report.* Washington, DC: EPA.

10

Creating Economic Incentives for Environmental Protection and Resource Management

Introduction

Broadly speaking, incentive regulation is concerned with the design of regulatory schemes that use economic instruments such as prices, taxes, subsidies, bonds, liability, or markets to align individual incentives with the common good. Many incentive regulatory schemes are indirect; policymakers control pollution emissions or other environmental standards indirectly by modulating incentives rather than through direct controls and standards. A common example is the can and bottle redemption deposit schemes used by states such as California, Michigan, and Oregon to promote recycling, thus limiting littering and landfill flows. In California, for example, when one purchases a canned or glass-bottled soft drink or beer, included in the purchase price is a return deposit, such as those charged by equipment rental firms to assure that the equipment is returned in good condition. This deposit is returned when the empty beverage container is taken to a recycling center. Glass and aluminum container deposits are a form of indirect control and can be contrasted with a direct-control requirement that mandates the recycling of glass and aluminum containers. Another example of incentive regulation is the German "take-back" system (discussed in chapter 14) whereby manufacturers are required to take back the products that they make once they are worn out. The take-back program gives manufacturers an incentive to design products for low-cost reuse or recycling and so is an indirect way

Table 10.1

Summary of Economic Instruments for Environmental Protection and Resource Management

Instrument	Effects and impacts
Allowance trading systems	Lowers the cost of complying with environmental regulations
Environmental bonds (such as deposit-refund systems)	Fosters deterrence and provides funds for clean-up, restoration, and mitigation; promotes recycling
Environmental liability systems	Fosters deterrence and provides funds for clean-up, restoration, and mitigation
Market-based reputations	Environmentally conscious consumers reward "green" businesses
Property rights systems	Allows for effective resource governance, may prevent tragedy of the commons, and can create an incentive for productivity-enhancing investments
Pollution or effluent taxes and use fees	Reduces market distortions by internalizing exernalities and causing price to reflect marginal social cost; promotes less-harmful alternatives
Subsidies, loans, and grants for environmentally friendly investments	Promotes investment in clean technology and voluntary overcompliance

of lowering the cost of materials reuse and recycling. Liability standards and the potential for civil and criminal penalties offer another form of incentive regulation, as described in chapter 8. Still another example of incentive regulation is offered by funding garbage collection based on per-bag charges rather than through a fixed fee. The per-bag fee creates an indirect incentive to reduce the amount of garbage created by households.

A summary of some regulatory schemes that use various economic instruments to foster more environmentally friendly behavior is given in Table 10.1.

It is beyond the scope of this chapter to provide a complete accounting of the various incentive systems. Instead, the chapter will focus on two prominent forms of market-based environmental policy instruments, namely, marketable pollution allowances and environmental taxes and subsidies. Some additional incentive schemes will be presented in chapter 15. The discussion on environmental taxes in this chapter builds on the theoretical foundation regarding externalities and Pigouvian taxes that was developed in chapter 4.

Early environmental regulation has been criticized for its lack of beneficial incentives. The common approach was to use direct controls, also known as "command-and-control" regulation. Command-and-control regulation specifies how pollution is to be reduced through the application of uniform standards for firms, most prominently technology-based ("technology-forcing") or performance-based standards. *Technology based standards* specify the methods and equipment that firms must use in order to comply with environmental regulation. *Performance-based standards* set uniform control targets for all regulated firms, but unlike with technology-based standards, firms are given some choice over how the target is actually met (Stavins 2000). An example of a technology-based standard is the regulatory requirement that automobile manufacturers install catalytic converters rather than allowing automobile companies to find the cheapest or most effective method of control. Performance-based standards that establish uniform control targets for particular industries and pollutants do not allow for the trading of allowed emissions across sources.

There are at least two problems with command-and-control regulation. First, command-and-control regulation tends to lock in specific environmental technologies, and therefore retards the development of new and improved methods of pollution control. Second, as we will see in the next section of the chapter, uniform performance standards imposed on an industry in which firms have widely different pollution abatement costs results in a higher cost for achieving a given level of aggregate control. The original Clean Air Act (CAA) of 1970 provides one example of the problems associated with using command-and-control environmental regulation (Ackerman and Hassler 1981). At the insistence of U.S. senators from eastern states with high-sulfur coal, the CAA required that costly scrubbers be installed on coal-burning electricity-generating facilities, even though many could have generated the same clean-up by shifting to low-sulfur coal. While this requirement was politically efficient—the CAA could not otherwise have passed Congress—it fails to be economically cost-efficient. In his survey of eight empirical studies, Tietenberg (1985) found that the ratio of aggregate pollution abatement costs under command-and-control regulation to that of a least-cost benchmark method of control ranged from 1.07 for sulfate emissions in the Los Angeles basin to 22.0 for hydrocarbon emissions at all U.S. DuPont chemical manufacturing facilities. Thus there are potentially large cost savings to be achieved from more flexible alternative regulatory systems.

The market-based environmental policy instruments described below differ from traditional command-and-control regulatory schemes in several ways. Stavins (2000) argues that market-based environmental policy instruments are regulations that encourage behavior through market signals rather than through explicit directives regarding pollution-control levels or methods. Marketable allowance systems are one type of market-based instrument that is embedded in the structure of an overall emissions reduction program, but which allows the degree of abatement to vary across sources in a manner that reduces overall compliance costs. Marketable allowance systems regulate the quantity of emissions but do not generally force the use of a particular technology. Environmental taxes, such as those on pollution emissions, regulate the price of emissions and give firms an incentive to reduce their tax liability by reducing their emissions, thus indirectly reducing emissions. In addition, pollution taxes result in market prices that more closely approximate the marginal social cost of production and so make cleaner alternative technologies more price competitive. Finally, since pollution taxes do not mandate a particular technology, they create a dynamic incentive for research and development in ways to reduce the cost of cleaner technologies.

This chapter will begin with a discussion of marketable pollution allowances and their cost-saving properties, and will then move on to describe various environmental taxes and emission charges.

Marketable Pollution Allowances

There have been a number of policy experiments with marketable quotas or allowances, including individual transferable quotas (ITQs) used in fisheries management (chapter 6), marketable development rights, and marketable pollution allowances. In the context of regulating pollution, there are two types of allowance markets. Tradable *pollution credits* are created when a pollution source reduces its emissions below some individual source-specific target. If pollution regulation caps aggregate rather than individual emissions, then emission permits or allowances take the form of quota shares that are assigned to individual polluters. This latter program is sometimes called a *cap-and-trade* system because it involves the establishment of an aggregate rather than an individual cap on emissions, and tradable allowances take the form of individual quota shares to the aggregate emissions cap. The emphasis in this section of the chapter will be on cap-and-trade systems. Allowance markets are designed to help reduce compliance costs for those firms that are operating under environmental regulations. The cost savings generated by allowances trading will be illustrated by considering pollution allowances trading systems. It is important to recognize that marketable pollution allowance systems do not directly reduce pollution emissions but are designed to reduce compliance costs in the context of an overall reduction in emissions.

The elements of a well-functioning cap-and-trade pollution allowance system include:

- An overall cap on pollution emissions.
- A partitioning of the cap into tradable quota shares assigned to the vari-

Table 10.2

Hypothetical Example of an Industry with Heterogeneous Marginal Abatement Costs

Firm	Marginal abatement cost ($)	Historical baseline, annual emissions
A	12	50
B	18	50
C	24	50
D	30	50
E	36	50
F	42	50
G	48	50
H	54	50

Note: For analytical simplicity, it is assumed that marginal abatement costs are constant, and that historical baseline emissions levels are identical across firms. Thus firms differ only in terms of their marginal abatement costs.

ous pollution sources; these allowed emissions are usually set as a fraction of historical emissions during a baseline time period; the sum of these allowances is equal to the desired level of emissions.
- A well-functioning competitive market for trading allowances.
- A requirement that new firms must buy allowances from existing firms.
- Effective deterrence against emissions in excess of firms' allowances (see chapter 9).
- Sufficient *policy stability* over time so that firms have incentive to invest in pollution-control technology and become sellers of allowances.

Now that we see the basic structure, let's look at an illustrative example of how an allowances-trading system can work to reduce the overall cost of attaining a given level of pollution control.

An Illustration of the Cost-Savings Potential from Marketable Pollution Allowances

Consider the highly simplified example in Table 10.2, which features an industry made up of eight polluting firms that have different pollution-abatement costs (i.e., the cost of reducing emissions, such as from smokestack scrubbers or alternative production methods). To keep the example analytically simple, at the cost of being a bit unrealistic, we assume that each firm's marginal abatement costs are constant. Normally we would expect that a firm's marginal abatement costs would be directly related to the level of pollution abatement (why?).

Using the data from Table 10.2, we can plot the marginal abatement costs

Figure 10.1   **Industrywide Marginal Abatement Costs**

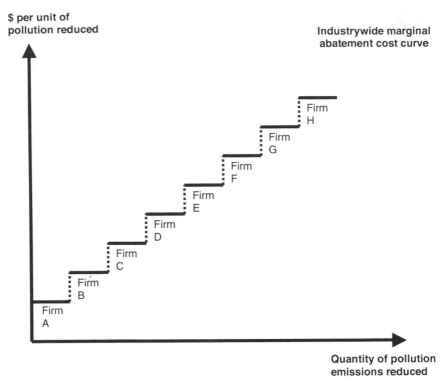

for all the firms in this industry, as shown in Figure 10.1. Each segment of the step function in Figure 10.1 represents the marginal abatement cost for one of the firms in the industry. The first segment of the step function represents the marginal abatement cost for firm A, the firm with the lowest marginal abatement costs in the industry. Once firm A has exhausted its potential for reducing emissions, the next segment on the industrywide marginal abatement cost function represents that of firm B, the firm with the next lowest marginal abatement costs in the industry. This process continues in ascending order of firms' marginal abatement cost.

Case 1: Traditional Uniform Performance Standard and No Marketable Allowances

Let's first assume that a uniform environmental performance-based standard of cutting emissions by 50 percent is applied across the firms in this industry based on their historical baseline annual emissions levels. Table 10.3 illus-

Table 10.3

Hypothetical Industrywide Cost of Cutting Emissions by One-Half Using a Uniform Performance-based Standard (Command and Control)

Firm	Marginal abatement cost	Historical baseline, annual emissions	Number of tons of emissions to be reduced	Total abatement cost ($)
A	12	50	25	300
B	18	50	25	450
C	24	50	25	600
D	30	50	25	750
E	36	50	25	900
F	42	50	25	1,050
G	48	50	25	1,200
H	54	50	25	1,350
Total	—	400	200	6,600

trates the industrywide cost of reducing emissions by 50 percent under this form of regulation. The total cost of reducing emissions by 50 percent is $6,600 per year under a performance-based standard in which each of the eight firms must cut its emissions by 25 tons.

Case 2: Cap and Trade

Now consider the same level of pollution abatement under a cap-and-trade system that features marketable pollution allowances. As before, each firm had been emitting 50 tons of pollution each year, and under the cap-and-trade system total industrywide emissions must be cut by 200 tons, or one-half of the 400 tons that had been emitted each year by the industry. This is accomplished by allocating a quota share of 25 tons to each firm, which is equal to one-half of their historical emissions. In the cap-and-trade system the 25 tons of quota per year that firms are allowed to emit are referred to as *pollution allowances,* and these allowances can be traded across the various firms in the industry. In our example, one allowance is equal to the right to emit one ton of pollution for one year. Thus, trading rearranges the level of clean-up each firm engages in but keeps the overall level of pollution reduction constant.

To determine the distribution of emissions across the regulated industry in a cap-and-trade system, we first need to predict the *pattern of allowances trade.* This means that we determine which firms will be buyers of allowances (purchasing the right to emit more pollution from other firms in the industry), and which firms will be sellers of allowances (selling the right to emit pollution to other firms in the industry). Going back to Figure 10.1, in general any firm in the industry would be willing to sell its allowances at a price above its marginal abatement cost. Recall from chapter 3 that each firm supplies along its marginal cost curve in a competitive market. Thus, we can construct a market supply curve for allowances, which in our example is equivalent to the industrywide marginal abatement cost step function in Figure 10.1, except that each step is only half as wide, since each firm only has allowances equal to one-half of its historical emissions. Moreover, in general any firm in the industry would be willing to purchase allowances at a price below its marginal abatement cost. For simplicity, we assume that only regulated firms in the industry can purchase pollution allowances. Thus, we can construct a market demand curve for allowances, where each firm's marginal abatement cost represents its maximum willingness to pay for allowances. The maximum quantity of allowances demanded by each firm in our example is 25 (the quantity of each firm's total emissions [50] minus each firms' allowed emissions [25]). The market supply and demand for allowances is shown in Figure 10.2.

As noted above, the predicted pattern of allowances trade involves firms with low marginal abatement costs selling allowances to firms with higher marginal abatement costs. For example, firm A's marginal abatement cost is only $12 per ton. If firm A were to sell an allowance to firm H for, say, $33, then firm A receives producer surplus $(33 − 12) = $21, and firm H receives consumer surplus $(54 − 33) = $21. Essentially, this allowance trade involves firm A taking on the task of cleaning up an extra ton of pollution emissions on behalf of firm H, and charges firm H $33 for this service. Recalling what we learned about the competitive market equilibrium in chapter 3, we can see in Figure 10.2 that the equilibrium quantity of allowances traded occurs where the market supply and demand curves intersect. At this equilibrium the firms with relatively low marginal abatement costs (firms A–D) are selling a total of 100 tons of allowance to the firms with relatively high marginal abatement costs (firms E–H). The equilibrium price of allowances will fall somewhere between $30 and $36 (why?), and with equal bargaining power on both sides of the market, an equilibrium price of $33 would be reasonable.

At $33 per allowance, firms E–H find it cheaper to buy allowances than to reduce their emissions, and firms A–D find it more profitable to sell their allowances and perform all of the pollution abatement for the entire industry. Table 10.4 illustrates how marketable allowances systems reallocate cleanup activity and reduce overall abatement costs.

In this highly simplified example, the industrywide cost of meeting the emissions cap—cutting pollution by one-half in the airshed—is $4,200, which

Figure 10.2 Market Supply and Demand for Pollution Allowances

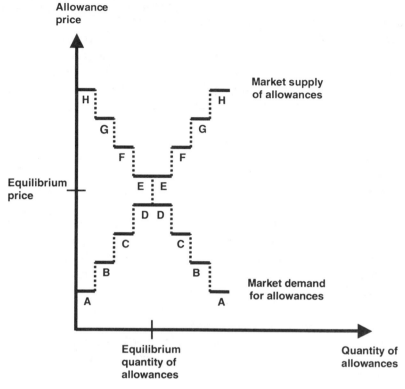

Table 10.4

Hypothetical Industrywide Cost of Cutting Emissions by One-Half Under a Cap-and-Trade System with Fully Tradable Allowances

Firm	Marginal abatement cost	Historical baseline, annual emissions	1. Initial tons of emissions to be reduced	2. Allowances sold	3. Allowances bought	4. Final tons of emissions to be reduced (1 + 2 − 3)
A	12	50	25	25	0	50
B	18	50	25	25	0	50
C	24	50	25	25	0	50
D	30	50	25	25	0	50
E	36	50	25	0	25	0
F	42	50	25	0	25	0
G	48	50	25	0	25	0
H	54	50	25	0	25	0
Total	—	400	200	100	100	200

is somewhat less than two-thirds of the cost of meeting the same overall pollution-control target under the performance-based command-and-control standard. However, what about the revenues and costs associated with the sales and purchases of allowances? Does the cost of buying allowances count as a part of the total cost of compliance with the cap? For an individual firm, the cost of purchasing allowances represents a cost of compliance, without a doubt. If only industry members are involved with allowance trades, as in this example, then the industrywide cost of allowances purchased by the demand side of the allowance market is, from an accounting standpoint, equal to the revenues from allowance sales by the supply side of the allowance market. In other words, intra-industry allowances trade has no aggregate net compliance cost impact, as purchase expenditures simply represent offsetting revenue flows to other firms in the industry.

We made the simplifying assumption that each firm's marginal abatement costs are constant, which resulted in firms with low marginal abatement costs selling all of their allowances, thus fully eliminating their emissions. Admittedly, it may be a bit farfetched to assume that the polluting facilities owned by firms A–D can completely eliminate their emissions, but this simple example illustrates the more general concept. The remarkable aspect of a cap-and-trade system is that it harnesses the cost-minimizing incentives of profit-maximizing firms and the competitive market process to reduce the costs of complying with pollution-control regulations.

More generally, if firms A–H each had different upward-sloping marginal abatement cost curves rather than constant marginal abatement costs, the *equimarginal principle* would come into play. To see this, consider Figure 10.3, which shows three firms, each with different, upward-sloping marginal abatement cost curves. To simplify this example, we focus on firms that supply allowances. If the horizontal dotted line indicates the equilibrium market price of an allowance, then one can see that firm 3 (with the highest marginal abatement cost curve) supplies the smallest quantity of allowances, while firm 1 (with the lowest marginal abatement cost curve) supplies the largest quantity of allowances. As the equimarginal principle would suggest, at the equilibrium allowance price, the marginal abatement cost of each firm for the last ton each cleans up is equal to the equilibrium allowance price. As a consequence, the firm with the lowest marginal abatement cost curve sells the most allowances and reduces emissions the most, followed by the firm with the next-to-lowest marginal abatement cost curve, and so on.

Figure 10.3 **Allowance Sales by Firms with Upward-Sloping Allowance Supply Curves**

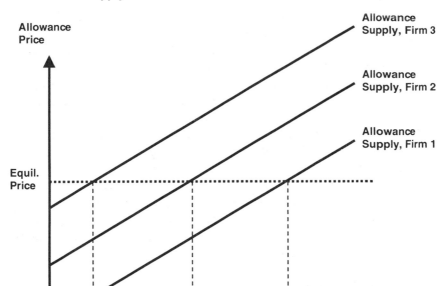

Case 3: Limited Allowance Trading

If the pollutant being regulated in the cap-and-trade system is not perfectly uniformly mixed in the atmosphere, there may be localized "hot spots" near point sources that, by buying up allowances, firms can continue to pollute as before. For example, in July 1997 the group Communities for a Better Environment filed a federal civil rights complaint against the South Coast Air Quality Management District (SCAQMD) and oil companies in the Los Angeles region. This group was arguing that the acquisition of pollution credits from buying and scrapping older, high-polluting cars violates the civil rights of lower-income and minority people who live near the oil refineries. Consequently, unconstrained trading of allowances may generate an asymmetry in the distribution of emissions that generates greater harms than if emissions reductions were more uniformly applied across the firms. In this case, there is a balancing of cost savings from allowances trading against the need for all sources to limit emissions.

Suppose that we cap trades at 10 tons for each firm. In the example below, we will cap sales as well as purchases, but if dealing with localized hot spots is the concern, it is only necessary to cap purchases by each firm. A cap on both sales and purchases is used here to illustrate the somewhat more realistic case in which all firms clean up to some degree, and yet no firm can completely eliminate its emissions. Table 10.5 shows what will happen under this constrained allowances-trading scheme.

Under this final case, all firms must cut pollution by at least 15 tons per year, which limits localized hot-spot effects. The result, however, of limiting trading is that the cost of meeting the overall standard of cutting pollution by half rises to $5,640, roughly intermediate between the cost with no trading ($6,600) and the cost with unconstrained trading ($4,200). Thus we can measure the opportunity cost of limiting localized hot spots by the foregone cost savings that would have been realized under more complete trading—in this case $5,640 - $4,200 = $1,440.

Advantages of Marketable Allowance Systems

There are both static and dynamic advantages associated with marketable allowance systems. A clear static advantage of marketable allowances is that substantial cost savings are realized from allowing low-abatement-cost firms to sell allowances to high-abatement-cost firms. Consequently, an overall pollution abatement target can be realized at lower total cost when allowances are tradable. Moreover, since firms with high abatement costs are paying someone else to do clean-up for them, this payment becomes a cost and so gives these firms an incentive to find a cheaper way to reduce emissions— R&D. A dynamic advantage of marketable allowance systems is that they give firms an incentive to invest in cleaner technology and cut their emissions below their allowance. The firms can then specialize in selling allowances to those that have not made a similar investment.

Disadvantages of Marketable Allowance Systems

When a firm has *market power,* such as with monopolies or colluding oligopolists, and lower abatement costs than potential entrants, and new entrants must buy emissions allowances from the existing firm, then the existing firm can use its dominant position to withhold allowances from potential rivals and so maintain its market power over time (Misiolek and Elder 1989).

Another possible problem occurs when there are few market participants

Table 10.5

Hypothetical Industrywide Cost of Cutting Emissions by One-Half with Limited Allowances Trading

Firm	Marginal abatement cost	Historical baseline, annual emissions	1. Initial tons of emissions to be reduced	2. Allowances sold (maximum of 10)	3. Allowances bought (maximum of 10)	4. Final tons of emissions to be reduced (1 + 2 − 3)
A	12	50	25	10	0	35
B	18	50	25	10	0	35
C	24	50	25	10	0	35
D	30	50	25	10	0	35
E	36	50	25	0	10	15
F	42	50	25	0	10	15
G	48	50	25	0	10	15
H	54	50	25	0	10	15
Total	—	400	200	40	40	200

and an ineffective market institution or other barriers to efficient market processes. In this case the *transaction costs* of exchanging emissions allowances may be larger than the value of the allowance itself, in which case allowance market failure results (Foster and Hahn 1995). For example, allowances-tracking systems are necessary so that regulatory agencies know each firm's allowed emissions, and there have been cases in which the cost of registering trades has been so high as to discourage otherwise mutually beneficial allowances transactions.

Policymakers must also be careful to make the allowances short-term in nature so that they do not become a permanent right that could not be adjusted further in the future if new scientific information comes along and policy makers decide to reduce pollution even more. This is part of the reason why the Environmental Protection Agency (EPA) has set the life of an allowance equal to one year.

Finally, as previously mentioned, a problem with unconstrained marketable allowances trading is that it can lead to hot spots of localized, high-concentration pollution (known as *concentrated pollution* as opposed to uniformly mixed pollution) occurring because the particular firm has bought an extensive number of emissions permits.

Marketable Pollution Allowances and the Clean Air Act (CAA) Amendments of 1990: The Acid Rain Program

Acid deposition occurs as a by-product of burning fossil fuels. Emissions of sulfur dioxide (SO_2) and nitrogen oxides (NOx) react with water droplets, oxygen, and various oxidants in the atmosphere, usually in cloud layers, to form solutions of sulfuric and nitric acid. These reactions are hastened by sunlight. Rainwater, snow, fog, and other forms of precipitation containing those mild solutions of sulfuric and nitric acids then fall to earth as acid rain. Interestingly, about half the acidity created through such atmospheric reactions falls to the earth's surface in the form of dry depositions, which are then carried by the wind or washed into waterways by subsequent rainfalls. While normal rainfall has a pH of 6, acidification of rain has lowered this pH in many areas of the northeastern United States and southeastern Canada to values ranging from 4.2 to 4.4, approaching the pH levels in cola soft drinks (National Acid Precipitation Assessment Program website). A reduction in pH values of the soil and water bodies that absorb acid rain results in damage or in extreme cases sterility to the associated terrestrial or aquatic ecosystems. Besides the northeastern United States and southeastern Canada, other primary deposition areas are associated with intense burning of fossil fuels in northern Europe and parts of East Asia. Terrestrial ecosystems particularly damaged by acid rain occur at high altitudes, as in the Appalachian and Adirondack mountains of the eastern United States, where acid rains and fogs frequently bathe and envelop the forests, meadows, streams, and lakes of the area and have made many of these waters uninhabitable to native fish and other aquatic life.

In the United States, electric utility power plants that burn fossil fuels generate about 75 percent of sulfur dioxide emissions. Many of these plants are concentrated in the Midwest. Emissions of the other major source of acid rain, nitrogen oxides, are somewhat more equally distributed between motor vehicles and electric utilities. Acids can remain in the atmosphere for weeks at a time and be transported by prevailing winds for hundreds of miles before they are deposited. In 1984 the U.S. Office of Technology Assessment estimated that in addition to the environmental damage caused by acid rain, acidic aerosols—small water droplets containing compounds of sulfur, nitrogen, and chlorine—may be responsible for as many as 50,000 deaths in the United States each year and pose a serious threat to people with respiratory illnesses.

When the U.S. Congress amended the Clean Air Act in 1990, the amendments included an experiment with the use of markets in reducing the cost of meeting sulfur dioxide emissions reductions. Title IV of the Clean Air Act addresses the control of acid rain and sets the overall goal of reducing annual SO_2 emissions to one-half of 1980 levels by 2010, or 8.95 million tons per year. These reductions were to be achieved through a two-phase process that places increasingly tight restrictions on the emissions of coal and other fossil–fuel-powered utilities. Information on the EPA's Acid Rain Program, some of which is summarized below, can be found on the Internet at www.epa.gov/airmarkets/arp/overview.html.

The first phase of the Acid Rain Program began in 1995 and affects 445 coal-burning electricity units located in twenty-one eastern and midwestern states. Interestingly, preliminary data reported by the EPA indicate that 1995 sulfur dioxide emissions at these units were reduced by almost 40 percent below their required level. The second phase, which began in 2000, extends restrictions to many smaller, cleaner plants and imposes a further tightening of the phase 1 standards on the larger and dirtier plants. The program affects existing utility plants having generators with an output capacity of greater than 25 megawatts as well as all newly built plants. The Clean Air Act requires that by 2010 the scope of the Acid Rain Program be broadened to include more than 1,000 U.S. electricity-generating facilities. The Clean Air Act also addresses emissions of nitrogen oxides, and requires a total reduction of 2 million tons relative to 1980 levels by 2000. The EPA claims that a significant portion of this reduction will be achieved by coal-fired utility boilers that will be required to install new burner technologies.

Under the trading system devised by the EPA, affected utility plants are allocated allowances based on their historic fuel consumption and emissions rate. Each allowance permits a plant to emit one ton of SO_2 during or after a specified year. Once a ton of sulfur dioxide is emitted in a particular year, the allowance is "retired" and can no longer be used. These allowances may be bought, sold, or banked. Any person may acquire allowances and participate in the trading system. The EPA must be able to keep track of the ownership of allowances in order to determine whether a plant has exceeded its allowed emissions. The EPA does so through the Allowance Tracking System, which monitors the transfer of ownership of allowances. As of 2003, firms that emitted more than their allowances permitted were fined $2,900 per ton, a figure that is indexed each year to inflation. Finally, regardless of the number of allowances a utility holds, the plant may not emit at levels that would violate federal or state limits set under Title I of the Clean Air Act to protect public health. This is a cap-and-trade regulatory system because the Acid Rain Program regulates overall emissions, and tradable allowances are quota shares.

An interesting phenomenon in allowance trading is the rise of groups that purchase allowances and simply retire them as a market-oriented strategy for cleaning the environment. For example, in the 2000 spot auction (allowances purchased for use in 2000), the Acid Rain Retirement Fund purchased 13 allowances, the Maryland Environmental Law Society purchased 10, and the Isaac Walton League, VA/Clean Air Conservancy purchased 5 allowances. Other groups purchased smaller quantities. Environmental groups have purchased and retired sulfur dioxide allowances each year since the EPA auction has been conducted. One of the largest such purchases was by the National Healthy Air License Exchange and the Glens Falls (NY) Middle

School, which raised over \$20,000 to purchase and retire nearly 300 tons of sulfur dioxide.

Between 1998 and 2003, the average price of an allowance fluctuated between approximately \$125 and \$220. In 2003, 4,200 individual allowance transfers representing roughly 16.5 million allowances (of past, current, and future vintages) were recorded in the EPA Allowance Tracking System. Of the allowances transferred, 8 million (49 percent) were transferred between economically unrelated parties. Most of the allowances exchanged between economically unrelated parties were acquired by electricity-generating companies. It is interesting to note that the price of allowances is substantially below the levels anticipated when the program was established in 1990. In particular, some originally anticipated that allowance prices would be around \$850, and the EPA originally estimated that allowances would trade at around \$750. These low allowance prices have resulted in a substantial cost savings for the SO_2 reduction target. In his survey of the literature on the cost of complying with the Acid Rain Program, Burtraw (1998) compares early and more recent studies to show how implementation has affected cost estimates. Early studies estimated annual compliance costs of between \$2 billion to \$5 billion (1995 dollars), while more recent studies, which have taken into account the actual performance of the Acid Rain Program, estimate annual compliance costs of approximately \$1 billion (1995 dollars). Carlson et al. (1998) attribute annual cost savings of approximately \$780 million to allowance trading, which represents an estimated 42 percent savings relative to command-and-control projections.

One concern regarding allowance trading is the potential for creating localized hot spots. Swift (2000) has found that in fact the largest coal-burning plants, with the largest sulfur dioxide emissions, reduced their emissions by the largest percentage under the Acid Rain Program. These firms are able to spread pollution abatement costs over a larger dollar value of capital. Consequently, Swift argues that the data allay concerns about localized hot spots under the Acid Rain Program. There have been some problems with implementation of the Acid Rain Program. For example, McCormack and Shaw (1996) report that the New York legislature tried to ban interstate allowances trades on the grounds that an electricity generator in New York might profit from selling allowances to generators in the midwestern United States, and with the prevailing wind pattern, increased midwestern emissions would result in increased acid rain deposition in New York.

Renewable Portfolio Standard (RPS)

A number of states have imposed an RPS on the electricity that is consumed at the retail level. The electricity consumed at the retail level (by households, commercial businesses, and organizations) is a generic commodity, but is gen-erated from a mix of generation sources such as coal-fired power plants, large-scale hydroelectric facilities, nuclear power plants, as well as various qualified renewable sources (photovoltaic, wind, small-scale hydroelectric, biomass, geothermal). An RPS works by setting a minimum percentage of generation that must come from qualified renewable sources. In most applications of RPS systems, this minimum percentage starts out relatively low and gradually in-creases over time, steadily decreasing a state's dependence on traditional en-ergy sources while simultaneously building a renewable energy infrastructure. As of November 2004, sixteen states have passed an RPS, and California's, which requires 20 percent of its retail electricity consumption be from renew-able sources by 2017, is the most stringent.

Some states allow retail energy companies to meet their RPS obliga-tions through the purchase of renewable energy credits (RECs). In these systems, generators of qualified renewable energy receive an REC for each megawatt of electricity generated from renewable energy sources. Retail energy companies can either meet RPS requirements through their own generation, or buy RECs from renewable energy generators. RECs can be tracked through establishment of certificate-issuing entities that are respon-sible for monitoring renewable energy generation. The tracking system will typically be an electronic database that tracks trades and ownership. There is an active market in RECs, also known as green tags and tradable renew-able certificates (TRCs).

Emissions Trading

So far, we have focused on cap-and-trade systems. Let's now consider a trad-able pollution credit system in which individual credits are created when a polluter reduces emissions below the maximum level allowed by law. The various EPA emission-trading programs have existed since the mid-1970s. These are regional, state-controlled programs designed and operated in co-operation with the EPA. Hahn (1989) estimates that cumulative cost savings created by the various emissions-trading programs range from $500 million to $12 billion. Target pollutants include volatile organic compounds, carbon monoxide, sulfur dioxide, particulates, and nitrogen oxide. Emission reduc-tion credits (ERCs) are earned whenever a polluter reduces emissions below the level required by law. ERCs are usually earned from exceeding compli-ance standards (usually resulting from either the installation of a new pro-duction process or a plant's closing down). An ERC gives the owner the right to emit one ton per year of the stated pollutant while the ERC is valid. ERCs can be transferred within a multiplant firm or by way of "external trading."

In highly impacted nonattainment areas (like Los Angeles), firms must acquire more than one ERC for every unit of emissions (typically 1.2 ERCs bought for every 1 ton of pollution) so that overall emissions are reduced. ERCs can then be traded in a number of ways.

ERCs can be used to *offset* new facilities (and their emissions) locating in "nonattainment areas" that have not met a specified ambient air quality standard. The CAA specified that no new emissions sources would be allowed to locate in nonattainment areas after 1975. Concern that the prohibition would stifle economic activity led the EPA to develop offset ERCs. An "offset" is a type of ERC specifically designed for new factories or other new sources of pollution to be built in areas that exceed emissions standards. Offsets can be traded internally within a multiplant firm or via external trading.

Another way that ERCs are traded is in a process called *netting*. Netting allows a firm that creates new sources of emissions in a plant to avoid the stringent emissions limits that would normally apply by reducing emissions from another source in the same plant. A firm using netting is allowed to obtain the necessary ERCs only from its own sources (internal trading).

Yet another way that ERCs can be traded is by way of trades within a given *bubble*. The bubble program is similar to the offsets program but applies to ERC trades involving existing factories rather than newly constructed ones. The term *bubble* refers to placing an imaginary bubble over a given plant, with all emissions exiting from a single outlet to the bubble. Thus, bubbles allow a firm to sum its total plant emissions and adjust individual sources of pollution within the plant so that the aggregate limit is not exceeded. This part of the program began in 1979. Bubble credit transfers have not generated a lot of transactions; some say this is because of regulator opposition, the nonuniform mixing nature of the pollutants, and thin regional markets, among others.

Finally, ERCs (unlike allowances in the Acid Rain Program) can be *banked* for future sale or use. States decide the specific rules and administer ERC banking. Foster and Hahn (1995) find that banking acts to reduce the *transaction costs* of ERC trading, especially for small-scale trades.

Other Experiments with Marketable Allowances

Fox River oxygen trading: Under this Wisconsin program, pulp paper mills and sewage treatment plants were required to purchase oxygen depletion allowances. See O'Neil et al. (1983).

Lead banking: In this pollution credit trading program, refiners were allowed to bank and trade lead allowances to meet a short timeline phase-out of leaded gasoline in a more cost-effective manner. Refiners that reduced lead content below the standard requirement received credits that could be "banked" and used in the future. Half of all refiners participated, 15 percent of allowances were traded, and 35 percent of production rights were banked. Hahn (1989) estimated $228 million in cost savings.

Chlorofluorocarbon (CFC) trading: As discussed in chapter 8, the Montreal Protocol was an international environmental agreement in which signatory countries agreed to a 1998 CFC cap equal to 50 percent of 1986 levels. Developed countries such as the United States later agreed to a complete phase-out of production. During the phase-out period, the U.S. EPA instituted a cap-and-trade system for the phase-out of CFCs. It is estimated to have saved several billion dollars in compliance costs. Similar production quotas were utilized in Canada, the European Union, and Singapore (Stavins 2000).

Heavy-duty motor vehicle engine emissions trading system: Engine manufacturers that produce heavy-duty engines that emit less nitrogen oxide that is required by law are granted credits that can be used to offset engines that fail to meet the standard. These credits can be used by the firm that produced them, or they can be traded to other firms. Credits can also be banked for future use.

Joint implementation of greenhouse gas controls: Countries that had ratified the Framework Convention on Climate Change established a joint implementation program in the 1995 Berlin Conference of the Parties. The 1997 Kyoto Protocol allows Annex B countries (countries that have an agreed ceiling on emissions) to meet their ceiling by way of emissions trading with other Annex B countries, and through joint implementation programs. In the pilot joint implementation program Annex B countries finance projects in other countries that reduce emissions of greenhouse gases, and these emission reductions are then credited toward meeting the Annex B country's ceiling. The U.S. Initiative on Joint Implementation has approved twenty-two such projects through 1997, and the worldwide total through 1999 was ninety-four (Stavins 2000). Most of these projects have funded the transition to less-polluting energy production processes or have focused on land use in Latin America and other lower-income regions.

Regional Clean Air Incentive Market: In October 1993 California's South Coast Air Quality Management District initiated a new cap-and-trade regulatory system for controlling emissions of oxides of sulfur and nitrogen, called the Regional Clean Air Incentive Market (RECLAIM), a prominent element of which features the trading of pollution allowances on the Internet. Anderson (1997) predicted that this cap-and-trade system would reduce compliance costs by 42 percent, the same percentage cost savings estimated for the Acid Rain Program allowance market.

Transferable development rights: As Convery (1998) observes, jurisdictions use transferable development rights in environmentally sensitive or unique areas where development should be limited or prohibited. Landowners in these "sending areas" are given development units that can be exercised only in a less sensitive "receiving area" such as within an urban boundary, and developers in the receiving area wishing to exceed density restrictions can purchase these rights. For example, Clallam County, Washington, has an ordinance that transfers development rights from agricultural land to receiving areas in the Sequim Urban Growth Area. Likewise, Seattle residential properties occupied primarily by low-income households with annual incomes at or below 50 percent of median income, and structures designated as Seattle landmarks by Seattle's Landmarks Preservation Board, became "sending sites" eligible to sell TDRs to office, hotel, and retail "receiving sites."

Environmental Taxes

Recall from chapter 4 that environmental taxes, such as those charged to polluters, are another form of incentive regulation in which something bad (pollution) is taxed in order to provide an incentive for it to be reduced. Pigouvian taxes are a particular form of pollution tax that is designed to internalize external costs, but given the difficulties in precisely measuring external costs and the vagaries of the political process, most pollution taxes are not designed to internalize external costs perfectly. Pollution taxes can take the form of a per-unit (excise) tax on inputs such as coal or outputs such as electricity that generate pollution. When monitoring data permit, pollution taxes and charges can be directly assessed on pollution emissions themselves (these are sometimes called *effluent taxes*). A negative environmental tax is a tax credit that subsidizes environmentally friendlier goods and services. For example, the Energy Policy Act of 1992 provides a 1.5 cent per kilowatt-hour credit for energy generated from wind or biomass sources, and solar and geothermal energy projects can receive up to a 10 percent tax credit. Jaffe and Stavins (1995) provide evidence that tax credits can be more effective than taxes in promoting environmentally friendly energy. As Barthold (1994) points out, systems of taxation have for a long time had consequences for environmental quality, though those consequences have oftentimes been unintended. The oil crisis of 1973–74 led to some of the first tax policies designed with the purpose of promoting energy conservation and use of alternative energy. In 1978, for example, the U.S. Congress passed the gas-guzzler tax, an excise tax that varies inversely with the EPA's fuel economy rating of automobiles.

Environmental Taxes in the United States

The list below describes a number of environmental taxes used by various states. This list is designed to be representative rather than comprehensive:

- *E-Waste Recycling Fee:* The state of California imposes a fee that ranges between $6 and $10 on the retail sale or lease of a new or refurbished video display device that has a screen size of more than 4 inches measured diagonally. The tax is used to fund the recycling of these products, which contain lead and other hazardous materials.
- *Hazardous Waste Tax:* The state of Vermont charges a tax of 11 cents per gallon of liquid or 1.4 cents per pound of solid for hazardous waste destined to be recycled for a beneficial purpose, or a tax of 23.6 cents per gallon of liquid or 3 cents per pound of solid for hazardous waste destined for any form of management other than recycling. The tax goes to an environmental contingency fund used to investigate and mitigate the effects of hazardous waste released into the environment. Minnesota also charges fees on hazardous waste. In 2004 it was $2.75 per gallon.
- *Oil Spill Tax:* The state of Washington imposes a tax (currently 4 cents per 42-gallon barrel of oil, with another cent per barrel that can be charged, depending on the fund balance in the oil spill response account) on the transportation of crude oil or petroleum products, by ship or barge, into navigable waters of the state and off-loaded at an in-state terminal. This tax is used for oil spill prevention, response, and restoration programs. Likewise, the state of Alaska imposes a 5 cent tax per barrel of oil, of which 2 cents go to oil spill response and 3 cents go to oil spill prevention.
- *Pesticide and Fertilizer Tax:* The state of Iowa imposes a tax of one-tenth of 1 percent on gross sales for pesticides at the retail level, and one-fifth of 1 percent of gross sales on the manufacturers of pesticides. It also imposes a tax of 75 cents per ton on nitrogen fertilizer. The tax is used to fund groundwater protection.

Environmental Taxes Around the World

So far, we have focused on market-based regulatory systems in the United States, but there is a wide variety of such systems in place around the world. In the case of the European Union (EU), the use of environmental taxes and charges is widespread and growing. These environmental taxes are imposed at the national level, as there is no international taxing authority, which results in concerns about the international competitiveness of the country imposing the taxes on their domestic industries. In the EU, environmental taxes and charges are imposed on products, such as pesticides, on services, such as sanitary landfills, on air and water pollution, and on resource use. An economic analysis of EU environmental taxes and charges found that, by and large, these were set at relatively low levels, and focused more on revenue generation than on the incentive effects of the taxes or charges (European Union 2001). This analysis indicated that while the "price signals" from the EU environmental taxes were generally quite modest, there was a disproportionately larger behavioral effect, which the report attributed to the role of the taxes in raising public awareness and creating moral concern about the environment. Moreover, due to the generally modest level of taxation, and the extensive number of exclusions, the impact of these taxes on economic competitiveness was found to be small.

The OECD (1997) provides a comprehensive list of environmental taxes in OECD countries (OECD members include the United States, Canada, Mexico, Australia, New Zealand, Japan, Republic of Korea, Turkey, Greece, and many European countries). For example, most OECD countries that still allow lead in gasoline also impose a differential environmental tax on lead that favors the use of unleaded gasoline. Denmark, Finland, the Netherlands, Norway, and Sweden impose an environmental tax on energy based on carbon emissions. Belgium, Denmark, France, Japan, Norway, Poland, and Sweden all have developed environmental charges on energy based on sulfur emissions. The Czech Republic, France, Poland, and Sweden impose a nitrogen oxide charge on energy. Eleven of the twenty-eight OECD countries utilize water effluent charges and impose noise charges on aircraft. France taxes water pollution and reinvests the revenues in pollution remediation, and Poland's stringent effluent fees include a penalty for emissions that exceed the regulatory standard. Belgium taxes disposable razors and cameras, Sweden taxes the production of various chemicals and uses the proceeds to fund monitoring and enforcement, and Iceland imposes a differential import levy to promote smaller and more fuel-efficient automobiles. Mexico has reduced taxes on new cars and increased them on older, dirtier cars in order to limit air pollution, and Argentina and Colombia offer subsidies for industrial pollution abatement investments, and tax rebates for those who adopt cleaner technology. Chile has developed a tradable permit system for particulate matter from stationary sources in the Santiago area, and Singapore has had a tradable permit system for ozone-depleting chemicals since 1991 (Stavins 2000).

Summary

- Incentive regulation refers to economic instruments such as cap-and-trade systems or environmental taxes that foster more environmentally friendly behavior and reduce compliance costs. Incentive regulation frequently operates indirectly by changing the incentives of firms, consumers, and government in a way that promotes the environment and public health.

- Command-and-control regulation specifies how pollution is to be reduced through the application of uniform standards for firms, most prominently technology-based ("technology-forcing") or performance-based standards.
- Technology-based standards specify the methods and equipment that firms must use in order to comply with environmental regulation.
- Performance-based standards set uniform control targets for all regulated firms, but unlike with technology-based standards, firms are given some choice over how the target is actually met (Stavins 2000).
- The original Clean Air Act of 1970 includes elements of command-and-control regulation. The Clean Air Act required that costly scrubbers be installed on coal-burning electricity-generating facilities, even though many could have generated the same clean-up by shifting to less expensive low-sulfur coal.
- Marketable pollution allowances are one form of incentive regulation. Marketable pollution allowances reduce compliance costs when polluters have different marginal abatement costs. Regulators give firms a reduced level of emissions as an "allowance" or permit and then grant firms the right to trade some or all of that allowance to other firms. The cost savings result when firms with high abatement costs purchase allowances from firms with low abatement costs, meaning that firms with low abatement costs subcontract to do some of the clean-up for the high-abatement-cost firms.
- In order for markets for pollution allowances to function, regulators must monitor and enforce the allowances so that firms cannot simply exceed allowed emissions, which would eliminate the incentive to purchase allowances.
- Tradable *pollution credits* are created when a pollution source reduces its emissions below some individual source-specific target. If pollution regulation caps aggregate rather than individual emissions, then emission permits or allowances take the form of quota shares that are assigned to individual polluters. This latter program is sometimes called a *cap-and-trade system* because it involves the establishment of an aggregate rather than an individual cap on emissions, and tradable allowances take the form of individual quota shares to the aggregate emissions cap.
- A prominent example of a cap-and-trade system is the EPA's Acid Rain Program, in which sulfur dioxide allowances are traded on the Chicago Board of Trade, and allowance prices are much lower than had originally been anticipated.

- One potential limiting factor for marketable allowances is the problem of localized "hot spots," which can occur when a firm buys so many allowances that it does not have to clean up at all (other firms have subcontracted for the clean-up). If the pollutant is not uniformly mixable in the atmosphere, then there could be substantial localized impact from this outcome. As a result, regulators may limit marketable allowance schemes to require all firms to clean up some minimum amount. While these restrictions limit the cost-savings potential, they can prevent localized hot spots from developing.
- Another form of incentive regulation is pollution taxes, also known as environmental excise taxes. A.C. Pigou and other economists have long argued for environmental taxes as a way to cause firms to internalize external costs and cause consumers to be confronted with prices that reflect the full marginal social cost of production. The incentive effect of pollution taxes is that they create a new cost that profit-maximizing firms then have an incentive to minimize. For example, pollution taxes make environmentally friendly technology more attractive and thus promote R&D and adoption of these technologies as a way to avoid the excise tax.
- Environmental taxes can be charged on polluting inputs such as coal, on goods and services such as electricity, or directly on pollution emissions. Direct taxes on pollution emissions are sometimes called effluent taxes or charges. Examples of U.S. environmental taxes include hazardous waste, oil, and pesticides. There are a large and growing number of environmental taxes and charges that are being used worldwide.

Review Questions and Problems

1. Go back to the tables and figures in the chapter for the illustration of the cost savings from marketable allowances.

    a. Redo the illustrative example of the cost savings from fully marketable pollution allowances relative to command-and-control regulation (case 2), assuming that emissions will be cut by 60 percent rather than 50 percent. It may help to redraw Figure 10.2. Calculate the cost savings from fully marketable allowances relative to traditional command-and-control regulation. Assume that a firm cannot clean up beyond its historical baseline emissions level.

    b. Independent of your work in part 1a above, redo the illustrative example of the cost savings from constrained allowances trading in the text (case 3) but now impose a constraint that no more than

15 tons of emissions can be bought or sold by a particular firm as a means of reducing the creation of localized hot spots of pollution. Calculate the total clean-up cost relative to unconstrained market trading and traditional command-and-control regulation. What is the opportunity cost of imposing the 15-ton trading constraint to limit localized hot spots relative to unconstrained market trading?

2. One of the criticisms of using indirect controls such as pollution taxes to limit pollution is that firms will simply view the taxes as a part of the cost of doing business and pass the cost along to their consumers while continuing to pollute as before.

    a. Explain the relationship between the size of a firm's marginal abatement costs and the pollution tax that is implied by the above statement.

    b. Describe the shape of the market demand curve implied by the above statement. For what industries might this condition come closest to being true?

    c. Might the shape of the demand curve for the industries you described above change over time if a pollution tax is imposed? If so, then why? (Hint: consider the dynamic incentives for developing substitutes.)

3. Draw a diagram in which firms A–H each have upward-sloping marginal abatement cost functions, as in Figure 10.3. Draw a uniform price for allowances such that the total quantity of emissions reduced sums to one-half of the industry's total emissions.

    a. Indicate on your diagram how much pollution abatement each firm will perform in equilibrium after complete market trading.

    b. Explain why the equimarginal principle results in cost-minimizing pollution abatement.

4. Download information on the volume of trade and allowance prices from the EPA's Acid Rain Program web page (www.epa.gov/airmarkets/arp/overview.html). How have allowance prices and the volume of trade changed from the numbers given in the chapter? What are the factors that led to the changes you have identified?

5. Access the Resources for the Future *Discussion Paper* 04–24 by Joseph Kruger and William Pizer, which provides a critical analysis and discussion of the European Union Emissions Trading Directive (www.rff.org/rff/Documents/RFF-DP-04-24.pdf). Note that the full paper is a PDF file, which requires the

free Adobe Acrobat program. (1) Summarize their arguments, and (2) relate the EU Emissions Trading Directive to the workings of the allowance trading system in the EPA's Acid Rain Program.

6. Access the European Union report, *Study on the Economic and Environmental Implications of the Use of Environmental Taxes and Charges in the European Union and Its Member States* (http://europa.eu.int/comm/environment/enveco/taxation/environmental_taxes.htm). Write a summary of one or more environmental taxes being used in Europe, including the purpose, the tax rate, and the effectiveness of the tax.

Internet Links

Acid Rain Program (www.epa.gov/airmarkets/arp/overview.html): Read about the trading of sulfur dioxide allowances at this EPA site.

Clean Air Markets (www.epa.gov/airmarkets): Learn more about allowances trading, the Acid Rain Program, and cap-and-trade systems.

Cost Savings, Market Performance, and Economic Benefits of the U.S. Acid Rain Program (www.rff.org/Documents/RFF-DP-98–28-REV.pdf): Resources for the Future *Discussion Paper* by Dallas Burtraw.

Environmental Policy Implementation in the Netherlands (www.rri.org/ envatlas/europe/netherlands/nl-inst.html): Read about the economic instruments used in the Netherlands to control pollution and improve the environment. Produced by the Resource Renewal Institute.

Experience with Market-based Environmental Policy Instruments (www.rff.org/Documents/RFF-DP-01–58.pdf): Resources for the Future *Discussion Paper* 01–58 by Robert Stavins reviews the use of economic-incentive or market-based environmental policy instruments around the world.

Harnessing the Tax Code for Environmental Protection: A Survey of Initiatives (www.rprogress.org/newprograms/sustEcon/taxcode.shtml): An accessible and comprehensive study by J. Andrew Hoerner of the Center for a Sustainable Economy that describes the rationale for environmental taxation and identifies 462 environmentally motivated state-level tax provisions.

Interactive Marketable Pollution Allowances Simulation (ftp:// sorrel.humboldt.edu/pub/envecon/module4.xls): A simple and informative interactive simulation produced by textbook author Steven Hackett that operates on an Excel platform. The user does not need to know anything about Excel to use the simulation. Be sure to enable macros when asked.

International Experiences with Economic Incentives for Protecting the Environment (http://yosemite.epa.gov/ee/epa/eermfile.nsf/vwAN/EE-0487–01.pdf): 2004 EPA report.

Pollution Allowances Audio Clip (www.humboldt.edu/~envecon/audio/ 3.ram): Audio clip provided by textbook author Steven Hackett on tradable pollution allowances.

Study on the Economic and Environmental Implications of the Use of Environmental Taxes and Charges in the European Union and Its Member States (http://europa.eu.int/comm/environment/enveco/taxation/ environmental_taxes.htm):

References and Further Reading

Ackerman, B., and W. Hassler. 1981. *Clean Coal/Dirty Air.* New Haven: Yale University Press.

Anderson, R. 1997. *The U.S. Experience with Economic Incentives in Environmental Pollution-Control Policy.* Washington, DC: Environmental Law Institute.

Barthold, T. 1994. "Issues in the Design of Environmental Excise Taxes." *Journal of Economic Perspectives* 8 (Winter): 133–51.

Boyd, R., K. Krutilla, and W.K. Viscusi. 1995. "Energy Taxation as a Policy Instrument to Reduce CO_2 Emissions: A Net Benefit Analysis." *Journal of Environmental Economics and Management* 29 (July): 1–24.

Bryner, G. 1993. *Blue Skies, Green Politics.* Washington, DC: CQ Press.

Burtraw, D. 1998. "Cost Savings, Market Performance, and Economic Benefits of the U.S. Acid Rain Program." *Discussion Paper* 98–28-REV. Washington, DC: Resources for the Future.

Carlson, C., D. Burtraw, M. Cropper, and K. Palmer. 1998. "Sulfur Dioxide Control by Electric Utilities: What Are the Gains from Trade?" *Discussion Paper* 98–44. Washington, DC: Resources for the Future.

Center for Global Change. N.d. *State Carbon Tax Model.* College Park: University of Maryland.

Convery, F. 1998. "The Types and Roles of Market Mechanisms." In *Using Market Mechanisms in Environmental Regulation.* New York: The Conference Board.

European Union. 2001. *Study on the Economic and Environmental Implications of the Use of Environmental Taxes and Charges in the European Union and Its Member States* (http://europa.eu.int/comm/environment/enveco/taxation/ environmental_taxes.htm).

Foster, V., and R. Hahn. 1995. "Designing More Efficient Markets: Lessons from Los Angeles Smog Control." *Journal of Law and Economics* 38 (April): 19–48.

Jaffe, A, and R. Stavins, 1995. "Dynamic Incentives of Environmental Regulations: The Effects of Alternative Policy Instruments on Technology Diffusion." *Journal of Environmental Economics and Management*, 29: S43-S63.

Hahn, R. 1989. "Economic Prescriptions for Environmental Problems: How the Patient Followed the Doctor's Orders." *Journal of Economic Perspectives* 3 (Spring): 95–114.

McCormack, C., and J. Shaw. 1996. "Emissions Trading: Clearing the Air." *PERC Reports* 14 (June): 10–11.

Misiolek, W., and H. Elder. 1989. "Exclusionary Manipulation of Markets for Pollution Rights." *Journal of Environmental Economics and Management* 16: 156–66.

National Acid Precipitation Assessment Program. http://www.oar.noaa.gov/organization/napap.html.

O'Neil, W., M. David, C. Moore, and E. Joeres. 1983. "Transferable Discharge Permits and Economic Efficiency: The Fox River." *Journal of Environmental Economics and Management* 10 (December): 346–55.

Organization for Economic Cooperation and Development (OECD). 1997. *Evaluating Economic Instruments for Environmental Policy.* Paris: OECD.

Roodman, D. 1996. "Harnessing the Market for the Environment." In *State of the World 1996,* ed. L. Brown. Washington, DC: Worldwatch Institute.

Stavins, R. 2000. "Experience with Market-based Environmental Policy Instruments." *Discussion Paper* 00–09. Washington, DC: Resources for the Future.

Swift, B. 2000. "Allowance Trading and Potential Hot Spots: Good News from the Acid Rain Program." *Environmental Reporter* 31: 954–59.

Tietenberg, T. 1980. "Transferable Discharge Permits and the Control of Stationary Source Air Pollution." *Land Economics* 5 (November): 391–416.

———. 1985. *Emissions Trading: An Exercise in Reforming Pollution Policy.* Washington, DC: Resources for the Future.

U.S. Congress, Office of Technology Assessment. 1984. *Acid Rain and Transported Air Pollutants: Implications for Public Policy.* Washington, DC: U.S. Government Printing Office.

11

Global Climate Change: Science, Policy, and Economics

Introduction

The earth's energy budget is the net result of a complex balance of energy flows over time, and exerts a primary influence on global climate. Light from the sun is absorbed by land, water, and vegetation on the surface of the earth, where it is transformed into heat and is reradiated in the form of invisible infrared radiation. Earth's atmosphere contains molecules that absorb this heat and reradiate the heat in all directions. These *greenhouse gases*—which include carbon dioxide, various halocarbons, methane, nitrogen oxides, nonmethane volatile organic compounds, ozone, sulfur hexafluoride, and water vapor—all have a molecular structure made up of more than two component atoms that are able to vibrate with the absorption of heat. Eventually, a vibrating molecule emits the radiation again, which is often reabsorbed by yet another greenhouse gas molecule. The absorption-emission-absorption cycle that occurs among greenhouse gases effectively holds heat in the atmosphere near the earth's surface, just as clear glass walls hold heat in a greenhouse, thereby slowing the process of heat being lost into space. Without the greenhouse effect, the mean surface temperature of the earth would be about 33 degrees Celsius lower than it is today, and most of the world's oceans would freeze over. As we can see, greenhouse gas molecules are responsible for the fact that the earth enjoys temperatures suitable for life as we know it in our complex biosphere.

Water vapor is the most abundant and dominant greenhouse gas in the atmosphere, but most attention is given to carbon dioxide due to increasing

Table 11.1

Global Warming Potential, Mean Atmospheric Lifetime, and Trend Growth in Emissions of Selected Greenhouse Gases

Gas	100-year global warming potential (relative to CO_2)	Global mean atmospheric lifetime (years)	Trend growth rate in the 1990's (parts per trillion per year)
Carbon Dioxide	1	5-200	1,500,000
Methane	23	8.4	7,000
Nitrous Oxide	296	120	800
Hydrofluorocarbon-134a	1,300	13.8	2
Perfluoromethane	5,700	50,000+	1
Chlorofluorocarbon-12	10,600	100	4.4
Hydrofluorocarbon-23	12,000	260	0.55
Sulfur Hexafluoride	22,200	3,200	0.24

Source: IPCC (2001).

atmospheric concentrations originating from human (*anthropogenic*) sources. The chemical properties of various greenhouse gas molecules result in differing capacities for absorbing heat in the atmosphere. The concept of global warming potential (GWP) was developed to compare the ability of each greenhouse gas to trap heat in the atmosphere relative to another gas, usually carbon dioxide. The definition of GWP for a particular greenhouse gas is the ratio of heat trapped by one unit mass of the greenhouse gas to that of one unit mass of carbon dioxide over a specified time period. There is an uncertainty of approximately +/- 35 percent in the GWP values listed in Table 11.1. Greenhouse gases also differ in their atmospheric lifetimes, as shown in Table 11.1. The case of hydrofluorocarbons (HFCs) is ironic because these chlorine-free halocarbons were largely developed as alternatives to ozone-depleting chlorinated fluorocarbons in refrigerant and other commercial and industrial applications (see the discussion of the Montreal Protocol in chapter 8 for details). Due to their roles as replacement gases under the Montreal Protocol, global emissions of HFCs are rising.

Anthropogenic greenhouse gas emissions are a part of the larger, naturally occurring global carbon cycle, which is illustrated in Figure 11.1. Note that it is customary to keep track of emissions in terms of their carbon content rather than their total molecular mass, in order to facilitate comparisons with other reservoirs and flows in the global carbon cycle in which the carbon may be in a variety of different chemical compounds. For example, the carbon content of carbon dioxide is found by dividing the weight of carbon dioxide by 3.67. It is also important to distinguish reservoirs (stocks) from

Figure 11.1 **Simplified Global Carbon Cycle Circa 2000**

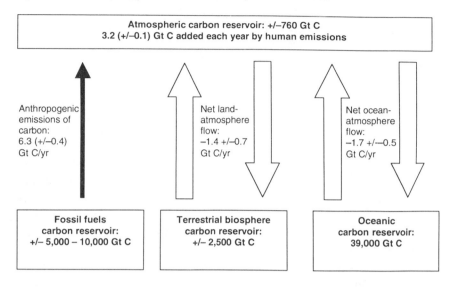

Atmospheric carbon reservoir: +/−760 Gt C
3.2 (+/−0.1) Gt C added each year by human emissions

Anthropogenic emissions of carbon: 6.3 (+/−0.4) Gt C/yr

Net land-atmosphere flow: −1.4 +/−0.7 Gt C/yr

Net ocean-atmosphere flow: −1.7 +/−0.5 Gt C/yr

Fossil fuels carbon reservoir: +/− 5,000 – 10,000 Gt C

Terrestrial biosphere carbon reservoir: +/− 2,500 Gt C

Oceanic carbon reservoir: 39,000 Gt C

Arrows represent carbon flows, while boxes represent carbon reservoirs. All numerical values are in billions of metric tons (gigatons) of carbon (Gt C). Positive flow values indicate carbon transport to the atmosphere, while negative flow values indicate carbon transport to the terrestrial biosphere and the oceans. Actual values vary based on different estimates, and numerical values shown here only serve as a simplified guide to the global carbon cycle. Note that more recent research by Sabine et al. (2004) suggests that the net quantity of carbon that is drawn out of the atmosphere by the terrestrial biosphere has been minimal until recent years, while the world's oceans have accounted for nearly all of the approximately 3.1 gigatons of human emissions removed from the atmosphere. *Sources:* Pewclimate.org, IPCC (2001).

flows (also known as fluxes) in this cycle. A very large reservoir of carbon is stored in the world's oceans and seafloor sediments, with smaller quantities stored in fossil fuels, the terrestrial biosphere, and the atmosphere. A very large flow of carbon is exchanged in the world's photosynthesis/respiration processes, and between the atmosphere and the world's oceans. Both of these naturally occurring gas-exchange systems are in near-balance. Approximately 3.3 of the 6.3 billion metric tons (gigatons) of anthropogenic carbon fail to be taken up by the terrestrial biosphere and oceans each year, and add to the accumulated stock of carbon (and other greenhouse gases) in the atmosphere. Dr. Robert Socolow, co-director of the Carbon Mitigation Initiative, has provided a useful mapping between carbon-equivalent emissions and increases in atmospheric carbon dioxide concentrations. In particular, every 2.1 gigatons of carbon-equivalent emissions (net of what is taken up by the earth's carbon sinks) results in a 1 ppm (part per million) increase in atmospheric carbon dioxide concentrations. Thus, the 3.3 gigatons of annual carbon-equivalent emissions that fail to be taken up by the earth's carbon sinks results in an annual average increase of about 1.57 ppm in the earth's atmospheric carbon dioxide concentration. It is this progressive rise in atmospheric greenhouse gas concentrations, caused by anthropogenic emissions in excess of the earth's capacity for uptake and sequestration, that results in a *climate forcing*—a mechanism that alters the global energy balance—that is widely expected to result in rising mean atmospheric temperatures and a complex of other changes in global climate.

Anthropogenic climate change represents perhaps the most significant and challenging global tragedy of the commons confronting the world's policy-makers. This chapter begins with a model that explains anthropogenic greenhouse gas emissions as a function of a number of economic variables, followed by a description of recent trends in global and U.S. emissions. Next, we turn to a summary of scientific predictions regarding future anthropogenic greenhouse gas emissions, and a review of the scientific evidence. We will then consider the record of international action on the problem of preserving the global climate commons. There have been a number of economic policy studies that estimate costs and benefits associated with the control of greenhouse gases, and after reviewing international action on global climate change, we will examine several economic studies of greenhouse gas control. Key elements of greenhouse gas control include the problem of industrialized countries curbing their emissions of greenhouse gases and the problem of developing countries "leapfrogging" from a less-industrialized status to sophisticated climate-friendly technologies. The chapter concludes with a discussion of climate-friendly technology transfer and the Clean Development Mechanism of the Kyoto Protocol, which address the latter of these two problems.

Greenhouse Gas Emissions and Global Climate Change

Modeling Carbon Dioxide Emissions

Human activity has increased concentrations of carbon dioxide in the atmosphere. There are several mathematical expressions that can be used to describe the primary factors driving anthropogenic greenhouse gas emissions, with emphasis on carbon dioxide. One of these is the *IPAT identity*:

Impact = Population × Affluence × Technology.

The IPAT identity relates a nation or other political unit's environmental impact (e.g., carbon dioxide emissions) in a given time period to the mathematical product of population, "affluence" (which can be measured as *gross domestic product* [GDP] per capita), and technology (which can be measured in emissions per unit of GDP). This relation can be expanded a bit more to yield the *Kaya identity* (Kaya 1990):

Carbon Dioxide Emissions = Population × (GDP/Population) × (Energy/GDP) × (CO_2/Energy).

These equations are useful in understanding the complex factors influencing changes in carbon dioxide emissions, though it is important to note that the elements are not entirely independent of one another. The Kaya identity tells us that, all else equal, a country with a small population, or with low per capita income (GDP/population) of energy, or with low *energy intensity* (energy/GDP), or with low *carbon intensity* (CO_2/energy), will have lower carbon dioxide emissions. A useful property of a multiplicative identity such as IPAT or Kaya is that the growth rate in energy-related emissions is equal to the sum of the growth rates of each component. Thus, for the case of the Kaya identity, we have:

$\%DCO_2$ = %DPopulation + %D(GDP/Population) + %D(Energy/GDP) + $\%D(CO_2/Energy)$.

Note that "%Δ" refers to growth rate in percentage terms. According to Watson, Zinyowera, and Moss (1996, hereinafter Watson et al.), worldwide energy-related carbon dioxide emissions have been growing at an average annual rate of approximately 1.7 percent since the middle of the nineteenth century. Using information from Nakicenovic et al. (1993) and Watson et al., this 1.7 percent rate of growth in annual emissions equals the sum of a 1 percent annual rate of growth in population, a 2 percent annual rate of growth in per capita income, a 1 percent annual rate of decline in energy intensity, and a 0.3 percent annual rate of decline in carbon intensity (sometimes termed "decarbonization"). The declines in both energy and carbon intensity are due to the fact that the intensities are mathematical quotients. So carbon intensity can improve (i.e., in the context of global climate change, decline) if, for example, a given quantity of electricity is generated from burning natural gas instead of coal (decarbonization). Energy intensity will improve (i.e., decline) if, for example, a given level of GDP is generated from more energy-efficient capital equipment. Yet reducing the carbon intensity of energy is not sufficient to assure a reduction in total carbon dioxide emissions. This is because while carbon intensity may fall, population growth and per capita GDP growth can swamp any improvement in carbon intensity. Projections for future carbon dioxide emissions usually assume continued decarbonization, though some experts believe that countries such as China, the United States, and India may "recarbonize" by substituting abundant coal resources for declining and more costly oil and gas resources.

Trends in Greenhouse Gas Emissions

Over hundreds of thousands of years of earth's history gathered from ice-core samples, atmospheric carbon dioxide concentrations have naturally fluctuated by 10 percent or more due to long-term orbital cycles that vary the quantity of solar radiation reaching certain parts of the earth. Ruddiman (2005) points out that these cycles in solar radiation in turn lead to the glacial and interglacial cycle, and that atmospheric concentrations of carbon dioxide naturally peak just before the ice caps fully melt at 275 to 300 parts per million. These carbon dioxide concentrations then naturally decline for perhaps 15,000 years or so to an average of approximately 245 ppm. Ruddiman argues that the earth should be in one of these long periods of declining carbon dioxide concentrations. Instead, ice core data indicate that carbon dioxide and methane concentrations have remained stable over the last 5,000 to 8,000 years, up to about 1780, a deviation from the natural trend that Ruddiman hypothesizes is due to the advent of human agriculture. Key culprits in this model are the clearing of forests and the irrigation and flooding of land. If his hypothesis is true, then by the late 1700s the cumulative effects of agriculture account for a 250 parts per billion (ppb) increase in methane, a 40 ppm increase in carbon dioxide, and an average warming of 0.8 degrees Celsius. According to Ruddiman's hypothesis, absent agriculture, average temperatures would be steadily declining, and would have passed below the glaciation threshold about 5,000 years ago. One interesting piece of supporting evidence is that during several historical periods of mass plagues that reduced agricultural activity for several decades or more, carbon dioxide concentrations actually declined by 5 or 10 ppm.

As of the mid-1700s, atmospheric concentrations of carbon dioxide stood at approximately 280 ppm. Starting in the late 1700s—the beginning of the industrial revolution and the rapid rise in human population—atmospheric concentrations of carbon dioxide began to increase, and as of 2005 had increased to 380 ppm. According to the Intergovernmental Panel on Climate Change (IPCC 2001), the present carbon dioxide concentration in the atmosphere has not been exceeded during the past 650,000 years, and likely not during the past 20 million years. The current rate of increase is unprecedented during at least the past 20,000 years. The IPCC (2001) also provides information on emissions trends for other greenhouse gases. For example, they report that the atmospheric concentration of nitrous oxide has increased by 17 percent since 1750 and continues to increase. The present atmospheric nitrous oxide concentration has not been exceeded during at least the past thousand years. Moreover, the atmospheric concentration of methane has increased by 151 percent since 1750, and continues to increase. The present methane concentration has not been exceeded during the past 420,000 years. About one-third of current nitrous oxide emissions and one-half of current methane emissions are anthropogenic

Trend data over the last half-century from the Mauna Loa Observatory in Hawaii indicate an acceleration in the rate of growth in the concentration of carbon dioxide in the atmosphere. In particular, between 1990 and 1999, atmospheric carbon dioxide concentrations increased at an average annual rate of 1.5 ppm. Carbon dioxide concentrations were only growing at a rate of 1.0 ppm a half-century ago, when observations were first made at Mauna Loa. Estimates of greenhouse gas concentrations by the year 2100 depend on changes in the energy-related emissions factors in the Kaya identity, as well as changes in land use, rates of deforestation, and emissions of sulfate aerosols, among other factors. Future change in these factors is difficult to predict. If the current 1.5-ppm growth rate were to continue for fifty years, for example, then by 2055 the atmospheric concentration of carbon dioxide would be a bit over 450 ppm, or approximately 1.6 times the pre–industrial revolution concentration of 280 ppm. Moreover, if the current 1.5-ppm growth rate were to continue for 100 years, then by 2105 the concentration of carbon dioxide in the atmosphere would be 528 ppm. In fact, if action is not taken, annual increases in atmospheric concentrations are likely to increase rather than stay the same.

The IPCC (1996) provides a "business as usual" (BAU) forecast for carbon dioxide concentrations. Under BAU, the world's population is predicted to reach 9 billion by 2050, global per capita income is predicted to be 3.3 times larger in 2050 than in 1990, and the energy intensity of economic activity is likely to have improved by 2050 to 60 percent of its 1990 value. Based on these projections, world energy consumption in 2050 would be three times larger than in 1990. If the carbon intensity of world energy supply continues to fall at its BAU rate of about 0.2 percent per year, this scenario would entail world carbon dioxide emissions from the energy sector being 2.7 times bigger in 2050 than in 1990. Continuation of this BAU scenario until 2050 would result in atmospheric concentrations of carbon dioxide reaching 550 ppm by 2050, and 715 ppm by 2100, or two and a half times the pre-industrial level and still rising steeply.

According to the U.S. EPA (2004), total U.S. greenhouse gas emissions in 2002 were 1.88 gigatons, measured in carbon equivalent GWP. Total U.S. emissions have risen by 13 percent from 1990 to 2002. Emissions rose slightly from 2001 to 2002, increasing by 0.7 percent. Annual greenhouse gas emissions by an average American are roughly equivalent to that of 18 Indians or 99 Bangladeshis. As the largest source of U.S. greenhouse gas emissions, carbon dioxide from fossil fuel combustion has accounted for a nearly constant 80 percent of global warming potential (GWP) weighted emissions since 1990. Emissions from this source category grew by 17 percent from 1990 to 2002, and were responsible for most of the increase in national emissions during this period. In 2001 Paul McCardle of the U.S. Energy Information Administration reported that during the period between 1949 and 1999, over 99 percent of the variation in U.S. carbon dioxide emissions could be explained by energy consumption, and over 85 percent could be explained by U.S. GDP. According to the U.S. Energy Information Administration's *International Energy Outlook 2004* (U.S. EIA 2004) reference case, world carbon emissions are projected to rise to 7.55 gigatons by 2010 and 10.1 gigatons by 2025. Much of the projected increase in emissions is expected to occur in the developing world, accompanying the increases in energy use projected for the region's emerging economies. Developing countries account for 61 percent of the projected increase in carbon dioxide emissions between 2001 and 2025.

Global Climate Change Predictions

It is more difficult and controversial to predict global climate change than it is to predict future greenhouse gas emissions. Climate models are extremely complex, and so as our understanding of the world's climate improves, so too will our ability to model and predict climate change caused by anthropogenic greenhouse gas emissions. Moreover, in addition to relatively smooth cause-and-effect relationships between greenhouse gas concentrations and temperature, there is the potential for abrupt and dramatic changes. For example, a report by Schwartz and Randall (2003), commissioned by the U.S. Department of Defense, indicates that there is the potential for freshwater runoff from melting glaciers to abruptly slow the North Atlantic Ocean's thermohaline conveyor (the Gulf Stream). This slowing could reduce average temperatures in Northern Europe by as much as six degrees Fahrenheit over a ten-year period, and generate as much as a 30 percent decline in rainfall as well as significant declines in agricultural production. Similar disruptions of thermohaline conveyors in other areas of the world's oceans make this a problem of potentially global concern. Schwartz and Randall note that these disruptions could persist for as long as a century, as they did the last time an ocean conveyor collapsed due to these effects 12,700 years ago, and again 8,200 years ago.

Consider the evolution of IPCC greenhouse gas and climate predictions during the 1990s. In 1990 the IPCC had estimated average increases in temperatures at the earth's surface ranging from 3 to 10 degrees Fahrenheit by 2050, with the most likely increase being nearly 5 degrees. The IPCC also issued a mid-range estimate for global warming in the longer term (several hundred years into the future) of 18 degrees Fahrenheit. In January 1996 the IPCC lowered the projected rate of warming over the next century by about 30 percent compared to its 1990 assessment. This downward adjustment occurred due to including more variables and interactive effects into the climate change model. For example, the new model included emissions of traditional pollutants such as sulfates and carbonaceous aerosols, which cool the atmosphere by reflecting incoming solar radiation and altering the reflective properties of clouds. These sulfates and aerosols may have masked one-half of the heat-trapping impacts of increased concentrations of greenhouse gases. The newer model also included increased carbon dioxide sequestration by forests whose growth will be stimulated by a more carbon-rich atmosphere. Another reason for the downward revision in the climate change forecast was the decline in projected chlorofluorocarbon emissions due to international control actions taken within the structure of the Montreal Protocol since 1990. The 1996 estimates for global warming, based on moderate population growth and economic expansion, and a lack of international greenhouse gas-control efforts, predicted a mean surface temperature rise of between 1 and 3.5 degrees Celsius by 2100.

Harris, Kattenberg, and Maskell (2000) provides climate change predictions drawn from an improved understanding of the factors driving greenhouse gas emissions and land use changes. This report describes scenarios drawn from four very different "storylines" describing possible future demographic, social, economic, technological, and environmental trends. While these storylines predict widely different carbon dioxide concentrations in the future, the midpoint of these predictions suggests atmospheric carbon dioxide concentrations of approximately 750 ppm by 2100, and a cumulative transport of approximately 1,500 gigatons of carbon dioxide into the earth's atmosphere. The midpoint of these storyline predictions suggests an approximate doubling of annual atmospheric nitrous oxide and methane emissions by 2100. Consequently, the globally averaged surface temperature is projected to increase by 1.4 to 5.8 degrees Celsius by 2100.

One direct implication of global warming and temperature rises in polar areas is the potential for large-scale melting of ice caps, resulting in a rise in sea levels (estimated in 1996 by the IPCC to be around 0.5 meter by 2100) and widespread flooding in low-lying coastal areas. Hansen (2004) argues that rising sea levels are the dominant issue in global warming, since a large share of the world's population lives within a few meters of sea level, along with trillions of dollars of infrastructure at risk. Levitus et al. (2000) reports that the heat content of the world's oceans has increased by about 10 watt-years per square meter in the past fifty years, and that the rate of ocean heat storage in the 1990s is consistent with Hansen's estimate that the earth is retaining between 0.5 and 1 watt per square meter. Hansen notes that the amount of oceanic heat needed to melt enough ice to raise global sea levels by approximately one meter is 12 watt-years. Given the current level of annual climate forcing, that amount of oceanic heat could be accumulated in twelve to twenty-four years. At the peak rate of ice melt during the time of greatest warming in the Holocene interglacial period, a one-meter sea level rise occurred in a twenty-year period.

If the predictions regarding global warming prove to be true, then the damage from rising sea levels will disproportionately harm poorer countries without the income to build dikes and other engineering works to counteract rising seas, and may result in large-scale refugee displacements (hundreds of millions or more people leaving Bangladesh, the Nile Delta, and coastal China, among others). While current models predict a global average increase in precipitation, this increase is not expected to be uniformly distributed. In particular, higher latitudes are expected to experience an increase in precipitation because of poleward transport of atmospheric moisture generated from increased evaporation in lower latitudes. This increased spring evaporation will tend to dry out many soils in lower latitudes, resulting in less moisture being available for evaporation and rainfall during the summer, and leading to sharper summer droughts (Karl, Nicholls, and Gregory 1997, hereinafter Karl et al.). More generally, the pace of the greenhouse effect is predicted to proceed more rapidly than the natural ability of many plant and animal species to adjust, hastening the rate of extinctions.

Karl et al. (1997) observe that small increases in average daily temperatures cause a disproportionate percentage increase in the frequency of extremely hot days and heat waves. Cold spells will still occur but will be less likely. Using the Chicago area as an example, Karl et al. point out that with "just a three degree C increase in the average July temperature, the probability that the heat index (a measure that includes humidity and measures overall discomfort) will exceed 49 degrees C (120 degrees F) sometime during the month increases from one in 20 to one in four" (p. 80). An interesting effect of global warming appears to be that warming affects daily minimum temperatures far more than daily maximums, thus lengthening the growing season in many temperate areas around the world. Dai, Del Genio, and Fung (1997) point out that this increase in daily minimum temperatures coincides with (and thus might be explained by) a global increase in thick, precipitating clouds, as might be expected from the greenhouse effect, and these clouds tend to reduce nighttime cooling. Moreover, while earlier analysis of global warming suggested an increase in the frequency and intensity of tropical cyclones and hurricanes, more recent work suggests that there will not necessarily be a significant global increase in tropical storm activity.

Hayhoe et al. (2004) provides climate change predictions for California using two different climate models (the Parallel Climate Model and the Hadley Center Climate Model) and several different future emissions scenarios drawn from IPCC (2000). These scenarios include a "low" atmospheric carbon dioxide concentration of 550 ppm by 2100 (scenario B1), and a "high" atmospheric carbon dioxide concentration of 970 ppm by 2100 (scenario A1fi). Under the "low" carbon scenario, the two models predict average annual statewide temperatures in California will rise by 2.3–3.3 degrees Celsius, the sea level will rise by 19–27 centimeters, and April 1 snowpack water equivalent will decline by 29–72 percent. Under the "high" carbon scenario, the two models predict average annual statewide temperatures will rise by 3.8–5.8 degrees Celsius, the sea level will rise by 29–41 centimeters, and April 1 snowpack water equivalent will decline by 73–89 percent. Earlier runoff may increase the potential for early-season flooding, and when combined with increased evaporation, may lead to a decline in late-season water availability.

The Hadley Center for Climate Prediction and Research in the United Kingdom produced a number of predictions regarding global climate change and its impacts in 1999. A summary of their predictions based on unmitigated anthropogenic greenhouse gas emissions is provided below. The Hadley Center predicts that with unmitigated emissions, global average temperature will increase by 3° C and mean sea level will rise by 40 centimeters by the 2080s compared to the present (Hadley Center 1999). Land areas will warm twice as fast as that of the oceans, and winter high-latitude temperatures will warm more quickly than the global average, as will areas of northern South America, India, and southern Africa. The 40-centimeter rise in mean sea level forecasted by the 2080s is estimated to increase the annual number of people flooded from 13 million to 94 million. Sixty percent of this increase will occur in southern Asia (along coasts from Pakistan, through India, Sri Lanka, and Bangladesh to Burma), and 20 percent will occur in Southeast Asia (from Thailand to Vietnam, including Indonesia and the Philippines). Large changes in precipitation, both positive and negative, are anticipated in the tropics. With unmitigated emissions, the Hadley Center predicts a substantial dieback of tropical forests and tropical grasslands by the 2080s, especially in northern South America and central southern Africa. Considerable growth of forests is predicted to occur in North America, northern Asia, and China. The

Hadley Center predicts that the absorption of carbon dioxide by vegetation will increase during the twenty-first century, but this sink is lost in the 2070s, with unmitigated emissions due to a dieback in tropical vegetation.

With unmitigated emissions, the Hadley Center model predicts that by the 2080s there will be large changes in the availability of water from rivers. Substantial decreases are predicted for Australia, India, southern Africa, most of South America and Europe, and the Middle East. Increases are seen across North America, Asia (particularly central Asia), and central eastern Africa. Climate change and carbon dioxide increases due to unmitigated emissions are forecasted by the Hadley Center to increase grain harvests at high and mid-latitudes, such as North America, China, Argentina, and much of Europe, by the 2080s. At the same time, grain harvests in Africa, the Middle East, and, particularly, India are expected to decrease. In terms of human health impacts, the Hadley Center forecasts that an estimated 290 million additional people worldwide will be at risk of *falciparum* malaria (clinically more dangerous than the more widespread vivax malaria) due to climate change from unmitigated emissions by the 2080s. The greatest increases in risk are projected for China and central Asia. Epstein (2000) reports that predicted increases in temperature will broaden the range of mosquitoes carrying not only malaria, but also dengue fever, yellow fever, and several kinds of encephalitis. Predicted increases in flooding events will not only create ideal mosquito habitat, but will also increase the spread of cholera and other water-borne diseases. The Hadley Center predicts that human-induced warming will reduce the risk of mortality in many large temperate-zone cities, as the estimated reduction in winter-related mortality exceeds the increase in heat-related summer mortality.

In 2000 the U.S. Global Change Research Program (USGCRP 2000) issued a national assessment of predicted climate change impacts on the United States, key elements of which are summarized below. The national assessment predicts that the warming in the twenty-first century will be significantly larger than in the twentieth century. Scenarios examined in the assessment, which assume no major interventions to reduce continued growth of world greenhouse gas emissions, indicate that temperatures in the United States will rise by about 5–10°F (3–6°C) on average during the twenty-first century, which is more than the projected global increase. This rise is very likely to be associated with more extreme precipitation and faster evaporation of water, leading to greater frequency of both very wet and very dry conditions. The assessment reports that natural ecosystems (as opposed to agricultural lands or timber plantations) are especially vulnerable to the harmful effects of climate change since there is often little that can be done to help them adapt to the projected speed and amount of change. Some ecosystems that are already constrained by climate, such as alpine meadows in the Rocky Mountains, are likely to face extreme stress, and may disappear entirely. It is likely that other more widespread ecosystems will also be vulnerable to climate change. One of the climate scenarios used in the assessment suggests the potential for the forests of the Southeast to break up into a mosaic of forests, savannas, and grasslands. Several of the climate scenarios suggest possible changes in the species composition of the Northeast forests, including the loss of sugar maples. Major alterations to natural ecosystems due to climate change could possibly have negative consequences for our economy, which depends in part on the sustained bounty of our nation's lands, waters, and native plant and animal communities.

The USGCRP assessment also includes an examination of the potential impacts of climate change on different regions of the United States. For example, rising sea levels will very likely cause further loss of coastal wetlands (ecosystems that provide vital nurseries and habitats for many fish species) and put coastal communities at greater risk of storm surges, especially in the southeastern region of the United States. Reductions in snowpack will very likely alter the timing and amount of water supplies, potentially exacerbating water shortages and conflicts, particularly throughout the western United States. The two models used in the assessment forecast annual average temperature increases ranging from 3 to over 4 degrees Fahrenheit by the 2030s and 8–11°F (4.5–6°C) by the 2090s. The two models project increased rainfall during winter, especially over California, where runoff is projected to double by the 2090s. In these climate scenarios, some areas of the Rocky Mountains are projected to get drier. Both models project more extreme wet and dry years. The melting of glaciers in the high-elevation West and in Alaska represents the loss or diminishment of unique national treasures of the American landscape. Large increases in the heat index (which combines temperature and humidity) and increases in the frequency of heat waves are very likely. The assessment argues that these changes will, at minimum, increase discomfort, particularly in cities. It is very probable that continued thawing of permafrost and melting of sea ice in Alaska will further damage forests, buildings, roads, and coastlines, and harm subsistence livelihoods. In various parts of the nation, cold-weather recreation such as skiing will very likely be reduced, and air conditioning usage will very likely increase.

The USGCRP assessment also predicts some positive impacts from global climate change in the twenty-first century. For example, crop and forest productivity is likely to increase in some areas for the next few decades due to increased carbon dioxide in the atmosphere and an extended growing season. The assessment states that some U.S. food exports could increase, depending on impacts in other food-growing regions around the world, and that a rise in crop production in fertile areas could cause prices to fall, benefiting consumers. Other benefits that are possible include extended seasons for construction and warm-weather recreation, reduced heating requirements, and reduced cold-weather mortality.

Finally, the USGCRP assessment points out that there are also very likely to be unanticipated impacts of climate change during the next century. Such surprises may stem from unforeseen changes in the physical climate system, such as major alterations in ocean circulation, cloud formation, or storms, and unpredicted biological consequences of these physical climate changes, such as massive dislocations of species or pest outbreaks. In addition, unexpected social or economic change, including major shifts in wealth, technology, or political priorities, could affect our ability to respond to climate change. Policymakers are confronted with the challenge of devising greenhouse gas policy in the context of uncertainty. Thus, we are conducting a *natural experiment* on the planet, the outcome of which may range from moderate to catastrophic, and which will last well beyond the human time scale of lifetimes and generations.

The Evidence Regarding Global Climate Change

There is overwhelming consensus in the peer-reviewed scientific literature that anthropogenic emissions are responsible for at least some of the observed warming trend on earth over the past fifty years. In particular, Oreskes (2004) reviewed the 928 peer-reviewed scientific articles on climate change that have been published in scientific journals between 1993 and 2003. Oreskes found that 75 percent of these articles endorsed anthropogenic climate change, while 25 percent addressed methodological issues and did not take a position on anthropogenic climate change. Most importantly, not a single peer-reviewed scientific article disputed anthropogenic climate change. As Oreskes notes, "[p]olicy-makers and the media, particularly in the United States, frequently assert that climate science is highly uncertain. . . . This is not the case" (p. 1686). To illustrate Oreskes's point, in June 2005, about six months after her paper was published in *Science*, the Government Accountability Project and the *New York Times* reported that Philip Cooney, the chief of staff of President Bush's White House Council on Environmental Quality, modified a number of government scientific reports to increase the emphasis on uncertainty regarding climate change. According to the *New York Times* (Revkin 2005), before being appointed to the Council, Mr. Cooney, a lawyer rather than a scientist, worked as a lobbyist for the American Petroleum Institute, which, like the Bush administration, opposes mandatory curbs on greenhouse gas emissions.

Hansen (2004) notes that while there are both natural and anthropogenic climate forcings affecting the earth's energy balance, anthropogenic climate forcings now dominate natural forcings. These climate forcings are measured in watts per square meter. Greenhouse gases and black carbon aerosols (small particles of dark soot that absorb heat from sunlight) contribute to radiative climate forcings, while reflective aerosols (e.g., sulfur dioxide from burning coal, aerosols from volcanic eruptions), declines in solar irradiance, and increases in the albedo effect from clouds reduce radiative climate forcings. While events such as volcanic eruptions result in significant interannual variation in climate forcings, and there is some question about the role of changes in atmospheric water vapor and cloud cover, the evidence suggests a discernable rising trend. According to the IPCC (2001), climate forcings due to increased concentrations of greenhouse gases from 1750 to 2000 are estimated to total 2.43 watts per square meter. Of this total, carbon dioxide accounts for 1.46 watts per square meter, methane accounts for 0.48 watts per square meter, various halocarbons account for 0.34 watts per square meter, and nitrous oxide accounts for 0.15 watts per square meter. Hansen (2004) argues that if recent greenhouse gas growth rates continued, the added climate forcing in the next fifty years would be approximately 2 watts per square meter, which is at the low end of the range of future scenarios given in IPCC (2001).

The IPCC reported in January 1996 that over the last 100 years, global mean surface temperatures have increased by between 0.3 and 0.6 degrees Celsius, and mean sea level has risen by between 1 and 2.5 millimeters per year. The IPCC concluded rather cautiously that it is unlikely that this rise in global temperatures is entirely due to natural causes, noting, "the balance of evidence suggests a discernible human influence on global climate." In April 2000 the IPCC issued a stronger draft message in which it stated that "that there has been a discernible human influence on global climate." The National Research Council (2000) reports that accelerated warming in the late 1990s has caused the IPCC (1996) to increase its warming estimate during the twentieth century to between 0.4 and 0.8 degrees Celsius. The World Bank (1999) reports that the twentieth century was the warmest in 600 years, and fourteen of the warmest years since 1860 have occurred in the 1980s and 1990s. The World Bank also reports that winter seawater temperatures in latitudes above 45 degrees north have risen by 0.5 degrees Celsius since the 1980s, and that in 1999 the International Ice Patrol did not report a single iceberg south of 48 degrees north latitude. In its assessment of climate change impacts on the United States, the USGCRP (2000) reports that the average annual U.S. temperature has risen by almost one degree Fahrenheit (0.6°C) during the twentieth century, and precipitation has increased nationally by 5 to 10 percent (mostly due to increases in heavy downpours). The assessment reports that these trends have been most apparent over the past few decades. The Hadley Center (1999) reports that the atmosphere at a height of 3–5 km above sea level has clearly warmed over the past thirty-five years, although not always in concert with the surface, and that the extent of Arctic Sea ice has decreased over the last three decades. As pointed out earlier, analysis of the observed rise in global temperatures indicates that the increase is due in large part to increases in daily minimum temperatures. For example, Easterling et al. (1997) find that while global daily maximum temperatures have been rising at a rate of 0.88 degrees Celsius each century, daily minimum temperatures have been rising at the rate of 1.86 degrees Celsius each century. Increases in cloudiness are believed to have caused much of this effect.

Improved methods of reconstructing and then explaining the earth's climatic history are essential to understanding the extent to which the current warming trend is anthropogenic. Methods of reconstructing the earth's climatic history include tree ring analysis, ice cores, corals and sediments, and borehole temperatures. As Overpeck (2000) describes in his review of the recent scientific literature on the world's climatic history, natural factors such as variation in solar output or volcanic eruptions that episodically reduce solar heating at the surface account for many features of the pre-industrial portion of the temperature record. Yet such natural mechanisms can explain only a fraction of the total warming that took place in the twentieth century, leaving us with the likelihood that human-induced warming is under way.

One source of controversy over the observed record of global climate change has been the disparity between rising surface temperature readings and steady satellite temperature readings for the lower and mid-troposphere (that portion of the atmosphere that extends from the surface to about 8 kilometers above the surface). Climate change models predict that the lower and mid-troposphere should warm at least as much as the surface, and therefore the satellite data appear to invalidate the models. The satellite data have been available only since 1979, which makes it difficult to infer any meaningful trend in the data. Nevertheless some have used this disparity to cast doubt on the reliability of the surface temperature record and the claims made by the IPCC that there is a discernable human influence on global climate. A special panel was assembled by the National Research Council to assess this disparity. The National Research Council (2000) reported that the warming trend in global mean surface temperatures is "undoubtedly real" and is "substantially greater" than the average rate of warming during the twentieth century. They go on to report that the disparity (which was reduced somewhat by corrections in the microwave sounding units used to gauge tropospheric temperature) in no way invalidates the conclusion that surface temperatures are rising. The panel stated that the lack of warming in the troposphere in the twenty-year period might have been due to natural causes such as volcanic eruptions, and human causes such as ozone depletion in the stratosphere.

Global climate change skeptics have also pointed to the fact that observed surface temperature warming has so far been very modest, less than some have predicted, thus arguing that dire forecasts of future warming are overstated. Climate modelers have responded that a good deal of the warming should be occurring in the world's oceans, though the historical temperature record was thought to be too spotty to get a definitive answer. Thus, the United Nations sponsored the Global Oceanographic Data Archeology and Rescue Project, which over the last seven years has resulted in an additional two million ocean temperature profiles being added to the historical record. Levitus et al. (2000) reported that these data show a marked warming in the world's oceans over the last half of the twentieth century. Kerr (2000) reported that the increased heat content found by Levitus et al. is roughly what climate models have predicted.

There is a variety of other regional sources of evidence for global climate change. Myneni et al. (1997) report that since the early 1980s the active growing season has increased by approximately twelve days in the Northern Hemisphere between 45 and 70 degrees latitude. Much of the increase is concentrated in the spring and appears to be associated with an earlier disappearance of snow cover. The USGCRP (2000) reported that during the twentieth century, temperatures in the western United States have risen by 2 to 5 degrees Fahrenheit (1–3°C). The region has generally had increases in precipitation, with increases in some areas greater than 50 percent. However, a few areas, such as Arizona, have become drier and experienced more droughts. The length of the snow season decreased by sixteen days from 1951 to 1996 in California and Nevada, and extreme precipitation events have increased. Epstein (2000) reports that the elevation at which temperatures are always below freezing has ascended almost 500 feet in the tropics, and mosquitoes carrying malaria and dengue fever now occur at higher elevations than before. For example, nineteenth-century European colonists in Africa avoided malaria by settling in cooler mountain areas, but many of these havens are now compromised. Epstein observes that insects and the diseases they carry have been found at higher elevations in Central and South America, east and central Africa, and Asia.

International Action on Global Climate Change

The political economy of global climate change exemplifies a global environmental policy dilemma:

- The steps required to make a substantial reduction in greenhouse gas emissions imply significant near-term transition costs that are concentrated on fossil fuel–related industries and their consumers.
- The estimated benefits of substantially reducing greenhouse gas emissions are diffuse across the globe, uncertain or unknown in terms of probability and magnitude, and primarily fall far in the future.
- Moreover, global warming has the characteristic of irreversibility from the perspective of the next few human generations; Maier-Reimer and Hasselman (1987) estimate that it will take approximately 1,000 years to remove 85 percent of the excess carbon dioxide from the atmosphere.
- With transition costs concentrated and in the present, and with benefits diffuse, uncertain, and cast in the future, the political economy of greenhouse gas control is "Olsonian" in the sense that this term is used in chapter 8. Thus, for example, current politicians may find it to be "political suicide" to deviate from a cheap energy policy and impose carbon taxes to limit emissions. Therefore coordinated international policies to slow or reverse global climate change will tend to be difficult to achieve and unstable.
- In order for global-warming policy to be effective, there must be international coordination and cooperation across countries that are highly diverse in income, extent of industrialization, culture, population growth rates and other demographic characteristics, educational attainment, and extent of democratic empowerment.
- The transnational characteristic of global climate change implies a concern about free-riding behavior by countries choosing to avoid costly greenhouse gas control efforts, which in turn creates a competitive advantage in terms of international trade.

The IPCC, which was formed in 1988, issued its First Assessment Report in 1990 in which the organization highlighted the importance of forming an international agreement on climate change. The Second World Climate Conference, also held in 1990, linked many who were advocating for international negotiations. As a result, the United Nations General Assembly opened negotiations on a framework convention on climate change in 1990, and created the Intergovernmental Negotiating Committee to conduct these negotiations. Thus, as early as 1990 it was recognized that the world's climate is a global common-pool resource (CPR), and that international action is necessary in order to avoid a potentially catastrophic tragedy of the commons. As with managing the world's marine fishery CPR's, lack of international coordination and cooperation will likely result in many countries failing to take adequate measures, thus free riding on the control efforts undertaken by other countries. The question of what level of greenhouse gas control is in the best interests of a particular country is very difficult to answer for a variety of reasons. Regional effects are known with much less certainty than global effects, yet in all likelihood, some regions and countries will be much more impacted than others. Moreover, northerly countries such as Canada, Norway, Sweden, Finland, and Russia may actually benefit from global warming. In addition, given the high degree of asymmetry between high- and low-income countries, diversity also exists in the extent to which countries can engineer around negative impacts of global warming. Countries also differ in terms of the educational attainment and political empowerment of their citizens. Thus, from an international relations perspective, countries are diverse and are unlikely to have national interests that are mutually consistent. Nevertheless, most governments see a benefit in at least some control of greenhouse gas emissions as a type of insurance against the risk of negative future impacts.

While the world contends with the challenging political economy of climate change policy, human emissions continue. In the past, most public discussion about climate change was focused on how to prevent anthropogenic changes from occurring, and as we will see below, international action has focused on reducing future greenhouse gas emissions. But even if we were to sharply reduce our emissions of greenhouse gases today, the stock of atmospheric greenhouse gases that has accumulated from anthropogenic emissions will result in further warming and rising sea levels for decades, even centuries to come. Consequently what is required is a two-tracked climate change policy strategy of (i) preparation for the impacts of climate change that are likely to come about due to past greenhouse gas emissions, and (ii) stabilization of atmospheric concentrations of greenhouse gases. As the IPCC (2001) notes, populations that inhabit small islands and/or low-lying coastal areas are at particular risk of severe social and economic effects from sea-level rise and storm surges. The impacts of climate change will fall disproportionately upon developing countries and upon the poor persons within all countries, and thereby exacerbate inequities in health status and access to adequate food, clean water, and other resources. Consequently, the first track will likely require an international fund to address the needs of "climate change refugees" displaced by the impacts of climate change. The IPCC (2001) estimates that the second track—stabilization of atmospheric carbon dioxide concentrations at 450 to 650 ppm—would require global anthropogenic carbon dioxide emissions to drop below 1990 levels within a few decades to about a century, and continue to decrease steadily thereafter. Eventually, carbon dioxide emissions would need to decline to a very small fraction of current emissions.

The Earth Summit

The idea of sustainable economic development was made prominent following the publication in 1987 of the World Commission on Economic Development (Brundtland Commission) report *Our Common Future*. Concerns for integrating biodiversity and climate change with sustainable development strategies led to representatives of national governments meeting in May and June of 1992 at the United Nations Conference on Environment and Development (UNCED), frequently referred to as the Earth Summit. The United Nations Framework Convention on Climate Change (UNFCCC), which the Intergovernmental Negotiating Committee had adopted by consensus in May of 1992 in New York, was opened for signature during the Rio de Janeiro meetings of the Earth Summit. A total of 181 governments and the European Community are parties to the Convention. To become a party, a country must ratify, accept, approve, or accede to the Convention. Parties meet regularly at the annual Conference of the Parties to review the implementation of the Convention and continue talks on how best to tackle climate change. The Convention set an "ultimate objective" of stabilizing atmospheric concentrations of greenhouse gases at safe levels. Such levels, which the Convention does not quantify, are to be achieved within a time frame sufficient to allow ecosystems to adapt naturally to climate change, to ensure that food production is not threatened, and to enable economic development to proceed in a sustainable manner.

The Convention divides countries into Annex I Parties and unlisted "non–Annex I" countries. Annex I Parties are industrialized countries, made up of wealthy Organization for Economic Cooperation and Development (OECD) countries and economies in transition (EITs) such as the Russian Federation and various central and eastern European countries that have historically contributed the most to climate change. The per capita emissions from these countries are higher than those of most developing countries, and they have greater financial and institutional capacity to address the problem. The principles of equity and "common but differentiated responsibilities" enshrined in the Convention therefore require these parties to take the lead in modifying longer-term trends in emissions. To this end, Annex I Parties committed themselves to adopting national policies and measures with the non–legally binding aim of returning their greenhouse gas emissions to 1990 levels by the year 2000. The OECD members of Annex I are also listed in Annex II of the UNFCCC. Annex II countries have a special obligation to provide "new and additional financial resources" to developing countries to help them tackle climate change, as well as to facilitate the transfer of climate-friendly technologies to both developing countries and EITs. A Global Environment Facility (GEF) was set up to coordinate the transfer of support from Annex II Parties to the non–Annex I developing countries and EITs in Annex I. The UNFCCC entered into force in 1994 after having been ratified by fifty countries. The UNFCCC also established a Conference of Parties, to which signatory countries agreed to report their current emissions levels and provide plans for reducing them. The Conference of Parties holds annual meetings.

The Kyoto Protocol

The implementation arm of the UNFCCC is the Kyoto Protocol, which was developed in December 1997 at the Third Conference of the Parties (COP-3) in Kyoto, Japan. In order to enter into force, the Kyoto Protocol had to be ratified by at least fifty-five parties to the Convention, including Annex I Parties accounting for 55 percent of anthropogenic carbon dioxide emissions from this group as a whole in 1990. Since the United States refused to ratify the Protocol, and since the United States accounts for a large percentage of total Annex I emissions (approximately 36 percent of emissions from Annex I Parties), the problem had been that the 55 percent rule could not be satisfied unless Russia ratified the Protocol. When Russia ratified the Kyoto Protocol at the end of 2004, that requirement was satisfied, and the Protocol entered into force on February 16, 2005.

From a political economy standpoint, Russia's ratification is believed to have been a condition imposed by key European countries in return for their support for Russia being admitted to the World Trade Organization. As with the Montreal Protocol on Substances That Deplete the Ozone Layer, the Kyoto Protocol is a "two-world" approach whereby rich industrialized countries are required to cut emissions, while lower-income countries can continue business as usual. Proponents view this as politically essential to allowing large industrializing countries such as India and China to catch up economically to richer industrialized countries before having to stabilize or cut emissions. Opponents, particularly in the United States, see this as putting industry in the richer regulated countries at a competitive disadvantage, and leading to a shifting of industrial production—and emissions—to unregulated lower-income countries.

The terms of the Kyoto Protocol call for Annex I countries (including most of the world's industrialized countries) to reduce their overall greenhouse gas emissions by at least 5 percent below 1990 levels over the 2008 to 2012 period. The Kyoto Protocol commits Annex I Parties to individual, legally binding quantified emissions targets to limit or reduce their greenhouse gas emissions. The individual targets for Annex I Parties are listed in the Kyoto Protocol's Annex B, and range from an 8 percent cut for the European

Union (EU) and several other countries, to a 10 percent increase for Iceland. Under the terms of the Protocol, the EU may redistribute its target among its fifteen member states. It has already reached agreement on such a scheme, known as a "bubble," whereby the larger and richer EU countries must cut emissions, while Spain, Portugal, and Greece could actually increase emissions. Starting in 2005 the parties to the Protocol began discussions about achieving greater reduction in a second five-year period after 2012 aimed at bringing emissions down to levels that will not affect the climate, considered to be at least a 60 percent global cut. Early discussions have focused on creative ways of slowing the rate of emissions growth in China, India, and other rapidly developing large countries around the world.

Despite its significant diplomatic importance, the first phase of the Kyoto Protocol will have only a minimal impact on improving the climate. The reductions called for under the Protocol by 2012 represent a modest first step for the nations of the world, but meeting these target reductions would not result in a reversal of anthropogenic climate change. Moreover, relatively few of the Annex I countries are likely to meet their emissions reduction obligations under the Kyoto Protocol. While industrialized countries cut their overall emissions by about 3 percent from 1990 to 2000, this was largely because of a significant decrease in the emissions of former Soviet-bloc countries caused by the transition of their economies. This decline in eastern European emissions masked an 8 percent increase in emissions among the other industrialized countries of the world. Overall, the industrialized world is not on target to meet the Kyoto emissions reduction goal, and is predicted to be about 10 percent above 1990 levels by 2010. As of 2004, only four European Union countries were on track to comply with the national targets that all pre-2004 member states had accepted in order to ensure that the EU as a whole fulfills its Kyoto commitment. The four are France, Germany, Sweden, and the United Kingdom. The United States is prominent in its failure to meet the Earth Summit target. In 1990 the United States produced 1.346 gigatons of carbon-equivalent emissions due to the combustion of fossil fuel, and by 2003 that figure had increased by 17.6 percent to 1.6 gigatons. Moreover, the United States also has the world's highest per capita emissions.

The Kyoto Protocol includes three incentive-based economic instruments that are designed to help Annex B countries reduce the cost of meeting their emissions targets. These instruments are joint implementation (described in chapter 9), emissions trading, and the Clean Development Mechanism (CDM). These instruments allow Annex I countries to meet their emissions target by either producing or acquiring emissions reductions in other countries, most commonly lower-income developing countries. Joint implementation projects allow an Annex I Party to receive emission credits for projects that reduce emissions or enhance emissions-absorbing sinks in other Annex I countries. It is specifically indicated in the Protocol that trading and joint implementation are supplemental to rather than a substitute for domestic actions. The world's first mandatory multinational carbon market—the EU Emissions Trading Scheme (ETS)—began in early 2005. As Michaelowa (2004) notes, the EU allocated generous quantities of carbon credits to various polluting industries for the 2005–7 period to help ease the transition. Moreover, in April 2004 the EU parliament passed the "linking directive," which allows participants in the emissions trading system unlimited use of emission credits from the CDM. The linking directive is the world's first large-scale incentive for companies to participate in the CDM. Michaelowa goes on to report that the EU, especially Germany and the Netherlands, is making significant funds available for CDM projects, in order to generate credits that can be used to help the EU meet its Kyoto obligations.

The CDM was envisioned to perform a three-fold function:

- to assist non–Annex I countries in achieving sustainable development;
- to contribute to the ultimate goal of the convention, that is, stabilization of greenhouse gas concentrations in the atmosphere;
- to help Annex I countries comply with their emission reduction commitments.

The CDM assists developing countries in achieving sustainable development by directing "environmentally friendly" investment into their economies from Annex I Parties and corporations. Two biomass examples included a sugarcane waste–fueled power plant constructed in Brazil, and a swine waste/methane–fueled power plant in Chile, both of which generated Certified Emissions Reductions (CERs) to the Annex I country funding the power plants. Environmental groups have been concerned that some CDM projects, such as large-scale hydroelectric facilities, fail to satisfy an "environmentally friendly" criterion.

Policy Studies: The Economics of Controlling Greenhouse Gas Emissions

The future costs associated with climate change manifest themselves in a variety of ways. A large portion of those costs would fall on farmers who would be displaced as formerly productive agricultural lands are taken out of useful production by climate change. Other costs include increased cooling costs for homes and offices, net of the decreased cost of heating, the costs associated with the displacement of people and infrastructure associated with rising sea levels, and premature deaths due to increased heat and disease epidemics. Much harder to quantify are the costs associated with loss of species, unique ecosystems, and the threat of catastrophic change such as that associated with displacement of the Gulf Stream. If action is taken to reduce anthropogenic greenhouse gas emissions, then some of these costs can be avoided. These avoided future costs can be considered the benefits of controlling greenhouse gas emissions today.

Since these harms are far into the future, applying a typical real discount rate of 2 to 6 percent would result in a miniscule present value of harms. As Cline (2004) notes, for example, discounting at even 3 percent annually causes $100 two centuries in the future to be worth only 27 cents today. As a result, spending more than 27 cents today could not be justified on benefit/cost terms to generate $100 in climate change benefits two centuries from now. Yet, as Cline points out, the essence of the global warming policy is taking potentially costly actions in the present in exchange for a reduction of potential climate damages far in the future. Climate change harms from today's emissions occur in the future due to lags induced by energy absorbed by the oceans, and the relatively long atmospheric life of many greenhouse gases. As a result, the use of typical discount rates can introduce a strong bias against any preventive action. Consequently, any economic analysis of the benefits and costs of greenhouse gas controls must confront the issue of selecting an appropriately low discount rate. Cline (2004) uses a discount rate of 1.5 percent (consistent with the social rate of time preference, which will be described in detail in chapter 13) in his benefit/cost analysis of various actions to limit greenhouse gas emissions.

According to Cline (2004), economically optimal abatement involves an aggressive program that cuts global carbon emissions by an average of about 45 percent from baseline during the twenty-first century, and 55 percent from baseline in the next century. He notes that this would require carbon taxes to rise from about roughly $130–170 per ton through 2015 to about $600 by 2100, and eventually $1,300 before declining again. Using a 1.5 percent discount rate, this policy strategy would generate a present value of global net economic benefits equal to $143 trillion (in constant 1990 dollars).

Nordhaus and Boyer (2000) estimate damage costs associated with climate change, expressed as percentage of GDP, including the risk of catastrophic damages such as those associated with displacement of the Gulf Stream. They find that damage costs as a percentage of GDP are initially negative (i.e., beneficial) for mean global temperature rises of up to 1.25 degrees Celsius. Damage costs as a percentage of GDP increase with mean global temperature beyond this point, however, and rise to 1.1 percent of GDP for warming of 2.5 degrees Celsius, 1.6 percent of GDP for warming of 2.9 degrees Celsius, 5.1 percent of GDP for warming of 4.5 degrees Celsius, and 10 percent of GDP for warming of 6 degrees Celsius. Nordhaus and Boyer (2000) find that meeting the greenhouse gas reduction targets contained in the Kyoto Protocol results in costs that exceed benefits, largely because the reduction targets are so modest as to result in negligible improvements in the future global climate.

Economic analyses of action to slow anthropogenic climate change are sensitive to the types of benefits and costs that are included. According to a study by Burtraw and Toman (1998), for example, climate change policy to reduce emissions of greenhouse gases may also reap environmental benefits by reducing emissions of other conventional pollutants. These ancillary benefits occur immediately, and could be approximately 30 percent of the incremental cost of greenhouse gas reduction. Along these same lines, Boyd, Rutilla, and Viscusi (1995, hereinafter Boyd et al.) sought to determine the level of energy taxation, conservation, and carbon dioxide emissions control that can be economically justified based on a net benefit criterion. The analysis by Boyd et al. offers a range of different scenarios, including low, medium, and high environmental benefits, and different assumptions regarding the extent to which firms can respond to higher energy prices by conserving on the use of energy in production. It is also important to point out that the Boyd et al. study utilizes a "no-regret" perspective in which the computed benefits of reducing carbon dioxide emissions are based on the *current* or *secondary* harms of fossil-fuel burning—particulates, sulfur dioxide, ozone, nitrogen oxides, and carbon monoxide—and not on the possible future primary harms from carbon dioxide emissions. This method of computing the benefits of carbon taxation is referred to as a "no-regret" measure because it is based on known current impacts of fossil-fuel burning rather than more conjectural future global-warming impacts. Thus, their study uses *current benefits* and costs associated with reduced use of fossil fuels to justify reductions in carbon dioxide emissions, which generate uncertain long-term benefits that are secondary to the analysis.

One of the interesting findings from Boyd et al. is that under the assumption that very little energy conservation is possible in production, reducing carbon dioxide emissions by up to around 7 percent imposes insignificant economic costs. Each additional 7 percent increase in carbon dioxide emissions imposes progressively higher economic costs. These costs "increase strikingly" for reductions beyond 35 percent. When substantial energy conservation is assumed possible, the economic costs of reducing carbon dioxide are much lower, and the cost of a 50 percent reduction is only around 1.4 percent of real gross national product (GNP).

The principal findings of Boyd et al. are:

- Energy prices are lower than socially optimal. Depending on the scenario used, fossil-fuel energy tax rates of between 20 and 70 percent are socially optimal. Even in the most conservative scenario, tax rates of 20 percent on coal, 10 percent on oil, and 5 percent on natural gas are socially optimal.
- Under the assumption that firms cannot easily reduce their use of energy in response to higher prices, the analysis finds that a 12 percent reduction in carbon dioxide is socially optimal, and a reduction of up to 20 percent can be accomplished before social welfare is reduced relative to the no-control (base) case.
- Under the assumption that firms can more easily reduce their use of energy in response to higher energy prices, a 29 percent reduction in carbon dioxide emissions is found to be socially optimal, and close to a 50 percent reduction could occur before social welfare is reduced below the no-control case.
- Carbon taxation is mildly regressive, taxing a larger proportion of the incomes of the poor relative to the rich, as is the case with most sales taxes, for example.

Thus, the Boyd et al. study indicates that relatively substantial reductions in carbon dioxide emissions are consistent with a net monetary benefit–based policy standard. Boyd et al. estimated that the total (excluding global warming) environmental harms caused by fossil-fuel burning in the United States range from 0.2 to 4 percent of real GNP, with a midpoint value of around 2 percent. Nordhaus and Yang (1996) estimate these economic costs to be in the range of 1 to 2 percent. As mentioned above, the Boyd et al. study computes the benefits of carbon taxation based on the current or secondary effects of fossil-fuel burning, rather than on the possible future or primary effects caused by carbon dioxide emissions. In a survey of this literature, Ekins (1996) finds that these secondary benefits of reducing carbon dioxide are of the same order of magnitude as the costs of medium to high levels of carbon dioxide abatement. Moreover, these secondary benefits are generally estimated to be higher than the primary benefit associated with less global warming. Clearly, the existence of these secondary benefits greatly reinforces the case made by environmental economists for current action on carbon dioxide emissions.

Following the approach of Burtraw and Toman (1998) and Boyd et al.

(1995) in their benefit/cost analysis of Italy meeting its Kyoto obligations, Gatto et al. (2002) included in their analysis the current or ancillary benefits from reducing carbon dioxide. These current benefits include lower emissions of sulfur dioxide, nitrogen oxides, carbon monoxide, mercury, and so forth, based on estimates of average external cost per unit of pollutant. In evaluating Italy's current fuel mix versus the mix that meets the Kyoto target, they included benefits derived from avoided external costs to human health, agriculture, material goods, and ecosystems. Damages to biodiversity and ecosystem services were not accounted for in the cited literature, and thus external costs in this study are likely an underestimation. Based on an average global cost of 30 euros per ton of carbon dioxide, Gatto et al. found that it would be economically advantageous for Italy to change its power generation strategy to comply with Kyoto. This could be achieved with a fuel mix using more gas, less coal, more renewable sources, and more co-generation (combining electric and formerly waste thermal energy).

Recent research on the costs of reducing carbon dioxide emissions has focused on emissions at power plants. According to Socolow (2005), stationary coal-burning power plants are the source of about one-quarter of the world's anthropogenic carbon dioxide emissions. It is anticipated that many new coal-fired power plants will be built during the first half of the twenty-first century. As a result, much attention is now being focused on capturing carbon dioxide emissions from these power plants and injecting the gas deep into geological formations for long-term storage. Socolow cites estimates of approximately $25 per ton of carbon dioxide as the prevailing view of the added cost of capturing the gas at a new coal gasification combined-cycle plant and injecting it into geological formations. Costs would likely be much higher at an existing coal-fired steam power plant. This cost translates into an increase of approximately 2 cents per kilowatt-hour for electricity. Passing this cost along to end consumers would raise the average retail electricity price (currently at around 10 cents per kilowatt-hour) by about 20 percent. If carbon dioxide injection became a mandate, then the extra 2 cents per kilowatt-hour cost would make wind power and perhaps other renewable sources of electricity price-competitive.

The U.S. Energy Information Administration (EIA) undertook an analysis of the cost to the United States of meeting its obligations under the Kyoto Protocol (U.S. EIA 1998b). The EIA considered a number of different scenarios based on the extent to which the reductions are achieved domestically rather than through the acquisition of emission credits through trading, joint implementation, or clean development. These ranged from the 1990+24 case, in which U.S. carbon emissions are 24 percent above 1990 levels and approximately 80 percent of the Kyoto reduction is accomplished from the acquisition of emission credits, to the 1990–7 case, in which the Kyoto reduction is entirely accomplished through domestic emission reductions. In its 1998 analysis of the Kyoto Protocol, EIA assumed that a carbon price would be applied to each of the energy fuels at its point of consumption, relative to its carbon content. The carbon price would not be applied directly to electricity but would be applied to the fossil fuels used for electricity generation and reflected in the delivered price of electricity. The EIA estimated that by 2010, the carbon price necessary to achieve the targets ranges from $67 per metric ton (1996 dollars) in the 1990+24 case to $348 per metric ton in the 1990–7 case. In the more restrictive cases such as 1990–7, the carbon price escalates rapidly to achieve the more stringent reductions but then declines over the next ten years of the forecast horizon.

Cumulative investments in more energy-efficient and lower-carbon equipment, particularly for electricity generation, reduce the cost of compliance in the later years. These carbon prices would in turn raise the price of energy based on relative carbon content. For example, delivered coal prices would rise by between 152 and nearly 800 percent, average electricity prices would rise by between 20 and 86 percent, average delivered natural gas prices would rise by between 25 and 148 percent, and average petroleum prices would rise by between 12 and 62 percent. Clearly we can see that the trading of credits, joint implementation, and clean technology options substantially reduce the economic impacts of compliance with the Kyoto Protocol.

Over the long run these higher energy prices would in turn lead to increased energy efficiency (as measured by reduced energy intensity, measured as energy per dollar of real GDP) and reduced reliance on carbon-intensive energy sources such as coal. Higher fossil-fuel energy prices also have implications for the macroeconomy. The EIA estimated the macroeconomic impacts of the Kyoto Protocol using the Data Resources, Inc. (DRI) Macroeconomic Model of the U.S. Economy. Using this model the EIA estimated that the average annual cost to the U.S. economy (in constant 1992 dollars) from compliance with the Kyoto Protocol ranges from $128–283 billion for the 1990–7 case to $77–109 billion for the 1990+24 case. Based on a projected real GDP of $9,425 billion for the 2008–2012 time period in which the reductions are to occur, these annual costs to the economy are estimated to range from a high of 3 percent to a low of 0.8 percent of GDP. The more restrictive cases led to a larger reduction in projected economic growth in the period between 2005 and 2010, though the economy was projected to quickly rebound so that impacts on economic growth during the longer 2005–20 time period are estimated to be minimal.

Nordhaus and Yang (1996) also take a general equilibrium approach to analyze the economics of climate change policy, but their economic model distinguishes costs, impacts, and policies for different regions of the world. They find the efficient global carbon tax to be around $6 per ton by 2000, rising to $27 per ton by 2100. Under this scenario, China and Russia will be confronted with much higher emissions controls than Japan and Europe, and Nordhaus and Yang acknowledge that in the current policy environment, the efficient level of control is unlikely to obtain. Nordhaus and Yang also find the discounted net economic gain from an international cooperative effort in climate change policy to be about $300 billion relative to noncooperative efforts by various governments and $344 billion relative to a "no-abatement" benchmark.

Azar and Sterner (1996) criticize the Nordhaus and Yang study and similar studies on several counts, including the use of what they consider to be an excessively high discount rate, and excessive pessimism regarding the rate of technical change in energy efficiency and alternative energy technologies. Other criticisms focus on ignoring unequal distributions of income and the marginal utility of money around the globe (implying unequal values attributed to statistical lives lost due to global warming), and the assumption that climate change will proceed "as a smooth and predictable process without risk for sudden catastrophic events" (p. 170). Azar and Sterner recompute the Nordhaus Dynamic Integrated Climate Economic (DICE) model with adjustments for these various shortcomings, with the exception that they could not model the possibility of catastrophic scenarios. They also used a 300- to 1,000-year time horizon. While Nordhaus (1993b) estimates the marginal cost of carbon dioxide emissions to be $5 per ton, Azar and Sterner estimate the marginal cost of carbon dioxide emissions to range from $260 to $590 per ton. The difference is almost entirely due to a weighting of costs in poorer regions of the world and a three percentage-point lower discount rate.

While these economic studies are helpful in understanding the trade-offs involved in climate change policy, what practical steps are necessary to extend these policies into lower-income countries? Blackman (1999) has surveyed the literature on the economics of technology diffusion and has related it to the problem of promoting climate-change policy in developing countries. Blackman states that there are seven types of policy instruments available to speed the diffusion of climate-friendly technology in developing countries: Information, factor prices, regulation, credit, human capital, infrastructure, research and development, and intellectual property rights. Blackman argues that the dissemination of information is critical in all economic models of technology diffusion. Some examples of policies that may enhance the flow of information about new technologies include demonstration projects, advertising campaigns, the testing and certification of new technologies, and subsidies to technological consulting services. Factor (or input) prices can also be important in fostering the diffusion of climate-friendly technology in developing countries. In particular, there is considerable evidence that investment in energy-efficient technology is spurred by higher energy prices. Since many developing countries subsidize energy prices, the removal of those subsidies is likely to trigger increased domestic demand for energy-efficient technology. Presumably, the regressive nature of removing energy price subsidies would need to be addressed elsewhere in the tax system. Regulation such as energy taxes or pollution taxes provides the same sort of economic incentives for investment in energy-efficient technology as the removal of subsidies.

Access to credit has also been identified as a barrier to the adoption of climate-friendly technology. As will be discussed in much greater detail in chapter 13, large-scale projects funded externally by agencies such as the World Bank have had mixed results at best. Perhaps a more effective approach would be to help develop domestic sources of credit for smaller-scale and better-managed initiatives. The diffusion of climate-friendly technology also requires investment in human capital so that local people understand the new technology and can make it function properly in their specific cultural context, and investment in necessary infrastructure such as energy distribution networks. Research and development (R&D) provides a direct impetus to technology diffusion, and therefore the promotion of climate-friendly R&D activities in developing countries will have an obvious beneficial impact. Finally, intellectual property rights can be a formidable barrier to technology transfer due to high licensing prices, and therefore subsidized licensing arrangements may be a critical factor in the diffusion of climate-friendly technology in developing countries.

Summary

- There is widespread consensus that anthropogenic emissions of greenhouse gases have altered the earth's energy budget. These include both anthropogenic carbon dioxide emissions that have imbalanced the earth's carbon cycle, as well as nitrous oxide, methane, various halocarbons, nonmethane volatile organic compounds, ozone, sulfur hexafluoride, and water vapor. These gases allow visible light to pass through but trap some heat and prevent it from being radiated into space, thus operating like a greenhouse. If there were no greenhouse effect on earth, the surface of the planet would be approximately 33 degrees Celsius colder than it is now, and most ecosystems would collapse.
- Concentrations of carbon dioxide in the earth's atmosphere—the single most important greenhouse gas—have increased from 280 parts per million (ppm) before the advent of industrialization to approximately 380 ppm in 2005. "Business as usual" forecasts (i.e., emissions growth

trends are unabated by attempts to limit emissions) suggest atmospheric concentrations of carbon dioxide rising to approximately 700 ppm by 2100. The United States produces approximately 24 percent of all anthropogenic carbon dioxide emissions. The Persian Gulf states of Qatar and the United Arab Emirates (UAE) had the highest per capita annual emissions of carbon dioxide, at 16.9 and 11.5 metric tons, respectively.

- The chapter presents a number of different climate change predictions. These predictions call for varying amounts of global average temperature increases, sea level increases, and changes in the geographic distribution of forests, grasslands, and deserts. There is also the potential for significant "discontinuities" and abrupt climate change due to factors such as displacement of important ocean currents.

- Today's costs of making a substantial reduction in greenhouse gas emissions are relatively large, concentrated on the current cohort of fossil-fuel industries and their consumers, and are relatively well known.

- The estimated benefits of substantially reducing greenhouse gas emissions are diffuse across the globe, primarily fall 100 or more years in the future, and are therefore diffused across future generations. Thus, from a political economy perspective, greenhouse gas control policy is "Olsonian" (as the term was used in chapter 8)—difficult to achieve and relatively unstable to maintain.

- Models of the global climate continue to be refined, and scientists are getting better at predicting global climate, yet the mechanics of global warming, particularly at the regional level, are tremendously complex. As a consequence, the geographical distribution of benefits from controlling greenhouse gas emissions are uncertain.

- One important source of uncertainty is the possibility that large amounts of methane now locked in Arctic tundra and permafrost could be rapidly released if some initial degree of atmospheric warming occurs (and polar areas are predicted to experience the largest temperature changes). Another source of uncertainty is the role of cloud cover and rainfall patterns and whether they will reinforce or attenuate warming.

- Global climate change necessitates international coordination and cooperation across countries that are highly diverse in income, religion, culture, population growth rates and other demographic characteristics, educational attainment, and extent of democratic empowerment.

- In 1992 the United Nations Conference on Environment and Development resulted in 150 countries signing the UN Framework Convention on Climate Change, which pledges Annex I countries (rich industrialized countries and economies in transition) to control emissions of greenhouse gases. Unlike the European Union, the United States is currently behind schedule in reducing greenhouse gases relative to the 1990 bench-mark, in part because cheap gasoline has increased the popularity of less fuel-efficient automobiles.

- The Kyoto Protocol commits Annex I Parties to individual, legally binding targets to limit or reduce their greenhouse gas emissions, adding up to a total cut of at least 5 percent from 1990 levels in the period 2008–12.
- The Kyoto Protocol also establishes three incentive-based economic instruments that are designed to help Annex I countries reduce the cost of meeting their emissions targets. These instruments are joint implementation (described in chapter 10), emissions trading, and the clean development mechanism.
- The United States has not ratified the Kyoto Protocol, and most action to limit greenhouse gas emissions in this country is limited to state actions (e.g., renewable portfolio standards, described in chapter 10) or voluntary controls.
- The U.S. Energy Information Administration estimated the macro-economic impacts of the Kyoto Protocol using the Data Resources, Inc. (DRI) Macroeconomic Model of the U.S. Economy. Based on a projected real GDP of $9,425 billion for the period between 2008 and 2012 in which the reductions are to occur, these estimated annual costs to the economy range from a high of 3 percent to a low of 0.8 percent of GDP.
- In a number of ambitious studies, environmental economists have found that vigorous control of carbon dioxide emissions can be justified today when the ancillary benefits of reductions in pollutants emitted with carbon dioxide that harm people today, such as sulfur dioxides, particulates, nitrogen oxides, and ozone, are included in the benefit/cost analysis. These studies make a very strong case for action on greenhouse gas emissions based on a "no-regrets" policy.

Review Questions and Problems

1. Write a two-page essay in which you summarize what is known about global climate change. Discuss how the complexity, the long-term nature of the problem, the diffusion of the benefits, the uncertainty regarding global-warming effects, and the international nature of any effective solution make this one of the most important, controversial, and challenging environmental policy problems we face today.

2. Review the concept of the prisoners' dilemma in the Appendix to chapter 5. Is it reasonable to model the international coordination problem for

control of greenhouse gases as a prisoners' dilemma game? If so, explain the payoff structure in a simple case of a two-country world.

3. What other environmental policy dilemmas have uncertainty, irreversibility, and potentially large long-term impacts similar to the global-warming issue? Carefully explain your reasoning. How might the policy and political economy implications be similar to those of global warming?

4. Access the report *Climate Change Impacts on the United States* on the Internet (www.gcrio.org/NationalAssessment/index.htm). Summarize the forecasted environmental and social impacts of global climate change for a region of the United States.

5. President George W. Bush argued against ratifying the Kyoto Protocol because the Protocol fails to require India and China to make binding reductions in emissions of greenhouse gases, and because of concerns about costs to the U.S. economy. Nevertheless, most other major industrialized countries have ratified the Protocol and will be required to reduce their greenhouse gas emissions. Does this mean that the United States will be a free rider when it comes to global action on greenhouse gas control? How will this decision by the United States not to ratify affect the international competitiveness of our manufacturing firms?

6. The European Union has a greenhouse gas allowance trading system in place. Go to their website (http://europa.eu.int/comm/environment/climat/emission_plans.htm) and write a brief summary that describes how this trading system works. To what extent will greenhouse gas allowance trading reduce the economic cost of compliance with the Kyoto Protocol?

7. Visit the website of the Copenhagen Consensus (www.copenhagen consensus.com), a group that attempts to prioritize action on various global problems, including climate change. Review the article by Cline (2004) on climate change, the articles refuting Cline's work, and Cline's rejoinder (www.copenhagenconsensus.com/Default.asp?ID=165). Summarize the key differences expressed by the authors regarding appropriate public action to stem future climate change, and write a one-page position paper outlining your position on this issue. Do you agree with the panel of experts' ranking of climate change in their prioritized list of global problems? Alternatively, your class could use this material as background research for a debate on appropriate action on climate change.

Internet Links

An Abrupt Climate Change Scenario and Its Implications for United States National Security (www.gbn.com/ArticleDisplayServlet.srv?aid =26231): A report by the Global Business Network for the U.S. Department of Defense.

The Benefits of Reduced Air Pollutants in the U.S. from Greenhouse Gas Mitigation Policies (www.rff.org/Documents/RFF-DP-98-01-REV.pdf): A study by Burtraw and Toman at Resources for the Future.

Climate Change 2001: IPCC Third Assessment Report (www.grida.no/ climate/ipcc_tar): A key authoritative source of information on the science of greenhouse gases, atmospheric chemistry, trend emissions data, and the science of global climate change.

Climate Change 2001: Synthesis Report Summary for Policy Makers (www.ipcc.ch/pub/un/syreng/spm.pdf): This summary represents the formally agreed statement of the IPCC concerning key findings and uncertainties contained in the Working Group contributions to the Third Assessment Report.

Climate Change Impacts on the United States (www.gcrio.org/ NationalAssessment/index.htm): The U.S. Global Change Research Program (USGCRP) established this national assessment in order to analyze and evaluate what is known about the potential consequences of climate variability and change for the United States.

Energy Information Administration Greenhouse Gas Emissions and Climate Change Publications (www.eia.doe.gov/environment.html): Lots of good information on current and projected future greenhouse gas emissions in the United States and around the world.

EPA's Global Warming Internet Site (http://yosemite.epa.gov/oar/ globalwarming.nsf/content/index.html): Comprehensive information on greenhouse gases and global climate change.

European Union Greenhouse Gas Allowance Trading Scheme (http:// europa.eu.int/comm/environment/climat/emission_plans.htm): Learn more about the European Union's greenhouse gas trading system.

Hadley Center for Climate Prediction and Research (www.metoffice. com/research/hadleycentre): The Hadley Center is jointly funded by the United Kingdom Department of the Environment and the United Kingdom Meteorological Office. The main objective of the Hadley Center is to provide an authoritative, up-to-date assessment of both natural and man-made climate change.

The Heat Is On (www.heatisonline.org): Internet site based on Pulitzer

Prize–winning investigative reporter Ross Gelbspan's book on greenhouse gas emissions and global climate change.

Impacts of the Kyoto Protocol on U.S. Energy Markets and Economic Activity (www.eia.doe.gov/oiaf/kyoto/kyotorpt.html): Comprehensive 1998 economic analysis of the costs of complying with the Kyoto Protocol, sponsored by the U.S. Energy Information Administration.

Interactive Atmospheric Data Visualization Website (www.cmdl .noaa.gov/ccgg/iadv): Access the most current data from the National Oceanographic and Atmospheric Administration's Climate Monitoring and Diagnostics Laboratory.

Intergovernmental Panel on Climate Change (www.ipcc.ch): Learn about the latest consensus information on the status of greenhouse gas emissions, global climate change, and international policy responses.

Intergovernmental Panel on Climate Change Special Report on Emissions Scenarios (www.grida.no/climate/ipcc/emission): Read the IPCC's Special Report on Emissions Scenarios here.

Pew Center on Climate Change (www.pewclimate.org): Probably one of the best websites for up-to-date science and policy studies.

Resources for the Future's Climate Change Economics and Policy Studies (www.rff.org/Climate.cfm): This nonpartisan environmental think-tank is a good source of objective economic policy studies on climate change and the environment.

The Scientific Consensus on Climate Change (www.sciencemag.org/cgi/reprint/306/5702/1686.pdf): December 2004 *Science* article by Naomi Oreskes.

United Nations Framework Convention on Climate Change (www.unfccc.de): Comprehensive information on the UNFCCC, the Kyoto Protocol, and other aspects of coordinated international action on the control of greenhouse gas emissions.

World Resources Institute Climate Change and Energy (http:// climate.wri.org/): World Resources Institute (WRI) is an environmental think tank that goes beyond research to find practical ways to protect the earth and improve people's lives.

References and Further Reading

Azar, C., and T. Sterner. 1996. "Discounting and Distributional Considerations in the Context of Global Warming." *Ecological Economics* 19 (November): 169–84.

Blackman, A. 1999. "The Economics of Technology Diffusion: Implications for Climate Policy in Developing Countries." *Discussion Paper 99–42.* Washington, DC: Resources for the Future.

Boyd, R., K. Rutilla, and K. Viscusi. 1995. "Energy Taxation as a Policy Instrument to Reduce CO_2 Emissions: A Net Benefit Analysis." *Journal of Environmental Economics and Management* 29 (July): 1–24.

Broecker, W. 1995. "Chaotic Climate." *Scientific American* 273 (November): 62–68.

Brown, P. 1991. "Why Climate Change Is Not a Cost/Benefit Problem." In *Global Climate Change: The Economic Costs of Mitigation and Adaptation,* ed. J. White. New York: Elsevier.

Burtraw, D., and M. Toman. 1998. *The Benefits of Reduced Air Pollutants in the U.S. from Greenhouse Gas Mitigation Policies. Discussion Paper 98-01-REV.* Washington, DC: Resources for the Future.

Cline, W. 1992. "The Greenhouse Effect: Global Economic Consequences." Report of the Institute for International Economics, Washington, DC.

———. 2004. "Meeting the Challenge of Global Warming." *Copenhagen Consensus Program.* Copenhagen, Denmark: National Environmental Assessment Institute. Available at http://copenhagenconsensus.com.

Congressional Budget Office. 1990. "Carbon Charges as a Response to Global Warming: The Effects of Taxing Fossil Fuels." Washington, DC.

Dai, A., A. Del Genio, and I. Fung. 1997. "Clouds, Precipitation, and Temperature Range." *Nature* 386 (April 17): 665–66.

Dansgaard, W., S. Johnsen, H. Clausen, D. Dahl-Jensen, N. Gundestrup, C. Hammer, C. Hvidberg, J. Steffensen, A. Sveinbjšrnsdottir, J. Jouzel, and G. Bond. 1993. "Evidence for General Instability of Past Climate from a 250-KYR Ice-Core Record." *Nature* 364 (15 July): 218–20.

Doyle, R. 1996. "Carbon Dioxide Emissions." *Scientific American* 274 (May): 24.

Easterling, D., B. Horton, P. Jones, T. Peterson, T. Karl, D. Parker, M. Salinger, V. Razuvayev, N. Plummer, P. Jamason, and C. Folland. 1997. "Maximum and Minimum Temperature Trends for the Globe." *Science* 277 (18 July): 364–66.

Ekins, P. 1996. "The Secondary Benefits of CO_2 Abatement: How Much Emission Reduction Do They Justify?" *Ecological Economics* 16 (January): 13–24.

Epstein, P. 2000. "Is Global Warming Harmful to Health?" *Scientific American* 283 (August): 50–57.

Faucheaux, S., and G. Froger. 1995. "Decision-Making Under Environmental Uncertainty." *Ecological Economics* 15 (October): 29–42.

Gatto, M., A. Caizzi, L. Rizzi, and G. De Leo. 2002. "The Kyoto Protocol Is Cost-Effective." *Conservation Ecology* 6: r11. Available at www.consecol.org/vol6/iss1/resp11.

Gelbspan, R. 1998. *The Heat Is On: The Climate Crisis, the Cover-Up, and the Prescription.* Cambridge, MA: Perseus Books.

Hadley Center for Climate Prediction and Research. 1999. *Climate Change and Its Impacts: Stabilization of CO_2 in the Atmosphere.* London: U.K. Meteorological Office.

Hansen, J. 2004. "Defusing the Global Warming Time Bomb." *Scientific American* 290 (March): 68–77.

Hayhoe, K., D. Cayan, C. Field, P. Frumhoff, E. Maurer, N. Miller, S. Moser, S. Schneider, K. Cahill, E. Cleland, L. Dale, R. Drapek, R. Hanemann, L. Kalkstein, J. Lenihan, C. Lunch, R. Neilson, S. Sheridan, and J. Verville. 2004. Emissions pathways, Climate Change and Impacts on California. Proceedings of the National Academy of Sciences 101:12422-12427.

Intergovernmental Panel on Climate Change (IPCC). 1996. *Climate Change 1995: The Science of Climate Change*, ed. J. Houghton, L. Meira Filho, B. Callander, N. Harris, A. Kattenberg, and K. Maskell. Cambridge: Cambridge University Press.

———. 2000. *Emissions Scenarios: A Special Report of the Intergovernmental Panel on Climate Change*, ed. N. Nakicenovic and R. Swart. Cambridge: Cambridge University Press.

———. 2001. *Climate Change 2001: The Scientific Basis*, ed. J. Houghton, Y. Ding, D. Griggs, M. Noguer, P. van der Linden, X. Dai, K. Maskell, C. Johnson. Cambridge: Cambridge University Press.

Jorgenson, D., and P. Wilcoxen. 1993. "Reducing U.S. Carbon Emissions: An Econometric General Equilibrium Assessment." *Resource Energy Economics* 15: 7–25.

Karl, T., N. Nicholls, and J. Gregory. 1997. "The Coming Climate." *Scientific American* 276 (1): 78–83.

Kaya, Y. 1990. "Impact of Carbon Dioxide Emission Control on GNP Growth: Interpretation of Proposed Scenarios." IPCC Energy and Industry Subgroup, Response Strategies Working Group, Paris.

Kerr, R. 2000. "Globe's Missing Warming Found in the Ocean." *Science* 287: 2126–27.

Levitus, S., J. Antonov, T. Boyer, and C. Stephens. 2000. "Warming of the World Ocean." *Science* 287: 2225–29.

Maier-Reimer, E., and K. Hasselman. 1987. "Transport and Storage of CO_2 in the Ocean—An Inorganic Ocean-Circulation Carbon Cycle Model." *Climate Dynamics* 2: 63–90.

Michaelowa, A. 2004. "Climate Policy Challenges After the Kyoto Protocol Enters into Force." *Intereconomics* 39: 332–36.

Myneni, R., C. Keeling, C. Tucker, G. Asrar, and R. Nemani. 1997. "Increased Plant Growth in the Northern High Latitudes from 1981–1991." *Nature* 386 (17 April): 698–702.

Nakicenovic, N., A. Gruebler, A. Inaba, S. Messner, S. Nilsson, Y. Nishimura, H-H. Rogner, A. Schaefer, L. Schrattenholzer, M. Strubegger, J. Swisher, D. Victor, and D. Wilson. 1993. "Long-Term Strategies for Mitigating Global Warming." *Energy* 18: 409–601.

National Academy of Sciences, National Academy of Engineering and Institute for Medicine. 1991. *Policy Implications of Greenhouse Warming*. Washington, DC.

National Research Council. 2000. *Reconciling Observations of Global Temperature Change*. Washington, DC: National Academy Press.

Nordhaus, W. 1993a. "The Cost of Slowing Climate Change: A Survey." *Energy* 12: 37–65.

———. 1993b. "Rolling the 'DICE': An Optimal Transition Path for Controlling Greenhouse Gases." *Resource Energy Economics* 15: 27–50.

Nordhaus, W., and J. Boyer, 2000. *Warming the World: Economic Models of Global Warming*. Cambridge, MA: MIT Press.

Nordhaus, W., and Z. Yang. 1996. "A Regional Dynamic General-Equilibrium Model of Alternative Climate-Change Strategies." *American Economic Review* 86 (September): 741–65.

Oreskes, N. 2004. "The Scientific Consensus on Climate Change." *Science* 306: 1686.

Overpeck, J. 2000. "The Hole Record." *Nature* 403: 714–15.

Revkin, A. 2005. "Editor of Climate Reports Resigns." *New York Times*, June 10. Available at www.nytimes.com/2005/06/10/politics/11cooney.long.html.

Roodman, D. 1996. "Paying the Piper: Subsidies, Politics, and the Environment." Worldwatch Paper 133 (December).

Ruddiman, W. 2005. "How Did Humans First Alter Global Climate?" *Scientific American* 292 (3): 46–53.

Sabine, C., R. Feely, N. Gruber, R. Key, K. Lee, J. Bullister., R. Wanninkhof, C. Wong, D. Wallace, B. Tilbrook, F. Millero, T. Peng, A. Kozyr, T. Ono, and A. Rios. 2004. "The Oceanic Sink for Anthropogenic CO_2." *Science* 305: 367–71.

Schwartz, P., and D. Randall. 2003. "An Abrupt Climate Change Scenario and Its Implications for United States National Security." Global Business Network (prepared for the U.S. Department of Defense). Available at www.gbn.com/ArticleDisplayServlet.srv?aid=26231.

Shoven, J., and R. Wigle. 1991. "Cutting CO_2 Emissions: The Effects of Alternative Policy Approaches." *Energy Journal* 12: 109–24.

Socolow, R. 2005. "Can We Bury Global Warming?" *Scientific American* 293 (1): 49–55.

U.S. Energy Information Administration (EIA). 1998a. *Annual Energy Outlook 1999*. Washington, DC: U.S. Department of Energy.

———. 1998b. *Impacts of the Kyoto Protocol on U.S. Energy Markets and Economic Activity*. Washington, DC: U.S. Department of Energy.

_____. 2004. *International Energy Outlook 2004*. Washington, DC: U.S. Department of Energy.

U.S. Environmental Protection Agency. 2004. *Inventory of U.S. Greenhouse Gas Emissions and Sinks: 1990–2002*. Washington, DC: US EPA. Available at http://yosemite.epa.gov/oar/globalwarming.nsf/content/ResourceCenter PublicationsGHGEmissionsUSEmissionsInventory2004.html.

U.S. Global Change Research Program (USGCRP). 2000. *Climate Change Impacts on the United States: The Potential Consequences of Climate Variability and Change*. Draft. Available at www.gcrio.org/NationalAssessment.

Watson, R., M. Zinyowera, and R. Moss, eds. 1996. *Climate Change 1995—Impacts, Adaptations and Mitigation of Climate Change: Scientific-Technical Analyses*. Contribution of Working Group II to the Second Assessment Report of the Intergovernmental Panel on Climate Change. Cambridge: Cambridge University Press.

World Bank. 1999. *World Development Report 1999–2000*. Oxford: Oxford University Press.

World Resources Institute. 1994. *World Resources, 1994–95*. Oxford: Oxford University Press.

———. 1996. *World Resources, 1996–97*. Oxford: Oxford University Press.

———. 1998. *World Resources, 1998–99*. Oxford: Oxford University Press.

Part III

Topics on the Economics of Sustainability

12

Introduction to the Concept of Sustainability

Introduction

There is a growing awareness of the increasingly sharp demands that human societies place on their economies and their natural environment, and of the corrosion of many social and political institutions. Many also recognize that the imperatives of a healthy, functioning economy, community, and environment are interdependent. Sustainability represents a vision of the future whose roots can be traced back to a variety of primary origins, including the Iroquois Confederation, which developed a standard of judging decisions based on the well-being of tribal people seven generations into the future. Many cultures over the course of human history have recognized the need for harmony between their economy, community, and environment. What is new is an articulation of these ideas in the context of the globalization of technology, information, economics, and environmental crises. The sustainability movement calls for a more sophisticated and inclusive view of development and well-being that explicitly takes into account ecological health, natural resource stocks, vibrant and just communities, and democratic processes. Sustainability has come to mean different things to different people, and by encompassing so many things there is the potential for its meaning to dissipate or to become appropriated. We will develop a definition of sustainability in this chapter that can be used as a standard for evaluating social, economic, and environmental policies.

How is sustainability viewed within the discipline of economics? As we will discuss in detail in chapter 14, traditional economic growth theorists see sustainability as an issue of intergenerational equity and as a constraint on economic growth, and see human-made capital as substitutable for natural capital. Somewhat more recently, but in the same vein, Arrow et al. (2004) view sustainability as an economic modeling problem, and interpret sustainability to mean that social welfare does not decline over time. Other economists are much less traditional in their views. For example, Daly and Cobb (1989) draw upon Aristotle's distinction between *chrematistics and oikonomia* to illustrate the difference between the mainstream of contemporary economic thought and the emerging sustainability economics. *Chrematistics* can be thought of as the process of managing economic affairs in such a way as to maximize the value of the decision maker's financial wealth, as measured in money. *Oikonomia* refers to household management, which in Greek times included a broad array of activities, a relatively larger number of people than we associate with modern households, and elements of a multigenerational perspective. Accordingly, Daly and Cobb argue that *oikonomia* differs from *chrematistics* in that (1) it takes a longer-term view, (2) it focuses attention on the well-being of the household community as opposed to a more individualistic perspective on financial wealth accumulation, and (3) it places a larger emphasis on use value, while *chrematistics* is more narrowly focused on money exchange values. Thus, *oikonomia* emphasizes the broader focus and longer time horizon that is more consistent with the sustainability perspective than is the prevailing economic focus on financial wealth, which is embodied in the concept of *chrematistics*.

Ecologists, environmental ethicists, and others argue that a sustainable society is premised on the integrity of the ecosystems that provide the basis for life on earth. As we shall see in chapter 13, ecologists are not particularly sanguine with regard to the ability of human-made capital to substitute for natural capital (for example, that the loss of natural wetlands can be mitigated by constructed wetlands). According to this view, the path to sustainability requires restoration and preservation of the stocks of natural capital embodied in the earth's ecosystems. Economists and other social scientists acknowledge the central role of ecosystem integrity but argue that sustainability also requires democratic processes and empowerment, and a vital economy to provide economic security and meaningful work opportunities and to promote resource-efficient technologies. According to this argument, restoration and preservation of natural capital stocks is more likely when economic systems are put into place that address the basic human needs of the world's poor. In addition, these sorts of economic systems in turn require democratic processes and empowerment so that all people have access to education, justice, a voice in governance, property ownership, and meaningful work opportunities. Sustainability encompasses both an ethic and a set of technical processes that relate ecological health and human well-being to an interdependent array of economic, sociopolitical, and environmental/ecological systems. In fact, as we will see below, sustainability occurs at the intersection of ecological integrity, economic vitality, and democratic systems and processes. The ethic of sustainability provides the common imperative and the shared values, and the technical processes provide the means of acting in a manner consistent with the sustainability ethic.

Sustainable Development

To sustain something means to maintain, support, or uphold something, to supply it with necessities. In the context of *sustainability* as the term is used in this book, the "something" that is being sustained includes the essential elements of a healthy, functioning economy, community, and environment over a long-term time horizon. To develop something means to expand or realize its potential, or to bring something to a fuller state. Economic development, therefore, is not the same as *economic growth,* the latter referring to inflation-adjusted increases in gross domestic product. Therefore, we can think of *sustainable development* as providing the support necessary for the functional elements of economy, community, and environment to achieve their full potential. While it may or may not be possible to sustain endless economic growth, it should be both possible and desirable to promote sustainable development. In this section, we will consider the evolution of the concept of sustainable development. In chapter 14, we will return to this concept in detail.

Modern international discussion of sustainability goes back at least to a United Nations Conference on the Human Environment, held in Stockholm in 1972, where the notion of sustainable development was put forward as a way of transforming conflicting objectives into complementary aspects of a common goal. Arising from this conference was the Stockholm Declaration, a set of principles that together represented the beginning of international dialogue between rich and poor countries regarding the links between economic growth, declines in global common-pool resource systems such as the air, water, and oceans, and the well-being of people around the world.

The momentum for sustainable development that started with the Stockholm Declaration increased due to the work of the World Commission on Environment and Development that was headed by Gro Brundtland, who served as prime minister of Norway in 1981 and again between 1986–89 and 1990–96. Between 1983 and 1987, what later became known as the Brundtland Commission facilitated a series of public hearings throughout the world, including many lower-income countries, to further develop the concept of sustainability. In a unanimous, report, the Brundtland Commission concluded that our common future depends on sustainable development. In 1987, the Brundtland Commission published the book *Our Common Future* (Brundtland, 1987), which "defined sustainable development and called upon nations of the world to adopt the objective of sustainable development as the overriding goal and test of national policy and international cooperation" (Tokyo Declaration). The Brundtland Commission defined and framed the imperatives of sustainable development, and focused on the "interlocking crises" implied by the fundamental changes through which the planet is passing. As pointed out in *Our Common Future,* more than 80 percent of population growth is forecast to occur in the urban areas of the world's poorest countries. As these people strive for the same standard of living enjoyed by people in rich countries, will their industrialization path doom the productive capacity of the world's biosphere? The problem of making the economy of an increasingly populous world environmentally sustainable is one of the central challenges that motivate the sustainability movement.

There are many definitions of sustainability and sustainable development. The World Commission on Environment and Development (the Brundtland Commission) provided the following definition of sustainable development in 1987:

> Sustainable development is development that meets the needs of the present without compromising the ability of future generations to meet their own needs.

While this is a very broad definition, the Brundtland Commission envisioned two key concepts associated with sustainable development. The first concept was that of *needs,* in particular the essential needs of the world's poor, which are seen as having overriding priority. The second concept is the idea of *limits* on the ability of the environment to meet present and future needs. The Brundtland Commission identified seven strategic imperatives for sustainable development:

- Reviving growth.
- Changing the quality of growth.
- Meeting essential needs for jobs, food, energy, water, and sanitation.
- Ensuring a sustainable level of population.
- Conserving and enhancing the resource base.
- Reorienting technology and managing risk.
- Merging environment and economics in decision making.

The Brundtland Commission saw sustainable development as a process of change rather than as a fixed state of harmony. Therefore, the exploitation of resources, the direction of investments, the orientation of technological development, and institutional change are made in a manner that is consistent with future as well as present needs. The Brundtland Commission's view of sustainable development was centered on promoting more appropriate and equitably distributed economic growth, and the imperatives of ecological integrity and democratic systems and processes did not play as prominent a role.

At the 1992 United Nations Conference on Environment and Development (the Earth Summit) in Rio de Janeiro, Brazil, representatives from governments and nongovernment organizations (NGOs) developed the Rio Declaration on Environment and Development, also known as the Earth Charter. In its original form, the Earth Charter contained twenty-seven principles covering a broad array of economic, social, and environmental issues. According to the 1992 Earth Charter, environmental protection constitutes an integral part of the development process and cannot be considered in isolation from it (principle 4), and countries must enact effective environmental legislation (principle 11). Moreover, principle 7 states that countries shall cooperate in a spirit of global partnership to conserve, protect, and restore the health and integrity of the Earth's ecosystem. The 1992 Earth Charter recognizes the importance of economics in sustainable development. It affirms the right of development (principle 3), the essential need to alleviate poverty (principle 5), the imperative of reducing and eliminating unsustainable patterns of production and consumption (principle 8), technology transfer (principle 9), and the promotion of a supportive and open international economic system that would lead to economic growth and sustainable development in all countries (principle 12).

The 1992 Earth Charter also addresses empowerment and democratic principles. For example, principle 10 states that environmental issues are best handled with the participation of all concerned citizens. Moreover, individuals are to have appropriate access to information concerning the environment that is held by public authorities, including information on hazardous materials and activities in their communities, and the opportunity to participate in decision-making processes. States shall facilitate and encourage public awareness and participation by making information widely available. Effective access to judicial and administrative proceedings, including redress and remedy, shall be provided. The 1992 Earth Charter recognizes the imperatives of empowering women and indigenous peoples. Principle 20 states that women have a vital role in environmental management and development, and that their full participation is therefore essential to achieve sustainable development. Likewise principle 22 states that countries should recognize and duly support the identity, culture, and interests of indigenous peoples, and enable their effective participation in the achievement of sustainable development.

Representatives from governments and NGOs were unsuccessful in securing adoption of the Earth Charter during the Rio Earth Summit in 1992.
The Earth Charter Initiative was created by the Earth Council and Green
Cross International in 1994, and an Earth Charter Commission was formed
in 1997 to oversee the drafting of a revised Earth Charter. At the conclusion
of the Rio+5 Forum in Rio de Janeiro in 1997, the Earth Charter Commission issued the Benchmark Draft Earth Charter. After considerable feedback,
a second Benchmark Draft was issued in 1999, and a final version was issued in 2000. The 2000 Earth Charter has sixteen main principles, various
supporting principles, and a conclusion. The principles are divided into four
parts: (1) respect and care for the community of life; (2) ecological integrity;
(3) social and economic justice; and (4) democracy, nonviolence, and peace.
The Earth Charter Initiative offers the following definition of sustainable
development on their Internet site (www.earthcharter.org/):

> The goal of sustainable development is full human development and eco-
> logical protection. The Earth Charter recognizes that humanity's environ-
> mental, economic, social, cultural, ethical, and spiritual problems and as-
> pirations are interconnected. It affirms the need for holistic thinking and
> collaborative, integrated problem solving. Sustainable development requires
> such an approach. It is about freedom, justice, participation, and peace as
> well as environmental protection and economic well-being.

In 1995 the World Summit for Social Development produced a declaration and program of action that is addressed to defining and articulating a
vision of sustainable development. The authors of the declaration and program of action articulated a deep conviction that economic development,
social development, and environmental protection are interdependent and
mutually reinforcing components of sustainable development, which is the
framework for efforts to achieve a higher quality of life for all people. They
argued that equitable social development recognizes that empowering the
poor to utilize environmental resources sustainably is a necessary foundation for sustainable development. Finally, the authors of the declaration and
program of action argued that broad-based and sustained economic growth
in the context of sustainable development is necessary to sustain social development and social justice.

Conservation-based Development

Multilateral doctrines such as the Brundtland Commission Report and the
Earth Charter are useful because they encompass the values and political

interests of both high-income industrialized countries and lower-income countries. A more local and applied perspective on sustainability is provided by what is known as *conservation-based development,* which refers to programs and policies that help entrepreneurs succeed in developing viable businesses that are environmentally sound and make a positive contribution to their local community. For example, Johnson (1997) surveyed a number of local conservation-based development efforts in the Pacific Northwest region of the United States. By looking at both successful and unsuccessful conservation-based development projects, Johnson was able to develop some basic themes that serve as practical design principles.

- "They engage residents at the local, community, or watershed level to *define and pursue a common vision* of long-term community, economic, and ecosystem health. In the process, they often help to reinvigorate local civic processes and build upon local knowledge and culture."
- "They seek to *maintain and restore healthy ecosystems* upon which the community and economy rely. Often this involves building a better knowledge base by engaging citizens in developing and monitoring indicators of community, ecological, and economic well-being."
- "They *develop economic opportunities* that provide for the needs of local residents while ensuring the long-term sustainability of the ecosystem upon which the community relies." (p. 14)

Johnson argues that analysis of conservation-based development projects identifies three key lessons. One lesson is the importance of trust and the ability of people from widely diverse backgrounds and interests to collaborate. Second is the importance of finding markets for niche value-added or sustainably harvested products. Third is the importance of addressing poverty and diversity, and expanding community-based development to include people of more diverse cultural and ethnic backgrounds.

A Working Definition of Sustainability

The definition of sustainability that will be used in this textbook draws upon many of the sustainable development themes articulated in the Earth Charter, and on conservation-based development themes identified by Johnson (1997). The definition of sustainability was developed by Viederman (1996, p. 46), and states:

> Sustainability is a community's control and prudent use of all forms of capital—nature's capital, human capital, human-created capital, social capi-

tal, and cultural capital—to ensure, to the degree possible, that present and future generations can attain a high degree of economic security and achieve democracy while maintaining the integrity of the ecological systems upon which all life and production depends.

Viederman's definition begins with a discussion of the *five capitals* of sustainable development that shape, and are shaped by, human society. Note that to economists, capital represents the stock of something that is capable of producing a flow of valuable goods and services. In economics, *capital* refers to the built environment—factories, offices, roads, power lines, water systems—as well as equipment, tools, and inventory. In general, the larger the capital stock, the larger the flow of goods and services that it can produce. As shown in Figure 12.1, a bathtub serves as an analogy of the capital stock. Its "water" level rises with investment that adds to the stock, and its level falls with depreciation or the harvest of natural resources. Analogously, a fortunate retiree may have a sizable stock of financial capital that she built up from careful savings over the years. The size of this stock of financial capital determines the sustainable flow of income that is available to support her retirement lifestyle. For example, the retiree may have her financial capital retirement savings in government bonds that pay interest income over time. If the retiree demands too large of an income from this stock, she will be spending part of the stock itself (e.g., selling bonds). As a result, the stock will decline, like the falling level of water in a bathtub, thereby reducing the flow of income that the stock can sustainably support in the future. As we will see below, this same process is at play in other forms of capital as well, especially natural capital.

Natural capital generates the flow of natural resources (e.g., harvest of fish from fisheries, harvest of trees from a forest, grazing of livestock on rangeland) and ecosystem services (e.g., oxygen from forests, freshwater filtration from watersheds, nutrient cycling in wetlands) upon which human society depends. As Wackernagel and Rees (1997) observe, "natural capital is not just an inventory of resources; it includes all those components of the ecosphere, and the structural relationships among them, whose organizational integrity is essential for the continuous self-production of the system itself" (p. 4). Costanza et al. (1997) and Daily (1997) argue that the various forms of *ecosystem services* such as climate regulation, soil formation, nutrient cycling, habitat, erosion control, and recreation are the benefits that flow from the stock of functional ecosystems that are an element of natural capital. Importantly, the emerging field of ecological economics focuses on determining the economic value of the stocks and flows associated with natural capital, and some of the pioneering work in this area indicates that natural capital has considerable economic value.

Figure 12.1 **The "Bathtub" Model of Capital Stocks and Flows**

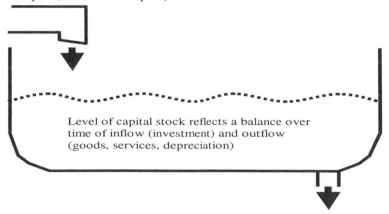

Inflow of investment: Examples include watershed restoration (natural capital), education (human capital), and construction or repair (constructed capital)

Level of capital stock reflects a balance over time of inflow (investment) and outflow (goods, services, depreciation)

Outflow of valuable goods and services: Examples include flow of natural resource goods and ecosystem services (natural capital), services of labor (human capital), and the services of constructed capital

Human capital is another term for the knowledge, skills, and capabilities of people that can be deployed to create a flow of useful work for their business, employer, family, or community. Education represents investment in human capital. By increasing the stock of human capital through education, a larger and more valuable flow of labor and volunteer services is obtained. *Created capital* (or constructed capital) is comprised of the technologies, productive facilities (e.g., factories, offices, laboratories, roads and other infrastructure), and inventory of products that economists traditionally think of as "capital stock." Business firms and government both invest in created capital, and this investment increases the stock of created capital, which in turn provides a larger flow of useful services.

Social capital, as the concept is used by sociologist James Coleman and political scientist Robert Putnam, refers to the stock of "civic virtues" and networks of civic engagement, involvement, reciprocity norms, and trust essential to democratic communities. In Italy, for example, Putnam (1993) argues that social capital was essential to the functioning of markets and government in the *comuni* of medieval Pisa, Siena, Lucca, and Florence. Social capital is sometimes measured through participation rates in voluntary service groups such as the PTA, unions, service clubs, and town hall meetings. There is economic value in social capital. For example, Trivers (1971) developed a theory of reciprocal altruism, contending that making a sacrifice for another yields a payoff in the form of a future return of the favor. As de Waal (2005) notes, researchers in the field of animal behavioral economics have found that norms of reciprocity and cooperation naturally evolve in nonhuman populations such as chimpanzees, and have documented many cases where today's gift (e.g., of food) is linked to a future reciprocal gift (e.g., of grooming services). In summarizing the findings of new agent-based cultural algorithms (models that simulate social and cultural changes), Kohler, Gumerman, and Reynolds (2005) note that kinship-based reciprocity norms enhance the ability of households to survive downturns in their economic circumstances, which indicates the economic value of social capital. Communities with large stocks of social capital enjoy a flow of economic benefits in the form of lower transaction costs, lower-cost dispute resolution, and more timely adaptive and cooperative responses to adverse shocks of various kinds (e.g., mill closures, natural disasters).

Cultural capital refers to the body of knowledge, stories, visions, myths, and languages shared by people and providing the framework for how people view the world and their proper role in it. Cultural capital can also include culture-specific place-based knowledge, including of locations and uses of medicinal plants and cycles of abundance for various resources. Of the five capitals, cultural capital is probably the most difficult to grasp and quantify.

It should also be noted that Viederman's (1996) definition focuses attention on *community* rather than on the individual. Private property regimes and market systems of allocation rest on an ethical foundation of individualism, which states that all values, rights, and duties originate in individuals and not in society as a whole. In contrast, the sustainability ethic holds the interdependent health and well-being of human communities and earth's ecology over time as the basis of value. Viederman's definition ends by providing guidance for how society should deploy the various forms of capital at its disposal. The *three pillars* of sustainability offered by Viederman (economy, community, and environment) are widely accepted as the central elements of a sustainable society, and these pillars illustrated in Figure 12.2. Note, however, that Viederman specifically refers to democracy when discussing the community pillar of sustainability. There is some debate over whether democracy is essential to the concept of sustainability. In the absence of constitutional protections, a tyrannical majority that preys upon minority interests can potentially hijack democracy. This was the position taken in Plato's *Republic,* which was partially a reaction against the injustice of the death of his mentor, Socrates. More recently, Fareed Zakaria, in his book *The Future of Freedom,* argues that under certain temporary circumstances a reformist au-

Figure 12.2 **The Three Pillars of Sustainability**

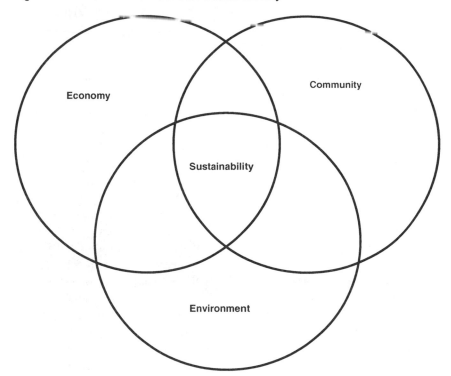

tocracy may be preferable to a democracy that lacks basic constitutional protections for minority interests.

In an earlier work, Viederman (1993) has emphasized that sustainability is an ethical standard as well as a technological, economic, and political problem to resolve. Building on this notion, Proops et al. (1996) argue that while sustainability is often seen as a scientific problem for which technical solutions can be developed, more important is the development of an ethic "to formulate the goals, the social will to achieve these goals, and the maturity of judgement to realize the goals" (p. 133). Developing this ethic requires a broad consensus in society regarding the basic values that underlie the concept of sustainability. Proops et al. also argue that sustainability is not a thing to be achieved but a constant process.

One of the challenges associated with learning about sustainability and developing specific policies is the presence of rigid disciplinary boundaries, which tend to promote rivalries and limit cooperation. The discipline of ecological economics has recently organized itself around the integration of ecology (nature's household) with economics (humankind's household), an integration that is central to the concept of a sustainable society. The journal *Ecological Economics* states in its aim and scope, for example, that "this integration is necessary because conceptual and professional isolation have led to economic and environmental policies that are mutually destructive." It is likely that these boundaries were a necessary part of developing a set of "best methods" for isolating, analyzing, and ultimately understanding the economic or the ecological or the sociological or the political elements of the world. The argument from the sustainability movement is that these best methods must be integrated now that we recognize the inherent interdependencies across these disciplines. There is a natural hesitancy on the part of some economists, ecologists, sociologists, and other experts in various disciplines to overcome their differences in terminology, analytical methods, and outlook. For example, Dasgupta and Maler (1996) point out that while it is self-evident that poor countries depend on the integrity of their environmental and natural resources—soil, forests, animals, and fisheries—for fifty years economic development models have largely ignored the health and integrity of environmental and natural resources as an element of successful development. Similarly, the discipline of environmental economics has largely ignored issues concerning poverty and its links to environmental quality. As the International Institute for Sustainable Development (IISD) has stated, the economics of a sustainable society "occurs at the intersection, or balancing, of three global imperatives: environmental integrity, economic efficiency, and the well-being of people [and community]" (www.iisd.org).

Summary

- Sustainability occurs at the intersection of three global imperatives— economy, community, and environment—over time.
- Ecologists, environmental ethicists, and others argue that a sustainable society is premised on the integrity of the ecosystem. Ecologists do not see the potential for substitutability between important life-support elements of the ecosystem and human or human-made capital. From this perspective, one can argue that sustaining the integrity of the remaining stocks of natural capital embodied in the earth's ecosystems is the path to sustainability.
- Social scientists and economists acknowledge the central role of ecosystem integrity but argue that sustainability also requires democratic process and empowerment to allow people to make good decisions, and a vital economy to provide economic security. Moreover, most economists to varying degrees argue that some forms of human-made capital

can substitute for declining stocks of natural capital and focus on maintaining human well-being as the path to sustainability.

- The international sustainable development movement provides insight into the historical development of the concept of sustainability. Prominent achievements of this movement include the Brundtland Commission Report and the Rio Declaration on Environment and Development.
- Conservation-based development represents a local and applied variant of sustainable development.
- Viederman (1996) has defined sustainability as being a "community's control and prudent use of" the *five capitals*—natural, human, human-made, social, and cultural—"to ensure, to the degree possible, that present and future generations can attain a high degree of economic security and achieve democracy while maintaining the integrity of the ecological systems upon which all life and production depends" (the *three pillars*).
- *Sustainability* is such an encompassing term that it easily loses its meaning. It includes a process of development, an ethical and a policy standard, and a set of technical processes that relate ecological health and human well-being to an interdependent array of economic, sociopolitical, and environmental/ecological systems.
- A central issue associated with sustainability has to do with the proper way of guiding and measuring the performance of development. As we shall see in chapter 14, there are competing theories for what sustainable development means and by implication what policies are consistent with moving us closer to a sustainable society.

Review Questions and Problems

1. Go back to chapter 7 and review the concept of benefit/cost analysis and the dynamic efficiency standard that is implied by such an analysis. Can benefit/cost analysis and dynamic efficiency be made consistent with a sustainability standard? If so, how might this affect the appropriate choice of discount rate and the sort of screens that might be applied to various projects that could eliminate projects or policies that generate current benefits at the cost of future generations?

2. Contrast the focus of sustainability on community and intergenerational equity with the individualistic focus of contemporary Western society. Explain why the greatest challenge of sustainability might involve human values and attitudes rather than the development of policies and technologies.

3. Access the Sustainable Development on Campus page of the International Institute for Sustainable Development website (www.iisd.org/educate) and familiarize yourself with the issues. Once you have done so, go to their

Sustainable Campus Policy Bank page (www.iisd.org/educate/policybank.asp) and review a number of the sustainable campus policies shown here. Next, form a group of students and develop a proposal for a sustainable campus policy at your college or university.

4. As international statements, the Brundtland Commission report and the Earth Charter reflect the interests of both high-income industrialized countries and lower-income countries. Access the 1992 Rio Declaration on Environment and Development (www.un.org/esa/sustdev/documents/agenda21/) and list what you think were the priorities of the high-income industrialized countries, and what you think were the priorities of the lower-income countries. Identify possible conflicts between these lists of priorities that might imperil sustainable development initiatives.

5. Read the paper "The Prosperous Community: Social Capital and Public Life" by Robert Putnam at www.prospect.org/print/V4/13/putnam-r.html. Write a half-page summary of what Putnam means by social capital, and describe several real-world examples of how the stock of social capital generates an economically valuable flow of services to a community.

6. Read the paper "The Value of the World's Ecosystem Services and Natural Capital" by Robert Costanza and his colleagues at www.uvm.edu/giee/publications/Nature_Paper.pdf. Write a half-page summary of what Costanza et al. (1997) mean by natural capital, and describe several real-world examples of how the stock of natural capital generates an economically valuable flow of ecological goods and/or services to people.

7. Can we achieve sustainability, as that term is understood in this textbook, in the absence of democracy? How does this relate to the role of Plato's philosopher-king, and to modern nation-states ruled by Islamic law? What sort of protections would need to be in place to assure that a democracy is consistent with sustainability principles?

Internet Links

Agenda 21 (www.un.org/esa/sustdev/documents/agenda21): Agenda 21, the Rio Declaration on Environment and Development, and the Statement of Principles for the Sustainable Management of Forests, were adopted by more than 178 governments at the United Nations Conference on Environment and Development (UNCED) held in Rio de Janeiro, Brazil, 3 to 14 June 1992.

ConservationEconomy.net (www.conservationeconomy.net): A project of Ecotrust, this website describes the elements of the conservation economy and provides a number of case studies drawn from the Pacific Northwest.

Earth Charter USA (www.earthcharterusa.org): A U.S. organization that seeks to promote the Earth Charter and sustainability.

Earth Council (www.earthcouncil.com): The Earth Council is an international nongovernmental organization (NGO) that was created in September 1992 to promote and advance the implementation of the Earth Summit agreements.

International Institute for Sustainable Development (www.iisd.org): Since its incorporation in 1990, IISD has worked to help decision makers understand the principles of sustainable development and how to put them into practice. This site contains an enormous volume of useful information.

IISD Sustainable Development Timeline (www.iisd.org/pdf/2002/ sd_timeline2002.pdf): Nice PDF file that provides a detailed timeline on the history of sustainable development.

SD Gateway (http://sdgateway.net): The SD Gateway integrates the on-line information developed by members of the Sustainable Development Communications Network. They offer more than 1,200 on-line documents related to sustainable development, a calendar of events, a job bank, the Sustainability Web Ring, a roster of mailing lists (listservs), and news sites dealing with sustainable development.

Sustainable Development on Campus (www.iisd.org/educate): IISD Internet site provides tools for making campuses more sustainable.

The Prosperous Community: Social Capital and Public Life (www.prospect.org/print/V4/13/putnam-r.html): Learn more about the value of social capital in this spring 1993 article by Robert Putnam published in the *American Prospect.*

United Nations Commission on Sustainable Development (www.un.org/ esa/sustdev/csd/csd13/csd13.htm): The Division for Sustainable Development provides leadership and is an authoritative source of expertise within the United Nations system on sustainable development.

Worldwatch Institute (www.worldwatch.org): A leading source of information on the interactions among key environmental, social, and economic trends. Their work revolves around the transition to an environmentally sustainable and socially just society—and how to achieve it.

References and Further Reading

Arrow, K., P. Dasgupta, L. Goulder, G. Daily, P. Ehrlich, G. Heal, S. Levin, K-G. Maler, S. Schneider, D. Starrett, and B. Walker. 2004. "Are We Consuming Too Much?" *Journal of Economic Perspectives* 18 (3): 147–72.

Berkes, F., and C. Folke. 1994. "Investing in Cultural Capital for Sustainable Use of Natural Capital." In *Investing in Natural Capital: The Ecological Economics Approach to Sustainability,* ed. A. Jansson, M. Hammer, C. Folke, and R. Costanza. Washington, DC: Island Press.

Bruntland, G. (ed.). 1987. *Our Common Future: The World Commission on Environment and Development.* Oxford: Oxford University Press.

Costanza, R., and H. Daly. 1992. "Natural Capital and Sustainable Development." *Conservation Biology* 6 (March): 37–46.

Costanza, R., R. d'Arge, R. de Groot, S. Farber, M. Grasso, B. Hannon, K. Limburg, S. Naeem, R. O'Neill, J. Paruelo, R. Raskin, P. Sutton, and M. van den Belt. 1997. "The Value of the World's Ecosystem Services and Natural Capital." *Nature* 387 (15 May): 253–60.

Daily, G. 1997. *Nature's Services: Societal Dependence on Natural Ecosystems.* Covelo, CA: Island Press.

Daly, H., and J. Cobb. 1989. *For the Common Good.* Boston: Beacon Press.

Dasgupta, P., and K-G. Maler. 1996. "Environmental Economics in Poor Countries: The Current State and a Program for Improvement." *Environment and Development Economics* 1 (February): 3–7.

de Waal, F. 2005. "How Animals Do Business." *Scientific American* 292 (April): 73–79.

Johnson, K. 1997. *Toward a Sustainable Region: Evolving Strategies for Reconciling Community and the Environment.* Seattle: Northwest Policy Center, University of Washington.

Kohler, T., G. Gumerman, and R. Reynolds. 2005. "Simulating Ancient Societies." *Scientific American* 293 (July): 77–84.

Meadows, D.H., D.L. Meadows, J. Randers, and W. Behrens (Club of Rome). 1972. *The Limits to Growth.* New York: Universe Books.

Proops, J., M. Faber, R. Mansetten, and F. Jost. 1996. "Achieving a Sustainable World." *Ecological Economics* 17 (June): 133–35.

Putnam, R. 1993. *Making Democracy Work: Civic Traditions in Modern Italy.* Princeton: Princeton University Press.

———. 2000. *Bowling Alone: The Collapse and Revival of American Community.* New York: Simon and Schuster.

Trivers, R. 1971. "The Evolution of Reciprocal Altruism." *Quarterly Review of Biology* 46: 35–57.

Viederman, S. 1993. "A Dream of Sustainability." *Ecological Economics* 8: 177–79.

———. 1996. "Sustainability's Five Capitals and Three Pillars." In *Building Sustainable Societies: A Blueprint for a Post-Industrial World,* ed. D. Pirages. Armonk, NY: M.E. Sharpe.

Wackernagel, M., and W. Rees. 1997. "Perceptual and Structural Barriers to Investing in Natural Capital: Economics from an Ecological Footprint Perspective." *Ecological Economics* 20 (1): 3–24.

Zakaria, F. 2003. *The Future of Freedom: Illiberal Democracy at Home and Abroad.* New York: W.W. Norton.

13

Recognizing Interdependencies and Thinking Long Term

Introduction

Moving toward a more sustainable society requires an understanding of the interactions between the elements of the three pillars—economy, community, and environment—over a long-term time horizon. This chapter will highlight a number of the more prominent factors and describe their relationship to the three pillars of sustainability. In the second part of this chapter, we will discuss the challenge of developing long-term policies for sustainability in political and economic contexts that tend to favor shorter-term approaches.

Recognizing Interdependencies

There is a tendency to approach fields of study such as economics, sociology, and environmental science in isolation from one another. This is the traditional way in which colleges and universities construct their major curricula. This approach tends to create isolated fields of expertise with relatively limited interdisciplinary skills. To some extent, this is necessary in order to build depth and core competencies. Nevertheless, sustainability studies demand an interdisciplinary approach. Moreover, economic, social, and environmental processes do not operate in isolation, which suggests that these discipline-centered boundaries are to some extent artificial and dysfunctional.

This section of the chapter describes a few of the better-known interdisciplinary topics that relate to the three pillars of sustainability.

The Industrial Revolution and the Agrarian Transition

The theory of path dependence suggests that where we are today, and where we are going to be in the future, can be explained in part by the particular series of events that make up our history. From this perspective, the human world is where it is today in large part because of our common experience with the industrialization process that transformed the way people live and relate to the world around them.

Prior to the industrial revolution, traditional agriculture was small in scale and labor-intensive. Both Mahatma Gandhi and Thomas Jefferson saw small-scale, traditional agriculture as being at the center of healthy and thriving local communities. As economies industrialize and make greater and greater use of capital equipment, the scale economies that are inherent to capital lead to unit production costs that are lower for large farms than for small farms. Farmworkers displaced by this process frequently move to urban centers looking for work. This process leads to a small number of large-scale, highly capitalized farms. These large farms specialize rather than having both livestock and crops, so chemical fertilizer, which is cheaper to apply, replaces the old system of spreading manure from the livestock onto the cropped fields. Food becomes relatively cheaper, and a large labor force is available for large-scale, low-wage manufacturing. In the United States, it took many years for workers to fully share in the gains created by the industrial revolution.

The agrarian transition can be accelerated by international trade agreements such as the North American Free Trade Agreement (NAFTA), which focuses on reducing barriers to trade, thereby more fully realizing the aggregate material gains from trade (more on this topic later in the chapter). In the case of NAFTA, Mexico was required to reduce barriers to U.S. and Canadian agricultural commodities. Since the time of Mexico's colonization, an elite class, descending from the Spanish colonists, owned most of the productive land in Mexico, thereby controlling most of the country's power and wealth, while the majority of the population worked in poverty. A key outcome of the Mexican revolution was land reform, which broke up the haciendas and ranchos and created the ejido, or farm cooperative program, that redistributed much of the country's land from the wealthy landholders to the peasants. The ejidos are still in place today and comprise nearly half of all the farmland in Mexico. With the advent of capital-intensive and highly subsidized agriculture in the United States, large U.S. farms are able to produce agricultural commodities in many cases much cheaper than on the under-capitalized ejidos in Mexico. As a result, removal of Mexican trade barriers has increased the flow of U.S. agricultural commodities into Mexico (from $2.9 billion in 1993, before NAFTA was implemented, to $4.2 billion in 2001), thereby displacing Mexican farmworkers and accelerating the process of migration into the urban centers of Mexico and into the United States. Many undocumented immigrants in the United States come from Mexican states that have been affected most negatively by the agriculture sections of NAFTA, including Guererro, Guanajuato, Oaxaca, Veracruz, Morelos, Puebla, Querétaro, and Michoacán.

The process of assimilating displaced farmworkers in increasingly industrialized urban societies is a significant challenge confronting low-income countries as well as the richer countries to which many of these people migrate for work. The results are seen in the squalor of growing shantytowns on the outskirts of many cities around the world, and both legal and undocumented immigration into more industrialized countries. The jobs available to undocumented immigrants are usually less safe, and in agricultural settings may involve exposure to harmful pesticides and other agricultural chemicals. Substantial steps are needed to improve the economic, social, and environmental conditions of these recent migrants.

Many recent migrants working in richer countries remit a portion of their income to their families back home. These remittances help sustain rural communities that have been impacted by the agrarian transition, and represent a significant portion of the economies of many lower-income countries. For example, in 2004 the Banco de México (Mexico's central bank) estimated that Mexicans living abroad remitted $17 billion to Mexico, larger than the revenues derived from either Mexico's oil exports or from foreign tourism into Mexico, and supporting an estimated one out of every ten families in Mexico. The Inter-American Development Bank forecasted that an estimated $30 billion in remittances was sent to Latin America in 2004 from the United States. The countries of Latin America and the Caribbean basin have contributed about one-half of the U.S. foreign-born population and receive almost one-third of the world's remittances. According to Inter-American Development Bank estimates, three-quarters of remittances to Latin America and the Caribbean originate in the United States. The World Bank (2004a) estimated that total world remittance flows to lower-income countries totaled $93 billion in 2003, dwarfing the $58 billion in official aid flows to lower-income countries. As of 2001, remittances to Haiti, Jordan, Nicaragua, El Salvador, and Jamaica represented more than 10 percent of their GDP.

Due to factors such as the agrarian transition, cities in lower-income countries are where the great majority of the world's population growth is forecast to occur in the twenty-first century. In particular, at the UN-sponsored Habitat II Summit in Istanbul in 1996, it was reported that 40 to 50 percent of the world's population lives in urban slums, and that people of the developing world continue to pour into these cities hoping to find a chance for a better life. By 2015, only one of the globe's ten largest cities (predicted to range in population from 19 million to 27.4 million people) will be in a rich country of the developed world. The process of providing energy, shelter, and transportation to these rapidly growing urban centers will strain the resources of low-income countries. Lack of access to cleaner technologies may result in an industrialization path that, like that of the rich countries before them, involves a period of intense pollution, which makes sustainable development in the cities of developing countries a global problem.

Income, Poverty, and Economic Growth

From the material perspective of income and consumption, poverty occurs when people lack access to economic resources sufficient for them to meet their basic material needs, and are therefore physiologically deprived. However, poverty also includes social deprivation, in which people are denied opportunities for improving their situation, and thus are robbed of dignity, confidence, and self-respect. The circumstances of those in poverty are often such that they have no choice but to live and work in the most polluted and degraded of environments. Moreover, those in poverty lack access to resources to meet their basic material needs, let alone to restore and conserve their natural environment. Poor communities are oftentimes politically disenfranchised and therefore are exposed to environmentally unjust policies.

In order to have a common reference point for estimating poverty worldwide, the World Bank uses reference lines set at $1 and $2 per day (adjusted for inflation), with the former serving as a threshold for extreme poverty. Based on these benchmark income thresholds, the World Bank estimated that in 2003 there were 1.2 billion people out of the developing world's 4.8 billion people living on $1 per day, while another 2.8 billion were living on less than $2 per day. The World Bank (www.worldbank.org) also reports that the proportion of people living in extreme poverty on less than $1 a day dropped by almost half between 1981 and 2001, from 40 percent to 21 percent of the global population. In terms of population numbers, these percentages imply that the number people living in extreme poverty fell from 1.5 billion in 1981 to 1.1 billion in 2001. The World Bank also provides information on poverty from a regional standpoint, elements of which are summarized below.

Among the regions of the developing world, East Asia is making the most rapid progress in poverty reduction. Dramatic economic growth in the region has pulled more than 500 million people out of poverty, and GDP per capita tripled. The proportion of people living in extreme poverty in East Asia fell from 58 to 16 percent. Huge regional disparities remain, especially in sub-Saharan Africa, where the number of poor people has increased significantly during the same time period and is projected to continue rising. In 1980 one out of every ten poor people in the world lived in sub-Saharan Africa. In 2000 the figure rose to one out of every three. Future projections predict that one out of every two poor people will live in sub-Saharan Africa. Between 1981 and 2001, the number of poor in sub-Saharan Africa rose from 164 million to 314 million, and real per capita GDP declined there by 14 percent. In Latin America the proportion of poor in the population has been almost unchanged since 1981, with about 10 percent living on $1 a day, while another 25 percent live on $2 a day. Finally, the percentage of poor in the overall population has also decreased in South Asia, although the numbers have not fallen by very much due a rapid population growth in the region. The number of people living on less than $1 a day dropped by just 34 million since 1990, to 428 million in 2001.

The United Nations Human Development Report (United Nations 2000) finds that about one-third of the world's countries experienced a drop in per capita GDP during the 1990s, including nearly one-half of those in sub-Saharan Africa and the majority of those in Eastern Europe. Thus chapter 4 of Agenda 21 from the Earth Summit concludes that high levels of consumption by the wealthy few results in excessive demands and unsustainable lifestyles among the richer segments, which place immense stress on the environment. The poorer segments, meanwhile, are unable to meet food, health care, shelter, and educational needs. Yet as the Human Development Report also observes, there is no automatic link between economic growth and progress in human development. Some countries have had fast growth and little improvement in human development, while others have had low growth and yet more rapid improvements in human development. The Human Development Report argues that in order for economic growth to improve the well-being of all people, it must prevent those who failed to gain from growth from falling into abject poverty, create jobs, ensure wide participation, protect the environment for future generations, and protect cultural traditions.

Economic growth has complex links to the sustainability of production and consumption. This is particularly evident in the case of energy and economic growth. On the production side, energy intensity—a measure of the quantity of energy required on average to produce the equivalent of a dollar of GDP—has declined in most countries around the world. According to the U.S. Energy Information Administration (EIA), the world's energy intensity declined an average of 1.3 percent per year between 1980 and 2001 (U.S. EIA website). In the case of China, the largest energy consumer among developing countries in Asia, the reduction in energy intensity has been attributed to improving technical efficiency associated with new capital. Economies with more rapid economic growth, such as China's, tend to have more rapid upgrading of production capital, which tends to be associated with improvements in energy efficiency. On the consumption side, however, economic growth tends to be associated with increases in energy consumption. For example, the U.S. Energy Information Administration reports that worldwide electricity consumption is expected to nearly double between 2001 and 2025 (U.S. EIA website). The strongest electricity-consumption growth rates are projected for the countries of the developing world, where net electricity consumption is forecasted to rise by 3.5 percent per year, compared with a projected average increase of 2.3 percent per year worldwide. The EIA argues that robust economic growth in many of the world's developing nations is expected to boost demand for electricity to run newly purchased home appliances for air conditioning, cooking, space and water heating, and refrigeration. There is a similar pattern for oil consumption and economic growth. There have been moderately successful efforts at decoupling energy consumption and economic growth, particularly in Western Europe. For example, in the United Kingdom over the last thirty-one years, GDP has increased by 106 percent, while total energy consumption in that same period rose by only 12 percent, and carbon dioxide emissions fell by around 20 percent.

Among the world's poorest countries, increased income is needed for those basic requirements that people in industrialized countries often take for granted—sanitation and water treatment, food storage, remediation of gross pollution problems, and fuel for heating and cooking. With water, for example, the basic need is to separate and properly treat drinking/cleaning water and wastewater. According to the World Bank (2004b), about one-fifth of the people living in the developing world were without access to safe water in 2000, while one-half lived without adequate sanitation, and 90 percent lived without their wastewater treated in any way. The World Bank reports that while there have been gains, some of which were associated with the United Nation's Decade for Water and Sanitation program, access to water and sanitation lags far behind the milestones set in the 1980s.

According to the World Bank, 5 to 6 million people die each year in developing countries due to waterborne diseases and air pollution. They estimate that the economic costs of environmental degradation have been estimated at 4 to 8 percent of GDP per year in many developing countries. The World Bank (1993) measured the present value of future years of disability-free life lost due to premature death or to disability from air or water pollution in a given year. Disability-free life expectancy is a key human capital indicator of sustainability. The World Bank study found that people in very low-income regions suffer much higher rates of illness and disabilities caused by bad air and water. The rate per 1,000 people in sub-Saharan Africa was 120, approximately 70 for India, more than 60 for the Middle East, approximately 15 for China, and approximately 7 for "established market economies." In countries with more than 20 percent of their population subsisting on $1 per day or less, at least 40 percent of children are affected by stunted growth, and people subsist on about half the amount of fresh water per capita as in richer countries (World Bank 1994). Half of the world's poor live in ecologically fragile rural areas and rely almost entirely on natural resources for day-to-day survival. Under these conditions, food insecurity leads to the development of agriculture on unsuitable terrain such as steep, erosion-prone slopes or nutrient-poor rain forest floors (Barrett 1996).

People who have inadequate food, water, and shelter for themselves and their children, and people, especially children, suffering from waterborne diseases and malnutrition, are under tremendous pressure to deal with today's crisis and may have to choose between protecting natural resources for the future and keeping themselves and their children fed today. Very poor regions and countries are the least resilient to stresses and shocks such as droughts, population booms, and political instabilities. When poor people live in ecologically fragile areas, the response to shocks may be to intensify deforestation, rangeland degradation, or displacement of wildlife habitat. In a very stark sense, the high cost of energy-efficient and cleaner technologies, and the opportunity cost of protecting biodiversity and wildlife habitat, may make important elements of protection and conservation a luxury good that only the rich countries can afford.

Population growth in lower-income countries has increased the scarcity of resources such as firewood for heating and cooking food, clean water for drinking and cleaning, fertile ground for raising food, and habitat for fishery resources. Industrialized countries have developed substitutes and energy-efficient technologies for overcoming the scarcity of these resources, yet these substitutes are costly. For example, pipeline infrastructure can be used to deliver natural gas and water to households, thereby reducing pressure on forests, freeing up labor for more productive activities, and improving sanitation. Similarly, relatively simple alternative energy technology, such as solar ovens, allows an even more complete move toward sustainability. The problem is that people in low-income countries may be priced out of the market for more sustainable production technologies.

There have been a number of economic studies that find evidence for an inverted-U-shaped relationship between levels of environmental harms (e.g.,

Figure 13.1   **The Environmental Kuznets Curve**

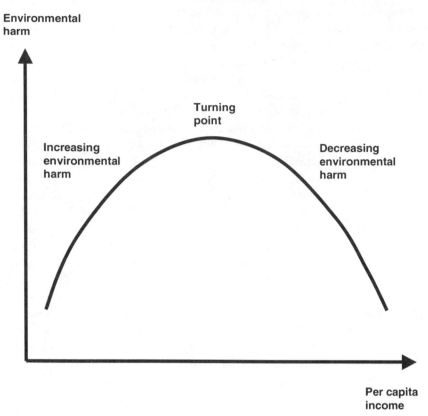

atmospheric concentrations of certain pollutants) and per capita income as measured by real GDP (Selden and Song 1994; Grossman and Krueger 1993; Hettige, Lucas, and Wheeler 1992; World Bank 1995). This inverted-U relationship follows a pattern similar to the hypothesis by Kuznets (1955) that income inequality first rises, and then declines, with economic development. Thus, the inverted-U relationship between pollution concentrations and per capita real GDP is usually referred to as the "environmental Kuznets curve" (EKC), such as the one illustrated in Figure 13.1. The idea is that as low-income countries industrialize, increased production and consumption is initially fueled by burning coal and other relatively dirty fossil fuels. Thus, as Kander (2002) found for the case of Sweden in the 1950s, carbon intensities tend to be high in this stage of industrialization. As a result, the world's worst urban air pollution tends to occur in newly industrializing low-income countries where ambient concentrations of sulfur dioxide, carbon monoxide, lead, particulate matter, and nitrogen oxides are high. As countries become richer, they purchase a cleaner environment through more stringent environmental regulations, change the fuels they use (i.e., replace coal with natural gas), use newer and more efficient capital equipment, and move the dirtiest industries to less regulated countries. This pattern would explain the difference in concentrations of atmospheric sulfur dioxide emissions between, say, a nonindustrialized country in comparison to China, and China in comparison to Germany.

An unfortunate implication of much of this empirical research is that countries such as China, India, and many countries in Latin America and Africa are on the left-hand curve of the EKC, meaning that incremental increases in income will create *more* rather than less pollution in the near future. Not all pollutants follow the EKC pattern. For example, there is a direct relationship between per capita income and garbage, and this direct relationship does not appear to decline at higher income levels. It has been found, for example, that a 40 percent increase in the GDP of countries belonging to the Organization for Economic Cooperation and Development (OECD) since 1980 has been accompanied by the same percentage growth in municipal waste. A similar pattern may also hold for carbon dioxide emissions. Moreover, not all economists accept the EKC relationship as a general metaphor for the relationship between income and sustainability. For example, in commenting on the EKC relationship, Nobel laureate Kenneth Arrow and colleagues (1996, p. 106) point out:

> While they [advocates for the EKC] do indicate that economic growth may be associated with improvements in some environmental indicators, they imply neither that economic growth is sufficient to induce environmental improvements in general, nor that the environmental effects of growth may be ignored, nor, indeed, that the Earth's resource base is capable of supporting indefinite economic growth. In fact, if this base were to be irreversibly degraded, economic activity itself could be at risk.

Along these same lines, Copeland and Taylor (2004) note that while there is evidence of an EKC in some cases, their skepticism remains about the existence of a simple, predictable, and general relationship between pollution and per capita income.

Arrow et al. point out that the inverted-U relationship has not been shown to hold for accumulated stocks of waste or pollutants involving long-term or more dispersed costs (such as CO_2), for resource stocks, or for systemwide consequences (for example, reductions in one country pop up as increases elsewhere). Finally, Arrow et al. argue that most reductions in pollutants are attributable to local institutional reforms such as environmental regulations, market-based incentives, and empowerment to reduce environmental impacts.

Another argument linking income growth to sustainability comes from a World Bank (1995) report indicating that most rich countries have fossil-fuel taxes, which discourage fossil-fuel use, while lower-income countries actually subsidize such energy use. We will discuss this point in detail below. Yet another point in favor of the argument that economic growth is needed for low-income countries to become environmentally sustainable is that rising incomes tend to be associated with declining population growth rates, which is also explained in greater detail below.

To summarize, then, economic growth produces income that raises many (if not all) people out of poverty, and higher incomes are associated with lower fertility rates, safer drinking water, and the prevalence of cleaner and less resource-intensive production technologies. Nevertheless, there are strong counterarguments to the idea that higher incomes move us closer to a sustainable society. One could argue that it is the rich countries, after all, that consume the great majority of the world's resources and are responsible for a disproportionate percentage of the world's trash, toxic emissions, ozone-depleting chemicals, and greenhouse gases. For example, with 5 percent of the world's population, the United States generates 19 percent of the world's wastes and consumes 20 percent of the world's metals, 24 percent of its energy, and 25 percent of its fossil fuels. International trade between rich countries and less democratic low-income countries that fail to honor land tenure and property rights can accelerate unsustainable resource harvest rates.

Can economic growth be sustainable? Free-market economists who focus on the self-correcting properties of well-functioning competitive markets will usually endorse this view. Others, particularly ecologists, take a more skeptical view (more on this in chapter 14). Ayres (1996) argues that "it is quite possible to have economic growth—in the sense of providing better *and more valuable* services to ultimate consumers—without necessarily consuming more physical resources" (p. 118). The flow of natural resources (e.g., wood, energy, plastic, metals, food) through extraction, the production and distribution of goods, consumption, and disposal is sometimes known as the material *throughput* of an economy. It can be argued that the problem of the sustainability of a macroeconomy is less about economic growth per se, and more about the nature of what is produced and how. A country with economic growth and declining material throughput could actually be making more progress toward sustainability than a society with no economic growth but rising material throughput. Declining material throughput in the context of growing real GDP could occur, for example, with a shift to production and consumption of high-quality services associated with long-lived, durable, and energy-efficient consumer goods that can easily be disassembled for reuse or recycling at the end of their product life. Hawken, Lovins, and Lovins (1999) refer to this as the "service and flow" economy, and describe straightforward ways—such as leasing rather than owning—to get there. Other ways that throughput can be reduced include the purchase of locally produced food and other products that embody less transportation energy, and a general shift from "quantity" to "quality."

Costanza and Daly (1992) argue that the term *economic growth* should be used when throughput is increased, while the term *development* should be used when economic growth occurs because of increased resource and organizational efficiency that does not increase throughput. Ayres (1996) observes that increasingly resource-efficient technologies allow for a de-linking of large elements of economic activity from energy and other material throughputs, a process sometimes known as *dematerialization,* which has occurred to some extent with computer and telecommunications technologies. By the same token, policies that focus on economic growth, as measured by GDP, will not necessarily improve the well-being of people or lead to a more sustainable society. We will discuss the relationship between GDP and sustainable development in chapter 13.

Education, Empowerment, and Justice

Sustainability is not simply restricted to the relationship between economics and the environment. Just as important is a variety of social, cultural, and political empowerment issues. Failures of empowerment lead to dependency, exploitation, and a wide variety of other ills. Important areas for empowerment include recognizing the rights of communities to manage the local common-pool resources upon which they rely, and giving women access to education, employment, land ownership, and influence over policies that affect them.

One indicator of empowerment is the adoption of democratic institutions in government. The World Bank (1999) reports that the number of democratically governed countries has grown steadily. Yet in many parts of the world, the empowerment of women remains largely unfulfilled. As of 1995, more than 60 percent of the world's poor were women, and growth in the poverty rate has been higher for women than for men. Estimates that are more recent reveal that approximately 64 percent of the world's illiterate are women and girls, up from 58 percent in 1960 (United Nations Development Program 2002, hereinafter UNDP). According to the United Nations, in countries such as Yemen, Iraq, and Senegal, more than two-thirds of all women are illiterate, and even in countries such as India more than half of all women are illiterate. Significant gaps continue to exist in school enrollment between boys and girls. According to the World Bank (1999), two-thirds of the children without access to even a primary education in lower-income countries are girls. The International Labor Organization reports that women are more likely than men to find employment in the informal economy, which lacks the same degree of legal and regulatory protections afforded by regular employment. Women own less than 1 percent of the world's property. According to Human Rights Education Associates, women held only a small fraction of the seats in the world's national congresses and parliaments, accounting for only about 14 percent of all legislative seats in 2002. As a final point, women and children experience high levels of rape and other forms of violence during periods of war and conflict, and represent a majority of the world's refugees and displaced peoples (Jazairy, Alamgir, and Panuccio 1992; Erlich, Erlich, and Daily 1995; Mehra 1996).

A strong inverse relationship exists between various measures of women's empowerment (educational access and attainment, access to jobs and employment, reproductive decision-making opportunities) and total fertility rates. For example, the relationship between female literacy and fertility rates is described in the following excerpt from a speech given by Federico Mayor, the director general of the United Nations Educational, Scientific, and Cultural Organization (UNESCO):

> Education has . . . been central to Thailand's dramatic success in reducing population increase. In a country where 90 percent of women are literate, the average number of children per woman fell from 6.1 in 1965–70 to only 2.2 in 1987 and was matched by a sharp drop in infant mortality and substantial economic progress. In Brazil, illiterate women produce an average of 6.5 children, while women with secondary education only 2.5. Sub-Saharan Africa, where female literacy averages only 15 percent, significantly has some of the highest rates of population growth. No one, of course, would seek to deny the complexity of population issues or the many factors involved in the reduction of fertility—including the socioeconomic context, the availability of family planning services and, in some cases, direct incentives to limit family size. However, it is clear from the World Fertility Surveys and many other studies that education, particularly of girls and women, is the key to reducing fertility, whatever the socioeconomic or cultural context. (www.un.org/popin/confcon/poped/anx3wp.htm)

Likewise, Martin and Juarez (1995, p. 52) offer the following insights into the relationship between female education and total fertility rates in Latin America:

According to data from Demographic and Health Surveys for nine Latin American countries, women with no education have large families of 6–7 children, whereas better-educated women have family sizes of 2–3 children, analogous to those of women in the developed world. Despite these wide differen tials in actual fertility, desired family size is surprisingly homogeneous throughout the educational spectrum. While the least educated and the best-educated women share the small family norm, the gap in contraceptive prevalence between the two groups ranges from 20–50 percentage points. Better educated women have broader knowledge, higher socioeconomic status and less fatalistic attitudes toward reproduction than do less educated women.

As well as having fewer children, educated women are more likely to have better fed, and therefore healthier, children—who will themselves be better educated. An increase in educational attainment by women is also generally associated with increased labor-force participation rates among women and decreased rates among children, with higher life expectancies, with increased use of contraceptives, and with safer drinking water. It seems clear, therefore, that the education and empowerment of women is closely tied to sustainability.

Mehra (1996) reports that the majority of poor women in developing countries support their families through farming and the raising of livestock, and thus are at the heart of where new and more sustainable practices must be implemented. In many parts of Africa, women provide the majority of the labor for food production, which in many cases results in nearly one-half the cash-equivalent value of household income. Women play a central role in collecting livestock feed and water and in providing labor for gathering fuelwood. Yet in many of these same countries, women are blocked from owning land and thus receive only a small fraction of development funds going to agriculture. By working land they do not own, women lack the incentive to make long-term investments that benefit the environment, such as the planting of trees. In fact, in some parts of Africa, Mehra reports that land tenure is linked to the planting of trees, and men prevent women from planting trees as a way to keep them from gaining land ownership and power. Moreover, women are frequently not given the same access to economic development and conservation resources. External aid organizations have in the past been unaware of the key role of women in agriculture and resource management and so have developed site-specific plans with men, with the result being misdesigned projects that omit those who are responsible for carrying them out.

Looking beyond the issue of gender, another manifestation of empowerment is the provision of secure land tenure to farmers. A lack of secure, long-term land tenure can reduce farmers' incentives to make beneficial long-term investments in the land that they work. For example, lack of secure land tenure in China has led to a reluctance by farmers to sink money and labor into land improvements such as terraces to limit erosion because farmers fear that they may not be able to keep farming the land long enough to realize a return on their investment (Prosterman, Hanstad, and Ping 1996). Securing land tenure may involve recognizing, and returning to, locally devised systems of private and common property.

Exploitation, which is obviously inconsistent with sustainability, is more likely to obtain when there is a substantial asymmetry in local power and a failure to recognize local property rights regimes and the right to local self-governance. For example, local communities and tribespeople of Ogoniland in Nigeria have little control over the massive oil development and collateral environmental degradation from corporations such as Royal Dutch–Shell in partnership with the Nigerian government. Income from oil development enriches the military regime of Nigeria, which has executed a number of dissident Ogoni tribespeople who protested the environmental degradation, including activist Ken Saro-Wiwa. Similarly, native Papuans have suffered because of the huge Freeport mine.

Multinational corporations might claim that if they did not do business with governments accused of extensive human rights and environmental abuses then others would, and those others would not have the same degree of ethical control. Moreover, multinational corporations might also argue that their presence generates income that will eventually raise local living standards. Both points can be argued, just as one could argue that these corporations could use their advantage to foster reforms and pressure the more repressive governments with which they do business.

Income inequality is both a cause and a manifestation of asymmetries in empowerment and educational access. As of 2003, the richest 20 percent of the world's population received 85 percent of total world income, or about 60 times the 1.4 percent of total world income received by the poorest 20 percent of the world's population. By way of comparison, in 1960 the richest 20 percent had only 30 times the income of the bottom 20 percent. The *Human Development Report 2003* (UNDP 2003) describes income inequality using a *Gini coefficient* (derived from a *Lorenz curve* diagram), where a value of 0 indicates perfect equality and a value of 1.0 total inequality. That report found that incomes are distributed more unequally across the world's people (with a Gini coefficient of 0.66) than within the most unequal countries (Brazil, for example, has a Gini coefficient of 0.61). The *Human Development Report 2003* also notes that the gap between the world's richest and poorest countries has been increasing, and that inequality had been increasing in many of the world's developing countries. That report goes on to note that the richest 1 percent of the world's population receives as much as the poorest 57 percent, and that the 25 million richest Americans have as much income as almost 2 billion of the world's poorest people.

Countries with the most unequal distributions of income also tend to be relatively poor, an issue investigated by Simon Kuznets (1955). More recently, Persson and Tabellini (1994) studied fifty-six countries and found a strong negative relationship between income inequality and growth in per capita income, which they attributed to government policies that failed to protect individual rights and appropriated the returns on effort and other investments. Similarly, World Bank researchers report that unequal distributions of assets such as land form an even greater impediment to economic growth (Deininger and Squire 1997). In many cases a political/economic elite controls most of these countries' income-generating resources and so gets most of the income. For example, the *Economist* (5 August 2000) reports that the Suharto family was alleged to have corruptly amassed a $45 billion fortune. Prior to his ouster in 1998, President Suharto's children were reportedly involved in almost every aspect of the country's economic life. When asked how Indonesia's economy is run, President Suharto reportedly replied, "my children are very good in business." Income inequality is not just a problem in the poor countries, however. The OECD recently reported that the United States has the most unequal distribution of income among the rich countries. Obviously, one implication of income inequality is that information on average *per capita income* is not very descriptive of the conditions under which most people live.

Highly unequal distributions of income, and the mass poverty that goes with them, are difficult to reconcile with a sustainable society. Economic systems featuring highly unequal distributions of wealth and income frequently result in the political disenfranchisement of the poor, which is inconsistent with the requirement for democratic process in a sustainable society. In addition, most revolutions around the world have been reactions to extremely unequal distributions of wealth and political influence, and blockaded access to wealth-generating resources. Countries with highly unequal distributions of income must spend substantial resources on building walled communities, prisons, and other defensive investments against crime and theft. Of course, no country has a perfectly equal distribution of income, nor would any country necessarily want to. There are two somewhat conflicting notions of fairness at work. One notion of fairness is that a person's income should match the value of the work he or she does, which naturally leads to some inequality but provides desirable incentives. Another notion of fairness is that of fundamental human rights, from which one might argue that it is morally wrong for one person to be a billionaire while another starves in the street.

Government failure in providing education and opportunities to all people has led to the emergence of NGOs—nongovernmental organizations—to deal with rural development, small-farmer rights, urban service provision, and protection of natural resources. NGOs include international development organizations (the International Monetary Fund [IMF], the World Bank), human rights organizations (Amnesty International), environmental organizations (Greenpeace, the World Wildlife Fund [WWF]), unions, and so forth.

A remarkably successful form of empowerment is the provision of microscale loanable funds to help people living in poverty start small businesses. Traditional banks will not lend to people who do not own valuable assets that can be pledged to secure repayment, and *venture capitalists* (those who capitalize entrepreneurs with funds from sources such as pension funds, university endowments, foundations, and wealthy individuals) rarely work with small or microscale entrepreneurs. A positive development in the area of women's empowerment and the alleviation of poverty is the creation of Bangladesh's Grameen Bank and similar organizations that specialize in microlending. In 1976 economist Muhammad Yunus went into the villages of Bangladesh to try to find out how the poor of Bangladesh could be helped. In one village, Yunus found forty-one people engaged in activities such as making bamboo stools and earning wages of only 2 cents a day. What they lacked was the equivalent of $26 to capitalize small businesses that would make them entrepreneurs capable of earning substantially more money.

Yunus created the Grameen ("village") Bank to provide microloans to the most impoverished and oppressed villagers so they could set up their own small businesses to produce goods such as baskets, fishnets, and food. As of 2005, 96 percent of Grameen's 4 million borrowers (in nearly 48,000 villages) were women. Yunus found that women proved to be more disciplined and resourceful borrowers, were more reliable in repaying their loans, and could be counted on to share profits with their families (Counts 1996). These microloans have played a surprisingly central role in alleviating poverty. Approximately 99 percent of the loans have been repaid, a rate higher than for traditional banks in the area that lend to wealthier people. A key reason for this high repayment rate, and for the success of Grameen-style banking, is that individual loans are made in the context of a peer group or solidarity group. Each member of the solidarity group assumes responsibility for guaranteeing the repayment of loans extended to every other member (Stix 1997). These solidarity groups serve as an alternative to collateral in guaranteeing loan repayment.

The Grameen Bank has elevated an estimated 48 percent of its women borrowers above the poverty line and 34 percent of the others very close to the line. Among a control group of similar families that had not been capitalized by Grameen, only 4 percent were above the poverty line. Both Bornstein (1996) and Counts (1996) report that the Grameen Bank has been substantially more successful in combating poverty than traditional foreign aid or other antipoverty programs. By providing very poor people, especially women, with access to credit, microcredit programs provide these people with the means to transform their own and their families' lives, providing better nutrition, education, housing, and health for themselves and their children. In impoverished parts of the world, there are few opportunities for wage and salaried employment, and the great majority of people are self-employed. In this context, a small loan of $150 or less, provided at a reasonable interest rate, can allow people to support themselves, thus breaking the cycle of poverty.

Grameen-style microcredit programs are rapidly growing, and there are microlending organizations in most countries around the world. A few of the many microcredit organizations include Trickle Up, Opportunity International, and SHARE. The United Nations made 2005 the International Year of Microcredit, and microcredit is now widely acknowledged as one of the most effective ways of elevating people out of poverty. Yet it is clear that Grameen-style microlending cannot function in a social and political vacuum—there must be substantial social capital within the solidarity group as well as sufficient business training and accountability among both borrowers and lenders. Moreover, microlending is not a panacea and should not be seen as a substitute for education and public health programs, among others. Performance up to now does suggest, however, that microlending is an important tool of more sustainable economic development.

International Trade

"Free" or liberalized international trade and its relationship with sustainability is another contentious subject. Free or liberalized trade means that there are no barriers to trade. Barriers to trade usually take the form of special taxes charged on imports (called tariffs), limits on the quantity of imports (called quotas), or technical restrictions (e.g., restrictions on the characteristics of products or how they are produced). The classical argument in favor of free and unimpeded international trade, which goes back to Adam Smith and David Ricardo, is that free trade allows for regions and countries to specialize in those activities that they do best. Specialization and trade create material wealth, and increased international competition promotes innovation and reduces consumer prices. Free trade and investment can heighten social and environmental exploitation, however, when governments engaged in trade, or the trade agreements they create, lack adequate democratic institutions and processes to protect the environment and exhaustible natural resources. For example, trade between wealthy and low-income countries can lead to a process whereby low-income countries with lax environmental laws, poor enforcement, or corrupt administration specialize in producing goods that are pollution-intensive or resource-intensive, and specialize in providing waste disposal services by accepting toxins and trash generated in wealthy countries. Trade agreements can also undermine local sovereignty and take away tools that can be used to assure compliance with labor and environmental standards when environmental or labor regulations are narrowly interpreted as trade barriers. In addition, multinational corporations working in partnership with corrupt government authorities can construct environmentally damaging projects that displace local communities and create benefits that are narrowly focused on the political elite. We will discuss these and other issues below. In chapter 14 we will look at the mixed record of success with international development lending.

The Argument for Free International Trade

The modern argument for free international trade derives from a model of trade developed by David Ricardo, which advanced even earlier work by Adam Smith. The assumption is that potential trading partners have fixed differences in natural resources or capital such that each can specialize in the production of a particular good (or set of goods) that they can produce at a lower opportunity cost than the others. Assuming that property rights are fully articulated and respected by trading parties, and that there are no large barriers or costs associated with trade, then specialization and trade will result in an increase in aggregate material prosperity. To see this, consider the following simple example. Suppose that an island has a coastal zone with a highly productive fishery, but with unproductive agricultural land. For example, suppose that on average a person working all day could catch 20 pounds of fish per day, or produce 10 pounds of agricultural products, as shown in Table 13.1. Consequently, resources such as labor and capital that are applied to agricultural production on the coast come at a high opportunity cost in terms of forgone fish production, since these resources can be more productively applied to fishing. In this example, a day spent in agricultural work generates an opportunity cost of 20 pounds of fish.

Suppose that the island also has an interior that has highly productive agricultural land. Therefore, resources such as labor and capital that are applied to fish production in the interior come at a high opportunity cost, since they can be more productively applied to agriculture. For example,

Table 13.1

An Illustrative Example of Bilateral Trade

Country	Fish production per person per day (lbs)	Agricultural production per person per day (lbs)
Coast	20	10
Interior	5	30

suppose that on average a person working all day in the interior could catch 5 pounds of fish per day, or produce 30 pounds of agricultural products, as shown in Table 13.1. Consequently, resources such as labor and capital that are applied to catching fish in the interior come at a high opportunity cost in terms of foregone agricultural production, since these resources can be more productively applied to agriculture. In this example, a day spent fishing generates an opportunity cost of 30 pounds of agricultural products. Suppose further that each zone is a separate country. In the absence of international trade, agricultural products will be very expensive in the coastal country due to their relative scarcity and high opportunity cost. Similarly, fish will be very expensive in the interior country due to the high opportunity cost of its production.

In the absence of trade, if people divided their time in half between fishing and agriculture in each country, then on average in a day a person on the coast would produce 10 pounds of fish and 5 pounds of agricultural products. In contrast, a person in the interior on average would produce 2.5 pounds of fish and 15 pounds of agricultural products. In total, these two people produce 12.5 pounds of fish and 20 pounds of agricultural products per day. Thus on the coast the *relative price* of a pound of agricultural products would be 2 pounds of fish, whereas in the interior the relative price of a pound of agricultural products would be only 0.17 pounds of fish. Since agricultural product prices are considerably higher on the coast than in the interior, entrepreneurs will recognize that an *arbitrage opportunity* exists and will have an incentive to export agricultural products from the interior to the coast where they are more valuable. Note that an arbitrage opportunity exists when there is a difference in prices in different markets that cannot be entirely accounted for due to differences in shipping and transaction costs, and which therefore promotes trade. We can also derive the relative prices of fish. On the coast, the relative price of a pound of fish will be half a pound of agricultural products, while in the interior the relative price of a pound of fish will be 6 pounds of agricultural products. Since fish prices are considerably higher in the interior than on the coast, an arbitrage opportunity exists and entrepreneurs will have an incentive to export fish to the interior where it is more valuable.

Bargaining and trade between the coast and the interior will cause the price of fish and agricultural products to equilibrate across the two countries.

Trade involves specialization, and in economics the *Law of Comparative Advantage* states that total material wealth can be increased when goods and services are produced by the country with the lowest opportunity cost. We have seen that a person in the coastal country can produce a pound of fish at an opportunity cost of only half a pound of agricultural products, whereas in the interior the opportunity cost of producing a pound of fish is 6 pounds of agricultural products. Since the coastal country produces fish at a low opportunity cost relative to the inland country, the coastal country should specialize in fish production. Their low opportunity cost gives them a comparative advantage in producing fish relative to the inland country. Likewise, we have seen that a person in the inland country can produce a pound of agricultural products at an opportunity cost of only 0.17 pounds of fish, while for a person on the coast the opportunity cost is 2 pounds of fish. Thus, the inland country should specialize in agriculture, where their low opportunity cost gives them a comparative advantage. With complete specialization and trade, a person on the coast can produce 20 pounds of fish a day, and a person in the interior can produce 30 pounds of agricultural products per day. Consequently, specialization and trade results in an extra 7.5 pounds of fish and 10 pounds of agricultural products each day relative to the scenario of no trade, where people divided their time between the two productive activities. This illustrates how trade increases material wealth.

Free international trade may move us closer to a sustainable society for several reasons listed below:

- By increasing material wealth, free trade can raise incomes, improve human health, move people out of poverty, and free up time for arts and culture.
- As wealth increases, poorer countries increasingly can afford costly but cleaner energy technologies.
- Trade exposes people to different cultures and can foster increased understanding and tolerance of diversity.

Of course, concerns regarding self-sufficiency, the cost of transporting goods, and cultural and religious incompatibilities can reduce the gains from free trade. Moreover, in the example given above, free trade generated cheaper imports that displaced those coastal people engaged in relatively high-priced agriculture, and those people from the interior who specialized in relatively high-priced fishing. There is also no guarantee that the gains from free trade will be distributed equitably within either country. Nevertheless, most human cultures over thousands of years have engaged in some degree of trade, driven by the basic incentive to exploit arbitrage opportunities and improve material standards of living. Attempts at heavily regulating or eliminating trade will usually result in the development of black markets. As economist Paul Krugman has stated, "[i]f there were an Economist's Creed it would surely contain the affirmations, 'I believe in the Principle of Comparative Advantage,' and 'I believe in free trade'" (1987, p. 131).

The Argument Against Free International Trade

When the idealized conditions identified by Ricardo and later trade theorists do not exist, the material gains from free trade may be overstated. Moreover, aggregate analysis of the gains from trade often ignores the distributional consequences of trade within a society, where some people lose their livelihoods due to cheaper imports. In addition, *globalization* has substantially increased the mobility of capital relative to Ricardo's day. To see this, suppose that country A has developed an automobile industry, while country *B* has developed a textile industry. Once these industries are in place, we would naturally expect that comparative advantage, specialization, and international trade in cars and clothes would proceed along the same lines as in the island example given above. Nevertheless, what if capital is highly mobile and labor or regulatory costs are substantially lower in country A? Ricardo's law of comparative advantage is premised on immobility of the factor of production that produces the comparative advantage, and does not hold if that assumption fails. While capital mobility improves profit and reduces consumer prices, it also can lead to considerable labor displacement, harm smaller communities that lose their factory, and force countries to reduce health, safety, environmental, and organized labor regulations in order to prevent their industry from going offshore. This latter effect is sometimes termed a "race to the bottom." Education and training that enhances worker productivity is essential to maintaining high wages under free trade and capital mobility.

As mentioned earlier in the chapter, free trade and investment can heighten exploitation when governments engaged in trade lack adequate democratic institutions and processes. Chichilnisky (1994), for example, models North–South trade between a high-income country with well-defined and enforced property rights to environmental resources and a low-income country with poorly defined and enforced property rights. The difference in the level of property rights enforcement is sufficient by itself to motivate bilateral trade, because the environmental resource is underpriced in the low-income country relative to the high-income country due to the exhaustion of Hotelling rents (discussed in chapter 5). She shows that the "tragedy of the commons" effect in the low-income country is worsened by trade and transmitted to the entire world economy. Overproduction of the environmental resource in the low-income country is matched by overconsumption of the resource in the high-income country. Thus, it is not necessarily efficient for countries in the South to specialize in dirty, resource-extractive production.

Along these same lines, the United Nations Environment Program (1999, p. 1) notes:

> Recently . . . there has been an increasing concern over the potential negative impacts of trade liberalization, particularly on the environmental and natural resources of developing countries and countries with economies in transition where trade has grown most rapidly. These countries have found that economic activities supporting, or supported by, rapidly expanded trade can result in serious environmental degradation when complementary environmental policies are not in place. Unless appropriate action is taken, such degradation can spark a progressive cycle of decline for national development. Pollution of air, water and soil, and unrestrained natural resource exploitation, grow to levels that jeopardize the viability of the economic activities they support. Trade thereby becomes unsustainable as the potential for future trade is significantly reduced.

UNEP goes on to argue that emphasis should be placed on enhancing the institutional and human capacities of developing countries for integrating environment, trade, and development policies—in other words, sustainable development. This issue is addressed in detail in chapter 14.

Copeland and Taylor (2004) use the phrase "pollution haven effect" to refer to the argument that an increase in environmental regulations will, at the margin, have an effect on plant location decisions and trade flows. This argument is strongly supported by economic theory and by recent empirical research. Thus, there is the potential for some countries to weaken their environmental regulations as a way to out-compete other countries for new production plants and to enhance their international competitiveness. In contrast, Copeland and Taylor offer a more stringent "pollution haven hypothesis" that a reduction in trade barriers (e.g., reduced tariffs or quotas) will lead to a shifting of pollution-intensive industry from countries with stringent regulations to countries with weaker regulations. They note that the theoretical support for this hypothesis is quite weak because, as they observe, trade theory suggests that there are many factors other than pollution regulation that affect trade flows. Moreover, the empirical literature suggests that these other factors are in fact more important in determining trade patterns. Thus, there appears to be less concern that trade liberalization will result in a "race to the bottom" in terms of environmental standards.

A related problem is that of rich countries exporting hazardous wastes and garbage. Increasingly tight regulation for the handling and disposal of hazardous waste has increased the cost of safe disposal in rich countries. In contrast, extreme poverty and corruption in very low-income countries often results in very low-cost disposal opportunities, thereby creating an unfortunate comparative advantage in hazardous waste disposal services grounded in poverty and failures of effective democratic governance. The 1989 Basel Convention on the Control of Transboundary Movements of Hazardous Wastes and Their Disposal addressed this environmental injustice. Amendments to the Basel Convention effectively banned all forms of hazardous waste exports from the rich industrialized countries to all lower-income countries. The ban amendment will come into force after sixty-two parties to the treaty ratify it, and only applies to those parties that ratify it. As of 2004, forty-four parties had ratified the amendment, with the notable exception of the United States. Yet illegal waste dumping has increased as regulations governing the safe and proper disposal of hazardous waste tighten.

For example, Somalia's coastline has been used as a dumping ground for tens of millions of metric tons of rich countries' hazardous wastes since the late 1980s, though the pace of dumping accelerated with the start of the civil war that followed the 1991 overthrow of the late dictator Mohamed Siad Barre. Local warlords, many of them former ministers in Siad Barre's government, were paid large sums of money by European firms in return for providing dumpsites for their hazardous waste, which included lead, radioactive uranium, mercury, cadmium, and various industrial, hospital, chemical, and other toxic wastes. Payments to warlords of approximately $8 per metric ton have been documented, which contrasts sharply with the cost of safe disposal in rich industrialized countries, which can exceed $1,000 per metric ton. The United Nations Environment Program announced that the massive December 26, 2004, tsunami waves washed up and broke open rusted barrels of hazardous waste. People living in northeastern coastal towns on Somalia's Indian Ocean coast were reported by the UN to be suffering from radiation sickness and higher than normal numbers of respiratory infections, mouth ulcers and bleeding, abdominal bleeding, and unusual skin infections.

Within the United States, the Supreme Court has ruled a number of times that garbage disposal services represent an "article of commerce" protected by the commerce clause of the Constitution from state-level restrictions on interstate commerce. As a result, wealthy communities export their trash by truck, barge, and rail to some of the poorest counties and American Indian reservations in the United States.

Yet another problem with international trade liberalization derives from the way we have structured international trade agreements. The General Agreement on Tariffs and Trade (GATT), forged in concert with the IMF and the World Bank at the Bretton Woods Conference in 1947, and renegotiated in Punta del Este, Uruguay, in 1986, may threaten the integrity of local, national, and international environmental improvement efforts. GATT requires signatory countries to follow the principles of multilateralism (trade is governed by international rules) and nondiscrimination. Nondiscrimination requires that foreign firms be treated the same as domestic firms ("national treatment"), and that firms from different countries be treated the same ("most favored nation" status). Thus if an exporter in country A cannot sell its *existing product* in country B because country B has environmental laws that constrain how the product is made or packaged, the exporter (or country A) can file a complaint with the World Trade Organization (WTO) that country B has a "nontariff trade barrier" that restricts free trade. It is then possible that the WTO will impose reciprocal trade and other sanctions on country B.

The WTO was formed in 1994 as a successor to GATT, and its primary activities are in resolving international trade disputes. WTO decisions are binding on the 125 member countries. Article XX of GATT states that GATT shall not be construed as preventing the adoption or enforcement by any contracting party of measures (1) necessary to protect human, animal, or plant life or health, or (2) relating to the conservation of exhaustible natural resources, if such measures are made effective in conjunction with restrictions on domestic production. Article XX has been the subject of a number of test cases having to do with disputes over environmental regulations as nontariff trade barriers. In most all cases, the GATT or the WTO has found against the environmental regulations. For example, Mexico filed a trade complaint against the United States under GATT in 1991 over provisions of the Marine Mammal Protection Act that required the United States to ban imports of tuna from countries that could not prove adequate dolphin protection measures were utilized. Two important issues emerged from this case. One issue was whether one country could tell another what its environmental regulations should be, and the other issue was whether trade rules allow bans or tariffs based on the method used to produce goods, rather than the quality of the goods themselves. The GATT panel said no to both questions. Based on this finding, domestic U.S. tuna fishers would be placed at a disadvantage over foreign fishers, and the United States would no longer have the sovereignty to limit imports produced in an unsustainable manner.

Another such case had to do with a complaint filed by Venezuela and Brazil against the United States. The charge was that U.S. regulations for evaluating a gasoline refiner's compliance with the Clean Air Act (CAA) of 1990 discriminated against foreign refiners. In particular, the EPA's "gasoline rule" allows a domestic refiner to use an "individual baseline" to evaluate toxic and other pollution emissions characteristics of its currently refined gasoline. In other words, if the refiner was producing gasoline prior to the CAA, then the refiner could evaluate its gasoline using an internal or individual baseline. The gasoline rule did not allow foreign refiners to use a similar individual baseline, but instead required them to use a statutory baseline. After final appeals were heard, in April 1996 the WTO found in favor of Venezuela and Brazil. The WTO stated that since "imported gasoline was effectively prevented from benefiting from as favorable sales conditions as were afforded domestic gasoline by an individual baseline tied to the producer of the product, imported gasoline was treated 'less favorably' than domestic gasoline" (WTO 1996). Importantly, the WTO panel agreed that clean air is an exhaustible natural resource and so is covered under Article XX.

In another important case, in October 1996 a complaint was filed by India, Malaysia, Pakistan, the Philippines, and Thailand [WT/DS58], challenging a U.S. ban on imports of shrimp caught without using turtle-excluding nets. Again, the WTO found against the United States, arguing that the ban was unilateral and thus violated the doctrine of multilateralism embodied by the WTO. Moreover, the WTO argued that the ban was not applied uniformly on all shrimp exporters. The WTO argued that the United States did not fully exhaust the potential for fostering an international agreement on turtle conservation methods. The emerging view at the WTO is that international agreements rather than unilateral import bans or tariffs are the preferred method of addressing international environmental issues. To date, the WTO has invalidated no international environmental agreements. In addition, following the Mexican tuna decision, the WTO has taken the position that trade restrictions (bans, tariffs, etc.) cannot be imposed on a product purely because of the way it has been produced. Thus, seemingly in conflict with the nondiscrimination doctrine of the WTO, domestic firms whose production methods are regulated to protect the environment, labor, and human health are placed at a disadvantage over foreign importers. Moreover, one country cannot use trade restrictions to reach out beyond its own territory to impose its standards on another country. Therefore, in the absence of an international environmental treaty, U.S. markets are forced to be open to foreign products that damage the environment in ways that domestic firms cannot. Taken together, it is clear that the WTO position has restricted the tools available for assuring environmental protection, and places downward pressure on domestic environmental regulations.

Starting in the 1990s, questions began to be raised about the legality of ecolabels under WTO rules. An ecolabel is usually awarded by independent third party certifying agencies, such as the Forest Stewardship Council (certified sustainable forest products), the USDA (organic food), or the Nordic Council of Ministers (Nordic Swan product life-cycle standards) to products that meet or exceed certain environmental criteria. These market-oriented environmental programs provide information to consumers and allow consumers to use their "dollar votes" in the marketplace to reward environmentally friendly products. Ecolabeling programs can be considered a type of technical barrier to trade (TBT), and WTO rules state that members cannot use technical regulations or standards to restrict market access or discriminate against imported goods unless there is an internationally accepted standard, or if the rules are necessary under Article XX. Currently, there is no single ecolabel standard worldwide. If an ecolabel applies to the characteristic of a product (e.g., made from recycled products) and countries apply the label equally across domestic and imported goods, it will not be a violation of WTO rules. Where things get difficult, however, is with regard to ecolabels that relate to processing and production methods (PPMs) that are not related to the product's characteristics (i.e., non-product-related PPMs). Under WTO rules, such ecolabels can be contested. For example, if a country adopts an ecolabel program lumber that is based on tree harvesting methods that are unrelated to the characteristics of the lumber, then this non-product-related PPM ecolabel could be contested in the WTO. As of 2005, the European Union and Canada support PPM ecolabels, while various developing countries (with different dominant values toward resource harvest) and the United States (concerned about discrimination against genetically modified agricultural and food exports) oppose them.

Finally, expanded international trade has put great pressure on certain endangered wildlife populations. The allure to some of rhino horns, pet reptiles, leopard skins, shark fins, bear gallbladders, or rare orchids has imperiled many threatened or endangered species of animals and plants. The United States is the world's largest market for wildlife and wildlife products. Because the trade in wild animals and plants crosses borders between countries, the effort to regulate this trade requires international cooperation to safeguard certain species from overexploitation. CITES (the Convention on International Trade in Endangered Species of Wild Fauna and Flora) is a multilateral international environmental agreement designed to address this problem. As of 2005, CITES accords protection to thousands of species of animals and plants, whether they are traded as live specimens or after they have been rendered into products. Nevertheless, a large illegal trade in wild fauna and flora still exists, and in some isolated cases, such as with African elephant ivory, parties to CITES vote to partially legalize trade. Some argue that CITES is excessively rigid and lacks accountability. For example, harvesting a few seed pods from a rare orchid can allow commercial growers to produce thousands of these plants and take pressure off of wild stocks, but CITES does not distinguish this form of harvest from large-scale black market trade.

To summarize, then, the argument against international trade from a sustainability perspective includes the following:

- When capital is highly mobile, this mobility strengthens firms' bargaining positions when negotiating with unions, local governments, and environmental agencies, eroding livable wages, undermining the fiscal base for local government, and putting downward pressure on health, safety, environmental, and organized labor regulations.
- Free international trade between rich and poor countries facilitates a pattern of trade in which rich countries export their trash, toxic waste, and the production of goods that generate especially high levels of pollution. While some argue that this pattern is simply a reflection of differences in the marginal utility of money and a manifestation of comparative advantage, others view it as unethical and a potential source of environmental injustice. By separating the consumption of goods from the pollution associated with these goods, the incentive to reduce this pollution is itself diluted. Moreover, if property rights and democratic systems are not in place in the low-income country, then free trade will hasten the destruction of the environment.
- The WTO has taken a series of positions that limit the tools that are available for protecting the environment, and that place domestic firms in countries with high standards at a disadvantage over firms in countries with lower standards, with the potential for promoting a race to the bottom.

While there are important questions regarding the extent to which countries should engage in international trade, the nature of the goods that should be traded, and the extent to which trade agreements should allow for trade restrictions based on production methods, it is neither practical nor desirable to eliminate trade completely. Trade has occurred between diverse human societies for thousands of years, fostering mutual understanding, the diffusion of ideas, and interdependence.

Population

Concerns regarding overpopulation and resource scarcity have been articulated at least as far back as ancient Babylon and Rome. These concerns may have been justified; there are indications that civilizations may have collapsed because resource degradation led to desertification and climate change in northern Mesopotamia, the Aegean, Egypt, Palestine, and the Indus (Weiss et al. 1993). It is estimated that about 50 million people lived on earth in 1000 B.C. Today's population is more than 100 times larger, and each year population rises by nearly twice the total number of humans who were alive in 1000 B.C. As Cohen (1995) reports, global population growth rates never exceeded 0.5 percent per year until approximately 1750, and never exceeded a 1 percent annual rate until about 1930. Since 1950, they have never fallen below their present level of roughly 1.33 percent per year. What are the causal factors that explain changes in population growth rates?

The Demographic Transition Model

In 1798 economist Thomas Malthus argued that rapid population growth would depress wages and result in higher mortality rates due to famine, disease, and war, and he referred to this as a "positive" control on population. He also argued that lower wages would cause people to delay marriage and promote vice that would ultimately limit fertility rates, which he referred to as the "preventative" check on population growth. Malthus believed that improvements in material standards of living were only temporary, since population would soon grow until once again misery and vice provided positive and preventative population checks. Thus, Malthus opposed providing economic support for poverty alleviation. Lee (2003) argues that evidence from preindustrial Europe generally supports Malthus's theory, in that real wage increases tended to be associated with reductions in mortality-related labor force reductions. Sen (1999) notes, however, that in the modern era there is significant evidence of declining fertility rates that is linked to social and economic development.

Since the work of Frank Notestein in 1945, demographers have recognized an empirical regularity in the data on the relationship between the stages of industrial economic development and population growth rates over the last several hundred years. The evidence generally supports what is known as the *theory of demographic transition,* which underlies the argument used by many economists that economic development is the key to overcoming the rapid population growth rates that we observe in many developing countries. This theory suggests that industrializing countries go through four distinct stages of population growth:

- *Stage I:* Prior to the industrialization process, both birth and death rates are high, with only modest population growth. In these traditional agrarian societies, children provide a valuable source of labor and are a form of social security in countries that lack adequate retirement programs.

There may also be powerful cultural or religious values favoring large family sizes and restricting the use of birth control methods.

- *Stage II (mortality transition):* At the start of industrialization, death rates fall (largely from improvements in medical technology that reduces contagious and infectious diseases, the rise of public health measures, and improvements in personal hygiene and nutrition that reduces child mortality rates), while birthrates remain stable or fall only slightly (perhaps because technology changes faster than cultural, religious, and social institutions). Stage II is marked by accelerated population growth.
- *Stage III (fertility transition):* This more mature stage of industrialization is marked by people shifting to raising substantially fewer children (due to economic factors such as female participation in the labor force, the rise of social security, the need for greater educational investment to assure a child's future economic success, delayed parenthood, and laws limiting child labor, as well as social issues related to the education and empowerment of women), resulting in the first sustained instance of the society experiencing declining birthrates. At the same time, death rates may continue to decline, or stabilize at a relatively low rate.
- *Stage IV (stabilization):* In this postindustrial stage of development, both birth and death rates are low. Net population growth rates once again are low.

These four stages of the demographic transition are illustrated in Figure 13.2. It has been argued that the stabilization characterized in stage IV may be incorrect. Many high-income countries have experienced what some demographers refer to as the second fertility transition, in which fertility rates fall far below the steady-state replacement rate of 2.1 children per woman. Lee (2003) reports that Western Europe's demographic transition from stage I to stage II—characterized by falling death rates and acceleration in population growth rates—began in approximately 1800. In contrast, in many low-income countries this same transition began in the early twentieth century and accelerated in the years following World War II. Declines in death rates have stagnated in some low-income countries, particularly in sub-Saharan Africa, that are struggling with increased mortality due to AIDS. The transition from stage II to stage III—characterized by falling fertility rates—began in Western Europe between 1890 and 1920. Some lower-income countries started this transition to stage III in the 1960s and 1970s, with dramatic reductions in fertility rates in East Asia, and much slower reductions in south Asia and Latin America. As of 2005, the average fertility rate worldwide is 2.65 children per woman, and there are sixty countries with 43 percent of the world's population that have total fertility rates at or below the replacement

Figure 13.2   **The Demographic Transition**

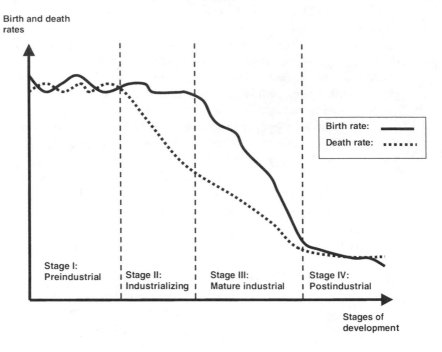

rate. In developed countries as a whole, fertility is currently only 1.56 children per woman, well below replacement. Lee reports that 17 of these 60 countries at or below replacement fertility rates are "less developed" countries, including countries such as China, South Korea, and Taiwan.

There is some debate over the relative importance of economic and female empowerment factors in explaining the fertility transition in stage III. Economic factors include labor force opportunities for women raising the opportunity cost of their time in child-rearing (which overlaps with female empowerment), pension and social security systems replacing one's children as providers for the elderly, the need for greater educational investment in one's children in an industrialized society, and rising per capita incomes. While few argue against most of these economic factors, there is question about the role of higher incomes. Erlich, Erlich, and Daily (1995) report that the evidence for a simple relationship between per capita income growth and declines in fertility is mixed; Mexico and Brazil, for example, have undergone periods of income growth with little or no reduction in birthrates. Erlich et al. go on to argue that fertility declines may be even more strongly related to the empowerment of women, access to maternity health programs and family-planning programs, and tax policies that encourage small families.

Likewise, Sen (1999) reports on empirical studies comparing various regions within India that differ in terms of both income and the level of female empowerment (including education, employment opportunities, social status, and property rights). Sen found that the level of real per capita income had almost no impact on fertility rates compared with the sharp difference made by the empowerment of women. Sen notes (p. 226):

> The view of "development as freedom" gets reinforced by these empirical connections, since—it turns out—the solution of the problem of population growth (like the solution of many other social and economic problems) can lie in expanding the freedom of the people whose interests are most directly affected by overfrequent childbearing and child rearing, viz., young women.

One of the key sustainability challenges associated with the observed trends in the demographic transition is that rapid reductions in total fertility rates result in a younger age cohort that is much smaller than the older age cohort. This imbalance is exacerbated by the rising life expectancy in these same countries. Many countries, including the United States, have "pay as you go" social security systems in which the current working age cohort is taxed to fund old-age pensions for the older cohort of retirees. The fiscal health of these systems is cast into doubt when the number of working-age people supporting each retired person shrinks, as has been occurring in most high-income countries. Solutions involve a combination of reducing benefits, increasing the retirement age, raising taxes, or promoting immigration by working-age people.

Population Forecasts

Thomas Malthus, the eighteenth-century economist, argued that human population growth rates would exceeded the rate of growth in agricultural production. As we have mentioned before, Malthus's model featured famine as a positive control on population. So far the evidence has not supported the Malthusian prediction. Two reasons present themselves. First, Malthus did not anticipate the demographic transition relating population growth rates to the stages of the industrialization process. Second, Malthus apparently did not anticipate the rate of technological advance. For example, what has been known as the "green revolution" in the 1970s was a period of rapid improvements in crop yields and methods of industrial agriculture. While a growing number of agricultural scientists questions the sustainability of the methods that grew out of the green revolution (pardon the pun), they are an example of the technological change that has so far allowed the human world to dodge the bullet of Malthusian decline despite enormous growth in human population.

Boserup (1965) offers an alternative to the Malthusian view. The Boserup hypothesis regarding population density and agricultural productivity states that increased population density, together with a greater reliance on market systems of allocation, will lead to improvements in the management of the land resource. There is evidence that Boserup effects result in an increase in the utilization of organic fertilizer and integrated crop–livestock systems that enhance soil fertility. A number of studies (Ruthenberg 1980; Pingali, Bigot, and Binswanger 1987; Tiffen, Mortimore, and Gichuki 1994) have supported the Boserup hypothesis. Heath and Binswanger (1996) argue that the evidence from Kenya, Ethiopia, and Colombia suggests, however, that the factors given in the Boserup hypothesis are not sufficient and that sustainable agricultural systems are more dependent upon social and economic policies that present farmers and others with the proper incentives. For example, some developing countries have instituted policies that promote large-scale, export-oriented cattle ranches over small, labor-intensive farms, pointing to the importance of factors other than population density and market capitalism.

While the predictions of Malthus and his followers have so far failed to manifest themselves, population growth can be difficult to reconcile with sustainability. Deep ecologists, for example, question the ethics of burgeoning human populations displacing a rapidly growing list of species and more generally appropriating what has been estimated to be approximately 40 percent of terrestrial biomass. Population growth contributes to the exhaustion of CPR systems. Examples include the decline of common grazing lands, deforestation in areas where too many people are trying to harvest fuelwood, declines in desirable species of fish in marine and freshwater fisheries, and excessive pumping from groundwater CPRs. The interdependence of agrarian and demographic transitions leads to congestion and squalor in the cities of many developing countries. As Pearce and Warford (1993) argue, the extent of overcrowding can be gauged in part by comparing population densities per square kilometer across industrialized and developing countries. While U.S. cities such as Chicago (2,500 people per square km) and Philadelphia (3,000) have relatively low population densities, cities such as Buenos Aires (15,000), Cairo (24,000), Lima (29,000), Mexico City (43,000), and Calcutta (88,000) in the developing countries have profound human congestion.

What will the global human population grow to in the future? According to the United Nations Population Division, world population is currently growing at the rate of approximately 1.22 percent per year and reached the 6 billion mark in 1999. From 1804, when the world passed the 1 billion mark, it took

123 years to reach 2 billion people in 1927, 33 years to attain 3 billion in 1960, 14 years to reach 4 billion in 1974, 13 years to attain 5 billion in 1987, and 12 years to reach 6 billion in 1999. The medium variant forecast of the United Nations (2005) projects world population at 9 billion by 2050. According to the assumptions in the medium variant scenario, by 2050 the population of the more developed countries as a whole would be declining slowly by about 1 million persons a year, while that of the developing world would be adding 35 million annually, 22 million of whom would be absorbed by the least developed countries. The medium variant population forecast is based on the assumption that average fertility rates decline from 2.6 children per woman in 2004 to slightly over 2 children per woman (i.e., replacement) in 2050. By way of comparison, if average fertility rates declined only slightly to 2.5 children per woman by 2050, world population would reach 10.6 billion, while if average fertility rates declined to 1.5, world population would reach 7.6 billion by 2050.

Undoubtedly, there will be unanticipated impacts that will affect population. As Cohen (1995) points out, even elaborate systems dynamics models have failed to predict population accurately ten or more years into the future. Predictions regarding upper limits on supportable human populations vary from the view that there is no limit to the view that the current population has exceeded the earth's carrying capacity. For example, from Kates et al. (1988) and Millman et al. (1991), we find that the 1989 primary food supply could feed up to 5.9 billion people. Millman et al. recognized, however, that further population growth will create price and other economic incentives for increasing the quantity of food supplied.

Taxes and Incentives

Taxes have been around since the early civilizations in Babylon, India, Rome, Greece, China, and pre-Columbian Central and South America. As Webber and Wildavsky (1986) report, early taxes were placed on food production and labor in the form of tithing and conscription. With the advent of more developed civil societies such as in Rome, taxes were placed on wealth and traded commodities. Thus for millennia human civilizations have taxed productive activities to raise funds for government services and operations. Roodman (1996) reports that in contemporary rich countries, such as the United States, Japan, and Germany, tax revenues primarily come from (1) profit and income taxes (roughly 30 to 40 percent of the total); (2) employment and wage taxes (roughly 30 to 40 percent); (3) sales, import/export, and value-added taxes (roughly 15 to 25 percent); and (4) property taxes (roughly 2 to 10 percent). Lower-income countries receive a larger share of their tax revenues from sales, import/export, and value-added taxes. Global taxes total approximately $7.5 trillion, or about one-third of the value of measured global economic output, and are a major factor in the world's economies.

In the absence of externalities to internalize, taxes and subsidies distort the incentives naturally produced by the market system. In addition to being the basis for public finance, taxes also have the effect of raising the cost of the taxed activity and thus to a greater or lesser degree creating a disincentive to engaging in the taxed activity. Thus, higher employment taxes dilute the incentive to create jobs; higher income taxes dilute the incentive to work hard or invest in costly specialized education; higher sales taxes mean that some low-income people will go without; higher property taxes reduce the affordability of homes for low-income people and can contribute to homelessness. As we learned in chapter 4, and discussed again in chapter 10, appropriately devised environmental taxes can discourage pollution and internalize negative externalities. Unfortunately, as noted in the preceding paragraph, most taxes are charged on productive activities, which leads to perverse incentives.

At the same time that societies find themselves using taxes to discourage productive activities, it ends up that they frequently encourage destructive activities such as resource depletion and pollution through a variety of different subsidies. For example, the International Center for Technology Assessment (1998) categorized and then estimated the subsidies and external costs (costs that are passed along to others through taxes, environmental harms, health expenditures, and prices in other sectors) associated with gasoline and diesel-powered motor vehicles in the United States. Categories for which estimates were generated included (1) annual federal and state tax breaks that support gasoline production and use ($9.1 to $17.8 billion); (2) government program subsidies supporting the extraction, production, and use of petroleum and petroleum fuel products ($38 to $114.6 billion each year); (3) military and other protection costs associated with oil transport and motor vehicle services ($88.5 to $140.8 billion); (4) negative externalities to the environment, human health, and other areas of society ($231.7 to $942.9 billion); and (5) other costs ($191.4 to $474.1 billion). Their analysis generated an estimated sum of subsidies and external costs totaling $558.7 billion to $1.69 trillion per year, which adds up to $4.60 to $14.14 per gallon of gasoline more than the price at the pump. A 2005 update of total annual U.S. military and protection cost estimates for oil ranged from $78.2 to $158.4 billion. Of this total, $39–$98.5 billion annually represents spending by the U.S. military to secure the production and transportation of foreign oil, not including the cost of the Iraq war. By way of comparison, the National Defense Council Foundation estimated in 2004 that the United States spends

$49 billion per year for the defense of oil production and transportation, which when summed with other costs associated with oil imports would add over $3 to the existing price of a gallon of gasoline. Such subsidies undermine the demand for alternative energy, the flow of private financial capital into alternative energy technologies and processes, and the incentives for consumers to conserve on petroleum consumption.

The basic argument of *ecological tax reform* (also known as environmental tax reform) is to shift some taxes from productive to destructive activities, and to shift subsidies from harmful activities to beneficial alternatives, thus more fruitfully employing the incentive effects of tax system. As Roodman (1998) observes, pollution taxes are the most direct way for governments to enforce the "polluter-pays" principle. By removing harmful subsidies and raising taxes on pollution and resource depletion, and reducing taxes on neutral or beneficial things such as wage income society receives many dividends. Ecological tax reform creates a disincentive to pollute, improves the economic basis for cleaner energy forms, and increases after-tax income for working people, while maintaining revenue neutrality. Taxes on resource depletion, such as for oil, gas, and coal, allow society to share in the Hotelling rents associated with their increasing scarcity (see chapter 5 for a description of Hotelling rents). Some of the first experiments with ecological tax reform have occurred in Northern Europe. The barriers to implementation of ecological tax reform include adjustment costs for people and industry, though perhaps the largest impediment is political pressure exerted by those industries and consumers whose tax burden would increase as a consequence of the change. Gradual change and a well-informed and empowered citizenry are likely to be key elements of successful transition. This topic will be addressed in greater detail in chapter 15.

Thinking Long Term: Discounting and Policy Making

Sustainability makes explicit a long-term time horizon. A central challenge is in bringing future impacts into present policy making. There are several problems with promoting the longer-term planning horizon required by sustainability. One of these is associated with government. In representative democracies, those running for office are most likely to succeed if they appeal to their current constituents' interests, even if it is not sustainable. For example, in the United States it is nearly impossible in 2005 to imagine a presidential candidate advocating for ecological tax reform in energy policy. Removing fossil-fuel subsidies and imposing pollution taxes would end the "cheap energy" policy that benefits current constituents at the cost of future generations, and most assuredly would end that candidate's prospects for being elected. In fact, whenever there is a public policy issue that requires a substantial up-front investment that generates future benefits, it will be difficult for politicians to support such a policy, as it imposes short-term costs on current voters. Possible solutions to this structural problem with representative democracy include educating the public about sustainability issues, inculcating an ethic of sustainability, and building support through successful pilot programs.

Aside from political feasibility, there is also the problem of economic feasibility that is related to benefit/cost analysis when there are flows of benefits and costs over time. As we saw in chapters 5 and 7, discounting is used to bring future flows of benefits and costs into a present-value context. Analysis of the present value of benefits and costs is used in public policy contexts to evaluate whether policy proposals make economic sense. Moreover, the world's financial markets use discounting methods to allocate financial capital to fund capital investments. In order for sustainability-related projects to attract funding, they must pass muster in a benefit/cost analysis for public funds, or on a rate-of-return basis for private funds. One of the questions addressed below is whether discounting is consistent with sustainability. If discounting can indeed be made consistent with sustainability, then the next question that arises is whether the discount rates associated with competitive financial markets are consistent with those required for sustainability. Since financial markets are central to contemporary market capitalism, this discussion of discounting brings us to the larger question of whether market capitalism is consonant with sustainability.

As we first learned in chapter 5, individuals discount future benefits and costs for a variety of reasons that are similar to why we must pay interest when we borrow money. Like many people, you are likely to have borrowed money for school, or to buy a car or a home. Likewise, governments borrow money when they issues bonds, and the people who buy those bonds are the lenders. When a lender allows you to use her money today, the lender is forgoing using that money now so that you can use it. What opportunities might a lender have passed up in order to lend the money to someone? Some options include:

- the ability to buy more goods and services now than in the future due to rising prices (inflation);
- the increased utility from consuming goods and services today rather than having to wait;
- the interest income that could be earned if those funds were loaned to someone else;
- the net income from a capital asset (i.e., skills gained from an educa-

tion, or all or part of a profitable business enterprise) purchased with those funds.

Thus the opportunity cost of lending someone money is either the forgone utility of current consumption, forgone purchasing power due to inflation, or the forgone income that could have been earned by loaning the money to someone else or by purchasing a capital asset. In the world's financial markets, the interest rate paid on borrowed money must be larger than the lender's (risk-adjusted) opportunity cost in order to generate a supply of loanable funds. For example, suppose that the lowest interest rate that a lender is willing to accept in order to make a one-year loan of $1,000 is 10 percent. This information tells us that the lender is indifferent between having $1,000 today (the present value) and being repaid $1,100 in one year (the future value). The future value of today's $1,000 will increase with the interest rate and with the length of time of the loan. There's another way of looking at this relationship. Suppose someone was going to receive $1,100 exactly one year in the future, but they needed money in the present. What is the smallest amount of money that that person would take right now in return for giving up the inheritance next year? The answer to this question is that person's present value of the future $1,100 inheritance. As we learned in chapter 5, economists use the more general term *discount rate* to refer to the rate of time preference (such as an interest rate) that equates present value and future value.

Recall from chapter 5 that if we know that an environmental policy today will generate a benefit equal to $B that will occur exactly T years from the present, and if policymakers use a discount rate equal to r (assume for simplicity that it is constant over time), then the present value (PV) of that future benefit today is given by:

$$PV_B = \$B/(1 + r)^T.$$

The hypothetical example below illustrates how discounting affects the dynamic efficiency of environmentally friendly investments.

The Effect of Discount Rates on Environmentally Friendly Investments and Sustainability: An Illustrative Example

Suppose that Samantha has just bought an older, uninsulated house. Samantha commissions an energy audit and finds that an adequate insulation job would cost approximately $3,000. Samantha's career usually requires her to move every five years or so, and realtors have told her not

Table 13.2

Hypothetical Example: Costs With and Without Home Insulation

Option	Year 0	Year 1	Year 2	Year 3	Year 4	Year 5	Total
Insulation added	3,000	1,000	1,000	1,050	1,100	1,100	8,250
No insulation added	0	1,800	1,800	1,890	1,980	1,980	9,450
Cost savings from insulation	−3,000	8,00	800	840	880	880	1,200

to count on recovering the cost of the insulation job in the resale price. Thus Samantha will conduct a benefit/cost analysis of the insulation job using a five-year time horizon. The $3,000 cost of insulating her home is paid at the start of the five-year time horizon (period 0), while the benefits are represented by the present value of the five-year annual flow of energy cost savings. Based on the energy audit and estimated energy prices, Table 13.2 indicates the costs associated with the options of insulating or not insulating.

Samantha's decision regarding whether or not to add the insulation to her home is based on whether the net present value (NPV) is positive over the five-year time horizon. The NPV of insulation (subscript "I" below) is given in the following equation:

$$NPV_I = -\$3,000/(1 + r)^0 + \$800/(1 + r)^1 + \$800/(1 + r)^2 + \$840/(1 + r)^3 + \$880/(1 + r)^4 + \$880/(1 + r)^5.$$

We can compare net cost savings from insulation based on a number of different discount rates, as shown in Table 13.3. Note that Samantha's dynamically efficient choice depends on the discount rate that she uses. As the rate at which Samantha discounts a future payment over a current payment increases, the financial advantages of home insulation decline. Somewhere between the 10 and the 15 percent discount rate, Samantha finds that the home insulation project fails to pay for itself. This example illustrates how discounting affects the net present value of environmentally friendly investments. In addition, two related issues are raised by this illustrative example. The first has to do with determining whether we can identify a discount rate that is consistent with sustainability, and the second has to do with relating this sustainable discount rate (if it exists) to the discount rates generated in financial markets. These issues will be addressed below.

Table 13.3

Hypothetical Example: Cost Savings from Home Insulation for Different Discount Rates

Discount Rate	Year 0	Year 1	Year 2	Year 3	Year 4	Year 5	Total
0 Percent (0.0)	−3,000	800	800	840	880	880	1200
5 Percent (0.05)	−3,000	761.91	725.62	725.64	723.89	689.49	626.64
10 Percent (0.1)	−3,000	727.27	661.16	631.10	601.50	546.82	167.85
15 Percent (0.15)	−3,000	695.65	604.92	552.32	503.14	437.51	-206.47

The Opportunity Cost of Capital and the Social Rate of Time Preference

The Opportunity Cost of Capital

As was alluded to above, the opportunity cost of lending money in financial markets is primarily generated by the income that can be earned by investing the money in some other income-generating asset. In economics, the term *capital* traditionally refers to the tools, equipment, factories, inventories, offices, and other human-made instrumentalities that generate income through their employment as factors of production. A profit-maximizing firm that is considering investment in capital (say, for example, to expand a factory or to add new equipment to a production process) evaluates this investment by comparing the anticipated flow of income generated by the particular capital investment under consideration to the various other investment opportunities open to the firm. In other words, each dollar invested in capital generates income known as the *rate of return on capital,* and a profit-maximizing firm seeks the highest rate of return on each dollar of invested capital. Of course, investment returns are not guaranteed. It is possible that invested capital will be lost if markets change or if firms fail. Thus, riskier investments tend to offer a *risk premium* in the form of a higher rate of return on invested capital. The opportunity cost of capital to a firm is the next best (risk-adjusted) rate of return that was forgone when a particular investment decision was made. When someone buys a share of stock, he or she owns a portion of a publicly traded firm and so owns a right to the net income generated by the firm. This investor can sell this share of stock if a better (risk-adjusted) rate of return can be found in some other form of investment, such as the interest generated on a U.S. Treasury Bond. Thus, the opportunity cost of capital generally refers to the prevailing risk-adjusted rates of return available in financial markets. A typical benchmark is an 8 percent rate of return, which is approximately the average rate of return on publicly traded shares of stock in the United States in recent history.

The Social Rate of Time Preference

While the opportunity cost of capital forms the basis for discounting by optimizing entities in financial markets, the social rate of time preference forms the basis for discounting in policies designed to enhance the well-being of society over time. The social rate of time preference has two elements—the rate at which a society's wealth-generating capital stocks grow and the pure rate of time preference. Let's first consider growth discounting. Consider a society with a stable population and no inflation that is committed to a sustainability standard. Suppose that this society accepts some degree of substitutability between the various forms of capital (as defined in chapter 11). Suppose a proposal is made to invest money in enhancing future natural capital by reducing emissions below the level at which they accumulate and thus pollute the air, water, or soil in the future. Suppose further that natural increases in productivity (e.g., from technological innovation) result in a 2 percent per capita annual growth rate for human and human-made capital. The implication is that diverting a dollar of investment in human or human-made capital today means that we must forgo a 2 percent social rate of return. Given the assumption that we can substitute human and human-made capital for natural capital, then the opportunity cost of social investment in natural capital is a 2 percent real rate of return on human or human-made capital. If various forms of capital are perfect substitutes, then the future benefits of an up-front investment in natural capital should be discounted at a 2 percent annual rate to make it comparable to the natural growth rate in the productivity of human and human-made capital.

Even if we allow for only one type of capital, if that capital stock is growing relative to population, then people in the future will have greater income than people will in the present. It is generally accepted that the marginal utility of income (broadly defined as the flow of benefits deriving from various forms of capital) declines as income grows. If a society has steady-state population and growing capital stocks, then its income is growing over time. Yet if income is higher in the future, then the marginal utility deriving from this income is becoming smaller (and so total utility is growing at a slower rate than income). Based on this argument, consumption of a given unit of income next year will generate a smaller level of utility than if consumption of the income had occurred today. This difference in utility can also be seen as the basis for growth discounting—in an increasingly wealthy society, future income is discounted because it will generate greater utility today than next year. Note that if population growth is occurring faster than capital stocks, then it is possible to have *negative growth discounting*.

Let's now consider the pure rate of time preference. The pure rate of time preference is based on factors such as impatience—people would rather consume now than in the future—and fundamental uncertainty regarding whether a person will be alive to consume in some future period. The pure rate of time preference forms the basis for consumers in markets applying positive discount rates in their consumption and savings decisions. If the correct growth discount rate is zero or negative, then the only basis for a positive social rate of time preference is the pure rate of time preference. Yet while it makes sense for individuals to have a positive pure rate of time preference, given the probability that an individual will die before future consumption can occur, this argument does not hold as well for an entire society. By the same token, it is not clear that impatience is a good reason to include a positive pure rate of time preference when constructing a discount rate for sustainability policy purposes. As Azar and Sterner (1996) argue, the choice of pure rate of time preference is a question of value judgments, and at the societal level, there is no good ethical argument for using a pure rate of time preference other than zero.

Thus it can be argued that sustainability policies can be made dynamically efficient through the use of the social rate of time preference, and the soundest element of the social rate of time preference is growth discounting. Yet if we relax the assumption that human and human-made capital can substitute for natural capital, then even the use of growth discounting can break down. Sustainability cannot generally be made compatible with dynamic efficiency under the low-substitutability scenario, which limits the applicability of benefit/cost analysis. Such a situation calls for alternative policy models such as the application of safe minimum standards to irreplaceable elements of natural capital such as biodiversity, wilderness habitat, and certain waste-assimilating functions of the earth's biosphere.

Are the Discount Rates Associated with Competitive Financial Markets Consistent with Those Required for Sustainability?

In contemporary financial markets in the United States, firms apply discount rates based on a risk-adjusted opportunity cost of capital that is several times higher than the social rate of time preference. This would seem to suggest that the investment decisions generated by financial markets will be biased toward projects and management plans that generate current rather than future benefits, and thus may not be consistent with sustainability. As the example below illustrates, financial markets treat natural and human-made capital as perfect substitutes when it comes to rates of return, implying that the opportunity cost of capital drives management decisions for commercial natural resources.

Recent developments with Maxxam/Pacific Lumber Company illustrate the difficulties associated with publicly traded firms managing their assets based on discount rates lower than those applied to similar assets in financial markets. The Pacific Lumber Company was founded in 1869 and owned approximately 190,000 acres of highly productive redwood forestlands in Humboldt County, California, south and east of Arcata. Albert Murphy, the grandson of the founder, at least implicitly recognized the need for sustainable forestry and set up a harvest plan in which the company would never run out of "old-growth" trees 150 or more years old. This form of conservative forestry management is consistent with a relatively low discount rate, since old-growth trees grow very slowly and thus add little additional commercial value over time. As a consequence of these conservative forest management practices, by the mid-1980s Pacific Lumber owned approximately 70 percent of the old-growth redwood in private hands, creating a virtual monopoly on the supply of extremely durable and valuable lumber from the heart of these old trees (Harris 1995). Apparently, the discount rate implied by Pacific Lumber's management plan was substantially lower than the prevailing discount rates for similar forestland assets. This made Pacific Lumber an acquisition target, because its management plan was inconsistent with maximizing the discounted present value of profits at a higher discount rate; Pacific Lumber was "undervalued" based on its conservative management practices.

Thus with financing arranged by Michael Milken, an expert in junk bond financing, Charles Hurwitz's Maxxam Corporation managed to acquire a controlling interest in Pacific Lumber. Management practices were changed to increase the logging cycle substantially and to cut the remaining inventory of old-growth trees, a process that ultimately led to one of the largest forest-related protests in U.S. history in September 1996. Soon after the protests, a deal was struck, and federal officials agreed to acquire 7,470 acres of the remaining old-growth groves at a cost of $380 million. The Pacific Lumber case illustrates the dilemma of "environmentally friendly" corporate management practices in the context of competitive financial markets; the firms that manage their assets based on below-market discount rates become takeover targets, creating a form of "market discipline" that undercuts more socially or environmentally sustainable practices. In this sense, our contemporary form of market capitalism may not be consistent with sustainability.

Rice, Gullison, and Reid (1997) offer a very similar account of the economics of tropical forestry practices in Bolivia. Dollar-denominated accounts in Bolivia offer real (inflation-adjusted) annual interest rates averaging 17 percent—a decent measure of the after-inflation opportunity cost of capital. Moreover, mature mahogany trees (and mahogany prices) grow slowly, and so delaying harvest for a year increases the value of the tree by only around 4 or 5 percent, much less than the 17 percent (inflation-adjusted) opportunity cost of capital. Finally, delaying harvest places the timber company at risk of policy reversal. Thus, Rice and his colleagues find that the financially optimal strategy is for loggers to harvest mahogany trees as quickly as possible and invest the proceeds in financial markets to yield high returns; unrestricted mahogany harvest is two to five times as profitable as forestry practices designed to sustain the mahogany resource.

If it is not always feasible for publicly traded firms to select environmentally friendly management practices that imply below-market discount rates, then might this same argument also hold for policymakers? Horowitz (1996) has identified a form of *time inconsistency* associated with just such a case. While a policymaker today may want to commit future policy makers to a sustainable policy path, when that future becomes the present, new policymakers feeling the pressure to generate current returns may have an incentive to deviate from the sustainable path and instead select policies that are dynamically efficient based on prevailing discount rates. This means that the original commitment was time-inconsistent. One way around this time inconsistency is to make a large capital investment in pollution control that cannot easily be reversed. Another is for policymakers to use a market discount rate but to assign a very high value on *future environmental amenities.* As Horowitz (1996) points out, "[a] high value of future environmental amenities, discounted at the market rate, will on paper look much the same as a low environmental discount rate. Yet this price approach avoids the inconsistency problem and, at the same time, ensures that future generations' interests are adequately represented in policy analysis" (p. 74).

Summary

- Technological advances that led to the industrial revolution and the agrarian transition have also contributed to dramatic changes in rural and urban populations. Countries undergoing these changes experience an accelerated recruitment of less technically trained former agricultural workers into the industrial labor force, which has an adverse impact on wages and presents difficulties in terms of providing adequate sanitation and other urban infrastructure to growing urban communities in lower-income countries. The agrarian transition can be accelerated by freer international trade, and can help explain patterns of both legal and undocumented migration into richer industrialized countries. Remittances from these foreign workers provide a large and important source of income for lower-income countries.

- Income and economic growth may have both pro- and antisustainability properties in the contemporary human world. Growth in per capita incomes raises people out of squalor and poverty, makes cleaner technologies available, and contributes to lower population growth rates. On the other hand, economic growth is associated with high levels of consumption and disproportionate emissions of greenhouse gases, ozone-depleting chemicals, trash, and toxic wastes. In a world of rich and poor, the rich can export dirty and destructive production practices to poorer countries that are more desperate for sources of income.

- The benefits of education and empowerment are much less ambiguous. There is clear evidence that education raises incomes in general, and increased social, reproductive, and economic empowerment for women results in higher family incomes, reduced child mortality, and substantially reduced fertility rates.

- Like economic growth, international trade has both pro- and antisustainability properties. Specialization and international trade along the lines suggested by comparative advantage has occurred for thousands of years of human history, and the resulting trade creates wealth that increases aggregate material standards of living. Ricardo's theory of comparative advantage assumes fixed capital endowments for different countries, which casts increasing doubt on the properties of this model of trade in the context of economic globalization and increasing capital mobility. Moreover, capital mobility creates a "lowest-common-denominator" effect in which communities with strong labor and environmental protections export their businesses and production facilities to those with weaker protections. When rich countries trade with lower-income countries for natural resource commodities over which property rights are poorly defined and enforced, free trade can accelerate the rate of unsustainable resource harvest. Others question the ethics of trade in the services of garbage and toxic materials disposal that are provided by lower-income regions and countries.

- Many environmental and social activists question the sustainability properties of the World Trade Organization (WTO). While the WTO allows for exceptions to its rules against trade barriers in the case of protecting exhaustible natural resources, actual dispute settlements regarding protections such as turtle-excluding devises for catching shrimp have sided against the protections. Moreover, the growing movement for ecolabels may conflict with WTO rules, particularly in the case of process and production method (PPM)-based ecolabels such as certified sustainable forest products and shade-grown coffee. WTO rules generally do not allow a country to restrict imports based on how those products were made.

- The demographic transition model provides a useful framework for understanding the economic, social, cultural, and technological factors influencing population trends. This model finds that high mortality rates transition downward before high fertility rates, resulting in a period of high population growth. This is thought to be because the public health, nutritional, and sanitary improvements associated with early industrializing countries proceeds at a faster pace than the social, economic, and cultural factors influencing fertility rates. Amartya Sen has argued that the fertility transition is most heavily influenced by the education and empowerment of women. For example, when women have access to an education and to the workforce, their opportunity cost of child-rearing increases.
- Taxes not only are the source of funds for public financing of government, but they also affect economic incentives. Traditionally most governments tax productive activities such as work and income, and subsidize politically powerful and entrenched interests such as fossil-fuel industries. These patterns create perverse economic incentives. Economists who study sustainability argue for ecological (also known as environmental) tax reform, shifting some taxes onto harmful activities, and shifting subsidies from harmful activities and to beneficial activities. A growing number of European countries are implementing ecological tax reform.
- Sustainability also requires that we think long term. A challenge to effective sustainability policy is that of "market myopia," namely, that the plethora of profit opportunities in contemporary financial markets leads to discount and interest rates that are inconsistent with sustainability. Another challenge to thinking long term is that elected politicians tend to have a short-term time horizon focused on satisfying their constituents' most immediate concerns and leaving future problems to future elected leaders to deal with.
- Arguments for the root causes of environmental degradation and failures of sustainability include rural poor living in ecologically fragile environments; government failures in selecting and enforcing appropriate property rights regimes; the concentration of power and lack of accountability associated with large multinational corporations and their

relations with corrupt local governments, particularly in developing countries; relatively unconstrained international trade in garbage and toxics, and trade agreements that treat legitimate environmental protection measures as trade barriers; failures of democratic process and local empowerment caused by discrimination against women and minorities, as well as concentrations of political power and political access; government or corporate control of major news media that limits news critical of corporate or government practices; the short-term orientation of markets and governments; perverse incentives created by taxing productive activities and subsidizing polluting and resource-depleting activities; and finally, the lack of leadership in fostering an ethic and a vision of sustainability.

Review Questions and Problems

1. Develop an international trade policy that allows trade yet also protects those who live in countries with relatively strict labor and environmental standards. How would your trade policy be different from that of the WTO? How would the leaders of exporting countries in the developing world feel about your policy?

2. Explain the relationship between income and the quality of environmental and natural resources in a given country. In particular, explain why one might expect an inverted-U-shaped relationship (an environmental Kuznets curve) between levels of per capita income and environmental degradation. Can you think of any situations in which this relationship might not always exist? What does the evidence suggest? You can find additional information at www.perc.org/publications/research/kuznets2.php.

3. Explain why empowerment, education, and opportunities for women and other disadvantaged groups are positively related to a more sustainable society. Your explanation should go beyond the issue of democratic process to include impacts on economic vitality and environmental integrity. Which countries have made the most progress in this area? Which have made the least? You can find information on this by looking at the Human Development Index at www.undp.org/hdro.

4. The bioregionalist movement argues for most goods to be produced in the same bioregion in which they are consumed, limiting the role of trade and the scale of production. Discuss the merits of this proposal, with attention to its benefits and its costs.

5. Access the United Nations Population Division's Internet site (www.popin.org) and find some examples of countries that have successfully reduced high rates of population growth. What policies or economic

Table 13.4

Hypothetical Example: Cost Savings from Purchasing a More Fuel-Efficient Furnace (in US dollars)

Option	Year 0	Year 1	Year 2	Year 3	Year 4	Year 5	Total
80% efficient furnace	1,000	1,200	1,200	1,300	1,300	1,400	7,400
90% efficient furnace	1,500	1,080	1,080	1,170	1,170	1,260	7,260
Cost savings from more efficient furnace	-500	120	120	130	130	140	140

trends do you think were responsible for reducing the growth trend?

6. Suppose that Clara just bought an older home. She expects that her employer will ask her to accept a new assignment and move in five years. Clara's house needs a new natural gas furnace. Clara is considering two options: an 80 percent efficient furnace and a 90 percent efficient furnace. The 90 percent efficient furnace costs $500 more than the 80 percent efficient furnace, but of course, the more efficient furnace will save Clara money over time because it is more fuel-efficient. Suppose that, after considering expected inflation, Clara projects the time-zero installation costs and operating costs over a five-year horizon to be as shown in Table 13.4.

   a. Determine which of the two furnaces has the smaller present value of total installation and operating cost when Clara discounts the future at (1) 5 percent, (2) 10 percent, and (3) 15 percent.
   b. Briefly discuss the relationship between discount rates and (1) the market viability of environmentally friendly products, and (2) the likelihood of sustainability policies' being implemented.

7. Use the Internet to research and describe an ecological tax reform policy or policy proposal. A good place to start is the Redefining Progress Internet site (www.redefiningprogress.org/programs/sustainableeconomy/other.htm).

8. Use the Internet to research and describe the extent to which international development programs are addressing the education and empowerment of women, and the protection of the environment. A good place to start is the World Bank's *World Development Report* Internet site (http://econ.worldbank.org/wdr) and the United Nations Development Program Internet site (www.undp.org/).

9. Use the Internet to learn about population pyramids, a way to present

information on the age profile of different countries' populations that is related to the demographic transition. Find two countries with regular pyramid-shaped populations, and two countries with square or even inverted pyramid populations, and use demographic transition theory to explain the causes and consequences of these age profiles. You can find these easily at the following U.S. Census Bureau Internet site: www.census.gov/ipc/www/idbpyr.html.

10. Access the Earth Track Internet site (http://earthtrack.net) and select a category of dysfunctional subsidy for environmentally harmful activity. Write a one-page paper that describes the environmentally harmful activity and summarizes the estimated dollar value of the subsidy. Be sure to fully cite the source(s) used in your paper.

Internet Links

Earth Track (http://earthtrack.net): Informative website that contains links to primary research studies that estimate subsidies provided to various sectors of the economy, including fossil-fuel energy subsidies.

Ecological Tax Reform (www.redefiningprogress.org/programs/sustainableeconomy/other.htm): Redefining Progress site with lots of useful material and links to on-line resources.

Environmental Kuznets Curves: A Review of Findings, Methods, and Policy Implications (www.perc.org/publications/research/kuznets2.php): A review of the literature from the Political Economy Research Center.

Grameen Bank (www.grameen-info.org): The Grameen Bank was started in Bangladesh in 1976 as an experiment on how a small amount of credit could affect the lives of the rural poor.

Human Development Report (www.undp.org/hdro): You can supplement and update the material in this chapter by accessing the United Nations Development Program's current *Human Development Report* on the Internet.

United Nations Development Program (www.undp.org): Learn more about the UN's view on sustainable development.

United Nations Population Division (www.popin.org): Access information such as the world population estimates and projections, as well as commissions on women and sustainable development.

World Development Report (http://econ.worldbank.org/wdr/): You can supplement and update the material in this chapter by accessing the World Bank's current *World Development Report* on the Internet.

World Resources Institute (www.wri.org): Nongovernmental organization whose mission is to move human society to live in ways that protect earth's environment for current and future generations. Publishes the *World Resources* report on-line.

World Trade Organization (www.wto.org): You can read the actual text of the WTO decisions regarding trade disputes over gasoline, tuna, and shrimp discussed in the chapter.

References and Further Reading

Adriaanse, A., A. Bringezu, A. Hammond, Y. Moriguchi, E. Rodenburg, D. Rogich, and H. Schütz. 1997. *Resource Flows: The Material Basis of Industrial Economies.* Washington, DC: World Resources Institute.

Arrow, K., B. Bolin, R. Costanza, P. Dasgupta, C. Folke, C. Holling, B. Jansson, S. Levin, K. Maler, C. Perrings, and D. Pimentel. 1996. "Economic Growth, Carrying Capacity, and the Environment." *Environment and Development Economics* 1 (February): 104–37.

Ayres, R. 1996. "Limits to the Growth Paradigm." *Ecological Economics* 19 (November): 117–34.

Azar, C., and T. Sterner. 1996. "Discounting and Distributional Considerations in the Context of Global Warming." *Ecological Economics* 19 (November): 169–84.

Barrett, C. 1996. "Fairness, Stewardship, and Sustainable Development." *Ecological Economics* 19 (October): 11–18.

Bornstein, D. 1996. *The Story of the Grameen Bank and the Idea That Is Helping the Poor to Change Their Lives.* Englewood Cliffs, NJ: Simon and Schuster.

Boserup, E. 1965. *The Conditions of Agricultural Growth: The Economics of Agrarian Change Under Population Pressure.* New York: Aldine.

Boulding, K. 1964. *The Meaning of the Twentieth Century.* New York: Harper & Row.

Brown, L., W. Chandler, C. Flavin, J. Jacobson, C. Pollock, S. Postel, L. Starke, and E. Wolfl. 1984. *State of the World, 1984.* New York: Norton.

Chichilnisky, G. 1994. "North-South Trade and the Global Environment." *American Economic Review* 84 (September): 851–74.

Cohen, J. 1995. *How Many People Can the Earth Support?* New York: Norton.

Copeland, B., and M. Taylor. 2004. "Trade, Growth, and the Environment." *Journal of Economic Literature* 42 (March): 7–71.

Costanza, R., and H. Daly. 1992. "Natural Capital and Sustainable Development." *Conservation Biology* 6 (March): 37–46.

Counts, A. 1996. *Give Us Credit.* New York: Times Books.

Daly, H. 1973. *Toward a Steady State Economy.* San Francisco: Freeman.

———. 1996. *Beyond Growth: The Economics of Sustainable Development.* Boston: Beacon Press.

Daly, H., and J. Cobb. 1989. *For the Common Good.* Boston: Beacon Press.

Deininger, K., and L. Squire. 1997. "Economic Growth and Income Inequality: Re-examining the Links." *Finance and Development* 34 (March): 38–41.

Erlich, P., A. Erlich, and G. Daily. 1995. "What Will It Take?" *Mother Jones* (September–October): 61–67.

Frederick, K. 1989. "Water Resource Management and the Environment: The Role of Economic Incentives." In *Renewable Natural Resources: Economic Incentives for Improved Management.* Paris, France: OECD.

Grossman, G. 1995. "Pollution and Growth: What Do We Know?" In *The Economics of Sustainable Development,* ed. I. Goldin and L. Winters. Cambridge, MA: Cambridge University Press.

Grossman, G., and A. Krueger. 1993. "Environmental Impacts of a North American Free Trade Agreement." In *The U.S.-Mexico Free Trade Agreement,* ed. P. Garber. Cambridge, MA: MIT Press.

Harris, D. 1995. *The Last Stand.* New York: Random House.

Hawken, P., A. Lovins, and L. Lovins. 1999. *Natural Capitalism.* Boston: Little, Brown and Company.

Heath, J., and H. Binswanger. 1996. "Natural Resource Degradation Effects of Poverty and Population Growth Are Largely Policy-Induced: The Case of Colombia." *Environment and Development Economics* 1 (February): 65–83.

Hettige, H., R. Lucas, and D. Wheeler. 1992. "The Toxic Intensity of Industrial Production: Global Patterns, Trends, and Trade Policy." *American Economic Review* 82 (2): 478–81.

Horowitz, J. 1996. "Environmental Policy Under a Non-Market Discount Rate." *Ecological Economics* 16 (January): 73–78.

International Center for Technology Assessment. 1998. *The Real Price of Gasoline.* Washington, DC: International Center for Technology Assessment.

Jazairy, I., M. Alamgir, and T. Panuccio. 1992. *The State of World Poverty: An Inquiry into Its Causes and Consequences.* New York: NYU Press.

Kander, A. 2002. *Economic Growth, Energy Consumption and CO_2 Emissions in Sweden, 1800–2000.* Lund Studies in Economic History. Stockholm: Almqvist and Wiksell International.

Kates, R., R. Chen, T. Downing, J. Kasperson, E. Messer, and S. Millman. 1988. *The Hunger Report: 1988.* Alan S. Feinstein World Hunger Program, Brown University.

Krugman, P. 1987. "Is Free Trade Passé?" *Journal of Economic Perspectives* 1 (Fall): 131–44.

Kuznets, S. 1955. "Economic Growth and Income Inequality." *American Economic Review* 45: 1–28.

Lang, T., and C. Hines. 1993. *The New Protectionism.* New York: New Press.

Lee, R. 2003. "The Demographic Transition: Three Centuries of Fundamental Change." *Journal of Economic Perspectives* 17 (4): 167–90.

Mander, J., and E. Goldsmith, eds. 1996. *The Case Against the Global Economy.* San Francisco: Sierra Club Books.

Martin, T., and F. Juarez. 1995. "The Impact of Women's Education on Fertility in Latin America: Searching for Explanations." *International Family Planning Perspectives* 21: 52–57.

Mehra, R. 1996. "Involving Women in Sustainable Development: Livelihoods and Conservation." In *Building Sustainable Societies,* ed. D. Pirages. Armonk, NY: M.E. Sharpe.

Milanovic, B. 1999. "True World Income Distribution, 1988 and 1993: First Calculations Based on Household Surveys Alone." Policy Research Working Paper 2244. Washington, DC: World Bank Development Research Group.

Millman, S., R. Chen, J. Haarmann, J. Kasperson, and E. Messer. 1991. *The Hunger Report: Update 1991.* Alan S. Feinstein World Hunger Program, Brown University.

Ohlin, B. 1933. *Interregional and International Trade.* Cambridge, MA: Harvard University Press.

Pearce, D., and J. Warford. 1993. *World Without End: Economics, Environment, and Sustainable Development.* Oxford: Oxford University Press.

Persson, T., and G. Tabellini. 1994. "Is Inequality Harmful for Growth?" *American Economic Review* 84 (June): 600–21.

Pingali, P., Y. Bigot, and H. Binswanger. 1987. *Agricultural Mechanization and the Evolution of Farming Systems in Sub-Saharan Africa.* Baltimore: Johns Hopkins University Press.

Prosterman, R., T. Hanstad, and L. Ping. 1996. "Can China Feed Itself?" *Scientific American* 275 (November): 90–96.

Rabl, A. 1996. "Discounting of Long-Term Costs: What Would Future Generations Prefer Us to Do?" *Ecological Economics* 17 (June): 137–45.

Radetzki, M. 1992. "Economic Growth and the Environment." In *International Trade and the Environment,* ed. P. Low. Discussion Paper 159. Washington, DC: World Bank.

Rice, R., R. Gullison, and J. Reid. 1997. "Can Sustainable Management Save Tropical Forests?" *Scientific American* 276 (April): 44–51.

Roodman, D. 1996. "Harnessing the Market for the Environment." In *State of the World 1996,* ed. L. Brown. Washington, DC: Worldwatch Institute.

———. 1998. *The Natural Wealth of Nations: Harnessing the Market for the Environment.* Washington, DC: Worldwatch Institute.

Ruthenberg, H. 1980. *Farming Systems in the Tropics.* New York: Oxford University Press.

Saint-Paul, G. 1995. "Discussion [of the Grossman–Kruger line of research]." In *The Economics of Sustainable Development,* ed. I. Goldin and L. Winters. Cambridge: Cambridge University Press.

Selden, T., and D. Song. 1994. "Environmental Quality and Development: Is There a Kuznets Curve for Air Pollution Emissions?" *Journal of Environmental Economics and Management* 27: 147–62.

Sen, A. 1999. *Development as Freedom.* New York: Anchor Books.

Stix, G. 1997. "Small (Lending) Is Beautiful." *Scientific American* 276 (April): 16–20.

Tietenberg, T. 1996. *Environmental and Natural Resource Economics.* 4th ed. New York: HarperCollins.

Tiffen, M., M. Mortimore, and F. Gichuki. 1994. *More People, Less Erosion: Environmental Recovery in Kenya.* Chichester, NY: Wiley.

United Nations, Department for Economic and Social Affairs, Population Division. 2005. *World Population Prospects: The 2004 Revision.* New York: United Nations.

United Nations Development Program. 1994. *Human Development Report 1994.* New York: Oxford University Press.

———. 2000. *Human Development Report 2000.* New York: Oxford University Press.

———. 2002. *Development Report 2002.* New York: Oxford University Press.

———. 2003. *Human Development Report 2003.* New York: Oxford University Press.

United Nations Environment Program. 1999. *Trade Liberalization and the Environ-*

ment: Lessons Learned from Bangladesh, Chile, India, Philippines, Romania and Uganda. New York and Geneva: United Nations. Available at www.unep.ch/etu/etp/acts/capbld/rdone/synrep.pdf.

U.S. Energy Information Administration. http://www.eia.doe.gov/.

Wathen, T. 1996. "Trade Policy: Clouds in the Vision of Sustainability." In *Building Sustainable Societies: A Blueprint for a Post-Industrial World,* ed. D. Pirages. Armonk, NY: M.E. Sharpe.

Webber, C., and A. Wildavsky. 1986. *A History of Taxation and Expenditure in the Western World.* New York: Simon and Schuster.

Weiss, H., M.-A. Courty, W. Wetterstrom, F. Guichard, L. Senior, R. Meadow, and A. Curnow. 1993. "The Genesis and Collapse of Third Millennium North Mesopotamian Civilization." *Science* 261: 995–1004.

World Bank. 1992. *World Development Report 1992.* Oxford, UK: Oxford University Press.

———. 1993. *World Development Report 1993.* Oxford, UK: Oxford University Press.

———. 1994. *Poverty Reduction and the World Bank: Progress in Fiscal 1993.* Washington, DC: World Bank.

———. 1995. *Monitoring Environmental Progress: A Report on Work in Progress.* Washington, DC: World Bank.

———. 1999. *World Development Report 1999–2000.* Oxford, UK: Oxford University Press.

———. 2004a. *Global Development Finance 2004.* Oxford, UK: Oxford University Press.

———. 2004b. *World Development Report 2004.* Oxford, UK: Oxford University Press.

World Trade Organization. 1996. Panel report on "United States—Standards for Reformulated and Conventional Gasoline" [WT/DS2/R]. http://www.wto.org/english/tratop_e/envir_e/gas1_e.htm.

Worldwatch Institute. 2000. *Vital Signs 2000: The Environmental Trends That Are Shaping our Future.* Wahington, DC: Worldwatch Institute.

14

Sustainable Economic Development

Introduction

The goal of economic development has been to improve the material well-being or welfare of society. Nevertheless, the focus on jobs and income that characterized economic development in the postwar period often failed to screen out projects and policies that harmed the environment, failed to address poverty and empowerment, and failed to sustain local communities and indigenous peoples. International development lending projects formed with corrupt host-country government leaders often left developing countries saddled with such large debt service requirements that essential investments in human capital such as domestic health and education programs had to be reduced or curtailed. These failings of traditional economic development served as the impetus for the sustainable development movement. The Brundtland Commission defined sustainable development as satisfying present needs without compromising the ability of future generations to meet their own needs (World Commission on Environment and Development 1987). The concept of sustainable development is broad and has come to mean different things to different people. For example, Pearce, Markandya, and Barbier (1989) document over sixty definitions of sustainable development. As Jaeger (1995) points out, the conventional economic and ecological approaches need to be integrated if we are to progress in conceptualizing sustainable economic development as a necessary precursor to operational policy.

In this chapter we will first consider the history and performance of conventional economic development and how some of the perceived failures of these conventional methods have provided the motivating force for work on more sustainable economic development concepts and strategies. We will then consider several competing theories of sustainable development and how particular indicators of sustainable development have been derived from these theories. We will conclude with several brief case studies that measure progress relative to various sustainable development standards.

Conventional Economic Development Strategies

The primary goal of conventional economic development has been to improve real per capita income, where income is measured from GDP. Increases in real per capita income have been a prized objective of development policymakers because rising incomes can lift people out of poverty and provide them with access to medicines, safe drinking water, and cleaner production technologies. Moreover, income can be relatively objectively measured, and so analysts can gauge the success of development policies and programs with objective performance data. As we shall see below, in the post–World War II period, international development assistance programs were modeled on the reconstruction of developed European countries and focused on large project-based lending designed to increase per capita incomes. Unintended consequences of these economic development programs have led to the movement for sustainable economic development.

Conventional Economic Development Assistance Programs

International economic development policies take the form of technical assistance, financial assistance, and development loans. Development loans have frequently been facilitated by either the World Bank or the International Monetary Fund (IMF) pooling funds from donor countries such as Germany, Japan, and the United States and then lending these funds out to developing countries. In the 1970s, however, it was large commercial banks from the United States and elsewhere that originated many of these development loans. In past decades, these loans tended to be focused on large-scale infrastructure projects such as the building of hydroelectric and other power plants, mines, irrigation networks, road systems, and port facilities.

Unfortunately, many of these debt-financed projects were economically, socially, and environmentally misguided. For example, loans have been used to fund large-scale resettlement of urban poor in rain forests in Brazil and Indonesia, with the result being displacement of indigenous people and massive deforestation. Loans have been used to fund large coal-fired power plants and open-pit coal mines in India, leading to massive sulfur dioxide and heavy metals pollution problems and the uncompensated displacement of thousands of local people. Loans have been used to fund large dam projects in Thailand, displacing numerous small, locally self-governed irrigation common-pool resource (CPR) systems in which local people sustainably managed the community forests that served as watersheds for the community rice paddy irrigation systems. As Ostrom (1990) remarks, "the failure . . . to develop an effective set of rules for organizing their irrigation system is not unusual for large-scale, donor-funded irrigation systems in Third World settings" (p. 166). Thus as Rich (1994) and others have pointed out, the record of large-scale international project lending has featured substantial environmental and local community destruction and dislocation.

World Bank and related lending programs have also failed from a financial perspective, as revealed by the World Bank's own "Wapenhans Report" in 1992 (World Bank Portfolio Management Task Force, 1992). The report found that the performance of the World Bank's $140 billion loan portfolio was deteriorating at an alarming rate, as measured by appraised rate of return on investment and on compliance with loan conditions. The rate of financially "unsatisfactory" projects increased from 15 percent in 1981 to 30.5 percent in 1989 to 37.5 percent in 1991. The report also found that World Bank staff used project appraisals as marketing devices to advocate loan approval rather than as unbiased assessments of project viability. It found that developing countries that borrowed from the World Bank saw the negotiation stage of a project as being a largely coercive exercise in which the World Bank imposed its philosophy on the borrower. Confidential surveys of World Bank staff indicated that substantial pressure was being exerted on staffers to meet lending targets and that this pressure overwhelmed all other considerations; the report stated that only 17 percent of the staff in the survey believed that their project analysis was compatible with achieving project quality.

Other problems encountered included a lack of democratic political institutions in some borrowing countries, which led to leaders who opportunistically appropriated development funds or project revenues for their own use, and an ignorance of local environmental, political, and social systems. Those projects that were successful in producing export commodities contributed to rapid growth in world commodity supplies that outpaced demand, resulting in a downward trajectory in commodity prices and repayment capability, as described below. Thus, the overall performance of large-scale international economic development lending was poor and led to a crisis in which developing countries were faced with staggering external debt and inadequate income for repayment.

Because about one-half of the development loans were held by large commercial banks, there was fear of a collapse of the international financial system. The World Bank and the IMF responded to this debt crisis by offering debtor countries an opportunity to restructure their debt through structural adjustment loan (SAL) programs, using concepts of economic development that later became known as the "Washington Consensus." Accepting a SAL also implied that the debtor country accepted structural adjustment plans (SAPs) crafted by the World Bank or the IMF. These plans instituted fundamental change in a debtor country's political and economic institutions. Economic restructuring included market-oriented reforms such as liberalization of foreign trade and finance (reduction of import/export tariffs and restrictions on foreign direct investment), reduced spending on government programs, and the reorganization of the domestic economy. Domestic economic reorganization was focused on privatization of state-owned enterprises, deregulation of industry, strengthening of private property rights, and a focus on export-oriented production capable of generating income from trade with rich countries for debt repayment.

The emphasis on export-oriented industry occurred in part because the exchange value of many debtor nations' currencies was in decline, and so exportation of goods to rich countries generated a source of *foreign exchange,* meaning acquiring the currency of countries such as the United States, Japan, and Germany, whose value was far more stable. This foreign exchange could then be used to repay old external development loans. The decline in the value of debtor nations' currencies occurred for a number of reasons. One reason is that wages and sales transactions in many low-income countries are "underground" and hence difficult to tax, creating a challenge to financing government. As a substitute for taxation, governments could secretly print money and make purchases before merchants and others learned that there was more currency chasing the same number of goods and services, and thus before knowledge of money printing led to higher prices. Eventually people catch on to this scheme, and the result is accelerated inflation. Another reason for declining currency values is that low-income countries imported many of the finished goods and services they consumed and had little other than raw commodities to export, leading to trade deficits and currency devaluations.

The rise of external development debt and the export-oriented policies mandated by structural adjustment programs were common across many low-income countries around the world and led to a substantial increase in raw commodity exports to high-income countries. According to the World Bank's *Commodity Trade and Price Trends* report (1986), natural resource–based export earnings in the early 1980s were 59 percent or more of the overall economy in countries such as Central African Republic, Ethiopia, Indonesia,

Nepal, Costa Rica, Mexico, and Paraguay. The increased supply of raw commodity exports resulted in a substantial decline in the price of these commodities, as would be suggested by simple supply-and-demand analysis. This is revealed in the *barter terms of trade,* or the ratio of export prices to import prices for low-income countries. According to the World Bank (1991), the barter terms of trade for low-income countries declined by 50 percent during the period between 1965 and 1988. The decline in the value of commodity exports relative to finished goods imports reduced the income that developing countries gained from commodity exports. In the case of Africa, for example, where a majority of export earnings came from basic commodities such as cocoa, coffee, palm oil, and minerals, Godfrey and Rose (1985) observed that "prices [fell] so rapidly with increased production and supply that increases in export volume actually result[ed] in a decrease in earnings" (p. 178). If these countries had substantial amounts of human or human-made capital, they could shift away from reliance on commodity exports, but expensive educational and capital investment schemes are beyond the reach of the very poorest of countries trying to cope with rapidly growing populations, urbanization, and hunger. In order to maintain adequate incomes to support both the national economy and SAL repayment schemes, more raw commodities would have to be harvested and exported.

The Brundtland Commission argued that the promotion of commodity exports in the manner described above has led to unsustainable overuse of the natural resource base for commodities such as forestry, beef ranching, ocean fishing, and some cash crops (World Commission on Environment and Development 1987, pp. 80–81). Thus the hypothesis is that as the barter terms of trade for commodity-exporting countries decline, these countries must increase such exports in order to maintain steady export income. This puts pressure on environmentally sustainable forestry, pasturage, and cropping systems in these countries. There is some evidence supporting this hypothesis. For example, Malawi has had ten SALs since 1979, and the Overseas Development Institute found negative outcomes resulting from those SALs. Similarly Ghana's SAP called for export-oriented cocoa production, which failed as an income-generating strategy following the collapse of world cocoa prices. In the Philippines, the World Resources Institute found that SALs encouraged overexploitation of natural resources, increased pollution, and urban decay. Moreover, analysis of tropical deforestation data by Bawa and Dayanandan (1997) uncovers a statistically significant and relatively large positive correlation between per capita external debt levels and annual tropical deforestation rates. In particular, Bawa and Dayanandan used World Resources Institute data for seventy tropical countries and looked at fourteen socioeconomic factors thought to be related to deforestation. Their multiple regression analysis of the relative magnitude of direct effects indicates that per capita external debt is the single most important factor explaining deforestation rates in Latin America and Asia, while in Africa the debt measure is ranked behind population density in importance. Interestingly, per capita gross national product (GNP) was not found to be a significant factor in explaining deforestation.

Looking back, structural adjustment programs can also be attacked on humanitarian grounds. Severely indebted low-income countries, having a present value of debt repayment obligations that are at least 80 percent of the annual gross national income or 220 percent of total export revenue, are effectively unable to repay their debt while at the same time providing for the needs of their citizens. For example, the World Bank (1992) indicated that interest payments on external debt in Latin America consumed up to 40 percent of these countries' national export earnings, leaving little money available for necessary imports, let alone health care, low-income assistance, job-creation programs, education, or the promotion of more pollution-efficient technologies. Oxfam International estimated that Uganda spends $17 per person on debt repayment annually but only $3 on health care. The U.N. Commission on Africa reported that expenditures on health in IMF/World Bank–programmed countries in Africa declined by 50 percent while these countries were under SAL programs in the 1980s, and education expenditures declined by 25 percent. To create income for repayment, SAL programs require reduced spending on imports, and one way that is accomplished is by allowing inflation-adjusted wage floors to decline, an explicit IMF/World Bank policy. As a consequence, income inequality and poverty have increased, even in countries such as Mexico and Chile, which are considered SAL successes. While SALs have been damaging to most countries operating under them, they have generated substantial benefits to the donor banks and countries. Not only did the SALs force loan repayments, but by increasing the supply of commodity exports, they contributed to lower prices for key commodities such as cocoa and coffee, which are disproportionately consumed in rich countries.

Case Studies

Brazil's experience with conventional international development lending assistance provides an instructive case study in the failure of such programs to address sustainability issues. In the 1970s international development lenders were providing project finance to build roads, dams, agricultural extensions, and to promote colonization of the Amazon rain forest. One of these projects was the Itaipu hydroelectric dam, which began in the early 1970s and was funded by the World Bank. The project was anticipated to cost $3.4 billion, but "skim-offs by the military rulers of Paraguay and Brazil and their colleagues contributed to the costs skyrocketing to around $20 billion" (Select Committee on International Development 2001). Another project financed by the World Bank was the $5 billion Carajás project, which was designed to promote agricultural and mineral exports by creating road, rail, and port infrastructure.

According to the Select Committee on International Development (2001) of the United Kingdom, the Itaipu dam displaced 42,000 people, and the World Bank acknowledged negative effects including prolonged idleness, incidents of intracommunal violence, alcohol abuse, family disintegration, and low morale (Danaher and Shellenberger 1995). Danaher and Shellenberger go on to note that the Itaipu dam flooded unique rain forest ecosystems and accelerated the spread of bilharzia, a water-borne disease. Along these same lines, the road network created by the Carajás project encouraged illegal settlements that depleted forests, degraded soils, polluted water, and resulted in land conflicts. Furthermore, road building in the Amazon enabled developers to gain access to dense rain forests and caused an influx in deforestation from logging, farming, mining, and other exploitative industries, which contributed to the permanent loss of unique functioning ecosystems. During the high-growth 1970s, a significant portion of foreign borrowing had been done by Brazilian state enterprises to fund various development projects. In 1991 the World Bank admitted in the Wapenhans Report that 44 percent of its projects in Brazil were failures because the World Bank ignored local inputs, adopted a negotiating rather than consultative role, and was more responsive to pressures to lend than a desire for successful project implementation.

The second oil price shock in 1979–80 contributed to a global acceleration in inflation rates, which in turn led to record-high interest rates on variable-rate development loans that ratcheted up debt service requirements among all debtor nations in the developing world, including Brazil. This oil price shock doubled the price of oil imports into Brazil, which substantially reduced the amount of funds available for Brazil to service its external debt. The IMF intervened in late 1979 with a structural adjustment program that imposed various austerity measures along with a restructuring of Brazil's external debt. At around the same time, Mexico was also entering into a problem servicing its external debt. In August 1982 the U.S. government provided Mexico with a $4.55 billion "rescue package" to give the Mexican government additional time to negotiate work-out plans with its creditors, most of which were private commercial banks, and to set up a restructuring plan with the IMF. Mexico's threat of default on its external debt contributed to an international debt crisis that substantially reduced the flow of private development finance to lower-income countries, including Brazil. As a result, after 1982 there was an increased dependence on IMF/World Bank/government–guaranteed loans. Danaher and Shellenberger (1995) note that in spite of a focused effort on external debt repayment, during this time Brazil's foreign debt grew from $64 billion in 1980 to $115 billion by 1989.

One somewhat more successful example of structural adjustment is offered by the case of Costa Rica, which was given an SAL following earlier development loan defaults. The Costa Rican economy had been primarily driven by coffee exports, and in 1982 Costa Rica experienced a crisis caused by the collapse of world coffee prices. SALs offered by the IMF and the Inter-American Development Bank, together with $2.7 billion in U.S. aid, resulted in substantial economic and social progress. Per capita income is $5,800, 93 percent of the population has access to safe drinking water, the rate of adult literacy is 94 percent, infant mortality rates have declined from 110 to 12 per thousand births, and fertility rates have declined from 7 to 3 births per woman. Moreover, Costa Rica has diversified its exports, and in 1995 nontraditional exports generated $1.4 billion in income and represented 57 percent of total exports. At the same time, Costa Rica has managed to preserve large tracts of rain forest.

Envisioning Sustainable Development: The Brundtland Commission Report, the Earth Summit, the Millennium Development Goals, and Beyond

A growing perception that conventional methods of economic development were failing contributed to an international movement to promote more sustainable methods of economic development. The Brundtland Commission is where the term *sustainable development* first began receiving widespread attention as an alternative to the widely publicized failures of traditional large-project international lending programs. These sustainability concepts were further discussed and refined in a June 1992 United Nations Conference on Environment and Development (UNCED), held in Rio de Janeiro, Brazil. This meeting, more commonly known as the Earth Summit, produced an international charter known as *Agenda 21,* a program of action for sustainable development worldwide. The Earth Summit also produced the Rio Declaration on Environment and Development, also known as the Earth Charter. From the perspective of this chapter, one of the most important products of the Earth Charter is the list of guiding principles for sustainable development.

The sustainable development principles contained in the Earth Charter represent an integration of conventional income-enhancement policies with a broad array of value statements that address social justice, poverty alleviation, and environmental preservation and restoration. These principles include international cooperation to help countries enhance their carrying capacity; policies to promote a more informed and empowered citizenry; a recognition of the needs of future generations; environmental laws that compensate pollution victims, limit the relocation of polluting activities or substances from rich to poor communities, and cause firms to internalize pollution costs; international agreements by which rich countries would assist poor countries in accessing clean production technologies; empowerment of local and indigenous communities to manage the resources upon which they rely; providing people with information and a voice in decision making; the promotion of peace. Thus, from the perspective of the Earth Charter, sustainable development policies differ from conventional economic development by acknowledging the interdependencies between economy, environment, and community, and thus more completely addressing the well-being of people.

A variety of different policies have been identified that are considered to be broadly consistent with the sustainable development principles articulated in the Earth Charter. Examples include policies to increase literacy rates; the provision of microloans, entrepreneurial skills, and marketing assistance to low-income people; the imposition of pollution taxes and liability on polluters, as well as information reporting such as the Toxics Release Inventory; the fostering of appropriate legal, political, and property rights reforms needed to protect local communities that have sustainably governed their local common-pool resources; the promotion of local small businesses to produce goods to replace imports that drain income from the community; family-planning programs; social and political reforms that empower women; the promotion of ecotourism, which generates income and employment from protection of nature preserves and biodiversity, and transforms poachers into guides and guards; and finally, direct monetary assistance and technology transfers from rich countries to promote environmentally friendlier production in low-income countries.

In September 2000, the United Nations sponsored the Millennium Summit. The result of this summit was the Millennium Declaration, which was ratified by 189 countries. The declaration includes eight broad development goals that are to be met by 2015, along with 18 specific targets, which are listed in Table 14.1. The declaration also includes forty-eight indicators of progress, which can be accessed on the Internet at http://millenniumindicators .un.org/unsd/mi/mi_goals.asp. The goals and targets are based on the ideas of promoting "sustainable economic growth" and focusing development resources on the poor, with human rights at the center of the development process. Environmental elements are more limited. The seventh goal addresses environmental sustainability, but only the first target in this goal

Table 14.1

Millennium Development Goals and Targets

Goals	Targets
1. Eradicate extreme poverty and hunger	• Reduce by half the proportion of people living on less than a dollar a day
	• Reduce by half the proportion of people who suffer from hunger
2. Achieve universal primary education	• Ensure that all boys and girls complete a full course of primary schooling
3. Promote gender equality and empower women	• Eliminate gender disparity in primary and secondary education preferably by 2005, and at all levels by 2015
4. Reduce child mortality	• Reduce by two-thirds the mortality rate among children under five
5. Improve maternal health	• Reduce by three-quarters the maternal mortality ratio
6. Combat HIV/AIDS, malaria, and other diseases	• Halt and begin to reverse the spread of HIV/AIDS
	• Halt and begin to reverse the incidence of malaria and other major diseases
7. Ensure environmental sustainability	• Integrate the principles of sustainable development into country policies and programs; reverse loss of environmental resources
	• Reduce by half the proportion of people without sustainable access to safe drinking water
	• Achieve significant improvement in lives of at least 100 million slum dwellers, by 2020
8. Develop a global partnership for development	• Develop further an open trading and financial system that is rule-based, predictable and nondiscriminatory. Includes a commitment to good governance, development, and poverty reduction— nationally and internationally
	• Address the least developed countries' special needs. This includes tariff- and quota-free access for their exports; enhanced debt relief for heavily indebted poor countries; cancellation of official bilateral debt; and more generous official development assistance for countries committed to poverty reduction
	• Address the special needs of landlocked and small-island developing states
	• Deal comprehensively with developing countries' debt problems through national and international measures to make debt sustainable in the long term
	• In cooperation with the developing countries, develop decent and productive work for youth
	• In cooperation with pharmaceutical companies, provide access to affordable essential drugs in developing countries
	• In cooperation with the private sector, make available the benefits of new technologies— especially information and communications technologies

addresses the environment as a value somewhat independent of human health. The overall objective of the declaration is to promote a comprehensive approach and a coordinated strategy to address improvements in the well-being of people, tackling many problems simultaneously across a broad front. Low-income countries that have suffered the most from the effects of poverty have been taking the lead in advocating for the declaration, especially the first seven goals that call for improvements in human well-being. The eighth goal includes steps that developed countries need to take in order to provide support to the efforts of lower-income countries.

Nevertheless, as Barraclough (2001) observes, while sustainable development is a term that is widely used, it conveys different and sometimes contradictory meanings for the different groups that promote it. He argues that part of the reason for the popularity of the concept stems from its ambiguous meaning. Even when applied with sincerity, sustainable development has been a term used to promote both reformist modifications of conventional economic development and technological modernization on the one hand, and more radical revisions that focus on social justice and the environment on the other. Barraclough offers the following explanation for why sustainable development was considered by some to be the best term to describe an integrated approach to combating environmental degradation and promoting social justice:

> Most important, [the term *sustainable development*] could help to open new space in international organizations for those convinced that environmental degradation and social polarization were not only closely linked, but were also symptoms of deep systemic malfunctioning. This would enable them to promote more effectively radical people-centered institutional and policy reforms at international, national, and local levels. Of course, vested interests would use this same space to try to maintain their privileges and power, but vigorous popularly based social forces could use it to improve their opportunities to counter them. (Barraclough 2001, p. 6)

The Millennium Development Goals represent a recent and significant example of some sustainability principles being promoted in the context of international economic development. Fully and conclusively satisfying sustainable development principles involves analysis of trade-offs that will be hampered by practical limits to the quantification and commensurability of the dissimilar factors under consideration, uncertainties relating to cause/ effect relationships, and the unknown preferences of unborn future generations. Given these practical policy challenges, it may be more productive to view sustainable development as a continuing process of education, advocacy, incremental change, and assessment. In order to use the concept of sustainability as a policy guide, it is important that we go beyond the definitions provided in chapter 12 and develop theories of sustainability from which we can extract policy implications. We turn to that subject below.

Theories of Sustainability

So far in this chapter we have seen that social, economic, and environmental failures of international development lending programs resulted in a call for more sustainable economic development, as articulated in prominent declarations such as the Brundtland Commission report and the Millennium Development Goals. Theorists in various disciplines have also made efforts to understand the concept of sustainability. These different approaches can be placed into two broad categories. One of these categories focuses on the primacy of ecological integrity, diversity, and carrying capacity, and identifying the quantity and quality of natural capital stocks that are necessary for sustaining the entire system. Performance indicators in this category transform human activities and impacts into physical measures of consumption or drawdown that can be compared to available flows of biophysical resources from the earth's stock of natural capital. The other category of sustainability theory focuses on the aggregate value of natural, human, constructed, social, and cultural capital stocks, and thus allows for trade-offs of one form of capital over another. Performance indicators in this category can be difficult to compare across types of capital. Attempts to produce single-number indicators in this category usually convert the flows of services from these capital stocks, as well as any harmful or beneficial human impacts on these stocks, into monetary values.

As Turner and Pearce (1993) point out, following the Brundtland Commission report, there was an evolution of the economics and ecology debate into two competing theories of sustainability, which we will refer to here as *weak* and *strong* sustainability (Pearce and Atkinson 1993; Pearce, Hamilton, and Atkinson 1996). While each of these two categories of sustainability theory tends to draw its own loyal advocates, perhaps a more useful way to think about them would be to consider the circumstances in which the assumptions that underlie them are true. For example, what are the essential elements of natural capital that lack any practical substitutes? The need to understand the functional characteristics and human impacts on these elements of natural capital makes the issues of carrying capacity and resilience in the first category of sustainability theory relevant. As we learned in chapter 12, sustainability must also include the economic and social needs of people that go beyond simply being represented as impacts on environmental integrity. The need to understand the flow of goods and services from all valuable forms of capital, and the practical trade-offs involved with meeting basic human needs, makes the second category of sustainability theory relevant.

Weak Sustainability

Weak sustainability theory has developed from economic models of growth and technological change in the context of limited resources. A central element of weak sustainability theory is the assumption that human-made capital can effectively substitute for natural capital and the services provided by ecological systems. The weak sustainability concept has developed from earlier work by Solow (1974) and his colleagues in understanding the conditions required for continued economic growth in a world with limited natural resources. Solow (1992) argued that a sustainable path for the national economy is one that allows every future generation the opportunity to be as well off as its predecessors. Likewise, Repetto (1986) states that "the core of the idea of sustainability, then, is the concept that current decisions should not impair the prospects for maintaining or improving future living standards" (pp. 15–16). The concern was that if natural resources are limited, and there is little substitution between different types of natural and human-made capital stocks, then per capita consumption may not be sustainable in a world with a growing population. Dasgupta and Heal (1979) found that if unlimited substitution of human-made capital for natural capital is possible, then exhaustible natural resources do not pose a limit to population and economic growth, even in the absence of technological advance. Hartwick (1977) developed a savings/investment perspective that, as Gutes (1996) points out, helps link economic growth theory with the concept of weak sustainability. Under the Hartwick rule, in order to sustain constant levels of per capita consumption, the gains that society today enjoys from utilizing an exhaustible natural resource must be reinvested in natural or human-made capital over time. Following the benefit/cost rule, such a substitution of human-made capital for exhausted natural capital is justified so long as the increase in the productive capacity of human-made capital more than offsets the loss in productive capacity from natural capital. As a result, a nondeclining aggregate flow of beneficial goods and services from all capital stocks is maintained over time. As Pearce (1994) alludes, a Hartwick-style savings rule underlies the Pearce-Atkinson concept of weak sustainability.

An implication of weak sustainability is that it allows for the mitigation of lost natural capital. For example, land conversion that eliminates an acre of wetland may be mitigated with a number of acres of constructed wetlands. Likewise, according to weak sustainability, the loss of natural runs of salmon may be mitigated through the development of fish hatcheries or aquaculture.

Strong Sustainability

Running down the stocks of natural capital and replacing these stocks with constructed substitutes is not universally seen as being consistent with the requirements of sustainable development, however. As Victor (1991) has argued, "the easier it is to substitute manufactured capital for depleting resources or a degraded environment, the less concern there needs to be about the capacity of the environment to sustain development" (p. 194). Strong sustainability theory has developed from ecological science. It emphasizes the ecological imperatives of carrying capacity, biodiversity, and biotic resilience. From this perspective, human-made capital cannot effectively substitute for the vital services provided by ecological systems. Arguments supporting strong sustainability theory include (following Pearce, Barbier, and Markandya 1990):

- *Uncertainty:* The consequences of depleting natural capital in terms of the functional characteristics and productivity of ecological systems are unpredictable, which suggests caution. Because of this uncertainty, we cannot determine the proper level of offsetting investment in human or human-made capital that is required by weak sustainability.
- *Irreversibility:* So many of our actions, such as species extinctions, large-scale ecosystem disruptions, and global climate change, cannot be undone. Unlike human-made capital, which can be rebuilt, destruction of certain forms of natural capital, such as biodiversity, is irreversible. While it is possible in theory to compensate future generations for permanently diminished natural capital, from a practical standpoint we cannot know their preferences regarding the trade-off between natural and human-made capital. As a result, as a practical matter we have no way of satisfying the weak sustainability standard.
- *Scale and Discontinuities:* Instead of the smooth and continuous cause-and-effect relationships assumed in models drawn from weak sustainability theory, natural systems often feature discontinuities and threshold effects. One of the best known of these is the potential for melting terrestrial ice sheets to disrupt the Northern Atlantic thermohaline circulation system. The temperate climate of Western Europe is dependent upon the transport of warm ocean waters northward, and evidence suggests that acute freshwater runoff events due to climate warming in the past have disrupted this flow, resulting in dramatic cooling and loss of agricultural production in Western Europe. Similarly, with uneven topography, each additional one-foot rise in sea level will generally imply highly uneven land inundation rates. As a final example,

loss of one species may have a small ecosystem impact, while loss of another may cause the same ecosystem to collapse.

To summarize, strong sustainability theory is distinguished by the view that there is very little substitutability between human-made capital and natural capital in terms of the flow of goods and services that they are capable of providing over time. Strong sustainability theory is therefore focused on the critical and irreplaceable life-support systems associated with natural capital. From a more technical perspective, another distinction is that weak sustainability theory is built on economic conceptions of smooth and continuous cause-and-effect relationships, while strong sustainability theory is premised upon an ecological systems approach that features discontinuities, discreteness, and thresholds in cause-and-effect relationships. Thus in strong sustainability the ecological systems approach provides the basis for guiding (or constraining) sustainable development, while in weak sustainability economic methods of analysis provide the context for evaluating sustainable development. While weak sustainability calls for the maintenance of the *sum* of human, human-made, and natural capital, strong sustainability calls for maintaining human, human-made, and natural capital separately (Costanza and Daly 1992).

There has been relatively little research that has attempted to evaluate the hypothesis of substitutability between human-made and natural capital on a comprehensive basis. Presumably, substitutability is possible in some cases and not possible in others, which would imply that the choice of weak or strong sustainability is situational and complex. Pearce (1994) points out that the waste-transforming capacity of the natural environment and the degree of biodiversity, for example, have no real substitutes (though the productivity of natural sink functions has been improved by technology, as illustrated by innovative new methods of using wetlands to transform various human wastes). Empirical evidence supporting high degrees of substitutability has largely been limited to the study of energy and mineral resources (see, for example, Brown and Field 1979).

Practical Policy Implications

Policies consistent with weak sustainability theory are those that view natural capital, human capital, and human-made capital as substitutes. Degradation of natural capital is acceptable if, and only if, it is accompanied by a mitigating increase in human and human-made capital. This view is reflected in various World Bank positions, as expressed in the *World Development Report, 1992,* and by Pearce and Warford (1993). Therefore, for example, it may be consistent with weak sustainability to build a hydroelectric dam that destroys elements of natural capital if the constructed capital that constitutes the dam generates an offsetting flow of benefits. A central concern that critics have for weak sustainability theory is that it does not necessarily provide for limits to the built environment, or for minimal preservation of wildlands and other attributes of natural capital.

In contrast, policies consistent with strong sustainability theory call for the application of a *safe minimum standard* that ensures the continued existence and at least minimal functional integrity of the various renewable resource stocks and ecosystem functions of natural capital from which flow the food, fiber, energy, and ecosystem services essential for a sustainable society. Consistent with the notion of minimal substitutability between natural and human or human-made capital, economic growth premised on development of human and human-made capital would be constrained when pollution and other waste by-products persist in the environment and significantly degrade natural capital. As Opschoor (1996) argues, strong sustainability requires preserving unique and vital natural capital stocks ("ecological infrastructure") and thus keeping human activity consistent with the earth's carrying capacity and the available environmental utilization space.

Stepping back a bit, it should be noted that one need not make an "either-or" choice of weak or strong sustainability as a guide to public policy. In most any complex society, we can readily observe policies consistent with both strong and weak sustainability theory. For example, most societies have sacrificed some natural capital in the process of developing human-made capital such as transportation infrastructure, agriculture, manufacturing facilities, hospitals, and schools. These same societies may at the same time have designated wilderness areas and wildlife refuges, regulatory systems to protect wildlife and ecosystem services generated from privately owned land, and programs to conserve agricultural lands and soil resources.

Sustainability Indicators

We will begin by discussing measures of weak sustainability and then address measures of strong sustainability. Weak sustainability indicators usually start with quantitative measures of human, human-made, natural, and perhaps social capital that are made commensurate in monetary terms so that they can be reduced to a single aggregated indicator that is roughly comparable to GDP. The Human Development Index (HDI) takes a somewhat similar approach of aggregating indicators of human capital and human-made capital, though the HDI number is not monetized. Moreover, the Millennium Development Indicators provide separate measures of human, human-made, and natural capital, though no attempt is made to aggregate them into a single indicator. Thus, before we consider some of the more prominent weak sustainability indicators, we should briefly consider the conventional means by which macroeconomic performance is measured.

Macroeconomics is the subdiscipline of economics that analyzes the aggregate performance of an economy, with particular attention given to the *business cycle* of expansion and contraction that leads to changes in inflation, unemployment, and income. The data that are used to measure macroeconomic performance are organized into *national income and product accounts,* which were first developed by Simon Kuznets and other macroeconomists for the U.S. Department of Commerce in the Great Depression. Before that time, policymakers lacked timely and reliable macroeconomic data and therefore were unable to take appropriate policy actions in response to current trends in the economy. Kuznets received a Nobel Prize in economics for his work with the national income and product accounts. A central element of national income accounting is *gross domestic product* (GDP). GDP measures the market value of all the goods and services bought by consumers, firms, or government agencies, those invested in to enhance production by firms and other enterprises, and those involved in net exports (export minus import expenditures) each year in a particular domestic economy. When people refer to the status of the economy, they usually mean GDP. GDP can grow over time due to a general increase in prices (inflation) or due to an increase in the productive capacity of labor and capital in the economy, or a combination of both. When one removes the component of GDP increase that is due to inflation, one is left with *real* GDP growth or GDP growth due only to increases in the quantity and quality of goods and services produced. Growth in real GDP is called *economic growth.* Finally, real GDP divided by population is per capita real GDP, or the average person's share of real GDP in the economy. To central government policy makers, the key macroeconomic policy goal is to promote the highest growth rate for real per capita GDP that is consistent with low inflation.

Consider the problem of adjusting GDP to take into account unmeasured (or incorrectly measured) changes in the quality of the social and natural environment. Many important qualities associated with a healthy natural environment or the safety and quality of our community, for that matter, are not bought or sold, and so are more difficult to quantify and have been ignored in conventional macroeconomic analysis. Macroeconomics simply tallies up the value of market transactions, and yet macroeconomic performance defines the issues that policymakers work to address. As degradation of sensitive environmental and natural resource systems accelerates, it becomes increasingly important to find a way to adjust GDP and our system of national income accounts so that they provide a more accurate picture of the well-being of people over time—macroeconomic sustainability.

Limitations of conventional GDP accounting include the following:

- Money spent deterring and remediating crime and other problems associated with the deterioration of communities is counted as economic gain and increases GDP, as is money spent after a natural disaster.
- Money spent remediating pollution problems is added to the income generated by the industrial process that originally created the pollution problem, thus creating the illusion that the industrial activity creates a double benefit to society.
- GDP is not affected by the degree of inequality in the distribution of income in a national economy, and per capita real GDP does not indicate the extent of inequality in an economy. Thus poverty can increase when real per capita GDP increases.
- GDP does not take into account moral, spiritual, or aesthetic values associated with biodiversity, wilderness, Native American religious sites, or unique aspects of the natural environment.
- GDP does not distinguish a dollar generated by sustainable harvest of a resource from a dollar generated in the process of exhausting a natural resource. From a business perspective, we can say that depreciation of the productive capacity of the *natural capital stock* is not taken into account in GDP.

Therefore, we can see that simple GDP accounting treats every transaction as positive, as long as money changes hands, and therefore real per capita GDP is inadequate as an indicator of progress toward a sustainable society. Let's now look beyond GDP to find indicators of weak and strong sustainability.

Indicators of Weak Sustainability

Recall that weak sustainability theory calls for the maintenance of a constant (per capita) level of capital stock, largely independent of whether it is human-made, social, human, or natural. A number of measures have been developed that attempt to take indicators of human-made, human, natural, and social capital and reduce them to a single aggregated indicator of weak sustainability. From the standpoint of weak sustainability, ideally the national income and product accounts would be extended beyond the market-mediated flows underlying GDP measurement to include all stocks of capital and both market-mediated and nonmarket flows of valuable goods and services. Moreover, ideally markets would accurately capture both negative and positive externalities in the sense described in chapter 4. Under these conditions, *net national product* (the sum of aggregate consumption spending and net capital formation) is equivalent to the maximum sustainable amount of consumption spending that an economy with zero population growth can indefinitely maintain (National Research Council 1999). *Net capital formation* refers to capital investment in excess of depreciation (or deterioration). Consumption spending and net capital formation would include traditional market-based consumption and investment as well as nonmarket consumption and investment not currently captured in the national income and product accounts. Nonmarket consumption would include the flows from resource stocks such as forests, rangelands, fisheries, and aquifers, as well as flows of ecosystem services such as oxygen exchange, temperature regulation, the hydrological cycle, and waste absorption. Accordingly, net capital formation would include investments in natural capital.

Presumably, one would also have to include consumption of the flow of services from social capital in this measure, as well as net investment in social capital. From the perspective of the National Research Council (1999), however, there is no satisfactory metric for measuring social capital, and no established methodology for valuing it in monetary terms, and therefore economists have not included social capital in some measures of augmented GDP. Recall that social capital is made up of factors such as trust, norms of reciprocity, volunteerism, and networks of support. Quantitative social capital indicators include trust in government, voter participation rates, memberships in civic organizations, and hours spent volunteering. Despite the concerns of the National Research Council, there have been some attempts at valuing volunteerism and other aspects of social capital, but before addressing them, we will first consider several relatively simple indicators of weak sustainability.

One method of GDP augmentation that applies some of these concepts uses the Hartwick rule to derive a measure of environmentally adjusted or *green GDP*. Green GDP is derived as follows:

Green GDP = GDP – Hotelling rent for nonrenewables – total expenditures on pollution control – other direct costs due to environmental degradation.

Recall that Hotelling rent reflects the excess of (price - marginal cost) from resource extraction and reflects the opportunity cost of current resource consumption. Scarce resources consumed today are not available in the future, and so Hotelling rent reflects forgone future consumption value. Hartwick and other growth theorists have shown that steady-state consumption can be maintained if Hotelling rent from consumption of nonrenewable resources is reinvested in some form of capital stock (natural, social, human, or constructed) to provide for future consumption. Thus, as nonrenewable resources are exhausted, the Hotelling rents generated by dynamically efficient consumption of these resources create a revenue source that can be invested to develop substitutes for the time when the resource is exhausted.

Along these lines, Arrow et al. (2004) proposed *genuine investment* as an indicator of weak sustainability, which they interpret as assuring that a nondecreasing level of social welfare is being maintained over time. Genuine investment refers to the sum of the values of investments or disinvestments in each of society's capital assets (i.e., human, human-made, social, natural, and cultural). Since under weak sustainability theory we can view the sum of these stocks of capital assets as society's genuine wealth, we can also view genuine investment as the rate of change in genuine wealth. While this is a helpful concept in understanding weak sustainability theory, it poses challenges from a measurement standpoint. For example, weak sustainability theory requires that declines in nonrenewable resource stocks over time must be offset with genuine investment in one or more of the five categories of capital stock. In order to maintain nondecreasing social welfare, however, society must assign values to the flows from each of these stocks, and direct genuine investment in a manner consistent with maintaining nondecreasing social welfare. Arrow et al. noted that the potential for substitution of one form of capital for another would likely vary depending on differing degrees of scarcity and characteristics of social utility.

A closely related and computationally identical indicator for weak sustainability, developed by Hamilton (1994), is *genuine savings* (also see Pearce, Hamilton, and Atkinson 1996). Hamilton and Clemens (1999) provided estimates of genuine domestic saving for nearly all the countries of the world in 1998. Their formula for estimating genuine domestic saving is given as follows:

Genuine domestic saving = investment + education – CO_2 damage – oil depletion – mineral depletion – net forest depletion.

Note that investment in the equation above refers to aggregate spending on human-made capital of various kinds, net of depreciation, while education refers to aggregate investment in human capital. Hamilton and Clemens (1999) measure CO_2 damage at US$20 per ton. The last three terms refer to depletion of oil resources, mineral resources, and depletion (net of regeneration) of forest resources. Hamilton and Clemens found that genuine domestic savings (or in Arrow et al. [2004] terms, genuine investment) was positive in all the rich industrialized countries of the world, as well as in most middle- and even lower-income countries, but was negative in thirty-three of the world's poorest or most oil-export-dependent countries. In particular, the Middle East, North Africa, and sub-Saharan Africa regions featured negative genuine domestic savings because the increases due to investment in human-made capital and in education were more than offset by depletion of oil and other natural resource stocks. Thus the large positive values for genuine domestic saving in rich industrialized countries is at least partially based on exporting their resource depletion to these oil-exporting countries.

Arrow et al. (2004) modify the genuine domestic saving calculation from Hamilton and Clemens (1999) to take into account the additional impacts of population growth and technologically based improvements in the productivity of human-made capital. Even with these adjustments, Arrow et al. still find negative genuine investment rates for sub-Saharan Africa, North Africa, and the Middle East, due to depletion of oil and other natural resource stocks. Moreover, countries such as Bangladesh, India, and Pakistan, which had relatively large positive rates of total genuine investment, were found to have near-zero rates of per capita genuine investment due to their high population growth rates. Arrow et al. conclude that for sub-Saharan Africa's -2.6 percent rate of genuine investment implies that this region's genuine wealth is declining by a factor of two about every twenty-five years.

While there are some challenges associated with adequately measuring genuine savings, it can be argued that it is the most widely accepted and best attempt at measuring weak sustainability so far, with considerable scope for future development and improvement (Dietz and Neumayer 2004). There are a number of other more ambitious measures of weak sustainability that include a wider variety of indicators, including some for social capital. Two of the better known of these socioeconomic measures of weak sustainability are the index of sustainable economic welfare (ISEW), developed by Daly and Cobb (1989), and the genuine progress indicator (GPI), developed by Cobb, Halstead, and Rowe (1995, hereinafter Cobb et al.) and maintained on the Internet at www.rprogress.org/newprograms/sustIndi/gpi/index.shtml. Computation of the ISEW begins with per capita real consumption spending (a major element of GDP), followed by the introduction of various adjustments to take into account a variety of socioeconomic and environmental factors. The following are examples of the large number of adjustment factors that Daly and Cobb (1989) include in their index:

- deduction of an estimate of the amount that society would need to set aside in a perpetual income stream to compensate future generations for the loss of services from nonrenewable energy resources such as oil and natural gas;

- deduction for estimates of pollution and other environmental damages, including noise pollution, and what they admit to be a rather speculative estimate of damage from global warming;
- deduction for income inequality;
- addition of the nonmarketed value of household production;
- addition of the value of government expenditures for education, health, roads, and highways;
- deduction for the higher cost of urbanized living.

The GPI is very similar to the ISEW. To compute the GPI, one starts with real personal consumption spending, adjusts for income distribution, and then adds or subtracts a number of different elements that reflect ecological and social benefits or costs. Adjustment factors *added* to traditional consumption spending to arrive at the GPI include:

- the value of household work and parenting, based on the cost of hiring out these services, based on the work of economist Robert Eisner;
- the value of volunteer work, using Census Bureau data and taking the opportunity cost of time at $8 per hour;
- services of consumer durables net of their costs (from making do with old things);
- services of government capital such as highways, streets, and other infrastructure, as a percentage of the total value of the stock of these assets.

Factors *subtracted* from traditional consumption spending to arrive at GPI include:

- cost of crime;
- cost of family breakdown, based on added expenditures;
- loss of leisure time;
- cost of underemployment, measured at opportunity cost;
- cost of consumer durables;
- cost of commuting (a defensive expenditure);
- cost of household pollution abatement;
- cost of automobile accidents;
- cost of water, air, and noise pollution;
- loss of wetlands;
- loss of farmlands;
- depletion of nonrenewable energy resources;
- other long-term environmental damage;
- cost of ozone depletion;
- loss of old-growth forests.

As you might expect, green GDP, genuine savings, ISEW, GPI, and similar weak sustainability measures are controversial, particularly among economists. Many economists are uncomfortable with them because they are not as concrete and objective as traditional GDP accounting. For example, the dollar values assigned to GPI elements such as family breakdown and loss of old-growth forests are to some degree subjective and open to debate, while the conventional national income accounting methods underlying GDP are widely accepted. In its description of augmented accounts for tracking economic sustainability the National Research Council (1999) excludes elements such as income inequality and the success and happiness of families. While both of these are included in the ISEW and the GPI, and in fact, inequality is a major factor explaining their trend, the National Research Council argued that such things are important but not amenable to economic measurement. Finally, despite the complexity of measures such as the ISEW and the GPI, they still exclude important factors such as risk and uncertainty. Should the path to sustainability be risk-free, or is society willing to accept policies or technologies that offer a good chance of a major improvement, but at the cost of a small chance of a loss in sustainability?

While the weak sustainability measures are clearly controversial and somewhat subjective, it is also clear that current GDP accounting offers a highly incomplete view of economic well-being and sustainability. There is a growing recognition of the need for augmenting the traditional national income and product accounts. For example, the National Research Council (1999) observes that "augmented national income accounts would . . . be valuable as indicators of whether economic activity is sustainable. . . . It is clear that the national productivity depends on many non-market elements, including not only the environment, but also such things as schooling, health care, and social capital in volunteer and civic organizations. It may not be possible to capture all these important facets of modern society in nation's accounts, but an attempt should surely be made . . ." (pp. 15–16). With time, a set of "best methods" may develop that will lend more precision and acceptance to measures of weak sustainability.

Indicators of Strong Sustainability

Indicators consistent with strong sustainability theory include measures of ecological resilience such as biological diversity and yield variability in agriculture, measures of carrying capacity, and ecological impact analysis. As Pearce, Hamilton, and Atkinson (1996) point out, under strong sustainability theory, sustainable development occurs by conserving key elements of the natural capital stock that preserve ecological integrity. Wackernagel, White, and Moran (2004) argue that strong sustainability has specific, definable requirements, including the need to avoid ecological overshoot, meaning the level of human resource demand that exceeds ecological carrying capacity. Two indicators of strong sustainability are carrying capacity based on net primary product (NPP), and ecological footprint (EF), each of which focuses on measuring the natural capital requirements of human society. NPP can be derived from the amount of vegetation produced annually over the land area of the country for which NPP is being calculated. Following Vitousek, Ehrlich, and Matson (1986), one can then divide NPP by the average amount of vegetable matter required to support a human per year to arrive at a measure of the human carrying capacity of the land area under analysis.

The EF is a more comprehensive measure of appropriated human carrying capacity, or the natural capital stock utilized by human society. The EF is approximated by the area of ecologically productive land and water per capita that is necessary to support existing human consumption and to absorb many human-generated wastes (see Rees and Wackernagel 1994). Some impacts are not quantified in EF analysis. For example, toxic pollutants and species extinction are not incorporated into the EF model. Wackernagel and Rees divide land into categories: arable land, pasture, forest, sea space, built-up land, and fossil energy land. Fossil energy land refers to land set aside to sequester carbon dioxide created from burning fossil fuels. Wackernagel and Rees report that only about 0.25 hectares per capita of arable land exists worldwide, and that nearly all is already under cultivation. According to analysis by Wackernagel and Rees, the world has only 2 hectares per capita of productive surface area, including sea space. They then subtract 12 percent of ecological capacity for biodiversity to arrive at their net figure of 1.7 hectares per capita of ecologically productive land. Since the world average per capita EF is 2.3 hectares, the implication is that humanity's consumption exceeds what nature can generate on a continuous basis by about 35 percent. As a result, the work of Wackernagel and Rees suggests a "sustainability gap," or overshoot, in which industrialized countries are drawing down natural capital stocks (or importing them from lower-income countries) rather than living on sustainable flows. The EF can be reduced by various combinations of more resource-efficient technologies, reduced population, reduced consumption, and increased ecological productivity.

Venetoulis, Chazan, and Gaudet (2004) show that while the global aggregate EF has been rising, average worldwide per capita EF has been slowly and steadily declining since 1980. Moreover, while there is a correlation between a country's per capita income and EF, there is not a direct linear relationship, indicating that some rich countries are able to foster far more sustainable societies than others. For example, Venetoulis and colleagues report that the per capita EF in the Netherlands was only 3.81 in 2000, while Italy's was only 3.26. In contrast, per capita EF in the United States is nearly 10 hectares, the highest in the world, and those of New Zealand, Canada, and Norway exceeded 8 hectares. In contrast, countries such as Haiti and Bangladesh have per capita EF values below 1.0. Wackernagel and Rees find that some countries are in an EF deficit, implying that they must import carrying capacity from another country (or from future generations), while others still have a surplus. Canada is one of the better examples of a country with surplus carrying capacity. Japan, on the other hand, has a significant deficit.

Case Studies in Measuring Sustainable Economic Development

Scotland

Moffatt, Hanley, and Gill (1994, hereinafter Moffatt et al.) used both weak and strong sustainability measurement techniques to answer the question of whether Scotland is on a sustainable development path. Some of their key findings are summarized below:

- *Approximate environmentally adjusted national product, 1988–92:* According to this measure, which is a measure of green GDP, Scotland is on a sustainable development path, as this measure has risen without break, with a start-to-finish rise of approximately 30 percent.
- *Index of sustainable economic welfare (Daly and Cobb 1989), 1984–90:* According to this measure, Scotland is unlikely to be on a sustainable development path, as this measure has declined in all years except 1989, with a start-to-finish decline of over 10 percent. Moffatt et al. classify this as a marginal case.
- *Carrying capacity:* This ecological measure indicates that Scotland is very close to its human carrying capacity, and so Moffatt et al. classify this outcome as being marginal.
- *Ecological footprint (appropriated carrying capacity):* Analysis of Scotland's ecological footprint indicates that its present patterns of energy and food consumption are unsustainable.

The results from Moffatt and colleagues are quite mixed, and they do consider theirs only a pilot study. Nevertheless, as one might expect, the weak sustainability measures are to some extent more likely to indicate a sustainable development path than measures of strong sustainability.

United States

Daly and Cobb (1989) offer an ambitious study of the sustainability of the United States's development path using the ISEW. Based on this analysis, Daly and Cobb find that the ISEW generally increased from 1950 (per capita ISEW value = 2,488) to 1979 (per capita ISEW = 3,776.4). Annual increases averaged 0.84 percent in the 1950s and 2.01 percent in the 1960s. Daly and Cobb argue that a major factor explaining the dramatic rise in the per capita ISEW during the 1960s was the increased equality of income that occurred during that period. There were also appreciable increases in net capital. Between 1979 and the end of their study in 1986, per capita ISEW declined by approximately 10 percent (1986 per capita ISEW value = 3,402.8). The decline during the 1980s averaged 1.26 percent annually. This decline occurs even when one removes the more controversial elements from their index, such as assumed impacts of global warming. This decline is driven by worsening income inequality, further heavily impacted natural resources, and inadequate investment in socially beneficial forms of capital.

As mentioned above, Cobb et al. (1995) have developed a genuine progress indicator (GPI) that includes a very broad range of environmental, social, political, and economic adjustment factors. Cobb et al. have computed GPI for the United States from 1950 to 1994. GPI is an adjusted dollar measure of per capita income. Their methodology is similar to that of Daly and Cobb, and their findings are somewhat similar. Cobb and his colleagues find that GPI was relatively constant during the period from 1950 to 1961, ranging between 5,658 and 6,346. From 1961 to 1969 the GPI rose from a value of 5,872 to 7,400, approximately a 25 percent increase. The GPI declined, with a few small upward blips, through the 1970s and by 1980 was at 6,369, a level comparable to that of the 1950s. By 1990 the GPI declined to a value of 5,304, a 17 percent drop. The 1994 figure for GPI is 4,068, showing a 23 percent decline in four years. As with the analysis by Daly and Cobb, much of this decline can be attributed to the increase in income inequality that has occurred in the United States since the 1960s. For example, while GPI declined by 45 percent from 1973 to 1994, if income distribution had remained the same, GPI would have declined by only 10 percent.

Venetoulis and Cobb (2004) provide an update on the GPI for the United States for the period 2000–03. They note that in the period between January 2000 and January 2003, real GDP increased by 2.64 percent, or $180 per American. Based on the GPI, however, the value of economic activity grew by less than 1 percent (0.12 percent) during the same period. On a per capita basis, from 2000 to 2003 there was a $212 decline in GPI, with the biggest reductions coming from the degradation of natural resources and a rise in the national debt. There was also an increase on the positive side of the GPI. In particular, the GPI increased by $600 billion due to the increased value of housework and volunteer work between 2000 and 2003, which is not counted in GDP. In terms of ecological footprint analysis, Venetoulis, Chazan, and Gaudet (2004) report that in 2000, the most recent year for which data are available, the United States became the country with the largest per capita ecological footprint of any country on the planet—9.57 hectares (23.6 acres) per person.

Sub-Saharan Africa, Latin America, and the Caribbean

The World Bank (1995) computed *genuine savings* for a variety of different developing regions of the world. While the World Bank acknowledged that this computation should also include investments in education (human capital) and health, its analysis did not include them. The World Bank's results indicate that sub-Saharan Africa has experienced negative genuine savings since 1977. Latin America and the Caribbean as a single region experienced periods of negative genuine savings from 1980 to 1984 and again in the period since 1989. Most developed countries experienced a genuine savings rate of between 1 and 10 percent annually. More recent measurements of genuine savings by Hamilton and Clemens (1999) and Arrow et al. (2004) indicate that while Latin America and the Caribbean have improved, sub-Saharan Africa continues to experience negative genuine savings.

Summary

- Sustainable development is about broadening the traditional mandate of economic development policies, which focused on increasing real per capita incomes in developing countries, to include social and environmental factors. The sustainable development movement is driven in part by the perception that conventional methods of sustainable development may result in serious environmental, resource, and community degradation, as well as fostering a dependency on resource-depleting commodity exports as a means of repaying past development debt.
- While conventional economic development policies have focused on fostering income growth, sustainable economic development policies also include improved education and literacy; family planning; the provision of information and democratic empowerment; the tailoring of economic development to local conditions, environments, and cultures; the promotion of ecotourism; and the fostering of environmental regulations, among others.

- Two broad categories of sustainability theory have become prominent. One of these, weak sustainability, derives from economic models of sustainable economic growth and is based on the assumption that technological innovation will allow for the substitution of human-made capital for depleted natural capital. The other of these, strong sustainability, derives from ecological models of carrying capacity and is based on the assumption that natural capital is usually unique and thus cannot be replaced by human-made capital.
- Traditional macroeconomic accounting techniques for measuring economic performance are inadequate for evaluating the sustainability of a national economy. A number of recent attempts have been made at adjusting GDP to take into account the environmental and community requirements and impacts related to the economy. These adjustments are very difficult because of the problem of quantifying social and environmental qualities that are not directly traded in markets.
- Indicators of weak sustainability include green GDP, genuine savings, the index of sustainable economic welfare, and the genuine progress indicator. These measures begin with conventional elements of GDP and make adjustments based on the monetary value of changes in the environment, natural resource systems, and a variety of social and political factors related to sustainability. While these measures are controversial both for the factors that are included and for the values assigned to them, conventional GDP accounting offers only a very incomplete picture of the well-being of people.
- Indicators of strong sustainability include carrying capacity, biodiversity, and ecological footprint. These indicators provide information on the ability of terrestrial ecosystems to support human life over time. They do not allow for improved technology or for the substitution of human-made capital for natural capital.
- Case studies indicate a substantial disparity between the trend in conventional GDP, weak sustainability measures, and strong sustainability measures. For example, while real per capita GDP has generally been rising in the United States at a slow but steady pace (with the exception of recessionary periods), both the ISEW and the GPI indicate a decline in sustainable economic welfare over the last twenty or more years.

Review Questions and Problems

1. Research the effects of traditional development lending and SALs in a country of your own choice and write a two-page essay describing your findings. Discuss the impacts of development debt on the domestic economy of

the country, poverty and income distribution, food security, social spending, and the integrity of environmental and natural resources.

2. Describe the conceptual differences between strong and weak sustainable development. What is the basis for disagreement over which of the two offers the better guide to sustainable development policy?

3. Make a list and describe some examples of situations in which there appears to have been a sustainable substitution of human-made capital for natural capital. Now make another list and describe some elements of natural capital that cannot be replaced by human-made capital. How might we combine elements of strong and weak sustainability theory into a unified theory of sustainable development that is consistent with the two lists you have drawn up?

4. Access the Compendium of Sustainable Development Indicators on the Internet (www.iisd.org/measure/compendium). Select an indicator of sustainability that has not been discussed in the textbook and critically evaluate how well it measures progress toward sustainability.

5. Access the Millennium Development Indicators website (http://millenniumindicators.un.org/unsd/mi/mi.asp), select a country, and produce a summary report of the trends in that country's Millennium Development Indicators.

6. Go to www.myfootprint.org and assess your own ecological footprint based on where you live and on your various life-style choices. Then consider several life-style changes and see how those would affect your ecological footprint.

Internet Links

Compendium of Sustainable Development Indicators (www.iisd.org/measure/compendium): Provides an overview of initiatives on sustainable development indicators being carried out at the international, national, and provincial/territorial/state levels. It has been prepared by the International Institute for Sustainable Development, Environment Canada, Redefining Progress, the World Bank, and the United Nations Division for Sustainable Development.

Dashboard of Sustainability (www.iisd.org/cgsdi/dashboard.asp): A free, noncommercial software package that illustrates the complex relationships among economic, social, and environmental issues. The visual format is suitable for decision makers and others interested in sustainable development.

Debt Relief for Heavily Indebted Poor Countries (www.worldbank.org/

hipc): Read about the World Bank's program for providing debt relief to heavily indebted poor countries.

Ecological Footprint (www.rprogress.org/newprojects/ecolFoot.shtml): Information and computation procedures for estimating ecological footprint, from the group Redefining Progress.

Friends of the Earth's Trade, Environment, and Sustainability Program (www.foei.org/trade/index.html): An advocacy group that is critical of "corporate globalization," and that promotes fair and sustainable economies based on democracy, diversity, reduced consumption, cooperation, and caution.

Genuine Progress Indicator (www.rprogress.org/newprograms/sustIndi/ gpi/index.shtml): Information and updates on the GPI from the group Redefining Progress.

Greening the GDP: Is It Desirable? Is It Feasible? (www.rff.org/Documents/RFF-Resources-139-greengdp.pdf): Article by Joe Darmstadter in the Spring 2000 issue of *Resources* addressing the National Research Council's study of the merits of measuring green GDP, published by the group Resources for the Future.

Human Development Reports (http://hdr.undp.org/reports): A good site to read global reports such as the annual *Human Development Report,* as well as regional and national reports, and to read the latest Human Development Index. Produced by the United Nations Development Program.

Index of Sustainable Economic Welfare (www.foe.co.uk/campaigns/ sustainable_development/progress): Information and computational procedures for estimating the ISEW, from the group Friends of the Earth.

International Institute for Sustainable Development (http://iisd.ca): One of the best and most comprehensive sources of information on sustainable development.

Millennium Development Goals (www.un.org/millenniumgoals): A framework of eight goals that relate to sustainable development. Maintained by the United Nations Development Program.

Millennium Development Indicators (http://millenniumindicators.un.org/ unsd/mi/mi_goals.asp): A set of forty-eight indicators that can be used to gauge progress toward the millennium development goals. Maintained by the United Nations Development Program.

Multinational Monitor (http://multinationalmonitor.org/monitor.html): Published monthly, the *Multinational Monitor* tracks corporate activity, especially in the Third World, focusing on the export of hazardous substances, worker health and safety, labor union issues, and the environment.

Social Capital for Development (www.worldbank.org/prem/poverty/ scapital/index.htm): This World Bank Internet site is a good resource for those studying social capital.

SD Gateway (http://sdgateway.net): Information gathered from the Sustainable Development Communications Network, including over 1,200 documents available in SD Topics, including a calendar of events, a job bank, the Sustainability Web Ring, a roster of mailing lists (listservs), and news sites dealing with sustainable development.

United Nations Division for Sustainable Development (www.un.org/esa/ sustdev): Internet site for the Division for Sustainable Development, Department of Economic and Social Affairs, United Nations.

United Nations Economic Commission for Africa (www.uneca.org): Lots of good information on development in Africa, including the African Statistical Yearbook.

World Bank Environmental Initiatives (www.worldbank.org/environment): Read about what the World Bank is doing to promote environmentally friendly development.

World Development Report (econ.worldbank.org/wdr/): An annual World Bank publication with articles and extensive indicators relating to development worldwide.

References and Further Reading

Arrow, K., P. Dasgupta, L. Goulder, G. Daily, P. Ehrlich, G. Heal, S. Levin, K-G. Maler, S. Schneider, D. Starrett, and B. Walker. 2004. "Are We Consuming Too Much?" *Journal of Economic Perspectives* 18 (3): 147–72.
Barraclough, Solon. 2001. "Toward Integrated and Sustainable Development?" Paper Number 1, United Nations Research Institute for Social Development. Available at www.unrisd.org.

Bawa, K., and S. Dayanandan. 1997. "Socioeconomic Factors and Tropical Deforestation." *Nature* 386 (April 10): 562–63.

Brady, G., and P. Geets. 1994. "Sustainable Development: The Challenge of Implementation." *International Journal of Sustainable Development and World Ecology* 1: 189–97.

Brown, G., and B. Field. 1979. "The Adequacy of Measures for Signalling the Scarcity of Natural Resources." In *Scarcity and Growth Reconsidered,* ed. V. Smith. Baltimore: Johns Hopkins University Press.

Cobb, C., T. Halstead, and J. Rowe. 1995. *The Genuine Progress Indicator: Summary of Data and Methodology.* San Francisco: Redefining Progress.

Costanza, R. 1991. "Assuring Sustainability of Ecological Economic Systems." In *Ecological Economics: The Science and Management of Sustainability,* ed. R. Costanza. New York: Columbia University Press.

Costanza, R., and H. Daly. 1992. "Natural Capital and Sustainable Development." *Conservation Biology* 6 (March): 37–46.

Cruz, W., and R. Repetto. 1992. *The Environmental Effects of Stabilization and Structural Adjustment Programmes.* Washington, DC: World Resources Institute.

Cumberland, J. 1991. "Intergenerational Transfers and Ecological Sustainability." In *Ecological Economics: The Science and Management of Sustainability,* ed. R. Costanza. New York: Columbia *University Press.*

Daly, H., and J. Cobb. 1989. *For the Common Good: Redirecting the Economy Toward Community, the Environment, and a Sustainable Future.* Boston: Beacon Press.

Danaher, K. 1994. *50 Years Is Enough: The Case Against the World Bank and the International Monetary Fund.* Boston: South End Press.

Danaher, K., and M. Shellenberger. 1995. *Fighting for the Soul of Brazil: A Project of Global Exchange.* New York: Monthly Review Press.

Dasgupta, P., and G. Heal. 1979. *Economic Theory and Exhaustible Resources.* Cambridge: Cambridge University Press.

Diefenbacher, Hans. 1994. "The Index of Sustainable Economic Welfare: A Case Study of the Federal Republic of Germany." In *The Green National Product: A Proposed Index of Sustainable Economic Welfare,* ed. C. Cobb and J. Cobb Jr. Lanham, MD: University Press of America.

Dietz, S., and E. Neumayer. 2004. "Genuine Savings: A Critical Analysis of Its Policy-Guiding Value." *International Journal of Environment and Sustainable Development* 3: 276–92.

Economic Commission for Latin America and the Caribbean. 1985. *Sustainable Development: Changing Production Patterns, Social Equity and the Environment.* Santiago, Chile: United Nations.

Eisner, R. 1985. "The Total Incomes System of Accounts." *Survey of Current Business* (January): 45–51.

Godfrey, M., and T. Rose, eds. 1985. *Crisis and Recovery in Sub-Saharan Africa.* Paris: OECD.

Gotlieb, Y. 1996. *Development, Environment, and Global Dysfunction: Toward Sustainable Recovery.* Delray Beach, FL: St. Lucie Press.

Gutes, M. 1996. "Commentary: The Concept of Weak Sustainability." *Ecological Economics* 17: 147–56.

Hamilton, K. 1994. "Green Adjustments to GDP." *Resources Policy* 20 (3): 155–68.

Hamilton, K., and M. Clemens. 1999. "Genuine Savings Rates in Developing Countries." *World Bank Economic Review* 13 (2): 333–56.

Hartwick, J. 1977. "Intergenerational Equity and the Investing of Rents from Exhaustible Resources." *American Economic Review* 67 (5): 972–74.

———. 1990. "Natural Resources, National Accounting and Economic Depreciation." *Journal of Public Economics* 43: 291–304.

Howarth, R., and R. Norgaard. 1992. "Environmental Valuation Under Sustainable Development." *American Economic Review, Papers and Proceedings* 82 (May): 473–77.

Jackson, T., and N. Marks. 1990. *Measuring Sustainable Economic Welfare: A Pilot Index, 1950–1990.* Stockholm: Stockholm Environment Institute.

Jaeger, W. 1995. "Is Sustainability Optimal? Examining the Differences Between Economists and Environmentalists." *Ecological Economics* 15: 43–57.

James, D., P. Nijkamp, and J. Opschoor. 1989. "Ecological Sustainability and Economic Development." In *Economy and Ecology: Towards Sustainable Development,* ed. F. Archibugi and P. Nijkamp. Dordrecht, Netherlands: Kluwer Academic Publishers.

Malthus, T. 1960. *An Essay on the Principle of Population, as It Affects the Future Improvements of Society. With Remarks on the Speculations of Mr. Godwin, M. Condorcet, and Other Writers* (1798), complete 1st ed. and partial 7th ed. (1872). Reprinted in *On Population,* ed. G. Himmelfarb. New York: Modern Library.

Moffatt, I., N. Hanley, and J. Gill. 1994. "Measuring and Assessing Indicators of Sustainable Development for Scotland: A Pilot Survey." *International Journal of Sustainable Development and World Ecology* 1: 170–77.

Munn, R. 1989. "Towards Sustainable Development: An Environmental Perspective." In *Economy and Ecology: Towards Sustainable Development,* ed. F. Archibugi and P. Nijkamp. Dordrecht, Netherlands: Kluwer Academic Publishers.

National Research Council. 1999. *Nature's Numbers: Expanding the National Economic Accounts to Include the Environment,* ed. W. Nordhaus and E. Kokkelenberg. Washington, DC: National Academy of Sciences.

Opschoor, J. 1996. "Institutional Change and Development Towards Sustainability." In *Getting Down to Earth: Practical Applications of Ecological Economics,* ed. R. Costanza, O. Segura, and J. Martinez-Alier. Washington, DC: Island Press.

Ostrom, Elinor. 1990. *Governing the Commons: The Evolution of Institutions for Collective Action.* Cambridge: Cambridge University Press.

Pearce, D. 1994. "Reflections on Sustainable Development." Paper presented at the European Association of Environmental and Resource Economists, Dublin.

Pearce, D., N. Adger, D. Maddison, and D. Moran. 1995. "Debt and the Environment." *Scientific American* 272 (June): 52–56.

Pearce, D., and G. Atkinson. 1993. "Capital Theory and the Measurement of Sustainable Development: An Indicator of Weak Sustainability." *Ecological Economics* 8: 103–8.

Pearce, D., E. Barbier, and A. Markandya. 1990. *Sustainable Development: Economics and Environment in the Third World.* London: Edward Elgar.

Pearce, D., K. Hamilton, and G. Atkinson. 1996. "Measuring Sustainable Development: Progress on Indicators." *Environment and Development Economics* 1 (February): 85–102.

Pearce, D., A. Markandya, and E. Barbier. 1989. *Blueprint for a Green Economy.* London: Earthscan.

Pearce, D., and J. Warford. 1993. *World Without End: Economics, Environment, and Sustainable Development.* Oxford: Oxford University Press.

Perrings, C. 1987. *Economy and the Environment: A Theoretical Essay on the Interdependence of Economic and Environmental Systems.* New York: Cambridge University Press.

Reed, D. 1992. *Structural Adjustment and the Environment.* Boulder, CO: Westview Press, World Wide Fund for Nature.

Rees, W., and M. Wackernagel. 1994. "Ecological Footprints and Appropriated Carrying Capacity: Measuring the Natural Capital Requirements of the Human Economy." In *Investing in Natural Capital: The Ecological Economics Approach to Sustainability,* ed. A. Jansson and R. Costanza. Washington, DC: Island Press.

Repetto, R. 1986. *World Enough and Time.* New Haven: Yale University Press.

Ricardo, D. 1951. *Principles of Political Economy and Taxation.* Sraffa edition. Cambridge: Cambridge University Press.

Rich, Bruce. 1994. *Mortgaging the Earth: The World Bank, Environmental Impoverishment, and the Crisis of Development.* Boston: Beacon Press.

Select Committee on International Development, UK Parliament. 2001. "Itaipu Hydroelectric Project, Brazil, Recent Cases of Corruption Involving UK Companies and UK-Backed International Financial Institutions—Appendices to the Minutes of Evidence." http://www.parliament.the-stationery-office.co.uk/pa/cm200001/cmselect/cmintdev/39/39ap06.htm

Simon, J. 1981. *The Ultimate Resource.* Princeton: Princeton University Press.

Simon, J., and H. Kahn. 1984. *Resourceful Earth.* Oxford: Basil Blackwell.

Solow, R. 1974."Intergenerational Equity and Exhaustible Resources." *Review of Economic Studies* (symposium): 29–45.

———. 1992. "An Almost Practical Step Toward Sustainability. Resources for the Future Invited Lecture. Washington, DC.

Turner, R., and D. Pearce. 1993. "Sustainable Economic Development: Economic and Ethical Principles." In *Economics and Ecology: New Frontiers and Sustainable Development,* ed. E. Barbier. London: Chapman and Hall.

United Nations Development Program. 2003. *Human Development Report 2003.* New York: Oxford University Press.

Venetoulis, J., D. Chazan, and C. Gaudet. 2004. *Ecological Footprint of Nations 2004.* Available at www.rprogress.org/newpubs/2004/footprintnations2004.pdf

Venetoulis, J., and C. Cobb. 2004. *The Genuine Progress Indicator 1950–2002 (2004 Update).* Available at www.rprogress.org/newpubs/2004/gpi_march2004update.pdf.

Victor, P. 1991. "Indicators of Sustainable Development: Some Lessons from Capital Theory." *Ecological Economics* 4: 191–213.

Vitousek, P., P. Ehrlich, and P. Matson. 1986. "Human Appropriation of the Products of Photosynthesis." *Bioscience* 36: 368–73.

Wackernagel, M., and W. Rees. 1997. "Perceptual and Structural Barriers to Investing in Natural Capital: Economics from an Ecological Footprint Perspective." *Ecological Economics* 20 (1): 3–24.

Wackernagel, M., S. White, and D. Moran. 2004. "Using Ecological Footprint Accounts: From Analysis to Applications." *International Journal of Environment and Sustainable Development* 3: 293–315.

Walter, G., and O. Wilkerson. 1994. "Information Strategies for State-of-Environment and State-of-Sustainability Reporting." *International Journal of Sustainable Development and World Ecology* 1: 153–69.

World Bank Portfolio Management Task Force. 1992. *Effective Implementation: Key to Development Impact.* Report, Washington, DC: World Bank.

World Bank. 1986 *Commodity Trade and Price Trends*. New York: Oxford University Press.

————— 1991. *World Development Report*. New York: Oxford University Press.

————— 1992. *World Development Report*. New York: Oxford University Press.

————— 1995. *Monitoring Environmental Progress: A Report on Work in Progress*. Washington, DC: World Bank.

World Commission on Environment and Development. 1987. *Our Common Future*. Oxford: Oxford University Press.

15

Issues in Sustainable Production and Consumption

Introduction

The role of production and consumption in sustainable development was a major issue discussed during the UN Conference on Environment and Development (more commonly known as the Earth Summit) held in Rio de Janeiro in 1992. Two important documents emerged from the Earth Summit. One of these, the Rio Declaration on Environment and Development (more commonly known as the Earth Charter) represents a statement of twenty-seven principles of sustainable development. Principle 8 of the Earth Charter addresses sustainable production and consumption: "To achieve sustainable development and a higher quality of life for all people, States should reduce and eliminate unsustainable patterns of production and consumption and promote appropriate demographic policies." *Agenda 21* is the other document that came out of the Earth Summit, and is a forty-chapter action blueprint on specific issues relating to sustainable development. Chapter 4 of *Agenda 21* is addressed to the subject of sustainable production and consumption. For example, section 4.3 of *Agenda 21* states that "the major cause of the continued deterioration of the global environment is the unsustainable pattern of consumption and production, particularly in industrialized countries, which is a matter of grave concern, aggravating poverty and imbalances." Accordingly, chapter 4 of *Agenda 21* states that action is needed to meet the following broad objectives:

- to promote patterns of consumption and production that reduce environmental stress and will meet the basic needs of humanity;

- to develop a better understanding of the role of consumption and how to bring about more sustainable consumption patterns.

Agenda 21 calls on industrialized countries to take the lead in developing sustainable production technologies and consumption policies, and to help in disseminating them among lower-income countries. These technologies and policies must be demonstrated to be resource-efficient, less polluting, affordable, feasible, and attractive. Moreover, these technologies and policies should not hinder the development efforts of lower-income countries.

There are several challenges associated with sustainable production and consumption. One challenge is that the capital costs of implementing cleaner production technologies often put these methods beyond the reach of low-income countries. The lack of social and political empowerment, the existence of fossil-energy subsidies, and pressures to export resources abroad in order to repay development loans have all reinforced problems of unsustainable production in the developing world. Another challenge in the industrialized world is the disconnect between product design and packaging on the one hand, which is driven by consumer preferences for convenience and styling, and the imperatives from sustainability to reduce waste, promote reuse, and reduce the cost of materials recycling on the other. High-income countries consume a disproportionate amount of the world's resources and are responsible for emitting a disproportionate share of the world's air pollution, toxic wastes, and trash. Market systems that are largely responsible for generating the wealth and cleaner production technologies enjoyed by high-income countries also reinforce the consumer culture and the problems associated with unsustainable consumption in the industrialized world. Our ways of production and consumption are embedded in our culture, which means that moving onto a path of more sustainable production and consumption requires a cultural change. Moreover, the value of most of our capital assets and infrastructure—homes, factories, roads and highways, layout of towns and cities, facilities for generating electric power, and modes of transport—are themselves dependent upon current ways of production and consumption.

Amory Lovins of the Rocky Mountain Institute has popularized the notion that there is a strong *path-dependence* aspect to investments in homes, factories, roads and highways, the layout of towns and cities, facilities for generating electric power, and modes of transport. Once started on a particular path, it becomes difficult to change. This commitment occurs for a number of reasons:

1. Once made, infrastructure investment (highways, water/sewer/power lines) is "sunk" into place, representing a substantial financial com-

mitment to the existing way of doing things, and making jobs and the economy itself dependent on existing methods.

2. Private R&D investment is more likely to be directed toward the security of existing systems than toward speculative alternatives, which reduces the cost of existing systems and makes them more difficult to dislodge.

3. As a technology diffuses through the economy, it becomes possible to produce at larger and larger scale. *Scale economies* (the drop in unit costs as scale or size of operation grows) develop in the chosen technology that put alternatives at a cost disadvantage.

4. The existing system becomes a standard upon which people come to rely when they make complementary investments. For example, the primacy of automobiles and extensive road networks as the transportation standard results in suburban sprawl. Those with investments contingent on a particular path (e.g., owners of suburban housing) have a strong economic stake in status quo policies such as subsidies for roads and petroleum.

Hart (2005) provides a useful analysis of automobile-centered transportation planning. She notes that while the population of the United States increased by about 17 percent between 1982 and 1997, the amount of land converted for urban development in that period increased by 47 percent. Public subsidies for gasoline (see chapter 13) and publicly funded road infrastructure encourage the use of private automobiles over public transit, and results in demand for low-density suburban and exurban automobile-dependent development. The United States Environmental Protection Agency (U.S. EPA 2001) reported that between 1980 and 1997, vehicle miles traveled (VMT) in the United States increased by 63 percent, a growth rate almost three times more rapid than population growth during the same period. A 1990 National Personal Transportation Survey (NPTS) cited in that EPA study found that 64 percent of the observed increase in VMT was attributable to increases in the number and average distance of automobile trips. Moreover, the 1995 NPTS found that from 1983 to 1995, the average length of work trips increased by 36 percent (from 8.5 to 11.6 miles), reflecting the fact that jobs and housing have become increasingly segregated from one another in recent years. From an economic standpoint, investment in highway capacity induces additional demand for automobile travel by temporarily reducing travel time and costs. Urban design that emphasizes the automobile, such as large surface parking lots, wide streets, and a lack of safe pedestrian or bicycle routes, makes automobile use more comfortable and safer than walking or bicycling, even for short trips.

Thus, we can see that there is also a problem with the political and so-cial feasibility of new and more sustainable approaches that is linked to the problem of path dependence. People who have made financial investments and life-style commitments to the existing pattern of the built environment are likely to join with automobile manufacturers and petroleum companies in supporting status quo policy in the United States. To be politically fea-sible, sustainable production technology must create profit opportunities for firms in order to create a supportive economic interest group. More sustainable products must provide approximately similar service quality as existing goods and not be too much more expensive, in order to gain con-sumer support. This is why there is so much interest in developing fuel-cell automobiles. Perhaps most important to the success of more sustainable production and consumption is for people to become convinced that exist-ing systems are destructive, that a change is warranted, and that they act on those convictions. Once this change begins, growth in markets for more sustainable technologies and products will allow for cost-reducing econo-mies of scale in production and also provide an incentive for cost-reducing research and development.

The discussion below will address some renewable energy resources and technologies. As the price of oil, natural gas, and other fossil-fuel energy resources increases, so too does the economic viability of the renewable, solar-based resources and technologies described below. Recall from chap-ter 4 that the imposition of Pigouvian taxes on fossil-fuel energy resources, or the provision of subsidies for renewables, also helps promote these alter-natives. Many Western European countries lead the way in the deployment of renewable energy resources and technologies due to their use of carbon taxes and various renewable energy subsidies.

More Sustainable Energy Resources, Technologies, and Processes

Solar Energy

Daly and Cobb (1989) have argued that low-entropy matter–energy (energy that is available for useful work) is the ultimate resource for human enterprise. Further, they state, "the feature of the industrial revolution whose implications are insufficiently appreciated is the shift to fossil-fuel energy and mineral ma-terials. This is a shift from harvesting the surface of the earth to mining the subsurface" (p. 11). Solar energy drives the earth's hydrological cycle, climate system, and photosynthetic process, which people have harvested in the form of water power, wind power, and wood/biomass fuel. Georgescu-Roegen (1971) referred to this transformation as a shift from dependence on energy currently coming from the sun to stored energy on the earth. Daly and Cobb point out that while solar energy is unlimited in stock, the flow that arrives on earth is strictly limited. In contrast, fossil fuels are strictly limited in stock but are relatively unlimited in available flow. Thus, the industrial revolution shifted the emphasis from low-intensity but abundant solar energy to high-intensity but more scarce terrestrially based fossil fuels.

Movement to a sustainable society will likely require a shift back to a greater reliance on solar energy in our economy. As Hoagland (1995) has pointed out, every year the earth's surface receives about ten times as much energy from the sun as is available from the total stock of the known reserves of natural gas, oil, coal, and uranium combined. This flow of solar energy is 15,000 times greater than current levels of energy consumption by humans. The first patent for a solar-powered motor was granted to Augustin Mouchot in 1861, but cheap and readily available fossil fuels stunted the development of solar energy technologies until a brief period in the late 1970s following the Organization of Petroleum Exporting Countries (OPEC) oil crisis. Yet by 2025, worldwide demand for electricity is forecast to rise by 265 percent. Hoagland estimates that solar energy could provide 60 percent of this electricity. A few of these renewable, solar-based electric energy resources, or the technologies developed to harness them, are listed below.

Biomass: According to the World Energy Council (www.worldenergy.org), biomass resources are potentially the world's largest and most sustainable energy source, though these resources are also relatively poorly documented. Sources include trees and other woody matter, agricultural products and by-products, and municipal solid waste. The World Energy Council reported in 2005 that there are millions of acres of dedicated energy plantations in countries such as in Brazil, China, Sweden, and the United States, where eucalyptus, willow, and other species are combusted for the generation of heat and power. Biomass is both a modern and a traditional fuel. In rural areas of lower-income countries, annual biomass consumption is estimated to be approximately 1 metric ton per person, with about one-half this level of consumption occurring in more urban settings. Sustainable energy-crop resource management and deployment of technology to limit air pollution are key policy issues. Agricultural and forestry wastes are currently the main sources of biomass energy. The United Nations estimated in 1992 that biomass could supply 55 percent of the world's energy needs, but the water-intensive nature of photosynthetic processes will limit the production of biomass in arid environments. Biomass fuels can be used in conjunction with intermittent sources (wind, photovoltaic) to maintain minimum steady energy ("baseload") supply.

Hydroelectric: The World Energy Council reports that hydropower accounts for 19 percent of the world's electricity supply, and estimates that about one-third of its economically exploitable potential has been developed. Hydroelectric power is created by channeling water through turbines. Large-scale hydroelectric development usually involves creating proportionately large dams and reservoirs that displace human and natural communities, and impact water quality and natural sediment transport in ways that can result in further displacements downstream. Hydroelectric facilities can be used to meet both peak-load demand and to offset more intermittent electricity sources, thus improving system reliability.

Hydrogen Fuel Cells: Hydrogen can be used to store solar energy for use in various energy applications including powering vehicles, and running turbines or fuel cells to produce electricity. For example, an intermittent wind turbine or solar photovoltaic system can be used to generate electricity necessary to remove hydrogen from water through electrolysis. The hydrogen can then be stored for later use in a fuel cell. Other ready sources of hydrogen include gaseous hydrocarbons such as methane or natural gas. A fuel cell directly converts chemical energy into electricity by combining the stored hydrogen with oxygen from the air. A common form of fuel cell consists of an electrolyte and two catalyst-coated electrodes (a porous anode and cathode) separated by a proton-exchange membrane (PEM). The PEM is derived from a thin, fluorocarbon-based (or hydrocarbon-based) polymer that serves as both the electrolyte and as a barrier to keep the hydrogen and oxygen separate. Each electrode is coated on one side with a catalyst such as platinum. Electricity is produced when the anode catalyst splits the incoming hydrogen into electrons and protons. The electrons flow through an external circuit to provide power to a drive motor. The hydrogen protons pass through the membrane to the cathode, where the catalyst causes them to combine with oxygen from the air and returning electrons to form water and heat, the only waste products from the process. Despite tens of billions of dollars in research and development since the 1990s, as of 2005 fuel cells are not commercially viable except in a few highly specialized applications. After considerable technical advance, most major automobile manufacturers have developed prototype fuel-cell vehicles. Nevertheless, commercial viability will require higher gasoline prices, the development of a hydrogen production and distribution system, and additional advances in onboard hydrogen storage, fuel-cell durability, and reductions in fuel-cell costs. In his survey of the state of the fuel-cell technology, Ashley (2005) cites various sources as indicating that commercial viability is unlikely to occur before 2015 at the earliest.

Methane: Methane is generated from animal and human wastes, biomass, and from municipal solid waste. Dairy and swine operations can produce large quantities of fecal matter that must be stored in lined ponds in order to protect surface and groundwater supplies from contamination. Animal feces and other biological waste sources contain volatile solids that are transformed by anaerobic bacteria into biogas that consists of methane (50–80 percent), carbon dioxide (20–50 percent), and trace levels of other gases such as hydrogen, carbon monoxide, nitrogen, oxygen, and hydrogen sulfide. The relative percentage of these gases in biogas depends on the feed material and management of the process. Some form of scrubbing is necessary in internal combustion applications to remove highly corrosive hydrogen sulfide, and commercialization of biogas may require scrubbing out carbon dioxide. Anaerobic digester systems include a pre-mixing area or tank, one or more digester vessels, a system for gathering the biogas, and a system for distributing or spreading the effluent (the remaining digested material), which can be a valuable fertilizer. Anaerobic bacteria thrive best at temperatures between 98 and 130 degrees Fahrenheit, and so some form of temperature control may be needed to maintain digester productivity. From an economic standpoint, the U.S. Department of Energy reports that when costs are high for sewage, agricultural, or animal waste disposal, and when the digester effluent has economic value, anaerobic digestion and biogas production can be profitable, as well as limit emissions of methane, a potent greenhouse gas (see chapter 11).

Ocean Tides, Waves, and Ocean Thermal Energy Conversion: According to the California Energy Commission, the three most promising ocean-related energy technologies are tidal power, wave power, and ocean thermal energy conversion. Wave energy is a potentially enormous resource in many areas around the world. Wave energy conversion technology is not currently commercially viable, though the prospects are promising. Extracting commercially valuable energy from ocean tides requires large tidal differences. For example, the Bay of Fundy in eastern Canada has a very large tidal difference, and this ocean energy resource is being harnessed at the Annapolis Tidal Generating Station, which feeds power directly into the Nova Scotia Power Corporation's utility system. Ocean thermal energy conversion makes use of the difference in temperature between warm surface water of the ocean and the cold water in depths below 2,000 feet to generate electricity. As long as a sufficient temperature difference (about 40 degrees Fahrenheit) exists between the warm upper layer of water and the cold deep water, net power can be generated. Ocean thermal energy conversion has been done in Hawaii, though as of 2005 the cost of producing electricity from this system exceeded that from conventional fossil-fuel sources.

Solar Dish-Engine Systems: Research at locations such as the Sandia National Laboratory in New Mexico is being directed at designing systems to convert solar energy into electricity by way of dish collectors and Stirling heat engines. The dish is used to collect and concentrate solar energy, which is converted into thermal energy and fed into the Stirling heat engine. The Stirling engine uses heat to move pistons and create mechanical power in a manner similar to that of internal combustion engines. This mechanical power is then used to generate electricity. According to information produced by Sandia Lab, solar dish-engine systems are being developed for use in emerging global markets for distributed generation, to produce certified "green power" for states with renewable portfolio standards (see chapter 10), to generate power in remote locations, and for grid-connected applications. Due to their high efficiency and conventional construction, the cost of dish-engine systems is expected to become price competitive with other energy systems.

Solar Ovens: Advocates of solar ovens see this simple technology as a remedy for deforestation that is induced by household demand for fuelwood. According to the World Energy Council, most of the world's fuelwood consumption occurs in Africa and Asia, and in those regions, most of that fuelwood consumption is for cooking and related household uses. For example, they report that more than 86 percent of total fuelwood consumption in Africa in 1994 was attributed to the household sector. Moreover, they estimate that 90 to 98 percent of all household energy needs are met with fuelwood in sub-Saharan Africa. According to the World Resources Institute (1994), about 2 billion of the world's poorest people rely solely on fuelwood as their energy source for heating and cooking. Various sources (e.g., Nandwani 1996; World Resources Institute 1994) indicate that the rate of fuelwood consumption in many areas exceeds the rate of reforestation and regeneration. In many areas of western and sub-Saharan Africa, for example, fuelwood consumption is running 30 to 200 percent ahead of the average increase in the stock of trees. High rates of sunshine in these same areas make solar oven technology a possible substitute for fuelwood. Various relatively inexpensive solar oven designs have been developed, some as simple as cardboard and aluminum foil. In order for solar ovens to be accepted by households in low-income regions of the world that are dependent on fuelwood, substantial training and continuing promotion and social support are necessary. While even the modest cost of a solar oven may be quite high for people living on the equivalent of $1 or less per day, the increasing scarcity of fuelwood is driving up the price that rural people must pay. Fuelwood expenditures account for perhaps as much as 25 percent of average household budgets in places such as rural China and Zimbabwe. Thus as Grupp (1996) argues, the availability of microloans for families to buy solar ovens may be critical, since the fuelwood savings can be used to repay the loans. Key limitations of solar ovens include the less than full reliability of the technology, due to the inability to store energy for cloudy days, and the longer cooking times required. Despite these limitations, Nandwani reports that about 525,000 solar ovens are in use around the world. Solar ovens are well suited as supplemental cooking devices and gaining acceptability in places such as Central America, India, Cuba, and parts of Africa.

Solar Photovoltaics: These systems directly convert sunlight into electricity with semiconducting materials such as crystalline silicon. The balance-of-system components include everything in a photovoltaic system other than the photovoltaic modules, such as mounting structures, tracking devices, off-grid storage batteries, power electronics (including an inverter, a charge controller, and a grid interconnection), and other devices. According to the International Energy Agency (IEA), by the end of 2003 a cumulative total of 1,809 megawatts (MW) of solar photovoltaic capacity had been installed worldwide. The top three countries accounting for about 85 percent of the world's installed solar photovoltaic capacity are Japan (859.6 MW), Germany (410.3 MW), and the United States (275.2 MW). Most new capacity in countries with subsidy programs is grid-interconnected, while in unsubsidized areas most new capacity is off-grid. As of 2005, photovoltaic systems are not price-competitive with most conventional grid-based electricity sources. In some off-the-grid locations a quarter-mile or more from power lines, stand-alone photovoltaic systems can be more cost-effective than extending power lines. Solar photovoltaic systems are also used in remote, environmentally sensitive areas such as national parks. Some state and national governments provide subsidies and tax rebate incentives in order to bridge the gap between the cost of photovoltaic technology and the cost of conventional grid-sourced electricity. Like wind, photovoltaic electricity is intermittent, and storage is costly, implying that photovoltaic electricity must be augmented with electricity from other sources in order to support baseload requirements.

Wind: About 0.25 percent of the sun's energy is transformed into lower-atmosphere wind, and areas that have average winds of more than 7.5 meters per second can generate electricity from wind farms for about 4.5 to 5 cents per kilowatt-hour (kWh). The implication is that in areas with sufficient wind resource, wind-generated electricity is at or near being price-competitive with fossil fuel and other conventional generation sources. The IEA reported that as of 2001, 86 percent of the world's installed wind capacity was located in just four countries—Denmark, Germany, Spain, and the United States. According to the Global Wind Energy Council (www.gwec.net), new wind power capacity installed in 2004 totaled 7,976 MW, a 20 percent increase over 2003. Total worldwide wind power capacity in 2005 was 47,317 MW. The top five countries with the largest total installed wind power capacity in 2005 were Germany (16,629 MW), Spain (8,263 MW), the United States

(6,740 MW), Denmark (3,117 MW), and India (3,000 MW). Installed capacity growth in the United States has been lagging in recent years due to uncertainty about the federal government's commitment to the production tax credit. Newer turbine design and better site selection have helped reduce bird and bat mortality associated with wind power. Offshore sites have also helped reduce visual impacts. Wind energy is intermittent, however, and storage is costly, implying that from a practical standpoint wind power must be augmented with electricity from other sources in order to support baseload requirements.

Industrial Ecology

While referring to something (or someone) as being "linear" is a popular disparaging remark, a central facet of industrial ecology is transforming linear production processes to ones that more closely mimic the circular processes in natural ecosystems. Hawken (1994) has used the phrase "waste equals food" to refer to the cyclicity of natural systems, where nothing, or almost nothing, that is produced by one organism as waste is not a source of food or useful material for another. In contrast, traditional production methods are linear in the sense that they produce waste materials that cannot readily be assimilated as inputs in some other productive process. The environmental and energy complementarities across production facilities that serve as the foundation of industrial ecology can be realized by way of a collaborative planning, site design, and business management approach referred to as eco-industrial parks. As the Smart Communities Network (www.sustainable .doe.gov/business/ecoparks.shtml) notes, eco-industrial parks use of ecological design to foster collaboration among firms in managing environmental and energy issues. In an eco-industrial park, each firm's production requirements and processes are coordinated so that production residuals from one firm become valuable inputs for another, following the cyclical "waste = food" principle of natural systems. From a managerial standpoint, eco-industrial parks enhance opportunities for collaboration on innovation and technological development, access to new markets, strategic planning, and financing. As with conventional industrial parks, site design allows firms to exploit cost-savings through the sharing of park infrastructure and a more streamlined permit process.

A good example of a renewable energy project that incorporates industrial ecology and eco-industrial park elements is provided by the winning project in the 2005 National Hydrogen Association Student Design Competition. Humboldt State University students designed the Evolution Energy Systems hydrogen power park to be located in the city of Eureka on the northwestern coast of California. The power park will be capable of providing about 442 kilowatts (kW) of electric power and 132 kW of thermal power as hot water to new businesses along the Eureka waterfront. In addition, the power park will be capable of producing 10.5 kg/hr of gaseous hydrogen for use as vehicle fuel. The industrial ecology element of the design involves the use of methane emitted from decomposition of municipal solid waste from a local landfill as feedstock to produce the energy and hydrogen at the power park. Landfill gas is considered an eligible renewable energy source in the Renewable Portfolio Standard of twelve states, including California (see chapter 10). The plan calls for the landfill gas to be scrubbed and then transmitted through the Pacific Gas and Electric (PG&E) natural gas pipeline system to the power park. One barrier that would have to be overcome is that PG&E does not allow third parties to inject gas into their pipelines. The team hopes to change that policy if this project moves forward. The gas will be internally reformed into hydrogen and carbon dioxide within two 250 kW fuel cells. The overall net efficiency of the power park will be an estimated 65.5 percent, which compares favorably to the approximately 33 percent average efficiency of electric power–generating facilities operating in the United States. The price of the electricity produced by the power park is $0.075/kwh, the price of heat produced by the power park is $0.60/therm, and the price of vehicle-grade hydrogen fuel produced by the power park is estimated to be $2.50/kg. Evolution Energy Systems' Eureka Power Park will reduce CO_2/kWh emissions by an estimated 40 percent relative to California grid electricity generation, not counting the emissions avoided through cogenerated heat and the use of hydrogen-fueled vehicles.

One well-known example of a large-scale implementation of industrial ecology is in Kalundborg, Denmark, where an oil refinery, an aquaculture facility, a greenhouse, and residential homes employ waste heat from a power plant. Both a chemical company and a wallboard producer utilize the sulfur waste from the petroleum-refining process. The wallboard producer uses the sulfur waste as a substitute for gypsum. Considine (2001) argues, however, that profitable waste exchange possibilities can remain unexploited for years due to high transaction costs from technical, regulatory, legal, and organizational constraints. Another source of inefficiency is information asymmetries. As an example of an information asymmetry that forms a barrier to the application of industrial ecology, Considine reports that firms typically do not know the quantity and quality of waste streams of other companies, or even of other divisions within a large corporation. Engineers and managers can overcome these information asymmetries and find ways to reduce transaction costs if they have the proper incentives. As an example of the importance of incentives, Considine reports that International Business Machines

(IBM) achieved substantial reductions in the concentrations of heavy metals in their water effluents from their disk plants when they included environmental performance measures in their annual performance reviews of production line engineers.

There is a growing interest in product *life cycle analysis* (LCA), which allows firms, consumers, activists, and policymakers to evaluate the environmental impacts of different products. In the first stage of LCA, a researcher creates an inventory of the energy and various material inputs involved with production, distribution, use, and subsequent reuse, recycling, or disposal. Typically, LCA inventories ignore "second generation" impacts, such as the energy required to fire the bricks used to build the kilns used to manufacture the raw material. The second stage of LCA is life cycle assessment. This stage is more difficult, since it requires the analyst to interpret data and evaluate trade-offs. For example, is it better to use a product that uses less energy, or that uses less water? Is it better to use plastic products that are derived from environmentally harmful and nonrenewable oil, or to use renewable wood products that may come from timber harvesting that creates other environmental harms? LCA might be conducted by a firm or an industry group to enable it to identify areas where cost-saving improvements can be made, or to provide an objective foundation to claims that their product is environmentally superior to competing products. Alternatively, the LCA may be intended to provide objective environmental information for environmental advocates, for the general public, or for government.

One interesting example of life cycle analysis was conducted by the Dutch Environment Ministry regarding the environmental friendliness of reusable porcelain coffee cups, disposable paper cups, and disposable Styrofoam cups. The life cycle analysis included extraction and processing of raw materials, production of the cups, and final disposal. The analysis took into account energy use at each stage as well as consumption of natural resources, hazardous materials by-products, and volume of waste. The biggest problem with reusable coffee cups is the water and energy required to clean them. The report indicated that washing a porcelain cup and saucer once, in an average dishwasher, has a greater impact on water resources than either a paper cup or a Styrofoam cup. In contrast, porcelain cups have less impact on air, energy consumption, and volume of trash. If a reusable coffee cup is used twice before being washed, then it becomes energy-efficient relative to Styrofoam cups after 114 uses, and takes less than 100 uses to be energy-efficient relative to paper. Even fewer reuses are required for the reusable mug to be more air pollution efficient and landfill volume efficient. An interesting finding of the study is that more attention needs to be given to energy requirements of dishwashers and to the environmental impacts of detergents (1992, p. 58).

Policies Promoting Sustainable Production and Consumption

Market forces will eventually provide very powerful incentives for cleaner and less resource-intensive methods of production and consumption as price responds to growing resource scarcity and mounting environmental degradation. The problem is that this sort of sudden and reactive change in the way people live could come too late, involve sudden transitions that are costly and painful, and lead to an irreversibly damaged environment. Interventions in the form of regulations, taxes, subsidies, and direct funding of clean technology research and development are necessary in order to prevent potentially even greater problems in the future caused by our inaction.

Extended Producer Responsibility (EPR)

Traditionally, manufacturers are only responsible for their immediate pollution and waste emissions, while end-users and municipal governments are responsible for reuse, recycling, and disposal of wastes. Extended producer responsibility (EPR) is a policy tool in which producers are required to be financially or physically responsible for their products after their useful life. Because the product design, manufacturing, marketing, distribution, and retail sales functions are economically separated from downstream reuse, recycling, and disposal costs, product and packaging design does not usually reflect downstream recycling and disposal costs. EPR is a policy strategy that is designed to shift the downstream costs of disassembly, recycling, or disposal onto the upstream producer. While costs are shifted, which makes EPR policy difficult to implement, more importantly costs can be reduced when profit-maximizing firms redesign their products and packaging to enhance profitability by reducing costs. This incentive to design for the environment is a key environmental economic benefit of EPR.

As Hanisch (2000) observes, EPR programs are rapidly growing in popularity among European and some Asian countries. Peter Lindhqvist developed the EPR concept at the Swedish Ministry of the Environment in 1990. According to Environment Canada, the core objectives of EPR are to (i) internalize downstream costs into the price of the product, (ii) reduce or divert waste and focus on increased reuse or recycling, and (iii) design for the environment. EPR requires that producers either take back waste products and packaging and manage them through reuse, recycling, or remanufacturing, or contract for this responsibility with a third party, known as a producer responsibility organization (PRO). EPR policies have been implemented by a variety of governments around the world, including Canada, some states in the United States, Taiwan, South Korea, and Japan. In 2001 the state of New

South Wales in Australia created legislation allowing for EPR to be implemented. Product stewardship is a concept that is closely related to EPR, and tends to be voluntary in nature. Examples of product stewardship projects in the United States include batteries, carpeting, computers, and other electronics. Examples of EPR policies include the following:

Green Dot: Germany initiated an ambitious take-back program in 1991 with the German Packaging Ordinance. As Hanisch (2000) reports, under the German Packaging Ordinance, producers of all kinds of packaged products are required to either individually take back their packaging or join the Duales System Deutschland (DSD), an industry organization for packaging waste. DSD charges a fee to license its Green Dot label to firms, and the licensing agreement allows firms to print the green dot on their packaging. Consumers can then dispose of green dot wastes in the DSD disposal system. Moore and Miller (1994) report that by 1993, 400 randomly surveyed German companies "had completely abandoned the use of polyvinyl packaging, plastic foams, and 117 other types of packaging" (p. 36). Between 1991 and 1998, the per capita consumption of packaging in Germany was reduced from 94.7 kg to 82 kg, a reduction of 13.4 percent. As of 1999, the ordinance requires that 60 percent of plastic packaging must be recycled. In 1998 the cost per ton for waste management in Germany was $360.80. The costs for the Green Dot program have been significantly reduced over recent years. In comparison to 1998, the license fee that companies from the industrial and commercial sectors paid for using the Green Dot on their packaging had fallen by an average of 23 percent. According to a study performed by the Gesellschaft für Konsumforschung (GfK) in May 1998, 94 percent of all Germans separate their waste. In their opinion, recycling is by far the best way of handling waste. In a GfK survey carried out in March 1999, more than three-quarters of the people questioned (77 percent) were in favor of collecting and recycling waste. In contrast, very low acceptance figures were recorded for waste incineration (17 percent) and landfilling (4 percent). Systems based on the German Dual System model have also been set up in Austria, Belgium, Czech Republic, France, Great Britain, Greece, Hungary, Ireland, Latvia, Luxembourg, Norway, Poland, Portugal, Spain, and Turkey. Work is currently ongoing to develop an environment-oriented product policy within the European Union (EU).

Ecocycle Society: Sweden has committed to the creation of an "ecocycle society" in which producers are responsible for life-cycle wastes associated with the goods that they make and for maximizing energy and materials efficiencies. According to the United Nations Commission on Sustainable Development, the Ecocycle Bill was passed in 1993 to reduce the environmental impacts of goods, particularly by reducing waste and promoting the recycling and reuse of goods at the manufacturing stage. Sweden's Ecocycle Commission has responsibility for defining new energy or environmental wastes that firms are responsible to reduce. The Public Cleansing Act (1979), administered by the Swedish Environmental Protection Agency, implements the legislative framework for a number of ordinances targeted at industry to reduce, reuse, and recycle waste material such as packaging, paper, and tires. The Ordinance on Producer Responsibility for Waste Paper was passed in 1994, and had a collection target of 75 percent for waste paper by the end of the year 2000. According to the Swedish EPA, the waste paper target was attained in 1997, and has increased since then to about 80 percent. The total weight of packaging consumed in Sweden declined by 20 percent during the period between 1991 and 1998 (Hanisch 2000).

Automobile Recycling Nederland: The Dutch created Automobile Recycling Nederland (ARN), which charges a waste disposal fee (45 euros as of 2005) and sets targets for recycling automobiles at end of life. As of 2005, 89 percent of all scrapped automobiles in the Netherlands were recycled, and industry set a goal of recycling 95 percent of all scrapped automobiles by weight by 2007. According to the ARN website (www.arn.nl), the number of different types of materials that car dismantling companies have been required by ARN to dismantle has increased every year. Nevertheless, ARN only requires that materials be dismantled from scrap automobiles if high-quality recycling processes are available for the material in question. Moreover, ARN reports that it conducts research on a continuous basis into what materials are present in scrap cars and whether those materials can be processed now or in the future. When it becomes feasible for new materials to be recycled, the dismantling companies are required to gather those materials.

Ecolabels

Ecolabel programs are designed to promote more sustainable production and consumption by providing an environmental standard for consumer goods. Typically, ecolabel programs set environmental standards (and sometimes labor standards) that exceed those set by law, and are administered by a government agency or a trusted auditing or certifying organization. Third party certification (the term "third party" refers to an entity other than the buyer or the seller) has developed as the most credible method for assuring compliance with meaningful standards because many people do not trust unverifiable claims made by corporations. Firms bear the cost of third party certification and in return can label their product as complying with the ecolabel standard. Ecolabeled goods are perceived by some consumers as being of higher quality than nonlabeled goods. Therefore, firms may find that participation in an ecolabel program increases the demand for their product and differentiates it from nonlabeled rivals.

According to the United Nations Commission on Sustainable Development (UNCSD), as of 1996 there were thirty ecolabel programs operating worldwide (UNCSD website). One of the more prominent examples of ecolabel programs is offered by Germany's Blue Angel program. This program has registered 4,000 products and is the oldest ecolabeling program. According to a study by Papastefanou (1996), the number of ecolabeled products in Germany increased from fewer than 100 in 1979 to over 4,000 in 1994. The number of ecolabeled goods dropped to approximately 3,400 in 1995, approximately the number for 1990. Papastefanou reports that people most open to ecolabeled goods in Germany tend to be middle-aged (38–42), employed part-time or in the home, living in small cities rather than rural or large metro areas, moderately or highly educated, middle or upper class, female, and with children under age six. Other countries are experimenting with ecolabel programs, including Taiwan's, whose Green Leaf program has registered 200 products, as well as Sweden, Norway, Iceland, and Finland, with its Nordic Swan program. In Sweden, the market share of ecolabeled detergents increased from 12 percent in 1992 to 80 percent in 1995. The U.S. EPA manages a number of ecolabel programs, one example of which is the Energy Star program for energy-efficient appliances and office equipment. Common ecolabels in the United States include Energy Star (electronic appliances), Forest Stewardship Council–certified lumber, USDA-certified organic food, and Fair Trade coffee. Recall that the issue of ecolabel programs (particularly those programs that establish standards for processing and production methods in the exporting country) in the context of World Trade Organization rules was discussed in chapter 13.

Factors Relating to the Success of Ecolabel Programs

- Both environmental nongovernmental organizations (NGOs) and industry members play a role in the development of ecolabel standards and support the standards.
- Ecolabel certification is done by "third party" agencies or organizations that consumers can trust and that are subject to periodic audits.
- A substantial number of people are educated about the impacts of their consumer choices on the environment, and perceive ecolabeled goods as being of higher quality than nonlabeled goods.
- Firms can make a profit by producing ecolabeled goods.

Three Examples of Ecolabeled Goods

Certified Sustainable Wood Products: The most credible of these programs utilize "third party" certification procedures. Third party certification involves an organization such as the Forest Stewardship Council (FSC), which establishes guidelines and standards, and accredits other organizations (such as the SmartWood program of the Rainforest Alliance) that certify professional foresters, forestlands, and lumber mills. In order for wood products originating from certified sources to carry the FSC logo, the wood products must be tracked from logging operation to log transport, milling, lumber transport, and the lumberyard in a process known as "chain of custody." Chain of custody assures consumers that the ecolabeled lumber they buy was harvested in a manner consistent with FSC standards. Certified sustainable forestry has spread throughout the world. According to the FSC (www.fsc.org), 50 million hectares in more than sixty countries were certified in accordance with FSC standards between 1995 and 2005. Between 2003 and 2005, the number of FSC chain of custody certificates increased at an annual rate of 25 percent, while the hectares of forest certified to FSC standards doubled. In addition, as of 2005 several thousand products are produced using FSC-certified wood and carrying the FSC trademark, and the size of the global market in FSC-certified products is estimated to be in excess of US$5 billion. FSC operates through its network of National Initiatives in more than thirty-four countries.

Certified Coffee: There are a number of different organizations that are certifying coffee based on environmental and social criteria. For example, the American Birding Association has collaborated with the Thanksgiving Coffee Company to produce Song Bird Coffee, which is certified to come from coffee plants grown in the shade of rain forests that provide habitat to a large number of migratory birds. The advocacy group Global Exchange has developed a "Fair Trade" certification for a variety of products, including coffee. According to their Internet site, to become Fair Trade certified, an importer must meet international criteria, including paying a minimum price per pound of $1.26, providing credit to farmers, and providing technical assistance such as help transitioning to organic farming. Starbucks has recently agreed to provide financial support for shade-grown coffee projects, and to market both shade-grown and Fair Trade coffees.

Organic Foods: According to Scheel (2004), the organic industry (food and nonfood) reached $10.8 billion in consumer sales in 2003. Organic foods, the largest segment of the organic industry, grew 20 percent in 2003, reaching $10.4 billion. Scheel goes on to note that sales of organics increased at an annual rate of between 17 and 21 percent each year since 1997. In contrast, total U.S. food sales increased at a 2 to 4 percent average annual rate.

As the Rodale Institute's New Farm Program (www.newfarm.org) notes, while the concept of organic farming is not new, a common legal definition of "organic" in the United States became effective in 2002 through the U.S. Department of Agriculture (USDA) National Organic Standard (NOS). These standards define how crops and livestock are grown, processed, and handled in the marketplace in order to be sold in the United States as "organic." The NOS is considered the "organic rule" that individual inspectors use to determine compliance by each entity in the organic value chain. While the USDA has responsibility for overseeing the NOS, it is up to inspectors representing third party certifying agents to decide which farms, processors, and handlers meet the USDA's current organic standards. Organic food certification excludes the use of most synthetic pesticides, herbicides, and fertilizers, as well as human sludge and irradiation. Land must have been clear of prohibited substances for at least three years. Organic meats come from animals that have not been given hormones or antibiotics, have been fed organic feeds, and have had access to the outdoors. As of 2000, there were approximately 10,000 U.S. farms that claimed to be organic, 6,600 of which had been approved by one of the 88 different state or private certifying entities. Sales of organic foods in the United States have increased at a rate of approximately 20 percent per year, and sales in 1999 were estimated to be $6.46 billion.

Taxes, Subsidies, and Ecological Tax Reform

Most countries tax productive activities such as work (payroll and income taxes), but implicitly subsidize destructive activities such as pollution and the exhaustion of critical natural resource systems. As was discussed in chapter 13, the notion underlying ecological tax reform is that countries should shift their taxation from productive activities such as work and income generation, and onto pollution and resource exhaustion. This scheme can be revenue-neutral, meaning that total tax revenues to government remain the same. Most important, taxing pollution and resource exhaustion raises the cost of these destructive activities, thereby discouraging them. By reducing taxes on productive things, such a scheme encourages employment and income generation. Sweden and Norway have established tax-shift commissions in their ministries of finance to analyze the problems and implications of shifting to more ecological taxation, according to the UNCSD.

Government Research and Development Funding

Direct, government-financed research and development (R&D) is critical to moving renewable energy technologies toward market viability. In the United

States, substantial increases in alternative energy and energy efficiency R&D occurred in the years following the OPEC- and Iranian-induced oil price shocks in the 1970s. For example, the U.S. Department of Energy's R&D spending on renewable energy R&D, including energy efficiency, was $1.4 billion in 1980. A combination of factors, including the collapse of oil prices and a change in priorities when President Reagan took office in the early 1980s, led to a sharp decline in renewable energy R&D. According to the Energy Information Administration (www.eia.doe.gov), total federal R&D spending on renewable energy in the United States was $327.2 million in 1999.

A study by the European Commission (2004) surveyed both government and private R&D spending on renewable energy in the EU. Total annual EU government spending on renewable energy R&D was estimated in 2001 to be 349.3 million euros, with private and other sectors contributing an additional 340 million euros. More than one-third of the estimated annual 689.3 million euros of total EU R&D investment, and the great majority of business and university R&D spending in the EU, occurred in Germany (where half of the EU's total research personnel are working on renewable energy R&D). Denmark and the Netherlands have the highest ratio of research spending on renewable energy R&D in comparison to their GDP.

International Environmental Certification

There are an increasing number of international voluntary environmental certification programs. One of these has been developed by the International Organization for Standardization (ISO), a worldwide federation of national standards bodies that has been providing voluntary technical, safety, and other standards for manufacturing and other production processes around the world. ISO standards are constructed through a consensus process and are highly regarded internationally. Following the formation of the World Trade Organization (WTO) in the Uruguay Round of the General Agreement on Tariffs and Trade in 1986, which established the principle of regulatory "harmonization," a need was recognized for developing international environmental standards. ISO 14000 represents a series of international standards on environmental management. It provides a framework for the development of an environmental management system and the supporting audit program within firms. According to the ISO (www.iso.org), ISO 14001 is the cornerstone standard of the ISO 14000 series. It specifies a framework of control for an environmental management system against which an organization can be certified by a third party. Other standards in the series are merely guidelines designed to help firms achieve registration to ISO 14001. According to the ISO 14000 website, these other guidelines include the following:

- ISO 14004: provides guidance on the development and implementation of environmental management systems;
- ISO 14010: provides general principles of environmental auditing (now superseded by ISO 19011);
- ISO 14011: provides specific guidance on audit of an environmental management system (now superseded by ISO 19011);
- ISO 14012: provides guidance on qualification criteria for environmental auditors and lead auditors (now superseded by ISO 19011);
- ISO 14013/5: provides audit program review and assessment material;
- ISO 14020+: labeling issues;
- ISO 14030+: provides guidance on performance targets and monitoring within an environmental management system;
- ISO 14040+: covers product life cycle issues.

According to the American Institute for Certified Public Accountants website (www.aicpa.org), environmental management systems help companies satisfy the expectations of a broad range of stakeholders. By way of ISO 14001, environmental management systems can help emphasize the strategic importance of global management, integrate environmental considerations into the decision processes of senior management, and provide an accounting mechanism to relate environmental improvements to increases in shareholder value. In addition, environmental management systems can increase a firm's revenue, reduce its costs, and improve the quality of both products and processes. Importantly, implementation of the ISO 14001 standard can produce environmental performance information that can reduce shareholder exposure to regulatory risk due to noncompliance.

Another emerging voluntary certification system—leadership in energy and environmental design (LEED)—sets performance standards for "green" buildings, and was developed in 2000 by the U.S. Green Building Council. While LEED certification started in the United States, it is spreading to other countries around the world, and there are currently LEED-certified and registered buildings in Australia, Canada, China, Guatemala, India, Japan, Mexico, Puerto Rico, and Sri Lanka. According to the U.S. Green Building Council (www.usgbc.org), LEED certification was created with the following goals in mind:

- to define "green building" by establishing a common standard of measurement;
- to promote integrated, whole-building design practices;
- to recognize environmental leadership in the building industry;
- to stimulate green competition;

• to raise consumer awareness of green building benefits;
• to transform the building market.

The LEED certification system provides performance-based standards for the entire building design (or renovation) process based on five categories: sustainable sites, water efficiency, energy and atmosphere, materials and resources, and indoor environmental quality. Standards range from LEED certified (level 1) to silver (level 2), gold (level 3), and platinum (level 4). While in most cases LEED certification is voluntary, in Portland (Oregon), San Francisco, and Seattle, municipal governments have adopted LEED standards for city buildings. The state of California's Sustainable Building Task Force commissioned a report (Kats 2003) to estimate the benefits and costs of constructing LEED-certified green buildings in California. This study took into account the construction costs of thirty-three LEED-certified buildings in the United States and adjusted these based on the cost of energy, water, and waste disposal in California. Kats found that LEED-certified construction standards increased construction costs over and above those of conventional construction methods. This "green" construction cost premium generally increases with higher levels of LEED certification: 0.66 percent for certified, approximately 2 percent for silver and gold, and 6.5 percent for platinum. The average cost premium for the thirty-three LEED-certified buildings was approximately 2 percent. In contrast, the quantifiable economic benefits of LEED certification—in the form of life-cycle cost savings tied to energy and water efficiency and reduced worker absenteeism and higher productivity—was estimated to be approximately ten times as large as the "green" construction cost premium. The human health and productivity benefits represent the great majority of the quantified total benefits of green buildings, according to the study, but are the most difficult to quantify. These health and productivity benefits were drawn from other studies on the effect of features such as natural lighting and local temperature controls on students and office workers. California recently mandated that all new building construction or renovation projects undertaken with state funds must achieve at least the silver level of LEED certification.

Consumer Preferences and Sustainable Consumption

According to the Worldwatch Institute (2004), while the United States, Canada, and Western Europe account for about 11.6 percent of the world's population, in 2000 they accounted for about 60.2 percent of the world's consumption expenditures. As we learned in chapters 1–3, consumer preferences are a primary component of demand, and thus of what is produced, in market economies. A key characteristic of rich industrialized market econo-mies is the vast array of choices available to consumers. Free-market advo-cates argue that these choices should not be limited through government regulation, and that if consumers want more socially and environmentally friendly products or services, then by exercising those preferences in the marketplace, firms will respond by providing more of those products and services. Advocates of sustainability argue that certain consumer preferences are better than others. For example, that the cause of sustainability will be furthered if people in rich industrialized market economies adopt preferences that result in the consumption of goods and services featuring low material throughput, minimal environmental impact and resource depletion, and sup-porting living wages and humane working conditions. Effective ecolabeling programs can provide the information required to make those choices. Nev-ertheless, ecolabeling programs will not work if consumers lack the prefer-ence for more sustainable life-styles.

The origin of values and preferences is complex. We live in a social con-text where individuals are influenced by cultural trends, including messages from various media, as well as interactions in social networks involving rela-tionships with family, friends, and organizations such as employers, govern-ment bodies, affinity groups, and religious institutions. Sophisticated psychological principles are increasingly being used in designing products and marketing strategies that respond to (or shape) broader cultural trends in order to promote consumption. In fact, we are surrounded by marketing mes-sages promoting an attachment to material goods. Advocates of more sus-tainable consumption have developed various affinity groups for mutual support, and one of these is voluntary simplicity, or simple living. Voluntary simplicity is difficult to define, and can be approached in different ways, but the idea is that a high quality of life is more likely to be attained with less of a materialistic drive to acquire consumer goods, and a greater focus on ful-filling relationships with friends, family, community, and the natural world. A common view among voluntary simplicity advocates is that there is a vi-cious cycle in which the materialistic drive to acquire consumer goods forces people to work long hours and sacrifice personal relationships. Moreover, this sacrificing of personal and other relationships for income creates a void that people attempt to fill, paradoxically, by acquiring more consumer goods. This vicious cycle was termed "affluenza" by de Graaf, Wann, and Naylor (2002) and in several Public Broadcasting System programs co-produced by de Graaf. Key advocates for voluntary simplicity, such as Pierce (2000), ar-gue that to live more simply involves working less, wanting less, and spend-ing less. This life-style is easier to maintain when it is reinforced through social interaction with like-minded people.

Another sustainable consumption movement is focused on food choices. The Worldwatch Institute (2004) notes that humanity devotes about 25 percent of the planet's surface to food production, a scale of ecological change that makes it impossible to separate the way food is produced from the health of rivers, wetlands, forests, and our living environment. For example, about 40 percent of today's world grain production is used to feed meat-producing livestock. Converting these grains into meat and other animal products involves significant loss of energy. It takes about 5 pounds of grain to produce 1 pound of beef, and advocates for a vegetarian diet argue that the environmental impacts of farming could be reduced if people ate less meat. It is argued that these dietary changes could also help alleviate world hunger by making more grains available to the world's poorest people. We have already discussed how organic food certification has made important strides in promoting earth-friendly farming methods, but other aspects of the food system are seen by some as remaining less sustainable. In particular, food activists are interested in promoting diets based on locally produced food. The Worldwatch Institute (2004) reported that in the United States in 2004, the average food item travels 2,500–4,000 kilometers, about 25 percent farther than in 1980. While consumers benefit from unparalleled choices of foods from around the world, these "food-miles" imply that a great deal of fossil fuel used for processing and transportation is embodied in the foods we eat. The local food movement is focused on making food more sustainable by reducing food-miles and promoting the local economy by purchasing food produced by small farms in the local "foodshed." In chapter 16 we will show how to quantify the way in which "buying local" can enhance local economies.

Summary

- The traditional view is that sustainable production is the problem of low-income countries that cannot afford cleaner production technologies, and that sustainable consumption is the problem of high-income, developed countries with the money to consume a vastly disproportionate share of the world's resources. For example, it is estimated that on average each person in the United States consumes the same amount of energy as ten people in developing countries. Practically speaking, however, all countries are confronted with the challenges of sustainable production and consumption.
- More sustainable production and consumption requires that the world's economies shift toward renewable energy resources and technologies. Most of these ultimately derive their energy from the sun, rather than

from fossil fuels. Of these renewable energy sources, wind energy is experiencing rapid growth in installed capacity.

- Policies such as extended producer responsibility, ecolabels, renewable energy subsidies, fuel efficiency standards, and direct funding of renewable energy R&D are consistent with more sustainable production and consumption.
- Japan, the European Union, and the United States are all actively engaged in R&D for renewable energy resources and technologies.
- ISO 14000 provides a voluntary set of standards for implementing environmental management systems in corporations. LEED certification provides standards for green buildings in the United States and around the world.
- The voluntary simplicity movement advocates for more sustainable consumption. Its philosophy that a high quality of life is more likely to be attained with less of a materialistic drive to acquire consumer goods and a greater focus on fulfilling relationships with friends, family, community, and the natural world. The local food movement focuses on more sustainable diets featuring foods produced in local foodsheds, which thus reduces the embodied energy associated with long-distance transportation of food.

Review Questions and Problems

1. Select a particular clean technology and find out where the technology was developed, where the products are produced (or if they are being produced), and where they are sold. What factors, if any, limit sales of this technology relative to traditional technologies?

2. In the absence of some sort of government policy promoting clean technology, what types of environmentally friendly technologies will the market process produce and sell, and why? In the case of recycling, why is it important that both government policies and markets be coordinated?

3. Go to your local grocery store or coffee shop and compare the price of standard and ecolabeled coffees. Is there a price premium for the ecolabeled coffees over and above what is charged for the standard coffee? Ask the manager if they perceive the ecolabeled product as being successful. You might also compare certified organic fresh produce with standard produce at your local grocery store. Write up your findings in a one-page essay.

4. Suppose that a hybrid automobile costs $3,000 more than a similar conventional automobile, but gets an extra 30 miles per gallon of fuel economy. Assuming that a car is driven 12,000 miles per year, the discount rate is 5 percent, and gasoline costs $2 per gallon, determine whether

or not the energy cost savings from the hybrid pays for the higher up-front cost over a five-year time horizon. In how many years would the hybrid's energy cost savings pay for the higher up-front cost if gasoline cost $3 per gallon?

5. Go to the 2003 study by Kats titled *The Costs and Financial Benefits of Green Buildings: A Report to California's Sustainable Building Task Force* on the Internet at www.ciwmb.ca.gov/greenbuilding/Design/CostBenefit/Report.pdf and write a summary essay on the life cycle cost analysis done on LEED-certified green buildings. If possible, trace back the research on human health and productivity benefits and critically evaluate the key findings.

Internet Links

Fair Trade Coffee (www.globalexchange.org/economy/coffee): Learn more about the Fair Trade coffee campaign from the advocacy group Global Exchange.

Forest Stewardship Council (www.fsc.org): Read more about certified sustainable forestry.

Green Building Council (www.usgbc.org): Learn more about LEED certification standards for green buildings.

Is Extended Producer Responsibility Effective? (http://pubs.acs.org/hotartcl/est/00/apr/hanis.html): Article by Carola Hanisch in the April 1, 2000, issue of *Environmental Science and Technology.*

ISO 14000 (www.iso14000.com): Learn more about this international system of environmental management standards for business.

National Organic Program (www.ams.usda.gov/nop): This USDA Internet site describes the revised national organic standards.

OECD Environment Website (www.oecd.org/env): Although OECD countries make up only 19 percent of the global population, they are the major consumers of the world's natural resources. Read about OECD member country initiatives, indicators, and sectoral studies related to sustainable consumption. Material is also provided on sustainable production topics such as increasing resource efficiency and sustainable transportation. Site maintained by the Organization for Economic Cooperation and Development.

Online Fuel Cell Information Center (www.fuelcells.org): Learn more about fuel cells and zero-emission power sources.

Solar Cooking Archive (http://solarcooking.org): Find out more about this environmentally friendly technology. The country reports are especially useful.

Sustainable Markets (www.iied.org/smg/index.html): Internet site provided by the International Institute for Environment and Development's Sustainable Markets Group, the goal of which is to influence the behavior of key market actors and institutions to support dynamic enterprise, local livelihoods, environmental regeneration, and accountable decision making by the private sector, particularly in the global South.

The Earth Council (www.ecouncil.ac.cr): The Earth Council is an international nongovernmental organization (NGO) that was created in September 1992 to promote and advance the implementation of the Earth Summit agreements. You can read the text of the Earth Charter and *Agenda 21* on this site, and learn about efforts at implementing the proposals generated at the Earth Summit.

UN Division for Sustainable Development—Publications on Sustainable Consumption and Production (www.un.org/esa/sustdev/sdissues/consumption/conprod.htm): Lots of good information on this site.

Worldwatch Institute (www.worldwatch.org): Lots of information provided on sustainable production and consumption.

References and Further Reading

Ashley, S. 2005. "On the Road to Fuel-Cell Cars." *Scientific American* 292 (3): 62–69.

Considine, T. 2001. "Industrial Ecology: Challenges and Opportunities for Economics." In *International Yearbook of Environmental and Resource Economics: 2001/2002,* ed. T. Tietenberg and H. Folmer. Cheltenham, UK: Edward Elgar.

Daly, H., and J. Cobb. 1989. *For the Common Good: Redirecting the Economy toward Community, the Environment, and a Sustainable Future.* Boston: Beacon Press.

de Graaf, J., D. Wann, and T. Naylor. 2002. *Affluenza: The All-Consuming Epidemic.* San Francisco: Berrett-Koehler.

European Commission. 2004. *European Research Spending for Renewable Energy Sources.* Luxembourg: Office for Official Publications of the European Communities.

Froesch, R. 1994. "Industrial Ecology: Minimizing the Impact of Industrial Waste." *Physics Today* 47 (November): 63–68.

———. 1995. "The Industrial Ecology of the 21st Century." *Scientific American* 273 (September): 178–81.

Georgescu-Roegen, N. 1971. *The Entropy Law and the Economic Process.* Cambridge, MA: Harvard University Press.

Grupp, M. 1996. "Solar Cookers—They're Better Than Their Reputation!" *Gate Online* (February).

Hanisch, C. 2000. "Is Extended Producer Responsibility Effective?" *Environmental Science and Technology* 34: 170A–175A.

Hart, K. 2005. "Energy Conservation and Community Planning." *Planning Commissioners Journal* 57 (Winter): 30–38.

Hawken, P. 1994. *The Ecology of Commerce.* New York: HarperBusiness.

Hoagland, W. 1995. "Solar Energy." *Scientific American* 273 (September): 170–73.

Kats, Greg. 2003. *The Costs and Financial Benefits of Green Buildings: A Report to California's Sustainable Building Task Force.* Sacramento: California Integrated Waste Management Board. Available at www.ciwmb.ca.gov/greenbuilding/Design/CostBenefit/Report.pdf.

Lovins, Amory. 1977. *Soft Energy Paths: Toward a Durable Peace.* Cambridge, MA: Ballinger.

Moore, C., and A. Miller. 1994. *Green Gold: Japan, Germany, the United States, and the Race for Environmental Technology.* Boston: Beacon Press.

Myers, F. 1992. "Japan Bids for Global Leadership in Clean Industry." *Science* 256 (May): 1144–45.

Nandwani, S. 1996. "Solar Cookers—Cheap Technology with High Ecological Benefits." *Ecological Economics* 17 (May): 73–81.

———. "A New Chance for Solar Energy." 1995. *Scientific American* 273 (September): 173.

Papastefanou, G. 1996. "Social Basis of Paying Attention to Eco-Labels in Purchase Decisions in West Germany." Working paper, ZUMA, Mannheim, Germany.

Pierce, L. 2000. *Choosing Simplicity: Real People Finding Peace and Fulfillment in a Complex World.* Carmel, CA: Gallagher Press.

Rhodes, S. 1995. "International Environmental Standards to Emerge as the ISO 14000 Series: Guidelines Will Influence the Way Companies Do Business in the 21st Century." *Tappi Journal* 78 (September): 65–66.

Scheel, J. 2004. "New Product Trends: Driving Organic Growth." *Prepared Foods* August. Available at www.preparedfoods.com.

Schneider, D. 1995. "Putting Greens: Clean, Hydrogen-Powered Golf Carts Hit the Streets." *Scientific American* 273 (December) (reprint).

Sperling, D. 1996. "The Case for Electric Vehicles." *Scientific American* 275 (November): 54–59.

U.S. Environmental Protection Agency. 2001. *Our Built and Natural Environments: A Technical Review of the Interactions Between Land Use, Transportation, and Environmental Quality.* EPA 231-R-01–002. Washington, DC: U.S. EPA.

World Resources Institute. 1994. *World Resources Report, 1994–95.* New York: Oxford University Press.

Worldwatch Institute. 2004. *State of the World 2004 Special Focus: The Consumer Society.* Washington DC: Worldwatch Institute.

16

Issues in the Economics of Sustainable Local Communities

Introduction

There has been growing interest in the sustainability of national economies and in promoting sustainable economic development at the macro-economic level. But there has also been a growing recognition that the principles governing a sustainable society may be most effectively applied to smaller local communities, which is the focus of the present chapter. For one thing, it is at the local community level that the scale of decision making is most consistent with democratic process and the empowerment of people. As Ostrom (1990) has found in her research, sustainable common-pool resource (CPR) systems appear to be linked to effective local self-governance, which connects community with its natural resource life-support system. Yet local communities cannot wall themselves off from national and international trends, migrations, and trade. Sustainable local communities must not only find equitable methods of governing themselves and their local commons but also develop strategies for relating with the forces of the larger national and international economy and with the dynamics of in- and out-migration. In this chapter, we will contrast sustainable local institutions for governing CPR systems, many of which evolved in pre-industrial societies, with the dilemma of sustainable local economic development in modern industrialized economies.

Sustainable Local Self-Governance of CPR Systems

For hundreds, perhaps thousands, of years, local communities have had rule systems for jointly managing and using those common lands and other resources that typically lay between deep wilderness and the farmstead and that were not suitable for cultivation (Snyder 1990). Common lands were typically used for grazing livestock, the gathering of fuelwood and building materials, and varying degrees of hunting and gathering of wild animals and plants. Local tribes or village communities governed the use of these lands (or fishing grounds). Typically, their rule systems limited access to people from outside the community and related the intensity and frequency of use by those in the community to the resource's carrying capacity. For example, as we learned in chapter 5, some tribes such as the Yurok in northwestern California utilized variants of both private property and common property systems depending on the nature of the resource in question. In a very important sense, "the commons" constitutes both the resource and the community institutions of self-governance that connect that resource to the people who depend upon it. As Gary Snyder (1990) has stated, the commons is the contract a people make with their local natural system. There is, unfortunately, a long history of centralized government authorities' failing to recognize locally devised traditional common property regimes. The result has often been the loss of local community rights and controls. One prominent example is the enclosure movement in England and parts of Europe, which resulted in many village commons being transformed into private estates.

As was shown in chapter 5, the salutary effects of Adam Smith's invisible hand—that self-interested behavior is transformed into the common good by way of decentralized markets—do not extend to common-pool resource systems. The central problem is that there is rivalry surrounding the consumption of the natural resource in question. For example, when someone adds more cattle to the communal grazing land, there is a disparity between the flows of benefits and costs. The benefits flow to the person who added more cattle to the communal grazing land and may take the form of greater income from selling more calves or dairy products. All who use the grazing commons, however, share the costs. These costs take the form of less feed and degraded range conditions. Thus, a self-interested maximizer sees an opportunity to increase his or her herd without limit, receive 100 percent of the income, and share only a fraction of the cost. This is the mechanics of what Garrett Hardin called the *tragedy of the commons.* In economic terms, we can describe the tragedy of the commons as the outcome of self-interested users of the CPR imposing *appropriation externalities* on all the other CPR users.

What is interesting from the perspective of this chapter is that there are sustainable, long-enduring local communities that have not succumbed to the tragedy of the commons. Ostrom (1990) provides some of the most comprehensive analysis of the nature of these long-enduring and sustainable local communities and their relationship to the local natural resource systems on which they depend. The enduring role of common property resources such as grazing land and forestland in these communities is perhaps surprising to resource economists, who see private property as the solution to resource degradation. What one observes instead is a lasting, parallel existence of both private and communal property in communities where people exercise control over institutions of governance and property. Drawing upon her field research, Ostrom (p. 61) observes,

> Generations of Swiss and Japanese villagers have learned the relative benefits and costs of private property and communal-property institutions related to various types of land and uses of land. The villagers in both settings have *chosen* to retain the institution of communal property as the foundation for land use and similar important aspects of village economies. The economic survival of these villagers has been dependent on the skill with which they have used their limited resources. One cannot view communal property in these settings as the primordial remains of earlier institutions evolved in a land of plenty.

The tragedy of the commons is a characteristic of open-access property regimes and of other property regimes where rule systems have failed.

Examples of Sustainable Local Communities and the Systems They Use for Governing CPRs

Törbel, Switzerland

As described by Netting (1981), for centuries the people of Törbel have relied on a combination of private and communal property. Privately owned plots are used to grow grains, vegetables, fruit, and hay. Five different types of common property have been acknowledged in written legal documents that date back to 1224:

- alpine grazing meadows
- forests
- wastelands
- irrigation systems
- paths and roads connecting private and communal property

In 1483 the villagers agreed to a system of self-governance to manage the use of communal property. A central element of this rule system limits access to the village's communal property. For example, regulations written in 1517 state that "no citizen could send more cows to the alp than he could feed during the winter" (Netting 1976, p. 139). Ostrom reports that many other Swiss villages use the wintering rule as a means for allocating grazing rights. Moreover, those with rights to use the village communal property are given the power to decide whether additional people should be admitted to community membership. The boundaries of the communal property are well defined. A local official is authorized to impose fines on those who put an excessive number of cows on the communal alp and to keep half the fine. Each family receives a share of the village's cheese in proportion to the number of cows it grazes relative to the total. Villagers with voting rights have created an alp association to hire staff, impose fines, and arrange for manure spreading and other necessary maintenance of the commons. Those who use the grazing commons provide labor in proportion to the number of cows they graze. Trees needed for fuel and construction are selected by the village and assigned by lot to households. Before the rapid rise in population in the nineteenth century, Netting reports that severe population pressure was held in check by measures such as late marriages, high celibacy rates, long birth spacing, and a great deal of emigration.

As Ostrom reports, Netting's major findings are consistent with experience in many other Swiss communities. Throughout the alpine region of Switzerland, private property exists for more intensive cropping, while common property is used for summer meadows and forests. In fact, 80 percent of the Swiss alpine area engages in some form of common property. Ostrom cites an unpublished work by Hartmut Picht that reports that all local regulations limit the level of appropriation from these commons. Overuse of alpine meadows is rarely reported.

Japanese Village Commons

McKean (1986) estimates that approximately 12 million hectares of Japanese forests and mountain meadows were managed as communal property between 1600 and 1867, and that about 3 million hectares are so managed today. As in Switzerland, villagers in the Japanese villages studied by McKean use private property for valuable land that is more intensively cropped for rice and vegetables and use common property for larger areas of less valuable forestland and grazing land.

Spanish Irrigation Commons

Irrigated agriculture has been critical in Spain, where limited and highly seasonal rainfall would otherwise severely restrict agricultural productivity.

Ostrom (1990) reports that Spanish towns and villages have had self-governed irrigation systems for at least 550 years, and probably for close to 1,000 years. These systems require farmers to construct and maintain canal and ditch systems, and to agree on how to allocate scarce water supplies. The irrigation areas that surround or are near the villages that govern them are referred to as *huertas*. Interestingly, farmers lost control over their irrigation systems during the Spanish Civil War and did not regain this power until 1950. Moreover, the freedom of farmers to self-organize was peculiar to the traditional region of Aragón in eastern Spain. As Ostrom (p. 81) points out:

> By the time the centralized monarchy based on the Castilian model came to dominate Spain and Latin America, the autonomy of the *huertas* was well established. The continuing willingness of the irrigators in these regions to stand up for their rights attests that they had greater autonomy than did those in other parts of Spain. One can only wonder if the course of history in Latin America might have differed substantially if the Spanish monarchy established by Ferdinand and Isabella had been modeled on Aragón and not on Castile.

Ostrom finds that similar communities with longstanding communal irrigation systems exist in the Philippines, referred to as *zanjeras*. As with the *huerta* system, village communities have retained substantial autonomy to determine their own rule systems, including durable methods for assigning water, monitoring rule conformance, and providing labor for canal and ditch maintenance.

Localized Self-Governance of Fisheries

Schlager (1993) evaluated the varying degrees of success experienced by thirty locally self-governed coastal fishing grounds around the world. Three problems that develop in these settings are *appropriation externalities* (tragedy of the commons), *technological externalities* (gear entanglement and other forms of physical interference from fishing boats working adjacent to one another), and *assignment problems* (boats' locating themselves inefficiently on the fishery, such as when too many are clustered in one place). Schlager points out that fishers organize themselves as a way to coordinate their harvesting activities. She finds that this coordination has successfully reduced assignment problems and technological externalities relative to cases in which self-governance did not occur. She also argues that it is extremely difficult for fishers to resolve appropriation externalities because of the problem of determining whether a decline in catch is due to overfishing of that species, overfishing of species that are lower on the food chain, environmental circumstances, or even how many fish are landed by other fishers. Accordingly, Schlager finds no instance among the sample of coastal fishing grounds she studied in which fishers utilized a quota scheme. Thus, fishers try to regulate the use of the space of their fishing grounds rather than the overall catch.

Sanctions of various kinds have been found to be associated with successful local self-governance of fisheries. For example, Acheson (1988) studied Maine *lobster gangs,* which are groups of fishers who make informal (but very real) territorial claims for harvesting lobsters. Sustainable harvest rates in these territories have been achieved in part by use of sanctions such as destruction of the equipment of outsiders who repeatedly enter the territory claimed by the gang. In their study of local fishery self-governance in the state of Bahia in northern Brazil, Cordell and McKean (1992) find an elaborate system of social norms and rules for ethical conduct on the CPR. These rules are devised to prevent exhaustion of the fishery and to distribute access rights equitably. Violation of these norms-based rules of conduct can result in sanctions such as ostracism and sabotage of fishing gear and equipment. Thus, mutual monitoring and sanctioning appear to have been important to sustaining local fisheries and the communities that depend upon them.

Fodder and Fuelwood Use in Panchayat Community Forests

The panchayat community forests occur in the mid-Himalayan Mountains in the Almora District of Uttar Pradesh, India. Agrawal (1993) studied 6 of the nearly 4,000 villages with panchayat forests. Local *van panchayats*— councils made up of five elected people who set rules for forest use—manage these forests. For example, Agrawal finds that most villages have allocation rules that limit the time in which villagers can harvest fodder, usually two to twelve weeks. When tree leaves are cut for fodder, at least two-thirds of the leaf cover must be left on the tree. While in some villages people are given equal allocations of fuel and fodder, in others the rights are proportionate to the contributions made by each person in maintenance (tree planting) and monitoring (directly, or indirectly by paying the salary of a guard). Agrawal finds a very strong link between the level of village investment in monitoring and dispute resolution systems, the degree of village commitment to sanctioning violators appropriately, and the resource conditions in the panchayat forests. In the less successful villages studied by Agrawal, panchayat officials did not emphasize monitoring. Moreover, two of the three less successful villages used rule systems that discriminated against lower-caste people, and monitoring was primarily used to punish these lower-caste people. In contrast, successful villages linked a guard's pay to performance, and panchayat officials monitored the guards. In one of these villages, violators were required to confess in front of the entire village, creating a strong deterrent to violating the shared social norm of sustainable use. The failure of these three villages to construct adequate rule structures for governing panchayat forests explains the subsequent resource degradation in these forests.

After extensive field research, Ostrom developed a set of *design principles* that she found to be consistently associated with enduring, sustainable CPR governance systems. These principles are also supported by the later studies of Schlager and Agrawal, as described above, and by Pye-Smith and Feyerabend (1994) in their case study analyses of successes in local community environmental management.

Ostrom's Design Principles Associated with Sustainable Local Self-Governance of Common-Pool Resources

1. *Clearly defined boundaries:* Boundaries regarding who has the right to appropriate from the commons, and regarding the CPR itself, tend to be clearly defined.

2. *Congruence between appropriation and provision rules, and local conditions:* The rules that govern withdrawal of resource units from the CPR are tailored to local conditions. *Local conditions* include culture, the biomechanics of the CPR, and differences between resource users, among others. Rules that govern the provision of human-made CPRs similarly match local conditions. This principle argues against the "one rule system fits all" approach to self-governance.

3. *Collective-choice arrangements:* All *stakeholders* (people who use or are impacted by the CPR) are included in the formation of appropriation/ provision rules and in rule adaptation over time.

4. *Monitoring:* Those who actively audit CPR use and conditions are accountable to the appropriator group or may be the appropriators themselves.

5. *Graduated sanctions:* Sanctions or punishments imposed for violation of rules reflect the extent of the harm imposed and the context of the offense, and are established by the appropriator group itself.

6. *Conflict resolution mechanisms:* Appropriators and their officials have rapid access to low-cost arenas in which to resolve conflicts among appropriators or their appointed officials.

7. *Minimal recognition of the rights to organize:* External government authorities do not block or hinder local self-governance.

8. *Nesting of small-scale governance systems within larger governance sys-*

tems when localized CPRs are part of larger systems: Layering of governance structures matches the interdependence and complexity of CPR systems.

Research by Ostrom, Agrawal, and others supports the idea that successful CPR governance must include clearly defined boundaries between the CPR and either private property or other CPR systems. For example, Agrawal (2002) notes that the design principle of clearly defined boundaries can be expected to influence both the level of certainty that individuals within an appropriation group will receive benefits from the CPR, and the costs that they can expect to face when considering new rules for resolving a commons dilemma. Gibson, Williams, and Ostrom (2005) note that the principle of clearly defined boundaries should reduce uncertainty as to who will benefit and who will pay the costs, while poorly defined boundaries should increase uncertainty and thus retard efforts to find or sustain a collective solution.

Rule congruence linking appropriation with local conditions and with provision of maintenance or monitoring effort is also linked to successful self-governed systems. In principle 3, Ostrom points out that successful CPR self-governance is linked to inclusive, democratic process, one of the key elements of a sustainable community. Principles 4 and 5 indicate the importance of enforcement efforts in promoting compliance with appropriation and (effort) provision rules—groups must provide for effective monitoring and must have credible sanctions that are appropriate to the extent of the transgression. Monitoring and enforcement systems may be based on formal rule systems (de jure), or based on informal customs (de facto). Gibson, Williams, and Ostrom (2005) evaluated the empirical importance of monitoring and enforcement on successful community-level governance of CPRs. They used data from 178 community-forest governance systems that were collected by the International Forestry Resources and Institutions (IFRI) research program in Africa, Asia, and the Western Hemisphere. Gibson, Williams, and Ostrom evaluated two hypotheses: (1) If rule enforcement is sporadic—even if a user group has high levels of social capital—forest conditions are more likely to be poor. (2) If rule enforcement is regular—even if a user group has low levels of social capital—forest conditions are more likely to be good. Their results show that rule enforcement and forest condition are correlated, regardless of the level of social capital. They also show that it is highly unlikely for forest conditions to be good if there is only sporadic rule enforcement, and that this relationship exists whether social capital is high or low.

Principle 6 illustrates the importance of mediation, arbitration, and other alternative dispute resolution methods to sustainable local communities. Dietz, Ostrom, and Stern (2003) note that sharp differences in power and in values across interested parties make conflict inherent in environmental choices. They argue that the benefits of conflict resolution in and of itself may be as important a motivation for designing community-based CPR governance systems as is concern with the resources themselves. While the varying perspectives, interests, and values that people bring to problems of CPR governance can escalate to the point of dysfunction, they can also spark learning and change. The failure of centralized governments to recognize the rights of local groups to self-organize to manage their localized commons (principle 7) has been a problem for inshore fishers in the United States, Canada, and elsewhere. Finally, principle 8 provides a hint for how these very small-scale success stories can be replicated on a larger scale. The idea is for larger and more complex systems to have a number of small, highly localized self-governing groups nested within them. Then the larger, more complex, and interdependent system can be self-governed by representatives from the various small-scale self-governing groups. Ostrom also makes the point that success in small-scale self-governance creates social capital and organizing skills that can then be used for larger and more difficult CPR problems.

Retrospective on CPRs and Local Self-Governance

Ostrom has argued that there are important similarities shared by various long-enduring communities and their systems of CPR governance. The natural environments in which villages are located feature important uncertainties such as unpredictable rainfall and snowfall, and so successful rule systems are adaptable to changing natural conditions. In these situations, community members share a common understanding of the merits of continuing the status quo relative to various feasible changes in rules and norms of acceptable behavior. Importantly, populations in these villages have remained stable over long periods. Well-defined social norms prescribe a rather narrow band of acceptable behavior that facilitates interdependence with minimal conflict. As one would expect, the costs of being ostracized are quite high and, together with mutual monitoring of behavior, lead to powerful reputational incentives, which promote conformance to shared social norms of sustainable use. Community members tend to be very similar in terms of wealth, education, ethnicity, and race, and this homogeneity also limits conflicts. People who live in these communities share a common history and can reasonably expect to have a common future together. Because the rule systems can accommodate generational transfers of rights and land tenure, people can expect that they are making decisions that will determine the quality of life of their children and grandchildren. As Ostrom points out, this promotes very low discount rates and thus leads to policies that are consistent with community sustainability.

The case study research described above points to the central importance of social capital, and the evolution of behavioral norms of restraint and co-operation, to sustaining local common-pool resources. Sethi and Somanathan (1996) have developed a theory that explains why norms of behavior that restrain the use of CPRs can persist in social settings that might otherwise favor self-interested behavior. They use the mathematics of evolutionary processes and apply them to social and economic institutions such as the rules that communities use to govern CPRs. Their theoretical analysis is consistent with the extensive case study literature, namely, that social norms that restrain overuse of the CPR and provide sanctions for those who violate these norms can remain stable over time even when there is occasional intrusion by self-interested people. They also show, however, that factors such as a rise in the market price of the resource in question, or diminution of the impact of available sanctions, can produce a fatal instability in sustainable local self-governance from which it is extremely difficult to recover.

Successful local self-governance appears to be associated with only modest asymmetries in the distribution of local power and influence, a factor that is also linked to the quality of local democratic process. For example, the villages studied by Agrawal that featured rather rigid caste structures and discriminated against lower-caste people were less successful in sustainable self-governance. Similarly, proposals for local environmental dispute resolution through collaborative, stakeholder-based self-governance cannot be expected to succeed in local settings where certain stakeholders have disproportionate power and influence. Thus, community economic development centered on attracting disproportionately large business or government operations may undermine the quality of democratic local self-governance and so ultimately may not be consistent with community sustainability. As we shall see in the discussion below, protecting the quality of local self-governance forms one of the arguments for community economic development strategies that instead focus on assisting local small businesses that produce for local consumption and substitute for goods that would have to be imported into the community.

Integrating Sustainability into Local Economic Development

This section focuses on the sustainable development dilemma confronting relatively small local communities in rich industrialized countries. These industrialized countries feature large and highly specialized industrial enterprises, an extensive reliance on inter-regional and international trade, and free migration of people from one community to another. As the term suggests, industrialized societies generate much of their wealth from industrial production and from services, and thus local governance of CPRs may be of only minor economic importance. Moreover, unlike traditional subsistence or agrarian communities, local communities in rich industrialized societies rely on extensive outside trade with other regions for most of the goods and many of the services that local people consume. Unlike traditional societies around the world, most rich industrialized countries are open societies in which residents are free to migrate from one community to the next based on economic, quality of life, or a myriad of other factors. In this context many of the design principles developed by Ostrom for successful local governance of CPRs are difficult to implement, and the property rights to community quality-of-life factors may be essentially open-access in nature. The challenge of sustainable economic development in rich industrialized societies involves a balance of economic, community, and environmental goals in a technologically and demographically changing landscape that features stakeholders with sharply different goals.

We will start out by considering a simplified model of a local economy, which emphasizes the inflows and outflows of income that are driven by the relationships between the local economy and the broader regional, state, national, and international economies. We will then explore how the proportion of local purchases relative to the purchase of imports affects the ultimate local economic impact of a given amount of income injected into the local economy. Once we have this basic understanding of the local economy we will consider different views of local economic development.

A Model of the Local Economy

Consider a local or regional economy in the context of a modern industrialized country. These local economies are usually centered on distinct towns or cities where people shop, work, and conduct business, and that serve as centers of production and distribution. These local economies interact in various ways with other economies and government entities that range from the local to the international. The various sources of income that flow into a local economy from outside are called *income injections*, and these injections occur due to trade with or transfers from entities outside of the local economy. The sectors of the local economy that in various ways generate income injections are collectively referred to as the *economic base* of the local economy. Elements of the economic base may be business or government entities, or even categories of people such as retirees. Examples of economic base activities include the export of local manufactured goods, agricultural commodities, or services by local firms, as well as income injected by tourist visitation, local state and federal employee salaries, and federal benefits for local retirees. Offsetting these income injections are income leakages that occur when local residents purchase goods and services

Figure 16.1   **Simplified Model of a Local Economy**

<u>Income injections</u>: Generated by activities such as
the export sale of locally produced goods and
services, by taxes or transfers paid to local entities,
or by tourist visits to the local area.

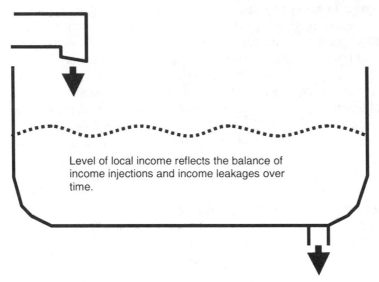

Level of local income reflects the balance of
income injections and income leakages over
time.

<u>Income leakages</u>: Generated by activities such
as the import purchase of externally produced
goods and services, by taxes or transfers paid to
outsiders, or by locals traveling outside the local
area.

produced outside the community, pay state or federal taxes, send money to family or friends in other places, or travel out of the area. Thus, we can see that many of these injections and leakages are the monetary flows linked to specialization and trade. In fact, many human settlements originated from some local comparative advantage, such as access to valuable resources or to advantageous ports and trade routes, which resulted in the formation of a base industry, export trade, and the rise of a town or city. Since the purchase of imports leaks income out of the local economy, then unless a local economy completely divorces itself from trade with the outside world, ultimately there must be some base industry in a local economy to inject income to fund the purchase of these imports and maintain a satisfactory level of local income. This relationship is illustrated in Figure 16.1.

A given dollar of income that is injected by the local base industry is usually spent more than once before it leaks out. Specifically, the income injected by the economic base of a local economy, net of the income that leaks out, flows to local businesses that support the base industry by providing various inputs or services, and to the households of those employed by the base industry. These businesses and households in turn respend a portion of this money locally at grocery stores, clothing and shoe stores, health care providers, restaurants, and for the services of those skilled in various trades, crafts, and professions. Thus, a dollar of net income injected into the local economy by export sales from the economic base is multiplied as it flows through the supporting businesses and through the spending of employee households. The size of this *multiplier effect* is determined by the extent to which the local economy imports rather than produces the goods and services that local people consume. In particular, the smaller the leakage rate, the larger the multiplier. Note that while we are speaking as if there is a single multiplier for the local economy, in reality each business, and each economic sector, will have a different multiplier. You can think of the multiplier, described below, as an average for the entire local economy, and representing the typical number of times a given dollar injected into the local economy is recycled as income for various members of the community.

To see how the multiplier effect works, consider the following simplified example. Suppose that a new lumber mill is opened in a community that generates $5 million in export sales. Before we proceed to the multiplier analysis, however, we need to subtract from this export income any initial leakage in the form of payments for imported factors of production used to generate the export sales, such as raw logs, energy payments, transportation services, equipment rentals or loan payments, stumpage taxes, or income paid to out-of-area workers or owners. Suppose that of this $5 million, $2 million flows out of the community right away as payments for imported production inputs and to owners from outside the community. Thus $3 million represents the (net) *initial injection* into the local community in the form of payments for locally sourced inputs, such as parts and hardware, wages, salaries, profits, and locally sourced equipment rentals and payments. The term *capture rate* is sometimes used to refer to the portion of gross export income that is initially injected into the local economy (in this example the capture rate is three-fifths or 60 percent). This initial injection is then spent by the people who received it as income, including workers at the mill, the owner of the hardware store, the equipment dealer, and any local owners of the mill. Some of this spending—say 50 percent—leaks out of the community on purchases of imported goods. For example, the hardware store owner spends some of this income on inventory orders from outside the community, and workers spend some of their income on car payments to dealerships in neighboring communities.

Thus, the initial $3 million injection generates an additional $1.5 million in local spending. This $1.5 million in second-round spending then spurs additional rounds of spending. For example, the workers and the hardware store owner spend money at the local grocery store, and the local grocery store spends some of that income on wages and locally sourced food, and some of it on food imported from outside. Thus, the third-round of spending is $750,000. Spending continues until leakages exhaust the process. The total increase in income is the sum of the initial injection and the additional income generated through each round of spending. The following formulas can be used to calculate this total increase in local income:

Initial injection = (gross export sales revenue) − (payments for imported factors of production)

Leakage rate = (total local expenditures on imports)/(total local expenditures)

Multiplier = 1/(leakage rate)

Total increase in income (economic impact) = (initial injection) × multiplier.

The initial injection of $3 million from the economic base can be thought of as the primary effect of the economic base activity. The multiplier is used as a simplified tool to measure the secondary effects of this initial injection. Secondary effects can in turn be divided into *indirect effects* (increases in income to the sectors of the local economy that support the base industry, such as locally sourced equipment rentals) and *induced effects* (increases in income to the entire local economy that occur due to increased spending by households that received income from the base industry or one of its support sectors). The total increase in income, or *economic impact,* generated by the initial injection of $3 million into the local economy is $6 million. This process is illustrated in Figure 16.2. The total economic impact represents the sum of the primary effect (the initial $3 million injection) and the secondary effects (the $3 million in indirect and induced effects) estimated by the multiplier. This formula is a simplified version of the more general case developed by Sirkin (1959) and assumes that savings by community members that leak out of the community in the form of loans (for example, money market mutual fund investments or savings in large national banks) are just offset by loan funds in the community that come from savings outside the community. There are other assumptions, such as the availability of excess production capacity and the relative sensitivity of imports and exports to income that go beyond the scope of the current presentation. Note too that while simple multiplier analysis is relatively crude,

Figure 16.2 **Economic Impact of Export Income on the Local Economy**

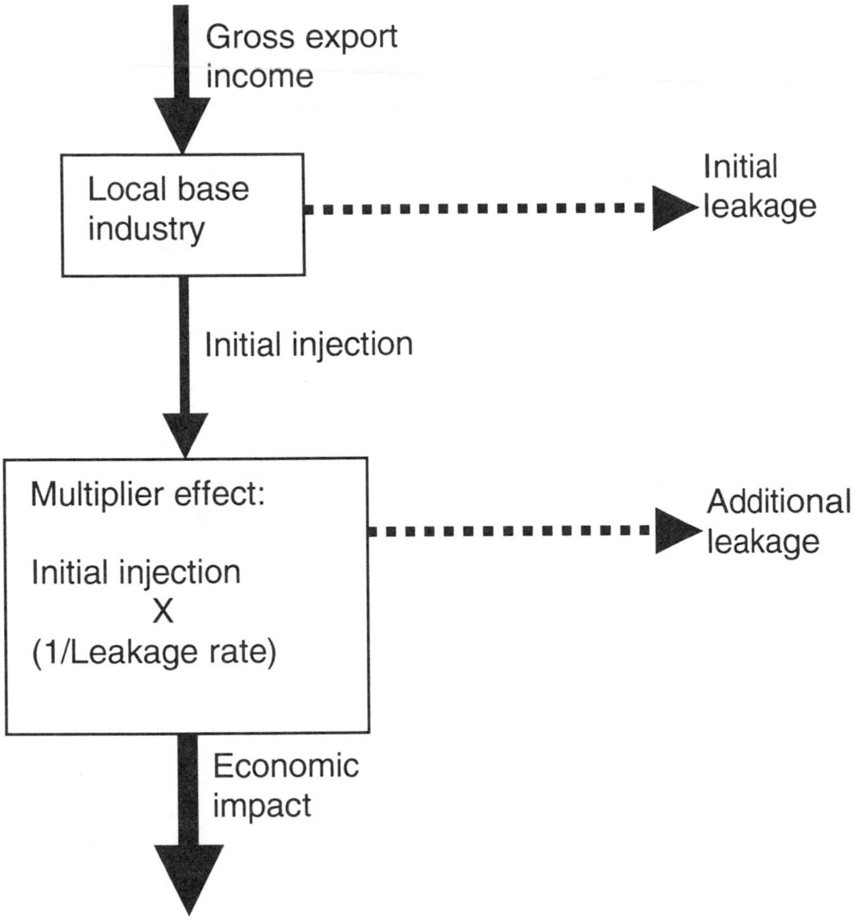

much more sophisticated input/output software programs can be used to much more comprehensively estimate economic impact.

Different Approaches to Economic Development

With this simplified view of the local economy and the economic impact of base industry sales in mind, let's look at economic development. A primary goal for conventional economic development has been to spur local economic growth in order to create jobs, enhance the vitality of commercial centers, and increase incomes for businesses and workers. An excessively narrow focus on job and income growth can lead to pathological results that undermine a community's sustainability. Perhaps one of the more notorious economic development strategies is termed "smokestack chasing," or more recently "microchip chasing." In this strategy, local or state governments compete with one another in order to attract large base-industry firms into their jurisdiction. The inducements used by these jurisdictions to attract these firms are property tax abatements, and free or subsidized land and site improvements. Unfortunately, winning the jurisdictional competition to attract a base industry can be very costly in terms of public resources expended, thus reducing funds available for schools, public safety, and other public services. These public resource inducements can be measured in terms of dollars per job. In one well-publicized example, in 1993 the state of Alabama paid the equivalent of $200,000 per job in order to attract a Mercedes-Benz assembly plant. According to the Rocky Mountain Institute (1997), during each year of the 1990s, the economic development agencies of approximately 25,000 U.S. jurisdictions bid for about 500 major base-industry plants. Note that there is no guarantee that the jobs promised will be forthcoming, or that the firm will not shift jobs and production elsewhere in the future. Meanwhile, pressure is often placed on local jurisdictions to offer proportionate inducements to existing firms, further eroding the foundation of public finance for infrastructure and public services in local communities.

More innovative local economic development strategies avoid the "winner's curse" of jurisdictional competition for footloose base-industry firms, and instead promote business development within their own jurisdiction. Some examples of these strategies include the following:

- streamlined "one-stop" development and business permitting processes;
- "specific plan" areas that have already undergone public hearing processes and have been zoned, pre-permitted, and designed for certain types of commercial or industrial uses;
- strategic infrastructure improvements such as broadband or telecommunications access in targeted commercial or industrial districts;
- marketing assistance, cooperative regional marketing programs, and creation of regional marketing images to assist export sales of locally made products and to promote tourism;
- training and business plan assistance for local entrepreneurs, as well as promotion of entrepreneurship in high schools and community colleges;
- microenterprise lending programs for new and poorly collateralized firms;
- organization of local base industry clusters that include base industry firms and associated suppliers and distributors; identification of local bottlenecks limiting further cluster development;
- formation of public redevelopment districts in blighted areas, or private

business improvement districts, that receive the increase ("increment") in property taxes resulting from successful economic development, with these funds going toward additional economic development efforts, infrastructure improvements, or marketing efforts;

- small-business incubators, which are facilities that provide space at below-market rates plus office management and marketing assistance; incubators usually require some form of subsidy;
- Internet-based information on permitting processes, local business conditions, and on-line databases of undeveloped commercially or industrially zoned parcels.

When economic development efforts cause local or regional economies to grow relative to those of neighboring areas, the growth in jobs and income attracts workers and other businesses, which in turn requires housing, office space, schools, and other infrastructure and public services. As a result, economic development cannot be done in isolation, but needs to be fully integrated with local and regional community planning. One way this can be done is to include an economic development "element" to the general plans of local and county jurisdictions. State and local tax policies, as well as the political influence of developers, can have a big impact on the incentives of local government policymakers regarding economic development and regional planning. For example, local governments in California can keep some of the sales tax revenue generated within their boundaries, but receive only a small fraction of the property tax revenue generated within their boundaries. Many local governments find that the property tax revenues they do receive from new housing development are inadequate to pay for roads, schools, public safety, and other public services that must be provided in support of new residential areas. As a result, while local governments in California compete for retail sales tax–generating businesses, they have less incentive to provide housing for new residents. So-called "big box" retailers understand this jurisdictional incentive to capture sales tax revenue from neighboring communities. While workers at some big-box firms receive such low pay and benefits that they depend on publicly provided health care and other subsidies, nevertheless these firms are able to succeed by offering consumers inexpensive goods produced elsewhere, and allowing small towns a chance to capture substantial sales tax revenue from neighboring jurisdictions.

The traditional laissez-faire approach to development by many local governments often results in a pattern of low-density suburban sprawl that is driven by the incentives and political influence of landowners, developers, and local business boosters, as well as the various subsidies for gasoline and personal automobile usage that influence preferred household locations (see chapter 13 for a discussion of these subsidies). Fodor (1999) refers to this setting as the "urban growth machine," and argues that the cost per housing unit of providing public services is inversely related to housing density. At the extreme, the result can be sprawled, automobile-dependent communities like San Jose, Denver, and Los Angeles. Low-density housing in areas with a strong economy but limited land available for development can lead to escalating housing prices and an affordability crisis, which in turn pushes people into cheaper housing in more remote areas, resulting in further sprawl, long automobile commutes, highway congestion, and loss of community identity. Increasingly, health care professionals see a linkage between automobile dependence and the growing proportion of people who are obese.

As a result, more recently some innovative communities are integrating land use planning and economic development in order to anticipate the housing needs of new workers in a way that preserves open space, reduces dependency on automobiles, and allows new development to "pay its own way" in terms of public services. One example is to provide development incentives and planning in support of "transportation oriented development" (TOD). The TOD community design concept features moderate and high-density housing combined with complementary retail, public facilities, and services. This mixed-use development is concentrated at various locations along regional public transit networks. TOD creates a pedestrian-oriented environment and reinforces the use of public transportation. Another example of innovative development planning is to integrate apartment or condominium housing units upstairs from retail or commercial operations in the center of cities and towns, and to design narrower streets with broader sidewalks that emphasize pedestrian uses. Other examples include open space requirements and urban growth boundaries. Many of these elements are drawn from successful Western European urban models. TOD projects are underway in a growing number of cities, including Atlanta, Boston, Charlotte, Los Angeles, Portland (Oregon), San Diego, the San Francisco Bay area, Seattle, and the Washington, DC, area.

An alternative approach to economic development is to focus on increasing the multiplier effect rather than on increasing the initial injection from the economic base (though there is nothing preventing a community from doing both). The multiplier effect is increased by reducing the income leakages associated with the purchase of goods and services imported from outside the local community. This type of economic development has been termed "import substitution" and was a dominant form of economic development in newly independent former colonies in Africa, Asia, and South America in the 1950s and 1960s. Many economists see import substitution as a less desirable form of economic development at the national level because it requires policies such as import tariffs and quotas that raise domestic consumer prices. Moreover, by limiting competition from foreign imports, import substitution policies are seen by some as government-sponsored protection for domestic firms, reducing their long-term competitiveness. At the local level, however, jurisdictions (at least in the United States) cannot levy import tariffs or quotas on goods and services produced outside the local economy, and so the economic distortions associated with import substitution policy are much smaller at the local level.

Thus, for the most part, economic development strategies based on local import substitution are less formal in nature, and usually amount to "buy local" campaigns and marketing assistance for locally made products or services. Another example is the development of a local currency, one of the most famous of which is the Ithaca Hours project (www.ithacahours.org). U.S. law allows local currencies or scrip as long as all appropriate taxes are paid on economic transactions mediated by local currency, and that U.S. money is not being counterfeited. If mostly locally owned businesses accept local currency, then use of the currency reinforces a "buy local" value system that increases the multiplier effect. Perhaps the most important benefit created by local currencies is the awareness that interactions linked to a local currency promote investment in social capital. Some jurisdictions have designed restrictions on "pattern restaurants"—restaurants that use a standardized menu and design at multiple locations—as a method of restricting large corporate chains and instead promoting local alternatives. In terms of sustainability, democratic and community values are enhanced by promoting local small business over larger corporate enterprises since the former are more likely to be politically responsive to the local community. Economically speaking, economic diversification—having many small businesses across many sectors of the economy—has the advantage of reducing a community's risk of economic dislocation due to one large employer going out of business. In some cases, large firms in small communities have used the threat of closing down to extract concessions from the community; this threat is less effective when employed by a small business.

One of the fundamental challenges associated with import substitution in small local communities is that of economies of scale in production. Mass-produced imports tend to be cheaper than local goods produced on a smaller scale. Those who support local small businesses often must be willing to pay a price premium. Those locals who are willing to pay a price premium for local goods and services may recognize the mutual benefits of buying locally, and a vibrant sector of locally owned businesses may serve as an indication of a community's social and cultural capital. The social and cultural aspect of buying locally is also manifested in the rise of farmers' markets and community-supported agriculture. Communities that are more isolated may find more success with the import-substitution development strategy, since relatively high shipping costs help work against the cost advantage of imports. In general, sustainable local economic development involves investment in the local stocks of natural, human, social, and human-made capital as a way of producing adequate flows of jobs, income, and quality of life to residents over time. As Power (1996) has argued, protection of the local natural environment and investment in the public commons and the arts provides a concrete way of enhancing local quality of life that also moves us toward what may be a more appropriate balance between the commercial and non-commercial aspects of life in local communities. Moreover, businesses make location decisions in large part based on these local qualities, and so an alternative to tax giveaways and erosion of community services is to enhance community services and protect local quality of life.

Case Studies

A number of strategies for more sustainable economic development have been discussed in Part III of this book and are summarized in Table 16.1. The case studies that follow help illustrate how these concepts can be applied in actual community settings.

Arcata

Some 275 miles from San Francisco and over 400 miles from Portland, the small city of Arcata, California, is located at one of the most remote sections of the U.S. Pacific Coast south of Alaska. Declines in the local forest products and fisheries industries have contributed to local unemployment rates substantially higher than in either California or the United States. Moreover, Arcata's remoteness makes it quite costly to export products and generate income injections into the community. In 2004, the City of Arcata created an Economic Development Strategic Plan that operates in the context of the city's General Plan 2020, a comprehensive planning template. The Economic Development Strategic Plan identified the economic development potential of the various districts in the city, and also articulated citywide strategies. The city has implemented many of the innovative economic development strategies described in the bulleted list in the previous subsection of this chapter. In addition to those measures given in the bulleted list, other citywide strategies include a focus on infill development for vacant, underutilized, and contaminated former industrial sites, "gateway" investment and signage for visitors at key entrances to the city,

Table 16.1

Selected Economic Instruments for More Sustainable Local Community Development

Instruments and Strategies	Description
Microlending	Very small-scale lending directed at low-income people lacking collateral. To receive a loan one must usually be part of a "solidarity group" of other borrowers who provide mutual support and help assure repayment. Microlending reduces dependency, promotes empowerment and entrepreneurship, and builds social capital among members of the solidarity group.
Promotion of local small business and entrepreneurship	Smaller communities need not compete away their tax base to attract large, export-oriented industry. An alternative strategy is to promote "home-grown" small businesses and entrepreneurs, some of which will be a part of the economic base that injects income into the community, while others will produce goods and services that substitute for imports from outside and thus stem leakages. Such development promotes a more stable and diversified local economy, and is more responsive to local democratic process. For example, farmers' markets and community-supported agriculture strengthen urban/rural ties and establish a connection between environmental quality and local economic vitality.
Ecotourism	Engaging local people as guides, guards, and hosts to tourists visiting adjacent ecologically important areas. Ecotourism provides a direct financial incentive for local communities to protect their natural areas and an economic alternative to poaching or extractive resource harvest.
Recognizing and enforcing land tenure rights and effective local systems of CPR self-governance	Securing land tenure and property rights, and recognizing effective local systems of CPR self-governance, helps avert "tragedy of the commons" outcomes and promotes a longer-term perspective to resource management.

cultural and environmentally based tourism, entrepreneurship, and technological spinoff collaborations with Humboldt State University faculty and students, complementary affordable housing measures, and a program for sustainability. The sustainability program includes implementation measures focused on promoting local organic agriculture and farmers' markets, energy conservation and the development of local renewable energy sources, revitalization of pedestrian-oriented neighborhood commercial centers, and preservation of key historical districts.

The City of Arcata has also promoted ecological tourism and related events such as the Godwit Days bird festival and the Arcata Bay Oyster Festival. These festivals both improve the quality of life of local residents and help make the area's ecological assets an integrated element of economic development. The Humboldt/Arcata Bay complex represents the largest embayment between San Francisco and the mouth of the Columbia River, is one of the most pristine bays in California, and thus is ecologically very important for bird migration. Thus, in addition to producing approximately 70 percent of all the oysters sold in California, it should be noted as well that mariculture creates a market-based incentive to protect water quality in estuaries such as Arcata Bay. Finally, the City of Arcata operates an industrial park that provides infrastructure for local manufacturing firms, many of which produce locally based food products and outdoor recreational equipment. Because of these efforts, Arcata's economy has become more diversified, and support of local entrepreneurs has increased economic vitality, created a higher degree of self-reliance, partially stemmed income leakages caused by reliance on imports, and created employment opportunities within the community.

The Cogtong Bay Mangrove Management Project

In August 1992 the World Wildlife Fund (WWF) and the International Center for Research on Women (ICRW) studied mangrove management in Cogtong Bay, which is on the island of Bohol in the Philippines. Mehta (1996) reports the results of this study, and elements of that report are summarized below. Mangrove systems act as nurseries and spawning areas for many animals, as erosion control, and as vital sources of food and fuelwood for people. Coastal mangrove forests have been cut down in many areas of the tropics to make way for fish ponds for aquaculture operations. Villagers in the Cogtong Bay area observed this same trend in their region, with newcomers from out of the area building fish ponds and unsustainably harvesting wild fish in Cogtong Bay. In 1990 the Philippine government empowered sustainable local community management of nonwilderness mangrove systems, one of which was Cogtong Bay. In Cogtong Bay 1,300 of the original 2,000 hectares of mangrove swamp remain, with the rest converted to fish farms. Approximately 52,000 people live in the Cogtong Bay area; per capita income is $228, less than one-half that of the Philippines as a whole; and wild fish yields were falling as mangroves were being cut down. Mehta reports that wealthy and politically well-connected entrepreneurs were conducting a disproportionate large proportion of the (largely illegal) mangrove logging, which was undermining the sustainability of local communities in the area.

The goal of the management project was to help the local people better control and protect their coastal mangrove resource, to promote sustainable resource use, and to improve the economic well-being of local people. Mehta reports that the plan was to (1) organize eight Cogtong Bay communities into resource self-governance organizations; (2) rehabilitate 400 hectares of mangrove forest; (3) install artificial coral reefs to replace those that had been destroyed; (4) begin a locally operated oyster and mussel mariculture operation to boost local incomes; (5) limit illegal fishing and more sustainably manage the fishery resource; and (6) award twenty-five-year individual "stewardship leases" to mangrove plots conditional on individuals' keeping the plots under mangrove cover. While only a fraction of the target number of reefs was developed, other project targets were generally reached or exceeded. The project is considered a prototype, and the Philippine government reportedly intends to place 150,000 hectares of mangroves under sustainable community management.

Sustainable Local Economic Development in South Africa

In 1994 a largely peaceful process of democratization and empowerment in South Africa resulted in the end of apartheid and the beginning of the presidency of Nelson Mandela. South Africa's parks have for many years been viewed as being among the best in the world. These parks have become among the largest remaining refuges for elephants, white and black rhinos, Cape buffalo, lions, and leopards, among others. South Africa has 17 parks, an additional 5 in the process of formation, as well as many provincial parks and private game reserves. Yet as Chadwick (1996) has pointed out, the South African government must also provide for the basic needs of the very poor, mostly black, people of South Africa, including medical care, water and sanitation, housing, and schools. Unemployment is estimated to be 40 percent, and South Africa's population is growing rapidly. How can park protection be made consistent with the pressures for economic development?

Part of the solution may lie in ecotourism and in finding ways of bringing the economic benefits of ecotourism to the rural communities adjacent to these parks. Piet du Plessis, South Africa's chief of tourism, pointed out that 730,000 people visit Kruger National Park annually, and that 77,000 of them are from overseas, compared to 56,000 when the international boycotts were still in effect prior to the transition to majority rule. Nationwide, the number of overseas visitors increased 52 percent from 1994 to 1995. The substantial income generated by Kruger National Park subsidizes other less well known parks that nevertheless harbor substantial biodiversity. Kruger and many other parks are fenced—what Chadwick refers to as a form of ecological apartheid—keeping local people from poaching and protecting local people from predators and their livestock from communicable diseases.

Perhaps most important is the work that is being done in linking the ecotourism income generated by the parks to the welfare of local communities. Chadwick (1996) quotes park employee Chris Marais as saying: "[T]he old idea of how to run a park was: Put up a BIG fence, get BIG guns, and keep the neighbors and their cattle OUT. . . . The new idea is to build support by making sure those neighbors benefit as much as possible from being next door" (p. 16). First, since independence, local chiefs are now empowered to meet with park staff to discuss common concerns. People displaced since 1913 can seek restitution. Most of Kruger Park's 2,700 employees are from the local communities. As Chadwick points out, "[T]he staff has established medical clinics, assisted with irrigation projects, and arranged to purchase local crafts and produce to sell in park stores. Neighbors pay only a nominal entrance fee now, and drivers of local bush taxis have been trained as tour guides" (p. 23). A portion of income from KwaZuluNatal parks is shared with local villages and communities. Chadwick reports that local villagers are considering establishing private wildlife reserves. Many local people retain traditional rights to gather building materials and some food, and some villages are developing camping facilities and guided tour programs. Since 1979, private reserves and game farms have increased from less than 2 million acres to more than 16 million. Most big South African parks are considered by their managers to be at carrying capacity, and many surplus animals go to private hunting reserves, where a rhino, for example, can generate $15,000 to over $40,000 in income. Other private reserves are primarily focused on attracting ecotourists.

The South African government recently passed up the opportunity to develop an estimated $3 billion in titanium, rutile, and zircon from the coastal dunes of St. Lucia Wetland Park, opting instead for preservation and ecotourism. This provides a strong indication of the commitment that South Africa appears to have to its parks and sustainable development principles.

Moving Toward Sustainable Urban Planning in Curitiba, Brazil

The capital of the state of Paraná in Brazil, Curitiba has grown from a population of 300,000 in 1950 to over 2 million in 1990. During that time Curitiba's economy has shifted from an agricultural base to one of industry and commerce. Yet the usual results of such rapid change in developing countries—high unemployment, squatter settlements, congestion, and environmental degradation—have occurred to a much smaller extent than in similar cities in Brazil. Herbst and Allor (1992) argue that Curitiba is a living laboratory for extensive public transportation, flood-plain parklands, citizen participation, and investment in appropriate technologies such as bicycle and pedestrian access. Mayor Jaime Lerner initiated this experiment in the late 1960s. During rapid growth in the 1970s, a public transportation system was already in place, and so growth occurred along a rationalized five-spoke public transportation network rather than the sprawl associated with private automobile transportation. According to Herbst and Allor (1992), three-quarters of all commuters are reported to use public transportation, so per capita fuel consumption is 25 percent lower than in comparable Brazilian cities, and the city has one of the lowest rates of ambient air pollution. City officials purchased land for conveniently located low-income housing prior to industrial and transportation construction when land was still relatively inexpensive. People wishing to build beyond the normal height limit pay a fee that goes into a low-income housing subsidy fund. Curitiba has a Free University for the Environment providing practical short courses for families, builders, shopkeepers, and others. These courses are a prerequisite for certain jobs, yet many take the courses voluntarily. Some 70 percent of households sort recyclable materials for collection, and employment opportunities are created for low-income people through labor-intensive reuse/recycling programs. To limit illegal dumping, low-income people can exchange garbage for free bus tokens or surplus food. Reportedly, Cape Town, South Africa, is following the Curitiba model.

Summary

- This chapter focuses on two different views of the economics of more sustainable local communities. One of these is based on institutions for local governance of common-pool resources (CPRs), many of which evolved in pre-industrial societies, and the other is based on a model of the local economy in the context of modern industrialized societies.
- Elinor Ostrom and her colleagues argue that carefully designed institutional structures are central determinants of sustainable and long-enduring community-based CPRs. These systems are based on inclusive, democratic policy processes, common visions of equitable ways of allocating work inputs and resource units harvested from the commons, effective monitoring and enforcement schemes, and adaptability to changing conditions.
- Ostrom has developed a set of design principles for local governance institutions for CPRs that are associated with sustaining both the resource system and the community that relies upon it.

- In industrialized countries, local communities must contend with free migration and extensive regional, national, and international trade. A local economy can be characterized by inflows and outflows of income. Income is injected into the local economy by the economic base, which sells goods and services to those outside the local community, or in other various ways injects income into the local economy. The purchase of imported goods and services, as well as other activities such as paying state or federal taxes or traveling out of the area, results in income leaking out of the local economy. The level of material prosperity in a local community is a reflection of the balance of these injections and leakages.

- Injections of income by the economic base, net of imported factors of production used to produce those exports, flows through local input suppliers and employee households to grocery stores, restaurants, and other elements of the local economy. Thus, an initial injection from the economic base generates a larger overall economic impact that can be estimated using multiplier analysis. A simplified multiplier can be derived from the inverse of the leakage rate. The leakage rate is the percentage of overall local spending that goes to imported goods and services.

- The economic impact of additional sales by the base industry of a local economy is equal to the product of the initial injection and the multiplier.

- Economic development strategies have traditionally focused on increasing jobs and income. One notorious economic development strategy is "smokestack chasing" (also known as "microchip chasing") where jurisdictions offer tax abatement and other giveaways in competition to attract a large base-industry firm. Winning local governments may end up spending hundreds of thousands of dollars per job.

- More innovative economic development strategies focus on improving local infrastructure, simplifying and streamlining the permitting process, and assisting local entrepreneurs in starting and growing local businesses.

- Alternative ideas for economic development focus on increasing the multiplier effect by sponsoring "buy-local" campaigns, promoting community currencies, and assisting local firms that produce local goods and services that substitute for imports.

- Economic development has substantial impacts on other aspects of community planning, including housing and transportation infrastructure. In order to prevent sprawl, economic development needs to be fully integrated with local planning.

- Local economic development can also focus on growing the natural, human, and human-made capital stocks in the community, thus increasing the flow of benefits to the community. Examples include education and training programs to improve the income-generating potential of local people, improved telecommunications infrastructure to promote decentralized cyber-commuting, promotion of farmers' markets (and thus local organic agriculture), and improving the noncommercial aspects of local communities such as parks, open spaces, and the arts.

Review Questions and Problems

1. Identify a local common-pool resource in the area where you live. It may be natural, like a lake or a fishery, or constructed, like a community pool. Research the property rights structure (who owns the resource) and the rules that govern usage, as well as who monitors and enforces these rules. Assess the success of these rules in sustaining the resource, and compare your results to Ostrom's design principles. Suggest any recommendations that might improve the condition of the common-pool resource.

2. Go to the E.F. Schumacher Society's Local Currency website (www .smallisbeautiful.org/local_currencies/currency_groups.html) and research one or more of the local currency projects described there. What was the purpose of the local currency project? How widely accepted is the currency, and how effective has it been in promoting locally owned small business and fostering the creation of social capital?

3. Suppose that a firm proposes locating a production facility in your community that would generate $25 million in annual export sales revenue. Suppose that $10 million of that revenue initially leaks out of the local economy as payment for factors of production from out of the local area. Assume that on average, 60 cents of every dollar of local expenditure goes to the purchase of imported goods and services, or otherwise leaks out of the local economy. What is your estimate of the annual local economic impact of this facility?

4. Interview someone in your local jurisdiction's planning or economic development department. Find out what strategies they employ for promoting the jurisdiction's economic development. To what extent is economic development integrated into community planning (e.g., zoning, housing, transportation)? Ask for one or two concrete examples of recent successful projects, and critically evaluate whether, in your judgment, these projects enhanced or undermined the sustainability of your local community. Justify your argument.

5. Devise a sustainable economic development plan for the jurisdiction that you live in or grew up in. Explain how your plan is consistent with sustainability and with improving the economic well-being of people in the community. What sorts of economic activities are most appropriate for your community and why?

Internet Links

Arcata Economic Development Strategic Plan (http://arcatacityhall.org/ econ_dev_strat_plan/final_plan/table_of_contents.htm): This site contains the entire economic development strategic plan for the city of Arcata, California.

Communities by Choice (www.communitiesbychoice.org): A national network of communities, organizations, and individuals committed to learning and practicing sustainable development. They define sustainable development as the process of making choices that consider the long-term economy, ecology, and equity of all communities.

E.F. Schumacher Society Local Currency Website (www. smallisbeautiful.org/local_currencies.html): Directory of local currency projects and other descriptive material.

International Association for the Study of Common Property (www.iascp.org): A nonprofit association devoted to understanding and improving institutions for the management of environmental resources that are (or could be) held or used collectively by communities in developing or developed countries.

Lincoln Institute of Land Policy (www.lincolninst.edu): A nonpartisan forum for discussion of the multidisciplinary forces that influence public policy regarding land and tax policy.

National Congress for Community Economic Development (www.ncced.org): Promotes, supports, and advocates for community development corporations and the community economic development industry, whose work creates wealth, builds healthy and sustainable communities, and achieves lasting economic viability.

New Urbanism (www.newurbanism.org): Promotes the creation and restoration of diverse, walkable, compact, vibrant, mixed-use communities.

Sierra Business Council (www.sbcouncil.org): A nonprofit association of more than five hundred businesses, agencies, and individuals working to secure the social, environmental, and financial health of the Sierra Nevada region for this and future generations. The council explicitly rejects the notion that Sierra communities must choose between economic and environmental health, and views environmental quality and resource conservation as key to the Sierra Nevada's economic prosperity.

Smart Communities Network (www.sustainable.org): The SCN website connects citizens with the resources they need to implement innovative processes and programs to restore the economic, environmental, and social health and vitality of their communities.

Sonoran Institute (www.sonoran.org): The Sonoran Institute works with communities to conserve and restore important natural landscapes in western North America, including the wildlife and cultural values of these lands. The Institute's efforts focus on creating lasting benefits, including healthy landscapes and vibrant livable communities that embrace conservation as an integral element of their economies and quality of life.

Sustainability Toolkits for Communities (www.iisd.org/comm/ default.htm): A directory of sustainability tool kits for communities that provides a listing of publications dealing with community sustainable development initiatives and "how to" guides. Provided by the International Institute for Sustainable Development.

References and Further Reading

Acheson, J. 1988. *The Lobster Gangs of Maine.* Hanover, NH: University Press of New England.

Agrawal, A. 1993. "Rules, Rule Making, and Rule Breaking: Examining the Fit Between Rule Systems and Resource Use." In *Rules, Games, and Common-Pool Resources,* ed. E. Ostrom, R. Gardner, and J. Walker. Ann Arbor: University of Michigan Press.

_____. 2002. "Common Resources and Institutional Sustainability." Chapter 2 of *The Drama of the Commons. Committee on the Human Dimensions of Global Change,* ed. E. Ostrom, T. Dietz, N. Dolsak, P. Stern, S. Stovich, and E. Weber. Washington, DC: National Academy Press.

Ascher, W. 1995. *Communities and Sustainable Forestry in Developing Countries.* San Francisco: Institute for Contemporary Studies.

Bartik, T. 1991. *Who Benefits from State and Local Economic Development Policies?* Kalamazoo, MI: Upjohn Institute.

Bromley, D., ed. 1992. *Making the Commons Work.* San Francisco: ICS Press.

Chadwick, D. 1996. "A Place for Parks." *National Geographic* 190 (July): 2–41.

Cordell, J., and M. McKean. 1992. "Sea Tenure in Bahia, Brazil." In *Making the Commons Work,* ed. D. Bromley. San Francisco: ICS Press.

Daly, H., and J. Cobb. 1989. *For the Common Good: Redirecting the Economy Toward Community, the Environment, and a Sustainable Future.* Boston: Beacon Press.

Dietz, T., E. Ostrom, and P. Stern. 2003. "The Struggle to Govern the Commons." *Science* 302: 1907–1912.

Fodor, E. 1999. *Better Not Bigger: How to Take Control of Urban Growth and Improve Your Community.* Stony Creek, CT: New Society.

Gibson, C., J. Williams, and E. Ostrom. 2005. "Local Enforcement and Better Forests." *World Development* 33: 273–84.

Herbst, K., and D. Allor. 1992. "Brazil's Model City: Curitiba." *Planning* 58 (September): 74.

Lammers, P. 1997. *1997 Humboldt County Economic & Demographic Almanac.* Eureka, CA: North Coast Almanacs.

McKean, M. 1986. "Management of Traditional Common Lands (*Iriaichi*) in Japan." In *Proceedings of the Conference on Common Property Resource Management,* National Research Council. Washington, DC: National Academy Press.

Maughan, J. 1995. "Beyond the Spotted Owl." *The Ford Foundation Report* 26 (winter): 4–11.

Mehta, R. 1996. "Involving Women in Sustainable Development: Livelihoods and Conservation." In *Building Sustainable Societies,* ed. D. Pirages. Armonk, NY: M.E. Sharpe.

Netting, R. 1976. "What Alpine Peasants Have in Common: Observations on Communal Tenure in a Swiss Village." *Human Ecology* 4: 135–46.

———. 1981. *Balancing on an Alp.* Cambridge: Cambridge University Press.

Ostrom, E. 1990. *Governing the Commons: The Evolution of Institutions for Collective Action.* Cambridge: Cambridge University Press.

Power, T. 1996. *Environmental Protection and Economic Well-Being: The Economic Pursuit of Quality.* 2nd ed. Armonk, NY: M.E. Sharpe.

Pye-Smith, C., and G. Feyerabend. 1994. *The Wealth of Communities: Stories of Success in Local Environmental Management.* West Hartford, CT: Kumarian Press.

Richardson, H. 1969. *Regional Economics: Location Theory, Urban Structure, and Regional Change.* New York: Praeger.

Rocky Mountain Institute. 1997. *Economic Renewal Guide: A Collaborative Process for Sustainable Community Development.* 3rd ed. Snowmass, CO: Rocky Mountain Institute.

Schlager, E. 1993. "Fishers' Institutional Responses to Common-Pool Resource Dilemmas." In *Rules, Games, and Common-Pool Resources,* ed. E. Ostrom, R. Gardner, and J. Walker. Ann Arbor: University of Michigan Press.

Sethi, R., and E. Somanathan. 1996. "The Evolution of Social Norms in Common Property Resource Use." *American Economic Review* 86 (September): 766–88.

Sirkin, G. 1959. "The Theory of the Regional Economic Base." *Review of Economics and Statistics* 41: 426–29.

Snyder, G. 1990. "The Place, the Region, and the Commons." In *The Practice of the Wild.* San Francisco: North Point Press.

Glossary

Absolute Resource Scarcity (chapter 5). Exists for those natural resources (or elements of an ecosystem) that have no substitutes and whose productivity cannot be enhanced by way of technology. An element of traditional Malthusian models of resource scarcity.

Acid Rain (chapter 10). Sulfur dioxide and nitrogen oxide emissions react with water droplets, oxygen, and various oxidants in the atmosphere, usually in cloud layers, to form solutions of sulfuric and nitric acid. Rainwater, snow, fog, and other forms of precipitation bring these acidic solutions into soil, streams, lakes, and rivers, lowering the pH of these soils and water bodies and damaging terrestrial and aquatic ecosystems.

Anthropogenic (chapter 11). An event, such as the emission of greenhouse gases, that is caused by human activity rather than "natural" nonhuman causes.

Appropriation Externality (chapters 5 and 16). Occurs when the act of harvesting ("appropriating") resource units from a common-pool resource by an appropriator subtracts from what is available to others, or results in damage to the current and/or future productive capacity of the resource. Therefore, appropriation from a common-pool resource imposes negative externalities on other appropriators, which is at the core of the tragedy of the commons. Also see the entry for "rule of capture externality."

Arbitrage Opportunity (chapter 13). A difference in prices in different markets that cannot be entirely accounted for due to differences in shipping and transaction costs, and which therefore promotes trade. Entrepreneurs have incentive to export products from low-price to high-price markets. Therefore trade tends to equilibrate prices across markets. For example, if apparel is cheap in China relative to the United States, then entrepreneurs will have an incentive to export apparel from China to the United States. Likewise, if alcohol taxes are considerably higher in one state than in another, then alcohol will tend to be smuggled from the low-tax state to the high-tax state.

Average Effort Cost (chapter 5). Total cost divided by total effort applied to resource harvest.

Average Revenue Product (chapter 5). Total revenue divided by total effort applied to resource harvest.

Base Industry (chapter 16). See entry for "economic base."

Benefit/Cost Analysis (chapter 7). An analytical technique that guides policy-makers by computing the present value of benefits and costs for each of a set of different policy alternatives. An application of utilitarianism.

Biodiversity (chapters 13 and 14). Refers to the number of different species interacting in a particular ecological system. Related concepts include biological complexity and ecological resilience.

Buyers (chapter 3). Those market participants who exhibit a willingness to pay for a certain number of units of a good or service offered through some form of market process. This willingness to pay reflects a combination of a preference for the good and an ability to pay.

Cap-and-Trade System (chapter 10). A regulatory system in which overall pollution emissions are capped, and tradable quota shares are assigned to polluters. The EPA's Acid Rain Program features a cap-and-trade system for sulfur dioxide allowances.

Capture Fishery (chapter 6). Marine or freshwater fisheries in which the stocks are wild rather than farmed by way of aquaculture or mariculture.

Capture Rate (chapter 16). In the context of economic impact analysis, the capture rate is the percentage of gross export income generated by a local economy's economic base, net of payments for imported inputs, that is initially injected into the local economy. Also see entries for "economic impact" and "economic base."

Capture Theory of Regulation (chapter 8). Based on the work of George Stigler and Sam Peltzman, the argument is that firms are able to form a more effective interest group than consumers or other more diffuse interests because each firm has a lot at stake, and small numbers make firms easy to organize. Therefore the interest group representing firms captures the regulatory process. This demand-side theory does not address the supply of regulation.

Carbon Intensity (chapter 11). Carbon dioxide emissions per British thermal unit (BTU) of energy.

Cartel (chapter 3). A group of colluding sellers who attempt to coordinate their behavior so as to collectively act like a monopolist.

Categorical Imperative (chapter 2). Presents an action as being of itself objectively necessary, or intrinsically right, without regard to any other end that may or may not result from the action. For example, it can be argued that the idea of equal protection under the law is a categorical imperative.

Climate Forcing (chapter 11). Mechanisms such as human greenhouse gas emissions or natural fluctuations in the earth's orbit that alter the global energy balance.

Coase Theorem (chapter 7). Named after economist Ronald Coase, the Coase theorem starts from the premise that a complete set of private property rights can be assigned to aspects of the environment, that polluters and those harmed by pollution can negotiate to resolve pollution problems at very low cost, and that "free-rider" effects among multiple parties on either side of the negotiation are minimal. Under these conditions the central finding is that private parties can negotiate a solution equally as efficient as that which would result from more centralized regulatory processes using benefit/cost analysis.

Collusion (chapter 3). An agreement among market participants to limit competition for mutual benefit. For example, a cartel of sellers colludes by coordinating a reduction in each firms' production output.

Command-and-Control Regulation (chapter 10). Specifies how pollution is to be reduced through the application of uniform standards for firms. See entries for "technology-based (technology-forcing) standard" and "performance-based standard."

Common Ownership (chapter 4). Also known as common property or communal property. A system in which the property rights of access, withdrawal, management, exclusion, and alienation are held in common by a group of individuals. Examples include communal farms, cooperative processors, wholesalers and retailers, and recreation facilities in a condominium development.

Common-Pool Resources (chapters 5, 8, and 16). Those resources such as groundwater basins, rivers, marine fisheries, and community forests for which (1) it is difficult to exclude multiple people from appropriating from the resource, and (2) the resource units appropriated by one are no longer available to others. Contrast with "private goods" and "pure public goods."

Comparative Advantage (chapter 13). In economics the Law of Comparative Advantage states that people (and by extension firms, regions, or countries) should specialize in those activities for which their productivity advantage is greatest, or their productivity disadvantage is least, relative to potential trading partners. As a result, the trading party with the lowest opportunity cost of producing something is said to have a comparative advantage in producing it. Comparative advantage answers the question of what people, firms, regions, or countries should specialize in producing.

Consequentialism (chapter 2). The moral worth of actions or practices is determined by the consequences of the actions or the practices.

Conservation-based Development (chapter 12). Refers to programs and policies that help entrepreneurs succeed in developing viable businesses that are environmentally sound and make a positive contribution to their local community.

Conservation Easements (chapter 4). A landowner sells a portion of her property right having to do with the right to develop or otherwise diminish the conservation characteristics of her land. The landowner can still engage in certain activities such as livestock grazing or selective timber harvest, but the owner of the conservation easement the landowner can charge for encroachment on the easement if the landowner engages in an activity that diminishes the conservation characteristics of her land. These easements are permanent transfers of rights that run with the land.

Constructed Capital (chapters 12 and 14). See entry for "human-made capital."

Consumer (chapter 3). A person who buys goods or services and uses them personally instead of reselling them.

Consumer Surplus (chapter 3). The gain from trade that goes to consumers when the maximum amount they are willing to pay for something exceeds the price that they have to pay. Geometrically it is the area between the demand curve and the price line in a supply/demand diagram. The experience of finding a bargain at a garage sale is an example of consumer surplus.

Contingent Valuation Method (chapter 7). Involves the use of survey questionnaires to elicit hypothetical willingness-to-pay information regarding alternative management practices or other contingencies, usually affecting environmental or ecological resources that are not traded in markets and so do not have a market price to provide an indication of value.

Cultural Capital (chapter 12). Refers to the stock and functional integrity of the body of stories, visions, values, history, language, and myths shared by people that provide the framework for how people come to view the world and their proper role in it. A source of the shared values that determine the nature of economic systems and the relationship individuals and communities have with the natural environment.

Deadweight Loss (chapter 4). A type of negative gain from trade that occurs when either too much or too little of a good or a service is exchanged in a market. Deadweight loss occurs in association with market failures, such as when pollution accompanies market transactions, or when there is a monopoly or cartel, or when consumers are misinformed about product quality. When there is deadweight loss, the total gains from trade in a market are not maximized, and so the market features an inefficiency that may justify some form of government regulatory intervention.

Decentralized Markets (chapter 3). When resource allocation occurs as a consequence of a set of individual market transactions rather than centralized allocation decisions made by government. Decentralized markets are a key element of capitalist systems.

Demand Curve (chapter 3). A graphical representation of the inverse relationship between price and quantity demanded. Points along a demand curve represent buyer willingness-to-pay values. See also the "buyers" entry.

Dematerialization (chapter 13). Refers to a process of reducing the throughput (see definition) of physical resources and energy required to produce a given dollar of gross domestic product.

Demographic Transition (chapter 13). A theory that relates the stages of the industrialization process to growth rates in population. Stage 1, prior to industrialization, features high birthrates and death rates, and thus low growth rates. Stage 2, the initial stage of industrialization, features a sharp drop in death rates but persistently high birthrates, perhaps because medical technology reduces child mortality but cultural values related to childbearing are slower to adapt. Much higher population growth rates are experienced in stage 2. Stage 3, the fully industrialized stage, features low birthrates and death rates, and thus a return to low population growth rates.

Deontological Ethics (chapter 2). Theories of action based on duty or moral obligation. Actions are judged by their intrinsic rightness and not by the extent to which they further one's own goals or aspirations.

Derby (chapter 6). In the context of marine capture fisheries, a derby is the race for fish that occurs when a total allowable catch (TAC) is set, and fishers compete with one another to catch fish before the TAC is met and the fishing season ends.

Deterrence (chapter 9). In the context of promoting compliance with environmental and resource management law, a risk-neutral firm will be deterred from violating the law when the expected penalty exceeds the cost savings or revenue gains from being out of compliance. The expected penalty is the penalty or sanction (such as a fine) weighted by the probability of the violator being detected and penalized.

Direct Compliance Costs (chapter 7). The cost of environmental regulation can be divided into direct and indirect costs. Direct compliance costs include pollution abatement and expenditures by firms, consumers, and government, as well as opportunity costs that can be attributed directly to regulation.

Discount Rate (chapters 5, 7, and 13). The rate of time preference that equates present value and future value. For example, one might say that $100 to be received twenty years from now has a present value of only $25. This is equivalent to saying that $25 invested today in a (risk free) financial asset paying an interest rate equal to the discount rate will grow to $100 in twenty years. Discount rates are embodied in interest rates charged on borrowed money and other investments in financial markets.

Dose/Response Relationship (chapter 7). In the case of risk assessment, the dose-response relationship for a specific pollutant or human activity describes the association between exposure and the observed response (health or ecological effect).

Dynamic Efficiency (chapter 5). A criterion for evaluating projects or decisions that generate a stream of benefits and/or costs into the future. When a set of alternatives is being considered, the dynamically efficient alternative generates the largest present value of net benefits, profit, or surplus.

Ecolabels (chapter 15). Programs designed to inform consumers of the social and environmental impacts of the goods and the services that they purchase. Ecolabels are most effective when an independent third-party agency establishes the standards and evaluates the extent to which products adhere to those standards. An example is the SmartWood certification for sustainably harvested wood products.

Ecological Tax Reform (chapters 13 and 15). The reform of public finance in which taxes are shifted from productive activities such as income and employment to destructive activities such as pollution emissions and the depletion of natural resources. Since anything that is taxed is discouraged, ecological tax reform can be a revenue-neutral way of promoting desirable activities and discouraging polluting activities. Also known as environmental tax reform.

Econometrics (chapter 7). The application of statistical methods to economic problems. Often involves use of regression analysis to estimate functional relationships between a dependent variable and a set of independent variables. Examples include estimation of demand, supply, production, and cost functions.

Economic Base (chapter 16). The sectors of a local economy that in various ways generate income injections are collectively referred to as the economic base of the local economy. Examples include the export of local manufactured goods, agricultural commodities, services by local firms (e.g., consultant services provided by locals to those outside the community), or the injection of income associated with tourism in the local area, or salaries at a local state university paid for by state taxes and out-of-area students.

Economic Development (chapter 14). The process of improving the well-being of society.

Economic Growth (chapter 13). The rate of increase in real (inflation-adjusted) gross domestic product (GDP).

Economic Impact (chapter 16). The total increase in income in a local economy that occurs as a result of an initial injection (see entry below) of income into the local economy from the base industry (see entry for "economic base" above).

Economic Rationality (chapter 1). Occurs when a choice is taken from among competing options that yields anticipated benefits exceeding opportunity cost.
Economics (chapter 1). The study of how scarce resources, goods, and services are allocated among competing uses.

Economies of Scale in Production (chapter 13). Occur when the average cost of producing a unit of a good or a service declines as more and more is produced at a given factory or office. For example, automobile and aircraft production features economies of scale in production because of the extensive amount of capital equipment required to produce cars and airplanes. The average cost of producing a car or an airplane declines as more and more are produced because the cost of the capital can be spread out over more and more units.

Ecosystem Services (chapters 5, 12, and 14). As Robert Costanza and his colleagues have observed, ecosystem services consist of flows of materials, energy, and information from natural capital stocks, which combine with manufactured and human capital services to produce human welfare.

Efficiency (chapters 3 and 7). Generally refers to the condition of producing something of value with a minimum of waste. Efficient *resource allocation* is realized under market exchange when all the available gains from trade are realized, while efficient *production* occurs when goods or services are produced at minimum cost. A proposed social policy is *Pareto-efficient* when it makes some people better off and nobody worse off in comparison to the status quo or some other policy option. In contrast, a proposed social policy is *potentially* Pareto-efficient (or *Kaldor-Hicks-efficient*) when it generates an increase in total net social benefits compared to the status quo and other policy options, and thus the potential exists for those made better off to compensate those made worse off.

Effluent Charges (chapter 10). Fees or taxes charged on the emission of a pollutant. Pollution taxes are a type of effluent charge.

Embedding Effect (chapter 7). In the context of the contingent valuation method, the embedding effect occurs when willingness-to-pay responses for a particular good (protecting a mountain lake) are approximately equal to the willingness-to-pay responses for a more inclusive good (protecting an entire mountainous region that includes the lake among other features). When it occurs, the embedding effect may indicate the nonexistence of individual preferences for the good in question, and the failure of respondents to consider the effects of their budget constraints in hypothetical willingness-to-pay surveys.

Emissions-Trading Programs (chapter 10). Started in 1976, these are regional, state-controlled programs designed and operated in cooperation with the Environmental Protection Agency. To understand the concept, see the "marketable pollution allowance systems" entry.

Energy Efficiency (chapter 11). In the context of a macroeconomy, British thermal units (BTUs) of energy per dollar of gross domestic product (or other relevant currency). In general, units of energy necessary to produce a given unit of something valuable.

Equimarginal Principle (chapters 4, 7, 9, and 10). The equimarginal principle simply states that an optimal allocation occurs when the marginal benefit (e.g., marginal revenue) equals marginal cost. If there are multiple sources of pollution emissions, each of which has a different marginal abatement cost curve, then the equimarginal principle would suggest that each source would have its own unique level of abatement where the marginal benefit from abatement equals marginal cost.

Ethics (chapter 2). A branch of philosophy that is concerned with moral duty and ideal human character.

Excess Demand (chapter 3). Occurs when price is below equilibrium in a competitive market, and represents the amount by which quantity demanded exceeds quantity supplied at that price. Also known as a "shortage."

Excess Supply (chapter 3). Occurs when price is above equilibrium in a competitive market, and represents the amount by which quantity supplied exceeds quantity demanded at that price. Also known as a "surplus."

Existence Value (chapter 7). See the entry for "nonuse value."

Expected Value (chapter 9). Relevant in the context of a risky choice, or gamble, where there are multiple possible outcomes, each with its own probability of occurring, the expected value of the choice is equal to the sum of the products of each possible outcome and its probability of occurring. For example, if you are offered a gamble where you receive a payment of $0 (heads) or $2,000 (tails) based on the outcome of the toss of a fair coin, where the probability of a "heads" or a "tails" is 50 percent each, then the expected value of this gamble equals $0*0.5 + $2000*0.5, or $1000.

Exposure Assessment (chapter 7). In the case of risk assessment, exposure assessment involves an estimation of the quantity of a pollutant that people breathe, drink, absorb through the skin, or are otherwise exposed to in a period of time. Exposure assessment also includes an estimate of how many people are exposed.

Extended Producer Responsibility (chapter 15). Refers to regulatory programs that make producers rather than consumers and municipal governments responsible for reusing, recycling, or disposing of packaging and worn-out products. Extended producer responsibility (EPR) programs give producers an incentive to design products with less waste and for easier and less costly reuse, disassembly, and recycling. Notable examples include the packaging take-back and recycling legislation in Germany, the Netherlands, Austria, Switzerland, and France, as well as end-of-life legislation and voluntary agreements concerning a number of complex products such as cars, batteries, electronic and electrical appliances.

Externality (chapter 4). Positive externalities are external benefits generated from production and exchange and enjoyed without payment by members of society. For example, when parents pay to vaccinate their children against infectious disease, they create an external benefit—the reduced likelihood of epidemic—that is shared by many in society. Negative externalities are external costs generated from production and exchange and borne without compensation by members of society. For example, when firms can avoid costly cleanup by polluting, they create an external cost—the harms created by their pollution—that is shared by many in society.

Fertility Rate (chapter 13). The average number of children produced per woman in a country. The fertility rate has been declining worldwide over the last fifty years, and is below replacement in almost half.

Fishery (chapters 5 and 6). The interaction of human harvest activities, environmental conditions, and the population dynamics associated with one or more species of fish.

Fishing Effort (chapters 5 and 6). The deployment of fishing inputs (vessel, gear, labor). May be measured as the dollar value of total inputs, or as the aggregate amount of time that inputs are deployed, with adjustments made for differences in the productivity of different vessel and gear types.

Fixed Costs (chapter 7). Those costs that do not vary with the quantity that a firm produces in the short run. An example is the cost of leasing office space or renting equipment. Even if a firm shuts down production, it must still pay fixed costs in the short run.

Free Rider (chapters 3 and 7). One who enjoys the benefits of a public good or common-pool resource without paying a share of the costs of providing for or maintaining it. Voluntary contributions will fall short of providing the socially optimal quantity of a public good or a common-pool resource when there are many free riders.

Fugitive Resources (chapters 4 and 5). Those resources such as marine fisheries, groundwater basins, oil and gas fields, or stocks of fresh air having the characteristic of being difficult or impossible to fence, brand, or partition. Such resources tend to be state property, common property, or open-access resources rather than private property.

Gain from Trade (chapters 3, 4, and 7). The positive net benefit to market participants that occurs as a consequence of trade. The gain to consumers, known as consumer surplus, is the difference between the maximum amount that consumers are willing to pay (consumer valuation) and the market price they actually have to pay. The gain to producers, known as producer surplus, is the difference between the market price and the minimum amount that sellers are willing to accept (producer valuation). Resources are said to be efficiently allocated in a market when all possible gains from trade are realized.

Genuine Investment (chapter 14). Refers to the sum of the investments or disinvestments in each of society's capital assets (i.e., human, human-made, social, natural, and cultural). Since under weak sustainability theory we can view the sum of these stocks of capital assets as society's genuine wealth, we can also view genuine investment as the rate of change in genuine wealth.

Genuine Saving (Domestic) (chapter 14). A method for measuring genuine investment that offsets positive investments in human-made capital and in education with depletion of natural capital stocks.

Gini Coefficient (chapter 13). A measure of inequality, often applied to national income distributions. The Gini coefficient is calculated as a ratio of areas on a Lorenz curve diagram (see entry for Lorenz curve). If we refer to the area between the line of perfect equality and the Lorenz curve as X, and the area underneath the Lorenz curve as Y, then the Gini coefficient is $X/(X + Y)$. A value of 0 indicates perfect equality, and a value of 1 total inequality

Globalization (chapter 13). A complex process associated with technological, economic, and social changes that have lowered the barriers to international connectivity and integration. This process has speeded up dramatically as technological advances make it easier or cheaper for people to travel, communicate, and do business internationally. Associated with increased international trade and the mobility of capital and labor, and decreased cultural differentiation. Results in downward pressure on wages and prices.

Government Failure (chapters 3 and 8). A circumstance in which policy makers fail to craft regulatory interventions that enhance the efficiency of market processes. For example, policy makers may attempt to craft regulations such as Pigouvian taxes to resolve market failures, but political influence may distort the regulation to such an extent that the regulation creates additional inefficiencies.

Greenhouse Effect (chapter 11). Certain gases such as carbon dioxide, nitrous oxide, methane, and chlorofluorocarbons allow visible light to pass through the earth's atmosphere but block much of the resulting heat that would otherwise radiate from the warmed surface of the earth and out into space. Thus these atmospheric gases act like the clear walls of a greenhouse, creating a warmer environment than would otherwise exist. Human activity has increased the atmospheric concentration of carbon dioxide, a key greenhouse gas, by about 36 percent in the last several hundred years, and this process is forecast to accelerate.

Green GDP (chapter 14). An adjustment to gross domestic product (see the "gross domestic product" entry below) that takes into account declines in nonrenewable resources, expenditures on pollution control, and external costs due to pollution. A method of integrating environmental impact into GDP.

Gross Domestic Product (GDP) (chapters 11 and 14). The value of the final goods and services produced in a country in a given year.

Halocarbons (chapters 8 and 11). Synthetic compounds that combine carbon and halogen atoms such as fluorine, chlorine, and bromine. They may also contain hydrogen. Examples include chlorofluorocarbons, hydrochlorofluorocarbons, hydrofluorocarbons, carbon tetrachloride, methyl bromide, and perfluorocarbons. Some of these halocarbons are ozone-depleting chemicals regulated under the Montreal Protocol, and others were developed as substitutes under the Montreal Protocol. Most are also potent greenhouse gases with global warming potential many times greater than that of an equivalent mass of carbon dioxide. Many are long-lived in the atmosphere.

Harvest Function (chapter 6). Relates harvest from a fishery to different levels of fishing effort and to different levels of fish stocks.

Hazard Identification (chapter 7). In risk assessment, hazard identification refers to identifying the health problems caused by a pollutant. In the case of human health risk assessment, hazard identification uses both animal and human studies to establish the likelihood that a pollutant will generate harm to human health.

Hedonic Regression Method (chapter 7). A method used to determine the value of aspects of the environment not traded in markets and thus lacking a price to indicate value. This method uses regression analysis, a type of statistical analysis, to infer the value of environmental qualities that are bundled together with things that are traded in markets. For example, the price of residential housing reflects not only the characteristics of the house, but also the community and natural environmental qualities of the place where the house was built. Hedonic regression analysis can be used to assign prices to units of these environmental qualities such as lower crime rates, views, distance to a park or green space, open space, or clean air.

Hotelling Rent (chapter 5). See entry for "rent."

Hotelling's Rule (chapter 5). States that the dynamically efficient intertemporal allocation of a resource occurs in an equilibrium state where the marginal profit (P - MC) in the current period will equal the present value of the marginal profit in future periods. Note that "marginal profit" in the sentence above is actually a marginal rent. If the present value of marginal profit was larger in the future than in the present, then it would be profitable for producers of the resource to reduce sales today in order to have more to sell in the future. When Hotelling's rule is satisfied, the market is dynamically efficient, meaning that the present value of the total gains from trade summed over all the years of resource production is maximized.

Human Capital (chapters 12 and 14). The stock of knowledge, skills, and capabilities of people that can be deployed to create a flow of useful work for community and economy.

Human-Made Capital (chapters 12 and 14). Also known as constructed, created, or manufactured capital. The stock of technologies, tools, equipment, productive facilities, infrastructure (e.g., roads, waterworks, electricity grids, telecommunications networks, and the like) and inventories of products that economists traditionally think of as the capital stock.

Import-Substitution Model of Economic Development (chapter 16). An alternative to the economic (export) base model (see the " economic base" entry above). Instead of offering tax giveaways to attract big exporting firms, which will then have disproportionate power over the local community, local incomes and jobs can be enhanced by promoting local small businesses that produce local substitutes for imported goods, which would otherwise drain income from the community.

Incentive Regulation (chapter 10). Regulatory schemes that use prices, taxes, subsidies, and other instruments to align individual incentives with the common good. This form of regulation controls pollution indirectly through incentives rather than by way of direct controls such as emissions caps and technology-forcing rules.

Indirect Costs (chapter 7). Changes in production and production costs due to environmental regulation can result in additional costs such as product market distortions, changes in market concentration, and reduced rates of economic growth.

Indirect Effect (chapter 16). In the context of economic impact analysis, the indirect effect of an initial injection (see entry below) represents the increase in income to the various sectors of the local economy that support the base industry that generated the initial injection of income.

Individual Quotas (chapter 6). In the context of a fishery, individual quotas (IQs) are shares of a total allowable catch (TAC) allocated to fishers, vessel owners, communities, or processors. Initial quota allocations are usually based on historical landings. Individual transferable quotas (ITQs) can be traded, sometimes with restrictions. A competitive quota market can be expected to allocate a quota to its highest-valued use. ITQ's are commonly used in fisheries that are overcapitalized and that have experienced problems associated with a race for fish (derby). Market forces resolve overcapitalization and promote efficiency by concentrating larger quota shares on a relatively small number of vessels. Fishers need not race for fish because they can fill their quota at any time during the season opening.

Induced Effect (chapter 16). In the context of economic impact analysis, the induced effect of an initial injection (see entry below) represents the increase in income to the entire local economy that occurs due to increased spending by households that received income from the base industry or one of its support sectors.

Inflation (chapter 13). The rate at which the overall price level rises over time. Inflation may be measured in the overall economy, for consumer prices, or for particular sectors such as health care or higher education.

Initial Injection (chapter 16). In the context of economic impact analysis, the initial injection is the portion of gross income generated by a local base industry net of any initial leakage in the form of payments for imported inputs used to produce the export. It is the initial injection, not gross export income, that is multiplied to get total economic impact. Also see the entry for base industry and capture rate.

Invisible Hand (chapters 3, 5, and 8). A term associated with economics pioneer Adam Smith that refers to the efficient way that well-functioning competitive markets coordinate the complex and interdependent allocation of scarce resources in an economy without the guiding hand of economic planners.

IPAT Identity (chapter 11). Human impact (I) = Population x Affluence x Technology.

Kaldor–Hicks Criterion (chapters 2 and 7). See the "efficiency" entry.

Kaya Identity (chapter 11). Carbon dioxide emissions = Population $\times$ (GDP/Population) $\times$ (Energy/GDP) $\times$ (CO_2/Energy).

Kyoto Protocol (chapter 11). International treaty to limit human emission of greenhouse gases that contribute to global climate change.

Land Tenure (chapters 4, 5, and 13). Also known as traditional or customary land tenure, often in contrast to "Western" property rights systems that commodify land. Land tenure refers to the rights, responsibilities, and restraints that individuals and groups of individuals have with respect to the use and occupancy of land. Customary land tenure is often linked to common property arrangements, and may include aspects of religious significance and of a permanent home attached to land. Formal land tenure systems are officially recognized and sanctioned, while informal land tenure systems are not officially sanctioned or recognized by the courts or government, but are practiced and accepted as an unspoken long-term customary practice. Land tenure may be of an indefinite or long-term duration, and instead of the right of alienation may have succession rules whereby when the tenure holder dies, the tenure rights either go to the holder's children or revert to a communal pool for reallocation by the customary authority. Many former European colonies have dual property systems of imposed Western-style property systems and indigenous (precolonial) customary land tenure systems.

Law of Comparative Advantage (chapter 13). Originally developed by David Ricardo, this law argues that countries specialize in those productive activities where their opportunity cost is lower than that of the other potential trading partners.

Law of Demand (chapter 3). Demand curves are downward-sloping.

Law of Diminishing Marginal Returns (chapter 3). In the short run some production inputs are fixed, typically capital (e.g., the lease on a production or sales facility). In order to increase output in the short run, therefore, the firm must add more and more variable inputs, such as labor. Eventually the fixed input becomes congested with the variable input (e.g., too many cooks in the kitchen, too much irrigation water or fertilizer in the field). When this congestion occurs, the marginal productivity of a unit of the variable input (e.g., labor) declines. For example, if a workplace is congested, then the next worker hired will make a smaller contribution to output than one who preceded her.

Law of Diminishing Marginal Utility (chapter 3). Each successive unit of a good that is consumed in a given time period generates less marginal utility than did the previous unit.

Law of Increasing Opportunity Cost (chapter 1). Is manifested when a society's resources (land, labor, capital, entrepreneurship) are at least somewhat specialized. As a result, successive increases in the production of a particular type of good or service entails higher and higher opportunity cost.

Law of Supply (chapter 3). Supply curves are upward-sloping.

Long Run (chapter 3). Time period for production over which all inputs can be varied, including land and capital.

Lorenz Curve (chapter 13). Illustrates income inequality in a population. Constructed on a diagram where the X axis represents the percentage of people in a population, arrayed from lowest to highest income, while the Y axis represents the percentage of the group's total income received by each percentile of the population arrayed on the X axis. If there were perfect income equality in the population, then the Lorenz curve would be a 45 degree straight line. With substantial inequality, the Lorenz curve takes the shape of the portion of a parabola that occurs in the northeast quadrant $(X, Y > 0)$ of geometric space.

Marginal Analysis (chapter 3). Economic technique used to identify optima. For example, the optimal output level for a profit-maximizing firm operating in a competitive market can be identified by comparing marginal revenue with marginal cost. Likewise in benefit/cost analysis, the optimal level of pollution abatement can be identified by comparing marginal benefit with marginal cost.

Marginal Benefit (chapter 7). The change in total benefit that occurs as a consequence of a small (one-unit) change in production or consumption.

Marginal Cost (chapter 3). See the entry for "marginal private cost" below.

Marginal Effort Cost (chapter 5). The increase in total cost from applying an additional unit of effort to resource harvest.

Marginal External Cost (chapter 4). The increase in total external cost (costs borne by society in the form of pollution harms) that occurs as a consequence of a small (one-unit) increase in output produced by a firm.

Marginal Net Benefit (chapter 7). Marginal benefit/marginal cost. When marginal net benefit is positive, then a small incremental increase in pollution control or other policy activity contributes to a larger total net benefit.

Marginal Private Cost (chapter 4). The increase in total private cost (borne by producers) that occurs as a consequence of a small (one-unit) increase in output produced by a firm.

Marginal Product (chapter 3). The increase in output generated by a one-unit increase in an input. For example, an additional pound of fertilizer input applied to farmland will result in an increased crop yield output from that land. The increase in crop yield is the marginal product of the additional pound of fertilizer. Also see "Law of Diminishing Marginal Returns."

Marginal Revenue Product (chapter 5). The change in total revenue from applying an additional unit of effort to resource harvest.

Marginal Social Cost (chapter 4). The increase in total social cost (borne by both producers and other members of society) that occurs as a consequence of a small (one-unit) increase in output produced by a firm. Marginal social cost equals the sum of marginal private cost and marginal external cost.

Marginal Utility of Money (chapter 7). The increase in a person's total utility or satisfaction that occurs as a consequence of a $1 increase in income. Economists generally assume that the marginal utility of money, like the marginal utility of most other valuable things, is positive but tends to become smaller as total income rises. Thus a billionaire would have a smaller marginal utility of money than someone living in poverty.

Market (chapter 3). An institution that coordinates trade between buyers and sellers. Markets determine how buyers and sellers communicate, how prices are set, and how money is exchanged for goods or services.

Market Capitalism (chapter 3). A socioeconomic system based on the use of a complete set of decentralized markets to allocate scarce resources, goods, and services. In this system, human-made capital is privately owned by individuals, and production and employment decisions are decentralized and thus made by firms. Contrast with centrally planned allocation of scarce resources and government (or community) ownership of human-made capital under socialism or communism.

Market Equilibrium (chapter 3). Occurs at a price at which the quantity of a good or service demanded by buyers is just matched by the quantity supplied by sellers, meaning that neither a shortage nor a surplus occurs.

Market Failure (chapter 3). Occurs when one or more of the conditions required for a well-functioning competitive market is not met in a substantial way. Examples include monopolization or cartelization of markets, the presence of significant positive or negative externalities, or poorly informed buyers.

Market Power (chapter 3). Exists when buyers or sellers can affect market price to their advantage by manipulating the quantity they purchase or sell. For example, a monopolist has market power if it can maintain a lower quantity of output than would otherwise be produced under competitive conditions, and thereby benefit from a higher market price. Likewise a monopsonist fish processor that buys all the fish in a local market has market power if it can maintain low prices paid to fishermen.

Marketable Pollution Allowance Systems (chapter 10). These systems are designed to work in conjunction with overall emissions-control schemes, with the objective being to reduce the cost of regulatory compliance. Polluters are issued quotas (usually a fraction of historical emissions levels), which represent their total emissions allowance under the emissions-control scheme.

If some firms can further reduce their emissions, and if their cost of emissions control is much lower than for others, then trade in allowances will result in the firms with lower emissions-control costs selling allowances to firms with higher emissions-control costs. Allowances trade shifts clean-up to firms with lower clean-up costs, reducing the industrywide cost of compliance with an overall emissions reduction target.

Maximum Sustained Yield (chapter 5). The maximum number or quantity of resource units that can be harvested without damaging the productive capacity of the resource stock.

Minimum Efficient Scale (chapter 6). The level of output where the long-run average cost curve stops declining. In other words, the level of output where economies of scale end. In a large market under long-run perfectly competitive conditions, minimum efficient scale will dictate the minimum size of firms.

Monopoly (chapter 3). The condition that exists when there is a single seller that dominates a market. When monopolies are protected from entry by rival firms, the incentive for profit maximization results in the monopolist supplying less to the market than would otherwise happen under competitive conditions, which causes price to be higher than under competition.

Monopsony (chapter 6). The condition that exists where there is a single buyer that dominates a market. When monopsonies are protected from entry by rival firms, the incentive for profit maximization results in the monopsonist buying less from sellers than would otherwise happen under competitive conditions, which causes purchase price to be lower than under competition.

Montreal Protocol (chapter 8). International treaty to limit human emissions of stratospheric ozone-depleting chemicals.

Multiplier Effect (chapter 16). In the context of economic impact analysis, the multiplier effect is the additional income created when income originally injected into the local economy by the economic base (see entry for "economic base") is respent and becomes additional income through the secondary effect (see entries for "indirect effect" and "induced effect").

National Income and Product Accounts (chapter 14). Accounts that are used to measure the total income and output of a national economy. Gross domestic product (GDP) is derived from data from the national income and product accounts.

Natural Capital (chapters 12 and 14). The stock of natural resources, together with the components and the structural relationships in the earth's ecosystems, that taken together serve as the foundation for life on earth. From the stock of natural capital flows the annual harvest of natural resources, ecosystem services, sink functions, and other benefits from a healthy environment.

Negative Externality (chapters 3 and 4). See the "externalities" entry.

Network Externalities (chapter 5). Positive network externalities occur when network use by one entity creates benefits for others. A classic example is the benefit of having everyone on a common telephone network, as opposed to having people on different telephone systems lacking interconnectivity. Negative network externalities occur when network use by one entity creates costs to others. For example, on electric transmission networks (grids), excessive withdrawals by one entity can create system problems such as blackouts on others. Similarly, excessive withdrawals of natural gas from a pipeline network can reduce system pressure and impair deliveries to other network members.

New Political Economy (chapter 8). An area of study that borrows economic approaches for modeling incentives as a way to understand the political and economic forces that shape public policy.

Nonrenewable Resource (chapter 5). A class of resource having the characteristic that the overall stock cannot replenish itself within the human timeframe.

Nonuse Value (chapter 7). Also known as passive-use value or existence value, reflects value that people assign to aspects of the natural environment that they care about but do not use in a commercial, recreational, or other manner. For example, someone might value the existence of grizzly bear habitat in Alaska but have no interest in actually visiting such wildland habitat. Existence values are controversial because they are difficult to measure.

Normative Economics (chapter 2). Identifies the economic elements of how things should be, based on a particular set of norms or standards, as opposed to objectively describing the current economic state of affairs.

Open Access (chapters 4, 5, and 6). A state of affairs that exists when there are no property rights systems recognized that constrain access to a resource or withdrawals of resource units, typically for a natural resource. Tragedy of the commons is the anticipated outcome when self-interested appropriators harvest resource units from an open-access common-pool resource.

Opportunity Cost (chapters 1 and 7). When a scarce resource, good, or service is allocated to one use, the opportunity cost of that allocation represents the net value of the best alternative that was forgone.

Opportunity Cost of Capital (chapter 13). When a firm is considering a capital investment, such as expanding production capacity, the investment is anticipated to generate a flow of additional net income. The opportunity cost of that capital investment is the net income that could be earned by investing the money in some other income-generating asset, like stocks, bonds, or alternative projects. For example, if the next best use of invested capital is to buy U.S. Treasury Bonds paying a 7 percent annual return, then every dollar invested in a particular capital project has an opportunity cost of generating a 7 percent return each year.

Pareto Efficiency Criterion (chapters 2 and 7). See the "efficiency" entry.

Performance-based Standard (chapter 10). A type of command-and-control regulation that sets a uniform emissions control target for all regulated firms. Unlike technology-based standards, however, firms are given some choice over how the target is actually met.

Pigouvian Taxes (chapter 4). A tax (named after economist A.C. Pigou) placed on firms that is equal to the marginal external costs resulting from their pollution emissions. For example, if each unit of a good or service produced by a firm generates $20 in marginal external cost, then a Pigouvian tax of $20 per unit of output would internalize the marginal external cost, thereby resolving the market inefficiency caused by the presence of the negative externality.

Political Economy (chapter 8). In contemporary usage, political economy is distinct from the discipline of economics in that it is more interdisciplinary in nature, draws upon related fields such as law and political science, and often has a broader scope. Within microeconomics, political economy is an approach used to understand how political and legal institutions influence the economic behavior of people, firms, and markets, as well as the economics of how interest groups influence the formation of laws and regulatory policy.

Pollution (throughout the textbook). Harmful human-generated (anthropogenic) waste emissions that exceed the assimilative capacity (sink functions) of earth's ecosystems.

Pollution Abatement (throughout the textbook). Reducing, eliminating, or properly disposing of unwanted human emissions or wastes that are harmful to the natural environment.

Pollution Credits (chapter 10). See entry for "tradable pollution credits."

Pollution Taxes (chapter 10). Taxes placed on firms based on their pollution emissions. Unlike Pigouvian taxes, however, pollution taxes may not be designed to fully internalize external costs. In other words, pollution taxes may be greater than or less than the theoretically correct Pigouvian tax. Also see the entry for "effluent charges."

Positive Economics (chapter 2). A method of economic analysis based on the Western scientific tradition of modeling the world and then subjecting these models to empirical test. Positive analysis seeks to explain the observable. Contrast with normative economics. (See the "normative economics" entry.)

Positive Externality (chapters 3 and 4). See the "externalities" entry.

Precautionary Principle (chapters 11 and 14). Suggests that precautionary measures should be taken when evidence suggests that an activity is generating costly or irreversible harms, even if there is still some uncertainty over the extent or the mechanics of the harms. An alternative to benefit/cost analysis.

Present Value (chapters 5 and 7). The value at present of a future benefit or cost. Because people (and thus firms as well) have positive discount rates (see the "discount rate" entry), the present value of a future benefit or cost is smaller than the dollar amount of the payment in the future. The higher the discount rate, or the longer the time period before the benefit or the cost is received, the smaller is the present value.

Primary Market (chapter 5). In the context of metals markets, for example, the market for metal directly smelted from virgin ore, as opposed to secondary markets made up of metal derived from recycled material.

Private Ownership (chapter 4). Also known as private property. An arrangement in which the property rights of access, withdrawal, management, exclusion, and alienation are held by a private company, partnership, or individual owner.

Producer Surplus (chapter 3). The seller's share of the gains from trade. The area between price and a seller's minimum sales price (usually marginal cost).

Property Rights (chapter 4). In the context of natural resources and the environment, one or more of the rights of accessing a resource, withdrawing or harvesting resource units, managing a resource, excluding others from accessing the resource, and selling to someone else.

Public Choice (chapter 8). A form of political economic analysis that treats politicians as any other self-interested maximizer having an objective function that might include current and discounted future income, reelection, ideology, or power and control. Thus the rational behavior of a politician is predicted to be of a manner that is consistent with his or her objectives, which may or may not be consistent with the public interest.

Pure Public Good (chapter 5). A good or service (1) that is used by multiple people, and (2) for which use by one does not subtract from what is available for others to use. The latter characteristic distinguishes pure public goods from common-pool resources. An example of a pure public good is public radio or public television broadcasts.

Quantitative Risk Assessment (chapter 7). Quantitative risk assessment involves four steps: hazard identification, exposure assessment, dose response, and risk characterization. Risk assessment for environmental issues often addresses impacts on human health or on animals and plants in ecosystems. Risk assessment data can then be monetized and used to indicate the value of environmental conservation and restoration in benefit/cost analysis.

Rate of Return on Capital (chapter 13). Net income generated from capital such as a factory or office equipment (also used for financial capital), expressed as a percentage of the total cost of the capital.

Rational Choice (chapters 1 and 8). From the perspective of economics, a choice is rational if it is consistent with the objectives and preferences of those making the decision, given the available information. An allocation choice is economically rational if it is seen as yielding a benefit that exceeds opportunity cost. What is economically rational for one person may not be seen as reasonable by another.

Relative Price (chapter 13). The price of one thing (usually a good) in terms of another in a barter transaction.

Renewable Resources (chapter 5). The class of resources that are capable of replenishing themselves over time. Excessive harvest can deplete the reproductive capacity of a renewable resource.

Rent (chapters 5, 6, and 14). A return or profit from a differential advantage in production. Also known as economic rent, Hotelling rent, resource rent, Ricardian rent, or scarcity rent. In the case of agricultural land, for example, rent represents the excess of the return from a given piece of cultivated land over that from land of equal area that has such limited productivity (or is so remote) that it is at the "margin of cultivation." Large rents may be evidence of a lack of competition, such as government-created monopolies, or of successful measures to limit harvest from a common-pool resource. In the case of a natural resource, due to fixed supply, consumption of a resource unit today has an opportunity cost equal to the present value of profit from selling the resource unit in the future. This opportunity cost limits current supply, which in turn elevates current price above marginal cost, creating the rent. Under tragedy of the commons, rents are dissipated because individual resource appropriators cannot find a way to limit current harvest and preserve the resource for future sale.

Rent Dissipation (chapter 5). Occurs when competition eliminates rents. For example, when firms compete for a government monopoly by offering kickbacks equal to the present value of the rents that would be derived from the monopoly. Rent dissipation may also be bad, such as in the context of common-pool natural resources, where dissipation of rents occurs when harvest rates exceed the dynamically efficient consumption rate. In the context of common-pool resources, this outcome has been described by Garrett Hardin as the tragedy of the commons. Also see the entry for "rent."

Resilience (chapter 14). As used here, the magnitude of shocks (flood, drought, fire) that an ecosystem can withstand before being pushed from one locally stable equilibrium to another. Shifts from one equilibrium to another can cause detrimental changes in ecosystems.

Risk Characterization (chapter 7). The final step of risk assessment, risk characterization presents risk assessment results in various ways in order to illustrate how individuals or populations in human or ecological communities may be affected by pollution or other harmful human activity.

Risk Preference (chapter 9). One's risk preference regarding a particular risky situation falls into one of three categories. To understand these, suppose you are offered the following choice: (A) $1,000, or, (B) based on outcome of the flip of a fair coin, either $0 (heads) or $2,000 (tails). Note that the expected value of (B) equals 0.5*$0 + 0.5*$2,000 = $1,000, which equals the guaranteed value of (A). A risk-averse person prefers (A) over (B), even though they have the same expected value, since choice (A) avoids risk. A risk-neutral person is indifferent between (A) and (B), as they have the same expected value. A risk-loving person will prefer (B) over (A), even though they have the same expected value, since choice (B) includes risk. A person's risk preference usually varies across different types of choices. It is usually assumed that large firms are risk-neutral.

Risk Premium (chapters 7 and 13). A payment provided in return for accepting higher risk, such as with riskier jobs or riskier investments. Lenders add a risk premium onto interest rates for loans to those with a larger likelihood of defaulting on loan repayment.

Rule of Capture (chapters 4 and 6). A part of our common law tradition, the rule of capture operates on open-access and common-property resources such as groundwater basins, oil and gas fields, and marine fisheries. The rule of capture states that resource units harvested from an open-access or a common-property resource become private property owned by the appropriator at the time the resource units are captured from the commons.

Rule of Capture Externality (chapter 6). A phrase used by some resource economists to refer to appropriation externalities.

Scarcity (chapter 1). The condition of not having enough of something to provide for all that is wanted. The condition of scarcity implies that not all goals can be attained at the same time.

Scarcity Rent (chapter 5). See the entry for "rent."

Secondary Market (chapter 5). In the context of recyclable resources such as glass and metal, for example, the secondary market is the market for salvaged or recycled resources, as opposed to the primary market for glass or metal produced from virgin resources.

Shortage (chapter 3). See entry for "excess demand."

Short Run (chapter 3). Time period of production in which at least one input, such as land or capital, is fixed. For example, once a farmer has planted a crop, land is fixed, and the short run is the growing season.

Sink Capacity (chapter 5). The capacity of the biosphere to absorb human waste and render it harmless. Pollution occurs when human emissions exceed the earth's sink capacity.

Social Capital (chapter 12). As the concept is used by sociologist James Coleman and political scientist Robert Putnam, it refers to the stock of "civic virtues" and networks of civic engagement, involvement, reciprocity norms, trust, volunteerism, and sharing essential to democratic communities.

Social Rate of Time Preference (chapter 13). A discount rate that can be made consistent with weak sustainability. A key element of the social rate of time preference is the per capita growth rate in the productivity of human-made capital. If the productivity of a unit of human-made capital naturally grows at a 1 or 2 percent rate because of technological innovation, then social projects that divert money from such investments and into improving future environmental quality (enhancing future natural capital) should use a 1 or 2 percent discount rate. Under weak sustainability the various forms of capital are substitutable for one another, and so the opportunity cost of in-

Tradable Pollution Credits (chapter 10). Also known as tradable emission credits, these are the product of regulatory programs that regulate emissions at the level of the individual source rather than setting an overall cap on emissions. Firms that reduce their emissions below their regulatory maximum are granted credits that can be traded. Tradable credit programs often allow firms to bank credits for future use. Contrast with a cap-and-trade regulatory program that sets an aggregate emission cap and allows emission quota shares to be traded among individual polluters.

Tragedy of the Commons (chapter 5). A term coined by Garrett Hardin referring to excessive appropriation from a common-pool resource under an open-access or dysfunctional common-property regime. Excessive appropriation occurs because (1) each user imposes appropriation externalities on the others, and (2) governance structures that might limit appropriation to sustainable levels are inadequate or lacking. The tragedy is that the rational appropriator knows that the resource should be conserved, but nevertheless depletes the resource because resource units conserved by one will simply be appropriated by another. The tragedy of the commons leads to the dissipation of rents and damage or destruction of the common-pool resource. Also see the entries for "appropriation externality," "rent," "open access," and "rent dissipation."

Transaction Costs (chapters 3 and 7). The costs of making, measuring, and enforcing agreements. Often times these are information costs. An example would be the cost of hiring a mechanic to inspect a used car to determine quality prior to purchase.

Travel Cost Method (chapter 7). In the context of measuring the value of aspects of the environment not traded in markets, the travel cost method assigns a dollar value to active recreational use based on observed travel costs borne by those who come to use the resource.

Use Value (chapter 7). Use value represents the utility enjoyed by people who directly use some aspect of the environment. For example, a bird sanctuary yields use value to bird watchers and to those who use the area as an open space (walking, jogging, observing the view). Likewise, a back-country area provides use value to hunters, hikers, backpackers, and equestrians, and the ocean shore provides use value to surfers and fishers.

Usufructuary Rights (chapter 4). Certain use and withdrawal rights to property that is owned by others. For example, treaties ceding Indian lands to the federal government sometimes include clauses granting Indian tribes usufructuary rights for hunting, fishing, and gathering on the ceded lands. Likewise "water rights" held by irrigators on navigable waterways are usufructu-ary rights, with the waterway itself being owned by government in a public trust capacity.

Utilitarian Ethics (chapter 2). A branch of ethics that considers a proposed social rule to be utilitarian-ethical if, after adding up the utility and the disutility that the proposed rule induces on people in society, a positive net social utility is realized that exceeds that of any alternatives being considered. This rule is sometimes (imprecisely) characterized as providing the greatest good for the greatest number without regard to the intrinsic rightness of the specific acts required to achieve the desirable end.

Utility (chapter 2). The principle that judges actions according to their tendency to increase or decrease an individual's happiness.

Weak Sustainability (chapter 14). A theory of sustainability that developed from economic models of growth. A key assumption is that declines in natural capital can be offset by increases in human, social, or human-made capital. In other words, one form of capital can readily substitute for another. While strong sustainability is concerned with the stock of each individual form of capital, weak sustainability is only concerned with the sum of the stocks of all forms of capital.

Willingness to Pay (chapter 3). The amount a consumer is willing *and* able to pay for a particular quantity of a good or service.

Index

About the Author

Steve Hackett is professor of economics at Humboldt State University in Arcata, California. Before coming to Humboldt, Hackett was an assistant professor and member of the graduate faculty at Indiana University in Bloomington. He has published in a variety of different scholarly journals, including *Journal of Law and Economics; Journal of Environmental Economics and Management; Journal of Law, Economics, and Organization; Journal of Economic Behavior and Organization; Economic Inquiry; Marine Resource Economics; Japan and the World Economy; Journal of Theoretical Politics; California Agriculture;* and *California Cooperative Oceanic Fisheries Investigations Reports.* His research has been supported by grants from the National Science Foundation and the California Sea Grant College Program.